Grasslands Grown

Grasslands Grown

*Creating Place on the
U.S. Northern Plains
and Canadian Prairies*

Molly P. Rozum

University of Nebraska Press
Lincoln

© 2021 by the Board of Regents of the University of Nebraska

All rights reserved

Library of Congress Cataloging-in-Publication Data
Names: Rozum, Molly Patrick, author.
Title: Grasslands grown: creating place on the U.S. northern plains and Canadian prairies / Molly P. Rozum.
Description: Lincoln: University of Nebraska Press, [2021] | Includes bibliographical references and index.
Identifiers: LCCN 2020045932
ISBN 9780803285767 (hardback)
ISBN 9781496226716 (paperback)
ISBN 9781496227966 (epub)
ISBN 9781496227973 (pdf)
Subjects: LCSH: Regionalism—Great Plains. | Colonists—Great Plains—Social life and customs. | Frontier and pioneer life—Great Plains. | Human ecology—Great Plains. | Cultural geography—Great Plains. | Grasslands—United States. | Grasslands—Canada. | Great Plains—Civilization—19th century. | Great Plains—Environmental conditions—19th century.
Classification: LCC F591 .R794 2021 | DDC 978—dc23
LC record available at https://lccn.loc.gov/2020045932

Set in New Baskerville by Laura Buis.

In memory of

my sister
    Ellen Clare Rozum (1956–74);

daddy,
    Leo J. Rozum (1904–75);

mother,
    Virginia Dugan Rozum (1922–2017);

neighbors who treated me as a daughter,
    Jeanette Coyne Culhane (1928–2012)
    and Donald E. Culhane (1926–2018);

and

mentor and friend
    John Herd Thompson (1946–2019)

Contents

List of Illustrations	ix
List of Maps	xi
Acknowledgments	xiii
Introduction: Looking Northwest from La Vérendrye Hill	1
1. Parents' Choice: Taking Root on the Northern Grasslands	17
2. Small Worlds: Animal Friends, Foes, and Place Rhythms	57
3. Sensing Prairies and Plains: Grasses, Grains, Waters, Woods, Rocks, and Snow	93
4. "The Purple Hills That Beckoned": Growing Up, Travel, Education, and Region	133
5. "Old Woman Who Never Dies" and *Old Man's Garden*: Settler and Indigenous Relations over the Generations	175
6. "All Is So Still—So Big, I Scarce Can Speak": New Literature and Settler-Society Aesthetics	219
7. "Surely, Grass Is the Great Mother of All Plains Agriculture": Agricultural Adaptation and Grasslands Conservation	261
8. "All That Vast Region of Grass Land": The United States, Canada, and Changing Cultural Geography	301

Conclusion: Looking across the Line from the Prairies and Plains	349
Notes	363
Bibliography	421
Index	449

Illustrations

1. Harriet "Hattie" Foster, 1913 — 2
2. Collage of animal drawings by Hale Humphrey, 1880s and 1890s — 64
3. Era Bell Thompson on horseback, early 1920s — 69
4. Antelope, bison, and geese drawn by Clell Gannon, 1927 — 89
5. Wallace Stegner along the Frenchman River, circa 1916 — 108
6. Walter Neatby and Leslie Neatby on farmland, circa 1917 — 117
7. Annora Brown playing outdoors, circa 1900s — 119
8. Field of grain stooks, mid-twentieth century — 127
9. Era Bell Thompson's classroom, 1917 — 140
10. Kjersti Raaen, circa 1890s — 149
11. Lulu Pickler, circa 1880s — 154
12. Edward Pitblado, 1915 — 160
13. Aagot Raaen, circa 1890s — 168
14. Mandan "Double Ditch" village site, 1905 — 170
15. Annora Brown with Herbert Stanfield in classroom, circa 1926 — 172
16. *Indian Encampment* by Annora Brown, circa 1950s — 184
17. Scattered Corn, 1920s — 187
18. Prairie anemone and purple avens drawn by Annora Brown, 1954 — 196
19. George Will, Clell Gannon, and Russell Reid, 1925 — 203
20. James Holding Eagle, circa 1910s or 1920s — 207

21. Effie Laurie Storer, 1885 — 210
22. Robert McAlmon with friends in Paris café, 1920s — 229
23. Wilfrid Eggleston in journalism classroom, Carleton University, 1958 — 235
24. Wallace Stegner in his California study, 1951 — 240
25. Laura Goodman Salverson, circa 1910s — 243
26. Robert McAlmon, William Carlos Williams, and Florence Williams, 1921 — 248
27. Clell Gannon on rock formation, 1923 — 257
28. Elsie Hammond and family, 1933 — 270
29. George Will standing in cornfield, 1917 — 274
30. Aagot Raaen on skis, circa 1916 — 280
31. Skeleton weed and wild rose drawn by Annora Brown, 1954 — 285
32. Peter Norbeck, circa 1920s — 290
33. Annora Brown with her *Foothills Village*, circa 1950s — 295
34. Thorstina Jackson Walters in Iceland, 1929 — 303
35. Oscar H. Will and Company catalog cover, 1936 — 311
36. Cover of *American Daughter* by Era Bell Thompson, 1946 — 339
37. Era Bell Thompson, circa 1946 — 341

Maps

1. North America's northern grasslands — xxi
2. Modern reserves and reservations on North America's northern grasslands — xxiii
3. Possible La Vérendrye routes on North America's northern grasslands — 5
4. Transnational origins of northern grasslands settlement, 1862–78 — 32
5. Settler-colonial "boom" and "bloom," 1879–91 — 39
6. The last best transnational northern Grasslands West, 1896–1917 — 50
7. Wallace Stegner's routes west, 1934–43 — 316
8. Walter Prescott Webb's *The Great Plains Environment*, 1931 — 321
9. Walter Prescott Webb's *Land Regions of the United States*, 1931 — 322
10. William A. Mackintosh's *Prairie Provinces Natural Vegetation*, 1934 — 324

Acknowledgments

Grasslands Grown is dedicated to six people who I wish had lived to see this history published. Each of them influenced me in unique ways and are present in this book: these few words will stand for all I feel.

Without the enduring interest of singular people, I still would have a manuscript-in-progress, not a book. Tom Isern, Jacquelyn Hall, Jim Naylor, and Alan Stern have been supportive mentors and friends for many years. My gratitude is deep. Tom Isern was the first resident on the grasslands I spoke to about my idea to study the region transnationally; his research and writing on the Great Plains has been a constant source of inspiration and on occasion made for calming reading that kept me grounded. Jacquelyn Hall very early on helped me recognize the originality of my ideas, which encouraged me to persist; her knowledge of the force of cultural regions in southern history added important depth to my thinking about the northern plains. Jacquelyn Hall and Bob Korstad opened their Chapel Hill home to me to work and write; I enjoyed especially their wonderful back porch, which looks out to a seeming forest and garden landscape hard to imagine in the dense urbanity of Chapel Hill. Walks and talks over dinners with Jacquelyn are cherished memories that enriched this study greatly; Bob offered important reflections on book writing. Jim Naylor read the entire manuscript carefully and discussed endless stories from the book with curiosity and insight; his critical suggestions helped make this a sharper, leaner, and all-around better book. During the final phase of this project, Jim offered expert advice for negotiating all facets of the academic world and more, with constant care. Alan Stern has helped me understand difficult aspects of progress and much else, and I thank him for his encouragement and advice over many years.

The late John Herd Thompson's mentoring helped me negotiate Canadian historiography. Although my questions led naturally to Canadian prairie history, I do not believe I would have attempted a walk across the boundary without him, into, as Tom Isern might say, the gumbo of transnational work. Roger Lotchin, urban historian of the California West, raised on the Illinois prairie, read all of my early work on the rural northern Grasslands West with attention and encouragement. My American studies undergraduate adviser at the University of Notre Dame, folklorist Barbara Allen Bogart, helped set me on the road to an academic career. I appreciate the intellectual foundation I received at Notre Dame and still recall ideas encountered in Professor Allen's American Folklore course (where I first read Wallace Stegner) and Professor Ronald Weber's Hemingway and American Journeys courses. Nancy Tystad Koupal, director of the South Dakota Historical Society Press, has been a role model since before I knew her personally and in recent years a valued mentor. Many thanks go to each of these individuals.

The support of friends is incalculable. Historian Jennifer Ritterhouse has been a close friend since graduate school; I have relished constant conversations with her about wide-ranging history topics and much else good in life. Jen's support has run among the deepest. Many circles of friends and colleagues helped me at different points in the research process, and I thank them all: scholars from my years at the University of North Carolina at Chapel Hill include Natalie Fousekis, Gary Frost, Pam Grundy, John Hepp, Erin Kellen, Laura Moore, Marla Miller, Kathryn Newfont, Karen Parr, Molly (Conrecode) Singer, Michele Strong, Regina Sullivan, Sarah Thuesen, Robert Tinkler, Lisa Tolbert, Michael Trotti, and Georgia Weir, and also Paige Raibmon then at Duke University. For providing interdisciplinary insight into the research process, I thank Charles Capper, Peter Filene, John Florin, Glenn Hinson, Dan Patterson, David Whisnant, and especially John Kasson, William Leuchtenburg, and Terry Zug; the last three read early versions of parts of this plains history.

My colleagues at Doane University in Crete, Nebraska, gave me important intellectual and social support, even after I moved back to my home state and the University of South Dakota. These friends include former Doane president Jonathan Brand and colleagues Danelle DeBoer, Lyn Forester, Maureen Franklin, Peg Hart, Tim Hill, Kim Jarvis, Brad Johnson, Heather Lambert, Betty Levitov, Les Manns, Kate Marley, Ned McPartland, Mark Orsag, Brian Pauwels, Rod Peters, Peter Reinkordt, and Phil Weitl. The community I had at Doane cannot be matched. The history department at the University of South Dakota in Vermillion offered me the wonderful opportunity of a little more time in my schedule to finish this history of South Dakota's region. I am grateful to the entire department, including Kurt Hackemer, Judith Sebesta, Dave Burrow, Steve Bucklin, Scott Breuninger, and especially Jenn Beermann, Elise Boxer, Niki Hamonic, and Sara Lampert for sustaining me with friendship. Sara's expertise in cultural history and Elise's thinking about the U.S. West and Indigenous history gave important nourishment to this project's final phase; their intellectual energy and dynamism have inspired me. Friendships with Clayton Lehmann, also in the history department, and Angela Helmer, in modern languages, aided my progress from my first days at USD. The graduate students in my Great Plains seminar have refreshed my thinking about the field's historiography. Dan Daily, archivist and dean of libraries at USD, provided friendship, welcome encouragement, and academic support. Many thanks go to all of you valuable friends.

I am grateful to several institutions that advanced this project with financial assistance in its early stages. My research received support from two George E. Mowry Awards and a Smith Graduate Research Grant from the University of North Carolina at Chapel Hill. The Canadian embassy encouraged my initial research with a Canadian Studies Graduate Student Fellowship. The Center for Rural and Regional Studies at Southwest Minnesota State University in Marshall offered me an in-residence fellowship that allowed me to nearly complete the initial phase of research; there my ideas benefited from the creative original thinker Joe Amato, then head of the center, and Geoff Cunfer (now at University of Saskatchewan) and his knowledge of agriculture and environmental history. Early on my research benefited financially from the Pauline Maier Award of the Historical Society. The Canadian embassy's Thomas O. Enders Fellowship program, in partnership with the University of Calgary, allowed me to soak in Canadian culture as a visiting professor in the history department. Sarah Carter, Walter Hildebrandt, Elizabeth Jameson, and Jewel Spangler made my Calgary experience a productive one. I thank Sarah for pointing me to Lula Short's Alberta girlhood diary. While I was in Alberta, Sheila McManus invited me to speak at the University of Lethbridge and since then has been an important ally in the study of regional history. Finally, a Doane University Faculty Research Grant supported my research at Yale University's Beinecke Rare Book and Manuscript Library.

Working in archives is one of the joys of being a historian. This book benefited greatly from the expert assistance available at archives across the region—namely, the South Dakota State Historical Archives in Pierre; the Richardson Archives at the University of South Dakota in Vermillion; the North Dakota Institute for Regional Studies Archives at the North Dakota State University in Fargo; the State Historical Society of North Dakota Archives in Bismarck; the Provincial Archives of Manitoba and the University of Manitoba Archives, both in Winnipeg; the Saskatchewan Archives Board, then located in Regina and Saskatoon; the BARD facility associated with the University of Alberta Archives in Edmonton; the Glenbow Library and Archives in Calgary (now located at the University of Calgary); and the Montana State Historical Society in Helena. I found important sources for this project at the Rockefeller Archive Center, located in Pocantico Hills, North Tarrytown, New York; the Beinecke Rare Book and Manuscript Library at Yale University in New Haven; the Newberry Library Archives in Chicago; and the Library and Archives Canada in Ottawa. The staff at ID Weeks Library at USD is wonderful. I will forever have gratitude for the many people at these invaluable, too frequently underfunded, cultural institutions who made the research for this book a very pleasurable experience over many years.

Historians interested in the northern plains are a supportive bunch; I wish to thank all of those I haven't already mentioned who offered various assistance: Ted Binnema, Kristin Mapel Bloomberg, Sterling Evans, Dee Garceau, Barbara Handy-Marchello, Jennifer Helton, Fran Kaye, Suzzanne Kelley, Renée Laegreid, Lori Lahlum, Michael Lansing,

Amy McKinney, Dave Mills, Mary Murphey, Paula Nelson, and Jeanne Ode. A workshop on the Great Plains environment at the University of Oklahoma organized by Kathleen Brosnan and Brian Frehner proved a good venue for some final reflections on the project, especially as I considered comments by geographer Robert Rundstrom. I thank Nicole Neatby for searching through family photographs to find one of her grandfather and great uncle on the Saskatchewan farm. Two anonymous readers for the University of Nebraska Press waded through—let's call it—an extended version of *Grasslands Grown* and offered insightful guidance for final revisions. Their suggestions for particular aspects helped me refine corollary pieces. Bridget Barry, my editor at University of Nebraska Press, is an expert at her craft. I am thankful for her constant interest, since well before I submitted the manuscript for review, in this northern Grasslands West regional study. She carefully read the entire manuscript and offered key suggestions for honing the final book, all expeditiously, with reassuring professionalism that always advanced my ideas.

Family and friends outside of the academic world reminded me of positive social and cultural values still important to the region, which grew out of the settler societies created by the people I studied for *Grasslands Grown*. My friendship with Donna Culhane-Eberenz has sustained me since we met as very young children as neighbors growing up in Mitchell, South Dakota, as has a long friendship with Becky (Blindauer) Alexander, also of Mitchell. I thank friends Wayne Eberenz, Mary Curtis, and Todd Darringer for constant interest and support and Stacy Wasson and Heather Artz Harpenau for supportive conversation. Additionally, I am grateful to the people who hosted me on long-ago archival trips: Linda Yeo and Corinne Enns in Winnipeg; Jeanne Simpson in Pierre; my sister Mary and brother-in-law Kent Anderson in Vermillion (while I researched at the University of South Dakota's archives, years before I began teaching at the university); and my sister Martha Pfeifle and her late husband, Paul (who dug me out of snowdrifts), the winter I commuted from our family cabin in Minnesota near their home for research in Fargo. They, along with my sister Anne and brother-in-law Keith Bailey, brother John and sister-in-law Tona Rozum, brother George Rozum, and cousin Nancy

Everist, all have shown constant interest in my history work. I thank family, friends, and colleagues for supportively inquiring about my research without vocalizing wonder at how long it takes (at least in this case) to write a history of the region. As Jim Naylor says, "It's a process." Thank you goes to all here mentioned and to many more people who undoubtedly provided me assistance during the research and writing of *Grasslands Grown*.

Grasslands Grown

Map 1. North America's northern grasslands. Modern ecologists recognize several ecoregions or zones within the historical northern grasslands consisting of tallgrass and shortgrass species and flowering herbs. Much of the area hosted complex mixtures of these plants, dependent on constantly shifting annual precipitation, temperatures, sunlight, soil conditions, and the lay of the land. Distinct grassland and forest parklands bordered the grasslands on the north, west, and east. Erin Greb Cartography.

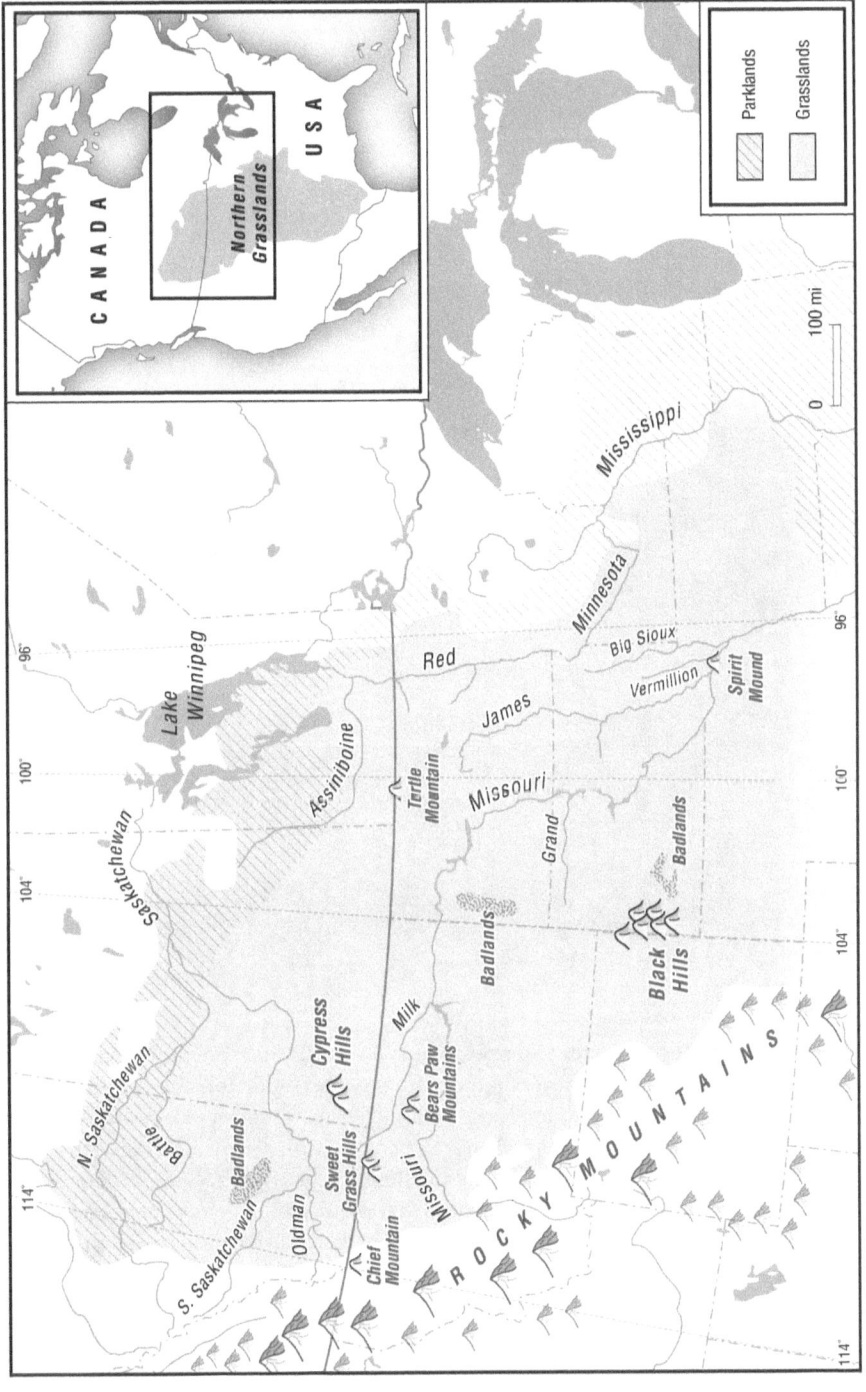

Map 2. Modern reserves and reservations on North America's northern grasslands. Today's pattern of large blocks of reservation territories south of the international border and scattered small reserves north of it resulted from distinct U.S. and Canadian policies. Concerned with removing Indigenous nations out of the way of settler-colonial traffic, the United States promised huge reservation territories in treaties that required Indigenous peoples to move onto them quickly. More concerned with acquiring titles to the entire area north of the border, Canada's Numbered Treaties did not require Indigenous nations to move immediately to reserves. Eventually, Canada assigned reserves to individual bands. Erin Greb Cartography; see also St. Germain, *Indian Treaty-Making Policy*.

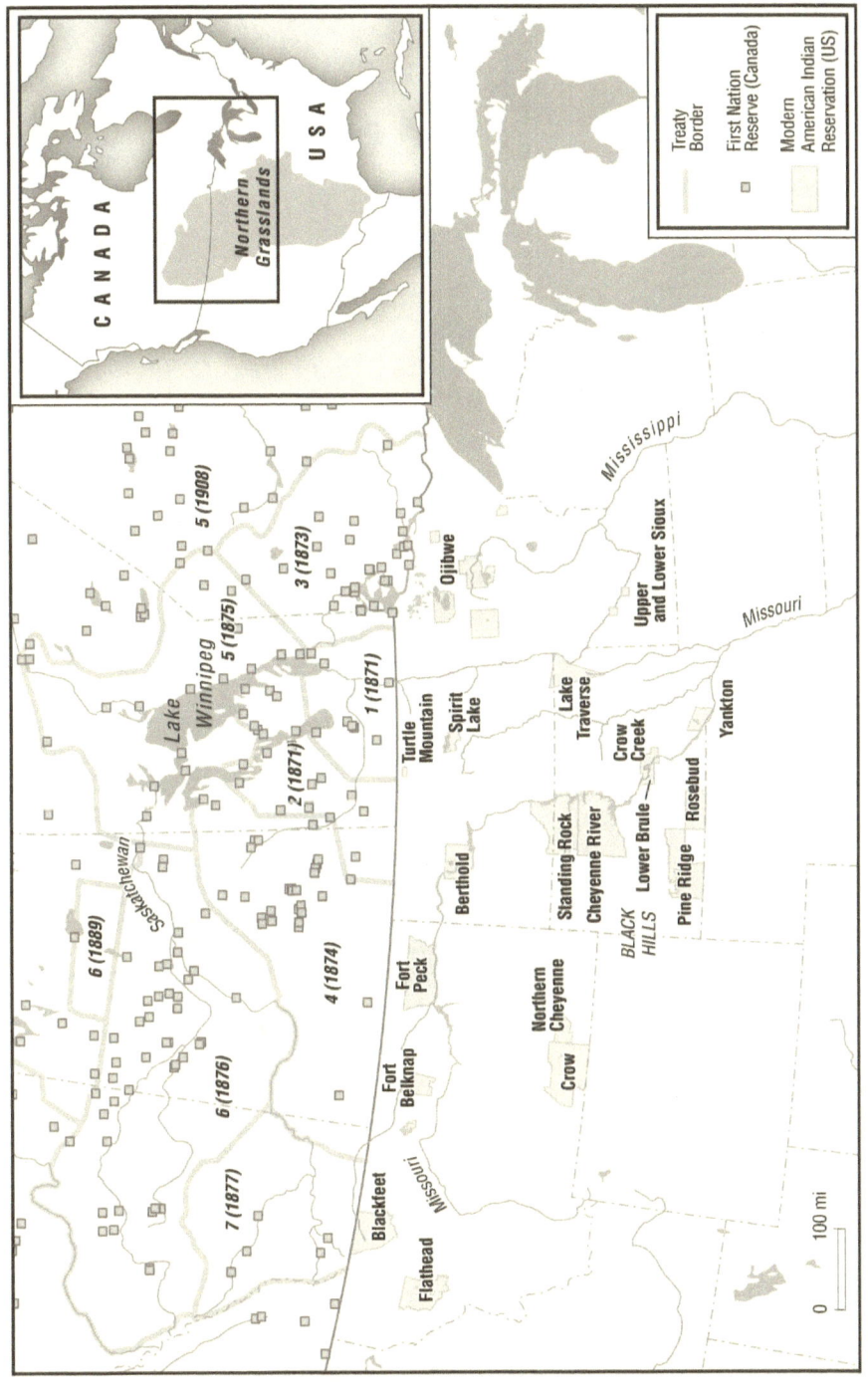

Introduction

Looking Northwest from La Vérendrye Hill

On a "balmy" February afternoon in 1913, Hattie May Foster and several other girls amused themselves on the undulating grasslands surrounding the village of Fort Pierre, South Dakota. "We girls were out walking, and went up on the hill," Hattie recalled. Nature delivered a spectacular view from this river-bluff hilltop: the twinned towns of Fort Pierre and Pierre lay tucked in the valley below, while the Missouri and Bad Rivers arched in different directions, shooting gray timbered bands into sepia-colored winter grasslands. The wide Missouri would soon flow in freshets from local snowmelt and distant spring thaws in the Rocky Mountains. A group of boys also made their way to the hill after a day of hunting. They often played war in a large earthen fortress shaped from the sticky gumbo soil.[1] These young people called the rise Harney Hill, after the highest peak in South Dakota's Black Hills, at the time named for the U.S. general William S. Harney and in 2016 renamed for the Lakota knowledge keeper Black Elk.[2] But on 16 February 1913, Hattie Foster made a discovery that changed the hill's name for a new generation of northern grasslands residents.

Years of walking on the earth and grass of this hill created the chance for Hattie Foster to rescue from oblivion a small, Latin-inscribed, lead plate. Telling the story of the day's events over and again, she later explained, "We were standing there talking, and I was scraping in the dirt with my foot. . . . When I saw it I kicked it out and picked it up." Buried with the intent of conquest in 1743 by François and Louis-Joseph La Vérendrye, North American–born colonial agents of France's North American empire, this lead artifact gave the hill a new identity. Harney Hill, a name memorializing U.S. conquest, became

1. Harriet "Hattie" Foster (*center*) stands with George O'Reilly (*right*) and another young man on a hill near the Missouri River at Fort Pierre, South Dakota, soon after 16 February 1913, the day they unearthed the lead plate the La Vérendrye brothers buried in 1743. South Dakota State Historical Society, South Dakota Digital Archives (2017-12-12-315).

forevermore La Vérendrye Hill, a monument to eighteenth-century French colonialism.[3]

The lightness of a day full of youthful rambling contrasts with the weightiness of the complex international colonial era in North America during which the La Vérendryes stood on a hill near an Arikara earth lodge village. No doubt, Hattie and her school friends were aware of the early French presence in North America, as their townlet took its name from French Missouri Fur Company traders. But it is unlikely they knew much about the La Vérendrye family's journeys into North America's grasslands nearly 170 years earlier, from territory by then located in Canada. Searching for the fabled Northwest Passage or—as the French called it, the Sea of the West—these French Canadians sought to secure a trade route to India for France.[4] King Louis XV hoped the La Vérendryes would lure the Assiniboine, Cree, Mandan, Arikara, and other Indigenous nations away from established trading patterns with the English at Hudson Bay to the north.

Most locals probably did not know of the 1743 report François La Vérendrye made to the governor-general of North America's New France, which explained, "On an eminence near the fort [an earth lodge] I deposited a lead tablet bearing the arms and inscription of the king and placed some stones in a pyramid.... I told the Indians [Arikaras led by Little Cherry], who had no knowledge of the lead tablet I had put in the ground, that I was setting up these stones in memory of the fact that we had been in their country." The French imperial intent was clear. La Vérendrye told the Arikaras "the Great Chief of the French wished all his children to live peaceably."[5] With a base in the Saint Lawrence River Valley and footholds in Illinois Country and Louisiana, acquisition of this vast northwestern interior territory might have wedged a French North American empire securely between those of England and Spain. By 1763, however, Great Britain had ousted France from the continent, thus burying, along with the lead plate, dreams of a French North American inland empire.[6]

In 1913 Fort Pierre's village residents found themselves in a "fever of excitement" over the discovery. Pioneers were trotted out to the site, their memories of Fort Pierre and "the hill" in the early days interrogated. Supposedly, the "oldest surviving inhabitant" remembered seeing a stone cairn on the hill. What happened to the pile of rocks marking the place where the La Vérendrye brothers buried the lead plate? A telephone call to the state historical society, conveniently located across the river at Pierre, finally revealed, in the words of local authority Charles DeLand, "to a moral certainty, the famous tablet of the La Vérendrye journal had at last been unearthed."[7]

For a moment North America's northern grasslands resonated nationally and internationally—in the United States, Canada, England, and France. Few had known of the exploits of the La Vérendrye family well.[8] Hattie Foster's discovery meant that part of the La Vérendrye route and the brothers' cultural exchange with an Arikara village now could be precisely placed. The director of the South Dakota State Historical Society, Doane Robinson, described the discovery in the pages of the Mississippi Valley Historical Association's *Proceedings* of 1914. Soon scholars began to conjecture the specific terrains traveled by the La Vérendryes and the probable Indigenous peoples they encountered. Local historians debated heatedly as they sought to place various routes in respective states; local experts wrote and debunked articles and erected and dismantled monuments as interpretations changed. The popular U.S. magazine the *Nation* emphasized the "romantic interest" of Hattie Foster's find and noted the route had "long vexed historians."[9]

DeLand, writing for the South Dakota society's biannual *Collections*, enthused, "What it means in the view of the people of the United States and to those of the Dominion of Canada cannot now be told. But that its resurrection after its long sleep *in the soil of the Northwest* will be hailed by all . . . citizens and subjects . . . from the Atlantic to the Pacific is certain." The Champlain Society of Toronto announced an edited collection of La Vérendrye reports with dual French-English translations.[10] Hattie's discovery became a landmark for her generation's understanding of North America's northern grasslands. The object served to remind residents of a *continental* northern grasslands without an international boundary and created new transnational connections as residents on both sides of the border worked together to reconstruct the La Vérendrye history.

Although members of North Dakota's state historical society took the occasion to inquire among Hidatsas and Mandans about the exact villages the father and son La Vérendryes visited near Bismarck—North Dakota's role in the story—published results of the inquiry do not mention the Arikaras. Yet by 1913 Arikaras lived with Hidatsas and Mandans on the Fort Berthold Reservation, located near Bismarck, some two hundred miles north of the Little Cherry village visited by the La Vérendrye brothers. Historically, Arikaras had lived near the Big Bend area of the Missouri and along the Bad and Cheyenne Rivers since the 1450s. Smallpox and cholera epidemics and conflict with Lakotas, however, pushed them steadily north and eventually into an alliance in 1862 with Hidatsas and Mandans. The directors of both Dakotas' historical societies exchanged letters on the subject but do not indicate benefit from Arikara knowledge.[11]

Hattie Foster's story is deeply telling for what it reveals about the complex ways individuals develop a sense of place. As the environmental historian Donald Worster claimed, "It is to *all* of the influ-

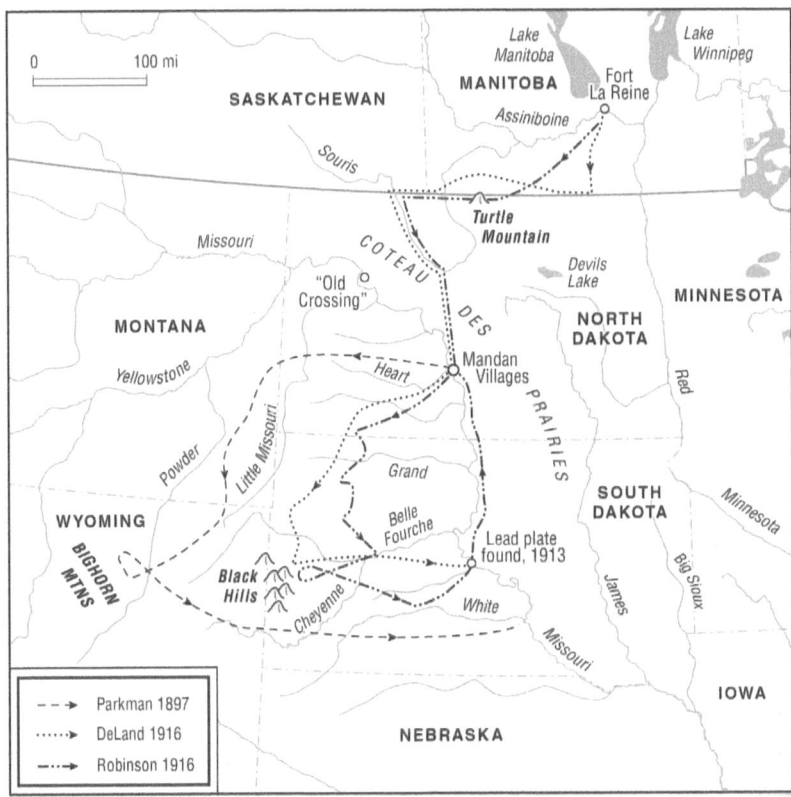

Map 3. Possible La Vérendrye routes on North America's northern grasslands. The account of François and Louis-Joseph La Vérendrye's 1742–43 journey is vague and uncertain. Francis Parkman concluded that the La Vérendrye brothers saw the Big Horn Mountains in Wyoming. South Dakotan Charles DeLand's 1914 route is considered to be the least reliable. The superintendent of the South Dakota State Historical Society, Doane Robinson, investigated more professionally to conclude that the brothers probably reached only the western modern Dakotas and the Black Hills. Experts agree only on the authenticity of the lead plate and that its 1913 unearthing means the brothers probably met with Little Cherry's Arikara band. Erin Greb Cartography; based on original in G. Smith, *Explorations*, 126.

ences of the land . . . that one must finally turn to understand the innermost history of the region."[12] Western historian Elliott West also once pointed to the West's "peculiar" physical settings as key to the "emotional and psychological dimensions of western history."[13] Young adolescents strolling across a land of hibernating flora lingering on a winter Sunday afternoon, hunting or perhaps chasing the area's prairie dogs and gophers: these activities on the grassed-over bluffs of the Missouri River suggest the tactile environmental experience common to children's play and the out-of-doors wanderings of young people in the era. Hattie Foster and her generation knew the northern grasslands well because their physical presence contributed to the shapes of those landscapes, which they perceived daily by sight, smell, touch, sound, and taste. The daily environmental encounter these children experienced constituted an informal sensuous education of place.[14] Children's experiences with the landscape, taken for granted as they reoccurred across the seasons, allowed them to grow invisible roots deep into complex historical soil: the roots of sense of place.

Hattie Foster's story also provides a clue to the cultural history of northern grasslands regional identity. In 1913 the La Vérendrye plate conveyed meaning, in the words of South Dakota lay-historian Charles DeLand, for "the soil of the Northwest." What the hill revealed that winter day conjures up some forgotten history of an older North American region—the Northwest—a label once applied widely to a *continental* northern grasslands space but which in 1913 referred to land long split between the United States and Canada. The first generations of settler-colonial society to grow up on the northern grasslands adopted many regional labels over time. Residents referred to the grasslands with historical language used by English, French, Canadian, and U.S. fur traders and by colonizers such as explorers and settlers. In the twentieth century residents on both sides of a border latched on to new terminology used by experts in agriculture, ecology, and archaeology. Uniquely national definitions of the same regional terms often worked to maintain the international border, but shared history and historical sources also gave Canadians and Americans a common intellectual foundation: the roots of regional identity.[15]

The stories of Hattie Foster's discovery and the La Vérendrye family's explorations evoke the major issues raised by *Grasslands Grown*, foremost among them, how the first generations born of settler-colonial society created modern regional cultures and senses of place from personal experiences. The surfacing of the long-buried "tablet" is an unusually striking example of the way history is recorded in the landscapes on which people live. The lead plate and place names show that Indigenous, French, and Canadian national histories simmered in the earth of the northern grasslands, threatening to challenge established boundaries of national thought, if not territory. By 1913 the intellectual and social cultures of settler society, General Harney and the U.S. nation, the Canadian La Vérendrye family and French colonialism, the Cree and Métis who guided the La Vérendryes to the Missouri River, and Little Cherry's band of Arikara *all* left cultural imprints on the Missouri River bluffs near Fort Pierre. Evidence from these cultures and many more northern plains Indigenous peoples might have risen—and may still rise—to the surface of the soil at any unexpected moment across the northern grasslands to spark commemoration of forgotten narratives.[16]

The La Vérendrye narrative also embodies the transition from an age of colonization on the northern grasslands, when European nations vied for control of North America's resources, to the era of settler colonialism, when new populations came to stay and root their own stories in the land.[17] By 1913 settler society had arrived everywhere on the northern grasslands, even the semiarid grasslands of the western Dakotas, eastern Montana, and southern Saskatchewan and Alberta.

The processes by which the transnational La Vérendrye narrative took shape suggest how the culture of settler colonialism strove to control narrative lines. When members of the State Historical Society of North Dakota made inquires to Hidatsas and Mandans about the La Vérendrye visits, they solicited Indigenous testimony on highly specific matters prompted by the records of the explorers instead of seeking to acquire Indigenous perspectives that might have provided larger historical insight or opened dialogue on modern concerns. Instead, the experts in the two Dakotas competed to place the La Vérendryes in their respective states and two men, who had old disagreements, rivaled as spokespeople for local Indigenous populations. Both argued vigorously for the value of Indigenous oral "testimony" but ended up burying such voices. None of the commentators considered the idea that Indigenous peoples might not volunteer all the information they knew.[18]

The public celebratory narrative also omitted the story of how one of the young boys quickly took "possession" of the plate from Hattie Foster and how his father kept the plate "in hiding" until its monetary value could be ascertained. The young man vied with Foster, who claimed ownership "by right of the discovery," and with the village, which claimed right by "ownership of the soil." Three years later, in March 1916, the young man's father relinquished any legal claim in the object for $500. A now-married Hattie Foster Moss did the same in February 1917, for $200. The state legislature refused to pass an appropriation to buy the lead plate, so the state historical society fund-raised among its members for the acquisition.[19] The ownership battle perhaps serves as a metaphor for the larger culture reorganizing the grasslands into private property: a settler-colonial commercial agricultural order.

Settler society's creation of senses of place and regions forms another stage in the centuries-long process of the expropriation of North American Indigenous land and expresses claims to cultural ownership of northern grasslands space. The grasslands, an environment itself constantly changing by deep-time geologic and atmospheric processes, also responds to short-term shifts in land use driven by cultural exchange. The physical boundaries and meanings of places and regions are always in motion, by turns intertwining and breaking away with multiple adjacent definitions espoused by diverse cultures. Grasslands-grown claims to space emerged in immediate postpioneer years, made by inheriting generations of "settler society" bound to stay on the grasslands or determined to explain their own relationship to a place they embraced and felt rooted to or profoundly affected by and yet left.

The continent's northern grasslands—one ecological region divided by two modern nation-states—provide a unique venue for assessing the interplay between environments and the cultures that create regions and places. Settler-society grasslands' experiences in Canada and the United States were not identical, nor one derivative of the other, but still the two countries became entwined through sharing common *northern* and *grasslands* experiences.

New patterns of settlement emerge from taking a continental view of northern grasslands space. From this view settler colonials from Canada and the United States moved into the northern grasslands from the outer borders of the region in a circular fashion into its center. Canada and the United States shared timings of settlement and similarities in climate that distinguished the northern grasslands of the two nations together from the central and southern continental grasslands located only in the United States.[20] Yet these northern grasslands have played different regional roles in the histories of Canada and the United States, providing settler colonials some different foundations for modern identities. People living on the northern grasslands or far off from the continental environment in national capitals on each side of the international boundary imagined the place differently. The Northern Great Plains states accrued little power within the nation, while, eventually, the Prairie Provinces wielded relatively considerable national power. Indeed, perhaps the Northern Great Plains states are the most Canadian-like in their relationship to the larger United States: the place takes up little consciousness in the minds of most Americans. But long-standing habits of unconscious neglect among Americans, according to historian John Herd Thompson, and national defensiveness in Canadians and the general difficulty of transnational analysis, according to Thomas D. Isern and R. Bruce Shepard, have kept many historians of the northern grasslands in their respective nations. Nationalist historiographies have obscured shared *continental* experiences rooted in similar historical climates and natural environments central to regional experience in both nations.[21]

Grasslands Grown asks rather than assumes where the people in this space at this particular time thought they lived and what they perceived about the environmental qualities they found. Places and regions are human constructions in the same way environmental historian Richard White has explained "Nature" to be "at once a cultural construct and a set of actual things outside of us and not fully contained by our constructions."[22] Indeed, no individual in this study used the label "northern grasslands" or referred generally to "North America's northern grasslands." Precisely because these individuals did not commonly use "northern grasslands" as a regional label during

Introduction 9

this period (although they would have understood its meaning immediately), the phrase allows the spatial, geographic, and environmental terms residents did use to appear, disappear, and move around free of the weight of present-day scholarly regional boundaries.[23] North America's northern grasslands serve here as both a *frame* for the region and as the main regional *question*, with the answers to the latter continually threatening to dissolve the former. The widely dispersed locations of the people studied suggest how individuals interacted with specific grasslands microenvironments to create senses of place but also allow for analysis of how each intellectually linked local life to the continent's northern grasslands as a whole to form geographic regional identities. Individuals and societies move through space always informed by multiple geographic scales of place. The selected body of individuals discussed in depth over broad spatial parameters suggests patterns of settler-colonial experience over generations and archetypical interactions with northern grasslands environments limited by the contours of the particular lives explored.

The first generation of individuals born or raised on North America's northern grasslands in settler societies in the United States and Canada further entrenched their parents' North American land claims. The concept of "generation" is employed broadly, as a generation actually separates the oldest and the youngest due to the graduated settlement of distinct areas within the northern grasslands from the 1860s to the 1910s. All the individuals explored represent the first generations of U.S. and Canadian settler-colonial societies to experience childhood and adolescence in particular locations within the transnational northern grasslands.[24] Recognition of these individuals as "settler colonials" helps to distinguish this generation from the many generations born to diverse Indigenous peoples—such as Lakotas, Dakotas, Bloods, Piegans, Arikaras, Mandans, and Crees—on the northern grasslands by the time "newcomer settlers" arrived.[25] The first resident-raised generations of settler-colonial society adopted regional identities and formed senses of place as a result of privilege ensuing from their parents' settler-colonial efforts.

The particular collection of transnational northern grasslands residents examined in this book represent children of white and

Black Americans and Canadians or of English, Icelandic, Norwegian, Swedish, and German immigrants. Most had more education than average for their generation, though they often worked very hard to get it. Many married, while others remained single or married later in life, especially women. Generally, these individuals came to enjoy middle-class lives. They established careers in agriculture, education, journalism, literature, politics, business, science, and art. Many gained positions of power within newly emerging institutions promoting ideas of place and regional meaning, such as historical societies, museums, colleges and universities, government, and newspaper agencies. These institutions were part of newly emerging settler-colonial infrastructures. Most were not well known nationally, but some individuals achieved recognition through their writings and advocacy within their state or province or particular professional or ethnic communities. Finally, these individuals, each investigated separately, turned out very often to have had varied contact with one another. This was as true *across* the international border as *within* Canada and the United States. They showed up at the same events. They corresponded. They frequently read the same historical literature and eventually one another's books and articles.

Grasslands Grown employs an explicitly postsettlement "regional" framework. The historian Elliott West once labeled regionalism "one of the most formidable challenges to confront western historians" and speculated that the people of North America's western settler societies who grew up in the immediate postconquest years might hold keys to understanding ongoing regional outlooks and cultural limitations.[26] Nevertheless, the tendency of scholarship on the North American West has been to challenge western myths rather than analyze how such myths played out in the lives of generations coming to their own terms with real western places.[27] Myths and embedded ideas concerning race, civilization, and land remained alive in the culture that shaped modern Grasslands West residents. The members of the settler-colonial generations studied here are important because they developed more realistic relationships with northern grasslands spaces and stayed or left; some remained associated with the place to advance interests of their nations. Their thoughts about the region influenced the entire twentieth century.

The postpioneer, but first grasslands-raised, generations of settler society possessed, as core experiences, contact with both native prairie and plains grasslands habitats and commercial agricultural fields and pastures. Children came to know the northern grasslands at a stage of life when physical stimuli proved especially powerful. Children's bodies soaked up the sights, sounds, smells, textures, and tastes of wild grasses, wildflowers, wild animals, and the tamed grasses of modern grain agriculture. These children wielded experiences and sensuous feelings into patterns of cultural expression, which followed them into adulthood, even as memory, adolescence, and subsequent experiences reshaped them. As the United States and Canada removed Indigenous generational counterparts from their homelands to boarding schools in an attempt to sever them from grasslands environments, these young generations of settler society gathered up sensuous environmental experiences they ultimately used to make the case for their own "indigeneity" to the northern grasslands.[28] These senses of place and regional identities on one level spoke to sincere personal attachments to grasslands spaces, but on another level they functioned to proclaim the successful transfer of the northern grasslands from Indigenous "Indian Country" to settler-society nations on the cultural plane of region.

A "grasslands-grown" status proves key to the importance of this generation's construction of place and region. Only this generation of many subsequent generations of settler society grew up in active association with *native* ecological grasslands habitats in ways that shaped their sensuous worldview *before* such habitats had been largely transformed by modern commercial agriculture and *before* the ways of industrial agriculture began to gradually filter corporal interactions with the land. However, the ecology of this interior continental space underwent major changes during their lifetimes. This generation participated in an environmental reality shaped by the long capitalist agricultural transformation of the northern grasslands. In contrast, succeeding generations of settler society had the texts and oral tales of only the first grasslands-grown generations to turn to for information that connected them, their societies, and cultures to northern grasslands ecological landscapes gone or supremely altered by the middle of the twentieth century.[29]

This generation of settler society created patterns of writing, language, and thought about the northern grasslands that would become important resources for subsequent generations of settler society more embedded in commercial agricultural landscapes. The northern grasslands in the United States and Canada saw some of the last nation-state–sponsored settler colonialism on the North American continent barely completed by the advent of a modern twentieth-century literary and artistic regionalist cultural movement. Modern regionalism is conventionally portrayed as broad cultural responses to industrialization, homogenization, and mass consumer culture in the 1920s and 1930s. *Grasslands Grown* suggests an element of this cultural regionalism also might have reflected another stage in the transfer of North American territory away from Indigenous hands to settler-society nations.[30]

The concept of intellectually carving the continent into cultural geographic regions is also one of settler society. The practice is a corollary to, but more than, the power implied in the everyday and official practices of (re)naming landmarks and geography by new national parameters. Regionalism in this sense at this place and time constituted a transformation of personal cultural and physical and psychological sensuous experiences with specific northern grasslands environments into intellectual and emotional geographic possessions. Expressions of experience reflected specific land claimed by individuals and the United States and Canada, but they also floated free of the land to proclaim cultural ownership to reading and traveling people everywhere.

In eight chapters *Grasslands Grown* explores regional identity and sense of place on North America's northern grasslands as both developed through settler-colonial generations and over the life span of core individuals. Chapter 1 introduces family contexts. It traces comparative historical background and recounts general treaty and land policies important to understanding the context of the late nineteenth and early twentieth centuries into which these settler generations were born. The common timing of the advent of settler colonialism, similar patterns of movement, and comparable infrastructures of settlement suggest why it makes sense historically to look at the northern grasslands as a continental North American region.

The next three chapters explore childhood and adolescent experiences of the northern grasslands environment with an emphasis on bodily immersion. Chapter 2 argues that domestic and wild animals often introduced children to grasslands ecology, and animal motion provided a historical tempo for this generation's experience of place and space. Historical big-game animals young people learned about primarily through story also contributed to how they imagined the northern grasslands. Chapter 3 examines particular microenvironments with which children formed close relationships, especially woods, waters, rocks, snow, native grasses, and commercial grains. Children's attachment to many of these particular features validated Indigenous understandings of the space at the same time they worked to dispossess them by reframing selected elements of the environment Indigenous peoples also held culturally dear. Chapters 2 and 3 together argue children's physical sensuous experiences during a stage of childhood development, as this historical moment shaped modern expressions of place still associated with the space. Chapter 4 follows adolescents as they expanded their geographic and environmental understandings beyond local attachments. Systems of regional connection began to emerge in part as the result of travel inside and outside the northern grasslands and because of the new intellectual concepts and skills individuals gained through education and wider life experiences.

A second trio of chapters examine adult relationships, activities, and careers as they related to place or regional questions. Chapter 5 investigates settler society–Indigenous race relations by describing a continuum of relationships, from denial to seemingly friendly, if not fully integrated, encounters between settler-society individuals and specific Indigenous individuals and nations, primarily from the perspective of settlers. Environmental habitat proved central to the potential for positive interactions. Chapter 6 examines aesthetic, social, and cultural experiences through creative literature and art. Aesthetic expressions sought to create a sense of place by restorying the northern grasslands with settler society at the center of the narrative. Indeed, the grasslands-grown generation—not their parents—wrote many of the family "pioneer origin" stories that inform chapter 1. Chapter 7 examines the ways individuals continued to interact with the land, especially under ongoing development of commercial agriculture and the seemingly contradictory impulses of a growing twentieth-century conservation ethic. The 1920s and 1930s brought new sensuous experiences in this generation's prime of life and added depth to the ways individuals understood the grasslands. Among those who "stayed" and those who "quitted," settler-colonial agriculture began to more clearly reference unique atmospheric and ecological grasslands qualities. Preservation of selected, sometimes reconstructed, habitats formed on-the-ground counterparts to what other settler-society grasslands-grown individuals in the generations tried to capture through literature, history, art, and memoir.

Chapter 8 concludes with an exploration of the currency of cultural geographic labels used by settler society's residents. Over the lifespans of this generation, the entire expansive northern grasslands moved in the regional imaginations of most people, from identification with a transnational Northwest or West to the Prairie Provinces or Prairie West in Canada, and the Northern Great Plains states and the West and Middle West in the United States. New regional lines came to divide the grasslands: the international boundary (the forty-ninth parallel) between the United States and Canada and lines of aridity (a line of longitude near the ninety-eighth or hundredth meridian and a triangle with the international border as its base). These lines spoke to the commercial agriculture key to settler society's plans for incorporation of the northern grasslands into the United States and Canada. The development of regional identities and senses of place in the grasslands-grown generations of settler society, however, began when their parents decided to immigrate to North America's prairies and plains.

1

Parents' Choice

Taking Root on the Northern Grasslands

"I think I am fairly entitled to claim that I was born to both printing and pioneering," boasted one-time *Moose Jaw Herald* employee Effie Laurie Storer in 1943. In 1907 Storer and two other "pioneer newspaper women of Saskatchewan" made a compact to spend their retirement writing about the province. This conversation came back to Storer on the day of the funeral of the second of the three women to die with "her book unfinished." She thought to herself, "I, too, have delayed." A rough-hewn draft exists, but Storer's life story never saw publication. The awkward, troubled manuscript told a "simple tale of the pioneer when I was young," but who was the pioneer, parent or daughter? "My Story," she explained, "after much re-writing emerged as 'The Queen's Printer,'" a narrative framed in her father's life. In 1878 her father began publishing the *Saskatchewan Herald*, the first newspaper in Canada's North-West Territories. In chapters placed throughout, Effie tucked in her life story. Effie Laurie Storer's struggle to tell her story and her emphasis on "pioneer" parents she idolized as paragons of white English "civilization" suggests a common generational impulse in the representation of growing up in settler society on North America's northern grasslands.[1]

The charismatic Republican senator from South Dakota, Peter Norbeck, after backing the successful 1936 reelection of the Democrat president Franklin Roosevelt, also "felt the need of a more complete record of the Norbeck family." A former South Dakota governor, Norbeck was famous for his work developing a state park in the Black Hills and finding federal funding for the then unfinished presidential busts carved into Mount Rushmore. Born in 1870 on a southeastern Dakota Territory homestead, he wrote from a sickbed until a few weeks before his death. His brother George finished the manuscript. The family history ends with the death of their Swedish Lutheran preacher father. Almost every chapter written by Peter either starts or ends with the patriarch. Even the chapter on "The First Born" (Peter) mentions his father in every paragraph, save one on his mother. Many Dakotans urged Peter to write an autobiography—and George a biography of Peter—but both brothers felt "these writings should deal primarily with our parents." Still, Peter interspersed memories of youth on his parents' homestead and George, the youngest, did the same for the new Dakota farm the family moved to in 1886.[2]

Northern grasslands residents such as Storer and Norbeck dutifully told family "pioneer origin" stories. Such narratives became part of this generation's claim to grasslands space. Family migration stories, rooted in oral history, styled by colloquial speech, and frequently written by the children of the settler-colonial movement's decision makers, formed one of the most widely shared creative expressions of the first setter-society generations to grow to adulthood on the northern grasslands. The continually circulating pioneer origin narrative formed an atmospheric pressure that asserted settler-society ownership of the region on the plane of culture. After their parents had used legal methods through homestead and purchase laws to create private property, this generation began storying their families into the landscape: two settler-colonial versions of rooting into the land that worked to displace Indigenous populations.[3]

Meaningful in their own right, the pioneer origin narratives also handily relate the diverse local places individuals grew up. The narratives contain enough cultural "truth"—impressions and feelings of families—to sketch out in this chapter the dates, details, and major players in the family migration. This chapter begins with a section on resident Indigenous peoples and their early formal negotiations and conflicts with the United States and Canada over grasslands homelands. Settler society's children knew of such affairs of state through the cultural air, though such negotiations and conflicts do not usually appear as parts of the pioneer-migration tale. The settler-colonial process encouraged narrative dissemblance within settler society. A second section on the agricultural potential of the region reviews international assessments of grasslands soil and climate from the 1850s to the 1870s, as both countries geared up for the settlement phase of this land's incorporation into their respective nations.

The last three sections sketch three general phases, between the 1860s and the 1910s, of transnational U.S. and Canadian settler-colonial migration, including discussions of shifting land law and Indigenous policy. Each section corresponds to when the children of the pioneers, settlers, and homesteaders, respectively, arrived or were born on the northern grasslands. Transnational northern grasslands settlement moved from an outer arc of more luxuriant grasses to the east, north, and west into mixed-grass interior spaces and then into the region's semiarid northwestern center. These three sections also suggest the general ways U.S. and Canadian development of the northern grasslands influenced and related to one another. Together the descriptions reveal the development of settler society on North America's northern grasslands as truly a transnational movement, if only for the long settler-colonial moment and its generational aftermath and if not always culturally synchronous or entirely cooperative.

The Geopolitical Importance of the Northern Grasslands

Long before the advent of settler colonialism, diverse Indigenous nations inhabited and controlled large expanses of the northern grasslands. All grasslands-grown generations of settler society stood on Indigenous ground—actually and figuratively—even when some of them never achieved full realization of how their presence supported international colonialism. In the middle of the nineteenth century, Sioux nations lived throughout the land that became modern western Minnesota, North Dakota, South Dakota, and Montana. The Sisseton, Wahpeton, Medawkanton, and Wahpekute Dakotas lived in a parkland-transition area between continental woodlands on the east, and the Yankton and Yanktonais were on the grasslands east of the Missouri River.[4] Most Lakotas (Brulé, Oglala, Miniconjou, Hunkpapa, Blackfeet, Two Kettle, and Sans Arc) dwelled west of the Missouri River in modern South Dakota and parts of North Dakota and ranged well west into Montana and south into Nebraska.

The agricultural Arikara, Mandan, and Hidatsa village nations long occupied the banks and bottomlands of the upper Missouri River and eventually confederated in a village in modern central North Dakota. Ojibwe nations lived in today's northwestern Minnesota and at one time in the Red River Valley connecting modern Minnesota, North Dakota, and Manitoba. Plains Crees and the Assiniboines of the future Canada lived out on the grasslands west of the northern Red River Valley, while Woods Crees resided north of the northern parklands between the continent's northernmost grasslands and broadleaf forest. The Blackfeet (United States) and the Blackfoot Confederacy (Canada)—including the Blackfoot (Siksikas), Piegan, and Blood Nations—lived east of the Rocky Mountains on land that became modern southern Alberta and northern Montana.[5] These and additional Indigenous peoples claimed territory and ancestral homelands throughout North America's northern grasslands at the advent of U.S. and Canadian settler colonialism.

Indigenous nations of the northern grasslands had well-accepted territorial homelands by the time U.S. and Canadian treaty processes aimed at dispossessing them began. The U.S. 1851 Fort Laramie Treaty accepted specific territorial claims made by Indigenous peoples.[6] In Canada the long operations of fur trade within the huge corporate domain of the Hudson's Bay Company and the Northwestern Territories resulted in a general acceptance of territorial boundaries defined by Indigenous peoples.[7] The decline of the continent's bison population and the fur trade and the ensuing need to shift economies proved the most important factor in the willingness of Indigenous peoples to consider land cessions with agents of the United States and Canada.

Despite some significant differences, as scholar Roger L. Nichols has argued, starting in the 1860s, with regard to "Indian" relations in the United States and Canada, "the actions of the two countries became more alike than at any previous time."[8] Both countries for different reasons desired a firm hold on their presumed shares of the northern grasslands, in part, as expressions of national identity. Canada desired control of the northern grasslands north of the forty-ninth parallel to create a transcontinental nation. For the United

States, control of the northern grasslands would complete its transcontinental hold and assert national power over resistant Indigenous nations, especially Lakotas and Blackfeet.

A series of settler-Indigenous conflicts in the 1850s and 1860s led the United States to shine a rare light of national attention on the northern grasslands. A incident on the Overland Trail grew into a major conflict between Lakotas and the U.S. military from 1854 to 1856 and established the first military forts well on northern grasslands, first at Fort Pierre in modern central South Dakota, then at Fort Randall in northeastern Nebraska. Drought, late treaty annuities, hunger, and indifferent U.S. bureaucrats led to the U.S.-Dakota War between some individuals of the Sisseton, Wahpeton, Medawkanton, and Wahpekute Dakotas and settler Minnesotans in 1862; hundreds of settlers died, and it ended with the largest mass hanging in U.S. history, when, a day after Christmas, crowds watched thirty-eight Dakotas hang. Increasing conflict between settlers and Indigenous peoples led to the Colorado militia massacre of a peaceful Cheyenne village at Sand Creek in 1864. The creation of the Bozeman Trail by miners headed to Montana across Lakota land led, from 1866 to 1868, to a successful defense against encroachment by U.S. military forts. A U.S. congressional commission tasked with studying the escalation of settler-Indigenous conflict concluded "most hostilities resulted from white encroachments or provocations." Phrased another way, by historian Jill St. Germain, the "long litany of violence on the plains was traced in every instance to white hands, often those of the military, but primarily of ordinary people, the pioneers."[9] These violent episodes encircled the eastern, western, and southern boundaries of the northern grasslands in the United States.

Such actions suggest implicitly the gradual growth of an informal northern "Indian Territory" on the northern grasslands of the United States. St. Germain has argued that U.S. officials in the mid-1860s "very deliberately" viewed spaces on the map north and south of Nebraska and Kansas as "empty" places—that is, without agricultural settlements—for the "concentration" of Indigenous nations to undergo "acculturation and assimilation."[10] Officials never issued a formal policy comparable to the land set aside for Indigenous peoples on the southern grasslands in modern Oklahoma, but official actions appear to have made it so—at least temporarily.[11] Indeed, one army officer who toured a parched Dakota Territory in 1866 suggested the U.S. Congress should "dissolve Dakota Territory" and turn the land into reservations.[12] In the aftermath of the 1862 U.S.-Dakota War, the U.S. Senate expelled Dakotas living on reservations fronting the Minnesota River with an act that stipulated the president choose a new place for them "outside of the limits of any state."[13] The sparsely settled Dakota Territory proved convenient, and Congress established Crow Creek Reservation on the east bank of the Missouri River in modern central South Dakota. In 1867, noting the usefulness of the Wahpetons and Sissetons as a "buffer between the white settlements and the wilder Indians to the west," the U.S. Congress authorized two Dakota reservations in eastern Dakota Territory.[14]

The establishment of the thirty-one-million-acre Great Sioux Reservation in modern western South Dakota for the "absolute and undisturbed use and occupation" by the many Lakota divisions and some Yanktonais by the terms of the Fort Laramie Treaty of 1868 also suggests the United States inched toward establishing a northern reservation for Indigenous peoples. An 1873 presidential executive order that established a twenty-six-million-acre Great Northern Reservation in the northern third of modern Montana for the Blackfeet, Gros Ventre, and River Crows furthered a de facto ad hoc northern Indigenous territory.[15] The United States' immediate interest in the northern grasslands seemed to be a containment of what leaders perceived as Indigenous threats to travelers and settlers moving elsewhere throughout the West.

The economic recession begun in 1873, and the 1874 confirmation of gold in the Black Hills began to change U.S. opinion about the value of its claim to the continent's northern grasslands. Then, as the United States celebrated its centennial in 1876, new headlines announced the decisive military defeat of Gen. George A. Custer and his Seventh Cavalry Company by Lakotas, Yanktonais, and Cheyennes in Montana Territory at the Battle of Greasy Grass, or, in the words of settler society, the Battle of the Little Big Horn. In retaliation the United States forced the Agreement of 1877 (to be found unconstitutional in 1980) on food-insecure Lakota bands. Lakotas had the choice of losing either rations and annuities promised by prior treaties or nine million acres of the Great Sioux Reservation, constituting all land west of the 103rd meridian, including the Black Hills.[16] Gold and national reputation caused the United States to seize control of a space theretofore found questionable. Few challenged the transcontinental status of the United States, but tight control of the northern grasslands solidified its transcontinental West in the wake of humiliating military defeats to Lakotas and Cheyennes.

Canada hoped to ensure the broad U.S. West would never include *all* of the continent's northern grasslands. Incorporation of the northern grasslands into Canada would create a transcontinental nation to match that of the United States. The idea of establishing an Indian Territory, or a Great Reserve, in Canada's Grasslands West seems never to have been considered. The idea of incorporating the land Britons and Canadians knew as Hudson's Bay Company (HBC) territory, or Rupert's Land, into a larger Canadian nation emerged in the 1850s with proconfederation advocates pushing for further independence from Great Britain. Many saw the acquisition of the resource-rich continental grasslands as key to confederation. With a Precambrian rock shield and northern climate, Canada had less access to potentially arable land than the United States. The British North American Act, which established the new Dominion of Canada in 1867, made special provision to ensure the eventual sale of HBC corporate land to Canada. This transfer happened in 1869. Moreover, in 1871, Canada promised British Columbia a railway to connect the province through the northern grasslands to the nation's east. The first National Policy of Canada aimed to bring settler colonialism based on commercial agriculture to the northern grasslands before the United States lassoed the territory in some capacity, whether simply for trade or, potentially as some feared, political incorporation as new states.[17]

The 1867 British North American Act also transferred responsibility of "Indians, and Lands reserved for the Indians" from the British Crown to dominion jurisdiction. Further, the HBC purchase agreement required Canada to extinguish Indigenous land titles. The sale produced a major crisis. Generations of mixed-race Indigenous

French Métis and Scottish Indigenous "country-born" peoples, many of them retired HBC employees, lived at the Red River Colony (in modern Manitoba) with only "customary" rights to the land. After 1859 a small but significant migration of English-speaking Protestant Ontarians migrated to the Red River Colony in anticipation of Canadian confederation. Many from these diverse groups in the Red River community rebelled under the French Catholic Métis leader Louis Riel over annexation without representation, with shifting levels of popular support. In response—the story is much longer—the dominion created a tiny province called Manitoba with parliamentary representation in Ottawa but without control of its public lands and natural resources. The Métis and country-born populations also won federal recognition of their land titles and a 1.4-million-acre set-aside to provided future land grants for generations to come. The Manitoba Act of 1870, however, did little to "extinguish" Indigenous rights in the new province, nor certainly in the rest of the former HBC territory, which became the North-West Territories to be administered by Ottawa. As Plains Cree chief Sweetgrass said after he heard about the transfer of HBC land to Canada, "We heard our lands were sold and we did not like it."[18]

Canada's grasslands remained largely isolated from the rush of settlers that caused steady conflict along the main U.S. approaches to the area. Nevertheless, Indigenous nations in Canada also resisted the encroachments of settler society. When negotiations for Treaty 1 commenced in 1870, however, the lieutenant governor of Manitoba made it clear "settlement was bound to occur." From 1871 to 1877 Canada signed a series of what Canadians have since called the Numbered Treaties with Indigenous peoples, including Ojibwes, Crees, Assiniboines, and nations of the Blackfoot Confederacy (Piegans, Bloods, and Siksikas) who lived on the northern grasslands and into the northern parklands. Treaty 3, for example, ceded over thirty-five million acres; Treaty 5 some sixty-four million acres; and Treaty 6 almost seventy-seven million acres. After Treaty 7 in 1877, Canada secured what it held to be the title to most grasslands (and more) north of the border.[19]

Canada's treaty provisions reflect the 1870s context. By then the United States had treated with Indigenous peoples on the northern grasslands for two decades. While in the 1850s and 1860s Lakotas believed treaties they signed might preserve wild game and bison, by the middle of the 1870s, many Indigenous elders in Canada (as well as in the United States) understood diminishing bison herds meant the collapse of their economy and way of life. Indigenous peoples in Canada seemed from the beginning to view treaty making as opportunities to establish working relationships with Canada, according to J. R. Miller, "that would guarantee them assistance in adjusting to the new order in the west." Similarly, the few Lakota leaders who signed the U.S. Agreement of 1877 did so, according to Jeffrey Ostler, because they "had reached the painful conclusion that if they did not give up the Black Hills, the government would carry out its threats to withdraw rations and they would perish."[20]

The signing of Treaty 7 with the Blackfoot Confederacy in 1877 suggests Canada's fledgling sense of sovereignty with regard to the international boundary on the northern grasslands, newly marked in 1873–74. While most Indigenous peoples of Canada's grasslands pressed for treaties, the Blackfoot Confederacy waited for Canadian officials to approach them. The latter worried the Blackfoot Confederacy might form an alliance with Lakotas, who by the thousands (after defeating Custer in 1876) had crossed the international boundary into Canada's sovereign space. "Such an alliance," according to St. Germain, might have led to a "real war" in Canada's "sparsely settled West." The young Canadian confederation little desired to test its national defenses. Moreover, the United States might violate Canada's sovereignty in pursuit of Lakotas north of the international boundary.[21] By the mid-1870s the northern grasslands for different reasons had become important to national identity in the United States and Canada.

The Agricultural Potential of Northern Grasslands

Any expansion of colonization by the United States or Canada on the northern grasslands meant reassessment of its economic value. Starting in the 1850s, a new generation of explorers and scientists began to evaluate the area's agricultural potential. The relative treelessness of the continent's grasslands had long confounded observers. Zebulon Pike's

1810 report to the United States on the southern grasslands predicted "these vast plains . . . may become in time equally celebrated as the sandy deserts of Africa." He noted "various places . . . on which not a speck of vegetable matter existed." The report of Maj. Steven Long's 1820 expedition inscribed "Great American Desert" on a map of his explorations on the southern grasslands; his geographer described the land as "almost wholly unfit for cultivation." Still, Pike had noted "Innumerable Herds of Buffaloes," and Long saw that the Indigenous economy rested on the "quest of game."[22] Both observations suggested productive land: big animals in large numbers required more than sterile sand. But if it was not an agricultural garden or a true desert, what was the real resource value of grasslands?

In the United States one of the first assessments of the continent's northern grasslands came from Lieutenant Gouverneur Kemble Warren, who traveled in 1856 and 1857 from Fort Pierre in modern central South Dakota to the Black Hills. He noted geologic connections between the "great mountain belt" and the Black Hills, the Bears Paw Mountains, the "Cyprus mountains, &c., in the British possessions" and predicted "continuous settlements cannot be made . . . west of the 97th meridian, both on account of the unfavorable climate and want of fertility in the soil."[23] The U.S. geologist Ferdinand V. Hayden, who had collected fossils in the badlands of Dakota in 1853 and accompanied Warren, offered more positive sentiments after conducting a survey of Nebraska's geology in the early 1870s. He lent support to the questionable idea: "with cultivation and the planting of trees on the plains would come increased rainfall." Although Hayden later suffered "scientific embarrassment" for his prosettlement boosterism, in an official 1872 U.S. government report, he suggested the Great American Desert "becomes narrower and narrower" with settlement.[24]

North of the border, in 1857, Britain and Canada funded two expeditions, the first led by Capt. John Palliser, a member of the Royal Geographical Society, and the second by University of Toronto professor and scientist Henry Youle Hind. Palliser's and Hind's reports drew an uncertain line around an "arid plains," eventually called Palliser's Triangle. Although today the area is considered to be the rough equivalent of modern southwestern Saskatchewan and southeastern Alberta, the report of 1857 actually outlined a much larger area, expanding, according to one Canadian historian, to an "irregular pentagon." Neither explorer thought that this, in Hind's words, "vast treeless region" would support agriculture, but their reports described a "fertile" grasslands "belt" that rose in a "giant arc from the American border at Red River northwest to the forks of the Saskatchewan [River] and from there along the North Saskatchewan to the Rocky Mountains," where it "turned southward" along the foothills to the international border. Hind and Palliser may have relied in part on new climate theory based on isothermal temperature lines that uncoupled the connection between climate and latitude. Isothermal lines suggested the continental northwest to be warmer than latitude alone implied.[25]

The Canadian geologist George Dawson, working with the 1873–74 International North American Boundary Commission, also saw grasslands suitable at least for "stock farming." Indeed, by 1877 dominion land surveyors had measured and assessed land beyond the so-called fertile belt and observed more "first class agricultural land" than before thought to exist. As the decade ended, the botanist John Macoun, under the auspices of the dominion government, argued the soil and the grasses of the "arid plains" signaled fertility, not desert. Macoun drew on new theories concerning "patterns of wind and rain." As both eastern and western winds blew into the center of the continent, they encountered high temperatures issuing from the southern grasslands, which supposedly stopped rainfall and ultimately pushed warm air north, where clouds would release their rain. The cutoff line for the "wind theory" lay somewhere in modern Nebraska, above the fortieth parallel (the international boundary lies at the forty-ninth parallel). As with Hayden's tacit approval of the rain-follows-the-plow idea, the rain-rides-on-the-wind theory had the stamp of authority of Canada's Department of Agriculture, which printed excerpts of the theorist that influenced Macoun in immigrant brochures.[26]

Reputable scientists contradicted these "aberrant" theories and the boosterism behind pseudoscientific ideas. Roscoe Pound, a botanist and early student of grasslands ecology, called one of the experts Hayden relied on, a biology professor from the University of

Nebraska, a "first class charlatan." Hayden's contemporary, the U.S. geologist John Wesley Powell, officially asserted in an 1877 report and in testimony before the U.S. Congress that agriculture unaided by irrigation would be impossible beyond the hundredth meridian. He proposed a drastically different organization of land, combining huge pastures (2,560 acres) and irrigated riverside homesteads (80 acres) as the ideal setup for development of arid lands, but the U.S. Congress rebuffed him. Even Henry Youle Hind publicly countered Macoun's exaggerated portrayal of the grasslands, accusing him of "falsehood and fraud."[27]

The contradictory information about the agricultural potential of the grasslands suggests the uncertain state of the science of the grasslands at the advent of settler colonialism, especially when considered from the average settler's ability to assess the scientific underpinnings of claims made by states, provinces, and U.S. railroad and Canadian railway companies promoting immigration. The historian David M. Emmons has argued the "ready willingness of the prospective immigrant to believe" such theories kept them alive and circulating.[28] If scientific men could be led astray by enthusiasm for agriculture, how much more convincing might such promotion be to hopeful settlers who had little experience with North America's northern grasslands?

Transnational Origins of Settler Colonialism, 1862–78

Nodes of settler society developed first along both the eastern and western edges of the transnational northern grasslands. At the same time as both U.S. and Canadian governments sponsored exploratory land assessments and treaty negotiations, transnational travel and exchange strengthened the near-simultaneous advance of agricultural settler societies. Canada's push to settle its Grasslands West encouraged settler-colonial development in Dakota Territory and Minnesota in ways disconnected to previous patterns of westward expansion in the United States centered on the Overland Trail. In short, Canada pulled U.S. settlement northward. Similarly, the population growth resulting from mineral rushes in the Rocky Mountains in modern Montana led to what Canadian historian Gerald Friesen called "the American origins of . . . [the Alberta] district" north of the forty-ninth parallel.[29] Transnational north-south corridors of travel and exchange, with roots in long-established fur-trade society, worked to build and bind small new settler populations across the international border during the 1860s and 1870s.

In the eastern northern grasslands, since the 1820s, settlers from a slow-growing Scottish colony, sponsored by the Earl of Selkirk and retired Hudson's Bay Company employees living near modern Winnipeg, forged trade routes to Saint Paul, Minnesota. By the early 1850s traffic between the two cities bore regular mail delivery, and by 1859 transnational traffic funded steamboat service on the Red River of the north. By 1871 a stagecoach operated. A hulking inaccessible rock shield that separated eastern and western Canada forced most settlers migrating from eastern Canada to travel first through the United States into Minnesota and then north into Manitoba, until at least the mid-1880s. As early as 1857, investors in Saint Paul and Minneapolis sent colonists to develop southeastern Dakota Territory, thus also drawing the grasslands of the Big Sioux River Valley into the same north-south settlement trajectory. Immigrants moved north from Iowa and Nebraska. In 1873 railroads reached Bismarck and Yankton in Dakota Territory but then stalled to remain solitary isolated lines. By 1878, however, the Manitoban (the Saint Paul, Minneapolis, and Manitoba) rail line connected with the Pembina Branch of Canadian Pacific Railway and ensured permanent travel between the gateway cities of Winnipeg and Saint Paul.[30]

In the western northern grasslands, gold and silver strikes in Montana increased steamship service on the Missouri River starting in 1862. Regular steamboat traffic in goods and passengers from Saint Louis and Omaha into the northern grasslands portal of Sioux City, Iowa—continuing on the Missouri through Vermillion, Yankton, and Bismarck in Dakota Territory—and on to Fort Benton, Montana, encouraged the development of a core settler population. Small ranches soon emerged to feed miners and grew into cattle, horse, and sheep "stock farming" operations in the transnational foothills. This population gradually edged eastward, pushing into the grasslands interior over the 1870s. U.S. bankers provided credit to Alberta ranchers, and Alberta's starter herds originated in Montana. After 1874 Fort

Benton serviced Canada's North-West Mounted Police, providing the force with, first, directions to the Alberta district; then, cattle, whiskey, beef, and commercial goods, as well as postal and even payroll services. This commerce wore south-north trails into the northern grasslands between Fort Benton and various destinations in Canada, including modern Fort Macleod, Calgary, and Lethbridge. Many of these communities, much as the eastern northern grasslands Saint Paul–Winnipeg route, had origins in the fur trade. Settler colonialism advanced only slowly on the northern grasslands in the 1860s and 1870s. North-south traffic nevertheless created outposts from which agricultural settlement launched.[31]

New legislation in the United States and Canada signaled the readiness of both nations to sponsor major settler-colonial movements. Prospective settlers in the United States could secure land through several government programs. By the time most individuals began to claim land in Dakota and Montana Territories, a male, age twenty-one, could systematically secure public grants of up to 480 acres. A male settler might file first for 160 acres under the 1841 Preemption Act, which could be claimed before an official land survey and purchased after only six months for $1.25 an acre. An individual, either male or female, could also claim another quarter section under the 1862 Homestead Act, after public notice of a five-year residency and "improvements": crops and a domicile. Finally, the revised Timber Culture Act of 1878 traded 160 acres of public domain for the cultivation of 10 acres of "living thrifty trees." Congress revised land laws continually, closing loopholes and defining and redefining terms, but these acts, the Homestead Act especially, provided the watchwords settlers in the United States used to speak about privatizing the grasslands, no matter how they finally acquired land.[32] These land laws successfully moved the grasslands one step further away from Indigenous hands, through public domain, to individually held private property.

Canadians too used the word *homestead* to describe the public land they claimed. Canada prepared for what it hoped would be the quick settlement of Manitoba and the North-West Territories by passing the Dominion Lands Act of 1872. The Canadian law featured the same gridline survey that divided 640-acre sections into four claims in the United States. Canadian law, however, required only three years of residence to "prove title" on 160 acres. Also, by the end of the 1873, age qualifications dropped to eighteen years. Canada did not require land claimants to publish repeated public notices in area newspapers as a part of the "proving up" process, but perhaps the most important difference in land law concerned women. The 1862 U.S. Homestead Act allowed single women and woman heads of household to acquire homesteads if they fulfilled the same duties as men, whereas in Canada, after 1876, only widows or the "sole head of a family" could secure a government homestead. Settlers in both Canada and the United States could purchase railway and school grant lands. Canadians could also buy land retained by Hudson's Bay Company.[33] As old fur-trade patterns and mirror land legislation suggests, settler colonialism arrived on the northern grasslands with mutually reinforcing transnational cultures, shored up by increasing cross-border trade and travel. Settlers had important individual reasons for migrating to the United States and Canada, but their presence constituted another step in Canadian-U.S. pressures to dislodge Indigenous peoples from the northern grasslands.

The first of the settler-society children explored in *Grasslands Grown* arrived in the 1870s, all in the region's eastern reaches. From southeastern Dakota Territory to the confluence of the Red and Assiniboine Rivers at Winnipeg, the children of the "pioneers," as they called themselves, landed in tallgrass land. To early arrivals precipitation signaled good agricultural prospects. The average twenty-five-inch annual rainfall had created rich dark soil out of the growth and decay of grasses such as big and little bluestem, switchgrass, and sweetgrass. Plants bloomed into goldenrod, cinquefoil, prairie clover, blazing star, and coneflowers. These grasses and flowers had roots so deep they survived drought, leading settlers to assess agricultural potential positively. The texture of the dark soil found in the transnational Red River Valley, in some places five feet deep, differed somewhat from that found in southeastern Dakota Territory because the glacial Lake Agassiz (ten thousand years before) nurtured its development. The Red River appeared a trickle compared to the 550-mile prehis-

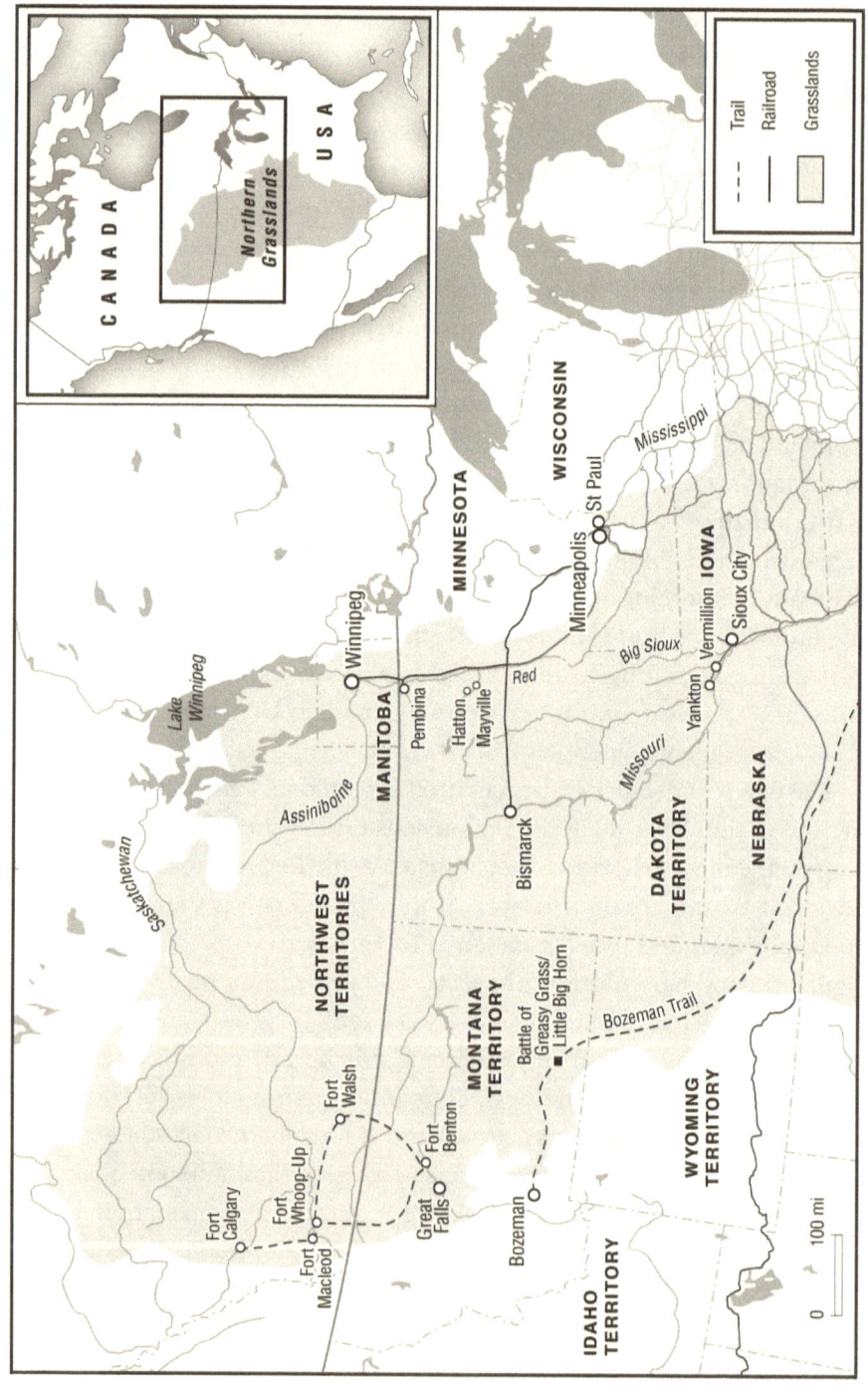

toric lake bed it ran through on its way north to Lake Winnipeg and Hudson Bay. The western edge of the valley rose in the transnational Pembina-Manitoba wooded escarpment.[34] The eastern northern grasslands watersheds flowed both north to Hudson Bay and south to the Gulf of Mexico. The "twenty miles of flat country with its ripe and unharvested wild grass five to six feet high" between Sioux City and Vermillion survived in oral history until Peter Norbeck recorded it in his parents' pioneer history.[35]

Peter Norbeck's mother never forgot that sight. His parents immigrated separately from Norway (though his father was Swedish) to Wisconsin and Sioux City, where they met and married in 1869, and then moved to Dakota Territory. As Peter told the story, he was born in a dugout cellar topped by a partially constructed frame house. His father had filed for a homestead located on "prairie, flat as the sea" and "in the center of a great plain" about eight miles north of the Missouri River village of Vermillion. The Norbeck claim lay in the eleven million acres of Yankton ancestral land ceded to the United States by treaty in 1858, not too far from geologic landmark Spirit Mound, or the "hill of little spirits" of importance to Sioux peoples. Family story recounted their mother's fear of "Indians" and a "land hunger" that at least matched her husband's. The Norbecks joined over 1,500 Scandinavians, predominantly Norwegians, but also Swedes and Danes, who lived in southeastern Dakota Territory by 1870.[36]

In 1874 Aagot Raaen, then a baby, traveled by wagon from Iowa with her parents, also immigrants from Norway, to the nearly one-hundred-mile-wide rich-soiled Red River Valley of the north. The family joined an almost systematic Norwegian settlement of the Dakota side of the Red River, land once claimed by the Ojibwes, who were by then living on reservations in northwest Minnesota. Aagot's father

---

Map 4. Transnational origins of northern grasslands settlement, 1862–78. As the United States and Canada negotiated treaties with resident northern grasslands Indigenous nations, the children of the "pioneers" arrived. Strong transnational north-south (Manitoba–North Dakota–Minnesota) connections in the area's eastern reaches and south-north (Montana-Alberta) ties in the western reaches nurtured settler-society development on both sides of the border, marked officially in 1873–74. Erin Greb Cartography.

Parents' Choice

filed for a homestead on the Goose River in the northeast corner of Steele County and built two log homes out of the river area's lush woods. He also brooded, drank, and signed a mortgage that Aagot remembered in two memoirs as "The Burden." She and her siblings worked half their lives to secure half the family homestead for the security of their mother and disabled sister. The Norwegian community grew to 14.1 percent of North Dakota's population by 1890, the largest immigrant group, followed by Canadians, who made up 12.6 percent of the population.[37]

Canadians headed to Winnipeg from Ontario through Minnesota often ended up staying below the boundary line. Effie Laurie's parents, however, did not stop. According to historian Walter Hildebrandt (and Effie herself), Effie's father, an "imperialist and ardent Canadian nationalist," preceded the family to the Red River Colony to begin printing for the zealously pro-Canadian *Nor'Wester* newspaper. He arrived in 1869, apparently almost at the moment when many of the Métis and country-born people already living there balked over the sale of Hudson's Bay Company land to Canada. Family story recorded that the Métis leader of the resistance, Louis Riel himself, asked Laurie to print flyers intended for the English-speaking community to explain the Métis position on nationhood. Instead, Laurie and his boss fled the country, recrossing to the U.S. side of the border at Pembina. After the creation of Manitoba, Laurie returned and waited for his family. At the age of four, in 1871, Effie Laurie made an "arduous trip to the west" from Windsor, Ontario, which she likely knew more from family story than memory. She traveled by railroad and stagecoach to and through Minnesota and, for the last leg of the journey, by steamboat downriver north on the Red River to Winnipeg.[38]

Transnational economic, infrastructure, and social connections in the 1860s and 1870s planted the seeds of settler society, such as the Norbecks, Raaens, Lauries, and many other settler newcomers on the northern grasslands. These nodes of settler society sat remote from both U.S. and Canadian power centers in the East. Each nation's territorial goals and the practical needs of would-be settler colonials required working together across the boundary, implicitly if not explicitly, to root relatively isolated outposts of settlement. The formal marking of the international border between Canada and the United States from 1873 to 1874 along the forty-ninth parallel signaled a cultural boundary to come.[39] Population increases and development in the 1880s would challenge the region's early transnational connections.

Settler-Colonial Boom and Bloom, 1879–91

By the end of the 1870s, settler colonialism began to gather momentum. By the 1880 census in the United States, some ninety-eight thousand settlers lived in Dakota Territory, with another thirty-eight thousand in Montana Territory. By 1881 Manitoba, with enlarged boundaries, had a population of some sixty-six thousand, but the population in the North-West Territories remained low and "less stable." Immigrants continued slowly to move into the districts, and at a faster pace after the Canadian Pacific Railway (CPR) began building across the grasslands in 1882.[40] Regular efforts in both Canada and the United States to reorient the transnational northern grasslands economy east to west accompanied population growth. A settler-colonial "boom" continued until the late 1880s in the United States, while a corresponding "bloom" in population occurred on Canada's grasslands during the same years.

The arrival of the CPR at Calgary in 1883 played a role in the final undoing of Montana's dominating economic influence north of the forty-ninth parallel. The location of the route through the southern area of Canada's grasslands reflected the National Policy and the railway's interest to keep settler trade from U.S. railroads. Indeed, the Northern Pacific Railway began building in 1879 from Bismarck west into Montana and reached transcontinental status in 1883. The Great Northern Railway connected through northern Dakota to the Pacific coast in 1887. Rail access reached the Missouri River in southern Dakota in 1880, but there halted at the border of the Great Sioux Reservation. A railroad extension moving north from Nebraska reached Rapid City, located in western southern Dakota Territory, by 1886.[41]

Other national policies and business decisions aimed to give meaning to border. In 1878, for example, Canada levied protectionist tariffs on imported goods to "foster interprovincial trade in place of international trade." High Canadian import duties mirrored high U.S. tariffs. In 1879 Great Britain gave impetus to the cattle industry of southern Alberta by placing an embargo on live imports from the United States, reducing the ability of Canadian ranchers to purchase stock in Montana. Similarly, the U.S. Congress attempted to limit British and other foreign corporate investment in U.S. cattle herds with a short-lived 1887 law that prohibited "aliens from owning any property in the territories." In 1883, when the North-West Mounted Police moved the site of Fort Walsh in the Cypress Hills to the CPR town Maple Creek, the Montana-owned I. G. Baker store moved too. In 1891, however, Baker sold all of its commercial concerns in Canada to the by then retail-oriented Hudson's Bay Company. Known for years by both Americans and Canadians as the "Manitoban" and located wholly south of the international boundary, the "St. Paul, Minneapolis and Manitoba" railroad became the "Great Northern" in 1890.[42]

Both the United States and Canada tweaked land laws in the 1880s. By then Canada competed determinedly with the United States for settlers. Canadian officials had spotted a troubling pattern. Many Canadian settlers, it seemed, sold their land upon achieving a formal title in three years and then dropped below the line to file for a five-year U.S. homestead. Canada revised its Dominion Lands Act in 1883 to allow entry on second claims "to prevent the drift to the western states." Canadian lawmakers also tinkered with easing standards for making final proof.[43]

Both the United States and Canada revised land laws to provide settlers opportunities to expand. The U.S. 1877 Desert Land Act allowed individuals to claim an entire section—640 acres—in return for paying $1.25 an acre and establishing irrigation works within three years. The irrigation requirements proved impracticable, but the law—without intention—provided three years of free grazing for the filing fee. Canada passed an 1881 law that set up an innovative one-one-one lease system to regulate access to pasture grasslands. Individuals could lease public land for grazing on contract for up to twenty-one years, not to exceed one hundred thousand acres, on terms of one acre, one cent, for one year.[44]

The increasing number of settlers correlated directly with continued expropriation of Indigenous territory. To clear Indigenous peoples out of the way, the United States strove to reduce huge tracts an earlier policy period had promised. An 1880 presidential executive order, an "involuntary cession," unilaterally moved the boundaries of the Fort Berthold Reservation, home to Mandans, Hidatsas, and Arikaras, reducing it from over 12.0 million to about 1.2 million acres, ostensibly so the Northern Pacific Railway could traverse northern Dakota Territory entirely outside the reservation. In 1882 the Indian Bureau, troops from Fort Totten, and officials of the General Land Office together seized, "without consulting the Turtle Mountain [Ojibwe] band," one-fifth of what became North Dakota. The Blackfeet, "starving and desperate," agreed in 1887 to a cession of some 17.0 million acres in Montana. Lakotas fought three commissions from 1882 to 1889 before questionable signature-gathering tactics and broken promises resulted in suspect "approval" of a new land cession. This "agreement" divided the Great Sioux Reservation into much smaller Pine Ridge, Rosebud, Lower Brulé, Cheyenne River and Standing Rock reservations.[45]

In Canada the growth of settler society in the 1880s pushed the government to officially survey land for Indigenous "reserves for farming" as outlined in the 1870s Numbered Treaties. Canadian policy created "reserves" usually around specific bands, not by Indigenous nations or major divisions within particular nations, as in the U.S. reservation system. Officials calculated reserve size by the number of individuals in each band, with each family of five allowed a 640-acre section.[46] Comparatively, then, Canadians created much smaller reserves than even reduced U.S. reservations but had more of them more widely dispersed.

Disappointment in Canadian fulfillment of treaty provisions during the 1880s, among Crees in particular, led in 1884 to an official meeting to formulate a plan to pressure Canadian government officials to renegotiate the Numbered Treaties. Crees hoped the Blackfoot Confederacy would join them in such conversations. In 1885, however, Canada's second major western crisis, the Northwest Rebellion in modern Saskatchewan, resulted in the defeat of the Métis, descended from the fur trade (who again fought the encroachments of settler society, as they had in the Red River Resistance of 1869–70 in Manitoba). Although Crees and the Blackfoot Confederacy did not ally with the Métis peoples, as the latter had hoped, violent incidents by individual Indigenous persons in combination with the Métis rebellion created widespread fear of an Indigenous peoples' war against settler society. The Canadian army rolled in from the east on the new transcontinental Canadian Pacific Railway; both underscored settler colonial presence on agriculturally transforming grasslands.[47] The conflict ended Canada's already tepid willingness to renegotiate treaties. The end of the 1880s left Indigenous peoples in Canada and the United States surrounded by settler-colonial families and dependent on national governments to deliver treaty promises and provisions with little recourse to protest misunderstanding, misconduct, and further land loss.

Settler colonials in the 1880s moved into the interior of the region, approaching from all directions: west from the tallgrasses of the Red River Valley and the Big Sioux River Valley in the United States; northwest and west from the fork of the Red and Assiniboine Rivers at Winnipeg; farther south from Canada's Fertile Belt; and east into the northern grasslands from the foothills of the transnational Rocky Mountains. Settlement moved from outer more luxuriant grasses and parklands into mixed-grass interior spaces. Settlers also moved north from grasslands in Iowa, Nebraska, and Kansas and from transportation hubs located in all directions outside the continent's northern grasslands space.

In the early summer of 1883 twelve-year-old Lulu Pickler Frad joined those headed into Dakota Territory. Many years later she recalled in a short account of the family migration how "numerous ponds and lakes" "vividly" speckled the land and that "the plain was beautiful and green." Her father, a Civil War veteran, migrated the

---

Map 5. Settler-colonial "boom" and "bloom," 1879–91. As Canada surveyed reserves for Indigenous bands and the United States negotiated for further reductions in (or expropriated) reservation land, the children of settlers arrived in increasing numbers, encouraged by a wetter climate and an expanding transcontinental rail network. National policies and laws began to make the international border on the forty-ninth parallel a cultural force. Erin Greb Cartography.

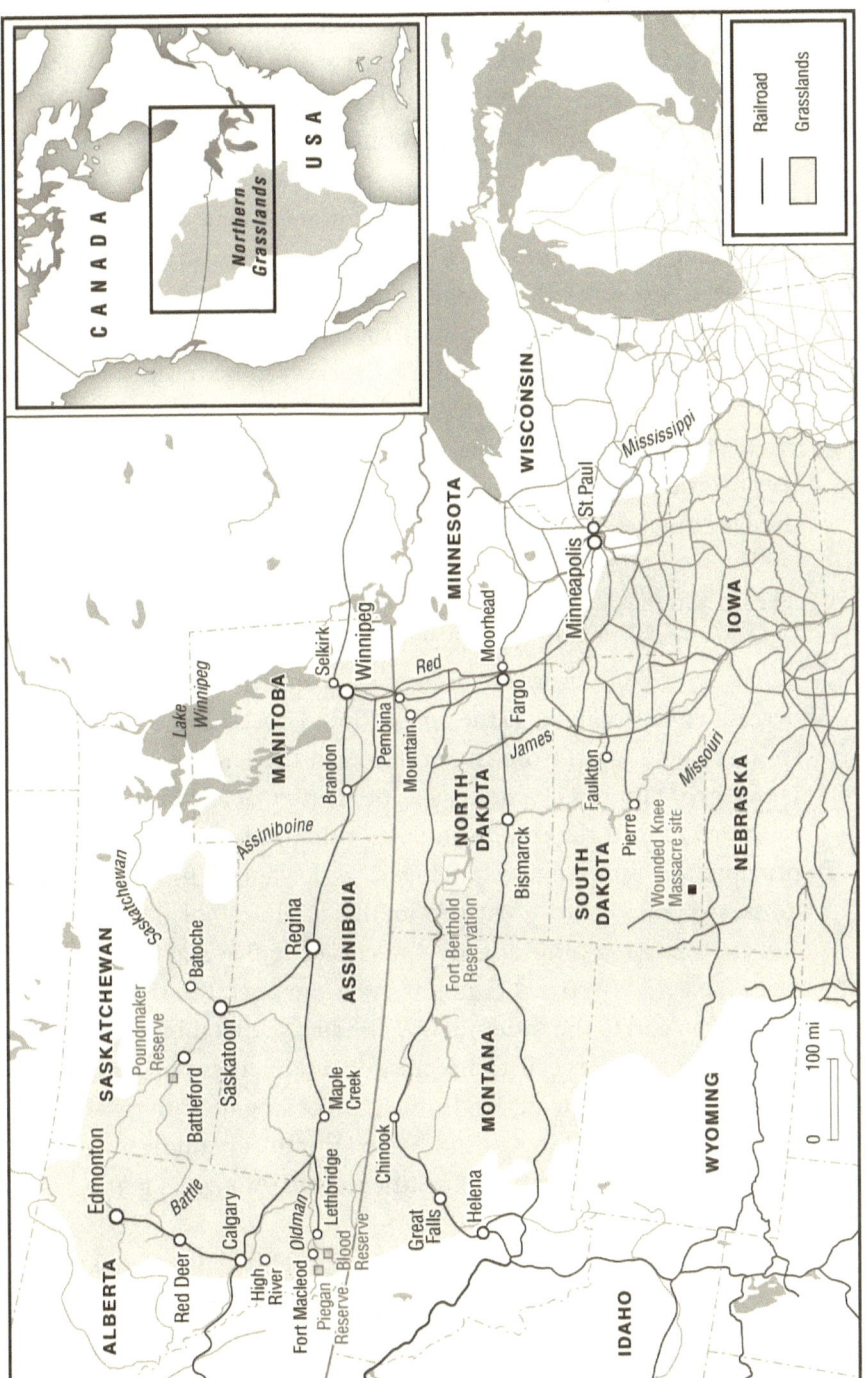

year before with a fellow Iowan, the father of Hale and Alice Humphrey. The next year Dakota Territory's population boom reached its peak, with almost 5.5 million acres claimed in a single year. The Humphrey children's father soon published the *Faulkton Times* and promoted the town both families hoped would become an "instant" great grasslands city. Indeed, both families hoped to benefit from boom-time ground-floor profits. Pickler, a lawyer soon involved in territorial and South Dakota state politics, established a land location and loan business. One of his advertisements promised settlers he had personal knowledge of railroad surveys to better locate "Good Government Lands" in the form of "Tree Claims, Preemptions and Homesteads." Humphrey stood to make "a good deal of money" on fees for the mandatory public declarations of residency required by the Homestead Act.[48]

Once churning glaciers and modern rain created the "ponds and lakes" Lulu Pickler saw. The town of Faulkton sat on snakelike banks, holding in the "beautiful, clear and sparkling water" of the newly christened Nixon River, one of several streams and creeks draining as decorative "festoons" into the James River. Locals bragged of artesian springs bursting up from the depths, but the land the Pickler and Humphrey families claimed lay at the center of a transitional zone westward toward the ninety-ninth meridian, where average annual precipitation sometimes challenged settler agriculture. To settlers grasses revealed the "great productive qualities" of the local soil: "on the sweeping prairies grow the choice native grasses which are unsurpassed," advertised Humphrey's newspaper. Residents thrilled to find "no end to the variety of wild flowers . . . blooming on the prairies." French traders called the "abrupt and picturesque" hummocks west of town the Coteau de Missouri, according to settlers "the best of grazing facilities." In April 1885 the Humphrey children's mother boasted, "We are having fine weather. Wheat up, grass getting nice and green."[49]

Some 50 miles west and 130 miles north of fledgling Faulkton, at Bismarck, Dakota Territory, George Will was born in 1884. His father, the son of German immigrants, had immigrated from Fayetteville, New York, in 1881 and met and married his mother, an immigrant from Dedham, Massachusetts. She had arrived with her parents in 1878, and her father planned to find work repairing steamboats. Will's father founded a seed and nursery business; the company's 1884 catalog highlighted the "hardy shrubs" and "forest trees and tree seeds" useful "For Planting Timber Claims, Etc." and offered "1 year"- and "2-years"-grown cottonwood, box elder, and honey locust trees; white willow and diamond willow "cuttings"; and seeds, all harvested from the Missouri River's bottomlands and the banks of its numerous "sluggish and aimless" tributary rivers and creeks. The "vast grassy plains" of the river bottom grew "rank with high grasses": big blue stem, western wheatgrass, and wild barley. The grasslands above the river valley stretched out to "grotesque" wind-eroded buttes some forty miles away. Buffalo grass, "curly sedge," little blue stem, and "lovely side oats grama" hid wild parsley, pasqueflowers, violets, and mallow, which bloomed into, according to George Will, "the glory and the color of the prairie land."[50]

The 1880s northern grasslands boom also saw Thorstina Jackson Walters born in 1887 to Icelandic immigrants. Her parents arrived separately in the Red River Valley in 1881. Her father, who immigrated first to the Icelandic settlement called Gimli on the west shore of Lake Winnipeg, traveled south across the border into northern Dakota Territory after five years residence in Winnipeg. Her mother traveled direct from Iceland to the United States and then to Glyndon, Minnesota, a town a few miles east of Moorhead, sister city to Fargo. Thorstina Jackson grew up hearing migration stories many times. This future social worker lived on a homestead on the Tongue River in Pembina County, near the Canadian border and the site of an old Métis community and fur-trade post.[51]

From 1870 to 1900 some twenty-five thousand to thirty thousand Icelanders immigrated to the United States and Canada, many of them to North Dakota and Manitoba. Like Jackson's father, Icelanders moved back and forth across the border. The North Dakota "colony," as Thorstina called it, grew considerable Icelandic-heritage populations. The painter Emile Walters, Jackson's future husband, was born in 1893 in Manitoba, but an Icelandic family in North Dakota raised him after he became orphaned.[52] The Icelandic parents of writer Laura

Parents' Choice 41

Goodman Salverson migrated to Winnipeg, where she was born in 1890, but the family moved among Manitoba, Minnesota, and Dakota. When writing about her parents' immigrant experience Salverson remarked, "I report from hearsay," but, she added parenthetically, "truth to tell, it seems odd I wasn't there," as if she knew the family migration narratives so well they became her own experience.[53]

As Dakota Territory settlers moved farther west, settlers in Manitoba began to move west into the North-West Territories. Effie Laurie's family was among those who left Winnipeg. Her father led the way in 1878, resettling in Battleford, the territorial capital. As Effie phrased it, "The wide plains beyond beckoned irresistibly to my father." Effie Laurie and her sister Minnie sledded into Battleford, an aspiring agricultural town on the flats south of the Battle River, near where it met the North Saskatchewan River, in the late winter of 1882. She later recalled that the "great expanse of prairie land" included sand hills, "honeysuckle and roses," poplar bluffs, and "high hills." Laurie crafted the experience of the "exciting adventure" as part of her family memoir. The grasslands crossing took fifty-two days, from February to April, and consisted of a party of eight, including Métis, or "half-breed drivers," as Effie called her guides. Showing a rigor she wanted emphasized, the traveling companions slept outside overnight for more than three-quarters of the journey. Actually, Effie and her sister rode the railway to Brandon, Manitoba, before taking up sleds (a fact frequently left out in her story). Their mother came most of the way by railway four months later. Since the age of twelve Effie wrote, her language sliding into romantic mythic West variety: "Always I saw myself on those vast plains, fording the swollen rivers, following the long dusty trails and camping by night under the stars while coyotes and Indians roamed around."[54] Indeed, Plains Crees had ancestral claim to the area and remained there her entire life. Elders selected reserves near Battleford by provisions of the 1876 Treaty 6.[55]

Directly south of the Laurie family, Elsie May Hammond's parents landed in the North-West Territories district of Assiniboia. The Plains Cree had ancestral claim to this area too. Most, but not all, Cree bands signed Treaty 4 in 1874. Her father, a carpenter from England, eventually settled near a budding cow town, established when the railway was built through it in 1883. Maple Creek sat on the northern edge of the semiarid grasslands south of the South Saskatchewan River and on an old glacial lake. The Great Sand Hills rose in the nearby north. The creek that gave the town its name ran north out of the Cypress Hills. This lodgepole pine oasis, about fifteen miles south of the Hammond home, had withstood the pressure of glaciers that ultimately swung around the hills. An extension of the Missouri Coteau hummocks of the eastern Dakotas rolled to the east. Ultimately, Elsie Hammond's father formed a partnership with a cousin under the "HP" brand on Hay Creek and purchased more property in 1896, four years after Elsie was born. She and her sisters and brothers grew up working on the family's farm-ranch operation.[56]

The same year the Canadian Pacific Railway founded Maple Creek, ten-year-old Julia "Lula" Short Asher flew through the town in a passenger car on her way from Selkirk, Manitoba, to Calgary in the Alberta district of the North-West Territories. What took Effie Laurie fifty-two days to go about half as far by sled for Lula added up to five days by rail. Lula Short Asher remembered the fast trip on the "crowded railway train" as stifling. She explained to her grandchildren in her memoir, "There were no grain elevators or wide fields of sprouting wheat at that time, only a boundless expanse of far-reaching grassland, enlivened by an occasional coyote or herd of antelope." From Calgary the Shorts made a two-day wagon trip "over the prairie" to the homestead near High River, a foothills ranch town. Her father had also attempted for a few years to take advantage of the 1881 revision to the Dominion Lands Act by securing a grazing lease. The Shorts claimed land made available by Canada's 1877 Treaty 7 with the Blackfoot Confederacy.[57]

Not far from the Shorts, in the Alberta district, lived Annora Brown at Fort Macleod, the site of an early North-West Mounted Police post (at the end of one of the south-north roads from Montana). The town sat on the Oldman River, a tributary of the South Saskatchewan River. Grasslands stretched out east from the Rocky Mountains. The Piegan Reserve lay on the outskirts of Macleod and the Blood Reserve, a few miles distant, both created according to the provisions of Treaty 7. Annora was born in 1899 on a homestead near Red Deer, but she remembered her father as a town clerk. Born and raised in London, England, he had "prove[d] ownership" in the mid-1880s on a homestead he claimed after working for a farmer who lived near Moose Jaw. He sold the claim and worked his way west as a member of the North-West Mounted Police. Annora Brown's mother, a schoolteacher with "adventure . . . in her blood," migrated from Ontario in the early 1890s. Though some sixty miles away, Brown felt "the massive, square-topped bulk of Chief Mountain" rising "sharply from the prairie" in the Montana part of her "world."[58]

South of the international line, Montana also experienced increased but limited homesteading activity in the 1880s, as more ranchers took homesteads and as former miners turned to ranching. The father and uncle of Peggy Olson Bell, born in Montana in 1887, for example, started out as miners, but the former became a cowboy and the latter a homesteader and smaller rancher, on land acquired from the Blackfeet in the United States by 1870s presidential executive orders. Her mother, an immigrant from Ireland, worked as a server in the mining communities of Helena and Great Falls. Olson's father immigrated from Norway. Peggy, without her parents early in life, recorded her parent's migration stories in two short paragraphs at the beginning of her memoir.[59]

Regional narrative tradition seemed to require an answer to the question: How did you arrive here? Farther east into Montana's grasslands, the father of five-year-old Lillian Miller purchased a 160-acre grasslands "ranch" in 1891 in the transnational Milk River Valley. The family moved from Iowa to near Chinook, a "bleak, tree-less little town." Lillian wrote of an "Empire" her father founded from that homestead. Family story held that land to be the beginning of his plan to set up Lillian's teenage brothers in the sheep and cattle business. Indeed, through purchases and leasing reservation land, her two brothers expanded the ranch into one of Montana's largest.[60]

Soon after the end of the boom period, the United States had admitted three new states, North Dakota, South Dakota, and Montana. The 1890 U.S. census recorded the settler society of South Dakota at almost 329,000 people; North Dakota at 191,000 residents; and Montana's population jumped to over 132,000. The Canadian bloom left Manitoba with a "stable community and reasonable prosperity" by 1891 and, according to Gerald Friesen, laid "the foundation for rapid growth." Some 220,000 settlers in total made the northern grasslands in Canada their home. Settlers had taken up some thirty-nine million acres in Dakota Territory. By the turn of the century, settlers in Manitoba and the North-West Territories had filed on roughly some twenty-five million acres. By 1886 some 664,000 cattle and 986,000 sheep grazed in Montana Territory. The Assiniboia and Alberta districts by then also had a "flourishing" livestock industry.[61]

Drought, tough winters, and economic depression from the late 1880s through the mid-1890s saw the settlement boom in the United States fizzle and the settlement bloom in Canada wilt. An eight-year drought parched southern Dakota starting in 1887. The Humphrey children's mother wrote from Faulkton, claiming, "This is a desolate place anyway." North Dakota recorded only four good harvests in the 1890s. The severe winter of 1886–87 in Montana came with "hideous" losses; some 60 percent of beeves perished.[62] In Saskatchewan the same winter "big die-up" caused similar devastation, and Canada ended its cheap grazing leases. Nevertheless, the boom and bloom of the 1880s allowed the United States and Canada to incorporate North America's northern grasslands more securely with infrastructure and commercial centers into the economic and political cultures of their respective nations.

The Last Best Transnational West, 1896–1917

Canadians have claimed the mantle the "Last Best West" to describe a boom in settlement that occurred north of the forty-ninth parallel in the early years of the twentieth century. This Last West had transnational reach. Settlement moved from the outer, more humid, rainier edges into the semiarid, semihumid grasslands—the Last Best West—at the region's northwestern center, an area shared by western North Dakota, western South Dakota, eastern Montana, southeastern Alberta, and southwestern Saskatchewan. Population statistics suggest the burst in settler society. In 1906 some 46,500 people lived in southwestern Saskatchewan; by 1916 the population had risen to over 178,000. Alberta's population increased more than five times from 1901 to 1911, from 73,000 to 374,000, many of the new residents taking land in that province's semiarid southeastern corner. In 1905 almost 58,000 people lived in western South Dakota; by 1910 the population had grown to almost 138,000. North Dakota grew, mostly in its western areas, by 250,000 people from 1898 to 1915. Individuals filed on more homesteads in Montana in 1910 than in the three previous decades combined.[63]

Warm-season, cool-season, and mixed dry and moist grasses covered much of this still "huge block of raw prairie."[64] Needle-and-thread and blue grama grasses, buffalo grass, June and Porcupine grasses, and fescue carpeted broad level land. Prickly pear cactus, the crocus (Canada) or pasqueflower (the United States), wild rose, sagebrush, and sumac commonly grew in the area's light-brown soils. Precipitation varied wildly across time and space: averaging 15.4 inches annually in western North Dakota, 14.0 inches in northwestern South Dakota, and 12.0 inches or below in southwestern Saskatchewan and southwestern Alberta. When agricultural settlers greeted these "great buffalo plains," huge two-foot-deep denuded circular wallows documented some of the twenty-eight million to thirty million bison that once grazed the grasslands. The Black Hills in western South Dakota and eastern Wyoming and the Cypress Hills straddling Saskatchewan and Alberta served as oases. Badlands in Alberta, Montana, and the Dakotas dazzled. Uplands such as the Sweet Grass Hills, Bears Paw Mountains, Belly Butte, Slim Buttes, and Porcupine Hills beaconed.[65] Only some homesteaders understood this land's meaning, not quite humid and not quite desert. Mixed messages of agricultural potential abounded.

Settlers frequently followed or anticipated new railroad lines that continued to expand across the northern grasslands. After 1900 the Canadian Northern and the Grand Trunk Pacific Railways joined the Canadian Pacific Railway north of the forty-ninth parallel. As above the border, the Northern Pacific and Great Northern Railways extended branches near almost everywhere settlers landed. In the Dakotas the Chicago and North Western, Milwaukee, Northern Pacific, and the Great Northern Railways webbed out into interior settlements. A rail line was built across the Missouri River to Rapid City from 1905 to 1907. That year the Milwaukee reached North Dakota's southwest and South Dakota's northwest at Lemmon, eventually to connect with a transcontinental line. State, provincial, national, and corporate railroad literatures continued to advertise for new settlers.[66]

Both the United States and Canada offered incentives to settlers by passing new homestead laws. To a degree the new laws acknowledged the semiarid nature of this environment and the corresponding need for larger acreages required to establish appropriate mixed-crop and stock-farming operations. In 1908 Canada passed preemption legislation, which allowed a man or head of household who had filed on land under the 1872 Dominion Lands Act to reserve a contiguous quarter section that could be purchased after securing title to the first property. In a similar manner the 1908 Purchased Homestead allowed a Canadian landowner to acquire a noncontiguous quarter section. Canada also ended its gigantic cattle-company leasing system, bringing more land to the market as early as the 1890s, especially after the winter of 1906. Also, after 1896, Canada's Department of the Interior forced railways to claim the land grants given as construction incentives. Unlike U.S. railroads, which received land grants of every other section along all lines built, Canada allowed railway companies to select land "fairly fit for settlement" anywhere on the grasslands. This meant a certain portion of the grasslands had been held off the market in a "land lock" during the 1880s.[67] This land could now be sold to settlers and the remaining land opened to the public.

In 1909 the United States implemented an Enlarged Homestead Act for Montana, allowing homesteaders to claim 320 instead of 160 acres. The law applied to North Dakota in 1912 (and later in South Dakota). If Canadian politicians passed panicked legislation in 1883 to stem the tide of homesteaders moving south across the border, U.S. politicians acted similarly in 1912. The Senate heard testimony that some 125,000 Americans emigrated to Canada in 1911, over fifty thousand of them located to Alberta and Saskatchewan; the next year, over another fifty thousand followed to the same provinces. In response, Congress reduced the residency requirement for homesteading from five to three years.[68]

In the early twentieth century, Canada and the United States continued to reduce reserves and reservations to meet the needs of ongoing settlement. Although treaties in the United States and Canada suggested reservations and reserves would be "permanent," according to Jill St. Germain, officials in both nations held "firmly" to the belief that "reserves were a temporary holding place until civilization dawned." Eventually, the logic went, Indigenous peoples would no longer need tribal homelands. With these beliefs in 1887 the U.S. Congress passed the Dawes General Allotment Act, which assigned parcels of reservation land to individual Indigenous people on the authority of the president. The act then allowed officials, in period language, to "open up" reservation "surplus" land to homesteaders. (Of course, the land was not surplus to Indigenous nations planning for the needs of future generations or to Indigenous farmers who desired to expand their operations.) Surveyors completed much of the allotting and final approvals thereof in the 1890s and early 1900s. As early as 1892 and 1895, the U.S. government "opened" to settlement Dakota and Yankton reservation lands east of the Missouri River. Official allotment of the Fort Berthold Reservation commenced in 1894, but the surveyed allotments received approval only in 1900.[69]

Further, between 1904 and 1913 the United States reduced by over 50 percent the Rosebud, Lower Brulé, Pine Ridge, Cheyenne River, and Standing Rock Reservations carved out of the Great Sioux Reservation in 1889. The settler-colonial demand for this land created a new wrinkle in land policy. The United States offered this land only by purchase and through a lottery system, although the law required claimants also to meet the provisions of the Homestead Act. In Montana, in 1907, in violation of an 1895 treaty that restricted the allotment process, the United States surveyed and divided the Blackfeet Reservation, releasing the "remainder" to settlers. Many settlers also convinced desperate Indigenous persons to sell or lease their allotments.[70] In the United States the general allotment process left what had been unified land blocks of reservation a checkerboard of Indigenous and settler-society ownership.

In Canada, amid the homestead boom, the minister of the interior expressed the idea that reserve lands in amounts "beyond their [Indigenous peoples'] possible requirements" were "seriously impeding the growth of settlement."⁷¹ Canada's Department of Indian Affairs also devised a plan to divide reserves into "individual lots," although land left unalloted could not be sold without consent of the band. Many Numbered Treaties, however, included provisions that allowed Canada, with compensation, to carve off "sections of the reserves" for "public works or buildings." Canadian officials pressured Blackfoot and Piegans to reduce reserves in southern Alberta for the specific purpose of opening up lands to settlers. Under pressure the Pasquah and Muscowpetung bands living in the lands of Treaty 4 surrendered thousands of acres in Saskatchewan, and the Passpasschase and Enoch/Stony Plains Reserves saw reduction in Alberta. Further, the desire to provide land to non-Indigenous veterans of World War I resulted in pressuring additional bands to surrender reserve land.⁷²

Despite such pressures, Indigenous peoples endured on the northern grasslands. By the middle of the twentieth century, from Minnesota to Montana, at least twenty reservations anchored Indigenous communities to ancestral territories. Manitoba, Saskatchewan, and Alberta hosted hundreds of reserves.⁷³ Indigenous peoples also remained culturally attached to the larger northern grasslands beyond reservations and reserves. The sense of place acquired by experiences with the land over the generations could not be sold or seized.

The last settlement wave on the northern grasslands resulted in the arrival of one final set of settler-colonial children. A generation of time separated these latter-day homesteaders' children from the small ones who trickled in with the pioneers at the edges of the northern grasslands in the 1860s and 1870s and came in a rush with 1880s settlers. Canada, perhaps, took the lead on advertising the Last Best West and competed directly with the United States to allure new settlers. Among other promotions, in 1897 Canada established immigration offices in cities such as Saint Paul, Kansas City, Omaha, Duluth, Indianapolis, and Saint Louis, as well as in Great Falls, Montana; Sioux Falls and Watertown, South Dakota; and Grafton, North Dakota. Homesteaders from the United States, not freighters carrying trade goods from Fort Benton, Montana, likely composed the wagon train Annora Brown and her parents watched move from the old "Fort Whoop-Up" Trail onto Macleod's Main Street in the early 1900s.⁷⁴

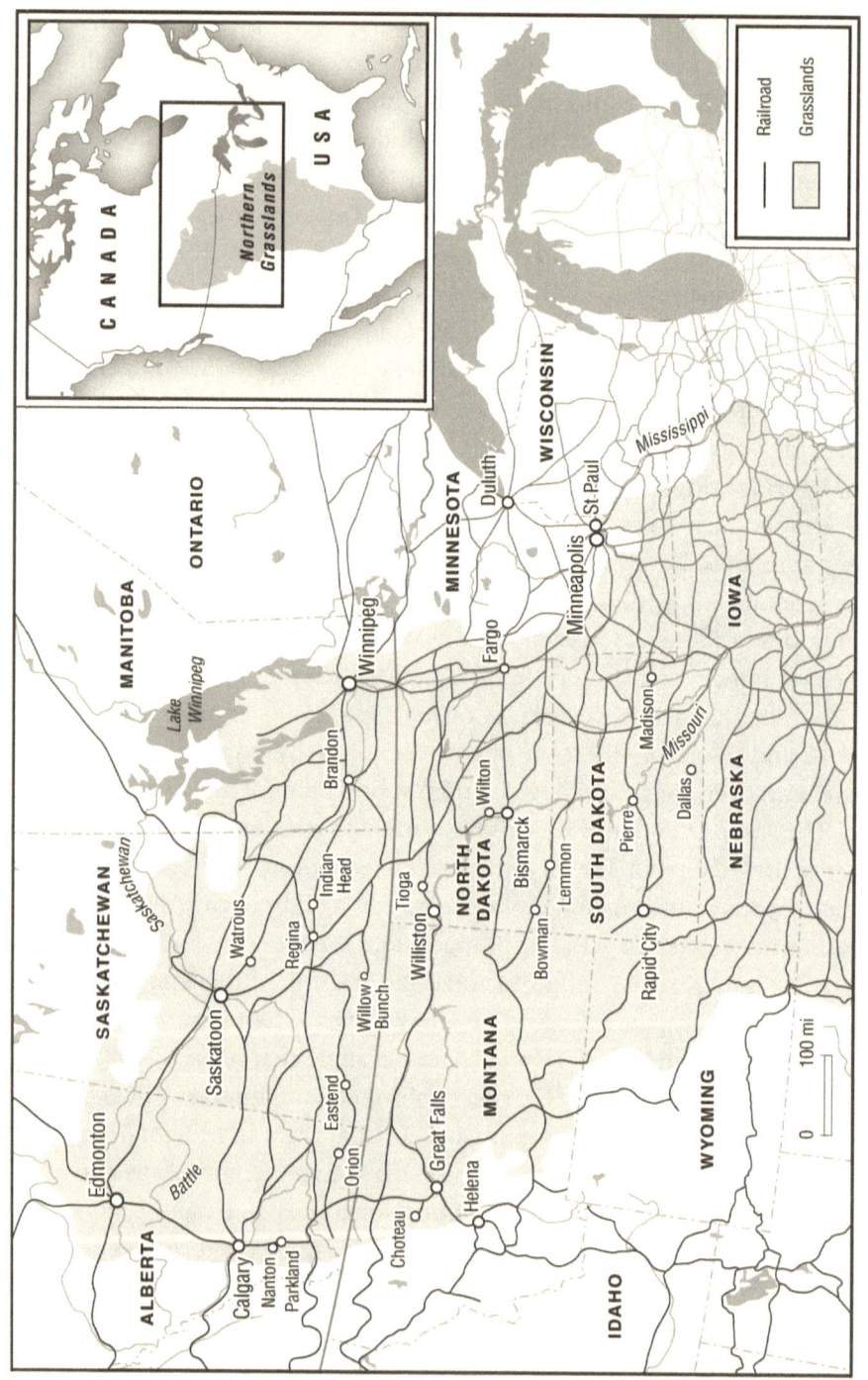

Indeed, many U.S. citizens and immigrants to the United States decided to move north of the line. Thorstina Jackson and her father were among those who left North Dakota for Saskatchewan in 1907. The same year a young Nell Wilson Parsons landed with her parents near Willow Bunch, Saskatchewan. An uncle lured north by "fabulous things" publicized in railroad literature had convinced Wilson's tenant-farmer father to move from Iowa to the "Canadian plains." After her mother died, Montana-born Peggy Olson Bell migrated north back "across the line" in the early twentieth century to live on a homestead in Alberta near her Canadian stepfather's relatives. The writer Robert McAlmon, who grew up in small eastern South Dakota towns, fictionalized his aunt's move north, citing a middle-aged widow who "began to talk of going to Canada to take a claim." In 1910 the Pickler children's aunt and uncle shocked the Faulkton family when they received word that "the *Whole bunch* are thinking of going to *Canada* to take land," including the single woman Hazel, who would "have to buy Soldiers Script." In 1914 the father of the future western writer and environmentalist Wallace Stegner moved his family from North Dakota to Eastend, Saskatchewan, and a homestead on the border with Montana. For the first time in Canadian-American relations, more Americans immigrated to Canada—990,000 between 1898 and 1914—than Canadians to the United States, some 591,000 to the northern grasslands.[75]

Ontario, England, and other European countries also sent immigrants to the new provinces of Alberta and Saskatchewan (organized in 1905).[76] Georgina Thomson arrived in Calgary with her mother and sisters in the early fall of 1904, after a long train ride from Ontario. The girls sat "fascinated by the prairie stretching away on every side." Thomson's father secured an abandoned homestead near Nanton, Alberta. Ralph Russell's parents moved in 1906 from Ontario to take

---

Map 6. The last best transnational northern Grasslands West, 1896–1917. The children of homesteaders arrived in the northern semiarid center of the northwestern grasslands as trains built numerous extensions and robust advertising attracted new settlers. Settler-colonial societies in Canada and the United States continued to pressure Indigenous peoples to cede land even as drought returned. Erin Greb Cartography.

up a homestead near Lipton, Saskatchewan. Wilfrid Eggleston's father filed on an Alberta homestead in May 1910, some thirty miles from Annora Brown. He remembered Montana's Sweet Grass Hills in the "skyline" as the "dominant and never-to-be-forgotten feature of our homestead." He was eight when the family moved from England to Alberta and eleven when the family moved to a homestead near Orion.[77]

This twentieth-century boom also reached seamlessly into the United States, even as it pulled Americans into Canada. Homesteaders flowed into eastern Montana and the western Dakotas. Canadian agents complained that state promoters from Texas to South Dakota constituted "formidable and unscrupulous rivals in the search for settlers."[78] In 1910 the five-year-old Olaf Olseth, in the company of his Norwegian tenant-farmer parents, railroaded from the Big Sioux River Valley in southeastern South Dakota (near where Peter Norbeck had grown up a generation before) to a homestead in northwestern South Dakota. The train stopped at Bowman, North Dakota; a wagon ride dropped the Olseths below the state line to live in a house made of the same buffalo grass Olaf would plow. A six-year-old Russian-born Sophie Trupin recalled "looking out upon the endless prairies" in 1909 to the "steel gray grass that covered the rolling hills and valleys" near Wilton, "Nordakota." In the "Old Country" her father "could not own even one acre because he was a Jew." The grasslands was a "promised land free from anti-Semitism and degradation." Her mother, however, sat "dismayed and horrified" as the view unfolded. Faye Cashatt's father won a lottery that allowed him to move the family from Iowa to "surplus" Rosebud Reservation land in South Dakota. Cashatt felt she participated in "almost the last frontier country of our West, a last chance to get a homestead in government land hitherto unoccupied." Unoccupied by settler colonials, she meant.[79] As the reservation origin of the homestead suggested, Indigenous people lived in the area once and still did.

Many children arrived with parents whose primary occupation centered on the infrastructure society needed in towns, although they also often took up land claims. Robert McAlmon arrived in Madison, South Dakota, in the early 1900s, when his father became the minister of the local Presbyterian church. Dorothy Johnson's family arrived in 1909 at Great Falls, Montana, but soon moved outside of town on the Missouri River after her father took a job as a timekeeper on a power dam under construction. Alfred Guthrie's father took a job in 1901, the year Alfred was born, as the principal in the high school at Choteau, Montana. Leslie Neatby and Kate Neatby Nicoll's father, a doctor, and mother immigrated from England in 1906. They tried to set up a medical practice at Earl Grey, Saskatchewan, before moving the family of eight children to a grasslands homestead near Watrous two years later.[80]

Participants in Last Best West land taking also included a strong contingent of young adults from settler society's first generation of grasslands-grown children. In 1908 Madge Pickler Hoy, the daughter of the founders of Faulkton, South Dakota, in 1883, took advantage of Lakota reservation land made newly accessible by the 1907 Milwaukee Railway extension to Lemmon, South Dakota. "Convinced" that northwestern South Dakota "is the best . . . in land," the couple wrote home to Faulkton about "good locations for ranches and places that have all the way from 80 to 140 acres of good plough land." Dale Pickler, along with four high school friends known collectively as the Happy Five, also moved to South Dakota's northwest. At least one of the Hammond boys purchased railway land to enhance family operations. Norris Hagen's father, the child of Norwegian immigrants, grew up in western Minnesota; only a baby, he and his parents arrived in 1907 to take up a homestead near Tioga, in northwestern North Dakota. A friend of Aagot Raaen's took a claim and built a "home on the new frontier" near Williston, North Dakota, and the Montana state line. When he was old enough, Walter Neatby took up land near his father's Saskatchewan claim. Edward Pitblado (whose grandparents migrated to Winnipeg from Ontario near the same time as the Laurie family) claimed homestead land in Manitoba during World War I.[81] The children of northern grasslands settler society of previous generations joined people coming from Europe, Canada, and the United States, with a new set of children who would become the first of settler society to grow up at or near the northwestern center of the transnational northern grasslands.

The Pioneer Pull and Their Own Chosen Work

The children of settler society grew up and lived with their parents' choices to represent Canada and the United States on still-contested terrain. The children of pioneers, settlers, and homesteaders felt the weight of the parental decision to take up land. As with Effie Laurie Storer of Saskatchewan and brothers Peter and George Norbeck of South Dakota, the pioneer pull worked strongly in the culture. A pioneer parental framework appears to have given unconscious shape even to the forty-year flow of Elsie Hammond's Saskatchewan diaries. Hammond kept day-entry diaries from 1910 to her last entry on 19 October 1949, her fifty-seventh birthday. The night before, she and her brother Les had attended an "Old Timers Banquet" in Maple Creek. He had returned from British Columbia to bury the body of their father next to their mother, who died a few years earlier. As Elsie watched her brother's midnight train pull out that night, leaving her the last, only, and youngest of her parents' six children to remain on the land, she paused. Something ended. She did not make another diary entry for over twenty years, until her seventy-eighth birthday. In that year, 1970, she confided to a new diary, "I am trying to reread all my old dairies. . . . for a book . . . as a record of our pioneers who came into our area before 1900." She hoped her diaries would "bring back . . . the early past of my life." Tellingly, her diaries *began* ten years after the projected end-date of her pioneer history. Her times spoke to the cultural hold of parental pioneers and point to often troubled, unprocessed meaning inherent in the myth-promoting laudatory "pioneer origin" narrative. Hammond's diaries, however, actually recorded *her* daily life growing up on the northern grasslands of Saskatchewan.[82]

Family migration stories began to implant northern grasslands settler societies into regional landscapes on the plane of culture, as the parents in pioneer tales had once used legal methods to create private property. Thorstina Jackson Walters's effort as a thirty-eight-year-old to finish her deceased father's three-volume chronicle of Icelandic immigration histories to North America also suggests the pattern. The task involved traveling from New York City, where she then lived, to North Dakota to conduct more interviews with "the pioneers and their children." She saw it through to publication in the Icelandic language by a Winnipeg press in 1926. Fellow North Dakotan Clell Gannon "dedicated in love" his first book of poetry "to my father and mother . . . pioneers of the Great Plains and builders of the West." Nell Wilson memorialized her Saskatchewan memoir to "papa and all those other forgotten homesteaders who *toiled* to make the Prairies the land of their dreams for future generations." Georgina Thomson's Alberta memoir honored "My Father and Mother," and Wilfrid Eggleston dedicated his first novel to "The Pioneers Who settled in 'Palliser's Triangle'—My parents among them." Olaf Olseth devoted his North Dakota memoir to the "memory of my beloved mother," and Sophie Trupin to "the memory of my parents and their neighbors, who braved the unknown and unfamiliar in search of a life with dignity." As the Montana writer Dorothy Johnson explained, "For a person living in Montana, having old roots in the state carries prestige."[83] These pioneer tales form one genre of vernacular literature created by the first generations of settler-colonial society that simultaneously spoke to the creation of this generation's sense of place.

These pioneer origin stories have formed primary sources for locating the children whose lives are the major concern of *Grasslands Grown*. Yet, as Icelandic North American Laura Goodman Salverson phrased it, her generation had to build new lives for the "genius of New Times."[84] This generation exhibited a distinct form of settler colonialism, storying themselves into the land and mythologizing pioneer parents. The culture of settlement pulled on Thorstina Walters enough so that twenty-five years after she published the Icelandic version of her father's pioneer histories, she published an English version with a regional press in North Dakota. Tellingly, she opened the volume with a personal essay, titled "I grew up with the Pioneers." As tellingly, although Walters's 1953 *Modern Sagas* grew out of her father's work, she transformed it with minibiographies of *her* contemporaries. Walters argued that she and her counterparts "realized" the "hopes and dreams" of their parents by moving from the "harsh environment" to an "eminent position in their own chosen work," from agriculture to art.[85] As Effie Laurie Storer's chapters tucked into

Parents' Choice 55

a biography of her father, and Peter and George Norbeck's paragraphs on boyhood into a family history, Walters had found a way to tell her generation's story while still nodding to the pioneers. The process of creating new senses of place and regional identities—a settler colonialism distinct from the parental generation's experiences and environmental contexts—began in childhood, when these initial grasslands-grown generations of settler society first dug themselves into prairie and plains landscapes.

2

Small Worlds

Animal Friends, Foes, and Place Rhythms

Nine-year-old Ira "Hale" Humphrey sat in a parlor on the grasslands at Faulkton, southern Dakota Territory, composing a letter to his older brother Alfred. "I send you and grandma four cattle and one mule. We went to the social Friday, and had lots of fun. We played blindmansbluff, Ruth and Jacob, grunt, and nosegames." These few sentences form almost the entirety of the letter young Hale composed in 1886; he spent most of his ink time drawing the detailed pictures of "four cattle and one mule" enclosed with the text. The renderings have expression, proportion, and distinguishing elements. The mule, for example, stands erect with tight triangle ears and a short stubby mane; a bull looks serious in his squat, extra-heavy, sagging shape; and a younger, trimmer cow scowls angrily out of the corner of one eye. The curves of their backs, rumps, and underbellies easily communicate the gait of these farm animals. Alfred, who lived with his grandmother in Iowa to attend school, already owned quite a collection of his brother Hale's "real cute" drawings. In a letter to his sister, Alfred instructed, "Tell Hale that Uncle said he was going to be an artist."[1] Sheets and sheets of Hale's penciled cattle flowed through the mail. His drawings suggest animals played a large role in his life and imagination.

Animal behaviors and activities combined with diverse environmental textures and surfaces to create childhood "experiences" of North America's northern grasslands in the late nineteenth and early twentieth centuries.[2] Hale Humphrey's brief letter suggests a child's unrealized beginnings of a personal sense of place, a set of feelings, and understandings about the environment. The "nosegames" mentioned could have introduced Hale to the smells of the prairie and bluffs of the Nixon River running near his family homestead. Grazing cows were the content of his daily life.

The wild and tame animals encountered by children helped them absorb the diverse ecologies that shaped their perceptions of the grasslands. The Humphrey children—Alfred, Alice, Hale, Kenneth, and Kittie—continually wrote of animals in their letters. Animals were ubiquitous, nearly as common in villages and towns as on farms and ranches. Children rode animals or moved in wagons and buggies by animal power. They appreciated animal companionship and partnered with animals in agriculture and exploration. Animal sounds patterned the air of the grasslands. The speed of animals in part shaped children's view and sense of distance. The species represented did not exist in the same balance and variety they did in the early 1800s or even the 1860s northern grasslands. Some species had all but disappeared, but settler-society culture also maintained connections to historical grasslands animals through storytelling. Narratives about grizzlies and buffalo, along with fur traders and big-game hunters, became the stuff of regional legend.

Everyday domestic and small wild animals helped introduce children to the life and rhythms of grasslands. Animals acted on instinct, and children followed them across the land. The needs of families and settler-colonial society together also shaped these encounters. Children interacted with local environments and animals in distinct ways. They traveled, played, worked, hunted, and, through family cooking, tasted animals of the grasslands. Some animals, children knew, were threats to successful agriculture. The historical nexus of animals, the continent's northern grasslands, and childhood cultural patterns distinguish this generation of settler society's senses of place from those generations that preceded and followed. Far fewer people in the future encountered native northern grasslands habitat in an expansive, unplowed expression in almost daily company with animals.

Small Worlds

The animal-child relationship offers one way to understand childhood encounters with the natural world. Most children of grasslands settler society grew up in different environments than their parents, which gave them unique associations with nature, including animals, and climate. Atmospheres helped shape the way bodies responded to environments in ways that competed with parental expectations. Moreover, children and adults also experienced the *same* place as fundamentally different. Children live in their own imaginary—"magical" or "other-dimensional"—worlds at the same time they live in larger, cultural historical worlds navigated by the direction of parents.[3] Animals played important roles in the ways grasslands children remembered and crafted memoirs, autobiographies, and fiction. Animals' impression is evident even in the metaphors they reached for, such as recalling "playing as if we were colts in a pasture on a spring day" and hail the "size of hens' eggs."[4]

Memoirs have been criticized for their inaccuracy and romanticism, but, in the context of actually conveying a child's perception of the world, aged nostalgic remembering also constitutes attempts by adults to express the imaginative worlds in which they, as adults, had long since ceased to inhabit but from which they had retained images and formative feelings.[5] The earliest, most resilient memories northern grasslands settler-residents claimed often involved animals, even when a person lived well beyond the age when animals were key to transportation and integral to daily life. In her elderly years the Canadian Annora Brown described the "flashing [of] several superimposed images on the mental screen," coming to her from a time "before I knew the meaning of any but the simplest words." One of these memories turned solely on the "soft nose" of a farm horse named Queenie. Brown did not remember the entire horse—only the *nose*, which she friendly "rubbed."[6] This snippet is the product of memory working for a lifetime on childhood experiences. Later she learned the context of the memory that helped her carry it forward in time: her parents sold Queenie to a "stranger" when they sold their homestead near Red Deer and moved to Fort Macleod, Alberta.

The story of childhood told from an adult perspective emerges *necessarily* incomplete because no longer can the adult have whole access to a childhood mentality. The inaccessibility of the meaning of the child's "small world" forms an obverse to the child's vague understanding of the migration dreams and life goals of parents;

that is, parents and children live in the same space but "experience" the same events uniquely.

The best of adult writers recognized the conflict that emerged from trying to convey accurately their childhood experiences and informed readers that their ensuing tales made sense only from a childhood perspective. One Icelandic Manitoban explained the childhood perspective as the glass fishbowl stage of life: "A child's mental life . . . revolves around its own emotions and sense impressions." A child's mind "swims about in the waters of . . . emotions as unconscious of the outer world as a goldfish in its little glass bowl." An African American North Dakotan wrote of "me and my child's world." A Montanan looking back from the middle of the twentieth century noted that the "mountains, fields, streams and woods" remained, but in "diminished" form because of "the boy" he "wasn't" anymore.[7]

After waxing on and on about trying "to raise a gopher as a pet," Wilfrid Eggleston of southern Alberta turned to the "blunt fact" of the "utter failure" of government policy and the semiarid grasslands to sustain his family. He wrote, "It gives me no pleasure, even after the passage of nearly seventy years, to recall that black era, so I shall be brief." The so-called black era he proceeded to describe, however, was indeed the *same* historical era he had just recalled so lovingly. The first half of his interpretation viewed his experience "as seen through the eyes of a romantic but ignorant boy." The second part of Eggleston's analysis flowed from his adult assessment of Alberta's semiarid grasslands intersecting with the "economic realities" of his parents' goals for the farmstead. Montanan Alfred Guthrie felt struck down "years later" when he finally realized the "hard, sore fact of parental struggle."[8]

Animals and Sense of Place

Animals mediated the way children first experienced the grasslands. Animal power dominated the daily routine of families attempting to establish a commercial agricultural order on the northern grasslands in late nineteenth- and early twentieth-century Canada and the United States. Everyone had "faithful oxen" and horses that seemed part of the family. Something about lumbering with animals over seemingly endless grasslands lodged the terrain in children's earliest memories. The constant repetition of the experience of animals' gaits provided distinct feels of the place. In a sense children rode the landscape as much as they rode horses or were pulled in wagons and buggies. They acclimated to the bumps, dips, swells, and cliff-like inclines and the mud, sand, early and late grasses, and seasonal growth. Landscape features shaped movement across space as absorbed by the body and had effects on legs and bottoms as well as in heads and stomachs, all mediated by oxen and horses. Animals provided historical rhythms to movement and the pace of travel that became a part of this era's sense of place.

Georgina Thomson remembered experiences from her perspective as a passenger in a wagon box in Alberta: the wagon "rumbled and bumped over the prairie" through wheel-matted "brown prairie grass." "I think you have missed a great deal," she informed modern readers. Manitoban Laura Goodman Salverson recalled feeling vibrations through the floor of her parents' wooden-wheeled buckboard wagon caused by the "rolling motion" of their team's "slow gait" over the "rutted trail." The "creaking noise" generated by the wheels, the "reedy sound" of horsetails "whisking" the dashboard, and the "clop-clop of their pounding feet" echoed. Thorstina Jackson Walters, child of Icelandic immigrants, cited the halting movements of "my first excursions into the world away from home" in the wagon, not the destinations. The terrain's human experiences included the smell of hay intermixed with ox odors.[9]

Winter required different skills and more equipment. Effie Laurie Storer recalled how she became "adept at jumping" on and off a sled pulled by "Indian" ponies as they trotted along at a "steady pace." She explained how handlers ensured the ponies worked together; the Métis attendants shifted the lead pony to the back at regular intervals, so all the ponies would share "the hard task of breaking [through the snow on] the trail." She noted the uniformity and efficiency of the pace as a plus: "each pony steps in the same hole and the sleigh will travel in the same rut." North Dakotan Era Bell Thompson wrote of sitting atop a "straw-covered bed of a big sled," "bundled" in horse blankets; she "could see very little" but "could smell the clean, fresh odor of straw and feel the sideways jolt of the runners as they bumped into rocks underneath the snow." The "steady, rhythmic beat of horses' hoofs" resonated in a particular way across open night air clarified by a thirty-five-below-zero temperature. The welcomed warmth of horse blankets and buffalo robes spoke to the smells of place and time.[10]

Animals interacting with topography pulled children's eyes down to grass level. What triggered that bump, caused that swing, or produced such a dip? Distant grasslands frequently collapsed the life and movement of the grasslands to a line of sight: a "plain . . . beautiful and green," a "vast land that stretched endlessly in all directions," or "prairie . . . always the same, mile after mile of sagebrush and cactus."[11] However, eyes have the capacity to catch grasses waving when in relative proximity. The experience of crossing the grasslands bounced, shook, and shuddered views, according to unique combinations of vehicles, terrain, and the inclinations of humans and animals. These early childhood experiences with animal transport came largely under the direction of parents and other adults busy with the business of life.

Animal Friends and Nature

Children spent a great deal of enjoyable time with animals on their own. Children relied on animals; learned their movements, manners, and moods; and understood the idiosyncrasies of animal individuality. Animals became "friends." While not exactly pets, some animals and their distinct personalities became highly associated with the family. Peggy Olson Bell of Montana claimed she "made pets out of all kinds of animals—prairie dogs, badgers, coyotes, porcupines, even a baby skunk," or, at least in her child's world, she thought she had domesticated these wild creatures. Wallace Stegner of Saskatchewan wrote of his "love" for animals, claiming, "Our pets were all captives from the wild—burrowing owls, magpies, a coyote pup, a ferret that I caught in a gopher trap and kept in a screened beer case."[12] Free movement of animals taught children about the landscape in ways less filtered than riding in a wagon or buggy.

Hale Humphrey from Faulkton, Dakota Territory, was not alone in his attachment animals, even in his own family. Special reports on the Humphrey family's barnyard residents and local wild animals formed a significant component of their rich correspondence, some writing in Dakota Territory, others reporting from Iowa. Hale drew chicks ensconced in a mix of grasses, with one large flowering, broad-leaved plant nearby. Two birds appear to fly off from the site, leaving five scurrying. Almost corresponding to his paper scene, he wrote, "We have one little chicken now, and I expect some more will hatch before night." Hale drew ducks or swans on the water, puffy clouds floating in the sky above, or a lone tree in proximity to a slough or creek. Tall cattail stalks and reedy grasses populate his water ponds. Hale's older sister Alice wrote in detail about "one little chicken": "it is real smart," she claimed with maternal affection. "This morning when I fed it, for the first time; it ate the meal from the dish and drank water from the spoon. It is in my hand now. It is all dark with a yellow dot on its head. I call it mine. Its name is Dot. . . . My chicks lungs are real strong." One modern observer of chickens suggests the "direct eye contact" with which children such as Alice Humphrey likely engaged formed a "crucial" element in a "trusting, friendly relationship." Dorothy Johnson, from Montana, recounted how she could "keep a hen's interest for a minute or so . . . by clucking and making soothing chicken noises while she stares at me with one eye."[13] Children such as Alice and Dorothy sought this "bond of friendship," which, without granting conscious intentionality, created a familiarity between "human and bird" that children often reworked into unique small-world stories.[14] These specific animal narratives maintained lifelong memories of particular chickens and experiences attached to specific places.

 Reading her 1880s Albertan diary over fifty years later, Lula Short Asher noticed entries on "Granny" and penciled in "Granny was our best mother hen." Most of the hens had names, and Lula enjoyed arranging adoptions between hens without chicks and attempted at least once to find a surrogate mother for duck eggs. Kjersti Raaen, living on the Goose River in the Red River Valley in northern Dakota Territory, cheered when her mother's hens starting "stealing their nests"—that is, laying eggs away from the nest; she felt the hens must "feel bad to have their eggs taken." Children often anthropomor-

2. The collage here shows animal drawings by Hale Humphrey, from Faulkton, Dakota Territory, that he enclosed with or drew on letters written to various family members in 1884, 1885, and 1886, and again in 1895, to his "wee" sister at home. Collage constructed by author for purposes of illustration. Humphrey Family Papers, State Archives Collection, South Dakota State Historical Society.

phized and felt protective of creatures, imbuing them with intentional action. Such memories also suggest that children's affection and prolonged attention made them keen animal observers. Indeed, modern chickens have been observed to plan particular places to lay eggs. Johnson recalled, "watching a hen take a dust bath" in Montana: the hen "shuffles her chest in the dry dust and works it into her feathers. She languidly stretches one leg and one wing, then the other leg and wing." Next the hen "digs with her beak at her itchy places." "She clucks with satisfaction [and] shuffles some more" and, finally, "shakes herself all over."[15] The creativity generated by children's small worlds and the time spent in sustained close contact with animals allowed children to believe in animal intentionality—and perhaps accurately observe behavior dismissed too easily as mere fantasy by adults.

Young girls, especially, saw themselves as mothers or directors of family flocks able to promote empathy among diverse creatures in their care. Era Bell Thompson snatched a piglet from a sow's litter for the doll buggy she pushed across North Dakota grass and named him Jerry; she cried when the family butchered him. In another letter to Iowa from the Humphrey place in Dakota, Alice reported, "Pet and Daisy [the horses] are both pretty, lively and plump"; "Snowball and Roan [the calves] are growing fast"; "The Kitties, Kitty Pride, Bonny [the bunny], Raby . . . and cow are all well." Bunny Bonny typically found kitten "friends besiting her," thanks to introductions made by Alice. The "little grey" kitten stayed with Bonny so much, Alice observed, "it will stand up on its hind feet and look around just like Bonny." Alice felt her descriptive power over the animals failed on the page and gave up: "I can't pen-picture it." Nevertheless, she felt animal relationships worth her attempts to detail for the family even if her mother could not wholly understand.[16]

Children assumed they had special relationships with animals unavailable to adults. The Montana-born Peggy Olson "always had one cow that was crazy" for her. Peggy never forgot one "big wild-looking dark red" cow distinguished by a "black neck and head." She felt cows paid attention to her appearance; they did not like new bright-blue dresses, only faded fabric. More interestingly, she insisted the cows liked her hair down, not tied back, and one in particular nipped off the string every time she tried to nap. Robert McAlmon's character, who lived in a fictionalized eastern South Dakota village, walked to a nearby farm because "he liked feeding the calves and petting them, and putting his face up against theirs." Portraying the special pact that seems to have been imagined by children across the grasslands, this boy felt sure the owner's "registered" cows, the "beautiful ones of them were friendly to him and caressed him as they never would" their owner. The adult memoirist or fiction writer often felt compelled to point out the animal relationships they took so seriously as children in the end offered only "simply live ears into which [any child] could say aloud his dreams and hopes."[17] But from a child's small-world perspective pigs and calves listened and comforted. Importantly, most of these acts of affection and the soft feelings they generated for animals took place outdoors, tying animals and children to area landscapes.

In the spring children hunted for wild birds, nests, and eggs, encountering common and "flamingly beautiful" robins, whippoorwills, golden orioles, goldfinches, rose grosbeaks, scarlet tanagers, olive kinglets, brown thrushes, loons, cardinals, and the turtle doves. Hundreds of bird species migrated annually north and south, using North America's Mississippi, Missouri, and Saskatchewan River systems and ponded, grassed wetlands as way stations. After spending a couple of days moving in and out of the house doing the washing and folding in April 1891, Alice Humphrey wrote her mother with an announcement. "The birds sing all day; I heard a meadow lark just now; they seem quite plenty this year, at least if one is to judge by the amount of song." The seven-year-old Dakotan Hale Humphrey reported to his mother that he "went hunting yesterday." "I found to nest with eggs in. An egg in each nest." Montanan Lillian Miller wrote of the distinctive brown curlew bird with long legs and an even longer curved bill that nested in a marshy area near one of their fences. In the evening a whole group would fly, "calling what sounded like their name." Era Bell Thompson mentioned meadowlarks, robins, "droves of raucous crows," and "white-winged sea gulls" that seemed to her out of place in a sea of North Dakota grass. Annora Brown recalled that the "call of the meadow lark and the song of horned larks and sparrows," along with grasshoppers, bees, and curlews, made her think "it was like listening to some great orchestra."[18]

As both a playmate and an older observer, one of Aagot Raaen's fond reveries involved her younger sister Kjersti "fairly bursting with questions" about birds and much else in Dakota Territory. In the spring the girls sat inside a vacant Goose River bluff dugout, letting the birds "come and go at will," "chattering, questioning, hopping all over them, eating out of their hands and laps." Kjersti dug worms with her hands to feed newly hatched birds and also protected birds from the cat. She called out in "bird dialect" from the bluff "Bird Home," as they dubbed the dugout, in tones of catbird, owl, whippoorwill, robin, and wren. Stegner forever remembered the specific "dialect" of the western meadowlarks that chirped in Saskatchewan. The sounds of nature invited children to move out to them to listen for whatever else they might hear and inspect the places from which sound resounded.[19]

Bird-nest hunting and bird sighting involved children scanning the sky and poking around through grasses, sloughs, shrubs, and tree stands. Lula Short remembered climbing a tree in Alberta to nab "a couple of young hawks or eagles" sitting motherless in a nest, though she found it "difficult" to "subdue" the younglings. Even greater disappointment ensued when her father forbade her to keep the birds as pets. That she could not distinguish many years later whether the birds were hawks or eagles may have been because of faulty memory, or she may never have known the exact species of the birds she knew by sight and sound. It was common for grasslands children to know animals and birds by sight, sound, and smell but not by taxonomic classification.[20] Where and when birds flew and rested also taught children about wind flows, atmospheric conditions, and the land across seasons.

The spring began when, according to Albertan Annora Brown's memory, scurrying gophers with "ramrod backs" appeared. The small wild-animal population of gophers, prairie dogs, jackrabbits, and coyotes thrilled and pulled children quickly through the terrain in chance ways. The Albertan Lula Short also remembered the wily nature of "hundreds of gophers," which she called "prairie squirrels," who

Small Worlds 67

"called . . . about us" near High River: "One would stand stiffly upright at the edge of its hole, whistle an invitation to approach till we came within a few feet, then dart out [of] sight underground, to reappear immediately at another opening and reiterate its merry defiance." Wilfrid Eggleston knew Alberta's gophers by variety of "alarm" and their pocket-like storage cheeks; he competed with gophers for wild onions, explaining "sometimes in the spring a whole hillside would be studded with the pits where the bulbs had been." Holes dug into the prairie brought a child to inspective attention. Once Wilfrid inched forward to burrows, belly down on the prairie, to take snapshots of particular gophers with his new Brownie camera.[21]

Horses and cattle received the most individualized attention; these animals brought commercial agriculture to the northern grasslands. Lula Short named one cow Diamond, though the reason is unclear, as the cow had "a mark on the forehead like a heart." One senses there was more to the story; Diamond seemed more logical than Heart in her small-world construction in a way that remains unavailable today—and probably to the adult Lula. One picture Hale drew included an action scene with a horse and its foal right behind, galloping at full speed over grasslands. The picture reflected one of his letters to Alfred: "The colt is weaned and is runing with Pet now. I have made a bridle and harness for her." Lulu Pickler Frad emphasized, "How we loved our horses and ponies. There was 'Jack and Jimmy' our two mules, Coalie a buggy horse, Bill and Kit our two Indian ponies who were our constant play fellows, and Old Prince Mamma's faithful buggy horse." "No memory is dearer than the affection we had for them [the horses] and their loyalty to us," insisted Lulu, looking back from the middle of the twentieth century.[22]

North Dakotan Era Bell Thompson remembered, "with my dog and my pony I was happy beyond the realm of people, for I had found a friendship among animals that wavered not, that asked so little and gave so much loyalty and trust," importantly, without noticing the color of her skin. Since her North Dakota schoolmates wanted to touch her hair (a school textbook informed her class, "Negroes were black folks with Kinky hair"), this recollection is especially poignant. The phrase "irrespective of color" followed fast on her claim of the

3. Era Bell Thompson rides on horseback in early 1920s Mandan, North Dakota. State Historical Society of North Dakota (00262-00003).

"loyalty and trust" of animals. Thompson also reiterated a feeling common among most children living on the northern grasslands: "Mother couldn't keep me from the horses." Fellow North Dakotan Thorstina Jackson may be the exception that proves the rule. Growing up, she received permission only "once in a while" to sit on the family's "plough horse." She marked her parents' rules as unusual (perhaps her parents proved overprotective because her only siblings, two sisters, died young in a scarlet fever epidemic).[23]

Letters from Lulu Pickler's neighbor and friend Alice Humphrey described horses that Lulu probably knew. Alice wrote as if her horse was a pal: "Daisy and I took a ride tonight. She feels splendid and enjoys a gallop as much as any one." Alice practiced all sorts of maneuvers on the horses: "I rode sidewise bare back" and at "a lope," as well as a "walk, trot, gallop and run," suggesting she spent quite an amount of time atop horses.[24] Anthropologists have noted that horses often choose to create friendships with unrelated individuals within their horse communities, but also with other species, including humans.

Small Worlds

Horses learn to sense particular riders' intentions; and riders, the characteristic needs of their horses. This interaction formed relationships of trust, suggesting that narratives of old friendly animals leading children and cooperating with their desires prove not far off, not merely anthropomorphizing.[25] Children formed attachments easily with horses because of their natures and the abilities and social needs of horses and, importantly, because of children's imaginations. Both interacted with the grasslands, teaching one another about the landscape.

George Will remarked that, during his Bismarck boyhood in the 1880s and 1890s, "a pony was an indispensable childhood equipment." He and his sister Mable shared their first pony, Dick, and the two quickly joined a "horsy group which comprised practically all the kids in town." Soon George and Mable rode "expert" bareback, ditching the gender-designated classic and sidesaddles their parents purchased to outfit the horse. The town became a board for children's games "enjoyed ahorse," including a version of night hide-and-seek. Will claimed that children rode horses more than they walked, even in town. Horses were so important to the daily lives of North Dakota children that they influenced George Will's memories of the 1893 Chicago World's Fair ("a mad whirl for us children"). He and his sister felt exhausted, he claimed, because there were "no ponies to ride" around the grounds. They were not in the habit of long walking on a daily basis.[26]

The power of the animal-child relationship can be seen in a particular moment of crisis recalled by Wallace Stegner. The death of one particular colt devastated him. A mishap (caused by Stegner's unintentional carelessness) injured Daisy's newborn foal. Stegner, in an act of mothering not often revealed in boys' memoirs, tried but failed to bring the colt back to health, feeding the animal by hand and attaching "iron braces" to the horse's legs. Whether it was kind or cruel of his father to try to hide the horse's fate from his son—the horse would need to be shot—he convinced "Wally" to believe the horse would live better if the family sold it to a local ranch. When Stegner later found the dead animal while scavenging the town dump, it traumatized him—it seems—for a lifetime. The small body, iron braces still attached, had been skinned and dumped. Although

Stegner as a boy excelled at earning cash by capturing and skinning animals, the two dollars he surmised the new owner received for his colt's skin seemed especially cruel.[27] Domestic or wild animals coaxed into friendships and caring relationships, when killed out of order, struck children at their depths.

The interconnections between children's emotions, animals, and the power parents had over children can be seen in the truly horrible incidents experienced by a very young Peggy Olson. She took refuge in horse "friends," shielding herself from a childhood full of neglect and abuse. Her love and knowledge of horses began by the age of two, when she claimed she first rode a horse. For a lifetime Peggy took pride for the way she—like her birth father—had a "way of getting on the good side of animals." One can only imagine, then, what the child said to the horses in the barn as she reached for the "heavy strap," a saddling tool that connected rider and horse. She knew her stepfather would soon use the strap in an attempt to lash out all of her affection. For failure at tasks too large for a little girl to do, Peggy's stepfather beat her to bleeding, insisting on at least one occasion that her mother also do the same. For the "strapping" weapon he chose the "belly band off the harness," which she recalled in emblazoned detail as "an extra-heavy strap, about two inches wide with no buckles." She used saddles and bridles almost daily. The sadism involved in instilling associations of pain and shame into a tool Peggy would encounter daily with her horses is astounding for its cruelty and perhaps more so for its presence—the unusual honesty—in Olson's memoir. She also witnessed her stepfather beat to death a gelding he had overloaded. She stressed the premeditated nature of the killing as she watched her stepfather methodically "carve a club out of an old cottonwood limb" with which he would beat the horse.[28] The child-animal relationship, as most relationships, could be manipulated in positive and negative ways. Since animals took up so much space in a child's life and in this period's cultures, the potential for parents or adults to issue abuse through animals increased in comparison to the emergent transportation age. The manipulation and emotional twisting of child-animal relationships occurred in proportion to the period, place, and proclivities of parents.

Work with Animals

Perhaps more typical, adults characteristically played along with child-animal friends because children who had good relationships with animals could transfer patterns of fun to work. Children often created play out of work, but they also worked hard. On a farm or in a small town—even the city—the skill of handling horses, ponies, and cows remained a necessity. As George Will explained, "The shortest trip or errand was performed aboard our willing pony." Although they lived in Bismarck, the Wills rode their pony to get groceries. The Will family's "big sorrel horse known as Grant" hauled for their tree and seed company store.[29] Most town families owned a milch cow and horses for buggies and wagons; most towns had commons pastures. The settler-society culture reshaping the northern grasslands valued such animals as essential to the local economy and a necessary component of the inland transportation network. Despite increasing railroad travel, animals dominated daily terrain and would remain in use in some capacity steadily until well into the twentieth century.

Many animals encountered as friends existed primarily for the commercial endeavors of profit and consumption. Alice Humphrey quickly caught on to the chicken factor in the overall family economy. Excitedly preparing for spring one year while back in Iowa with her mother, she wrote her father, "Do any of the hens want to set yet? Mama said I could raise all the chickens I could this year; and sell them (not all of them)." Another time, when Alice was in charge at home, she signed off one report to her mother saying, "It will take all my 'chicken money' to pay postage on my *letters to you.*" She acknowledged an acceptance of the commercial purpose of her chickens, once, if not still, her close friends. Chickens could contribute significantly to a family economy, as Lula Short's Alberta diary suggests. From 1885 to 1888 she collected eggs, noting the daily take, from 9 in February 1885 to 113 the next May. "So far this year have had 800 eggs," she recorded on 31 May 1888. By then Lula sold her eggs and butter in the nearest town, recording prices she earned per dozen and pound. Farm families and agricultural experts alike thought children's emotionally satisfying work with animals that also realized economic contributions helped attach them to the farm.[30]

Three letters from Hale, Kenneth, and Alice Humphrey, announcing the birth of a new calf in March 1886, suggest the connection between period, place, animals, work, and environment. "Durham's calf came in a snow storm and so we named it snow-drop," wrote Hale. He made an effort to connect the triple serendipity of birth, weather, and the physical attributes of the new little being. The younger Kenneth, in almost the format of a children's poem, simply printed: "Durham has a little calf, it is as white as snow." Only the eldest, Alice, pushed beyond naming to make connections between animals and work. She instructed her brother Alfred, "*If* Jersey's calf is a steer you will have the pleasure of breaking a pair of young oxen," Snow-drop, and another expected calf.[31] The letters nicely demonstrate the children's growing awareness of the essential role of animals to the family enterprise (and children's growing expressive skills). The birth of Snow-drop immediately paired with an unborn but hoped-for bull, and the acts making that bull into a steer and of "breaking" the two calves eventually to work and yoke anticipated a future agricultural role. Snow-drop and many of the animals the Humphrey children held dear existed to emboss a new commercial agricultural order on the grasslands.

Herding led children deep into the grasslands environment and connected children explicitly to commercial agricultural production. Growing up in southeastern Dakota Territory, Peter Norbeck, born in 1870, guided the family's small cattle herd and also milked cows. The chore suited children, as it required knowledge of animal behavior and a lot of energy but not an overabundance of physical strength. A boy from North Dakota's Icelandic communities hired out locally to herd wild "*cayuses*" for a cowboy "veteran of the old West." The same boy, in hopes of finding some "Wild West" experiences, herded cattle at a point far enough away from his home that it required staying overnight on the prairie. Instead of a "thriller" set in the "loneliness of the wide unsettled areas" he was hoping to find, however, he found jackrabbits and "relentless" mosquitoes.[32]

Small Worlds 73

Herding animals allowed boys to act out mythic Western fantasies of cowboys, but in the process they worked.

Free grazing animals often led their owners to encounter new grasslands spaces. In Alberta Lula Short's diary recorded the numerous times "we girls got in the cows and milked them" and searched for horses in the countryside. In mid-April 1886 Lula's brother Charlie rode horseback searching for cows for two days before finding them on the evening of the second day. One of the Short's horses made it all the way from High River to Macleod; the horse Polly had been gone for two weeks before the family received a letter indicating the distance she wandered. Lula cared enough to note once in her diary, "Polly's shoulder very sore from Ploughing," so her disappearance must have been distressing.[33] The pattern of children exploring the grasslands through herding remained persistent over many decades. In all the herding and searching for wandering animals, children covered a lot of ground to allow for continual observation of grasslands over the seasons. The accumulation of experiences with animals in the landscape affected ways of orienting in space, which contributed to forming senses of place.

Alice Humphrey explained implicitly to her brother Alfred that her level of work changed with spring snowmelt, as "there is water in the sloughs East of here and the cows drink there." Another time, however, Alice pushed on "to the river to water the ponies," as they "do not like the water" in the sloughs and would not drink it. Although Alice did not explain what she learned, her words suggest she closely watched the changing spring grasslands and observed patterns of growth. She may have learned about good drinking water from the actions of the cows and horses under her change. On occasion she directly revealed her observations. In April 1891 she informed her mother, "The pasture east of town is nearly done; there is quite a large herd in there now." Alice had learned enough about grazing cycles to judge a "done" pasture. She must have also noticed which species of grass her herd grazed the most, which plants they left alone, and, ultimately, the regrowth of a formerly "done" grasslands pasture. Scanning the terrain and making judgments about its qualities became a commonplace activity—a way of seeing developed by the requirements of time and place. Other children easily recognized "dry, hooftrod grass" and grass that had been "nipped close to the earth" by animals. Nell Wilson learned to distinguish among grasses by their effect on stock; she judged grasses with "irritating spears" of low quality and noted animals preferred "redtop" grass from near coulees. Olson's stepfather taught her to picket the horses at the creek, "where the grass was good and there were no rocks."[34] In a child's ability to read the landscape lies evidence of growing environmental knowledge, an intimacy gained only by daily interaction over the seasons that shaped senses of place.

Animals were of great use and concern during prairie fires. One 1880s fire threatened the fledgling town of Faulkton. Alice Humphrey, who "had a nice ride . . . out to where they were back firing," wrote about the fire in her usual report format: she tracked the towns the fire "cleared," the fire's "diagonal course," and, finally, how the fire "stopped at the road." She viewed the scene atop her horse. The "nice" ride she had seems out of place in the context of grasslands afire but may reflect her trusting relationship with her horse. The protection proved mutual, as Alice explained how, after the second day of the fire, the schoolteacher let Hale and her "go over on the flat and get the ponies" to the barn. Noting how gale winds spread the fire, she explained, "The wind nearly blew me off my pony when we went after the ponies, and I grabed the mane." "Now this is no tale," she added to rebuff any suspicion her mother may have had of her exaggerating the wind. When Hale told of the fire, he concluded by assuring his mother, "The ponies are all right." Implicit are observations Alice and Hale could not have missed over the ensuing months of recovery to the next spring.[35]

Peggy Olson came to understand the relationship of horses and cows to Montana and Alberta grasslands very well. She knew all the breeds of stock and most brands and could pair up mares and cows with their young "by their build and action or that certain way they had of looking me over, even to the three and four years olds." She knew what a picketed "shivering horse" would do to keep warm on a cold night (walk in circles). She knew how to distinguish a "milk cow from a dry cow." In the face of mosquitoes, she knew the cows would "graze facing the wind," moving against the gale no matter how far it took them away from their accustomed range. While herding her stepfather's cattle in Alberta, Olson learn to recognize "cozy tunnels" built of "tall grass arched over deep buffalo trails." She slept nestled in these spots, protected from mosquitoes. Since she might be beaten if the cattle got away from her while she slept, she made sure the cattle lay down to sleep before she did, so they would "imprint in the tall grass." She needed the proof of the "imprint" to protect herself from a charge that she acted carelessly. Once, when the cattle sought better pasture beyond recently burned-over grasslands, Olson could not find them for two days. For punishment her stepfather strung her naked to the house ridgepole and beat her until he made her "blood run." She recalled candidly, "my entire body was covered with stripes." Moreover, "snow-blindned" from herding in winter her eyes remained "troubled" for life.[36] As she and the cattle embossed the grasslands, the grasslands environment imprinted itself on Peggy's body, as it shaped her senses in many ways.

It was absolutely necessary to understand animal mannerisms and interactions with the landscape; horse work was especially risky. Studying Canadian grasslands children, Sandra Rollings-Magnusson found animal work required children to have riding skill, endurance, agility, plant knowledge, and the ability to assess animal health. Lula's horse, Dick, "bucked [her] off" after walking and trotting "around the barn," because the "stirrups were far to[o] short." She would not be thwarted: "I got on him again and though he jumped and tried hard to buck he didnt get me off." Two days later, one of the longest entries in her diary explained, "I rode Dick again.... He tried hard to buck but I kept his head up so he couldnt. So he tumbled down all of a sudden on his knees and put his back up. Then I went over his head. He got up and I got on him again. He tried to buck but he couldnt. So he rolled over onto his side and on my legs. So I put him into the barn (at Mama's command)." She suffered a "stiff" and "sore" neck for the next two days. A horse dragged one of Lula's brothers to his death.[37]

Faunal Extermination

When rodents and small furbearers intersected with agriculture or curious children, they frequently lost the battle. While wild creatures could be intriguing in their behaviors, children might also be instructed to either keep clear of or kill them. A few song and game bird eggs cracked by a child posed little ecological threat, but the sanction of other tasks by adults prepared children for more serious extermination efforts and to accept an ethic of species control. In the first half of the twentieth century, residents of the northern grasslands viewed animals through an economic lens, a common attitude for settlers societies until the middle of the twentieth century. The mix of experiential knowledge from action on the landscape and that acquired by children by observing parents' actions and hearing their ideas as filtered by small-world imaginations masked children's senses of their own impact on ecological habitat. Some of children's small-world actions did not conform to ethics they later developed as adults, after the idea of animals having intrinsic worth and important roles in ecological health became more popular in the mid-twentieth century. Still, animals seemed a valued and dynamic part of grasslands settler societies. National, provincial, and state laws developed, but—difficult to enforce in any case—they also often exempted private property owners or farmers seeking subsistence.[38]

Children often disrupted native grasslands ecology out of simple curiosity. Wallace Stegner of Saskatchewan fed his "live gophers" to his pet "big weasel." Really the pet was a black-footed ferret, Stegner learned much, much later. Stegner's sacrifice of one type of prairie animal, live gophers, to another, a ferret, once thought practically extinct, fits a common pattern of intimate but unscientific knowledge. Thorstina Jackson Walters noted a changing environment in 1890s North Dakota: the "wolves and foxes took a last stand, so to speak, often entering the barns and carrying off chickens and sheep." When she was a child, this seemingly indiscriminate snatching scared her, but her adult "last stand" comment suggests she linked a decline of native habitat and its wild animals to the rise of domestic creatures.[39]

Grasslands children grew up amid orchestrated state, provincial, town, and individual efforts to exterminate animals that threatened agriculture, especially gophers and prairie dogs but also rabbits. Systematic plans for extermination did not suggest the same sense of innocent childhood curiosity. One of Elsie May Hammond's later diaries opened with the following statement: "No. of gophers caught by Sask. Children up to May 15 1918 was 864,000." George Will recalled, "A favorite expedition for the boys was to ride out in the prairies, picket our horses, and spend an hour with a long string snare catching gophers." Settler society encouraged most children to kill. Eggleston explained, shifting some inkling of guilt to his parents, "Homesteader's children were expected to wage war on them—trap them, shoot them, drown them out in the spring when water was available, [and] poison them with strychnine-treated wheat kernels." Hammond's diary reveals young women hunted gophers too. Kate Neatby Nicoll recalled spooning grain laced with "Kill 'em Quick" poison into gopher holes. Nell Wilson Parsons recalled learning how to set dirt-covered snares at gopher holes and waiting patiently until she could jerk the string to capture the gophers when they appeared. Women's memoirs, however, almost never mentioned violent exploits, but men frequently recast their hunting of small animals with detail, emphasizing creative capture strategies.[40]

Stegner and his brother carried guns for summer fun as early as the age of eight and "spent hours of every day trapping, shooting, snaring, poisoning, or drowning the gophers that gathered in our wheatfield." "We poisoned out the prairie dogs," he recalled, now understanding how in doing so they "incidentally did in the black-footed ferrets that lived on them." He and his friends were "experts in dispensing death." They "knew to the slightest kick and reflex the gophers' ways of dying: knew how the eyes popped out blue as marbles when we clubbed a trapped gopher with a stake, . . . knew how an unburied carcass would begin within a few hours to seethe with little black scavenger bugs, and how a big orange carrion beetle working in one could all but roll it over with the energy of his greed."[41]

A boy from southwestern Minnesota outlined how he caught a "striped one" on his family's 880-acre sheep and cattle ranch. His capture technique used fish line to make a noose set over a gopher hole. He waited "quietly" for the animal to "pop his head out of the hole to see if all is safe around him" and then "jerked the string tight around his neck." Then, he explained, "I . . . swing him around my head and strike him on the ground till he is dead." Considering how many of these gophers existed, and the time this technique involved, the effort to catch this one small animal suggests a boy's small world of meaning. Yet another boy pretended to be a "horse doctor" and tied down "each leg" of a gopher and also performed "premature Caesarian on a prospective mother gopher."[42] The hours these boys laid on the ground waiting and planning—that in turn allowed many hours of close observation of the ground, insect life, and all matter of grasslands habitat activity—suggest how children absorbed place in daily activity, even with faunal extinction as the goal. Adults saw such activities as healthy ways of interacting with a land undergoing transformation, teaching one to handle blood and guts and the knife necessary for agriculture on the ranch or farm in preparation for the market.

Coyotes appear to be among the most feared animals among this generation—mostly because of their yowl. Coyote fur had monetary value, but the coyote appears foremost as the key nighttime soundtrack to the grasslands. Lula Short noted, "The weird howling of coyotes at night, once heard, is never forgotten." Peggy Olson, when living in Montana, felt vulnerable to coyotes and wolves on the open grasslands. One time trying to make her way two miles from her mother and stepfather's homestead to her uncle's and grandmother's homesteads, as a girl not yet ten, she lost her way with two still younger sisters in tow. She had taken a "road . . . . used so seldom that the grass wasn't worn off." Immediately she feared "wolves or coyotes might attack." Another time her stepfather left her "on a steep and icy" hill with a stalled wagon and a dead horse. Peggy heard the "howling" of the coyotes as they picked up the scent of the dead horse. The volume and chorus told her to expect many. Olson and her sister "shook with nervousness and fright." Her stepfather also forced her to check his coyote traps daily during the winter; if she found an animal she had to club it to death. In executing such violence Olson thought about "the dirty work of coyotes, killing little calves and lambs and how often they scared me when I was alone on the prairie at night. A man might kill a coyote without a qualm," she reflected years later, "but I dreaded it." She had to skin the coyotes too. Tellingly, Dakota boys George Will and Birlea Ward did not have qualms about racing "bareback," each with a "stout stick" in an effort to "ride down a coyote." Chasing down animals successfully suggested growing control over nature.[43]

One-time eastern South Dakota resident Robert McAlmon fictionalized a "Jack Rabbit Drive," witnessed by a six-year-old boy. He focused on the boy's struggle to understand an overlapping context: magnificent strong rabbits leaping on the grasslands overlaid by greedy, nasty rabbits feasting in a field. The local village of the plot sponsored the drive on behalf of its surrounding farms because the rabbits and "their burrowings and nibblings destroyed too much grain and property." Despite the fact that his mother told him the drive would be too "brutal" for him to see, he stole away to the edge of town. There he could hear the drive coming: "the resonance of the noises became continually louder." Finally, the dogs, women, men, and older children arrived at the designated fence, armed with guns, clubs, and tree limbs. Instead of the sound associated with cute bunnies—like Alice Humphrey's bunny "Bonny"—the "thump, thump, thump" the little boy heard corresponded to the "thump of clubs against the light-boned heads of the rabbits." "Tearing along, panic-struck huge white jack rabbits catapulted across the prairie towards the fence corner," wrote McAlmon, continuing in his realistic story. "The rabbits hurled themselves on at leaps of twenty, thirty, or even forty feet in the case of the huge-sized jacks." (Wilfrid Eggleston measured the leaps of jackrabbits in southern Alberta to be some twenty feet, "as footprints on the snow testified.") "Shrilly, above the pandemonium a shriek of rabbit pain sounded now and then as some dog captured a jack and ripped it to bits." To the boy, "It didn't seem that what he was seeing was actual. The jack rabbits looked so powerful and electric as they came across the prairie, and so limp, like damp besmudged cotton, as they lay torn upon the ground with the yellow of their hides, and the red of their interiors, showing." McAlmon concluded the story with a pileup of a thousand rabbit bodies and the boy "dizzy within himself," his mind "stalled."[44]

Through extermination practices children of the grasslands learned about the land and its native faunal life. McAlmon's fiction shows sensitivity to children's inner conflicts, desiring to participate in adult work and enjoying the challenge wild animals posed. Nevertheless,

McAlmon shows the effect animal violence could have on children—even when they sought it out and felt proud of their participation in ridding the land of threats to commerce and society. "Nobody could have been more brainlessly and immorally destructive," confessed Stegner years later. "And yet there was love there, too. We took delight in knowing intimately the same animals we killed." Stegner never forgot the time he drove a pitchfork through a ferret in the chicken house; it "sickened" him "by its ferocious vitality, dismayed by how hard the wild died."[45] Complex feelings surrounded children's relationships with wild animals. Animals were pets and threats: lives to admire and control.

The Taste of Animals

Children tasted the grasslands through native faunal life; grasslands taste came in part from a "shooting" tradition, which served to provide needed food for many families. Over time shooting also became a sport. Dakotan Hale Humphrey tasted the ducks and prairie chickens he once drew, flavored by wild grasses and the new commercial grains growing in the fields surrounding Faulkton. Hale described an 1880s Home Harvest picnic that suggests wild game as standard fare: he consumed "7 kinds of cake, 3 kinds of pie, wild duck, prairie chicken, dish of pudding, 1 tart, bread and butter, biscuit and butter, brown bread and butter, and a cookie." He added, "Was that not enough for any ordinary person?" The description of the ritual harvest dinner suggests how wild fare became the cuisine of place.[46]

Settler children ate enough wild game for the animals to become unforgettable elements of the seasonal routine, even as over the course of the twentieth century hunting for subsistence became unnecessary most of the time.[47] Everyday tasks of shooting, skinning, plucking, carving, dressing, cooking, canning, and tasting worked together to lodge animals commonly perceived as edible in the culture, time, and place. Regular entries in Lula Short's diary describe eating wild prairie chickens, ducks, and geese brought home by her brother and uncle for use on the family table. In October 1885 Short family hunters carried home a "wavy" or "Brant" small goose and eighteen ducks. One September expedition netted seventy-five ducks, thirty-two of which came home with Short hunters. The Saskatchewanian Elsie Hammond, in her 1910 diary, recorded her brothers and friends "gone shooting" for geese, duck, swan, turkey, and chickens. In late October "the boys" carried home "5 geese 12 swans and 30 ducks"; in November her brother Fred's hunting crew "got 4 turkeys." Another October her brother bagged "altogether 10 swans, 4 geese and 12 ducks."[48]

Nell Wilson remembered "rich and savory" jackrabbit stew with pleasure. She recalled in winter they kept up to "two dozen dressed rabbits hanging in a frozen row" in their coal storage shed. Lula Short recalled that "bush rabbits" in the foothills of the Rocky Mountains made "good eating" and were "plentiful most winters and easily snared." Lula herself participated in "snaring." Wilfrid Eggleston from Alberta claimed, "One of my own proud moments as a boy was the time I killed a jack rabbit with my .22 rifle and brought it home for rabbit pie." To provide food for his family and skill with a gun communicated dual forms of manliness: provision and protection. Members of this generation regularly ate wild food for dinner, taking the nutrients of the grasslands inside their bodies through wild game, while learning grasslands tastes.[49]

Many boys hunted for food, but at that stage of life hunting might fulfill developmental cultural markers. Eggleston's pride of one shot exudes a boyishness not represented in bringing thirty ducks home. When Wallace Stegner recalled his Saskatchewan boyhood, he believed that "Nothing . . . could have prevented us from hunting, fishing, trapping, and generally fulfilling ourselves as predators. I think there was not a boy who did not have a .22 by the time he was ten or eleven." Stegner remembered having "our own savage feasts out in the willows, dining upon sage hen or rabbit broiled on sticks over the fire." He even ate bullfrog legs. His language suggests boys' play in the challenge of capturing edible animals for immediate consumption rather than contributing to the family economy. Purportedly, it took Will and his boyhood friends only "an hour or so . . . to fill the cart with prairie chickens and ducks." Alfred Guthrie recalled "the joy of hunting . . . beyond accounting" in Montana, continuing, "I loved to bring birds down, to take quick aim at mallards, pintails, teal and prairie chickens on the wing and feel the twelve-gauge bounce against my battered shoulder and see the flight stopped short and the broken target fall." Eventually boys grew away from the developmental playtime aspects of shooting. Some adults gave up hunting. In the mid-1960s Guthrie revealed, "No longer do I like to kill or see things killed," but he also confessed he "would not give up my recollections," including "the good, wild smell of blood and feathers and exploded powder."[50] Boys grew into a multifarious shooting tradition that included ingestion of prey, and much play.

While women seemed to rarely mention their own hunting in their memoirs, Elsie Hammond's Saskatchewan dairies suggested young women grew up also with some shooting tradition. One July she went with her brother "shooting gophers" for two and a half hours, then bragged to her diary, "I shot 3 in 4 shots." In October 1914, on Canadian Thanksgiving, sisters Elsie and Rose Hammond and a guest "went up the creeks shooting" after breakfast. She explained, "Osie got four chickens but we [the girls] did not even get a shot at one." Again, on Halloween that year, she and her sister "went to shoot some prairie hens but did not get any." In later years a shooting accident killed Rose Hammond when she was out with a friend "coyote and hawk shooting up the creek."[51]

A letter home from England to Winnipeg, written by Edward Pitblado, suggests that his younger sister Edith hunted with the family at their "shooting lodge" fifteen miles north of Portage la Prairie. Edward asked her, "Did you manage to shoot any ducks yourself this year?" Two seasons later Edward wrote Edith, "I hear reports that you developed into a crack rifle shot. Hope you cleaned the gun after!" Apparently, Edward's mother also took "pleasure in the shoots." While residents far out into the grasslands often contributed to family food supply out of economy, the wealthy, city-located Pitblado family suggests tasting grasslands through prairie chickens to be part of a broad culture of place too.[52]

Fish, a subsistence strategy that also grew into big sport, provided another historical grasslands taste for the dinner table. When Hale Humphrey recounted the "hard" rain of 1885, he also mentioned, "There are lots of fish in the river now." Wallace Stegner used to "snare" suckers with "nooses of copper wire." The Alberta diary entries of Lula Short record her family's regular fishing, catching anywhere from two to five, twelve, and twenty-four fishes. One time she recorded, "caught 45 fish." Her autobiography explained the family enjoyed "fresh fish" and salted the "larger ones" for winter fare. Elsie Hammond's diaries record eating "fresh suckers" for supper. She fished in a nearby creek and captured "little live ones" in a box "in the creek" close to home to stock the beaver dams.[53]

Shooting and snaring, and fishing, brought welcome food home for the table and provided some fun in natural environments for children. The meat infused with grasslands tastes allowed children to take place inside their bodies in the way a combination of small animals and agriculturally transforming grasslands historically configured tastes of the era. Outings to hunt suggest exploration in grasslands habitats: scaring game birds out of high grasses and wetlands, fingering the ground to find successful shots. Fishing excursions suggest watching grasslands animals interact with water sources. Some of this grasslands-infused cuisine, particularly game birds, still survive but taste different, reflecting the agricultural terrain on which birds feed. Moreover, when eaten, game on the dinner table of the future came more as the result of ritualized sport rather than the everyday, even required, family dinner fare that landed on the Shorts' table. Native grasslands animal life over time played simultaneously reduced and intensified roles in regional food life, from everyday foodways to special-occasion meals and ritualized regional fare.

A food culture that cherished tastes of animals increasingly rare on the grasslands took root early in settler society. Tastes common before the settler era grew into the exceptional taste of later years in ways that connected settler society to both the fur-trade and colonial-exploration eras. The process helped create a deeper sense of place by attaching largely presettler society experiences to settler society. An experience with pemmican stew forged such a connection for Effie Laurie on grasslands north of the border. She ate what she called the "Indian delicacy" after a ritual "poetic effusion" detailing the recipe: basically, chop up a dense dried bison-berry slab with an "axe" and add water. The poem warned not to forget the task of "picking out the hair" embedded in the meat because of storage in a "bag of buffalo hide." Laurie "treasured" the poem as a "souvenir," including it in her 1940s memoir. Although he does not mention when he first had pemmican, no doubt grasslands stories piqued the interest of Manitoba-born, North Dakota–raised, Arctic explorer Vilhjalmur Stefansson in the "Chicago pemmican tests" in 1947. Conducted by a scientist of the American Federation of Biological Sciences, the tests gauged vitamin content; one man "had been on the pemmican almost thirty days" in "some very well controlled laboratory evaluations of (true) pemmican." Laurie's story of an unusual food experience and Stefansson's attention suggest how taste and story might work over lifetimes in those who absorbed historical stories of taste, if not actual fare, in childhood.[54]

George Will included in his unpublished autobiography a family story about a signal Bismarck event during the 1880s boom time that suggests the state of grasslands animal cuisine common to his generation's childhood. The political elite of the newly located Dakota Territory capital at Bismarck hosted a grand banquet in September 1883 to honor the laying of a cornerstone for a new capitol building. A "special train from the East" on its way to drive a golden spike in the tracks at Gold Creek, Montana, to celebrate the advent of "through traffic to the west coast" on the Northern Pacific Railway dictated the timing of the banquet. Born in 1884, Will did not actually remember the banquet; he knew it through family story. The cornerstone-laying ceremony including former president Ulysses S. Grant, Northern Pacific president Henry Villard, New York "financial leaders," a "choice assortment of the really great and the not so great from the seat of government in Washington," "celebrated Indian chiefs and members of their bands," reportedly including "Sitting Bull," and diplomats from Great Britain and Germany. Will explained, "Hunters had scoured the plains and hills" so dignitaries could feast "on every type of native game."[55] The plated dinner evoked a sense of place. The meats included both white tail and mule deer, elk, antelope, "grouse, prairie chicken, duck, geese and every other imaginable variety of game bird," and even badlands grizzly bear and mountain sheep. Will's use of the word "scour" suggests both his

Small Worlds 85

own sense of the difficulty of this culinary feat and the precipice on which grasslands big game stood by the 1880s. The menu reflected the native ecology but simultaneously suggested the success of the railroad in conquering the territory. Agricultural transformation of the land pushed many grasslands faunal tastes to the brink of extinction.

Steel tracks symbolized control of nature; the railroad reigned in space, narrowing traverse time—that is, lessoning the threat of expansive grasslands space to settler societies. The visit of a former president signaled the rare importance of the northern grasslands to the United States, and the inclusion of foreign diplomats showed the value of the United States to the world. North American animal cuisine symbolized the natural abundance of the continent. Ingestion of threatening animals of an older waning ecological order suggests the same emergent power over space felt by settler societies.

The inclusion of Sitting Bull and additional unnamed "celebrated Indian chiefs and members of their bands" spoke further to settler society's desire to manage Indigenous populations in a cloak of introducing "civilization" to them through a grand banquet and settler ceremonies. To celebrate the taste of the basic food supply of Indigenous peoples, also resources for them for spiritual practices and numerous lifeways, as a frill amenity communicated the same consuming power expressed in the coming of the Northern Pacific Railway.

Manufacturing and engineering feats, including a bridge across the Missouri River completed the year before, which in settler society's eyes could not fail to impress Indigenous peoples, communicated a similar message about the perceived benefits of the new cultural order inscribing the grasslands. Indeed, an earlier banquet attended by "notables" celebrated the completion of the bridge, remembered in story because the railroad company commissioned George Will's green-house-owning father to create "a mammoth floral piece, an exact model of the bridge to grace the banquet table."[56] Grand occasions worked to reassure settlers of their power and nourishing beneficence. The stories of celebratory game dinners, as told in his autobiography, linked Will through family to founders and pioneers to reassure him of his own place in settler-society history.

Animal Stories

Many, especially big-game, animals and their favored habitats would be reduced to almost extinction or pushed into protected pockets within or out of the northern grasslands altogether by the late nineteenth and early twentieth centuries. The architecture of the landscape still bore patterns—dips, swells, depressions, mounds, holes, and bones—of beaver, bison (often called buffalo), and other fauna of the presettler-colonial era, but the needs of modern agriculture began to refashion old animal-carved landscapes. By the time most of these children arrived on the northern grasslands, in the particular places they grew to know, the faunal framework for the land had changed drastically. However, settler society raised its children in a culture that kept historical grasslands animals in mind even when they were out of sight, if not entirely gone.

A 1948 list of extinct or endangered animals once prevalent on the grasslands included buffalo, grizzly bear, elk, mountain lion, a species of bighorn sheep, pronghorn antelope, mule deer, the white wolf, and, even "rarer each year," the coyote, lynx, bobcat, and fox. Gone were the herds of bison and "upwards of 100 elk" or "wapiti" seen by the Irish gentleman John Palliser on the Yellowstone River during his trip throughout the preterritorial grasslands that became Dakota and Montana. Palliser wrote the 1847 *Solitary Hunter*, a book read by George Will, ten years before his better-known 1857 report on his explorations of the grasslands north of the international border (in which he identified the Canadian "triangle" of arid plains named after him). Palliser recounted how he killed a seven-and-a-half-foot grizzly bear with four-and-a-half-inch claws in the Turtle Mountains of modern North Dakota. He recorded sightings of the "large white wolf, or buffalo wolf, the grey wolf, and the kit wolf," diverse wolves prowling the grasslands reduced in language by Will's day, by lack of experience, to "wolf" or simply "coyote."[57]

Notably, bison *did not* make the Northern Pacific Railway banquet menu Will claimed served "every type of native game." Bison numbering twenty-eight million to thirty million once thundered across North America's grasslands; by the mid-1880s only "a few hundred" grazed in Yellowstone National Park, with "other scattered survivors" elsewhere. Indeed, Elwyn Robinson noted the construction of the Northern Pacific Railroad led to the "wholesale destruction of game" in North Dakota, particularly bison; in the fall of 1883, badlands resident Theodore Roosevelt had trouble finding "a single buffalo." Even those settlers who moved to the grasslands before the near extinction of the bison went to areas where the bison no longer resided. Peter Norbeck grew up after 1870 a few miles away from Spirit Mound in eastern Dakota Territory—a point from which in 1804 Meriwether Lewis and William Clark viewed "herds of buffalow"—but he probably never saw a bison in Dakota until he was middle aged, around 1913, the year the New York Zoological Park shipped fourteen to start a bison herd in Wind Cave National Park in the Black Hills. Saskatchewanian Nell Wilson remembers searching for bigger, bluer blooms hiding by buffalo skulls; in Montana Lillian Miller had a buffalo skull nailed on the barn; in southern Dakota Laura Bower Van Nuys recalled her father used a "buffalo overcoat" to dress up as Santa Claus. Buffalo hides and pemmican made from bison meat once formed the economic base of the international border town of Pembina, but, born there in 1887, Thorstina Jackson heard only neighborhood "pioneer" Icelanders tell stories of buffalo "hides so plentiful that they flooded the market." Saskatchewanian Elsie Hammond might have seen her first "buffalo" at Woodland Park in Seattle, Washington, while on vacation; to her the bison looked "lon[e]ly." Over ten years later, in 1928, Hammond noted she "tasted buffalo for first time" at an "Old Timer's Banquet" in Maple Creek.[58] Later generations on the northern grasslands would see more of the bison after the species rebounded than these first generations of settler society, who grew up in the aftermath of their near extinction.

Pronghorn antelope also had turned into a rare sight during this generation's childhood. Lula Short's 1884 Canadian Pacific Railway trip across the grasslands from Manitoba to Alberta offered no sight of bison and only "an occasional coyote or herd of antelope." Nell Wilson Parsons mentioned seeing "three antelope leap away" in Saskatchewan. Of the "beautiful and graceful antelope," the adult North Dakotan George Will could recall only "one or two on the hills north

4. North Dakota artist Clell Gannon illustrated many of his poems with animal and nature scenes. This 1927 image nicely suggests the complex ecology of northern grasslands space. Antelopes take center stage, with distant bison herds grazing and geese flying in the sky. Plants dominate the foreground, while buttes mark a faraway horizon. Original image from C. Gannon, *Ever and Always*, published posthumously by Ruth Johnson Gannon and with permission from Grael Gannon.

of the Capitol as a boy." He noted an antelope hide earned a dollar in his boyhood, but "since then they were very nearly exterminated." An elderly Annora Brown remarked to an interviewer, "Isn't it strange that I lived on the prairies so long but I never saw an antelope." Yet Brown explored southern Alberta extensively during the first half of the twentieth century. Thought to perhaps outnumber bison on the grasslands in the presettlement era, at least in southwestern Saskatchewan, by 1913 only an estimated 1,500 antelope existed.[59]

Children heard stories of once-more-prevalent wild game from the first generation of settlers, growing older and telling more stories. George Will listened to "rough, uncouth, often bearded, gruff and rough talking" trappers and cowboys who had used Bismarck as a base before his boyhood. His father hired them to work at the family seed and nursery business.[60] Stories kept historical animal ecology alive in the culture and also suggested to children that settler society controlled the land, as indicated by the absence or rarity of animals that might threaten agricultural ways of life. Chance linkages between big animals once numerous on the northern grasslands and the settler society present suggests how animal narratives worked to imbue a sense of place that included historical fauna.

From Gallop to Gasoline

The first generation of setter-society colonials grew up on North America's northern grasslands hand in hand with the expansion of railroad tracks throughout the region, whether they settled during the Dakota Boom, the Canadian Bloom, or the era of the transnational "Last Best West." Most persons who lived on the northern grasslands in the late nineteenth and early twentieth centuries, however, traveled by "horse and buggy" the majority of days. As people began to note the "miracle of locomotion," whether railroad or increasingly the automobile, they spoke implicitly of much slower, animal-propelled experiences.[61]

The rise of the automobile and tractor after the turn of the twentieth century transformed the native grasslands ecology faster than children had time to grow. The Albertan Wilfrid Eggleston's first job in a new railroad town nicely suggests the dual nature of the times. One day his boss asked him to dig postholes for customers who wanted to hitch cattle or horses that pulled buggies; the next day his boss asked him to dig a hole for a gasoline tank the general store planned to install to serve automobile customers. A diary entry, made by Elsie Hammond, of an otherwise routine southwestern Saskatchewan April also spoke to the internal combustion change creeping over the grasslands: "Got Car," she titled her activities for 17 April 1916. As she incorporated the Ford automobile into her daily routine, she struggled to incorporate the new experience into her diary entries. "Had a rough ride each way," she wrote, adding "in car" above the sentence, and another time, "I drove each way," inserting "By Car" as an afterthought to distinguish the different propulsion from the way she had moved under the power of horses. For Elsie "driving" remained more securely associated with the animate. Horses trained specifically to "drive" constituted the drivers she knew (not all horses were "drivers"). Finally, Elsie settled on "motored" or "motoring" to connote a drive that took place without animals.[62] The automobile would add a new layer of sensual experiences and new perceptions to her sense of place.

The experience of traversing over the land with animal behavior and power provided a different sensual experience that encouraged intimacy with the surface of the land because of the body's more intense physical exposure to the land and sky. This generation would always remember the grasslands from the perspective of what they learned from riding, chasing, and watching animals travel over, around, and through its diverse terrain.

All bodily senses interacted with the shape of the landscape, fashioned and filtered by the movements of animals, according to instinct and training, as well as the cultures of settler society. The level of bodily containment in travel and speed provided the view and the limits of that view's detail, as much as the flora and fauna, the earth and sky, by themselves accounted for the viewing experience. The growing separation between humans and animals caused by inanimate locomotion began to change the qualities of that relationship, away from dependence on animals for work and travel as well as for economic prosperity to bonds based on commercial or entertainment value. The change would be slow, but, for many reasons brought forth by modern life, animals would have less influence on how the physical senses of subsequent generations of children took in the content of the grasslands. The affective power of South Dakotan Lulu Pickler's "dear" "ponies and horsies," experienced intensely and daily in her childhood, however, still had the capacity in the middle of the twentieth century to evoke in memory a ream of associations among animals, people, and place.

3

Sensing Prairies and Plains
Grasses, Grains, Waters, Woods, Rocks, and Snow

Annora Brown's mother frequently turned her and her sisters "out for an airing" to roam the family homestead near Red Deer, Alberta. One day, to great surprise, one of the sisters "became firmly embedded in mud." This chance happening, one of Brown's earliest memories, clung to her throughout life as much as sticky "gumbo" mud clung to her younger sister. The panic in her two-year-old body remained salient: "There stood Helen," she later recalled of her sister, "screaming with helplessness, rooted in gumbo. There I stood, rooted to the path, in terror of I knew not what."[1] The scene of a toddler and two young girls—the eldest *not* strong enough to pull the smaller out of trouble—venturing out to create their own entertainment is archetypal of childhood settler-society experiences on North America's turn-of-the-century northern grasslands. Brown's experience introduced her to prairie soil science on the toddler skill level.

Children often met the grasslands environment through immersion in its soils. They wallowed playfully in the mud and dirt, feeling the textures, smelling the tones, and seeing soil qualities through color and size. Aagot Raaen and her sisters came of age awash in the North Dakotan soil, digging "toes into the cool moist earth" and sinking "hot, tired feet . . . into the good earth, so soft." North Dakotans Era Bell Thompson and her brother "walked behind the plow in the shallow, trenchlike furrows, watching for earthworms, or sat on the velvety, upturned soil and let its warm earthiness seep up into our bodies." Gradually, through hands-on, feet-in, interactive experiences, grasslands-grown children learned to distinguish properties of soil, sand, and gravel.[2]

What Thompson observed about the "warm earthiness" of soil, that it had the power to "seep up into our bodies," was true for the "experience" of place generally at this historical moment on the northern grasslands. Place entered the body through daily, physical encounter with the grasslands, grafting smells, touches, views, sounds, and even tastes of the land to the body and mind. The cultural geographer Yi-Fu Tuan argued "human feeling" emerges from a "selective and creative process in which environmental stimuli are organized into flowing structures" that, with the aid of "memory and anticipation," "wield sensory impacts into a shifting stream of experience."[3] Historian Mark Smith has emphasized that the human body—itself always shaped by culture—mediates all environmental experience *reciprocally*, that seeing, hearing, touching, smelling, and tasting are together a "product of place and, especially, time."[4] Nell Wilson described what she felt as a child standing on the grasslands of Saskatchewan as "hear[ing] with your skin" or a "sort of feeling magic through your feet."[5] The children of settler society experienced grasslands environments with "small world" wonderment, producing feelings and sensitivities that remained powerful for lifetimes.[6] But those experiences would speak to the times—the late nineteenth century and the early twentieth century, when the northern grasslands underwent agricultural transformation.

Daily landscape encounters interweave inherited cultures and environments into senses of place. The narrative here follows children to the eve of young adulthood, as they explored prairie and plains spaces under their own power, interests, and imaginations. Children's interpretations implicitly reflected family influence and can be explicitly seen in the way children peopled the landscape with characters reflective of old world and mythic West cultures. Young people found certain features particularly compelling. In addition to the soil and wild plants of the grasslands, children formed special relationships with waters, woods, and rocks. Such facets, each in turn explored here, had the power to evoke the entire grasslands of this period, as if isolating particular elements allowed one to get ahold of an unmanageable whole. Children with fear and wonder also marveled at snow. Winter, as one of two primary seasons (along with the growing season from spring snowmelt to fall frost), in particular marks northern grasslands experience. As daily life interwove children into the grasslands environment, however, they—and their settler, agriculturist parents—changed the ground they walked on. Children of settler society viewed tame agricultural grasses as of a piece with wild native grasses. As the last section reveals, children described agricultural tasks and products with the same enthusiasm they did for native grasslands habitat.

Grasslands, Earth, and Sky

The youngest generation of settler society frequently pointed to the physical experience of roaming outdoors as key to their sense of place. Albertan Annora Brown remembered explicitly how she could "still recall my sensations as a child." One day she "met *myself* and the *prairie*" and later felt this *the* moment of her becoming "one with Nature." Brown punctuated her memoir with recollections of sensuous experience. She recalled the sights and feels of "summer haze" and "mirage-like heat waves." She remembered almost uncountable textures: soft, stiff, and rubbery petals and blades of grass; coarse, fine, stiff, and sticky stems; the pricks of pointy leaves and thorns; and seed-laden spent color blooms. Cold days made Brown think of the "rustling of dry winter grass" and the taste in her mouth after she "nibbled the pith of a rosehip" found in the snow. (Brown recalls rosehip as a treat, but another young girl ate rose hips to ease hunger pangs.) Come spring Brown noticed the "scent of wild roses and wolf willow boiled up" from the riverbanks and breezed out to the grasslands.[7]

George Will's rendering of childhood buggy drives his family took in the countryside of northern Dakota conveys the same sensual awareness: "The fall . . . with the blue sky, softened by the autumn haze overhead, the light breeze rustling through the dying grasses along the road, and vistas of soft rolling hills in all directions. Often the golden rod and wild asters brightened the yellows and tans of the autumn prairie."[8] The auditory "rustling" of grasses; the strong visual memory of "verdant" or "brightened" splashes of wild flowers; the haptic "weight" and "haze" of air; atmosphere that carried nature's scents over long distances; all these "experiences" noted by both Will and Brown suggest the way individual senses worked together with culture—signaled here by a buggy ride and shoeless walking—and grasslands habitat to wield multidimensional memories. These passages show a "tangling" of sensual stimuli that became impressions of grasslands experience.[9]

Such descriptions suggest the now-dominant North American grasslands place maxim "earth and sky" as manifested in lived experience. When Brown evoked "blue sky" and Will "sunset clouds," they spoke to actions of looking out, across, and up. The "rustling" grasses and Will's "wild asters" communicate the strength of terrain to pull eyes downward. Annora Brown once referred to "blue distance" as a summary experience, and this phrase neatly serves as a contraction for earth and sky. In Will's "vistas of soft rolling hills," the broad horizon of his view softened the hills so bits of earth and sky dip down and rise up into each other, stitching the two together. As North Dakotan Red River Valley resident Thorstina Jackson Walters phrased it, the "shadows that the clouds cast upon the prairie, seemed . . . to unite sky and land." Wallace Stegner also referenced a unity in earth and sky, when he observed that in a wet season "there is almost as much sky on the ground as in the air." Nell Wilson recalled "wind ruffled pools," each "blue as the sky." Stegner called the intermingling earth and sky "fusion"; he recognized "this sky would not be so spectacular without earth to change and glow and darken under it."[10]

Nighttime reinforced children's conception of the interwoven unified nature of earth and sky. For example, Kjersti Raaen's favorite nightspot lay atop a slope, down which she could see stars above and hundreds of fireflies blinking in the meadow below. Kjersti, as Aagot told the story, thought the fireflies were "stars" at "play" on the ground: the sky had come to "dance" on the earth. The story shows an imagination in which it made sense to connect earth and sky. After she had lived with her self-created story for some time, her father revealed the so-called stars as fireflies. Aagot recast this jarring news once again by telling Kjersti such fireflies looked like stars because they each carried tiny lanterns "so that the elves, gnomes, and fairies could find their way in the woods and meadows after sundown."[11] The

Raaen girls created ways to make sense of the enveloping spacious grasslands they felt while interacting with family culture, in this case Norwegian stories of gnomes and fairies.

The winds sweeping across the grasslands also encouraged the growing child's imagination to envision synchrony between earth and sky. Wind blew ubiquitously. When George Will recalled his life, especially "impressions of those early years," he noted, "the wind [was] always background." The wind dipped down to the ground, lifting up the earth and snow and casting it free to fly in the sky. No black-topped or concrete locked down roads. Stegner saw the sky—through wind—permeate even the "marvelous curly prairie wool [held] tight to the earth's skin." People wrote of "withering winds" that had the power to increase the effects of the sun and heat on grass and grains. Saskatchewanian Nell Wilson argued the wild rose, grass, *and* space all scented June wind, a smell also influenced by the "dazzling brilliance of the sun." Space acted as sensual stimuli. Wind gusts entangled sun and plants: sky and land by other names. Stegner recalled the wind's "push" and how the "wind fingered my face." Nell Wilson claimed a strong wind made "skin and muscle ache." Both Stegner and Brown also wrote of feeling the "weight of the sun" on their bodies.[12] This culture highlighted the sky and earth in ways that used the body and its senses as connectors to encase individuals in the environment.

The earth and sky invocation—now grown to popular cliché—spoke historically to a sense of spaciousness and envelopment individuals perceived. Feeling the sky, however, was not always a comfortable experience. Stegner, who moved to Saskatchewan as a boy, noted feeling uncomfortable as a "challenging upright thing" on the grass-lands, a "sense of being foreign and noticeable, of sticking out. I did not at first feel even safe," he recalled. As Annora Brown said, recalling her growing awareness of place, "I seemed to grow very small and the world of prairie vast around me." Isolation and exposure sometimes triggered primal fears felt in the body and mind. But, as Stegner explained, after a person "submitted" to the place "with all the senses," one's associations became more complex: "You become acutely aware of yourself." The grasslands "dwarfs the little—I!" wrote North Dakotan Clell Gannon in a poem.[13] While North Americans came through popular culture to know "earth and sky" as a place tag for the continent's grasslands, such an understanding remained incomplete without the daily experience of four seasons punctuated by the elements. Residents of settler society became part of the multidimensional interlocking exchange of earth and sky.

Wild Grasslands

Absorbed developmentally with small-world imaginative powers, curious children played with, or created fun using, the fiber and flora of their environments, as much as the setting surrounded them. Children came to know the details of the grasslands through hands-on, close-up interaction. Wallace Stegner was flat on his stomach when he eyed curly buffalo grass straining in the wind. Nell Wilson found a block of Saskatchewan sod her father cut from the ground "so fresh and moist on one side, so tough and grassy on the other." Children routinely across seasons and years roamed over larger areas of the grasslands and saw more than they could inspect. They made some sense of the unfathomable space surrounding them by generalizing according to colors. Grass might be "green" in the spring and "tawny beige" in the summer. Sophie Trupin colored the grasslands of North Dakota "steel gray," almost all "one hue," except for new "green shoots" in the spring. Montanan Lillian Miller remembered that "low" buffalo grass started out in the spring as "gray-green" but turned "rusty brown" in the fall. Others remembered the grasslands tinted blue or "tinged" purple with pasqueflowers or a "lemon-yellow color" when cacti bloomed.[14] Ecological waves of cool-to-warm-season grasses, shrubs, and bushes flowering, dying, or cycling into dormancy, over the seasons and years and climactic vagaries, all multiplied grasslands space.

Owning land for children meant knowing the environmental life within the boundaries of four property stakes that marked their parents' claims. To the boy Wilfrid Eggleston, when he took a pail in search of water, he crossed over to the lands of "Shangri-La" or "Sherwood Forest," not only southern Alberta. When he found a "limpid oval pool" and a deeply carved coulee, it was as if he entered a "Castle in Spain," and King Arthur had given him water from the "Round Table" itself. Nevertheless, he labeled the first pond from which he drew water "Gooseberry Pool," for its supply of "low gooseberry bushes." This childhood-level act of settler colonialism mirrored the formal, legal land-claim process used by his parents. Wilfrid continued to map and name the land about him: Saskatoon Hill, Mound Builders Mound, Sleigh Hill, Miniature Coulee, Verdant Coulee, North Hill, and the Orchard, became a vocabulary of place of his own devising. Implicitly, new names displaced Indigenous place names in ways that matched grasslands organized by a grid system of land alienated from the "public" domain by policy in the United States and Canada.[15] Settler-society adults, who did not have ready names for their surroundings, tracked spaces, activities, and whereabouts of family often by children's local labels. The act of naming landmarks began a process of naturalizing settler society's presence in the region.

Children understood marks on grasslands as claims made by settler society to establish a new cultural regime. Wallace Stegner loved the trails on the prairies that had their origins in settler wagons—a collective settler-society mark of ownership. Stegner "loved" even more the "privately made . . . paths" that emerged with "our daily living work in the prairie." These marks into "the earth's rind" felt to him as "an intimate act, an act like love." He recalled, "I scuffed and kicked at clods and persistent grass clumps, and twisted my weight on incipient weeds and flowers, willing that the trail around the inside of our pasture should be beaten dusty and plain." These paths spoke to ownership. Stegner's specifically masculine conception of forced "love" showed how power worked in a boy's ability to destroy grass and flowers.[16] Marks left in settlement's wake suggest children's grasslands roaming as analogous (for this stage of childhood development) to nation-backed explorations.

Children observed, interacted, and often creatively answered their own questions developed on roams. Aagot Raaen communicated the dearth of knowledge felt by children by recalling her sister Kjersti's "face was a question mark when she brought in the first crocus." Despite her mother's incredulity at thinking the ubiquitous sagebrush plant "pretty," the discovery of the "flat-like," "twisted, slivery green" sagebrush thrilled Nell Wilson; she liked the "way it leans against the wind," and her father teased about the wind-strummed music sounding from the plant akin to a harp. After doing the washing and folding one April, Alice Humphrey wrote her mother with an announcement: "The flowers are out." Two days later she wrote to ask, "Did Grandma ever see these flowers?" implying such flowers were new to her. She did not list the flowers by name. Many recognized pink wild roses by their smell, but those who lived there long enough recognized these roses grew inches above the ground on dry hills and into "bush proportions" with plentiful water in low areas. Laura Goodman Salverson recalled "picking flowers" on the prairie near Selkirk, Manitoba, near a local "insane asylum." Nestled in the "high prairie grass, with tiger-lilies like flaming swords at our backs," listening to stories—imagined or rumored?—about inmates, Salverson suggested a fantasy quality to her childhood interactions.[17]

The notable inability to name specific flora was not unusual. Individual children created entire folk floral taxonomies for grasslands plants. Wallace Stegner never forgot the look of what he later learned were white anemones that appeared in Saskatchewan only in "the dapple of the woods." He argued, "I . . . could not possibly have found out." Parents did not know, and textbooks did not include grasslands plants. He called primroses "wild tulips" because they appeared at summer's start, and Albertan Georgina Thomson called wild lupine the "umbrella plant" because "tall blue spikes" had "leaves that fanned out in spokes like stays of an umbrella." She and her friends called shooting stars "duck heads" because the "pointed yellow centre . . . reminded us of a duck's yellow bill sticking out." In Saskatchewan Nell Wilson called one "plumy spray" of flowers "snowflakes."[18] Knowing a plant by the senses and not by formal scientific classification suggests a child's way of knowing. Understanding the properties and phases of growth of a flower by experience—one's sensual intake over the seasons—and knowing the same plant by intellectual training represent two different forms of knowledge. Lacking scientific expertise or even adult-world nomenclature also freed children from such limitations.

Annora Brown became famous for recording the plant names her community of southern Alberta childhood playmates created. After the "crocus" or "pasque flower" appeared with the advent of spring, the child Annora expected the white-matted bloom of "may flowers," as she coined the "dainty" hood's phlox, to appear soon on the scene. She preferred to use "mayflower" even after she knew the "real" name of these small clusters of bloom. Similarly, Annora and her friends did not actually call an anemone by its English (crocus) or French (pasque) name but instead called these low-growing "downy buds" with furry leaves "goslings," because the flower reminded them of young geese. Brown recalled "tomato flowers" and "Dog-Fennel" that smelled like "pineapple freshly cut." She told tales of "bird bills" and the "elephant head" flower. Children called the white flower that bloomed only at night the "moon flower"; lucky children might be allowed to stay up past bedtime to see what in daytime appeared as a "shrivelled mass of brown petals and dusty sharp-pointed leaves." Kate Neatby Nicoll called wild yellow-and-orange snapdragons abloom on sunny Saskatchewan slopes "butter and eggs."[19] By adulthood one-time grasslands children knew layers of names, from colloquial and popular to the scientific.

As the children roamed, objects they found on the grasslands that related—or were imagined to relate—to Indigenous lifeways often became their first "contact." Lulu Pickler Frad and her siblings scraped and polished "buffalo horns" to a "glistened" appearance. Seventy years later Eggleston laughed a bit at himself over the incorrect stories he and his childhood friends told themselves over "Mound Builders Mound," realizing that, while it looked like ancient aboriginal sculpture, the mound was likely sculpted by prehistoric glacial action.[20] Children might have evaluated their "finds" accurately, or such treasures might have been figments of imagination that fit into a life caught in settler society's West. Objects had the power to spark questioning about nearby peoples who lived on reserves and reservations and their relationship to wider meanings of their family's colonial project (without formal language). Kept objects continued to hold the potential to spark new thinking about Indigenous lifeways.

New seasons brought new surveillance. After recounting a day of croquet playing, an offhanded comment Alice Humphrey made to her mother in April suggests she regularly observed the land: "The ground is in nice condition." Another reference, when a series of September grassfires made it "very smoking," suggests an ongoing

Sensing Prairies and Plains

accumulation of knowledge about grasslands ecology. The smell of burning grasslands; the sight of smoke and wind-driven, grass-fed fire; and the wake of blackened earth all lie ensconced in Alice's telling, as does the environmental cycle of regrowth succession that ensued on the land in the days and months following the fire. The burned-over area would have had grass growing for two weeks before the surrounding area began to sprout. After a fire ran through near High River, Alberta, Lula Short Asher noted, "We saved quite a lot of grass," suggesting a similar cultural sensibility to the grasslands as a resource constantly observed.[21] Ways of knowing the land are often so atmospheric, so much a part of daily living, that their expression can be caught only in glimpses here and there on the pages of letters and memoirs. In children's abilities to read the landscape lies the evidence of a specific place of knowledge growing inside of them.

New Settings, Old Stories

The multilingual narrative base of the northern grasslands population provided much material for children's imaginations to create stories out of and with the landscape. The many evenings, especially in winter, families spent reading and listening to stories fed the imaginations of settler children and suggest the larger racial, ethnic, class, and occupational cultures shaping children's interpretations of their surroundings. Children of immigrants to Canada and the United States and from places such as England, Ireland, Germany, Iceland, Norway, and Sweden grew up surrounded with cultural cues they invoked when trying to make sense of the northern grasslands. Peter Norbeck remembered winter as "story-telling" time among the Swedes in southeastern Dakota Territory, and Lillian Miller's father taught her the German songs he knew growing up and told her stories of Germany. The Pickler and Neatby families in Dakota and Saskatchewan, respectively, carried huge libraries to the grasslands. The Humphrey family regularly read stories out loud from magazines such as *Youth's Companion* and *Western Rural* and classic books during evenings in the parlor. George Will cherished fond memories of his mother reading aloud to the family from Mark Twain and "enjoyed" his father reading to them from a "fascinating volume of bible stories" each Sunday.[22]

Laura Goodman's first remembered experience of the "Dakota prairie" night sky suggests the influence of culture related to both family and the child's "small world." From her child mind's perspective, the family migration within the grasslands from Manitoba to Minnesota, now to Dakota, had no "reasonable meaning." From an adult perspective she recognized her mother's relief when the family reached an Icelandic home. The little girl she was then remembered a story her father told her and the "stories that mamma read to me"; she concluded the destination must be a "troll's house." In her parents' friends she saw "two bent gnomes" and finally believed the old woman to be a "witch." In an act of resisting comfort for the terrors of her childhood imaginative world, she remembered how "I could not and dared not explain" to her parents what she understood.[23] The insistence shows how deeply a child's loyalty can be to maintaining a coherent but other-dimensional world in addition to the adult world in which they *must* also traverse. The vignette reveals a child's intense immersion in traditional Icelandic narratives, heard in Icelandic tongue (the only language Goodman knew until the age of ten), by which her personal interpretation of that dark "Dakota prairie" night occurred.

Folk characters from Europe, the "old world," or the "big world across the sea" populated many stories these children heard. Goodman's mother, while sewing or spinning, told her stories of twisted "Tröll-karls" and "Tröll-skessur" and other fun tales of "Laufey and Lineik." Goodman also heard versions of "Snow White and Red Rose and the Seven Dwarfs," though in Icelandic language and style. When Aagot Raaen wanted to wander alone, or the girls wanted their younger brother to stay home, Aagot told "fantastic stories" of "mountain folk" hidden in the bluffs beyond the homestead or about a big, "scary old woman" who lived in the woods. One of her mother's more didactic stories told about a troll in the woods who safeguarded his berries from child trespassers. Fellow North Dakotan Thorstina Jackson recalled "rímur," or ballad singing, and listening to the sagas, while Salverson recalled that the "sagas were our chief entertainment." Her grandfather, born in Iceland, told her folk tales about "ghosts," "elves," and "Hidden Folk," who had moved from Iceland and now lived "in trees on the Dakota prairie." Thorstina recalled, "when I had to run some errands after dark . . . the supernatural characters of the folk tales seemed to be lurking everywhere."[24]

Children listened to tales of prior experiences in the North American West, a mix of myth, rumor, and history. Era Bell Thompson listened to her cousin sing "sad cowboy laments." Laura Bower Van Nuys, whose family became famous as a band touring the Black Hills, remembered "singfests" that featured songs such as "My Little Old Log Cabin in the Lane" and "O Bury Me Not on the Lone Prairie," sung "in true western style." The youngest generation heard Western stories—that some of the oldest children experienced firsthand—of the Métis rebellions in Manitoba and Saskatchewan, George Custer in the Black Hills, "Buffalo Bill" Cody in the Dakotas, and Jesse James in Minnesota. Dorothy Johnson listened to tales of mountain men, miners, outlaws, and Cheyennes. Annora Brown liked to look at the photograph album that showed her father dressed as a North-West Mounted Police officer and never tired of hearing police stories. In a portrayal of a South Dakota blizzard, author Robert McAlmon's boy character lay so "wakeful with a dumbness and numbness of consciousness of all the space surrounding him" that "no stories would come."[25] Nothing better captures a child's fright than the inability to tell or imagine a story.

Waters

Water forcefully connected the land and sky in the lives of grasslands children. Drama flavored water. As one of Robert McAlmon's characters explained it, "There wasn't a drop of water; there was a torrent falling in masses from the sky for a period of three to five minutes." Water became well understood over seasons of watching local patterns unfold, always present on the grasslands in conversation, if not by the inch. Wallace Stegner recalled a "whole folklore of water" circulating on the early twentieth-century Saskatchewan grasslands of his boyhood. The Rocky Mountains created a shared transnational regional life based on river systems and water flows astride a continental divide. Only beaver dams, dead trees, and ice—not cement, quarried rock, and dam architecture—blocked north and south flowing rivers draining the region to either the Hudson Bay or the Gulf of Mexico. Unplowed and predrained pasturelands hosted "pot," "kettle," and "pan" depressions left behind from the sluggish churning of ages-ago glacier retreat. Patches of wind-eroded groundcover also collected water.[26]

That Brown remembered mud first, rather than grasses or flowers, should not be a surprise. Gumbo slicks of loamy clay and alkali flats—the latter, where ponds of water collected, then dissipated into the arid air, leaving shining white blemishes—pocked the landscape. Experiences involving some*one* or some*thing* getting stuck in gumbo or some muddy mixture constitute almost a grasslands tale genre. Wilfrid Eggleston, who grew up in Alberta near Brown, explained how "the slope up the hill of our coulee . . . greasy from recent showers" made their horse "sprawl" and "slip awkwardly." Towns and even cities were not immune. Rain transformed turn-of-the-century Winnipeg into a city of "gummy spume, through which horses and men slithered and slipped, and often enough . . . sank half-way to their knees." Laura Goodman could still hear the "smacking sound" of mud's adhesive suction and the "feet of the horses glug-glug-glugged endlessly"; after a rain a trail "became a river of slippery glue."[27]

Spring snowmelt reinvigorated the landscape. Summer crops and arid transpiration changed the coat many times more. When snowmelt water from the Rocky Mountains began filling the three-foot trench cut out of a valley surrounded by twenty-foot banks, Eggleston knew spring would soon come to their homestead. "For a few days" the dry coulee "contained a swift flowing brook, even sometimes a raging torrent in places." Such water soon evaporated, first "into a series of pools connected by barely perceptible runnels" and then nowhere in evidence by June. This network of drains and pools left a wake of dry areas of exposed sand and water-worn stones, with "marsh grasses" and "water weeds" persisting in moister areas. Water marked the grasslands when present *and* absent.[28]

Hundreds of miles southeast of Brown and Eggleston, the same springtime found Era Bell Thompson balancing atop ice blocks on the Missouri River near Bismarck, North Dakota. Era relived the events of *Robinson Crusoe*, "flirting with death" in the frosty air. In

Sensing Prairies and Plains

early summer she watched the Missouri River occasionally take down trees lining its banks and "great chunks of land" collapsing into the water as the "treacherous current" cut into them. Thorstina Jackson recalled standing "tearfully on the wrong side" of Tongue River for school in spring, "the bridge . . . completely out of sight, covered with surging waters," flowing at the command of the Red River of the North.[29]

Nearby in North Dakota Aagot Raaen recalled one season in particular when water filled the "valleys and gulches . . . almost level with the bluffs." The snowmelt combined with rain made a sound so loud it would compare to the "roar" of "many thunderstorms." This noise came from the tiny Goose River that emptied into the Red, itself full with foaming "water way' up on the trees," with swirling mud and floating "cakes of ice" and trees. Laura Goodman Salverson recalled how the very same north-flowing Red River caused "dangerously high" water levels at Winnipeg and refreshed local marshes long after. George Will noted the "slush ice . . . running in the [Missouri] river" near Bismarck as the country lurched toward winter.[30] Mid-twentieth-century damming changed the soundscape, but the sounds of freely flowing rivers, icy water, cracking ice, and gushing roars became part of this generation's sense of place.

Grasslands children understood the power of water; it caused some of the most intense emotions in their society: fear and anxiety. When talking about the "grimmer realities" of adults, Wilfrid Eggleston remembered one of their neighbors "lost his whole farm" from digging wells for water. The money he invested in wells without reaching a water source left the farmer indebted, without credit to continue farming. June morning rituals involved scanning the sky for "thunderheads." By July settlers turned suspicious of clouds for the hail they might create. Eggleston never forgot the look of drought on his neighbors' faces.[31]

Annora Brown did *not* recall "even the glimmer of a memory of falling into the river at Fort Macleod, of being pulled out, [and] dried off," an event that happened in her first couple of years of life. Perhaps her much stronger memory of a river's roar covered for the personal experience of bodily immersion. The incident recalled in

Brown's autobiography also demonstrates the significant role stories told by others about oneself play in constructing a sense of place. Fear caused remembering as well as forgetting: Lula Short told a story of how one day she *almost* fell into the river; she did not know how to swim. Sometimes what did not happen was as memorable as what did happen. A girl who fell in and one who did not spoke to the same fear and the notable magnitude of rivers in this culture.[32]

Local rains from spring to fall added to the shifting patterns of terrain, starting water flow and drainage patterns at almost any point throughout the year. Raaen recounted one storm that started with "big raindrops" and became a "white sheet of water," then hail sounding like sand, soon pebbles, dropping on the roof. Thorstina Jackson recalled how her "childish mind" made sense of the "strange behavior of nature" after a rain. She thought of the "mud running on a rainy day down the hillside south of our house" in North Dakota as akin to "Mt. Hekla's molten lava," as it flowed in her grandfather's stories of Iceland, "although much less destructive."[33]

Wallace Stegner mentioned that the "unbearable recognition" of his home village came "partly from . . . the river's quiet curve." The valley of the Frenchman River hosted the copious growth of the wolf willow, whose scent he is more famous for recalling. Willows on the grasslands always existed in association with a water source, often absent on the "blistered and crisped" grasslands. The way Stegner felt about the valley and its wolf willows grew from the cultural force of frequently dry grasslands. He dreamed of the scent of the "gray leafed bush," which bloomed with small yellow flowers. Implicitly, when Stegner dreamed of wolf willow, he dreamed of water. He even evoked the images that powerfully called to mind his boyhood with a metaphor of water: the green—hence, well-watered—images of the valley, he explained, "lie in me like underground water; every well I put down taps them." Similarly, suggesting quiet river bends play a pattern in this generation's sense of place, Laura Bower also called the "grove in the bend of the creek" near their ranch one of her "favorite spots."[34]

As these children lived through countless turnings of the day, they discovered the grasslands had a paradoxical relationship with water.

5. Wallace Stegner called the Frenchman River "Whitemud" in his fiction. As a boy living in Eastend, Saskatchewan, Wally Stegner, here circa 1916, swam the river in summer and skated it in winter. When he grew up, the smell of riverbank wolf willows carried him back to childhood in memory. Original image housed at J. Willard Marriott Library, at the University of Utah. Used by arrangement with Brandt and Hochman Literary Agents, Inc.

The subsurface contained water mysteries. The Raaen household discovered a freshwater spring where "only two feet deep, the water bubbled" up to the surface; she remembered how they "drank deep" from the spring through a reed picked nearby. Dakotan Laura Bower drank from an "oasislike spring." Such artesian water sprung forth from below the parched land by a unique layering of gravel and clay. Hale Humphrey mimicked optimism of the time when he wrote his brother Alfred how "Papa says the new Huron artesian well is the greatest well in the country." Although rain tasted good, Nell Wilson Parsons recalled how "acrid" and "sloughy" most Saskatchewan water tasted. Much of the available water grew so "stagnant and brown" it discolored clothing washed in it; it had to be strained for "wrigglers"; and settlers concocted a genre of folk additives involving ginger, vinegar, spices, and soda to enable drinking water.[35]

The landscape reflected water's presence and absence. One August Elsie May Hammond searched for a "swimming hole but the creek was nearly dry." Grasslands swimming ended after a short period between the spring's rushing waters that filled creeks and the accumulation of summer's heat. In a distinct grasslands variation on going to the lake in the summer, Nellie Humphrey wrote of a special visit the family took one summer to "the *dry lake* up north west" of Faulkton. Evidence of a previous grand prehistoric sea once located across the expanse also left its imprint, creating an ancient relationship between historical grasslands and water. One young North Dakota boy, while digging a well, found what he held to be a peculiar stone with a "petrified butterfly" in it. The "butterfly" turned out to be a prehistoric sea animal from an ocean that once occupied the place where grasslands now lay. Nell Wilson pulled a "drab, clay-colored rock the size of a huge watermelon" out of a well that turned out to be full of an "iridescent mass of petrified sea shells." Lillian Miller found fossils in "milky stone."[36] Evidence of past water bodies added depth to the sometimes paradoxical relationship of grasslands and water.

Seeing the landscape change daily over seasons, children gained a complicated sense of the region's frustrating relationship with water. Water present and absent, but signaled everywhere, proved integral to the senses of place adopted by the grasslands-grown generation because the success of settler society's commercial agriculture depended on access to water.

Woods

Woods—even a single tree—proved a special place of comparative, natural luxuriance for grasslands children. A solitary tree emphasized the comparative lack of trees. Perhaps because trees signaled distinct places within the larger northern grasslands, they drew particular notice. Boyhood South Dakota resident Robert McAlmon phrased one tree stand aptly when he said it constituted "*for that space* a green avalanche which flooded the landscape." The larger northern grasslands enveloped significant stands of genuine forest—the Black Hills, Cypress Hills, Bears Paw Mountains, Wood Mountain, and Turtle Mountain. The view of trees from a distance distinguished them as isolated units: an openness so broad that one could never mistake trees for a forest. Wooded groves ribboned periodically flooded river bottoms so that a "green line of trees" in the distance often signaled rivers' courses. Dorothy Johnson recalled that on the "rolling prairie" of early Montana "to see a tree we used to walk half a mile on Sundays to a clump of cottonwoods." Nell Wilson could see only four cottonwood trees, which she called "fingers," about four miles away from their Saskatchewan homestead.[37] Oaks, ash, elms, box elders, and willows in the east; birch, black poplars, aspens, and maples in the north; spruces in the west; and cottonwoods everywhere signaled shade, rivers, lakes, wetlands, and, over time, farms, ranches, and towns.

As settler society took root on the northern grasslands, riverine trees found their way as transplants to homes, field shelterbelts, or U.S. "tree claims." Annora Brown prized the "tops of the trees in the river bottom" she could see from the rooftop of her home in Fort Macleod. Children soon learned to recognize the advent of towns by a clump of trees in the distance. When Era Bell Thompson, who grew up in a small town just east of Bismarck, visited Jamestown, she could hardly believe the sight and never forgot the "beautiful tree-lined streets, whose heavy foliage interlocked far overhead." "Surely this could not be North Dakota," she thought. "Surely less than two hundred miles could not make such a difference. But it did," she told her readers some thirty years later. Time magnified the result of such planting. As Wallace Stegner recalled of Eastend, Saskatchewan, "My town used to be as bare as a picked bone, with no tree anywhere around it larger than a ten-foot willow or alder." His memory did not conform to the 1950s, when he noted, "Now it is a grove."[38]

Trees and woody bushes found scattered throughout the larger grasslands habitat offered children resources for play. To Annora Brown a riparian forest became a "tree world," distinct from "my dry prairie" and full of special delight. Thorstina Jackson accompanied her mother in the woods that lined the Tongue River in North Dakota to "admire the flowers."[39] While her mother sought rest from the day's work, Thorstina was thrilled by the woods. Amid the melting snow, Aagot Raaen recalled how they "always played in the woods" of their North Dakota homestead on the Goose River. They ran barefoot all day and "ate what nature had to offer—young shoots of grapevines, fresh sorrel from the ground, tender budding basswood leaves, the bark of young branches on the chokecherry bushes," and a variety of nuts. As the summer moved on, the Raaen siblings sipped "sweet drips from the box elders" out of tree-bark cups. They gathered "moss, hulls of green hazelnuts, and several kinds of leaves, and bark," which their mother used to dye their own lamb wool. Using discarded cloth, Aagot sewed together a doll using the needle of a hawthorn bush, stuffing it with the "silky down from the milkweed." This interaction echoed Lakota girls who played with dolls made of forked limbs of cottonwood trees wrapped in buckskin, although of course the cultural context differed. Settler girls began to absorb the textures of plants and trees and of shaping these resources into positive experiences through play by which they came to feel comfortable in the place, as settler-colonial policies aimed to distance Indigenous girls from these resources.[40]

The process of absorbing the land and creating a sense of place through bodily experience shows especially clear in Annora Brown's memories of Alberta. Brown spent "two idyllic weeks at the girls' camp in Jerry Potts' Bottom," the broadest of the "fertile flats" created by the "Old Man's River," as Brown insisted on calling what most Albertans called the Oldman River. (She preferred the "Old Man" derived from the Blackfoot spiritual being of the river's namesake.) Brown believed cottonwoods, poplars, and willows "talked" to her "in their own language." She learned the scent of "hot sun on green leaves" there and enjoyed the unique experience of "walking in the woods." She "explor[ed] the site where decaying Indian graves sagged from age-old balm of Gileads."[41] Riparian graveyards directly conveyed the human contest over resources represented by the growing town of Fort Macleod a few miles away from Oldman River. Brown would

Sensing Prairies and Plains

have known that tenders of those graves lived nearby on Blackfoot, Piegan, and Blood Reserves. The sight suggested prior use of the local natural resources and indicated the spirituality Indigenous peoples attached to certain landscapes rather than the commercial or recreational use usually conjured up by trees along rivers when seen through settler-colonial eyes. Wooded play had the potential to provide children with noncommercial, question-provoking attachment to landscape separate from parents.

A particular "play" homestead built in the woods by Aagot Raaen and her sisters demonstrates the depth such creative play could achieve. Basically, the girls built a house *out* of the woods rather than simply *in* the woods. The corner posts of the main play "house" consisted of four large, leafy oak, ash, and elm trees that grew in a near square. Using "dry stumps" pried loose and "dry branches," they built walls by filling in the spaces between the corner-post trees with twigs fashioned after post-and-rail fencing they had seen. The leafy overhang of the branches shingled the "roof" and created natural openings, sky lights, as Kjersti explained, so "we can sometimes see the stars or a bit of red sunset." Small, "fallen and dried out" trees, bark, and bits and pieces of scrubby brush became household furnishings and food.[42]

From the nearby grasslands the children dragged back sun-bleached "buffalo bones of many shapes and sizes," which became oxen, cows, calves, sheep, lambs, and chickens inhabiting a "dugout" stable the girls hollowed out themselves. Kjersti clung to her imagination and "insisted" the bones "moved," although she admitted helping them shift back and forth between the make-believe "pasture" and "stable." The children played farm, complete with three sets of neighbors imagined in the "queer growths" of dead, dry branches they found in the woods. Through house play the children reenacted the conversations, community squabbles, rituals, and farm routines they witnessed daily. The site even included a "well-kept graveyard."[43] The Raaen girls' cherished "tree house" showed creative use of area ecology and role replication that communicated settler-society cultural norms.

The Raaen children's playhouse demonstrated as much about new cultures transforming the landscape as, on the surface, about how 1870s and 1880s children learned North Dakota ecology. As the Raaen children's parents turned their patch of the Red River Valley into commercial pastures and wheat fields, Aagot and her sisters turned the sun-bleached remnants of the last wild bison into domesticated "farm animals," and the brittle, sepia-gray trees into a "home." Imitating through body and behavior, cloaked in play, the Raaen children unconsciously learned a reason for their migration to the grasslands. The girls cleared the home-place environment of buffalo bones (a necessary task for preparing commercial agricultural land). With their mother the children harvested the fruits of the woods. The Raaen children's own footpaths penetrated into the earth, digging themselves into the history of grasslands ecology. Whatever the grasslands would become because of their presence, their touches and disturbances became part of the place. Twentieth-century ecosystems began to transform the nineteenth-century ecological formations Indigenous nations created based on bison, grass, river-bottom agriculture, and riverine forests.

The ruins of the Raaen girls' play overlaid and laid next to cultural traces of Ojibwes and Dakotas also marking the land, even if the European immigrant–heritage girls did not read about or understand that prior grasslands history in the landscape.[44] Indeed, their play echoed that of Lakota children who made horses out of "adobe mud" with willow branches or "slough grass for the legs" and envisioned "manure chips" as buffalo. Lakota girls made "little tipis from the leaves of the cotton wood tree, and fasten[ed] them together with a small twig." Eggleston and his childhood friends, perhaps showing some unconscious notion of trespass or apprehensiveness about Indigenous resistance, thought that the willow branches they found "sliced across with sharp knives" meant "Indians recently gathered material for baskets" on property his family now claimed. Indeed, Indigenous peoples—Piegans, Bloods, Crees, or Métis—may have had a continuing sense of resource ownership that transcended settler society's land law. Having settler children dig themselves into the landscape simultaneously worked to detach Indigenous children from grasslands resources.[45]

The Raaen family lived in an everyday world where only degrees in states of refinement existed between unfettered and crafted "nature."

Sensing Prairies and Plains

The same river-bottom trees formed the resource base for the Raaen family's *real* log home and the children's *make-believe* playhouse. The elemental vegetation the Raaen sisters played with in their imaginary house became the furniture, utensils, and food in the family's real log home. Raaen's father, a carpenter, constructed much of the family's furniture and hand-carved many spoons, bowls, and brooms out of local trees.[46] This childhood environment was less mediated by manufacturing and processing than the larger colonial agricultural community foretold. Living inside and outside, surrounded by essentially the same environmental materials, created a general melding of ideas and feelings about such spaces among many settler children.

Children furthered their timber knowledge through work. The Albertan Lula Short's diary recorded, "Us children cutting sticks in the morning for fence." She lived in the foothills of the Rocky Mountains, so trees formed a part of her regular view, but she also had a relationship to the expansive grasslands. While she built a fence with "small palings" the family hoped would protect the garden from chickens, her father prepared and hauled "rails to make the cross fence," which would keep their horses' pasture separate from "crop-planted land."[47] The Raaen girls knew how to build the walls of their playhouse and play fences from witnessing such work.

Without surprise, given his father's nursery business and in particular the company's focus on "tree claim candidates," one of George Will's earliest memories conjured "the smell of the clean yellow straw after it was well wet down and the earthy, woodsy smell of the seedling trees all neatly put up in bundles of one hundred and tied with a diamond willow shoot." In the spring and fall, Will claimed he spent "every out of door moment" helping pack trees for the family business, an experience, perhaps only with hindsight, he characterized as "delightful and fascinating." Oscar H. Will and Company "tree pullers"—former buffalo hunters, fur trappers, and cowboys—looked for work outside of the farming economy. According to Will, "They knew all the country like an open book," including the location of tree stashes on the tributaries of the Missouri River, which sprouted thickly after flooding in particularly wet seasons. Such jobless men "more than rejoiced to find that there was a market for the millions of little tree seedlings."[48] Sporting narratives told by former trappers and cowboys taught George about the larger patterning of grasslands trees and fueled his imagination.

A favorite and more universal grasslands wood-stand activity, berry picking, merged work and play. Children looked forward to picking berries, but berries also provided important nutrients for health or a source of cash income. The Raaen girls made gooseberry sauce and sold berries by the quart in town. Stegner knew he could make ten cents a quart from picking saskatoons, pin cherries, and gooseberries to sell to the town's "home-canning housewives." The "children of the early pioneers," Thorstina Jackson recalled, "rejoic[ed]" in the tastes of "abundant wild fruit in the woods": raspberries, pin cherries and wild plums. She remembered her favorite spot for what her grasslands generational cohorts north of the forty-ninth parallel called the Saskatoon berry: over "near the corral" where "the service-berry bushes grew to wondrous size due to the abundant, rich fertilizer" from family cows.[49]

Some seventy years later Annora Brown could still taste the "mouth puckering but edible" chokecherries, Saskatoon berries, and "vermilion" bull berries, which she knew were "ripe for picking" when the "bitter smell of frosted leaves" filled the air. "Holding a basket of freshly picked berries . . . is a physically satisfying sensation," she recalled, adding, "One feels the joy of cupping yet untasted richness," as if she could touch the tangles of bush, a plump berry, and the same basket at the moment of remembering.[50] Preserved berries, tasted in winter, recalled afresh the smell of bloom and the touch of berry skin ballooned with juice. Berries proved integral to memories of beloved woods, suggesting the force of taste on body and mind.

Rocks

Piles of rocks grew all over the northern grasslands during this time, from Alberta to the Dakotas. "Alfred, Hale and Kenneth are carrying stones off the plowing," sister Alice Humphrey wrote in one of her many report-on-the-home-front letters from 1880s southern Dakota Territory. The Thompsons of North Dakota, according to daughter Era Bell, found their first farmland, rented while under the cover of snow, a "horny earth" upon the first spring snowmelt. "Everywhere" the family looked "there were rocks, millions of rocks pimpling the drab prairie: large blue-gray boulders, free and bold in their shallow pockets; long, narrow slits of rocks surfacing the soil like huge cetacean monsters; sharp stone peaks jutting" from the earth. Even purple crocuses in spring "blossomed reluctantly." The Hammonds could be found "digging rocks" out of Saskatchewan grasslands well into the twentieth century.[51]

Knowing the grasslands during this transitioning era meant encountering rocky ridges, glacial moraines, gravel pits, sand hills, and outcroppings of shale or sandstone. Annora Brown recalled a time in Alberta when she dug down in her yard through the geologic strata with her hands and a shovel, from "soft earth" through to "glacial gravel with rocks worn round and smooth." A child even might have encountered one of many boulders or "great blocks weighing many tons" lying on the grasslands, "as though they had been dropped there by some gigantic force." Montanan Lillian Miller found a "lone boulder on a sea of green prairie" baffling. Many of the northern prairie boulders and rocks, as far south as southern Dakota, had moved with glaciers from North America's great Laurentian Shield in Canada. Elsie Hammond noted a destination rock, "the big sandstone" in her locality, "a great rock with many names carved on it."[52]

A whole system of strategies and tools such as log chains, crow bars, shovels, and stone boats grew for the rock work of grasslands farming. On the Eggleston, Alberta, homestead, piles of rocks soon outlined plowed fields. The land showcased a variety: "small loose stones" scattered about; "embedded but still visible" stones easily pried out; and "really troublesome stones" that had to be "turfed" out by the walking plow. Nell Wilson recalled rocks that had to be "dug in" by carving a "pit large enough so that the tumbled rock would be out of the way [deeply below the surface] for the plow for all time to come."[53]

Children were frequently assigned the task of removing rock and often transformed the work into play. Wilson played a "grand game of pretend," envisioning in differently shaped rocks a stove, "Indian hammer," "petrified blobs of table syrup," and a diamond; the Neatby boys suffered a "test of manhood" when lifting rocks and played

6. Brothers Walter Neatby (*left*) and Leslie Neatby pose, in or around 1917, on the family farm near Watrous and Renown, Saskatchewan, southeast of Saskatoon. Courtesy of Nicole Neatby.

"marksmen" by throwing rocks at targets. Lillian Miller built castles, barns, and ranches with the "beautiful rocks and stones" she found on the hills.[54]

Providing unique insight of the small on the smaller in roaming mode, a young Alice Humphrey wrote her mother one fall of a "found" treasure involving her younger brother. Hale had become enthralled with a rock he picked up on their property. A skeptical Alice informed her mother, "Hale said it would be nice if they could move the rock to some museim and have it for a curiousity. Was not that funny, he said it so sober," she shared her big sister mirth. This incidental evidence suggests Hale built a special story consistent with his small-world perspective around—in his mind—a museum-quality rock.[55] Questions and ideas gained from imaginative activities on the land attached to specific items such as rocks helped maintain overall feelings about the place.

Sensing Prairies and Plains 117

Children did not always understand the complicated nation-to-nation incidents that made the land they farmed or ranched homesteadable. But they knew Indigenous peoples had made their home on the broader northern grasslands before their parents or they arrived and that Indigenous people lived nearby on reserves and reservations. Children truly sighted, or imagined they saw, in the placement of rocks evidence of Indigenous presence, even if they were wrong about the rocks. Wilfrid Eggleston took pride in his ability to correctly size up "perhaps a dozen rock rings" along the rim of the local coulee; he identified these past tepee locations, along with "flint arrowheads," as evidence of former Blackfoot possession of his family homestead. Eggleston also "identified" what he imagined to be a type of aboriginal "relic of man's activity," consisting of a "mosaic of small glacial boulders and smooth granite stones," deeply embedded but, he thought, purposefully arranged.[56] The adult Eggleston was not so sure. Even the memory proved to be about *his own ability to judge* origin, not what it meant for a boy to find evidence that might challenge his own occupation of the land. Finding and identifying such Indigenous identified items—real or imagined—proved part of the way children claimed and occupied grasslands space.

Annora Brown lived in a small town with a "Stone Pile" that represented evidence of the growing commercial transformation of the grasslands. She said her "life was spent with rocks. Rocks to throw, rocks to break for the colours and patterns inside, rocks for building playhouses, rocks for games—smooth rocks, rough rocks, coloured rocks. I loved them." The pile of glacial-worn rocks grew into a "heap on the prairie" as people cleared the land and expanded the town of Fort Macleod, Alberta, she explained from an adult perspective. Remembering her childhood imaginative play she insisted, "There *is* something about rocks. . . . They talked to me in their own language." Her child's imagination mixed the stones, birds, rodents, grasses, "bigger and brighter" blue violets, sunflowers, and long-plumed red avens into what Annora called, some seventy years later, a "magic playground."[57]

The rocks of the town's "Stone Pile" also symbolized profound environmental experiences with grasslands habitat. The flowers Annora

7. Annora Brown (*center*) played outside in the 1900s, frequently ranging far onto the grasslands. Notice the rubble in the back, unearthed from a ditch she likely explored. University of Alberta Archives (UAA-1983-116-016-002).

remembered were of course "bigger" and "brighter" in her favorite place simply because she was smaller and also because memory has the capacity to embellish. But *they were vivid* too, because the snow in rock-shaded crevices melted slower and provided water catchments that lasted much longer than snow and rain would provide for flowers scattered out in distant grasslands. The optimism Brown found in this experience is the child's hope that her very presence could make her favorite flora secure and fixed. The existence of a community rock pile acknowledged metaphorically, however, in its growth with the expanding town of Fort Macleod, the displacement of one ecosystem for another. The "piles of rocks in heaps" in every North Dakota field Sophie Trupin noticed communicated the same development: agricultural fields that drove the economies of agricultural towns. The turn-of-the-century homestead rush and expansion of commercially cropped agriculture increasingly modified older landscapes of corporate-ranch graze lands, already reconfiguring Blackfoot Confederacy and Cree grasslands territories.[58]

Perhaps on some instinctual, unconscious level, the mix of ecological and cultural change spreading across the land made its way into the young Annora Brown. One of her fondest memories described how she and her sister once "found a meadow lark's nest under a clump of tall grass and brush" tucked between rocks; each day the girls "sat patiently" watching for the hatching moment. Ultimately, the girls found the birds dead, under a new load of rocks someone from town dumped on the pile. The two girls "cried together, sharing our sorrow." Sorrow helped lodge the experience in Annora's mind to recall again, as she thought about at her favorite site through the elderly "inward eye of memory." Brown also acknowledged, from her adult narrator's perspective, that the stone pile no longer existed at all; it had "long given way to homes and gardens," which were the very same reasons the stone pile she "loved" existed at all.[59] Further development had destroyed her childhood sense of the lay of the land. Brown's later-life telling of this childhood experience betrayed a relationship to the region and its natural life, seldom directly acknowledged but often implicitly present within the expressed experiences of her generation. Brown's little-girl play with rocks, she realized as an adult, signaled the transformation of the grasslands she held so dear.

Snow

Wintertime muffled the life of the rivers, tree stands, and snow-covered rocks scattered across the grasslands. Snowfall and freezing temperatures reshaped the landscape to provide a new setting for the long winter season. The power of snow and cold to create distinct landscapes and to impress on physical bodies, and the varying abilities of built environments to mediate temperature, marked these childhood grasslands experiences as *northern*. Annora Brown captured what winter did to the grasslands: "I went out into a brand-new world," a "strange white world."[60]

Snow in the sky lent itself to deepening the sense of vastness children felt. Sophie Trupin from North Dakota recalled on overcast days sensing "endlessness" and feeling "suffocation, as though one were swallowed up in some huge void."[61] Eddies and drifts aligned to topographic features. The built environment—houses, barns, haystacks, fence lines, and roadways—tailored snow into shapes and patterns on the ground. In a northern-latitude grasslands region, the transnational settler society shared winter temperatures, snow, ice, blizzards, and strong sharp winter winds different from North America's southern grasslands.

Differences between adult- and child-constructed experiences of the same events can be seen in some divergent reactions to winter. Era Bell Thompson knew winter neared when tumble weeds or "huge Russian thistles, ugly and brittle now, free of their moorings, roll[ed] across the prairie like silent, gray ghosts, catching in fence corners, piling up in low places." Laura Bower noted how Russian thistle transformed fences into hedges. While parents "looked grim and worried" at the approach of winter, as Era Bell recalled it, children were often "filled with the excitement." Similarly, Aagot Raaen recalled how the girls looked forward to blizzards for tasks saved for such enclosed times: soap making, knitting, spinning, tallow-candle making, and *flatbrød* baking. The children all fought to be in front of the log cabin's single window to see the wind push a "cloud of snow." Their father just paced. George Will enjoyed "Sunday afternoons in the winter," when he and sister could "buzz around the kitchen while our parents popped and mixed a big dishpan full of popcorn, after which we all adjourned to the sitting room to eat apples and popcorn in the evening to listen to Mother read aloud." Increased sociability and attention left children with pleasant memories of times their parents knew presented danger. Still, Will never forgot the druggist in town who died "by freezing on a thirty below zero night," trying to get home from Main Street.[62] In their own small-world way, children knew the danger of cold, but the workings of childhood imaginations allowed individuals to override some signals and later to soften memory with better moments.

The built environment, animal-based travel, and the nature of climactic knowledge—in an era before radar and professional weather forecasting—ensured high levels of bodily exposure to life-threatening winter elements.[63] Lumber-board shacks and chinked log and frame houses provided little insulation from thirty-degrees-below-zero temperatures, blizzards, gale-force winds, and windchill factors. Many children understood the warmth of grasslands sod when winter commenced. Alice Humphrey wrote her brother with a touch of fun, "We live in town now but it is not so warm in this home as it was in 'the little old sod shanty out on the claim.'" As her note of song title suggests, by the 1880s grasslands settler society knew well the insulating qualities of a house built with sod bricks.[64] Lumber houses required special dress for winter in this era: new mounds of dirt, extra sod walls, or "manure" banked around, rag chinking at the windows, and rugs rolled up at the doors.

Heat for the body, whether in town or in the countryside, came hard on the northern grasslands. Annora Brown's floor iced over, and she recalled how "our breaths form[ed] steam wreaths about our heads." "A thin coat of ice covered the north wall of the living room behind the couch where I slept," recalled Era Bell Thompson of one North Dakota home. One of Robert McAlmon's boy characters described a night spent in a claim shack during a blizzard: "It was as though the stove sat out in the open prairie trying to warm all the universe of outdoors." Even a home with coal and wood heat offered only partial protection. Cold winds "shook" Aagot Raaen's home. Elsie Hammond's Saskatchewan diary recorded everyone moving into the kitchen during a cold snap.[65]

The auditory scape of winter—winds, precipitation, and the way cold atmospheres shaped sound—marked this generation's childhood experience. Walking through the snow sounded like "crushed glass": "scrunch," "squeak," "scream." A blizzard sounded like, according to Robert McAlmon, a "cold blue symphony" or "weird snow music, snow wind clamour, shrill shriek of cold whiteness shattered by a high moaning vermillion calliope wail." He thought such sounds similar to "thousands of cats [that] might have been snarling in fury at the night." Thompson's North Dakota memoir matched McAlmon's interpretation of wrath in winter winds: "wind whistled along the floor, and the thin house creaked with the cold." Winds arrived "perpendicularly down across the vast gray plains they swept, increasing in intensity and coldness, howling and shrieking in fiendish anger until the very prairies echoed their savage refrain." Sophie Trupin described a blizzard as the equivalent of "pursuing wolves" on the Russian steppes, complete with "white fangs and bloodcurdling howls" and a propensity "to pounce without warning."[66] Winter sounds often felt assaulting.

The ubiquitous level of exposure is historically significant. Children helped care for farms and ranches and traveled to school and church amid snow, ice, and low temperatures, often in open-air modes of transport. Alice Humphrey complained to her brother Alfred of the winter chores, reporting, "Hale's hands got awful cold; I nearly froze my nose." One has the sense she was still thawing out or dreading evening chores, when she wrote "It is 5 o'clock P.M. and 7° below zero," ending, "I wish you was here to help us." Thompson remembered a "bitter, aching cold that hurt your forehead, stiffened your face, made you speak low." Wilfrid Eggleston remembered, "freezing my cheeks, ears, fingers, and toes" while walking to school. "Once my right ear swelled to several times its normal size," he recalled, emphasizing from his adult perspective; "I was probably lucky to escape gangrene." McAlmon brought attention to a "sting in the eyes" caused by bright sun on new fallen snow. The "hard-frozen snow" had "blinding brilliance." Cold air "stabbed into lungs." Nell Wilson Parsons recalled how winter blinded, stabbed, and "goaded" her.[67]

Despite the trials of cold weather, children looked forward to winter for play as they did other seasons: hands-in with full-bodied involvement. Alice Humphrey described, "Hale made a snowman the other day, and Kenneth made some snow-balls." Then, in typical child's play, Kenneth, "first . . . knocked the head off. He took the head and hit the stomack till it came off; and that was the last of hales snowman." Brown recollected making "angles" in the fresh snow and how children "tread out circles with spokes for games of fox and geese." Stegner played this game too.[68]

Any ponds that remained on the grasslands after the heat of summer and fall iced over to become skating rinks in winter. Era Bell Thompson "skated on the slough and skied down the pasture hill." One nice day Nellie Humphrey took her sons Hale and Kenneth out to the "lake bed back of our office" and "had a find time coasting" with a wind so strong, she explained, "it would take us across the pond on the sled." Kittie Humphrey described a "big sleigh ride" with a horse that "prances" in a way that "would through [*sic*] snow balls" at them as its hooves clopped up wet, sticky snow. Wallace Stegner recalled "moonlit winter nights" with children on sleds hitching a ride behind "a team and a bobsled full of straw" as it pulled through town for a winter version of crack the whip. Some children "made rude skis" to use on coulees and even built a "few ski-jumps." Tosten Raaen used barrel staves. Leslie Neatby recalled much fun "sleighriding," "tobogganing," and "spill[ing]" into the snow on "mild" days, knowing their "uproarious noise and showing could be heard for miles over the snowing moonlit plain."[69] These out-of-doors wintertime activities suggest the same high level of sensual, corporeal immersion that children experienced in more temperate times of the year.

Children took pleasure in watching snow's effects on the landscape and in describing the changing textures and colors of snow. They referred to freshly fallen snow as "clean white," recalled snow "sparkled" in the sun and under the moon, and remarked on its "gloss and dazzle." Dust "dulled" old snow into a "dirt crusted" "gray whiteness." Children remembered the process of snow "packing solidly." They experienced fine snow, "damp snow," "big, dry flakes, light and feathery," and numerous textures, as precipitation interacted with space, land, and atmosphere over the seasons and years. It might snow "as though a pillow had burst open." Kenneth Humphrey wrote to Alfred explaining, "the snow drifts though not high are hard. Papa says the snow was so damp when it fell that it helped it to pack and freeze hard," which made a better surface for travel. As a southwestern Minnesota pen pal of the Humphrey children in Dakota explained, "The snow does not drift here . . . for there are no fences except wire ones[.] ours are all wire, the buildings make it drift a good deal, but on the prairie it is only one or two feet deep." The boy's note about how snow swept uninterrupted across the grasslands suggests a growing understanding of the vastness of the grasslands environment. After one North Dakota storm, the Thompsons opened the front door to "a drift as high as the house," except the wind interacting with the building and snow carved out a small foyer, so the door opened to a patio before a wall of snow. Era's brother joked, suggesting growing knowledge about regional boundaries, how the Rocky Mountains had moved to North Dakota overnight. She noted the grasslands became "white-capped" like the sea.[70]

More than a timeless notion of the blizzard and winter snowfall makes these examples important. Significance flows from the interchange of blizzards as filtered by permeable built environments and cultural patterns. McAlmon suggested much when two of his novel's boy characters move from one side of the house to the other during a blizzard because "it was quieter there, on the side of the house away from the gale." Annora Brown, looking back, expressed the difference after considering the renowned 1906 winter: "There have been other such winters since but preparedness, snowploughs, tractors, trucks, and helicopters have made of them a different story." Living in the grasslands during the late nineteenth and early twentieth centuries meant bodily exposure outside and inside, regularly and daily. Though snow, freezing temperatures, and blizzards remained constant, with each passing decade of the twentieth century, the built environment, including innovation in home heating, changed the multisensual experience of winter. Transportation became enclosed. Weather monitoring helped residents prepare.[71] Winter sights changed because snow accumulated differently according to new built environments. Cold felt differently because of new cultural contexts for bodily exposure.

Tame Grasses

Springtime signaled the prime agricultural year, lasting from snowmelt to snowfall. The "scent of wheat" joined the "smell of melting snow" filling the air, recalled Annora Brown. When Aagot Raaen recalled North Dakota, she thought of the "endless stretches of wheat fields." In addition to activities in the native northern grasslands habitat, children became immersed in the cultivated smells and textures of agricultural land: wheat, oats, corn, barley, flax, and imported grasses. These landscapes resonated with parental design. Agriculture placed limits on children's interactions with the land. After watching the straight brown furrows fold away from her father's Saskatchewan plow, Nell Wilson recalled she finally "understood the difference between grassland and crop fields!"⁷²

Most children, especially boys, started early in work to raise the family's commercial crops. Dakotan Alice Humphrey reported enthusiastically one April, "Everything is growing." One neighbor had "100 acres of wheat . . . up about two inches," while another local had "wheat higher than that—a number of bushels stored several feet above ground, you know." Showing a booster's level of support and expectation for the family agricultural enterprise in a different year, Alfred Humphrey told his mother that one of the neighbors in Iowa suggested he "had better send for a bushel of good hard Dak. wheat flour to save grandma some board." Era Bell Thompson remembered the delight of an "overnight" bloom of their twenty-acre field of flax. The field "burst into delicate blue flowers." In Saskatchewan Nell Wilson recalled the difficulty of "tell[ing] where flax ended and sky began" when the plants bloomed. Children could not tear down the stalks, spears, and fruits of the agricultural endeavor for use in creative play, but they delighted in the growth and bloom of crops.⁷³

Thompson recalled distinctly that her brother left "my child's world" when he "took the plow" at thirteen. The young women represented here also often worked in fields or with products from them. Era Thompson's father, as a sign of growing maturity, eventually allowed her to drive the family's flax crop to the local elevator. The task made her feel like a "big girl now." North Dakotan Sophie Trupin recalled the "blisters on my palms and aching muscles" after helping with haying. The Albertan Lula Short "got in three loads of hay. I drove for them on the last load." Another time she "helped" her "uncle and papa to load on another load of hay. At least I drove the horses while Uncle loaded up and Pap raked up," she clarified. While her brother Leslie Neatby took part in both the "heavy labor of stooking" and in "building a load of sheaves" to prepare for threshing, Kate Neatby recalled helping to "'build' the load" on the hayrack—"that is to push the fast-coming contributions evenly over the rack" as others pitched "forkfuls" on the pile growing "ever higher." Not all young women worked directly with field crops, but those who did expressed

8. This field of grain stooks (which Americans call *shocks*) sits near Saskatoon. The mix of an agricultural field plowed out of still-visible "prairie" grasslands, along with the South Saskatchewan River and forest habitats, nicely communicates primary elements of the senses of place expressed by this generation of settler colonials. The company Gowen Sutton, in operation from 1921 to 1960, originally published the image. Courtesy of Saskatoon Public Library, Saskatchewan (PH-2015-4).

satisfaction and invoked the language of "helping" as they stepped away from gendered-assigned tasks.[74]

Although children worked many hours in the field or at other agricultural tasks, if given the chance, they played. Era Thompson "ate the shiny coffee-colored [flax] seeds or scooped them up in my palms and let them run through my fingers like millions of tiny sequins." She also recalled how she and her best neighbor friend "played in the mammoth loft of the big barn, rolling down mounds of hay, sliding through floor chutes into the mangers of startled horses." Wallace Stegner recalled jumping into the "enormous clean sandpiles" of wheat, even after "constantly being warned about the danger of drowning in the grain." Sophie Trupin knew a boy who died doing so. Stegner and his friends also stopped by the grain elevator in search of a "cone of spilled grain" to provide free mouthfuls of "glutinous, sweet-tasting mass" of wheat; it chewed like "gum."

(Stegner speculated the vitamins he gained from the wheat probably helped him live longer.) One hungry boy ate green wheat stems.[75]

Experiences with hay connote nicely the experience of growing up surrounded by both wild and tame grasses for these turn-of-the century children. Hay was ever present in town and country. Hay was wild, unplowed grasslands but also grew from seeds bred commercially and planted seasonally. Looking back, Lula Short recalled, "Hay seemed to be our surest and best-selling crop. It grew wild on the prairie and in the summer and fall we all worked hard at gathering it into stacks." In the 1880s the Short family hauled load after load, over thirty-five loads one year and thirty-eight the next, back to their ranch. They sold extra hay to neighbors. Lula explained that most of the hay the family cut and hauled was "wild grass which that year grew close at hand in low spots out on the benchland." The family also grew imported grass, as she noted, "Papa drawing in Hungarian," a reference to an Asian grass thought to do well in droughty areas. When Lillian Miller listed the "good grasses" for grazing animals, she mentioned imported timothy, along with native buffalo, gramma, and blue joint grasses. Many also recalled the "odour of alfalfa from fields" and the look of "late growth of uncut alfalfa."[76] The children of settler society lived among multiple grasses—wild, domestic, harvested, and grazed—and this mixing became important to the senses of place expressed by them.

Lying back on a pad of matted grasses and resting in shade created by agriculture brought one into full-bodied, intimate contact with wild and commercial grasses. All was not pleasant. Short recalled only the "hordes of mosquitoes" or "occasional swarms of flying ants" that could mar the "pleasure" of haying. North Dakotan Era Bell Thompson mentioned horseflies, mosquitoes, flying ants, botflies, and ground ants associated with haying, along with "hay needles" and dust that constantly irritated. Still, she noted "haying time, to me, was the happiest time of the year," as "our whole family took to the field."[77]

Experience with haying reflected an agriculturist's own cultural crafting. The "shade of a hay rack," "shock," "stook," or haystack were shadows of the society's own agricultural remaking of the land. The stacks and conical mounds and twisted upright bundles of wheat waiting in the fields for harvesting refashioned the grasslands. Thompson recalled how "there is an art in shocking grain" and that "it was a creative thing this building of a stack," the "piling-on, the spreading-out, the trampling-down" of it all. Her whole body partook: her hands held tight, and her arms pitched. The weight of her body bouncing strained her feet and physical frame. The bounce released smell and tossed fragments in the air. According to the Raaen family recipe, a haystack grew to "twenty feet long, fourteen feet wide, and twelve feet high." Then the family frosted the massive mound with "coarse grass" and laid a "network of willow branches," in turn decoratively "weighted with stones." They created an objet d'art. Hay sculpted.[78] This crafting or refashioning of the landscape provided a historical aesthetic sensibility. Even the shape of the shade cast on the land by haystacks changed over time. Eventually, the artful view that haystacks and grain fields shocked and stooked changed, as small commercial fields industrialized with standardized bales.

Knowing Grasslands, Inscribing Agriculture

As settler society's children came to know native grasses and flora, they came to know commercial agriculture. Wild, grazed, and cultivated fields had all suffused children's small worlds, seeming complementary, not contradictory or competing. Settler children experienced both an Indigenous, nineteenth-century landscape design of the grasslands and a modern, twentieth-century settler-society agricultural design. This mix of landscape shapes appeared ordinary to settler children: the landscapes of daily life lived in intense sensual awareness around the seasons amid the woods, waters, rocks, and grasses, wild and tame, during the growing season and the long snowfall-to-snowmelt season.[79]

Consider the work and play routines of the child Aagot Raaen and the level of bodily immersion she experienced in the place of her times. Raaen recounted the pervasive "berrying" experience as a highly tactile one, describing differences between the open grasslands and river bottoms in terms of their vegetational effect on the human body. As soon as the snow melted, Aagot ran barefooted through the woods, before any berry bushes bloomed. She and her sister fingered the pump bulbs until the day when berries finally could be picked. While Aagot picked berries, the air softly resounded with the "swish" of the sickle (an extinct sound on the grasslands today) and the odor of "new-mown" grasses that wafted up first from the meadow (grazed land), then from the grasslands (open wild). By the time she and her siblings *began* to pick gooseberries during July, "the skin was thick on the heels and soles of their feet" from other work and play outdoors. In essence Aagot's feet callused to a toughened, cork-like sole, as if she grew her own shoes. If one wore shoes "in the field," Aagot attempted to explain to her possibly surprised mid-twentieth-century readers, those scarce commodities would "wear out" too soon.[80]

As gooseberry picking continued, the "small sharp needles" on the bushes "stung and scratched" the Raaen girls' bodies anew. Toothed, stinging hairy leaves of "nettles burned their bare legs." In turn, the newly hardened skin, a sheath of protection for exposed limbs, served them for hand raking the ripe-smelling meadow grasses into conical-shaped "haycocks." When the family moved to haying beyond grazed meadows, the "sharp grass and stubble" of the little disturbed grasslands began to "hurt their arms and legs" once again.[81]

By the time winter set in, Aagot and her siblings had literally grown a bodily coat *from* and *for* work. "Scratched" bodies and thickened skin from haying, berrying, and playing all lingered as reminders of these environments, long after snow consigned berry season to the past. The skin reacted to the pressures of this annually repeated experience. Feet grew large, spreading wider. Like the visual, auditory, olfactory, and tactile nature of their memories, the thick, wide soles of grass-formed feet would be with northern grasslands children, not only for a single season, but for a lifetime. Aagot Raaen indicated she had trouble finding shoes to fit her large feet well.[82]

Historical-cultural and ecohistorical forces together filter sense of place. Growing up with a high level of sensual immersion, children created a series of first feels and first smells, the specific collapsed to the general by memory and time. High levels of bodily immersion, in combination with a porous built environment, marked the historical senses of place gained by this generation. The multisensual experiences and childhood patterns of interaction with the land changed for later settler-society generations rising in the region.

Children's sensuous absorption of prairies and plains grasslands followed the logic of settler colonialism. An Ojibwe elder, Gambler Tanner, a negotiator for Canada's Treaty 4 in the 1870s, described "our land" as "the earth, trees, grass, stones, and all that I see with my eyes." So he would have understood immediately the attachments these settler-colonial children had to northern grasslands features. At the same time settler society's children sensuously absorbed the grasslands, however, the United States and Canada sent Indigenous children off to boarding schools to *sever* their environmental ties to the northern grasslands habitat.[83] Legal systems of land alienation and treaty making expropriated Indigenous land, but the sensuous experiences of settler children suggest how bodies, living with the land, aided settler colonial claims down the generations. These first settler-society generations *felt* and carried for life on their bodies and in their minds memories of the historical multisensual experience of turn-of-the-century grasslands and grainlands localities: they carried senses of place.

4

"The Purple Hills That Beckoned"

Growing Up, Travel, Education, and Region

"This is so different from going just to Grand Forks," Kjersti Raaen wrote home in 1895. She wrote as if she were yet stealing glimpses of some seven hundred miles of grasslands from her train window. But Kjersti, eighteen years old, had already arrived in Helena, Montana. It was the first time she had traveled farther than fifty miles on the train. Sleep failed to relieve her on the all-night trip. "The next day I was so dizzy and my head ached so that I wished I had stayed home," she complained of motion sickness. With the next breath she again wrote of the view: "Through the train window we saw hundreds of sheep." Her estimation makes clear how vast such spaces appeared. She began to grow out of a mentality of locality in which the space of place consisted of a few sheep to shear. For the first time Raaen realized her village, Hatton, North Dakota, lacked unique styling. She did not yet understand how railroads shaped and reflected larger patterns of people on the grasslands. "There are small towns all along the railroad, and the train stopped at every one," she explained, admitting, "They are so much alike that I could not tell one from the other." Two days of travel provided Kjersti Raaen with a regional lesson in modern standardization, space, and place.[1]

Though most days people remained within the orbit of a horse-and-buggy world, by the late nineteenth century, railroads provided relatively easy access to the entire urbanizing continent. The railroad reached Hatton in 1884, shortening Raaen family trips from weeks to hours. Back then the girls had little conception of railroad travel. When the two "saw smoke in the distance" while haying one day, they mistook it for prairie fire but soon "saw a huge black something moving forward" and froze "rooted to the ground." Kjersti had a nightmare about a train chasing her into the woods, so her sister Aagot slipped away to find out how the "huge black thing they call a train" worked: no worries, the machine could not leave its tracks. Now, when she boarded at Hatton, Kjersti knew the trip would be quick. "[Helena] is far out west, but it doesn't take long to get there on the train."[2] At the same time, though the train window let Kjersti take in miles and miles of grasslands space, the view permitted *less detail* than her six-mile walk from the homestead to the railroad depot. The new geographic perspectives she gained from train travel and Helena, a western grasslands-edge city, spoke to the end of childhood small-world local life.

Kjersti Raaen's adventure beyond locality suggests how maturing young people began to understand regional concepts. This chapter follows grasslands-grown children as they moved into adolescence and away from home to visit friends and family and for work, pleasure, and education. Adventures of travel and intellect worked in tandem to propel adolescents and young adults over increasing amounts of landscape. From dreaming within the shade of a haystack, thinking, "I'd go there some day," these children went: by foot, horse, railroad, and automobile.[3] Young people's expanding sense of geography can be seen in moments when they came to understand previous environmental experiences as personal and local. Having absorbed cultural cues, such as the regional labels circulating in their communities and stories of travel, young people began placing what they had sensed and heard about ecological patterns into geography. Growing knowledge combined with memory to craft lasting versions of childhood experiences. They also gained new intellectual tools with which to view the grasslands anew and made friends and associations that enhanced their understanding of geographic difference. The senses of place children formed growing up with untutored immersion in local northern grasslands habitats informed new geographic and environmental experiences in mind and body to create regional sensibilities in young adults.

Down the Path to School

The world beyond home began sometimes just down the path, when this generation of children began their education. Many of them attended for part of the year, when rural schools popped up in newly established settler communities, others in town. These children spent much more of the year outdoors than children who grew up on the grasslands after school standardization and attendance laws became both mandatory and easier, logistically, to fulfill.[4] The patched, brief nature of the region's common educational experience during this period may account for some of the lifelong force of this generation's early sensuous experience with local landscapes. Local schools often formed one of the early *non*–home places to which prairie and plains children ventured independently.

Formal education occurred unevenly in settler society, in short several-month summer or winter school terms, at home informally, or in religious settings. Children in towns or living close to towns, such as Annora Brown, George Will, Edward Pitblado, Robert McAlmon, Alfred Guthrie, Dorothy Johnson, and Wallace Stegner, had greater access to formal education. The older Humphrey children remained in schools back in Iowa while staying with relatives, until the newly established Faulkton, Dakota Territory, opened schools, which younger Humphrey and Pickler family siblings attended. Children who lived isolated on newly opened homestead lands found regular school attendance difficult. Effie Laurie Storer's formal education ended at age fifteen, when she moved from Winnipeg to Battleford, Saskatchewan. A generation younger, Montanan Peggy Olson Bell received little education, though she read and wrote well. Laura Bower Van Nuys's parents, who had another daughter in Rapid City, sent Laura from the ranch to the city to attend fourth grade. To attend high school, the Hammond girls lived off the ranch and farm in a house the family owned in Maple Creek. Georgina Tompson and her sister waited two years for a school district to be formed in their Alberta area and later boarded in Calgary for high school. Faye Cashatt moved from her family homestead into Dallas, South Dakota, for high school.[5]

Many children also left school for long periods based on the agricultural calendar and other idiosyncratic reasons. As Leslie Neatby put it, "demands of the farm took precedence," so he spent spring school terms grazing the "thirty or forty head of stock" on public domain near their homestead; his brother Kenneth left school for periods to harvest and thresh. Leslie Neatby eventually enrolled in grade ten at the Saskatoon Collegiate Institute with a group of "latecomers from the country," as did several of his siblings. Peter Norbeck, raised in southeastern Dakota Territory, attended a rural school about one mile and a half away from his family homestead for an average of three months during the winter. In one session he attended school only 70 days of a 110-day term. Later, in 1887, Norbeck enrolled in a few sessions of the University of Dakota in the "Students not in Regular Courses" program and finished in the "sub-freshman department." Aagot Raaen attended Concordia College, in Moorhead, Minnesota (across the Red River from Fargo), where, as she put it, "so many grown-up people go who haven't been to school much."[6] Nevertheless, notably, this particular group of northern grasslands settler-society children shared educational achievement, notwithstanding long uncertain struggles.

The local school's importance lay not so much in promoting a regional identity, though teachers introduced students to basic geographic concepts. School instead formed a site of competition to children's environmentally engaged life, as a return home for farmwork suggests. Many children recognized the oak, cottonwood, and other wood grains in the logs or locally sawed boards of the walls, roof, desks, and benches of the first schools they attended. Their bare feet felt oiled wood flooring, similar to what they walked on at home. (Kate Neatby Nicoll never forgot the smell of fresh lumber in her school.) The nature of school, the built environment, and the curriculum, however, imposed new order on childhood ways of interacting with the environment. Looking back, Aagot Raaen explained of her neighborhood, "Children knew how to work with their hands. They lived an active life in the house, in the fields, in the woods," and "to sit still, in an unnatural position, on a hard bench, staring either at the blackboard or at a book, trying to learn a new language, was a hard task." Kjersti and Aagot Raaen never again played in their imaginary Goose River tree house after they began school.[7]

School stood out as a distinct place. "I learned to spell 'hippopotamus' when I could not spell 'gopher' and 'veldt' when I could not spell 'slough,'" recalled Annora Brown of her "haphazard" early

Alberta education. She wondered about the natural world around her but found few adults who could teach her about the nature of the grasslands. When she called a small yellow flower a "buttercup," adults said "no" but at the same time could *not* identify the flower. What about purple flowers lacing the grasslands? No. Not Scottish heather. Riverine berry bushes: no, not an orchard. As she put it, "I was passionately loyal to my own country." She felt the adults around her pined for the "Old Country," whether Ontario or some other place in Canada, the United States, or Europe. Even schoolbooks did not include material for the "proper study of Canadian plants," especially grasslands plants.[8] Children did not study local environment or history.

Wallace Stegner shared Brown's frustration, but only when he looked back on his childhood. He had not learned about the place's history *before* the advent of settler society or really even that a prior human history of the place existed. "Our education" explained Stegner, "did not perform its proper function of giving us distance and understanding by focusing on our life from outside. Instead, it focused on the outside from inside." In other words, no one taught him the history of the Métis people who once lived near him or about the Royal North-West Mounted Police once stationed there or that Sitting Bull and his Lakota followers exiled from the United States camped near where he played. Instead, schooling focused on world and national events "outside" the place Stegner lived. Similarly, Lillian Miller had no conception she grew up in Montana near where in 1877 the U.S. Army caught up with the Nez Perce leader Joseph heading with his people to the border and Canada.[9] Teachers covered history, literature, and science with examples set anywhere but the northern grasslands.

Lack of knowledge implicitly served the settler-colonial process. By the time this generation fully realized the history of the grasslands prior to the advent of settler society, they too had history in the place, setting up a plane of emotional conflict fundamentally different than settler-Indigenous conflicts endemic to their parents and nations. The lack of Indigenous history in local schools reinforced cultural ownership of the place in settler society's children.

Schools began to communicate regional geography, which also may have been taught at home or suggested in stories of travel. Geographic connections beyond home now could be imagined and charted by academic rules. Hale Humphrey, for example, explained another of his boyhood letter enclosures: "I have drew the map of Faulk County and are drawing the map of Dakota."[10] Since his parents homesteaded land and helped found the town of Faulkton, he may have seen a map of Dakota Territory at home. Hale's map is crowded with his town and nine comparable town dots, the winding Nixon River, section gridlines, and compass-direction points. The drawing speaks to organizing space, natural resources, and environmental experience by settler-society norms. Local schools served primarily as spaces for learning political, national, and international information, but formal education also helped children organize sense of place feelings into geography. As Hale Humphrey moved from drawing his county to the "map of Dakota," he likely learned about new landmarks, forming intellectual expectations for geographic space beyond locality without personal physical experience.

Once at school children became conscious, perhaps for the first time, that their well-known locality, bound by ethnicity or former parental place ties, formed only a component of a larger area, region, or nation—diverse in race, ethnicity, and class. Aagot Raaen revealed part of the reason why early rural schools took settler society to new places. She spoke Norwegian at home; her mother never learned to speak English even after living in the United States for more than fifty years. Similarly, Peter Norbeck, in southern Dakota Territory, heard Norwegian and Swedish at home. When Laura Goodman Salverson, born into the Winnipeg Icelandic community, finally attended a common school in Duluth, Minnesota, at the age of ten, she "understood nothing of English," except "a few words and phrases picked up." She felt "un-American" and claimed "our foreignness shrieked at me." Translation felt "very queer," but she vowed to make "this language . . . my own" to join "modernity and American culture."[11]

European immigrant or immigrant-heritage children learned of the United States and Canada in school. Thorstina Jackson Walters remembered teaching her eager Icelander parents and grandparents about the U.S. Revolution, particularly the "Boston Tea Party," the Civil War, and famous presidents. Salverson studied the "Pilgrim

Fathers" and the "Great Republic." Kate Neatby recalled pictures of "King George V" and "Queen Mary" on the walls as well as "King John signing the Magna Carta."[12] North American background, English-speaking children met Norwegians, who met Icelanders, who met children of Irish, English, and German descent. Sam Doughty of Heron Lake, southwestern Minnesota, wrote to the Humphrey children, explaining "there is so few Americans" in his locale and "most of the people are Swede, Norweigian [sic], Germans[?], Bohemian, Austrian, and Hollanders."[13] Grade schools for this generation could be sites of far-off travel when diverse children shared personal and family history.

Diversity encountered in school challenged many children. The Raaen girls and their brother, Tosten, suddenly became aware of class distinction. Walking to school on the grass to keep their feet clean did not keep them from being marked. Clean feet might communicate self-respect, but they did not cover poverty. Some children came to school wearing shoes, factory-made garments (not "homespun"), and ribbons (not "thread") in their hair. African American Era Bell Thompson found herself scrutinized because of skin color rather than the sound of her language or garb of poverty. She recalled feeling relieved to be wearing shoes, not because it elevated her class but because she did not want anyone asking her to explain why "the color ran out" on the soles of her feet and toes. Thompson heard herself demeaned with a Norwegian-accented epithet and called "Skunk" (for her mixed ancestry), while Laura Goodman Salverson heard the names "Eskimo" and "blubber." As an Icelander in a Minnesota school, and despite some shared heritage, Salverson recalled fighting with both Swedes and Norwegians. Laura, the "dirty Icelander," in turn made friends with a Polish Catholic girl she called a "dirty Polack." She recalled they "stood together against our common enemies" (including parents, who lacked appreciation for a mixed-religion friendship) as "two awkward foreign creatures."[14]

Few settler-society children met or exchanged personal stories with Blood, Piegan, Blackfoot, Lakota, Dakota, Cree, Arikara, or Mandan children. Indigenous children lived on reservations and reserves, carved out of, but segregated within, the region. Moreover, both

9. Twelve-year-old Era Bell Thompson, the only African American at the school, sits in the center of a 1917 class of young students (*center, third row from the front*) in Driscoll, North Dakota. She lived on a rented farm about a mile and a half away from the town until her mother died. Then her father moved the family to Mandan and later Bismarck. State Historical Society of North Dakota (00032-BL-39-00009).

Canada and the United States sent many Indigenous children to boarding schools as a way of forcing assimilation and settlers' ideas of "civilization" on the first generation of reserve and reservation children. Indeed, official U.S. and Canadian policy strove to break Indigenous children's ties to nation, parents, home, and place. Even when local schools for Indigenous children existed, they remained segregated. Effie Laurie Storer noted the "Indian Industrial School" in Battleford. Era Bell Thompson met her first "Indian girls" in Bismarck while visiting the playground at the "Indian school." Lillian Miller in Montana mentioned attending school with Métis or, as she termed them, "half-breed," children in rural Montana; she seemed to tolerate them only for the "courtesies and gallantries" she—thinking herself racially superior—was "sure they knew nothing about" but, she implied, could learn from her. As her response to local diversity—she the daughter of a German immigrant—suggests, racist attitudes about local Indigenous and Métis peoples still existed in settler-society culture (even though a new consciousness about the nation's problematic racial history and racism emerged around Miller as she wrote in the 1960s). The United States and Canada aimed to acculturate and assimilate both Indigenous peoples and European immigrants, but in ways that reinforced a racially tiered society.[15]

Expanding the Geography of Home

Children on the home place sensed being part of a bigger geographic entity. Intimately known grasslands home places, the ever-reconfiguring mix of wild and commercial flora and fauna swallowed up by distance and the sky, suggested an organic attachment between locality and an inchoate place. Locality ("here") and a larger diffuse area ("beyond") formed two basic geographic spaces. "The purple hills . . . beckoned" the young North Dakotan Era Bell Thompson "from the rim of another world." The Albertan Annora Brown could see "distance and more distance" all the way to Montana from her "favourite perch . . . on top of the house, near the chimney." The impulse to rise higher to see deeper suggests how children developed a visual claim to all seen, even if they had not experienced the landscape up close. One mid-February day, after taking a "long walk along the track," Elsie May Hammond and a friend looked out into the Saskatchewan distance from atop "the roof of the house while a train went by." The comings and goings of trains and distant views together suggest ways young people began to sense geography beyond locality. The middle distance pulled growing children's thoughts away from the immediate world of the home place.[16]

Children heard tell of landmarks, towns, and cities and stories of prominent locations long before they visited such places. Lillian Miller recalled in her childhood that "'Montana' meant the Bear Paw Mountains and the little town of Chinook." She knew well "a radius of thirty miles or so" but had only heard of the nearby "Little Rockies." A thirty-mile-round Montana reveals a child's local sensibility. In a two-day wagon ride from their homestead beyond the "four fingers"— single cottonwoods—bounding Nell Wilson Parsons's small world in vast Saskatchewan, her father directed her sight to the "curves of the trail, looping over and around hills and rocks" to reveal only apparently flat "gently rolling" terrain.[17]

Natural elements in the landscape also suggested connections to the world beyond. As Wallace Stegner phrased it, the flow of a river became pathways that "might bring us out" of the locality to somewhere but with "no notion where." Effie Laurie Storer recalled sitting near the Battle River with a "great fascination . . . watching the water flow by and picturing all that it saw in its windings." She felt these "dreams" to be a "valuable part of every girl's youth." Alice Humphrey implicitly learned a regional relationship when a "branch" prairie fire from Bismarck threatened Faulkton. Hundreds of miles separated the two towns, but wind, fire, smoke, and grass connected them. The meaning of smoke in the air, whether it came from prairie fire or a railroad, suggests ways children began to expand geographic sensibilities. Aagot Raaen imagined "an endless stream of carloads upon carloads of beautiful animals from the open plains of the West poured in" to Chicago, drawing regional connections based on the cattle market, so strong she toured the stockyards soon after arriving in the city for the first time.[18] This generation chose an imagery of rivers, railroads, and trails—historical features—as metaphors for growing up. Such imagery showed basic geographic awareness in ways unrelated to state, provincial, and national boundaries.

Favored childhood outdoor spaces became places for growing adolescents to spend time with friends away from parents. The rounds of bloom and fade received no childish awe or wonderment, only expectation for seasons' passing. Individuals knew the terrain so well they could now take its environmental features for granted, as adolescent concerns occupied their minds. Continued direct interaction with the surrounding terrain, however, reinforced associations of place first gathered in childhood.

Two June evenings outside, recorded in Elsie Hammond's diary, suggest a young woman who has moved away from childhood but was still linked deeply to activities on the landscape first experienced in childhood. One typical summer evening found Elsie with her cousin Daisy "out to see 'birds' nests." Finding none, they "laid on the hill at big Bend and read, I, history, till dark," she explained. Schoolwork soon turned into child's play. Under creeping darkness Elsie recorded how the two "turned some 'summers[a]ults' and with Sis, ran down the hill on the high lope." Soon "the boys [her brothers] hea[r]d us cross the bridge and came out to see us run." "Daisy jolted her hair all down." The very next evening Elsie recorded planning again to "read till dark, then have some fun as on previous night, but it was very cloudy and soon began to rain." The first evening showed how young women could enter into the landscape for serious adult forms of leisure and at the same time allow their limber bodies the freedom to roll, run, sweat, and play in expressiveness on the hills and grasses they knew so well. The summersaults suggest how mundane outdoor activity (here recorded by chance) imprinted people physically with place ecology in repeated, complicated processes.[19]

A similar situation suggests both the importance of everyday experience for the development of sense of place and how memory packages experience. Near the end of March one particular year, Elsie recorded how she and her cousin "went to look for crocuses." She must have looked annually for the first signs of spring since before she could remember. The time of year and something about the recent atmosphere must have suggested blooming crocuses. But "as we could not find any we lay on the hills and sunned ourselves," she explained. "We stopped at the creek and pushed ourselves around on boards on the ice and water as we had done *years before.* . . . We also broke in the ice with sticks and had a royal time." Since it had just "snowed hard for an hr." *that very day* and "then came out warm," the two friends probably did not leave overly disappointed at not finding crocuses. Indeed, only a few days prior, the two young women had gone "for a walk to the cut bank and there slid down snow banks as we had done *years before.*" Still, the feel of the air, the warmth of the sun, and the "creeks running over the ice" indicated crocuses would be along any day.[20]

With the children no longer in a continually present-tense world, daily life began to take on a comparative past-future dimension. Another diary entry records Elsie "talked of old times" with a close neighbor "and planned our summer riding." This entry suggests both the routine nature of "summer riding" and Hammond's own sense of maturity: she was old enough to have "old times." The phrase "years before" and the reassurance to her diary that breaking ice with a stick was a "royal time" nevertheless communicated a slight uneasiness. The snow with the water, thin ice, and earthy smell of thawing ground caused the two young women to remember and to try to enact prior childhood activities. Elsie's diary entry reveals this day of tromping occurred merely as a one-time re-creation, for fun and nostalgia. Such times were *past* daily recurrent pleasures, and not regularly part of her young adult everyday world. The stress on "years before" allowed her to feel secure in her adult body and let the child in her win out for the moment, because she could remember and her body sensed old feelings. The young women grafted childhood memories onto more mature—now twice environmentally told—bodies.[21]

Since Daisy planned her wedding at the same time, these women's jaunts in the ice, snow, and grass seem almost as symbolic good-byes to youthful friendship. Four years later, at twenty-two, Elsie Hammond could still play a game of "leap frog" with a girlfriend, in which they "jumped the currant bushes." When body in touch with land stimulates memory, the child inside occasionally won out, especially in the privacy of close friends and a personal diary. The memory and reexperiencing of an old, familiar movement provided continuity to one life, with many historical selves. Bodily retellings of environmental experience consolidated the landscape's textures, smells, and sounds to suggest these might be outdoors activities that would survive in Hammond's memory as well as her diary.[22] The intimacies with friends in relationship to grasslands environments implied in these two unexpected exchanges point to young people retreating from parental realms and growing to a new independence outdoors.

Local river trees surfaced repeatedly in Aagot Raaen's memoir, as she charted how she and her sisters grew more independent from their Norwegian community and rural North Dakota. Those old, scraggly, common trees—cottonwoods, elms, poplars, and oaks—framed the many scenes an aged Aagot crafted into the significant points and places in her autobiography. After her first term in teacher training, unsure of her success, Aagot "roused herself and went to the woods. The elms and oaks stood strong and majestic." She took inspiration from these trees, which "had withstood the storms of years." She practiced aloud before an "audience" of elms, oaks, and tall poplars the senior thesis she planned to read at graduation. She retreated alone or with her siblings to the woods of Goose River to make most of the important decisions of her adult life. She rejected a proposal for marriage in the poplar grove. Three of the Raaen children met in a secret conference in the same grove to plan how to save their parents' twice-mortgaged homestead.[23]

Young people also met friends on the land to talk and plan. Elsie Hammond and her friends went out walking and talking "in the field to pick flowers and see nests" and "to the cutbank and picked some upsidedown flowers." One time Hammond and a friend "went up to *the* little hill where [they] lay and talked till" quite late. Another time Elsie went up to meet a friend at "their hill." When a new teacher moved to the locality, the Hammonds entertained at the ranch, and Elsie took the teacher "up the little hill and picked some cactus flowers." During high school Elsie and a friend (who boarded at the Hammond family farm operated by Elsie's brother Lester) took a study break "up to the little hill," where they "picked roses and flowers." Another time they walked "down the fence north," where they "picked some violets."[24] Hammond regularly visited particular locations, having learned earlier what ecological life such spots hosted. Now young people's talk—growing insight into relationships and situations—not play, consumed her observational skills, the ground now taken for granted.

Aagot Raaen took one of her first major trips from the Red River Valley across the grasslands to Williston, North Dakota, to visit friends who had moved west to homestead. The trip ended with a five-mile walk, on which she "tarried so long" to figure out what made the "peculiar barking" she heard. Prairie-dog villages, like many regional features, did not populate every locality. It took travel beyond the Red River Valley for Raaen to understand the pulsing of prairie-dog villages across space. For two days more she and her friends "roved the hills" on horseback, "exploring the country," giving her a better understanding of western plains terrain as compared to the prairie of the Red River Valley.[25] Travel allowed new place perspectives, as each variation of grasslands ecosystems added complexity to the local world first sensed physically and imagined as children.

Elsie Hammond's diaries provide rich detail on the journeys she made to destinations that expanded her home geography. One July saw Elsie and three of her girlfriends set out on their horses, two picking up a third and a fourth along the way: their horses "got off the trail" several times; in one area one woman served as the "guide on horseback." About two weeks later Elsie and a longtime friend started "for the Bench" to harvest berries, but they rode beyond their usual picking spots. Her diary recorded the adventure: "We went up to Bob's and had a great hunt. Had to walk a long way thro' speargrass hay to get a drink." The two had gone so far out of the territory of their usual knowledge that they "got almost lost to find the trail off the bench. We began to think we were lost, but got home at 9." The feel of battering through "speargrass hay" and the taste of creek water added new layers of place experience. Another time she went "to see the beaver dams" and remarked, "It was quite dark coming home but we kept the trail without much trouble."[26] Excursions created environmental knowledge, added complexity to an individual's sense of locality, and tested one's independence.

Outings show how Hammond increased her knowledge of the environment, both its ecological content and cultural history. One September Elsie, her sister Kay, and two neighborhood gals "all [went] riding to the hills." They "galloped through the bushes" to another friend's place, and "from here we rode to the Indian grave-yard and winter quarters where no one was living; then to the coal mine" and on to another friend's home. Traveling to the "bush" for wood and to the "mine" for outcroppings of lignite coal, rarely, if a young woman had a brother or a father, fell within the realm of her duties (though she readily accompanied males on such trips and offered key help). Visiting Indigenous winter campsites and riverine spots evident with funerary traditions also might satisfy or spark Hammond's curiosity. Her ability to identify Indigenous cultural history on the landscape suggests at least implicit knowledge about her culture's displacement of Indigenous peoples. However, Hammond's diaries lack reflection. Using only the generic term "Indian," she does not personalize Indigenous culture sensitively. For many years she visited such sites, another time taking a "walk up to French Georges Butte to see the Indian graves." In the 1920s Hammond entertained her three nieces, walking them "up to the Indian graves and trees."[27] The graves suggest a regular destination, perhaps a site to see, the gawking certainly trying to the living relatives and tribes of the dead or ancestors. The traditional burials also suggest Indigenous persistence on the land and in the culture, growing difficult for settlers to deny.

The Hammonds regularly visited friends in the Cypress Hills. Elsie records going "up to the Pine hills. and to see the old mill site and the old boiler." There she also saw "the trail where the C.P.R. hauled out their pine ties for the track." Another time, while her parents went "shooting," she and her sister "went for some pine tree boughs and had a terrible climb" and later "took a run down to the spring" to read. Elsie's diary recorded one of the journeys as a "rocky ride" and one of frequent in and outs, as she "rode and opened gates[,] about 10." Another trip had a memorable ending when all "laughed at us getting lost." Although locals had "put us on the right road," Elsie explained, "we soon got mixed up." Finally, "we climbed up a long, long hill" to gain an orientation of the surrounding terrain "and thus got on the Bench."[28] The growing number of gates mentioned by Elsie suggests the rising population of families, such as those of Wallace Stegner, Wilfrid Eggleston, Leslie Neatby, and Ralph Russell, who claimed new homestead land in the early twentieth century. As she opened and closed gates, Hammond learned the recent history of the land. Grid-section lines materialized more boldly than the expansive open look of unmarked lines Hammond had gathered into herself as a child.

Hammond occasionally noted times when she "got off the trail" or "got mixed up," suggesting settler-society trails remained faint or contested by paths created by Indigenous peoples, fur traders, and bison. As fellow Saskatchewanian Ralph Russell would point out decades later, before paved roads, settlers confronted a "veritable network" of choices "running in all directions," making it "most confusing" to select the "proper trail to follow." Frequently, people well on their way unexpectedly confronted a "vanishing trail." Travel beyond the home place did not take too much distance to reach uncertain terrain. Even though Elsie Hammond was born and raised in Saskatchewan, she could get lost close to home, especially in preelectric darkness. Once Hammond even "nearly got lost while crossing *our stubble and ploughed field*," surely familiar territory; in the end she "had to trust Flotilla [her horse] to keep the trail which she did very well."[29] The knowledge that one could not know the grasslands completely proved part of what Hammond's generation came to realize. Getting lost in a terrain one knew so well suggested the spacious grasslands had some control over humans struggling to control the land. Individuals grew up with grasslands knowledge tempered by lifelong experience (if here brief by actual age), while their parents had to replace preconceived expectations about land and, at least at the start, their presumed power to wrest control of the place.

Travel and Sifting Memory: Recrafting Home I

The experience of viewing "distant" grasslands, a mysterious geographic space to the child's eye, shifted as individuals became increasingly aware, intellectually and experientially, of a larger geographic world. More adult—experienced and educated—eyes became trained to discern how home ecologies fit into larger physical-geographic contexts. Education and work frequently required traveling beyond home. Travel-born experiences informed individuals of elements that distinguished their location from other places. The process of figuring out the contours of regional space also comingled with the task of charting differences between city and countryside that occurred within as well as beyond the northern grasslands. Overlapping contrasts created new insights into home and region.

Work created opportunities for children to fit their well-known locality into a larger geographic conception. Paid work might supplement, support, or replace educational goals or become stepping stones for long-term goals or to leave the farm or ranch. Wilfrid Eggleston worked as a "store boy" in towns popping up along new railroad lines in Alberta and Saskatchewan and eventually held a clerk's position in a small-town bank. Aagot and Kjersti Raaen hired out as domestic servants, to "nurse" the ill and to help with births.

10. Aagot Raaen's autobiography recorded many of her sister Kjersti Raaen's activities, including her travel out west to Montana to be a cook, to Northwood for a position as a servant, and to Grand Forks to become a dressmaker. Kjersti (pictured here, probably in the 1890s) dreamed of becoming a nurse but became ill and died before she could carry out her plan. North Dakota State University Archives, Fargo, North Dakota.

Both also worked as cooks during the threshing season and sewed for neighbors. Tosten Raaen worked as a "separator man and engineer" during the threshing season. Era Thompson worked as domestic servant for an Englishwoman in Minneapolis and later returned to write for a "colored Minneapolis weekly" newspaper. Laura Goodman Salverson hired out for "housework" but also worked in a drug store and dancehall, sewed dresses and awnings (the latter, with a "big power machine"), pieced together horsefly nets, and nursed informally. Temporary jobs added income to family agricultural operations and sometimes funded independent adventures and formal education. Shifting locations came with opportunities, most of them unconscious and unrecorded, for learning new spatial and environmental configurations.[30]

When individuals traveled away from home places to work, study, and travel, they selectively used the content of childhood environmental experiences to form adult selves. Personality, experience, class, race, location, and a host of other social characteristics affected the elements of flora, fauna, space, and place individuals chose to remember. The ecological content that already suffused bodies and minds bubbled up in the context of latter-day experiences in new places by chance physical labors and intellectual endeavors. Away from but thinking of home, young people selected particular memories from masses of past daily life to maintain connections to home. A contemporary sensuous experience might echo past experience and stimulate memory anywhere: the combination of past experience and present encounter crafted "home." Adults carried consolidated moments of childhood into the future through such twice-telling and later recalled them in memoirs and autobiographies. Early environmental experiences, idiosyncratically selected, cannot be easily erased in part because they remained open to recall throughout life.

Aagot Raaen eventually enrolled at the Normal School in Mayville, North Dakota. She also attended the University of Minnesota and earned her bachelor's degree from the University of Wisconsin, later enrolling in at least a year of graduate school in Germany. Raaen's memoirs revealed she remembered the scenes of the Goose River locality many times as she began her teaching career at the turn of the century. Each time she remembered those childhood scenes, a new layer of meaning carried them forward in a constantly developing identity. During one of her first lengthy stays away from home, she worked for a term at the all-female Oak Grove High School outside Fargo. She felt comforted by the "forest of natural trees—oaks, elms, ash, box elders, [and] familiar bushes" against the Red River; they had been her "friends as far back as she could remember." While working on her bachelor's degree at the University of Wisconsin, she often "stole up on the campus [after midnight], threw herself on the cool grass, listened to the wash, wash, wash of Lake Mendota and looked at the stars overhead till she was calmed and rested." Aagot could touch, hear, and see the things that comforted her most: the feel of the grass, the sounds of water, and a view of stars—even lying near a lake in Madison, not beside Goose River. In darkness sensual clues and memory cloaked a place in the beyond with home. Similarly, on a visit to Chicago, Raaen retreated from "cracking" horsewhips, "clanging" streetcars, shouting hawkers, and a fast-moving, harried, "well-dressed mob" to Lincoln Park, where she found that "the friendly trees had never seemed more friendly, the gay flowers never so gay, the good earth never so good and the scent of green grass never as welcome." Here "nature's comrades from her *home* community" hailed her in from the storm of the city.[31]

Similarly, when attending the University of North Dakota in Grand Forks, Era Bell Thompson came to view grasslands landscape as a comfort. City bloom grew into "green velvet lawns and long hedges . . . [with] robins and bluebirds, iris buds and lilacs." On the other side of the railroad tracks, near the "back road where prairie grass was soft and warm," grew "sage, buffalo grass and purple crocuses." Thompson made her way to college classes by walking down the "back road" to school "to escape" the "ordeal" of "facing a new student body"; she felt people in the town stared at her Blackness. After she became a known figure on campus, however, she recalled, "I didn't walk down the back road so much any more, only when I wanted to think or when I got lonesome for the prairie grass and the floating clouds."[32] She spoke to differing city and country environments. Thompson's memoir used imagery characteristic of the grasslands to explain a shift to young womanhood and a wider world, in which her Blackness formed a social question for some people of whose answers she felt uncertain.

Aagot Raaen's similar craft at merging old experiences into a new setting shows how much the body and its senses transport the comforts of home even when the body is far away from home. Comfort does not imply total happiness. Aagot wished more than ever to be away from that home place to obtain education. She was bitter over her father's alcoholism, the family's poverty, and the lack of intellectual life and opportunity in her own locality. She realized *not* how sweet, innocent, and lovely her childhood had been but rather how it had been "starved" from bodily nutrients to intellectual life.[33] Nevertheless, past deeply known environments comforted her: old feels, sights, smells, and sounds. Aagot did not recall her labors, sore skin, and aching body during the moments she found environmental comfort on the grass at a Wisconsin lake. The mysteriousness of memory, mind, and body interacting allowed for such nostalgic moments.

To make sense of new environmental encounters, individuals placed them with reference to aspects of home they knew well. Raaen compared the "hard streets" of Minneapolis to the "soft earth" of the homestead. She yelled from the pages of her autobiography: "crowds, noise, confusion!" She could describe the city only as "one snarled web" of "everything and everybody . . . moving in all directions at the same time." If the space of the grasslands made one feel exposed and small, the space of the city gave one the feeling of being lost in a crowd.[34] As Raaen's train approached Boston at night she compared the approach of the city to a "dim light like the afterglow of a sunset"; the "many sparks" soon became "countless stars" and finally just "big lights." The "vastness" of Saint Petersburg, Russia, she compared to the "spaciousness of the Dakota prairies." On a long train trip across Argentina's pampas, she experienced awe and boredom at the view "all day long" of "grassy plains." A grasslands tall tale came to mind, in which an Englishman traveling by train across the United States queries a conductor in the morning, at noon, and again that evening about location. Each time the conductor replies with increasing impatience and volume: "In Montana."[35] Aagot's humor suggests a personal knowledge about the reputation of her broad home region. Such stories circulated among her generation and showed affection for and understanding of northern grasslands regional space.

Going east from Minneapolis by train for the first time, Raaen had felt somewhat disturbed because she could not "see any of the life of the prairie." Viewing the blur of a passing landscape, Aagot understood the rural countryside to be "plains" and "prairie," wild grasses in formation but now dotted with familiar commercial agricultural fields. No doubt the Indiana viewed from her train window was flat and carved agriculturally as the landscape of her home locality. But Aagot sensed a distinction. This Indiana "country shows age quite different from Dakota." Densely clustered farmsteads, tree-cleared flatlands, dense populations, and the historical detail and building shapes and styles in small towns east of the northern grasslands ultimately distinguished this agricultural countryside from Dakota's landscape and false-front, railroad-town atmosphere. Brick homes anchored many Illinois and Indiana farmsteads, which boasted old, thick stands of trees nearby.[36]

When Lulu Pickler Frad began attending the Dakota Territorial University at Vermillion in the spring of 1889, she also expanded her place knowledge. She adjusted quickly to college life, weeks "flitting swiftly by," but her early letters suggest longing for Faulkton. She enrolled in botany, Latin, and music classes; joined the chapel choir; and advocated on behalf of women's suffrage (she met Susan B. Anthony on the street one day) and temperance. Near the end of her first year, she attended the class picnic and recounted, "We went down to the boat ride on the Missouri which was not very far distant. Crossing the river we spent a very pleasant time in Nebraska; while there I got some very pretty flowers which reminded me of the woods at Grandpa's." While she possibly encountered some more southerly flora species, some of these new-to-her "pretty flowers" probably dotted grasslands wooded river bottoms generally.[37]

Pickler reached a sort of environmental epiphany about Vermillion after attending a "prayer meeting." "It seemed almost an ideal night," she tried to explain. "The trees being here make it seem almost like another state when compared with the prairie." More than once she

11. Lulu Pickler (pictured here, probably in the 1880s) lived at Faulkton, Dakota Territory, before she attended Dakota University, in Vermillion, where in 1889 she lived in East Hall. Pickler Family Papers, State Archives Collection, South Dakota State Historical Society (H91-074).

went "boating," commenting that "the river is very nice now and the trees are so pretty and green." Indeed, the Missouri River allowed for some of the thickest woods within the northern grasslands, much thicker than she would have experienced along the smallish "Nixon River" at Faulkton. Lulu remained within a larger, abstracted orbit of a state, but now trees fit into her conception of "prairie." At college, along with botany and music, Lulu Pickler learned environmental boundaries did not correspond with those of political lines. Traveling to and from Faulkton taught her about region.[38]

The sensuous textures of favored childhood places, not surprisingly for this generation, remained intertwined with animals and show in the craft of remembering over time and space. In the early 1890s, when Alice Humphrey attended South Dakota's Agricultural College at Brookings, some one hundred miles east of her home, she missed *her* animals. She asked after them in letters: "Is Daisy alright[?] I wish I could have a ride on her. . . . Does 'Jersey' ever kick and spill all the milk[?]" Alice could not wait to climb on Daisy, when school let out: "She will have a little (!) exercise when I return," she informed the family at home. Implicitly, she wrote of riding fast across the open country, her body taking in the weight of atmosphere at horse speeds. Certainly, Alice was not thinking of the frigid winter horse "runs" she complained of a few years earlier. She remembered no feelings of irritation or frustration, presumably part of her first reactions to a cow's kicks and spills (which she told about in childhood letters). These animals instead conjured Alice's home place. Her memory began to select favored animals and telling work and leisure patterns for shuffling into long-term memory. Thoughts of past experiences at this point in her life—recalling as one step away from firsthand experience—made the experiences more available for later recall. Such animals often ended up sentimentalized into "ponies and horsies" who could "almost express themselves without words."[39] Along with sentiment, however, children's former attachment to animals brought to life the ground on and atmosphere in which children and animals walked, rode, and played.

Arriving by train to Illinois in December 1894, Hale Humphrey's years in the "Commercial Class" at the Dixon Business College found him commenting on atmosphere as much as coursework. Quite possibly revealing the opposite feelings, Alice Humphrey's brother explained, "I feel quite at home at our [dinner] table as [the leader of the table] came from Clark, S.D.—he used to live in Redfield, S.D. [near Faulkton]—and one of the girls is a South Dakotan." Hale wrote of going "out walking" in the town and on campus grounds with fellow Dakotans. After receiving his father's newspaper, he wrote, "It seemed like an old friend" when "I received the '*Times*' this morning." Keenly, he tried to keep track of the home places and faces. "Has Faulkton grown any? Is the new mill running much of the time[?]" Some nine months after arriving in Dixon, he worried to his mother, "Faulkton will seem like a *strange place* to me the next time I see it—so many great changes having taken place."[40]

Hale Humphrey's environmental experience in Illinois, from the perspective of his surviving letters home, differed from Faulkton. The air felt different with humidity. In June he wrote of a "very bad cold." He continued complaining, "am very careful but the weather changes so that it is a difficult job. It is so damp, too. Quite different from Dakota atmosphere." Six months later he concluded, "We are having queer weather for winter. It has rained more or less for a week, and is foggy and disagreeable. The snow has all disappeared." Rain dashed Hale's expectations for winter. This shifting of rain and snow seemed untimely from his Dakotan perspective. Since Hale noted these complaints while alone at Christmastime, cultural atmosphere—not only climate difference—probably affected his propensity to complain; yet his observations of the atmosphere remain true. Similarly, after viewing a Swedish film that featured "rough white snow country," South Dakota novelist Robert McAlmon wrote his spouse that "the sight of snow country made me want it." Perhaps a rain-soaked Paris influenced his memory, for he reflected further, "Haven't had it for years though I grew up amongst it." Later the same year, McAlmon wrote from Stockholm, a city then "covered with snow," albeit not Dakota "rough": "A little soft and slushy but I like it."[41]

The unexpected contrast, as with Lulu Pickler encountering river-edge flowers and woods, taught Hale Humphrey and Robert McAlmon as much about Dakota open grasslands climate as it did about Illinois,

Paris, and Stockholm. In another letter Hale seemed thrilled to note a wind "blowing a perfect gale. I almost imagine that I am in Dakota once more." Whatever was in the wind that day, the tingle on his body, the tilt of his walk, and the toss of his hair reminded him of Dakota, where he first experienced consistent gale-force winds. Another time Hale charged his mother, "Tell Kenneth I am glad he is having some sport with the rifle. . . . I would like to take a day off to go with him after the 'Jacks.'" "I saw some rabbits the other day that were killed near Dixon. They were poor excuses for rabbits, too. You could have put one of them in your vest pocket . . . without any trouble."[42] Dakota boasted bigger animal life. Environmentally informed cultural expectation rarely rises to the surface of expression (even more rarely is recorded). Atmosphere is usually taken for granted until bodily expectation meets difference. Then, as in Hale Humphrey's examples, air became concrete and animal size spoke to environment. Insight and feelings simultaneously disrupted, reminded, and confirmed his knowledge of known places and differences between places.

Soon Hale Humphrey's letters home from school in Illinois ask after his horse. "Did you have any trouble with Selim?" he queried his mother. Perhaps trying to communicate on a level his five-year-old sister, "Kittie Wee," could understand, Hale began to depict the same animals *he* drew when a little boy. Mirroring the impulse, when the North Dakotan Era Thompson's older brothers left the North Dakota farm for Minneapolis, they sent her a "folding camera," and she "sent them pictures of all the animals so they would not forget." To Thompson and Alice and Hale Humphrey, the animals equaled place and home. Hale Humphrey also seemed to have understood what would be meaningful in Kittie's local world. He regularly sprinkled his letters home with animal pictures noted especially "for Kittie." Hale also peppered Kittie about the farm animals that he sensed could be meaningful to her: "Do you ride Daisy now? How is daisy's lame foot?" On Kittie's sixth birthday he asked, "How is Selim? Do you help water him any more?" Hale's questions suggest his own recalling of an intersection of land, animals, and seasonal weather. His efforts to communicate with his "wee" sister, however, probably provided himself with as much comfort as they did Kittie. As he drew again what he knew from childhood, surely Hale reflected on his own boyhood in the same place. In doing so Hale likely added weight to his remembered past experiences, helping to ensure survival from of all the things memory sifts out.[43]

One of Hale's first young-adult jobs, on a railroad crew in Texas and Mexico, at first alienated him with landscapes of "nothing but sand and sand hills," which he described in a letter. But he took comfort in "one thing here that reminds me of Dakota—meadow larks. I hear them every day—possibly the same bird will be up there next summer," he projected, then adding, "I would like to come with them." The next letter home related, "Coyotes are as thick as hornets in a hornet's nest." But he contrasted the situation for Faulkton folks: unlike in Dakota, "nobody shoots them because ammunition costs so much and it would take a regiment of soldiers to kill them all."[44] The workings of memory and prior attachment to animals show here in a transition to young adulthood.

When Kjersti Raaen remembered the labor of the home place from within the city of Grand Forks, where she lived a short time to train as a dressmaker, the atmosphere on the farm seemed inviting and fluffy nice to her compared to the "sun-baked" city and its close living quarters. Indicating certain unease in not experiencing the country seasonal routine, she longingly asked, "Have the wrens come back to their nests in the poplar trees?" In one letter she inquired, "How many new calves have we? What colors are they?"[45] Implicitly, animals attached her to the terrain and air. The sounds of the leaves of poplar trees came with birds chirping and the smells of calves and sheep nosing the ground. Sounds and smells could not be separated from Raaen's tactile experience and the soil and grasslands under her feet.

When Era Bell Thompson visited the Minneapolis–Saint Paul Black community, she—as did the Raaen sisters—ended up feeling "hemmed in, apart from the rest of the world." After a summer of working, she recalled, "I was glad to leave St. Paul, glad to get away from grocery stores and restaurants. . . . I was willing to give all the beautiful flowers in St. Paul for one ragged tumbleweed, all the beautiful lakes in Minnesota for one alkaline slough." She enjoyed the Black community and returned again to live and work there for a weekly newspaper; it was the low intensity of the built environment, the low concentration of people—a sparser atmosphere she missed. Until that time her world had been rural. Eventually, after attending the University of North Dakota and earning a bachelor's degree from Morningside College in Sioux City, Iowa, she moved to Chicago. When she returned to Mandan after her father died, the town now seemed "toylike" in comparison to Chicago skyscrapers. Her characterization of towns as "toys" displays not only a detachment from the earth that came with urbanization—the stuffiness and blotting out of nature felt by Aagot Raaen and Kjersti Raaen—but the particular way towns looked on the grasslands. Towns looked set down on the land whole: the effect of the broad land and sky on sense perception.[46]

Letters written by Manitoban Edward Pitblado from England and France during World War I, from 1916 through 1917, to his family in Winnipeg suggest the importance of regional game birds to at least his sense of stability. Pitblado joined Elsie Hammond's brother Bill in service. Thorstina Jackson Walters worked for the YWCA and YMCA in Europe during the war.[47] The war marked many in this generation, but Pitblado's growth in understanding region is especially telling. From London Pitblado wrote, "Today is just like a Canadian summer day with lots of dust from the road. The only difference is that there are thousands of soldiers awalking out of leave." He noted, "People call them 'rough' but it would be a comfort at home to have roads as good. They are perfectly plastered with signposts and you couldn't get lost."[48] The Pitblados lived on the wealthy and fashionable Wellington Crescent, fronting the Assiniboine River in Winnipeg, but Edward probably thought of all the countryside roads he traveled in Manitoba. (When Elsie Hammond visited Winnipeg, she toured the Wellington Crescent neighborhood as a must-see "sight.")[49]

Edward Pitblado's first views of the war-torn French countryside came from the perspective of subterranean "trench living." At one location he observed, "The country is wonderful and in a few respects resembles Southern Manitoba. It is slightly rolling and very green. Hop fields . . . very symmetrically planted . . . grain fields with excellent crops."[50] Born in 1896, Edward had Manitoba eyes and agricultural eyes; his view of southern Manitoba combined elements of grasslands

12. Canadian Edward Pitblado (pictured here, in 1915), from Winnipeg, served in France and England during World War I and eventually joined the Royal Flying Corps. University of Manitoba Archives and Special Collections, Pitblado Family fonds, MSS 48, PC 58, box 3, file 7, item 99.

landscape in agricultural dress. Pitblado's first time far from home caused him to see "home" in new landscapes to create comfort in an undoubtedly fearsome situation.

Much of Edward Pitblado's correspondence while serving in the Canadian Field Artillery in France concerned seasonal bird hunting.

Game birds made almost every letter he sent home. With the days of September 1916 marching on, Edward wrote to his father, "I was just remarking . . . that the ducks ought to be plentiful this year without such a gathering of men to kill them." By the end of October, his mind turned to prairie chickens. "Have been wondering how you made out in the opening chicken shoot." Having "seen what war really is" by this time, however, he became aware of the oddness of his desire to hunt. "Little I ever thought that this year's shoot would be so far fetched as the one we are now engaged in. I came up to the guns yesterday and have had quite a little excitement enough to last me for a few days at least," he admitted. Another letter spoke of a "rather eager longing to take another whack at the game birds as a change from this game."[51]

Spirits sagging, Edward's mother apparently decided to send a comfort that surely spoke to home at a deep level. She mailed a taste of the prairie—bottled! Ten days later the package had not arrived. "Have not received any of Mother's parcels yet," Edward wrote with an expectant anxiety, "that is of those she mentioned beginning with the prairie chicken." A week later Ed was "wonderfully happy over the results of the last two days' mail": five letters, his mother's "bottled chicken," a new pair of boots from his father, magazines, cake, nuts, candy, "fancy oddments," and a "parcel of notepapers." He and his captain had "sampled the eats in good style but we are holding the chicken for a grand feed," he emphasized.[52] There was something special about the idea of tasting prairie chicken. The expectations of taste buoyed him until the preserved meat arrived. But Ed held it back to savor. He could show the bottle to his friends, telling them all about hunting prairie chickens in Canada.

A week later he revealed to his father, as it turned out, the unfortunate results of the "grand feed." "Alas!" he sighed, "I nearly had ptomaine poisoning as a result of my appetite. The . . . wax sealing on the bottle had become detached with the result that the air had been allowed to enter." "It smelt rather queer but I was so eager to have a go at the chicken that I had to try it. The next day I had a bad session of pains but got [cleaned?] out with salts and was all right in a few hours." The prairie chicken gave him mental as well as intimate physical comfort and connected him to home landscapes. Though Edward Pitblado fought as a Canadian for the British Empire, his identity demonstrated a northern grasslands flavor. Shooting ducks and prairie chickens connected the young man to family, boyhood, and region, as the war gun gave him new connections to the British Empire and his Canadian identity. One could almost forget that Edward first learned his skill with the gun as a boy walking the landscape to hunt game birds. Another letter, however, recalls his comparative youth: he wrote home saying, "I am still growing so my size in tunics is steadily changing."[53]

Having graduated from the University of Manitoba with a bachelor's degree, Edward Pitblado returned to England on a Rhodes Scholarship to study law at Oxford University from 1921 to 1924. He lived close to London, and he occasionally visited museums and attended theaters or Charlie Chaplin movies. Still, he suffered continually from the "fever," as he called it, "to go shooting." His consciousness of the grasslands as a place seemed even greater. It felt "strange" to him, "that there are so few species of birds over here—hardly even see any at all." After "discussing shooting with an Englishman from the North," an unimpressed Edward wrote his mother how he "really had to smile to myself when I heard all of the particulars," although he did not "of course . . . tell him what good bags we get as that would long be rubbing it in."[54] Edward grew up with annual shooting sprees, "bagging" twenty during a single day's hunt. The abundance of birds using the grasslands migration corridor permeated life in that place and time. His ideas of place show the growing culture of thinking large in terms of size and abundance, a characteristic of bigness growing as a part of a northern grasslands aesthetic—such as Hale Humphrey's larger Dakota jackrabbits.

Edward thought consciously about the taste of his ducks. When he visited the coast of England, he noted the ducks he viewed were "somewhat similar in species" but speculated, "I can't imagine that they are as good eating with so much salt water about." The next year he wrote of mallards "hanging in the butcher's windows," saying, "I don't think they have been feeding on barley, and I know they have never seen Hudson's [sic] Bay." Grain crops began to change the taste of birds, but Pitblado's sense of taste remained bound to place. The taste of the birds depended on culture and available edibles in the native grasslands soil. The culture of grasslands hunting conditioned Edward's body and mind for expectations of taste. Together, wild and tame grain suggest taste both conformed to and shaped northern grasslands settler-society culture. He asked if his family had enough success to "lay in our winter supply of chickens." The wealthy Pitblado family did not depend on the seasonal gamebirds to supply daily sustenance, as the birds Lula Short Asher's family brought to the table. Nevertheless, a supply of fresh, wild meat did provide the Pitblados—and the Short, Will, Hammond, and Humphrey families—with the nourishment of place.[55]

The "dampness" of England also struck Pitblado. "As for scenery and beauty this place is certainly by itself but one cannot really appreciate it when it is so grey and cold," he opined. "I feel this dampness far more than a $-30°$ day at home[.] I never seem to get warm throu[gh] out." The climate seemed even worse to Edward after a couple of months' return to Winnipeg during the summer of 1922. Back in Europe again he felt "quite disgusted with the usual dirty climate. It was surely a sudden change after being at home and on the ocean, where there was always more air than any one person could possibly breathe up. Here it is much different and the feeling is that somehow or other the fresh air has all been used up leaving nothing but a musty smell of rivers, beer, or smoke." Similarly, Wilfrid Eggleston, who in 1926 traveled to England—where he lived as a young boy—scoffed at his first view of Liverpool ("masked under heavy smoke"), noting the "immense tract of houses crowded together like nothing ever seen in Canada, hideous, grimy, exactly alike." Unlike Pitblado's observations, from Eggleston's perspective in steerage, by the time his cattle boat approached the coast of Ireland, he "had grown tired of an ocean-locked view." Both young men here commented on difference between the city and countryside and, implicitly, the northern grasslands social and environmental atmosphere.[56]

Wilfrid Eggleston had traveled to the "British Isles" from Alberta, paying his way by feeding 741 stalled beeves "baled marsh hay... and sacks of grain—oats and Indian corn." Eggleston had earned a bachelor's degree from Queen's University, Kingston, Ontario, completing his first two years by "correspondence" while teaching high school history and English in the Rocky Mountains of Alberta. His first sight of land took him aback: "It was like nothing ever seen on the prairie." However, he immediately qualified, "though some prairie dawns match any pageant of nature anywhere displayed. But here were elements and hues not to be found elsewhere." He felt his "vagabond" status and hard work with cattle in the bowels of the ship earned him the view. Eggleston jumped in thought to the way the weather rewarded those attending to "business," not "pleasure," the way "nature . . . smiles on the farmer boy ploughing in the fields" (not those out for a mere "picnic"), as it did now for "the cattleman crossing the ocean." Backhandedly, here Eggleston expressed a regional identity based on day-to-day experience with the prairies. He understood the way human culture and emotion conspired with daily life to create experience: "one recalls," he explained to the readers of his *Lethbridge Herald* column, "the same air of unreality about certain sunsets, about certain mountain spectacles, about certain emotional moments in which not nature, but human nature, was the conditioner and creator." Big moments earned from hard times infused the culture of place thinking. Seemingly mundane activity allowed truly exceptional environmental imprinting.[57]

Eggleston also "noticed what every traveller from new crude countries notices" when traveling to England: "the trim, carefully-kept appearance of every foot of ground, as though we were passing through the grounds of some private park." The "thickly-grassed slope, studded with heavily-leafed umbrageous trees, . . . looked to me like a . . . sylvan fairyland" or a painting. Only Salisbury Plain reminded him of "the prairie" and "was as welcome as a breath of wolf-willow fragrance would have been." He had heard of "English green"; now he knew what people from the "prairies" meant by that color. The built environment of "substantial brick farmsteads, neat farms, budding hedges, [and] luxuriant green trees everywhere" he compared implicitly to the shacks and farms and the tawny greens he knew from Canada's grasslands.[58] As Raaen noticed differences between Indiana and Dakota farmland, Eggleston sensed a historical northern grasslands configuration of natural and built environment.

The environmental comparisons implicitly and explicitly made in travel for pleasure, work, and education during the young adult phase of this generation resulted in more sophisticated understandings of regional boundaries and place-distinguishing characteristics. Educational needs propelled this settler-society generation across much terrain within and beyond the northern grasslands and taught them, regardless of curriculum or career choice, about local and regional spaces.

Education and Transforming Thought: Recrafting Home II

Formal education often resulted in the acquisition of new intellectual tools that allowed this settler-society generation to see childhood favored grasslands spots anew. New ideas added layers of meaning to a young adult's expanding feelings about place without completely destroying memories of small-world affection. The new concepts and skills gained by formal education joined memory's crafting processes and travel insights to help these young adults reframe and add depth to environmental and regional knowledge.

Many in the first generations of settler society found their way to college and university degrees; as a group they shared educational aspirations. Thorstina Jackson Walters graduated with a bachelor's degree in modern languages from United College in Winnipeg and eventually took courses at Columbia University in New York City. Laura Bower headed for the Agricultural College in Brookings, South Dakota. Fred Hammond attended what his sister called "Edmonton College." Georgina Thomson graduated with bachelor's and master's degrees from the University of Alberta and became a librarian in Calgary. Faye Cashatt Lewis earned a medical degree at Washington University, Saint Louis, after graduating from the University of South Dakota in Vermillion. Leslie Neatby earned a bachelor's degree from the University of Saskatchewan and at the age of forty-five began and soon earned his doctorate in history from the University of Toronto. His sister Hilda Neatby earned a doctorate in history from the University of Minnesota. Suggesting the growing role of science in agriculture as a way of life, two Neatby brothers enrolled in an "associate course in agriculture" at the University of Saskatchewan, while another specialized in plant breeding, where Ralph Russell became interested in plant pathology related to agricultural crops.[59] As children, this generation read nature from a wholly untutored perspective and then, as young adults, used intellectual tools gained with higher education to read anew the northern grasslands.

Many in this generation turned first to teacher-training institutions, as one-room schools proliferated across the grasslands with settler-society growth over the decades. Teaching offered one of the few nonagricultural employment sectors with demand open to maturing young adults. The profession permitted a person as young as fourteen, without a high school diploma, to become minimally certified to teach. Aagot Raaen and her brother Tosten taught in North Dakota. Nell Wilson Parsons and sisters Elsie and Kay Hammond all taught in Saskatchewan. Annora Brown, Wilfrid Eggleston, and Georgina Thomson attended Calgary Normal School and taught in Alberta; Thorstina Jackson Walters taught in Manitoba. Dorothy Johnson taught in Montana. Laura Bower and many of her siblings attended Normal School at Spearfish, South Dakota.[60] Full credentials could be achieved between teaching sessions.

The well-worn path taken by many in this generation to rural or "permit" teaching suggests a settler-society order making its way across the grasslands. An educational infrastructure rose and fell over the lifespan of these first generations born to settler society. Increased settlement resulted in more and more small rural school districts with a corresponding need for teachers. However, many in this generation in turn leapfrogged teaching from rural school to rural school until they earned enough to exit the countryside, if not the region. Their departures mirrored a depopulation of the countryside caused by northern grasslands climate patterns and the slow rise of large-scale farming over the decades of the twentieth century. Regional school consolidation soon followed, as fewer farms meant fewer children to teach. In this way the rise and fall of rural teaching proved pivotal in charting the transformation of setter society on the northern grasslands. Many of these individuals used teaching as a stepping-stone to another career or to earn money for college and university degrees.

Aagot Raaen made teaching a life career. She taught all over North Dakota, served as Steele County superintendent of schools, and left the state for some years to take a job as an educational supervisor in Honolulu, Hawaii. However, she wrote the most about her intellectual development with reference to the Normal School, where she read again, now with academic skills, the nature she sensed as a child. Raaen favored literature and philosophy, but she remembered her classes in geology, botany, and astronomy with verve. On weekends, which she spent on the Goose River homestead, Aagot "would rise at dawn" to greet what she recalled as "childhood friends," the violets, trilliums, and wood anemones. She took the opportunity the microscope her botany class offered to gather and examine "specimens of all the growing things she could not name." Flower "friends" of childhood became "specimens" when she matured intellectually. The enthusiastic natural sciences professor Daniel E. Willard taught students to see the forces creating regional features such as glacial moraines, buttes, rocks, prehistoric lakeshores, and the ancient forest to be seen in lignite coal deposits. After taking Willard's classes in geology as well as a botany class, Aagot wrote, "landscapes took on a new meaning." Information on ecological processes, the formation of river systems, and "volcanic mountains" all "became regions in the making." In the late 1940s Raaen explained to Willard "how his teaching had helped to set me free."[61]

Raaen also recalled feeling compelled to take an extra astronomy class, a course not a part of the regular teacher-training program. This simple story corresponds to what Annora Brown referred to as unanalyzed "impressions" from childhood lying "dormant" but always available to be used for a continuum of elastic meanings. As Aagot stood staring at the posted course listing that day in early 1900s Mayville, "pictures etched into her memory long ago came to life. She heard herself once more making up stories about the stars to satisfy Kjersti." She recalled how her father had "helped them locate the Big Dipper, the North Star, and the Pleiades." Standing there "she saw herself again lying flat on her back on top of the haystack looking

13. Aagot Raaen (pictured here, probably in the 1890s) attended many educational institutions, including Concordia College, Mayville Normal School, University of Minnesota, and University of Wisconsin, where she earned her bachelor's degree around 1913. She also attended the University of Berlin. Raaen probably had this formal graduation photograph taken in Fargo. North Dakota State University Archives, Fargo, North Dakota.

up at the sky." The experience of remembering girlhood wonder as a college student led Aagot to astronomy to learn more about "the heavens" she once thought about often. Remembering reinforced already "etched" pictures in the mind, transferring them and their meaning to an adult context. Further, the new, more scientific understandings of the sky she learned in her astronomy class supplemented imaginative girlhood sky stories. The astronomy course added another layer of meaning, without destroying the old; she carried both meanings forward some fifty years and committed them to her 1950 memoir.[62]

168 *"The Purple Hills That Beckoned"*

Two of the Hammond sisters, Elsie and Kay, also trained as teachers at the Regina Normal School (their sister Rose attended "business college" in Winnipeg). The 1915 Regina Normal School course notes that Elsie Hammond recorded in her diaries suggest how educators attempted to shape the subjects and instructional methods of young teachers. She took a broad range of subjects: literature, history, grammar, and mathematics. One of the first lectures she heard in Regina covered the "Present War." She also attended a "fine" lecture on birds, reinforced by an in-the-field "Bird Tramp."[63]

Hammond's course in "Nature Study," a subject trending at Normal Schools in the early twentieth century, suggests that educators asked her to think about Saskatchewan from new perspectives. Not surprising, Aagot Raaen also enrolled in a Nature Study course. Georgina Thomson too recalled teaching a practice Nature Study lesson at the Calgary Normal School on "The Gopher," using a taxidermic stuffed animal (but she could think about the animal only as a "pest"). Hammond's notes explained that Nature Study "aims to train both the head and heart." Proponents, such as Wilbur S. Jackman—an expert Hammond mentioned in her notes—argued students could learn the scientific method by studying "their immediate environment in its relation to themselves." The theory hoped to turn the "knowledge of nature" children had already "gathered by a more or less careful observation of [their] surrounding landscape" into a "fuller recognition of natural laws."[64]

Nature Study recognized that imagination had an active role in "the story told by the pupil's senses" that sometimes produced "erratic and fanciful" images. A good teacher started with images produced by a child's "untrained senses" and turned those remembered experiences to lessons in natural science. Elsie summarized the goal in her notes: to "develop one's senses so that one will see, hear, feel and think more." In psychology she learned about the complexities of the senses—taste, smell, sight, and touch—working together to provide the "foundation of all knowledge." Hammond noted, "Children who have been well directed in N.S. do not wantonly trample upon wildflowers[,] mutilate trees or destroy animal life."[65]

The Regina Normal curriculum also included "home geography" and related subjects: "the Prairie Provinces," agriculture, and garden-

14. George Will took this 1905 photograph of the "Double Ditch" or "Bourgois" historical Mandan agricultural village site the summer he and his Harvard University friends conducted an archaeological dig on land north of Bismarck. The grasslands clearly show the indentations of former earth-lodge home sites, what the young men called "house rings" in their 1906 study called "The Mandans." State Historical Society of North Dakota (00105-00108).

ing. According to Hammond's notes, educators stressed that "the most important geography to the individual today is his local geography." Knowing one's environment, she heard, "should increase our pleasures by arousing our interest in natural scenery." Hammond listened to "Grain Growers Lectures," including a two-and-a-half-hour "Illustrated Lecture on soil and grain," until she was "nearly sick of it." In geography she outlined the natural regions of Saskatchewan, noting the province had "almost every kind of soil" and no doubt observed with pleasure "for the most part Sask. soils are among the richest in the world." Hammond's notes read antiseptically. Nevertheless, she returned to the ranch carrying a list of books to buy, including *How to Teach Nature Study*, *Birds of Canada*, and *How to Know the Wild Flowers*, suggesting she planned to implement some of the ideas.[66]

Similar to Aagot Raaen's remembered awe of Professor Willard's course, in North Dakotan George Will's words, Harvard University's American Anthropology 5, taught by Dr. Roland B. Dixon, "very greatly affected my entire future life." Dixon arranged a meeting between Will and the curator of Harvard's Peabody Museum, Professor Frederic Putnam, a founder of modern archaeology, who led excavations all across the West. Putnam's daughter lived in Minot, North Dakota, and Will thought it might explain why he treated him "always most kind," but Putnam and Dixon also must have sensed the chance to direct the unearthing of potentially important new archaeological findings.[67]

Soon a plan and a grant launched a summer archaeological dig in North Dakota, conducted by Will and three Harvard friends. That 4 July found Professor Dixon and Will riding horseback along the Missouri River, evaluating possible archaeological sites. Dixon delighted Will by helping him see the earthworks of an old Mandan village site on a bluff located on the family farm of his longtime friend Birlea Ward—landscapes Will thought he already knew well. Working nine-hour days, the young men dug and screened tons of dirt for six weeks during the summer of 1905 on farmland thirteen miles north of Bismarck. Although mosquitoes sounding "like a giant kettle boiling" plagued them, the boys had fun camping out, drinking, swimming in Missouri River water, and eating fried prairie chicken. Will's parents and younger sister, Mable, and her friends visited. Will showed off riding a "bronco" at a local ranch and interpreted roots, seeds, and vegetable remains. Six weeks gone, the young men packed their specimens for Harvard. After graduation with a bachelor's degree, George Will returned to Bismarck, began working at Oscar H. Will and Company, and used his archaeological skills to read the landscape for the rest of his life.[68]

The design and technique classes Albertan Annora Brown enrolled in at the Ontario College of Art in Toronto also caused her to see the grasslands anew. Long interested in art, and encouraged by her mother, Brown quit teaching. She arrived in Toronto as the city inaugurated its new Art Gallery with an exhibit of international paintings.

15. Annora Brown (*left*), a student at the Ontario College of Art in Toronto in the mid-1920s, stands in a classroom with design professor Herbert Stanfield (*right*). Designs on the wall behind are attributed to Brown. University of Alberta Archives (UAA-1983-116-016-001).

"My inexperienced brain was completely swamped with so much beauty," she recalled, but by her third visit she had taken refuge in the "paintings of Tom Thomson."[69] Brown worked directly with some of Thomson's colleagues associated with the avant-garde Canadian nationalist Group of Seven school of painters.

Brown was not alone in her desire to paint scenes from the northern grasslands. Painter Emile Walters, the Icelandic-heritage Manitoba-born, North Dakota–raised future husband of Thorstina Jackson, acquired similar skills at the Art Institute of Chicago. He painted landscapes of Iceland and North Dakota's badlands. Fellow North Dakotan, painter and poet Clell Gannon, also attended the Art Institute of Chicago and focused on grasslands landscapes. Eventually, while living in Bismarck, Gannon painted scenes of the agricultural village life of the Arikaras, Mandans, and Hidatsas for the Oscar H. Will and Company seed house, by then managed by his friend George Will.[70]

Brown reflected on her formal training in ways that suggest how it allowed individuals from this generation to use paint to reinterpret grasslands they already knew well.

No doubt Annora received encouragement in her self-proclaimed identity as a "lover of the country" from her teacher Arthur Lismer. One of the Group of Seven landscape painters, Lismer's own interests centered on the nature of Canada's North Country. Brown credited him with having the greatest influence on her overall artistic development. "Be yourself," he encouraged students. Brown completed possibly her first official wildflower painting, one "prairie cone-flower," for Robert Holmes, who painted Ontario varieties "in their natural settings." He shared with her his distress over disappearing Ontario wildflowers, while she in turn effused over the "myriad flowers of the West." Almost twenty years later Brown gave credit to Holmes for having "taught her to see in the wild life of Canada subjects for her painting."[71] Grasslands and Rocky Mountain wildflowers became the genre for which Brown, by the end of her career, would be most remembered.

At art school Brown made fast friends with a group of young female "westerners," one also, like her, born at Macleod. She recalled Lismer, who focused on foreground in his painting, often teased, "You Westerners" would miss anything valuable "lying at your feet. You would be too busy looking at the distance." Emphasizing how she felt a moment of self-recognition in his observation, she reflected back in her mind's eye: "All that met our eyes was distance." She must have thought anew about her favorite perch on the house roof. The "stretch of far horizons," where the grasslands flowed east from the foothills of the Rocky Mountains, had shaped her perception. In 1929, with a "new and unexpected self," Brown graduated as an "Associate of the Ontario College of Art" and returned to Alberta to teach at Calgary's Mount Royal College of Art.[72]

Regional Geography

The acquisition of regional knowledge did not have an endpoint. Rather, the northern grasslands on which the first generations of settler society had experienced childhood and adolescence remained with them. From walking to horse travel, they grew to experience many rhythms and perspectives on the place. Slow-moving trains traveled ten miles from one town's grain elevator to another elevator. Soon their automobiles struggled along muddy, narrow roads edging the grasslands, increasing the range, if not the rate, at which they could move from locality to locality. All modes of covering northern grasslands terrain included sweeping views and frequent stops to allow for observation of communities and landscapes beyond familiar environments. New sensuous experiences added layers of meaning to a young adults' feelings of place, bringing emotional texture and intellectual understanding to childhood memories of home places.

The experience of viewing "distant" grasslands, somewhat mysterious to the child's eye, shifted as individuals became increasingly aware of (as their more adult eyes became trained to discern) how home ecologies fit into larger physical-geographic contexts. Patterns of local life became connected. New experiences and new skills informed individuals of the elements that distinguished their home. The modern education and geographic knowledge they gained moving across grasslands and through national, and international spaces—at speeds and ease created by industrialization—allowed them to overlay the ecological North American northern grasslands with new regions designed to meet the needs of settler society for rootedness on the continent.

5

"Old Woman Who Never Dies" and *Old Man's Garden*

Settler and Indigenous Relations over the Generations

The early years of World War I found North Dakota–born George F. Will making "personal visits" to new Mandan and Arikara friends on the Fort Berthold Indian Reservation near Bismarck. He sought information on the "old native varieties" of corn, from planting to use in ceremonial traditions. Will found out that Mandan women once grew thirteen varieties, including soft yellow, soft white, soft red, hard yellow, hard white, blue, spotted, clay red, pink, black, "Society," white or red striped, and an apparently untranslatable type called "Keika." In 1917 he and another young man, George Hyde, who grew up in Nebraska, published their considerable investigation in *Corn among the Indians of the Upper Missouri*. They identified fifty varieties of "native" corn with—to them—a "surprising number" in "pure or almost pure strains." Will and Hyde laid out all they knew about Indigenous corn in many cases—again to their surprise—then still raised along the Missouri River. Will had come to deeply admire Indigenous women farmers, who planted each spring when the "Old Woman Who Never Dies" sent geese flying north.[1]

The businessman George Will had good reason to be excited about the potential of Indigenous corn on the northern grasslands. In 1917 the thirty-three-year-old Will also became the president of his father's agricultural and garden seed house, Oscar H. Will and Company. He assured customers the business would thrive under his leadership, saying that he "was born and grew up in North Dakota." He stressed his "practical experience with North Dakota soil."[2] Will saw potential in Indigenous corn for settler society. Amid the U.S. government "campaign . . . urging everyone to plant" for the Allied effort in World War I, the Will Company advertised it would "do [its] part in helping forward the feeding of our allies and our soldiers." From the beginning of his leadership at the company, Will urged farmers to invest in "recovered" Mandan and Arikara corn.[3] Will spent the next forty years breeding and selling seeds and reading the landscape, especially Indigenous archaeological sites. Will followed corn down a path to a more complex understanding of Indigenous cultures and grasslands environments.

The first generations born to settler society often made an implicit argument that they had a claim equivalent to Indigenous peoples, by their life history in the place and by the sensual immersion that grafted the land to their bodies. They rarely felt responsible for, even very involved in, what they considered parental and national-policy choices. As Lorenzo Veracini has theorized, such thinking equaled another form of settler-colonial claim to land: a created "identity" rooted in the land consistent with the larger colonial project of displacing North American Indigenous populations. It is undeniable that these grasslands-grown members of settler society knew little or not at all any other place as "home." Yet these postsettlement generations carried out unspoken and inchoately realized cultural imperatives of settler colonialism.[4]

George Will is notable for the depth with which he understood, gradually, over the course of his lifetime, the entwined consequences of conquest for Indigenous peoples and the ecology of the northern grasslands. This chapter explores settler-society–Indigenous relations as they intersected with ideas about land. Examining these relations through ideas, attitudes, and behavior provides a better understanding of the way older racial ideas tied up in issues of land survived and shifted in the modern era and over the postsettlement generations. Settler-society and Indigenous nations grew some tangled roots together in postsettlement culture.

Settler individuals of this generation expressed a range of attitudes, from complete silence, indifference, and a racism born in ignorance or the "scientific," religious, and mythic popular West ideas of their day to a friendliness rooted in courtesies of day-to-day encounters. A few individuals grew to respect and believe in the equality of cultural difference. When the most thoughtful of this generation of settler residents sought Indigenous knowledge, they did not seek "Indians" or "Indianness" to "flee" their worlds—similar to "popularizers" of Indigenous cultures active in their day—but, rather, so they could stay and build a better setter society.[5] Many settlers, however, interacted only superficially, if at all, with Indigenous peoples. The "reserve" and "reservation" systems in Canada and the United States—though indeed because of the agency of Indigenous leaders they became the seeds of modern tribal national sovereignty and self-determination—in this period often encouraged daily settler-society denial of Indigenous peoples, especially for settlers distant from these segregated social spaces.[6]

Remembering "Indians" from Childhood Years

Did the children of northern grasslands settler society's first generations interact and come to know nearby Indigenous children and their parents or communities? How did the first grasslands-grown generations of settler society look back on their childhoods to understand settler society's impact on Indigenous peoples still living in the region? Did they even look back or acknowledge Indigenous presence?

When George Will excavated the historical Mandan village site for Harvard University's Peabody Museum in 1905, he seemed to be "less" familiar, rather than "more" familiar, with the local Indigenous peoples he later said he "more or less" knew "in rather early childhood." Will wrote of knowing Indigenous peoples from "ever since I can remember" and claimed to "remember a number of encounters" but elaborated little. "I . . . particularly remember *my father's account* of the Hidatsa Chief, Son of a Star, who called on him at the little red potting shed attached to our small greenhouse" in the 1880s, explained Will in this family foundational business story. Son of a Star "very ceremoniously presented" his father with seed that Will and Company eventually sold as the "Great Northern Bean." Will, born in 1884, would "also remember *my father telling* of the first Indian Corn which he received in 1881 or '82."[7] Far from firsthand encounters with local Hidatsas or Mandans, Will seems to have adopted his father's personal relationships with specific Indigenous individuals as *his* own.

Moreover, many of Will's father's relationships with local Indigenous agriculturalists seem to have been secondhand, through the fur-trapper community members who had married Indigenous women. In the 1930s George Will stated that "one of the officers at Fort Stevenson" (possibly married to a Hidatsa woman) gave his father the first corn seed. Similarly, a former trapper named "Holbrook" employed at the Will store, who had a "Chippewa" Métis wife, put Oscar Will on to Indigenous melons, which became "Will's Sugar Watermelon." While George Will may have "interacted with Indian people from a young age," it seems unlikely he developed close relationships with members of the Three Affiliated Tribes during his childhood.[8]

The one specific memory George Will recalled from boyhood involved his awareness on the periphery of events leading to the massacre of Lakotas at Wounded Knee Creek in 1890. A boy of six years that December, Will recalled the "panic" set off in Bismarck at the sight of a "long cavalcade of ponies and wagons which was unmistakably Indians." Finally, someone realized the "big party" to be "merely . . . friendly Sioux," explained Will years later, on a return trip to Fort Totten after "visiting their cousins at Standing Rock."[9]

Around Thanksgiving Day a businessman had introduced the young George Will to Buffalo Bill Cody while walking the streets of Bismarck, something a six-year-old boy does not forget. Cody, under orders from the U.S. Army, hoped to speak with his friend and one-time "Wild West" performer, the Hunkpapa Lakota Sitting Bull, about reigning in the Ghost Dance—the reason for the nervous edge in Will's Bismarck. Cody never reached Sitting Bull. Soon Sitting Bull was killed, and by the end of December, the Miniconjou leader Big Foot and his band lay dead near Wounded Knee Creek. Recalling fifty years later, Will characterized these events as the "massacre in South Dakota." Will used an ironic tone to depict the Bismarck population; he stressed townspeople's fear and overreaction, creating humor out of the local militia pulling out a cannon normally used for Fourth of July celebrations. Will ends with the serious word "massacre," at a time when many in settler society might have used the word "battle." The interpretation reflects the path he had taken from young adulthood through the prime of his life, probably not his boyhood reactions. The juxtaposition of Buffalo Bill Cody, Sioux from Fort Totten, Sitting Bull, and the events at Wounded Knee communicate the cultural crosscurrents acting on Will and his generation.[10]

When a reporter asked Annora Brown if she knew any of southern Alberta's Indigenous residents "on more than a passing basis," Brown replied, "I don't really remember any particular Indians very well *but my father did*." She explained, "Many of the Indians *my father knew* from his days on the [North-West Mounted] police force." When scholars wrote letters to Brown inquiring about the "legendary figure" Jerry Potts, the Métis man who guided the North-West Mounted Police to the site in 1874 of what would become Fort Macleod, Brown could tell them only that her "*father spoke* of him [Potts] as a fine man and a helpful interpreter between the police and the Indians." As a very young girl, she had lived across the street from the Potts family, but "Jerry himself had died some years before." "To me," she said, "his name was familiar chiefly for the wonderful picnicking and camping in a spot we called Jerry Potts's Bottom," the fertile flatland carved by Oldman River.[11]

Brown's accounts of early encounters with local Bloods and Piegans carry the same general tone as those of George Will's. "I suppose I was four or five when I first remember . . . the Indians coming in [to town]," she told one interviewer. Brown associated her Blood and Piegan neighbors with horses: "They nearly always came on horseback." Brown also recalled individuals who stopped "door to door" to "sell berries" and "little articles, such as small baskets, made of sweetgrass. We had little circles of sweetgrass to hold our table knapkins [*sic*] at home," she recalled fondly.[12]

Brown grew up unafraid of "Indians," a frequent comment also made by members of her generation. She made this message clear in a story she told of her most intimate early contact. The future artist "left alone in the house" looked up from her playing blocks to find a "tall Indian, with red kerchief, long braids, rumpled brown suit, and beaded moccasins" standing nearby. The two exchanged no words; he departed through the back door. Her parents apparently dismissed the incident easily as one of curiosity: "We like to see how they lived in their tipis and they like to see how we live in our houses." Brown emphasized the encounter as one of "friendship, understanding, trust."[13] At once she argued against and contributed to an emergent Western mythology of her generation. Brown took a stock story—the peeping Indigenous man who scared the pioneer woman—and used it to project racial attitudes she desired to promote. She located conflict in the past.

Laura Goodman Salverson told a story that also projected an enlightened attitude on to the parental generation in the Winnipeg of her day. Walking the streets, her Icelandic immigrant father pointed out a particular Indigenous character named "Laughing Joe." The man, "a tall, sardonic Indian who was strutting up and down the river bank," supposedly waited for a crowd to gather with their coins before performing what her father explained she would hear: "the Red Man's version of Paleface mirth." Salverson caught on that Joe's laughter mocked happiness; he imitated "the white man's cruel laughter," and her father explained, "it is always cruel to laugh in the face of misery. . . . But that is something conquerors never trouble to know." Salverson suggested immigrants had special insight into Indigenous troubles, but, in showing her father in this light, she distanced immigrants from the settler-colonial project. Another story involved her aunt, who settled at Gimli, Manitoba, and attempted to sleigh her injured husband to Winnipeg in a blizzard. As her aunt explained, "Before I was overcome, an Indian found us, and took us home to his tepee." The man's wife "massaged" her frozen feet, fed the two, and dressed them in warmer clothing. The "fierce-looking brave" soon saw the two onto the correct road. The aunt (or Salverson) concluded, "Ah they were good, those two brown people."[14]

These narratives suggest sympathy for Indigenous people but also display as much about how later generations of settler society wished to convey their attitudes and those of the "pioneer" generation. Tellingly, the Indigenous couple in Salverson's story had no agency; "a miracle of God's mercy" had saved her uncle's life by, according to her aunt, "working through the simple heart of a savage."[15] The infantilization of Indigenous people and their innate natures lurks behind such positive stories. Both Indigenous and settler cultures might be curious, as Brown's parents explained to her, but only an innocent lack of sophistication led an Indigenous person—like a child—to peer into a home's windows. The compassion in these renditions of childhood encounters with Indigenous peoples, looking back, became self-selected seeds used to demonstrate later understandings and the desire for better relations.

The Icelandic-heritage Thorstina Jackson Walters framed racial encounter as a positive lesson taught by her mother. She wrote little about Métis people, or "French-Canadian half breed[s]," as she called them, who had lived in her area near Pembina, North Dakota, for more than a half century before her arrival. She recalled accompanying her mother on midwifery trips in Pembina and Cavalier Counties. Once Walters encountered "dark skinned children" that "frightened me" and asked, "Did God make those black children?" Remembering the incident in the middle of the 1950s, after she had "seen and heard so much of racial inequalities in different parts of the world," she felt proud, relating "in a split second my mother settled the matter of racial equality," replying, "certainly He did. If God chooses to make some children with fair skins and others with dark, it is not for you to criticize. All are God's children."[16] The miasma involved in this generation's positively remembered encounters pushed settler displacement into the background, though the episode also suggests that attitudes had changed enough for some in this generation to want to project enlightened behaviors on the past. Potentially positive small steps that suggest rising consciousness, but without action, could turn to the denial of settler society's role in the expropriation of the grasslands.[17]

The "Indian girls" Era Bell Thompson met outside the Bismarck Indian School disappointed her: "There were no wigwams, no squaws, no warriors, only big wooden buildings with little girls in pale blue dresses, their faces stolid and sallow, not red; their bobbed hair straight and black. Some of them ran to blue eyes and blonde tresses." As an African American girl, she "baffled" young Indigenous girls. She recalled how they ended up "touching [her] lightly with their fingers and giggling." Thompson had expected to see "Indians" of the mythic West; she saw instead Indigenous girls undergoing assimilation policies focused on dress, hairstyles, and boarding schools.[18]

Eventually, Thompson did make friends with Indigenous children. She had an epiphany at the Mandan rodeo while conversing with her Sioux friend Priscilla Running Horse, who explained her mother did not know how to speak "American." Thompson recalled having to correct herself on thinking Priscilla's mother must be from the "Old Country," similar to the parents of her immigrant friends, who also did not know English and dressed in "native [European] clothes." The German, Czech, Norwegian, and Icelandic immigrant communities suggested the complex cultural diversity of grasslands society. The insight Thompson made (whether in the 1910s or reflecting back in the 1940s as she wrote) from the perspective of a Black woman suggests how, in addition to skin color, markers of language and dress communicated race and cultural distance. Part of the "civilization" policy for Indigenous peoples—attacks on dress and language—point to ways the sounds and cadence of speech and the textures and tones of clothing operated generally in racialized relations and hierarchical thinking of the early twentieth century.[19]

Wallace Stegner recalled seeing "Indians," probably Plains Crees or possibly Métis, "once a year when a family or two in a rickety democrat wagon came down from somewhere and camped for a few days in the river brush" near Eastend, Saskatchewan. Townspeople tightened the temporal and geographic range of children and locked up in response to the appearance of an Indigenous camp. Rather than a positive lesson in race relations, the actions of his parents conveyed to Stegner "that an Indian was a thieving, treacherous, lousy, unreliable, gut-eating vagabond, and that if anything a halfbreed was worse." Looking back, he thought of the "dignity" and "helplessness" of Crees he had then harassed and made the center of an imagined Wild West shootout with his boyhood friends. Although members of this generation preferred to look back on their peaceful relations with Indigenous peoples and positive lessons taught by families, Stegner makes clear what many chose to bend in their narratives: children "inherited without question or thought" the "fully developed prejudices" parents and other settler adults had carried to the place.[20] Shedding or altering these attitudes caused struggle within.

Many children from this generation gained a sense of Indigenous culture from the annual town fair or rodeo or holiday that ritualistically celebrated past "frontier violence" and promoted "national mythologies."[21] George Will recalled attending the "colorful Mandan fair," in particular highlighting the summer of 1903, after which he left Bismarck to attend Harvard University: "Several hundred Indians from Cannon Ball came and camped on the fairgrounds." The most influential meetings Brown had with the local Piegan and Blood Natives during childhood happened during annual 1 July Dominion Day celebrations—what Brown recalled as "essentially Indian Day for me." She recalled that Indigenous families built tepees in the town square, donned traditional garb, walked the parade route, and drummed and danced far into the night. She took in patterns that would later appear in her paintings.[22]

Local settlers loved the pageantry of holidays, fairs, and rodeos and the high festive accoutrements Indigenous peoples displayed. In October 1913 Elsie May Hammond wrote of "Fair Day" in Maple Creek, Saskatchewan, where she attended the "Indian pow wow." In mid-July 1923 she visited Calgary's fair and "took some pictures of the Indian on 8th Ave." Performing "Indians" suggested control and safety. Holidays and stampedes, the latter a combination of annual agricultural fairs and Wild West shows that celebrated and mythologized ranchers and select Indigenous cultural traditions, allowed settlers to secularize Indigenous spirituality and culture. Such celebrations often turned sacred ceremony into dance and song and traditional dress and custom into craft and performance. Many settlers, such as Montanan Lillian Miller, assumed all the dances "were really war dances"; settlers found it difficult to imagine Indigenous peoples danced for religious, social, and political reasons. Indigenous people, from another perspective, took festivals as opportunities to make money, compete in feats of sport, and display skill. Some Indigenous participants saw tourist venues as spaces to "spread knowledge" of their "culture and spirituality" to a broad settler-society audience. Such performances, however, only reflected rituals and traditions; "actual sacred ceremonies" remained private and continually practiced.[23] When they encountered Indigenous individuals, these young

16. Annora Brown, who grew up in Fort Macleod, Alberta, near Piegan and Blood Reserves, became well known for her paintings of Blackfoot scenes, such as this work, titled *Indian Encampment* (watercolor on paper), painted probably in the 1950s and purchased by the Glenbow in 1957. University of Alberta Archives (UAA-1983-116-017-012); with permission of the Glenbow Museum, Calgary, which holds the original.

people of settler society did so primarily in the spaces controlled by settler society—Macleod's town square, Bismarck's streets, Mandan's rodeo, or Maple Creek's annual fair.

"Glad to Have Met You Folks": Everyday Cultural Exchange

Attendance at town celebrations and rodeos, parental family stories, and tales of prior days in history suggest the limited, formal nature of the experiences of many in this generation of settler society with Indigenous peoples. Over time, in some places, however, mutual contact of a more informal or direct nature increased. The beginning of exchanges in everyday work and social life among some in settler society and some in Indigenous communities suggest the slow development of hybrid—shared—spaces, sometimes uncomfortable and full of uncertainty but potentially rewarding for improved relations down the postsettlement decades.

After college George Will continued his study of Mandan, Hidatsa, and Arikara agricultural village tribes by digging deep in historical documents. He also began to reach out to experts, many of them associated with the State Historical Society of North Dakota. Will soon "got in touch" with the Nebraskan George Hyde, who within a decade would become his coauthor, to inquire about Indigenous seeds issuing from the Omaha hearth of the Missouri River cultural area. He corresponded with George Bird Grinnell on similar interests. Will formed a friendship with Gilbert Wilson, who began working on Missouri River agriculture near Bismarck the same year Will returned from college. Over the next fifty years or so, George Will surveyed over 140 Indigenous earth-lodge village sites along the Missouri River, acquiring "voluminous field notes," which he turned into publications for academic journals and popular magazines.[24]

George Will met many Indigenous persons in his documentary and historical work. The "young Mandan Indian" named James Holding Eagle, from Elbowoods on the Fort Berthold Reservation, north of Bismarck, probably had the most influence on Will's changing ideas. Will's diary records the day, 5 March 1910, he met Holding Eagle. The next evening Holding Eagle sat down to dinner in the Will family house. Will recalled seeing "quite a bit" of him while the latter worked at the historical society museum. Holding Eagle, the child of a Mandan mother and a Hidatsa father, began to teach Will the Mandan language. He eventually gave Will "samples of old native varieties of corn," which must have thrilled Will.[25]

It is unclear whether Will requested the seeds or Holding Eagle brought them to Will because of the latter's interests. Will recorded that he received "one variety" of corn and "some" squash seeds from Holding Eagle's mother, Scattered Corn, whom Will identified as his "principal informant." After testing, he concluded the squash seeds proved to be a "hybrid mixture of most of the Indian types." From the variety of seeds "still . . . pure" that Will eventually described thriving on the reservation in 1917, Scattered Corn—or her son—seemed to have shown caution in this early limited offering. Will acknowledged the "shrewd, suspicious, and sometimes even rapacious" reception of such requests among Indigenous peoples due to "long years of dealing with white traders," implying both the unscrupulousness of such trades and Indigenous resistance to colonial interventions in lifeways. Will, however, felt Indigenous peoples had treated him with generosity in the "samples of different plants and varieties" he acquired, either free or for minimal fees because of the "understanding of the purposes for which I wanted them." Knowledge of the language, probably, and Will's "interest in agriculture gradually established" him "as a 'mashshihsh,' a 'good white man' to the Mandans," he claimed.[26]

Will achieved some level of trust with the Holding Eagles. He had a genuine interest in Indigenous agriculture and also had information from his own research to share with local modern tribes. Somewhere in the years between 1911 and 1913, he received a welcome on the Fort Berthold Reservation to visit the Holding Eagles "for several weeks, getting not only further information on language but as complete a story of the Mandan agriculture as I could from Scattered Corn." Will identified "Scattered-Corn Woman" as "one of the few living full-blood Mandans." James Holding Eagle and George Will, as well as Scattered Corn, according to Will, all shared a "deep interest" in having Mandan agriculture "properly understood and presented."[27]

17. Russell Reid, a friend of George Will's associated with the State Historical Society of North Dakota, took this picture of Scattered Corn holding a shoulder blade hoe in the 1920s. George Will learned about Mandan agricultural traditions and culture primarily from Scattered Corn, James Holding Eagle's mother. State Historical Society of North Dakota (00200-6x8-00523).

Will must have visited regularly that summer to observe when Scattered Corn initiated new agricultural tasks. He recorded information from planting to processing for his study with Hyde and took note of her rituals and reasoning. She evidently felt comfortable enough around Will to both sing and discuss the field songs "handed down from mother to daughter." She showed him how she dried wild fruits, corn, and squash for storage and recalled for Will times of eating "just as much as they could" during the fresh "green corn season." By 1917 Will fully understood, "A few of the more careful people still preserve pure strains of the old varieties and they can yet be obtained by diligent search and careful inquiry."[28]

From the 1920s to the 1940s, George Will's archaeological mapping along the Missouri River in North Dakota and South Dakota brought him into contact with many Indigenous people. While acknowledging the "difficulties" of linking oral knowledge with specific locations, Will took "tradition" seriously and interviewed many Indigenous elders. He cites specific Hidatsa and Mandan traditions and includes the "interesting story," important landmark, and Indian map of occupants of one village in his catalog of archaeological sites. The results of his 1938 and 1939 summer "seasons" in the field (most likely funded by New Deal programs through the state historical society), for example, referenced current property owners, many who farmed. Last names and other identifying information suggest the owners were a mix of settlers and Lakotas, as well as Mandans, Hidatsas, and Arikaras. The report included a discussion of places "under cultivation by Indians for about 50 years." Some Indigenous families ranched or farmed on "allotment" acreages assigned as part of the break up of larger reservations under the Dawes Act of 1887 (or on land retained by other treaty provisions). Will noted that "Indian CCC [Civilian Conservation Corps] workers uncovered three burials" while landscaping. He explored the site—whether with permission or unaware or in spite of cultural prohibitions—with Dan Eagle and Abe Rough-Surface, "two Indian boys who had been detailed to help us." Will confirmed another village site on Bede Uses His Arrow's land; the evidence lay across acreage "under cultivation" and the "ranch yard of the owner." Uses His Arrow told Will about cache pits and lodge floors he once unearthed while "constructing fences and buildings."[29] These acquaintances and associations gave Will insight into Indigenous cultures and exposure to a range of individual life choices made by local Indigenous persons given the various assimilation pressures and shifting U.S. Indian policies.

By 1944 George Will believed enough in Indigenous oral tradition to include the location of a possible village site "because the Indians from the Standing Rock Agency across the river claim that an ancient earth lodge village was located near Cat Tail Creek." Will identified no physical remains on the site farmed for well over fifty years, but he believed it "possible that the Indians are correct." Archaeological fieldwork and historical accounts validated many of the "statements of the older Indians." Will formed working relationships with many Indigenous persons, mentioned by name in his works, such as James Young Eagle, "Stella Bear (Mrs. Eagle)," "Mrs. Floyd Bear," Crow Ghost, Bear's Belly, Willie Dean, John Hunts Along, Alfred Simpson, Pat Star, and Four Rings.[30] Will's research interest lay in archaeology, but he worked day to day with resident Indigenous peoples, whom he valued as contemporary authorities, also making their livelihoods, preserving and adapting their ceremonies and traditions, and remaining interested in their own history.

While George Will documented historical Indigenous agricultural villages, Elsie Hammond and her siblings worked on farm and ranch properties to support the family agricultural enterprise. Her daily diary entries allow rare glimpses into the ways farmers and ranchers interacted with Indigenous peoples on a day-to-day basis. Hammond, who rarely referred to "Indians" or "half breeds" by name or gender (but generally used male pronouns), mentioned only an unidentified "reserve" nearby, but it must have been Cree. Having resisted removal to a northern reserve, Nekaneet's Crees remained in the Cypress Hills area until Canada in 1913 begrudgingly granted the band a reserve.[31] Métis peoples also lived in the area.

A picture emerges of generally friendly, occasionally skeptical, and distant relations among the Hammond family and Indigenous peoples. Indigenes stopped by to telephone or wait for a doctor; many "halfbreed kiddies" and Indigenous persons grazed their "ponies in the field"; and in winter "Indians" stopped by on their way home to the reserve or to Maple Creek to "warm up." A couple of diary mentions of specific names suggest ongoing relationships. A person called "Skunk" had supper in 1913 and 1922. In 1926 the "Indian Stanley" helped her with the berry patch. Other entries suggest the Hammonds served meals to less well-known individuals, as in "Had an Indian in for D[inner]." In the summer of 1931, "An Indian came with [a] little tin of blueberries" that Hammond combined with rhubarb in a desert. She did not indicate if she purchased the berries, but Annora Brown, who lived not too far—plainswise—from the Hammonds, but in Alberta, also noted a local "Indian family" making the rounds selling berries in Macleod.[32]

Other diary entries suggest raising and working with horses in particular lent common ground on which local Indigenous peoples and the Hammond family interacted. Many Métis grazed their horses in Elsie Hammond's fields. More than once she recorded helping "an Indian run down his horse." Another time she "finally ran it [a wayward spirited horse] in the stable." Work with animals among Hammond, Indigenous persons, and Métis suggests a basis on which friendliness or at least personal knowledge *may* have been built. On occasion she apparently at least considered the value of Indigenous traditions. Once she recorded that two "Indians . . . came for the dead colt," and another time she went "down to see the old dead cow which the Indian had skinned." The entries suggest a modicum of understanding about Indigenous skill in the use of animal resources.[33]

The Hammonds hired local Indigenous individuals to work for and alongside them at various endeavors. An Indigenous person showed up to supply "green cut wood" for one of the schools at which Elsie Hammond taught; to put "sand on the road"; to "cut wood"; to sell "willow posts"; and to plant, with her father, "raspberry and blackberry vines," and with her, the potato crop. The Hammonds appear to have hired Indigenous workers regularly for seasonal work, as similar entries continued in the 1930s. Alfred Guthrie recalled "Indians" who left the reservation in Montana to work during harvests and haying, calving, and lambing seasons. Agricultural work and product sales seem to have formed a space where interactions took place to possibly lay groundwork for future Indigenous–settler-society relationships, friendly or not.[34]

The Hammond diaries show settlers and Indigenous peoples interacting on a day-to-day basis on the Hammond properties. The diaries never record Elsie or her family visiting a reserve. Hammond's diary entries on occasion also indicated discomfort and suspicion. When once an Indigenous person used the Hammond telephone, she stated cryptically, "Some of us sat outside and watched him and heard him talk." Another time she grew impatient at an unspoken boundary crossed by a "half-breed" who stopped by the house, which caused Elsie and her mother to delay leaving for town because they did not want to leave her sister Rose "home alone." Finally, Elsie took matters into her own hands, as her diary records, "So at last after waiting one hour for him to go I told him to go."[35] Hammond's diary entries suggest how Indigenous peoples and typical settler families focusing on day-to-day, mundane tasks met and learned about each other through work. The diaries also suggest distrust, suspiciousness, and social limits.

During the same decades George Will and Elsie Hammond made their living on the northern grasslands, sometimes working with local Indigenous peoples, Annora Brown could be found "motoring through the south collecting wild flowers" in southern Alberta. Known especially for her flower paintings, Brown also painted Indigenous cultural scenes, especially of Bloods and Piegans. Her first town exhibit included the portrait of a "well-known Indian chief," tellingly unnamed in the newspaper article and exhibit. Her early work included the batik paintings *Indian Encampment* and *Indian Legend of Autumn Leaves.* Brown went into nostalgic reverie, writing at the end of her life about a time she saw a sun dance: "I enjoyed again the originality of tipi design, the beauty of wall hangings and beadwork done in the geometric patterns traditional to the Blackfoot nation, and in the sighing rhythm of the Grass Dance I recognized once again the ancient poetry of the prairies." By the early 1940s Brown had achieved enough notice in Alberta art circles to become a feature story in the *Calgary Herald Magazine.* The article explained that Brown lived near the Piegan Reserve, "which gives her an opportunity to observe the habits, the types, learn the legends of these Indians, members of the Blackfoot Confederacy."[36]

Brown, however, seems to have approached contemporary Indigenous people less directly than George Will or Elsie Hammond. Brown made the round of local fairs. There she questioned accessible Indigenous individuals about traditional aesthetics and once painted right then the "Black Buffalo teepee" she saw, absorbing a transnational relationship between the North Piegans and the South Blackfeet of Browning, Montana. She apparently discussed "teepee" symbolism with one Eddie Merry Horse at an "Old Timers' celebration" held at a southern Alberta stampede. Merry Horse evidently told Brown about the beaver the tribe permitted his father to paint on his tepee to honor "courage." She learned the meaning of symbols (prairies, mountains, foothills, stars) and colors (red, green, black) painted on tepees. She thought the decoration, color, and drawing "sensitive"—really "worthy of a great master"—but nevertheless attributed the results to the "innate sense of design of primitive people." In a newspaper article published ahead of the Calgary Stampede on the same subject, Brown explained that the design represented the "nature of the country which was their home." The language designating a country that "*was their home*" also placed Indigenous peoples in the past and reinforced the idea that settler society now controlled space. Brown does not appear to have known Merry Horse, as she recorded his departure with his salutation: "Glad to have met you folks."[37]

To increase her knowledge, Brown seems to have taken advantage of friends who had connections to local Indigenous populations. For example, she accompanied a friend and professional portrait photographer on trips he arranged to local reserves to snap images of Blood and Piegan leaders. On one of these occasions she visited with Blood Reserve resident Rosie Davis, whom Brown characterized as a "clever woman" and a "fountain of information about the reserve and its people." When the same photographer visited the local Piegan Reserve during a "sports" and "festivities" week to capture pictures for a magazine article on young people, Brown tagged along. She "wander[ed] at will" to view "tipi design" before such "beauty and 'rightness'" would be "put away for safekeeping."[38]

It speaks volumes that in 1949, Annora Brown reached out to Archdeacon Samuel Henry Middleton, who had lived for some forty years on the Blood Reserve as head of its residential school, for advice and information regarding the grasslands plant history and lore book she had been working on for at least fifteen years. Middleton had been a friend of her father's, and she on occasion had driven him to the reserve. Brown sent him the manuscript and apparently a list of questions. In response he wrote he found her manuscript "very interesting" but was "sorry" he could not provide "any definite information regarding the Blackfoot origin of these names and subjects." He apparently spoke with "several of our older people, but other than the 'Mase'—'Turniproot'—they appear to be utterly oblivious of this culture of the early beginnings," he concluded. That Brown turned to Middleton suggests her connections with local Indigenous peoples remained weak, even as she grew older and more interested in Blackfoot traditions.[39]

Another source for Brown's work also suggests the limited nature of her contact with Indigenous peoples. Instead of trying to paint on the Piegan and Blood Reserves, Brown and her art school friend Gwen Hutton turned to what Brown described as a "second-hand dealer of questionable local reputation"—clearly a pawnbroker. Brown explained, he "proved to be an ally in our search for information about native cultures." Indigenous artifacts taken in exchange for ready cash apparently filled his store shelves. Brown and Hutton took artifacts home on some type of approval basis, though occasionally, it seems, the women purchased items. The admission of such indirect cultural exchanges suggests Brown's distance to the Indigenous cultures she became known for painting and explaining to settler society.[40]

When Alberta celebrated its Fiftieth Jubilee in 1955, the provincial government chose her painting *Prairie Chicken Dance* as one of eight paintings to be included in an anthology of prose, poetry, and art designed to showcase Alberta's culture. Brown's scene depicted Blackfoot traditional dance and costume in bright orange, yellow, turquoise, brown, and green, with touches of pink. Geometric lines, triangles, and diagonals shape the picture. The inclusion of Brown's painting suggests her notions of Alberta and depictions of Indigenous people found wide resonance in settler society. Indeed, Brown had seen many traditional Indigenous dances and probably more than one "Chicken Dance." Inclusion acknowledged Indigenous residency but placed a settler-society frame around Piegan, Blood, and Blackfoot Nations.[41]

Annora Brown's drawings suggest she looked at Indigenous people as skilled individuals who created beautiful traditional objects and worked in modern professions. In 1955 she illustrated a book for non-Indigenous children designed to teach *Stories of Canadian Indians*, with information on "Indians of Yesterday" but also a chapter on "Indians of Today," including vignettes on a rancher; a farmer; steelworkers; professionals in religion, art, medicine, law, military, science; and a modern "Chief." Her art generally provided settler society with dignified, complex images, no matter her actual complicated distance to the Indigenous people she depicted.[42] Her open-mindedness in seeing beauty, skill, and sophisticated cultural significance in the expression of design and ritual among the peoples of the Blackfoot Confederacy, however, centered primarily on her own artistic yearnings. These encounters and her research apparently also provoked her to think.

"Wapee's First Thought Had Been for the Flower": Annora Brown

By the time she published *Old Man's Garden* in 1954, Brown had been reading and taking notes on the history and natural history of the grasslands for almost twenty-five years. Reviewers celebrated the "fun" book for its "new approach" in combining history, botany, and Brown's own pen-and-ink illustrations. For those "accustomed to thinking of them in terms of their nuisance value only," the stories Brown told about roadside "flowers and weeds" provided a "fascinating" fresh view. One reviewer described her work as a "strange combination of factual botanical details, combined with how that flower fitted into the Indians' life or legends and was part of the West's early explorers."[43] Brown presented anecdote, scientific fact, and tribal legend alongside her original drawings of plants, grasses, shrubs, and trees. Brown attempted to explain the importance of her book on prairie plants: "Old Man created all this variety for the use and pleasure of his people, and we who have inherited it take full measure of enjoyment from its wonder." Her prose unconsciously revealed what it meant to be among the first generation of settler-colonial children to grow up on the northern grasslands. The study showed an inner conflict swirling in the air of her generation. Born "in region" but a child of "invaders," how does one become at home in a place so obviously stressed and troubled by one's very cultural presence?[44]

A small but telling description of the prairie anemone, a "little purple flower with a furry stem," illustrates her vision of cultural alliance. Botanists accompanying early grasslands explorers classified the early spring flower technically as an "anemone" after Greek tradition with the descriptive "prairie" to denote its western North American location. "Literally, flowers of the prairie wind," she translated. The English viewed the furry flower as similar to a "crocus" back home, while the French and "other European travellers" called it "pasque flower" because of the likeness of its Easter-time bloom to a European variety. In Brown's view, one of the best names came from her generation of settler-society "prairie children." They called the flower "gosling" because of its soft, "downy buds." But she thought "even better" the Indigenous name, "Ears of the Earth." This name derived from the shape of the buds lifting amid melting snowdrifts: "the prairie thrusts up to listen for the first faint rustle of summer." Subtly, perhaps unconsciously, Brown set those born into and raised with grasslands nature—settler children and Indigenous peoples—against those adults who tried to impose outside traditions on the grasslands. Only children and "Indians" knew no other environment to hamper them in their joy. At the same time both children and Indians were unformed intellectually, free of "civilization." But Brown and the other white children grew up, while local Indigenes in this construction seemed to stay the same developmentally. Brown always remembered the "gosling" and "Ears of the Earth" names, but when she painted as an adult, she painted the "crocus."[45]

The story surrounding the prairie anemone showed the creativity of Indigenous culture Brown admired in using nature to impart social values. She published her first wildflower piece, "How the Prairie Cro-

PRAIRIE ANEMONE

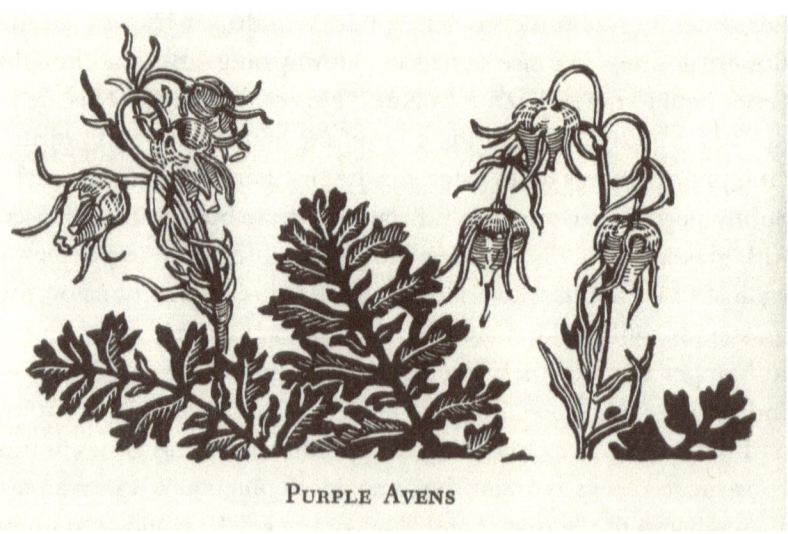

PURPLE AVENS

18. Annora Brown used the prairie anemone and purple long-plumed avens to show cultural diversity on the grasslands. Original images from A. Brown, *Old Man's Garden*, 11–15, 20–21; reprinted here by permission of the Glenbow Museum, Calgary.

cus Got Its Fur Coat," as a newspaper article in 1935 and repeated it almost word for word in the book. In addition to lexicography Brown told the story of "Wapee," an Indigenous boy who encounters the prairie anemone in a coming-of-age ritual. Sent out to seek dreams when the "snows of winter had but lately melted," Wapee slept out several nights "with dark space and loneliness and fear" amid a "*great emptiness.*" But when a flower showed itself "white as the snow" and "swayed and nodded" in his direction, he felt he "found a friend." Over the next three nights the flower helped Wapee find wisdom. Before leaving, Wapee asked the "Great Spirit" to grant the flower three wishes. As Brown told, "pleased that Wapee's first thought had been for the flower," the Great Spirit answered Wapee's prayers. Soon purple and yellow colors and a fur robe coated the flower so it "may face the cold winds that blow from the melting snow and bring men comfort and the hope of warmer winds to follow." Brown suggested flowers had great wisdom if one listened to their messages. The Great Spirit rewarded those who put nature first.[46]

Brown unconsciously implied that reward will come to those who place the grasslands first. A seeming "great emptiness" turned out to be full of life if viewed closely. Lying full-bodied on the ground, Wapee saw the anemone. The point about close-up ground-level growth she made continually. The uncommon yellow violet "grows on dry prairies," she explained in another entry, but its blooms hugged the ground so one had to look closely to see its beauty.[47] The insider, grasslands-grown person, she implied, injected details unseen to the outsider's view of the grasslands. Where the visitor saw monotony, because of day-to-day experience with the grasslands, residents saw infinite variety.

Brown recorded happy remembrances of beloved flowers, yet conflict emerged in her discussion of nomenclature and aesthetics. Long-plumed avens, red stemmed and red flowered, were "truly western" and "loved as much by the Indian children as by the children of the settlers." The former called them "lies-on-his-belly," while the latter used "Old Man's Whiskers" or "Prairie Smoke." In choosing "Old Man's Whiskers" as a name, Brown constructs prairie children as readily accepting "Old Man" as their own. Settler society's children and Indigenous children grew up both "truly western." The title of her book corresponds, then, not only to an Indigenous conception of the region but to her appropriation of the concept.[48]

Brown's interpretations of grasslands plants brought the conflict of her time and generation down to ground level. She wrote as if speaking to her English mother. The "many kinds of violets in *our* country," purple, white, and yellow, are "much loved in spite of the fact that they lack the fragrance of the English variety," for which her mother and other English neighbors pined. Contests took place on the soil. Silverweed, traditionally harvested by Blackfoot, lost out to settlers' potatoes. This nutritious root became "weeds that the white man hoed out with merciless determination." During the "famine years" of the late nineteenth century, when starvation tactics helped Canada complete its conquest of the grasslands, Indigenous peoples took "revenge" at night by digging out settlers' seed potatoes. Indigenes wondered, Brown explained, why white people planted such "valuable food into the ground instead of taking it out." Absconding with potatoes also had the positive effect, from an Indigenous perspective, of causing the fitness of the land for agriculture to be questioned. What worth is a "place where potatoes would not even come up"? Brown presents the potato caper as a clash based on mutual "ignorance": whites did not know clearing a field meant destroying nutritious tubers Indigenous peoples valued, and Indigenes thought of their stealth harvests only as "several meals for his hungry family," not the destruction of profit from a fully matured potato crop desired by settler society.[49] Potatoes and silverweed symbolize cultural conflict.

"Sweet grass," once used in sacred bundles, purification ceremonies, and dream-seeking traditions by Blackfoot and other grasslands Indigenous peoples, transformed under the pressures of agricultural conquest from "sacred" grass to a "noxious weed." Brown acknowledges cultural differences when she discussed many nutritious roots of prairie plants, staples of Indigenous diets, such as the bracken fern, the "spring beauty" tuber, "Indian bread root," and the "prairie turnip." Indigenes ate both the stem and the root of the bracken fern. The stem could be chewed raw as a "substitute for a drink" if necessary or "boiled and treated like asparagus." The inner root, she thought, tasted and looked similar to the "dough of wheat" after roasting, but a "bitter, astringent quality" meant whites failed to appreciate it. The flowering "turnip" held a "tiny drop of nectar." "Children of the prairie love to steal the nectar, sipping it from the bottom of the tube and then, perhaps, swallowing the whole flower," Brown told all of this knowingly. And further, "the sweet-nectar–filled tops, which the children of the prairie so soon discovered, were not overlooked by the original inhabitants, for they were dried by the Indians and used for incense." Again she argued children and Indigenes loved and valued the same plants.[50]

Whites tried to place edible grasslands plants new to them into familiar categories. Brown acknowledged settlers and explorers frequently ended up ill after initial forays into the "Indian diet." She did not attribute this to primitive taste on the part of Indigenous peoples. "It might be well to say that the vegetables used commonly by the Indians of a generation ago are not always agreeable to stomachs accustomed to the over-refined foods of the white man," she admitted, but "it worked both ways." She cited the "disdain" expressed by "prairie Indians" over the "food of the white man," which she argued, "invariably affected the health of the Indian." She reminded readers that it took the disappearance of buffalo for Indigenous peoples to "make the white man's food their own."[51] Brown's critique of "over-refined foods" implicates modern agriculture and the growth of industrial food; this subtly, if unconsciously, questioned the presence of settler society. The comparison also suggested the cultural foundation of Indigenous foodways. The juxtaposition challenged notions of primitive and civilized that had patterned the rationale for settler society's advent on the grasslands.

Many of Brown's vignettes pushed readers to see what whites and Indigenous peoples had in common. She noted, for example, the similar meal "complement" of "mint jellies and . . . our mutton roasts" and the mint leaves that lined Indigenous parfleche bags filled with dried meats. Her prose suggested similarity and a common humanity but also a developmental lag in Indigenous peoples. She compared "the medieval European" to "the Indian of a half century ago." Her chapter called "Old Man's Medicine Bag" addressed readers' skepticism, saying, although "the healing powers of some of them should be purely imaginary and mixed with superstition," these beliefs were not all that different from former English medicinal "recipes" that "called for grass grown in a churchyard, leaves picked by the light of a full moon, or roots dug by the seventh son of a seventh son." She explained many of the old cures "have gone rather out of fashion now" among modern Indians, but it is also true that many of the old remedies "may be found on the shelves of the modern dispensary."[52]

Although Brown rarely addressed religious concerns, she noted Indigenous peoples and settlers both found it necessary to pray with "urgency" for rain on the grasslands. The former prayed for bountiful berries, while the latter prayed for wheat. Farmers might offer a Christian prayer, such as, "Send us we beseech thee, in this our necessity, such moderate rains and showers, that we may receive the fruits of the earth to our comfort." The Backfoot with "as much dignity and urgency," she argued, prayed, "Listen Sun! Listen Thunder! Listen Old Man! All Above Animals and Above People, listen! Pity us! Let us not starve. Give us rain during the summer. Make the berries large and sweet. Cover the bushes with them. Look down on us all and pity us. Let us live." Brown implied similarly in impulse and sentiment. George Will came to the same conclusion about expressive religious values. Looking back about 1950 on the Arikara ceremonies he had observed in the early 1920s, he concluded "sleight-of-hand" ceremonies compared "somewhat like our own old miracle plays." The "medicine bundle" with its "mysterious contents" to Will now corresponded to a "sort of ark of the covenant."[53]

An article in a 1951 *Saturday Evening Post* on the "Sun Dance" on the Blood Reserve near Annora Brown (who saved the article) suggests she probably found many challenges to her thinking about settler-society–Indigenous conflict. Ranchers or "the whites who lived close" to the Bloods thought the ritual a "damn waste of time" in "the busy summer season when there is haying to be done and preparations to be made for the fall harvest." According to a rancher interviewed, "Pay 'em better to get their work done instead of laying around like that." The reporter, using the language of color difference rather than national identity, explained to readers, "the whites . . .

see their red brother as both improvident and utterly indifferent to his responsibilities as a landholder." An "Indian" retort to such thinking asked, "Does not the white man . . . also go to church? Does God Punish him for worshiping Him?" Others at the public part of the ceremony suggested to the reporter, "We can help the Indian by getting to know him. . . . We'd be wrong to force him exactly into our pattern. We'd be better advised to encourage him to retain the tribal arts and morals that make him an individual—an interesting guy."[54] The latter sentiment corresponds closer to attitudes grown in Annora Brown over her varied exchanges with Indigenous peoples over many decades.

"Another High Native Civilization Here in Our Northern Plains": George Will

Both Annora Brown and George Will wrote about North America's northern grasslands in ways that drew them into thinking more deeply about Indigenous cultures. No one called George Will and George Hyde's *Corn among the Indians of the Upper Missouri* "strange," as they did Brown's *Old Man's Garden*, yet reviewers noticed the book's unique combination of scholarly synthesis of "information of the living" and the authors' "own experiments" in "breeding and crossing of native corns." Reviewers understood this research to be "of immense value to modern agriculture." While the book gathered ethnographic material about threatened ceremony and religious and planting rituals, the study did not focus solely on yet another vanishing Indigenous tradition. Instead Will and Hyde announced that Indigenous corn thrived; Indigenous women preserved diverse corn seeds despite disease, warfare, and racial and cultural intolerance. Indeed, professional reviews noted the authors "have brought to light much that was believed to have been irrevocably lost."[55]

Corn among the Indians, for which Will claimed lead author, suggests much about Will's concerns and those of his generation over what it would take to live on the grasslands. Although he was born in 1884, Will had grown up not in the glow of the Dakota Boom; he thought of that population explosion as a "debacle." Boom seemed preposterous to him given all he knew about the place. He grew up in empty Bismarck, so overbuilt that after fifty years and more people still hung on to property and abandoned buildings hoping to realize a return some day.⁵⁶

By 1944 Will concluded, "The white man was *indirectly* responsible for the summary destruction of a people who were on the road of progress in culture and the arts which might have culminated in another high native civilization here on *our* northern plains, had it been allowed to develop naturally over another hundred years or so." Will could use only the words "indirectly responsible" for the role he felt "white people" played in the destruction he had spent a lifetime documenting. Showing some cultural possession of the grasslands, Will bemoaned the cultural wealth lost to "our northern plains." He believed agricultural village nations held the keys for everyone to live "happily and prosperously" on the northern grasslands. As early as 1928, he regarded the agricultural achievements of the Mandan people to be the "highest civilization of the plains." "We white people have lived only a scant 70 years in the Dakota Plains and we have not as yet fully accommodated ourselves to Great Plains conditions and learned to live with them in the best way," he argued. He thought white people should "study [Indigenous peoples] and learn more of their way of life."⁵⁷

George Will saw part of the problem as generational. With his links to James Holding Eagle and his mother, Scattered Corn, and other friends, he—as Brown did—aligned himself implicitly with multiple generations of Indigenous peoples against the parents of settler-colonial society. The annual Will and Company seed catalog suggests generational divergence in understanding. The company not infrequently referenced "Indians," but when George Will took control, its Indigenous touch points changed. The predominant imagery of pioneers, covered wagons, and Indians gifting mottled, many-colored "squaw corn" to settlers, characteristic of the company catalogs under his father's leadership, shifted to one portraying dignified, complex, historically accurate Missouri River Indigenous agricultural villages. The 1919 catalog cover featured a painting drawn by local artist and his friend Clell Gannon of a *Village of Corn Growing Indian Tribe in North Dakota*, complete with bluff-top, earth-lodge homes. An inset

19. In 1925 North Dakota seed seller and lay archaeologist George Will (*left*), artist and poet Clell Gannon (*center*), and historical society member Russell Reid (*right*) boated down the Little Missouri River from Medora to Elbowoods, and the Missouri River to Bismarck, camping along the way to explore the grasslands. State Historical Society of North Dakota (10190-00640).

identified as *North Dakota Pioneer Agriculturalist* pictured a Mandan woman hoeing corn.[58]

Will's father took great pride in "improving" what he called "Squaw or Ree Corn" in the company's turn-of-the-century sales catalogs, calling it a "very insignificant grain of many colors" on a short two-to-three-foot stalk. Will Sr. assured customers his "improved" version of the inferior aboriginal seed, what the company now called "Will's Pride of Dakota White Flint," grew even-rowed and pearly white on multieared, six-foot stalks, while maintaining the hardiness and early maturity of Indigenous varieties.[59] By 1917 George Will took issue with how "white people" used the term "squaw corn" "contemptuously" both to degrade Indigenous women and to diminish the importance of Indigenous agriculture generally. To George these farmers were always "women," not "squaws." (By the 1930s he referred to Scattered Corn also as "Mrs. Holding Eagle.") He insisted contemporary "badly mixed" corn varieties did *not* accurately represent traditional Indigenous farming skill. Impure corn products resulted instead from the effects of severe stress from years of disease and invasion brought on by white culture. By this time Will also knew Indigenous women had held back pure varieties from white hands.[60]

Will calculated that these women farmers cultivated on average about one acre per person, which he called "quite a respectable field to till with the rude implements they had at hand." For those who disparaged Indigenous women farmers, Will argued they should look more closely at their own farming tradition. Village plot size, about six acres per family of six, Will computed, compared favorably to the "American backwoodsmen" along the Ohio River around 1800. Indeed, the total acreage grown by "very large" backwoods families turned out to be less per person than that cultivated by an Indigenous family. Basically, Will argued Indigenous agricultural village nations ended up frequently more food independent than the famed U.S. backwoodsmen. He extended the comparison over time, with some of the same implicit note of developmental lag in Indigenous communities Brown also conveyed. Compared to "Celtic and Anglo-Saxon Farmers" of England's distant past, say the "twelfth century," he postulated, even with "oxen and plows," those Anglos "did not cultivate much more ground than did the Indian women of the Upper Missouri, and sometimes even less."[61]

Will recognized that convincing farmers of the expert nature of Indigenous agriculture required teaching white people about the cultural origins of gender roles. "Misleading" statements will need to be "considerably modified," he explained. Although "the women's work was severe," Indigenous women were not "drudges . . . forced to perform most of the heavy labor, including that of the fields," as the dominant "conception of the position of Indian women" from early historical accounts asserted. Rather, women "performed their tasks willingly and took great pride in doing their work well." He argued that an Indian woman "loved her work." Corn gave Indigenous women high status and expressed women's creativity. Will and

Hyde wrote in the present tense, explaining, "The spring ceremonies of the Mandans begin after the ice had gone out of the river and when the geese and ducks have returned," adding to be clear, and buried in a footnote, "We here employ the present tense, but the government has put a stop to all of these old Mandan rites and ceremonies." Will mocked the "systematic campaign against" the Three Affiliated Tribes by the "U.S. Indian Office" that stopped "Indian women" from sending offerings with the migrating geese to the "protectress of their fields," the "Old Woman Who Never Dies." Will, with a note of paternalism, said the women's rituals constituted "innocent beliefs and practices."[62]

Further, he argued—against popular conceptions—Indigenous men were not "sitting around smoking and chatting while the woman toiled." Men hunted and gathered driftwood. During the spring, while women planted, men pulled in drowned buffalo from "among the floating ice cakes in the Missouri." If danger threatened women's work, men formed an "armed guard in the vicinity." Will admitted, in an article written for Canadian audiences, women did not hold their acreage plots "by title and deed" according to white legal systems, but nevertheless Indigenous men understood Indigenous women oversaw the fields and crops they planted and harvested. Women also controlled the earth-lodge homes they built, directing their men when they needed assistance.[63] Will took on an enormous task to change settler-society thinking on foodways and gender, two intimate ways of organizing families and home life.

George Will wanted white people to understand that most Indigenous women were "very good farmers." Perhaps thinking of himself, Will compared the Indigenous woman farmer to "the modern market gardener or greenhouse man" who gave intense scrutiny to his vegetables. Will also worked against what farmers had seen with their eyes: many colored, mottled, stunted, and incompletely filled-out corn. These had been his assumptions as a young man undertaking his first archaeological excavation. Now he told settler society that Indigenous women had "rules" to ensure "purity" of breed and the maintenance of "good seed ears" that "differ very little from the scientific requirements as given at the present day by corn specialists."

Scattered Corn's family grew only three varieties to protect the purity of the plant.[64]

One of the most difficult hurdles Will faced involved convincing settler-society farmers their cultural presence—if not any one of them personally—destroyed the crops so carefully tended and selected over hundreds of years by Indigenous women farmers. Invasion disrupted traditional farming, as did the consolidation of the Mandan, Arikara, and Hidatsa at Like-a-Fishhook Village and Fort Berthold Reservation. With the coming of white people, village nations no longer had freedom to move along the Missouri River, seeking new village sites to tend crops in their own ways. Will cited Gilbert Wilson's work with Hidatsa women farmers, which revealed the "abundances of weeds" imported by "white men" that made tending fields more difficult for Indigenous women. At one time Indigenous women removed "all dung of the horses from the field in the spring," as they believed it to be the source of new weeds. Nevertheless, despite the stresses of the reservation and bureaucracies of the Indian Office, Indigenous corn varieties had survived.[65]

Will's respect for Indigenous women farmers actually helps to explain his surprising take on the U.S. Dawes Act of 1887, which ordered the "breaking up of the old village." Although he noted that "the government compelled" these moves, "he saw the establishment of each family on its own piece of land" as a way for women farmers to once again take control, away from "the most vicious white men among them" and from the brutal centralized authority of agency institutions. He blamed the reservation and its agencies, not tribal village culture, for the "physical and moral degeneration" of the Three Affiliated Tribes. Officials working for the U.S. Indian Office had manipulated Indigenous families by "favoring" the families with "Indian men who could be induced to work." Agents gave families with male farmers "more supplies" and even "cut off all supplies from the men who refused to engage in agriculture."[66] He speculated that varieties of corn planted too crowded together on reservations explained the source of the mixing that created some of the mottled cobs. Will concluded settlers' commercial farming had resulted in an overall increase in acreage planted, but quantity came with

20. James Holding Eagle (Mandan and Hidatsa) assisted George Will with the latter's research on historical corn varieties produced traditionally by Mandan, Arikara, and Hidatsa women farmers. He introduced Will to his mother, Scattered Corn, an expert farmer. Holding Eagle grew wheat successfully on the Fort Berthold Reservation, as is evident in this 1910s or 1920s photograph. U.S. government policy pressured Indigenous men from Missouri River village tribes to farm, though traditionally men hunted, harvested bison, and protected crops of corn, beans, and squash grown by village women. Holding Eagle and George Will, both born in 1884, forged a long friendship over the first half of the twentieth century. State Historical Society of North Dakota (A1469-00001).

a corresponding lack of control by Indigenous women over their agricultural processes, which resulted in the diminished quality of well-adapted varieties.

George Will drew a complicated picture for the overlapping traditions of the postsettlement generations of settler society and Indigenous peoples. He seemed to say the two could be blended in the future, each culture influencing the other. Indigenous women should be allowed to continue to practice their beautiful ceremonies and rituals surrounding corn and to plant the crop and make food according to their own traditions. However, Will placed white farmers in a position of dominance over Indigenous women, referring to white farmers as "successors of the Mandans." On occasion he even rhetorically completely dispossessed Indigenous farmers, pleading that "their memory be revered in their former land."[67] He argued that settlers did not have to adopt Indigenous traditions surrounding corn. White farmers should appropriate the corn-seed varieties of Indigenous women farmers for use in their own cultures.

In the last decade of his life, in 1948, George Will's writings questioned "our own smug superiority" that required Indigenous people "to see, admire and imitate our white man's civilization with the firm conviction that it is the self-evident only way to all rightness and goodness in human life." The Christian convert James Holding Eagle, Will's friend for decades, undoubtedly had influenced his thinking. Holding Eagle told Will "he could not altogether forget and give up the old Mandan philosophy and cosmogony." He instructed Will about the many "Mandan beliefs which he could carry with him into Christianity" and pressed Will about the right to "judge what is best, what is true and what is false." Now Will asked the larger reading audience of *North Dakota History*, "Just why must the white man make everything to the pattern of his desire and try to enforce upon every people the ugly, machine made garment of his civilization?" Will did not speak with turn-of-the-century antimodern sentiment that romanticized the primitive. He referenced instead a modern diversity of cultural pluralism, not an idealized oversimplistic primitivism. He referred to pressures placed on the "Chinaman," East Indian and African, as well as "American Indian." At this point in his life, he concluded, "Surely, America would be a more interesting place if we had interspersed over the country native Indian communities, willingly taking the really good things that the white man offers, hospitals, doctors, schools, but with education to the white man's way of living only if they wished it." The Mandan and Arikara lived fine in their "communal way," with their "ancient and certain crops" and "knew how to conserve ['pasture'] better than their white brothers." Now Will thought it "negative" to have "condemned [them] to scatter out onto lonely farmsteads away from the society of their people which meant so much to them."[68]

"The Advance of Civilization Would Be My Story": Effie Laurie Storer

Unlike George Will and Annora Brown, Effie Laurie Storer's ideas about Indigenous peoples of the northern grasslands changed little over the course of her lifetime. In 1946 she could still begin an essay on "Indian Life" with the sentence, "Prior to the advent of civilization our prairies were peopled with thousands of warlike Indians." To her, "Indians possessed a mysterious and almost uncanny sense of the land, most closely resembling the contrast of migratory animals." In her mind's eye, writing in her autobiography, "Indians roamed around" with coyotes on the "vast plains." She *viewed herself* as *sympathetic* to Indigenous peoples in that she formed an "interest" in them from an early age; in Winnipeg, the family "had no fence to keep them off of our premises," she wrote without insight. Storer's ideas by the 1940s, when she did most of her autobiographical writing, however, did not change very much from the racist framework her staunch conservative, "Empire building," annexationist-advocate father had when he immigrated to Manitoba amid the Red River Resistance of 1869–70. Effie Laurie Storer knew in 1947, settlers who "lived in the advance of civilization would be [her] story."[69]

She never freed herself from her father's shadow: to her he had "shrewd powers of judgement." Though he thought in terms of "lesser breeds," she thought her father an "unfailing champion" of the "underdog" and "Indians." He was a "Queen's Printer" to her, a symbol of high Anglican British civilization, a territorial posi-

21. The grand setting for this Duffin and Company 1885 portrait of future journalist Effie Laurie Storer (1867–1948) suggests the Anglo-Ontarian cultural aspirations of the Laurie family, who lived in Winnipeg before migrating to Battleford, in the Canadian North-West Territories. Courtesy of Saskatoon Public Library, Saskatchewan (PH-2006-202).

tion her father held for only a few short years. She wanted to write "historically from personal knowledge" particularly of the "opening up of the 'Last West,'" but she wrote little of her life experiences, nothing compelling or distinctive. Save for the pact she made with her fellow "pioneer newspaper women of Saskatchewan," she wrote little about her life as a journalist. Conventions of writing for women had shifted by the middle of the twentieth century, allowing freedom from nineteenth-century essentialist conceptions of women's sphere. Anthropological thought by then had long challenged racialized and hierarchical organization of diverse cultures. The Crees who lived near Battleford posed little threat to settler society. Nevertheless, Effie Storer's core ideas showed little change.[70]

Storer saw herself, her mother, and her sisters as white female carriers of civilization. Her whiteness and early arrival in Battleford, in the North-West Territories, meant something to her. Incredibly proud, she and her sister were "the first white girls to make the trip [across the prairies from Winnipeg to Battleford] in winter by land." Apparently she and her sister were numbers eleven and twelve of "white wom[e]n and girls" at Battleford by 1882. Her mother made thirteen, and "five more arrived that summer and the next year the number rose to twenty." The charting of white women's presence in the North-West Territories in the 1880s became a way for Effie Laurie Storer to claim a stake for herself in the West and Canada's "civilization" mandate. In her telling bravery and courage were attached to the outnumbered white women willing to endure isolation to bring a "civilization" they represented to the West.

She remained almost solely within the tradition of nineteenth-century thinking about civilization based on gender and racial hierarchies. Even in the middle of the twentieth century, she wrote of the "noble Red Man" and repeated the impressions of old-timers who believed the Indian to be "naturally stoical, brave and withal very kind to children." She had thought the "Indians" she saw outside her house in Battleford "terrifying," their faces "painted most hideously": black, yellow, crimson, green—"diabolical." Storer found Indigenous drumming and singing "monotonous," "very wearying," and "monotone." The "little" she experienced of the 1884 "Thirst

Dance" near Battleford, she explained, "satisfied my curiosity to a sickening sense." Crees had continued to perform these dances by tradition. Storer welcomed when "management adopted the civilized method" in 1935 for a newly conceived Thirst Dance.[71] Perhaps Storer's response also reflected her own insecurity. She did not reflect.

Storer's status as a woman limited her to the North-West Mounted Police stockade for what she considered the most important event in her life—the Northwest Rebellion of 1885—so she cited her father's diaries and articles written for his *Saskatchewan Herald* territorial newspaper. She relied too on her brothers William and Richard and their reminiscences. Sidelined, she attached herself to male actions and emphasized, if not embellished, the roles of male family members in the event. In the rebellion's aftermath Effie and her mother went "east to recuperate." When they returned on the train to Battleford the following October, they encountered a "weary" "little French woman," a "Metis of Manitoba." The two helped tend her two children, an infant and a small child. Storer claimed the woman turned out to be the wife of "doomed" Métis leader Louis Riel (who shortly, for his role in the rebellion, would be hanged in Regina).[72] Here Storer groped awkwardly to express an insight about women generally in the West that transcended a male Western frame. She did not. Or she could not.

When Effie Laurie Storer wrote of the efforts of "Old 'Squaces,'" a Cree woman, to teach her about prairie plants, she recalled only dislike for "wild turnips" and that "wild onion" gave her bad breath. In a superior tone she condescended that "Squaces" found "infinite satisfaction to herself" in conversations about the grasslands. Storer wrote proudly of escaping "unfortunate experience with wild berries" by taking her father's advice never to taste wild fruit "we did not know." There would be no trusting of "Squaces," only of her father. At their best, to Effie Laurie Storer, Indigenous people were innocent and childlike; at their worst they were "warlike," with men who made "slaves" of their women (here she did not apparently reflect on the role Indigenous women played in the Laurie household as domestic workers hauling water and chopping wood). Such men, if given the chance, would "save all white women . . . [to] be apportioned among the braves," a racist assumption she repeated in her narrative of the 1885 Northwest Rebellion.[73]

Storer's attitudes seem to have remained nearly the same by 1946, when she wrote the essay "Indian Life." She focused on the 1880s period. Yet by then she knew the fear she experienced witnessing Cree dancers in Battleford prompted "quite a needless precaution" of locking the front door. She understood the Thirst Dance to be less "barbaric as it might appear" because a "Medicine Man" oversaw the ritual from start to finish. Moreover, she even understood authorities called dances "cruel" after the Northwest Rebellion "in reality to prevent the congregation of large numbers of Indians."[74]

From the perspective of the mid-1940s and World War II context, Effie Laurie Storer looked back and concluded, "Things have changed in recent years." She then listed items symbolizing change, unfortunately leaving her meaning implicit. Indigenous people wore "shoes and hosiery" and "bought Victory Bonds." She imagined that Indigenous "lads" adopted "broad brimmed hats" in imitation of the North-West Mounted Police officer "with his Stetson" and that "young Indian women on the reserves imitate a measure of the styles worn by their white sisters." She credited "farm instructors and their wives" for "introducing useful ways" to the "squaws." "Now she can operate a sewing machine," Storer wrote brightly before recounting a 1946 conversation with an unnamed "young Indian woman" about modern needle and beadwork. Effie seemed surprised: the Indigenous woman "spoke so naturally, in the best of English, that I marveled at her intelligence in the matter" of wartime shortages of beads produced in Germany. Storer suggested a lack of civilization in the old "squaw" who used "a little oil" from her hair on the needle and saliva and her teeth to process "hard and dry" leather. Storer may have related this detail correctly, but her disdain shows; she seemed repulsed by the bodily fluids of Indigenous women having anything to do with sewing—as if a modern white woman had never put a thread in her mouth to meet the eye of a needle. She concluded the essay oddly, as was her norm. About modern Indigenous peoples she observed, "All, especially the children, have shown a fondness for ice cream, fancy biscuits and cold drinks."

But alas, she concluded, "they do not patronise the popsicles."[75] Indeed. Her meaning is unclear.

Effie Laurie Storer had an interest in Indigenous life, but it centered not on what she might appreciate or understand from Plains Crees or Métis about a regional environment they knew much longer and better than she. Instead, her interests related to her and her family's roles in "civilizing" the West, including forced acculturation of Indigenous peoples and transformation of northern grasslands habitat with commercial agriculture. From her perspective she served as a racial and female role model for settler society's "civilization." "Contact with the pioneers" and "tales of frontier life never failed to enthrall" Effie Laurie Storer.[76]

Reconfiguring Social Space Down the Generations

When George Will met James Holding Eagle, Elsie Hammond met the "Indian Stanley," and Annora Brown met Eddie Merry Horse, each operated in the space of everyday social hybridity. These day-to-day common meetings suggest examples of a new space emerging in the settler-colonial–Indigenous encounter, as articulated by Walter L. Hixson, in which a "hybridity" occurs. Hixson argues that understanding and "colonial ambivalence" occurred among settlers who, for example, "empathized with Indians, [and] condemned treaty violations and aggression against them" and Indigenous persons who "went a long way toward accommodating Euro-Americans by trading and interacting with them, negotiating and allying with them in warfare, converting to their religions, and showing a willingness to share space." Diverse peoples, with varied interest and personalities, "reconfigured" themselves in response to living with but also resisting one another.[77] On the northern grasslands care about the environment, from diverse even divergent Indigenous and settler-society perspectives, proved central to the *potential* of hybrid, third-space exchanges to be—if they were not always—positive. When Effie Laurie Storer met the Cree woman "Squaces," potential existed, but the exchange had to have mutuality as a goal, even if, as often occurred even in positive exchanges, unaltered assumptions of power remained in the air. Settler-society and Indigenous relations grew tangled roots down the generations. Annora Brown, George Will, and Elsie Hammond suggest understanding grasslands environments, even in agricultural dress, aided movement toward possibilities for positive, if flawed, cultural entanglement.

As Annora Brown wrote about "inherit[ing]" the northern grasslands from the Blackfoot peoples created by "Old Man," George Will wrote with similar blinders about "our red predecessors" and "white successors." Brown wanted settler-heritage residents to value grasslands ecological habitat. But it is clear she thought in terms of colonial possession and advocated habitat preservation primarily for the enjoyment of settler-society culture. Brown remained committed to friendliness and to her art and aesthetics. She also showed sincere appreciation for artistry evident in Blood, Piegan, and Blackfoot cultural tradition. Will desired the setter society his family company served to value the "agricultural achievements" he told his customers "we have received" from Mandans and Arikaras. Indigenous peoples "have given us a valuable foundation for our own agriculture." Indigenous crops had been "passed on as the gift of the Red people," as a "free gift," he enthused.[78] Will valued Indigenous women "farmers" and their agriculture deeply. However, he showed little insight into anything problematic in the transfer of Indigenous corn to settler commercial agriculture or even the possibilities of forming equal business partnerships with Indigenous women that would give them (some) control and income to thrive in the modern world of the socially and agriculturally transforming northern grasslands.

Will's friend Clell Gannon, who painted Mandan women agriculturists sensitively for the covers of many Will and Company annual seed catalogs, also wrote a 1924 poem that consigned "Redmen" to the past. The poem asks the Missouri River to speak of actions that occurred on its banks, from its creation by the "slow hand of God" to the recent advent of the United States, "a nation Founded on Justice." History unfolds in each stanza, from "the Indian," Sitting Bull, George Armstrong Custer, "the pioneers," Lewis and Clark, and "the ones that proved up on the claim."[79] Possession by succession thinking—the so-called inevitable march of history—persisted in settler society. It served to distance settler individuals such as Gannon,

Will, and Brown from a sense of their own and their larger culture's agency in shifting land from Indigenous peoples to settler society.

Will's and Brown's flawed sensitivity revealed possibilities on the positive end of a continuum of settler-Indigenous cross-cultural connections in their generation. Perhaps it is not a coincidence both Brown and Will lived in proximity to reserves and reservations. One legacy of segregation by reserves and reservations—in their original iterations, not as Indigenous peoples have transformed them to be centers of sovereignty today—meant settlers far removed from them could take the option to live with little thought about or contact with Indigenous peoples.[80] Effie Laurie Storer's attitudes suggest, however, that proximity might result in the opposite. She lived close to several Cree reserves. Old racial hierarchies remained in place in Storer's mind long after segments of the larger North American population had begun to absorb new insights from archaeologists and anthropologists that fostered tolerance and cultural pluralism and long after some of her contemporaries began to shift their ideas as a result of experiences in place with Indigenous peoples. Storer's ideas matter precisely because she suggests the long persistence of older notions of the West that claimed certainty about superior settler-society "civilization." Storer's mid-twentieth-century thinking revealed racial hierarchical thinking still lodged deeply in continental culture. The ideas of Brown and Will suggest modern cultural pluralism taking hold. Racial thought and settler society's attitudes toward Indigenous peoples lay on a continuum with Storer, Hammond, Brown, and Will representing various points, not equally distant from one another or in any ideal spot generally.

George Will and Annora Brown did not in some old-fashioned, romantic way view the Mandans or Blackfoot peoples as *part* of the grasslands environment. They saw similarities—real and imagined—between their own appreciation for the nature of the place and that of Indigenous peoples' attachments to the grasslands environment. The connection helped them grow to respect and value Indigenous knowledge, but primarily as keys to creating happier, healthier, more prosperous lives on the northern grasslands for the descendants of settler society. They were grasslands grown. Brown and Will desired to live better on the grasslands with their own culture dominant but informed by what *they considered* the best of Indigenous lifeways. They did not see their appropriation of aspects of Indigenous practice and culture as further colonial actions. They saw the desire for knowledge as complimentary to Indigenous peoples they grew to know better, if not fully, even after lifetimes of reaching out. Neither thought Indigenous peoples would disappear, if they did see older traditions fading. Both saw Indigenous people claiming modern rights to northern grasslands space through a longer culture and history in the place.

6

"All Is So Still—So Big, I Scarce Can Speak"
New Literature and Settler-Society Aesthetics

Wintering in Austria with his wife, Hadley, the novelist Ernest Hemingway wrote to fellow expatriate writer Robert McAlmon about the latter's novel: "Village is absolutely first rate and damned good reading. We've all read it down here and everybody thinks it's a knock out. It is swell." In 1924 McAlmon's own Paris-based Contact Publishing Company issued *Village: As It Happened through a Fifteen Year Period*. Set in the fictional town "Wentworth, North Dakota," the autobiographical novel evoked the lives of turn-of-the-century residents of Madison and Wentworth in eastern South Dakota that McAlmon, born in the mid-1890s, knew growing up. "I can't tell you how damned good I think Village is," Hemingway signed off. "Write me a letter and tell me all the dope."[1]

Hemingway's praise of *Village* may have been mere support designed to encourage a fellow writer, his friend and publisher. That year McAlmon's company published Hemingway's first collection of fiction, *Three Stories and Ten Poems*, when he was still unknown. But the opinion was probably sincere. The poet Ezra Pound offered essentially the same judgment, "a good piece about the American West," he said of *Village*. From Paris Gertrude Stein wrote McAlmon, "I have been reading VILLAGE. I find your young people to be as I knew them and as I know them and America as I know it." The Stockholm writer Ludvig Nordström praised *Village* and McAlmon for the "new aspect of America you are giving," which might "give to the world . . . pictures of the very mixed soul of America." Nordström thought the novel a "piece of history work" and compared McAlmon favorably with Hemingway, Sherwood Anderson, and Sinclair Lewis.[2] Although Robert McAlmon used every place he lived—Paris, the French Rivera, New

219

York City, Berlin, Los Angeles, the U.S. desert West, and a northern Mexican village—as material for fiction, he repeatedly returned to northern grasslands society, the Dakotas where he grew up and the city of Minneapolis where he moved as a young man.

Individuals of this generation of setter society came to terms with northern grasslands space in diverse ways: watching native grasslands habitats change over the seasons and years, studying agriculture scientifically, delving into Nature Study teaching methods, shifting crop and stock strategies, writing memoirs of childhood experiences, or painting the environmental scene. Another group of individuals came to terms with the land by crafting prose and poetry. This chapter considers creative works that emerged in the search for sense of place and regional identity among this particular group of individuals, rather than from weighing literary merit. Successful or not, the prose and poetry of many authors from the northern grasslands nicely reveals early struggles to create a literature that spoke to their generation's environmental and social experience. Literary scholar Robert Thacker has observed it took a generation who had grown up with the "overarching presence" of grasslands landscapes "incorporated into" their "very being" for a literature of place to emerge.[3]

Authors added regional nuance to the early twentieth-century literary critique of small towns by use of railroad and railway culture. These authors implicitly and explicitly commented on popular old western "pioneer" tales (which they sometimes also wrote) by creating alternative Grasslands West stories. Authors critiqued social life centered around small towns, but also life related to homesteads in the countryside rooted in personal northern grasslands experiences. These writers acknowledged consumer conformity, but geography and grasslands environments had as much power in their prose. The novels explored reflect a region rising with unique spatial-social organization related to the agriculturally adapting northern grasslands context.

More than a lack of literary quality slowed the emergence of artistic expression within the region from the northern grasslands-grown settler society—that is, beyond the better-known and enduring works of one-time Dakotan Hamlin Garland or Nebraskan Willa Cather and perhaps Nellie McClung of Manitoba.[4] A close look at Robert

McAlmon's struggles with the literary establishment suggests issues facing the region's would-be creative writers, including a rudimentary publishing infrastructure and editors open to the unique aesthetics emerging out of settler society on the northern grasslands. Some writers and artists saw the emergence of aesthetic expression rooted in landscapes as expressions of their own indigeneity, implicitly—perhaps unconsciously—designed to "dismiss" or supersede Indigenous claims to space. As Elizabeth Cook-Lynn has reminded us, "Literature can and does successfully contribute to the politics of possession and dispossession." New stories of place competed with ongoing Indigenous narrative traditions attached to the land, imagined differently.[5] Where their parents had claimed land by purchase and government grants, this generation of settler society began to claim land through literature and art on the plane of culture.

Revolt from "Coyote"

New fiction and poetry by grasslands writers shared some of the preoccupations of their modernist literary counterparts with World War I, consumerism and changing social and moral values, but northern grasslands writers used a distinguishing postsettlement, next generation, place-centered framework.[6] Modern grasslands writers began to publish when the culture of small towns preoccupied intellectuals across the continent. In a 1921 article for the *Nation* magazine titled "Revolt from the Village," literary critic Carl Van Doren commented on the recent novels of young writers, suggesting they wrote with less optimism and more "candor" and used new forms, subjects, and language. In *Contemporary American Novelists* he critiqued the former "local color" novelists by revealing how the new writers evoked the "stubborn depths of human life."[7] Modern literary historian Ronald Weber has argued this new literature grew from those who came of age to realize "the Fall from pioneer perfection" in their communities.[8] Subtle critiques of the "pioneer" are important for the grasslands "village" variant.

Van Doren highlighted *Main Street* (1920) by Sinclair Lewis, which he said had reached "hundreds of thousands" of readers. The action of the novel satirically, if more lovingly than often recalled, portrayed the culture of his boyhood hometown, Sauk Center, Minnesota, located at the eastern edge of the northern grasslands (called "Gopher Prairie" in the novel). Van Doren argued Lewis had his "revenges to take upon the narrow community in which he grew up." The "dullness militant and prospering" that Lewis depicted exposed his fictional town to "ridicule."[9] The potential for vacuous culture in small towns that concerned modernists such as Lewis received increased depth and nuance when joined with the question of town survival and agricultural adjustment on the northern grasslands; troubled towns led to railroad tracks.

The railroad, or railway, town received particular attention in northern grasslands literature of the village. In the 1910s the southern Albertan Wilfrid Eggleston referred to one of his rail-siding fictional villages as a "mushroom settlement." His boy character watches "every gesture by which a field of buffalo-grass is converted into a prairie village," a place where only three months before he had hunted jackrabbits. Railway companies laid out almost all grasslands town space across the region according to business plans. The Manitoban Edward Pitblado worked during the summer of 1913 staking out the path of a new "railroad line" across the grasslands, including the layout of small towns. He recalled the swift nature of a new town's progress: "Two towns behind us would be what you would call a thriving little center after just two weeks['] time!" Unfailingly, a Chinese restaurant and the Beaver Lumber Company became the first two businesses on a town site. In the process of atrophying from their first days, many grasslands railway towns became symbols for a faltering, or at least struggling to adapt, regional culture as much as small-town mediocrity.[10]

When Wilfrid Eggleston set out to give a "composite picture" of a "prairie town" in a five-part series in the *Lethbridge Daily Herald*, he remarked, "Coyote has its Main Street too, though no Sinclair Lewis has yet arisen to make it immortal." Rural homesteaders dreamed of all the businesses "coming" to the main street, often the only street of activity: the flour mill, shoe repair, photographer, grain elevators, Chinese laundry, bank, post office, and "the most remarkable building in town": the grocery store. The railway company built Eggleston's

1923 fictional town and even settled debate about the correct pronunciation of its name. Was it "Ki-oot" or "Koy-o-tee"?[11] Showing detachment between the broader community and railway companies, since the train clerks used *three* syllables, the railway decided the matter, despite the predominant local pronunciation. As if talking back to his publisher and to his readers, North Dakota poet Clell Gannon explained that he knew it "might be better usage" to use *three* syllables for "coyote" but instructed readers to use *two* ("ki'ot") "because it is the form most in use among the Westerners of the real Plains."[12] Eggleston suggested the alienation of grasslands communities from the same corporate railroads, on which they depended for market access and consumer goods. Communities did not have power enough to demand the primacy of regional language, an early suggestion of the struggle for regional literary expression.[13]

Echoing Eggleston's note of the power of railway companies, Edward Pitblado, with a tone of latter-day incredulousness, recalled how he and his fellow pathway workers placed signage on the newly staked out railway town plats at random, suggesting the interchangeability and "monotonous uniformity," to use Carl Van Doren's words, characteristic of grasslands rail-line towns. The town name had little meaning flowing up from a community: "at night when it was dark somebody would grab a sign from a pile in the box car and that became the name of the town." Town naming had become a corporate endeavor without having the weight of people to hold the place down or build it up. The railway-town style that rose across the northern grasslands below and above the international line suggested a regional flimsiness inherent in the newly built environment of settler societies. Railroad towns offered their own version of "dullness militant," though for many decidedly not "prospering."[14]

Nell Wilson Parsons's central character, Tory Jarvis, in *The Curlew Cried* (1947), describes how in anticipation "everyone spoke of the rails as STEEL—important, capitalized." She and her husband, Lane, physically traced the *intended* route of the impending railway, after which Lane shouts, "Pioneer days are over!" The Icelanders central to Laura Goodman Salverson's novel, *Viking Heart* (1923), "burned [with] the hope that some day the railroad would come and with it prosperity."

Two of the three families in Salverson's Icelandic settlement left (and all the children did) for work in Winnipeg or a better "prairie" farm. They tired of waiting for the railroad, because "until it comes we can't gain anything through either grain or stock." Eggleston devoted a chapter in his first novel, *The High Plains* (1938), to the arrival of the railroad and "The Village" that soon "transformed the life of Wolf Willow community," formerly an area of scattered homesteaders. The arrival of a railway town, as in Coyote, causes "long-suffering pioneers" to go "wild with the fulfillment of long-deferred hopes." In reality, the "great days" lasted only as long as construction, leaving settlers soon "hard up again."[15] On the grasslands, towns that secured a railroad had the best opportunity to endure, yet many of them never incorporated or lasted. Failure to rise to permanence signaled that more was going on than standardization and mediocrity in northern grasslands modern fiction.

When cactus, sagebrush, and tumbleweed replaced "finer grasses and flowers" around the countryside of Eggleston's "Wolf Willow" community, the railway "villages shriveled in sympathy" with struggling settlers on whom their prosperity depended.[16] Lane's romantic rival for Tory in Parsons's *Curlew Cried* anticipates the ten- to fifteen-year "boom" that would come and go with the arrival of railroads and plans to build a general store in every other town along the route. In imagery that precisely reflects settlers' conflicted relationship with "the rails," Tory decides the storeowner who made his real money on futures on the Wheat Board might best be seen as an "obnoxious" "tumbling mustard" weed. "There had been no such weeds before settlers and the rails came," she thinks. The store-owner speculator is a "weed," an "exploiter of the soil," while she distinguishes her husband as "one of the tilling farmers, laboring . . . from sheer love of the land." But her thought, perhaps unconsciously, implicates both settlers and the rails in bringing weeds to the grasslands.[17]

Motivation for farming mattered; Parsons argued that weeds grown with crops raised from "love" of the soil differed fundamentally from the weeds planted by corporations. Nevertheless, her link between weeds and settlers communicated the conflict of her generation thrilling to both agricultural and native grasslands habitats. Parsons grew up thinking sagebrush beautiful, even though the plant's spread commonly conveyed grasslands distress. The rural community indicted government land policy, railway corporations, and market and trade issues in the struggle for success. Parsons, a child who grew to love the grasslands, nevertheless knew from an adult perspective that plowing created some of the environmental problems the tumbleweed symbolized.[18]

The excitement of the popup railroad town lay in the "frontier" dream of settler-colonial advance on a perceived "wilderness." As Eggleston fictionalized, optimism ruled Coyote's one hundred residents, who all agree, "Coyote is a town with no past, an insignificant present, but with a magnificent future."[19] Robert McAlmon used almost the same line in a short story he wrote, probably about his own experience working in a railroad "surveying party." An older hand explains to a young summer hire, "There used to be some big ranches around here, but now that the government gives away claim lands, there aren't any great sized ranches." The young man exclaims, "That's the bloody trouble with this country; everything has been, or is going to be, but there's never anything here in the present."[20] The mythic West always looks to the past of "cowboys" (in McAlmon's story) or "suffering pioneers" in the "wilderness" (in Eggleston's tale), while unrealistic boosterism looks to the future. The present could seem the least real or defined to the rising grasslands-grown children of settler society.[21] Many northern grasslands towns remained more ephemeral and could not host the population necessary to create the communities envisioned by the founding generation of settler society.

Robert McAlmon's young summer railroad worker describes a "weird experience" he has while working on the construction crew: "Two miles away, across the flatness, his eye discerned the speck, which as he watched became an undulating line of train that continued headlong and smoothly past his vision and out of sight to another horizon line." He contemplates, "It was a shock to see a train passing and know it contained people—many people"—but only "passers."[22] As Diane Quantic has observed of Great Plains literature, the train meant goods, employment, and a "link to the outside."[23] The train also symbolizes the people one would need to create communities in spacious northern grasslands settler society, but who never arrived. In this story trains people the grasslands, if only with people passing by to get across. As Sophie Trupin wrote in her memoir, "There is no more solitary sight than that of a train speeding in the night through an endless prairie, its lighted windows glimmering in the vast darkness."[24] This generation, living through homestead busts and the droughts and insecure markets of the 1920s and 1930s, gradually realized that the spaciousness would remain in whatever settlement survived in ways their pioneer parents had not expected.

Wallace Stegner thought of his own hometown, Eastend, Saskatchewan, the "Whitemud" of his fiction, as "one of the ones that will last." He judged its location on a river and role as railroad-division point to have survival advantages over the stop-off sidings such as Eggleston's fictional Coyote. But Whitemud does not grow—much. Looking back, Stegner felt "failure was woven into the very web" of many grasslands towns. The rise and fall of his town could have happened "anywhere" in North America, he thought. But the "frontier curve from hope to habit, from optimism to a country rut, from American Dream to Revolt against the Village" had been "nearly inevitable on the Plains, because on the Plains the iron inflexibilities . . . limit the number of people."[25] As northern grasslands society over decades adjusted to increasingly understood inflexible environmental constraints and industrial "power farming," small railroad towns began a retreat. Stegner made clear that for the northern grasslands a "Revolt against the Village" meant revolt from Western mythology, which the rise and fall of railroad towns suggested, and also a departure from the dreams of settler society's parental generation.

Alternative Westerns from the Northern Grasslands West

The life spans of the writers considered here covered a broad period in literary history that saw national trends shift from romantic and "local color" fiction of the late nineteenth century to narratives of realism and modern forms and themes in the first half of the twentieth century. Hamlin Garland's collection, *Main Travelled Roads* (1891), with many stories set in South Dakota, and Willa Cather, author of important Nebraska novels, among others, *O Pioneers!* (1913), *My*

Ántonia (1918), and *One of Ours* (1922), rooted a northern grasslands critical literary tradition for both Canada and the United States.[26] Garland, by critic Van Doren's reading, offered "dissent from average notions about the pioneers" (such as the many heroic "pioneer origin" migration tales written by this generation to honor their parents). Van Doren thought Cather focused uniquely on "human character," conveying both uneducated people and a "higher type" with a notable "balanced independence" from all literary forms.[27] Literary historian Robert Thacker argued that Cather's "view of the land . . . commingles a romantic fancifulness" with "stark realities."[28] Popular grasslands tradition, according to Canadian literary historian Dick Harrison, included "mounting skepticism about the romance of pioneering" while holding on to an optimism in which characters might successfully be restored to a "harmony with nature."[29] The mixing of romantic, popular, realistic, and modern genres seems key generally to an emergent northern grasslands literature in the first half of the twentieth century.

Garland and Cather also inspired younger writers from their region interested in portraying the northern grasslands in literature—even if these writers frequently missed their marks! The young Albertan Wilfrid Eggleston noted that Garland's stories "might have been drawn from Alberta farms" instead of Dakota or Iowa. He hoped "more than one Canadian Garland" might emerge from the "thousands of boys on our Canadian prairie" to "fix the image of our pioneer days." Wallace Stegner cited Cather's *One of Ours* for its focus on a grasslands-raised young man's struggle for "cultural aspiration."[30] Robert McAlmon, Wilfrid Eggleston, Nell Wilson Parsons, Wallace Stegner, and Laura Goodman Salverson wrote alternative Grasslands West stories that commented on family relationships and personal experiences in Manitoba, the Dakotas, and Saskatchewan. Thematically, identity formation, personal crisis, and anguished grief shows in their explorations of postpioneer relationships to the northern grasslands.

Although Van Doren in 1921 viewed Sinclair Lewis's best-selling *Main Street* as the center of a new modern literature, South Dakotan Robert McAlmon and Albertan Wilfrid Eggleston both thought that novel missed part of the small towns they knew. Their towns reflected northern grasslands space as much as material and cultural conformity. Commenting on Lewis in a newspaper column in 1924, Eggleston thought "the author saw and depicted everything that a man of talent can see and depict of Gopher Prairie . . . but . . . there are realms either beyond his vision or beyond his power of expression." For Eggleston *Main Street* did not "suggest that last note of wonder."[31] He insisted, "Sinclair Lewis tells the truth, but it is not the whole truth." "There is another world beneath the world of 'Main Street.'" Lewis's characters could "be made lovable," like Eggleston's Coyote residents.[32] McAlmon knew Lewis and compared himself directly, claiming, perhaps with envy, "Our backgrounds were not unlike." He "conjectured that he [Lewis] didn't know a bit more about Main Street, or Minneapolis, or Babbitts, than did I." McAlmon argued that Lewis "chose to write the dullest aspect of small-town life and types, while I had memories of rather alert and lively people."[33]

Robert McAlmon's novel *Village* (1924) centers around the population of a northern grasslands small town in the model of Sinclair Lewis's "Gopher Prairie," established in 1880s Dakota. The town is bigger and more stable than Stegner's Whitemud and certainly Eggleston's Coyote, and McAlmon set out to "sociologize" the village, to "close in upon its heart, if villages have hearts." The dominance of cropped acres, shrinking wetlands, and "prairies covered in high dried weeds" signals the post-1900 eastern northern grasslands location. Now farmers ship "great quantities" of commodities to "the cities." Settlers seemingly control space; Indigenous peoples are consigned to reservations. Settlement is both a generation old and ongoing. Characters seek homesteads once again farther west in the Dakotas, eastern Montana, and Canada, unlike in the late 1880s and 1890s "famine years," when "climatic hardship" caused mass exodus of families from farm and village. Implicating the grasslands and settler culture that grew his "North Dakota" village, McAlmon argued that village "morality based on property and sex" limits the "social condition" of the then entwining townspeople and farmers. Key to McAlmon's tone: children and young people observe it all.[34]

The village revolves around the machinations of an "it" crowd, signaled by young women. Beauty qualifies one to be "it" but is judged

22. Robert McAlmon based his Contact Publishing Company in Paris, where he frequently could be found at cafés and bars. His biographer, Sanford J. Smoller, identified this 1920s photograph as showing either Le Dôme or La Rotonde in Paris. McAlmon is on the left, with Renée Claire[?], Tristan Tzara, Sylvia Gough, and Kiki (Alice Prin). Original image from Robert McAlmon Papers, folder 135, Beinecke Digital Collections, Beinecke Rare Book and Manuscript Library, Yale University (3600329).

by the "cornfed-health look," with family wealth, occupation, and religion mixed into the calculation. The achievements and activities of the young (before they leave or if they stay) substitute for a mature community with established and professional cultural institutions. McAlmon rendered what literary critic Diane Quantic has called "strong" children of the grasslands, who question and seek their potential, while Lewis described, in part, "weak" children who turn into conforming adults. McAlmon drew weak young characters too but accomplished his modern revolt looking with bite through the eyes of bright young people looking to their future, not those who returned to live as the next middle-aged generation of leading families in town (such as Lewis's central characters). Peter Reynalds (Robert McAlmon's teenaged alter ego), who speculates he would "kind of like to be only a hobo—a highclass one, and travel all over the world" (very much like McAlmon, who lived in Paris at the time he wrote the novel), relates much of the activity in *Village*. His close friend is Gene Collins (a fictitious Eugene Vidal, the father of the writer Gore Vidal), who desires an appointment to a military college (West Point for Vidal). Both are "alert and lively" and eventually move away from the village and the northern grasslands.[35]

Townspeople have invested in the countryside, and wealthy farmers have taken over the villages. "Better financed" settlers achieve success because of timely farmland purchases during droughts. A mere five families dominate the countryside around McAlmon's village. One farm family already operates as "equals" with the townspeople by inviting them out to "their homestead farm" (the original land claim, as opposed to land—at one time entire farms—acquired later). Another family "virtually owned and controlled all of the business and production of the village and farm community about them." Soon retiring farmers become the most reliable source of new village residents. The wealthy Angus family challenges the town's social order by moving from the farm into a big, old, deteriorating house in the neighborhood, where the "best Protestant" families live. The substantial "ten room brick mansion" built in town by long-gone pioneers from the East represents only a "*legend* of New England culture and respectability" that settler society once thought could be transplanted to the grasslands. Settler society now has a "revised idea of what wealth meant." The general property relations presented by McAlmon (and Garland and Eggleston) echo reformer Henry George's theories about the unearned increments of rising land values and other economic problems noted by turn-of-the-century farm movements.[36]

McAlmon also used youth to discuss his second limitation on the "social condition" of people, property being the first, sex the second. Traditional, value-instilling pioneer tales of migration and hard work still circulated, but McAlmon revealed young people concerned about sex and sexual identity. His emphasis on sexuality, and especially the emotional lives of boys, put him in the company of those new authors cited by Carl Van Doren for an "especial candor in affairs of sex," or, as another critic phrased it, McAlmon generally "dispensed with prudery."[37] He moved beyond the romanticized by revealing a village fully connected to grasslands countryside, a place where the young easily learned the facts of life. As McAlmon phrased it, "The spaciousness of the country and the freedom of young animal life about, permitted school children to escape the too cramping influences of petty minds if they had instincts of there being a larger-minded world outside the village."[38]

Interactions with animals that led children to discover the details of the environment and imprinted their bodies sensually also allowed them to know their bodies better. In one *Village* scene two boys take Daisy the cow out to be "serviced" by Othello the bull. One of the boys notes that Daisy "always had to be forced." The older farmer jokes, "Some females are that way," and goes on to discuss another young "little brown heifer" that "uses the bulls up." The two thirteen-year-old boys "laughed and looked sheepish," as they "weren't used to being talked to so frankly by older men, *as though they* understood everything and there was nothing to be self-conscious about." The boys *do not* actually understand everything and, perhaps projecting their feelings, see a "sour look of distaste" on Daisy's "bovine countenance, as if she wishes to throwup, and thinks the whole procedure disgusting to her higher cow nature." The story suggests how some rural men conveyed masculine culture aiming to shape the next generation in their relationships with women. The joking trivializes masculine power and sexual consent and also plays on stereotypes of the pure woman (Daisy) and fallen woman ("little brown heifer"). McAlmon countered "white church" morality by speaking plainly with everyday language and scenes from his Dakota childhood. In another scene a younger boy muses about "jacking-off a dog" as a neighborhood boy taught him to do, recalling "the expression on the dog's face." Sexual talk *was* part of traditional rural culture, but it took an indirect form—here in animals—of which McAlmon made modern literary use. The story is an implicit critique of "limiting" sexual relationships.[39]

In a short story called "A Boy's Discovery," McAlmon explored reproductive knowledge, depicting an awkward relationship between two boys about town. Harold (the McAlmon character) and Harry (a sickly boy) decide to visit a farm near the village. There the boys have the opportunity to view breeding. They "saw the excitement of the stallion, heard him neigh and whisper groaningly." Harold announces to Harry, "So there will be a colt. That's how young things are always made." Harry counters that doctors bring babies; Harold retorts, "Rats, that's a fairy story like Santa Claus. Men and women do that same thing,—only a man's thing isn't quite as big as a stallion's." Harry, now nauseous, replies that God sends a baby after praying. Harold insists, "A man puts his thing in a woman somewhere, I don't know where, and then after nine months she has a baby." McAlmon suggested Harold's ultimate innocence in his own lack of knowledge of where on a woman's body sex takes place.

The boys' discussion spins out over a few days into a community-wide, but children-only, discussion under the adult radar, eventually to include girls, on "how babies are made." Soon the boys and girls conspire in a hayloft to "show us what you have, and we'll show you."[40] Wallace Stegner recalled such boyhood "show parties in haylofts," and "gang diddling of complaisant little girls happened now and then"; he saw such memories as a mix of "conventional prudery and barnyard freedom."[41] McAlmon populated his village with children and young people not stultified by genteel sexual propriety, as if to place a point on the power of culture intersecting with the life cycle to shape values. He transferred natural curiosities of childhood into modern subjects and form.

McAlmon's prose reveals young people's innocent sexual questioning very much alive in turn-of-the-century villages of the northern grasslands, as they were part of the conversations occurring in Greenwich Village when he lived there and wrote of these people and the grasslands. McAlmon's teenaged characters, Peter and Gene, for example, have discussions about adolescent hormonal changes and sexual maturity. Peter even contemplates his "affection" for Gene. Still, he wonders whether the attraction might be only part of adolescence. Another college-aged friend of Peter's dreams of kissing a male friend and wakes up feeling life "mystifying, and not pleasantly so." The grown-up young people, both male and female, discuss ("countrified looking") farm girls who "fuss and cuddle," birth control, sex between people perceived to be "elderly," adulterous affairs and suicides, and indicate the occurrence of abortion.[42] McAlmon's literature engaged in the new attention to sex encouraged by modern naturalistic writers in ways that resonated with his grasslands upbringing. Although these individuals grew to adulthood in an agricultural economy in a region rising rural, McAlmon's work reminds us that they were not isolated from ideas percolating across the continent.

McAlmon's literary strategy united a modernist's turn away from the prohibition against discussing sex and tried to make the subject accessible through the eyes of innocent but realistic children and adolescents. One critic for the *Philadelphia Public Ledger* who read *Village* seemed to sense the originality of the subject matter and insisted the book was not "freakish and overburdened with sex and ultra-modern."[43] McAlmon's boy-girl talk matched the modern experimentation among adult men and women who self-consciously discussed sex with a new freedom in Greenwich Village.

Moderns, according to historian Christine Stansell, "thrilled" at the mere "lobbing" of "sex into the middle of common conversation."[44] While living in New York City, McAlmon first began to write about his grasslands boyhood and adolescence, sometimes earning money posing nude for artists. In his Greenwich Village–set novel called *Post-adolescence* (1923), he recorded himself walking the city's streets with writer Mina Loy and artist Marsden Hartley, on the way to the writer Marianne Moore's place. Triggered by the mention of "white peacocks," the McAlmon character begins thinking to himself about "white music. White winds; white with every colour in the world in it. He'd write something about that. White and purity. What is purity? . . . White winds blowing, cool and fresh through the white sky. Like the days far back in North Dakota when the blizzards hurled white sleet snow across the snow-covered plains. How tired he was of apathy; how primitively clear those winds, that snow, had been; and all the while through the whiteness to the eye the winds had shrieked out a cold blue symphony . . . something went on storming inside him."[45]

He brings the "plains" in its most northern guise to bear on the storming of early "manhood," waging the apparent "purity" of white snow against the reality of "every colour" wrought by the wind. He aligns clarity of thought and the energy to act with wind, snow, and sky, suggesting all the while the aural, tactile, and visual imprints grasslands space and place make on his body. McAlmon made use of regional experiences to convey universal truths in modern form.

Another McAlmon short story, called "A North Dakota Surveying Party," directly confronts the heroic-male frontier-Western narrative tradition. A frontier survey gang lays railroad tracks across western North Dakota in a largely homosocial male world. One evening the men attend a dance, where they mix with ranchers' daughters, schoolteachers, and cowboys. One of the more "brutal" men, a known rapist, eyes a schoolteacher who had that "Scandinavian hip movement," wondering, "what could I get out of [her]." He complains to the young men about the cold weather by dropping lines about how it made his "prick stand up" and his "worm" freeze. Because of his known prior behavior, the men, this time, do not let the rapist escort the teacher home. Once "when the gang was surveying about fifty miles back he saw her shack, and went up 'to get a drink.' He tried to stay and talk with her but she wasn't very friendly, or maybe she was, I don't know," muffled the narrator. "Anyway he threw her down and forced her." (Eventually the rapist departs the crew for Sioux Falls, South Dakota.)

McAlmon highlighted the phrase "to get a drink" with quotation marks to suggest the man's common ruse and an unspoken underside of legendary pioneer Western hospitality. Anyone could stop by for a drink of water or food or for safe harbor during a storm, but danger lurked that had nothing to do with "Indians," who—the older men in the story told the younger—"used to be around here, not more than ten, or anyway, twenty years back."[46] McAlmon's male West showed unspoken dangers for women. He spoke to the reality of many young teachers hoping to launch away from the grasslands, whose shacks would have populated the landscape. He also addressed young male initiation into sexual violence in the West or at least into knowledge of sex generally. McAlmon suggested sexual experimentation came with new responsibilities involving bystander ethics and consent.

In *Village* three years passed before the town would send its *first* boy to college, but the novel ends with a coterie of college people who claim "Wentworth" as a hometown, if not a current address.

23. Wilfrid Eggleston made his adult home in Ottawa, working as a journalist and, after World War II, as a professor in Carleton University's journalism program. Eggleston here teaches a 1958 class of Carleton students. The author of the novels *The High Plains* (1938) and *Prairie Symphony* (1978) and of a literary history, *The Frontier and Canadian Letters* (1957), Eggleston never lost touch with Alberta, where his brother, sister, and parents lived. © Malak of Ottawa. Image courtesy of Heritage Photograph Collection, Archives and Special Collections, Carleton University Library.

Prefiguring by more than three decades Stegner's comments about the "intelligent and talented young" having only two choices, "frustration" or "escape," McAlmon's characters continually bemoan "the dullness of Wentworth" and fear they will "petrify" if they stay. If they stay, young men inherit professions from their fathers, find brakeman or locomotive engineer work on the railroad, or become salesclerks or traveling salesmen. Marriage, Normal School teacher training, and stenographic or secretarial work are the adult opportunities for most young women. Those of the "it" crowd who stay wear the mantle of "old-time young people," reflecting the cultural capital of the phrase.[47]

"*All Is So Still*" 235

In his novel *The High Plains*, set in early twentieth-century Alberta, Wilfrid Eggleston used fiction to track his own failed family homestead. In the form of a boy's adventure story, he created an alternate reality in which farming success came from understanding the true nature of the grasslands, not only "pioneer" hard work. Newly opened "all rolling prairie" lures the Barnes family—as it did the real Eggleston family—from England. In the character Eric, one reviewer recognized the "looking-glass portrait" of Eggleston, a well-known figure to Albertans long after he left for a Toronto journalism career. Foreshadowing the failure of the family's efforts, a classic northern grasslands blizzard almost kills the boy's father while he is walking to town to file, sight unseen, for a homestead at the nearest land office. The fictional and real family had trouble participating in consumer culture, let alone becoming "rich," "vain," and mediocre, like the self-satisfied residents of Lewis's Gopher Prairie. They afforded a mere shack and "free land" and earned loans and taxes. Yet when the Barnes family first glimpsed "Wolf Willow country," as Eggleston called the area, "the landscape seemed a beneficent one."[48]

A murder entwines with the family homestead story and the boy Eric's life choices. Someone shoots the Swede Olaf Bjornson and everyone suspects the "hermit" Sylvester Huck, who collects rocks and shells on long grasslands walks instead of farming. Eric Barnes plays a role in both helping Huck flee from the scarlet-coated Mounted Police across the border to Montana and in exonerating him, after Huck's arrest in Arizona. Neither the boy nor the man—in the end both suspected by Mounties—turn out to be guilty.

As Eric frees Huck through his detective work, Huck plays a role in releasing both Eric and his family from the failed homestead. Huck receives a several thousand-dollar government settlement for his unwarranted arrest, half of which he gives to Eric, who had early on told his parents he would not farm. The boy in turn provides a down payment on a new eighty-acre irrigated Alberta farm for his parents, which allows his older brother to return to farming. Meanwhile, Eric—similar to Eggleston at this point in his life—leaves to travel and plans maybe to go to "University some day."[49] The ending mirrors the real-life "Big Move Out" of southern Alberta in the 1920s, when many of those who settled on the semiarid short grasslands, including Eggleston's parents, left after years of drought.[50] Eggleston thought the provincial-backed irrigation project a type of restitution for the faulty official land policy that lured his parents to the grasslands.

The Canadian literary critic Dick Harrison classified Eggleston's novel as a "sentimental comedy" in the "popular" tradition, written counter to the works of grasslands realists who stressed alienation from the environment. Harrison suggested Eggleston presented the possibility of "harmony with nature" and did not "seriously challenge popular values either literary or moral."[51] The end of Eggleston's *High Plains*, however, makes clear the government's responsibility for opening up land for row-crop farming more properly deemed rangeland, thereby exonerating the family—specifically Eggleston's father. Racked by grief and internally conflicted, Eggleston used fiction to resolve the conflict over his attachment and his father's situation. One reviewer for the *Edmonton Journal* recognized "Alberta's dust-bowl" and characterized *The High Plains* as "the tragedy of a wasting land[,] the blighting effect on the people who have settled within its boundaries."[52] Wilfrid's sympathetic pain and resentment over his parents' failure resulting in difficult career prospects for himself comes across indirectly. The characters have limited depths of feeling, however, almost the opposite of the agony Eggleston felt.

Eggleston's parents never visited their actual homestead again (though they lived nearby), while Eggleston visited in the 1930s, the 1950s, and later.[53] *The High Plains* highlights Eggleston's attachment to the northern grasslands he experienced as a boy without decision-making responsibility. The overriding tone of his novel is joy—a type of cultural ownership of the space. Eric loves the prairie landscapes of southern Alberta and the "strange country down there near the border, like a miniature Painted Desert, such as they have in the Dakotas." More than anyone, Eric identifies with Huck, the retired geologist who, as a young man, had worked on the boundary survey between the United States and Canada. In "secret visits" Huck opens for Eric the "fascinating worlds of geology, astronomy, paleontology and archaeology." Huck is the man Eggleston wished he would have known while growing up.[54] Eggleston inhabited both the boy Eric, attached to the prairie but who refuses to farm, and the man Sylvester Huck, who understands intellectually and scientifically the northern grasslands and who has the knowledge Eggleston acquired by study.

Similar to Eggleston's *High Plains* family homestead story, Nell Wilson Parsons's novel *The Curlew Cried* entwines fiction with the history of her family move from rented land in Iowa to "the Saskatchewan plains between the American border and Regina" forty years before. In the novel Victoria, or "Tory," marries the farmer and horse breeder Lane Jarvis under a romantic haze of meeting him on a ship destined for Canada. The change from Englishwoman to "plainswoman" begins when both the name "Victoria" and the Belleek tea set she brought from England seem immediately out of place in a one-room shack. Parsons suggests the difference between the two newlyweds in their views of "rotting" snowdrifts. Victoria thinks "left-over signs of winter ugly and severe," and Lane thinks them "beautiful, the way they cuddled the ground." Almost leaving for England several times, including once with an old beau, Tory eventually decides she too will "grow with the country."[55]

The novel offers a more optimistic end to Parsons's family story, revealed in a memoir published twenty years later. The fictional family moves into a long-abandoned sod house, symbolically and promptly embraced by their daughter, nicknamed Pony. By the novel's end the soddy, with a "breath-taking vista of distance," also symbolizes Tory's adaptation to the grasslands. In reality Parsons's father died within a year after her parents quit an indebted homestead to rent a farm "up north [in the fertile belt], where crops have always been better." His death "haunted" the Normal School–trained Nell Wilson Parsons, who had vowed to send home part of her salary to save the homestead. Similar to Eggleston, Parsons also "felt tightly bound" to a place where she "had seen the fields carved out of raw prairie" and where she "knew every stone on the land" and "each remaining sagebrush." The novel weighs a daughter's need to understand the devastation her father felt over the loss of "his own acres." For Parsons, "grief [wa]s memories" of her father's "vanished dream."[56]

Wallace Stegner's *On a Darkling Plain* (1940) explores the same family homesteading experiences but focuses tightly on the effects of a boyhood spent on a southwestern Saskatchewan homestead on his intellectual development. On the surface Stegner's first full-length novel—his least favorite, never allowing it to be published again—centers on the existential struggles of a World War I veteran from British Columbia.[57] The character Vickers exiles himself to a "remote prairie" on the Montana border (the site of the Stegner homestead) and visits the village of "Whitemud" (the town of Eastend) some fifty miles north of the claim. Vickers's angst comes vaguely from war experiences in France and ill-defined modern forces of cultural conformity.[58] Scholars Richard Etulain and Jackson J. Benson argue, in Etulain's words, that Stegner's emphasis on "relationships between individuals and the community" aimed to demythologize an individualist West. On a deeper level *On a Darkling Plain* also allowed Stegner to work with boyhood memories of Saskatchewan's semiarid grasslands to explore his own 1930s inner turmoil about a place he felt marked him. He struggled to "accept" that experience.[59]

The novel's title came from a Matthew Arnold poem: "And we are here as on a darkling plain / Swept with confused alarms of struggle and flight." Vickers thinks the poem "matched, somehow, the way he felt and the country he lived in."[60] Vickers embodies both the boy Stegner experiencing the grasslands (projecting from memory) and the young writer Stegner contemplating that experience. Stegner bent age, time, and memory, switching and swapping his perspectives on place in one person. Eggleston toggled back and forth between the older man Huck and the boy Eric to work through the same feelings. Parsons struggled with similar thoughts and conveyed what she recalled from childhood and how she felt as a girl through the character Pony. She also portrayed what she understood from an adult perspective through Pony's mother, Tory, perhaps musing on perceptions of her mother's experiences on the homestead.

Stegner has Vickers consider the negatives of his childhood in the "lotus land" home of Vancouver. By having Vickers conclude his childhood in such a "green" vegetated place would be "too quiet, probably too sheltered. No chance to get hurt." "Too ready to lull the noises the mind made." Instead, Stegner suggested the benefits of his own "aloneness" in a grasslands childhood. A lush place like Vancouver

24. Wallace Stegner began teaching for Stanford University's creative writing program in 1945. Here, in 1951, Stegner sits at his typewriter in a study in the home he and his spouse, Mary Page Stegner, built in Los Altos Hills, California. An environmentalist and literature and history writer, Stegner won a Pulitzer Prize for his novel *Angle of Repose* (1971) and a National Book Award for the novel *The Spectator Bird* (1976). Original image © Art Frisch, housed at J. Willard Marriott Library, at the University of Utah. Used by arrangement with Brandt and Hochman Literary Agents, Inc.

sheltered a boy the way ash and maple trees sheltered the "lawn." Stegner later recalled that the actual sight of his "first lawn" in Great Falls, Montana, almost stunned him. He "stooped down and touched its cool nap in awe and unbelief." A moment of self-realization about the existence of a refined life he had not imagined came to him in a touch. Thick orderly grass might be safe but foreign and confining to one accustomed to a treeless grasslands aesthetic.[61]

The sun "blistered and crisped" grasses in Stegner's boyhood. At first the open grasslands made him feel unsafe, but he ultimately concluded that "the prairie taught me identity by exposing me," something a boy who grew up too protected might lack. At one point Vickers explains, "One thing was sure. There was no anonymity possible here. You got a good look at yourself." As critic Robert Thacker has pointed out, grasslands "landscape forces introspection."[62] In Stegner's later work, *Wolf Willow* (1962), set in the same land and town as *Darkling Plain*, green was the "color of safety." An adult Stegner felt sure that occasional lifelike dreams dominated by the most "brilliant metallic greens" represented the sheltering valley of the Whitemud River and a "jungly dead bend" created by a dam—a constructed place—which became his "sanctuary."[63] The vastness of the grasslands combined with a burrow for retreat he appeared to conclude offered rich developmental possibilities.

Stegner seemed to be working against negative "darkling" feelings. He wondered about the "deculturation" of settlers (and himself) on the northern grasslands. In *Darkling Plain* Stegner discussed self-hatred but softened to "self-contempt" in *Wolf Willow*. Thinking of his boyhood "utterly without" painting, sculpture, conversation, travel, libraries, bookstores, books, even language, and "almost without music or theater," he said, "I was charged with getting in a single lifetime, from scratch, what some people inherit as naturally as they breathe air." Similarly, Eric Barnes, Wilfrid Eggleston's character in *High Plains*, unaware "what he had lost in being reared on the crude frontier," feels transformed upon hearing a mere live pipe organ recital. Eggleston also referenced a grasslands cultural landscape "barren" of books, music, and art. He mail-ordered classics from Everyman's Library and art posters of "great masters" while working his way off the grasslands.[64] As Stegner phrased it, "the dream of the founders is often the dream of the full life as well as the dream of material success." As much as Stegner loved the grasslands, he thought it only "as good a place to be a boy and as unsatisfying a place to be a man." In the 1950s Stegner did not think it would be possible for the town of Eastend to go beyond "marginal or submarginal in its community and cultural life" because of ongoing depopulation.[65]

Stegner also felt industrialization and urbanization had eliminated a valuable part of the childhood experience. Ultimately, Stegner took solace in the time he spent with the "raw continent," which had given him knowledge and experiences useful in a world overrun with consumer materialism. Stegner and Eggleston argued that rural isolation mitigated cultural conformity, ironically because the lack of success prohibited conforming consumerism. Well on his way to becoming the environmentalist and preservationist for which he would become well known, Stegner felt lifelong ambivalence. As Canadian literary critic Dick Harrison argued, Vickers, as Stegner, remains attached to "the soil" but questioned "union with nature." As Vickers finds that the grass on his soddy's roof did not grow to "tie the soddy into the earth," Stegner realized his boyhood disappointment at his father's choice of an "ugly" tarpaper shack to be a fantasy. Parsons symbolized adaptation to the grasslands with a sod house. Stegner realized that, in transforming the grasslands to wheat lands, his family actually "convert[ed] it into the lamentable modern world."[66] A sod house would not have changed the central aim of the settler colonial endeavor especially as modern agriculture became increasingly industrial.

In *The Viking Heart* (1923) Icelandic-heritage Laura Goodman Salverson asks, What will the "rising generation," the descendants of Icelandic immigrants, contribute to the development of Canada?[67] Born in Winnipeg in 1890, Salverson charted three families and five children who settle first on marshy homesteads, though the fisheries of Iceland had not prepared them for peasant life. Most of her characters migrate to Winnipeg and its environs for education and work, leaving homesteads with little of the remorse and longing expressed by Stegner, Parsons, and Eggleston. The central characters, immigrants Borga and Bjorn Lindal, move to "good prairie land . . . with a timber house nearly new" close to a high school.

Salverson explored the burden Icelandic-heritage children felt to raise their ethnic group's stature beyond the "average Canadian" view of the Icelander as "some wild northern savage." An Icelandic minister in the community preaches that although a "few" will "lose" in the new country, "the greater part will succeed . . . because of the children and because of that indestructibility of Norse Character" which "will remain unchanged" even after they become Canadians. Icelandic children must be prosperous and contribute to the culture

25. Laura Goodman Salverson (pictured here, probably in the 1910s), born in Winnipeg to Icelandic immigrants, won two Canadian Governor General's Awards, the first in fiction for *The Dark Weaver* (1937) and the second in nonfiction for *Confessions of an Immigrant's Daughter* (1939). Laura Goodman Salverson fonds, Library and Archives Canada (1971-03, e010764581).

of Canada to "claim *a part* in this country." The character Thor, leaving for the battlefields of World War I, believes he "can best prove my Norse blood by honoring this country which is mine." Fellow North Dakotan Thorstina Jackson Walters argued Icelandic whiteness or "Viking blood and its pristine purity" would give "the best in the Icelandic racial inheritance to the adopted country." To Walters Icelanders belonged in Canada and the United States because the ancient sagas told that "Leif Ericsson and other Vinland heroes" became the first Europeans to visit North America. Influenced by racial theories of the early twentieth century that question the fitness of some immigrants, Walters argued that Icelanders strengthened settler-colonial whiteness on the continent.[68]

Of the children in the fictional Lindal family, two are the critic Diane Quantic's "strong" children: Elizabeth becomes a successful fashion designer, and Thor, a surgeon, dies in World War I. The red-haired, most beautiful Ninna, a Quantic "weak" pioneer child, marries wealth and disowns her family. Balder, born lame, becomes a renowned solo violinist, bringing honor to the Icelandic community. Neighbor Tomi, who survives World War I, builds a successful construction company during a Winnipeg boom. Successful career contributions tie these children and their parents to Canada.[69] Walters's history mirrored Salverson's fiction in its list of "successful" children of Icelandic "pioneers" to the northern grasslands, who rose to "eminent position in their own chosen work," from agriculture, medicine, law, and engineering to music, poetry, painting, and sculpture.[70]

Salverson and Walters in their respective genres suggest Icelandic children led the adaptation of the parental generation to the northern grasslands. When Salverson's character Thor decides to serve in World War I, Borga begins to think of "Canada as a dear and precious possession." She tells Thor that hard work has kept her from "time to think of Canada as a country." It had been "wilderness" and "prairie" and "then—a farm." "This is your country, Mother," argues Thor. Salverson presaged the adaptation of the parental generation by having an Icelandic woman at a community event reflect casually, "It's strange how there seems to be something here to bind one." Borga's close Icelandic friend, Finna, responds, "Why, I declare, it's a long time now since I had to watch my rubbers—you know how it was with rubbers in the muddy days. It's even the mud here has a love for me, I used to tell my Einar, its sticks so!"[71] Land—symbolized here by soil, a prominent and historical metaphor—for immigrants, Salverson suggested, means both regional adaptation and national affiliation, whether Canadian or American. Writing a novel or a history, as Salverson and Walters did, respectively, paralleled the achievements of the characters they sketched. The two women's achievements aligned with the same cultural aspiration valued by Stegner and Eggleston, to which their literary and historical works also contributed.

McAlmon, Eggleston, Stegner, Parsons, and Salverson wrote to work out intellectual problems related to aesthetic crafting for the northern grasslands and to consider relationships with regional environments, homesteading, pioneer immigrant parents, and quality-of-life issues. Together these writers commented on popular "pioneer" tales by making known their own generation's alternate Grasslands West stories. If not rising to artistic heights, these examples explore complex feelings rendered in at least some insightful turns of phrases, metaphors, and imagery that—eagerly read by their regional counterparts—helped the grasslands-grown generation of settler society lay claim to space by expressing sense of place.

Placing the Northern Grasslands in Literature

Robert McAlmon's (unsuccessful) struggle to create modern literature using the northern grasslands is suggestive for what it might reveal generally about a generation struggling to assert place identity through literature and is therefore worth examining more closely. He unmistakably portrayed a grasslands or prairies and plains or Western place, although, according to his biographer Sanford Smoller, he "was not a regionalist."[72] McAlmon probably would have resisted the label "regionalist," but only because he wanted to create a distinctly national literature, prose in which critics accepted grasslands locations and peoples as representative of "American" culture. Nevertheless, he had some belief that geography influenced the physical, emotional, and intellectual senses that produced modern perceptions. In *Village* Peter Reynalds (McAlmon's alter ego) spouts off to his friends that he "will live out my own temperament . . . because it's more interesting than letting a set of social conventions which change with every *generation* and *geographical* situation dictate one's actions."[73] The reference to generation can be read as part of McAlmon's sense of being a part of a "Young America"—the modernists in New York City and the Paris expatriates with whom he would come to associate—and creating new modern literature to contrast with European and nineteenth-century forms.[74] His reference to geography is more enigmatic. McAlmon had insight that transcending literary conventions might require both checking and drawing on forces of geographic determinism. Throwing off—or reorganizing—select elements of place embedded in established forms and topics might allow for the creation of new literary forms.

McAlmon's works did not become well known until the late twentieth century, and then mostly in academic circles, so his influence on a northern grasslands literary tradition has been almost nonexistent. Generally, critics have seen him as "no more than a footnote to twentieth-century literature."[75] Scholars still debate why his work did not reach a wider audience. Most of his poems, novels, and short stories, with a few exceptions, came out in limited number by his own publishing company.[76] Few people but the avant-garde read his work, in part, because U.S. customs authorities seized (under obscenity laws) most of the books McAlmon published. Additionally, literary jealousies, competitiveness, and sexual-identification innuendo and homophobia led to divides between McAlmon and F. Scott Fitzgerald and his old friend Ernest Hemingway, at a moment when McAlmon had his best chance to sign with their publisher, Scribner's.[77]

Nevertheless, most of the major writers and the arts communities of the Paris expatriates and New York City's Greenwich Village found the Dakotan Robert McAlmon promising. The writer William Carlos Williams, who knew McAlmon in the early twenties (both his age and the period) as part of bohemian New York, described him as an "abortive genius who believed good writing driven home would do much to make life worth living." Williams noted McAlmon's "fearless[ness] in his attack on false standards." Critics debated at the time and since whether laziness, carelessness, talent, bad luck, ill timing; impatience with and an artistic prohibition against revision; or problems of the literary establishment held back McAlmon. Sanford Smoller suggested the then current "standards of judgment" gave less value to the aspects on which McAlmon shined: "subject matter, content, statement" as opposed to "polished style, precise word choice, intricate forms, and well-wrought structures."[78]

Regardless of critics, McAlmon saw himself as part of a new wave of American modern literary expression. In 1920, after wandering from Minneapolis and the Dakotas to Winnipeg and California (where his mother moved after his father died), McAlmon headed east to New York City. Growing since the 1890s, the Greenwich Village community by 1910 had "made modernity local and concrete, tangible to a popular American audience" throughout the continent, according to historian Christine Stansell. Despite the many "portraits of stultifying communities" in the hinterlands, argued Stansell, many small towns boasted a "high-minded provincial life." At places where Populism among other reform movements found support, "serious and varied culture sometimes thrived" and even took in trends issuing forth from bohemia New York.[79] Indeed, McAlmon likely would have heard his older activist sister discuss Progressive farm and labor politics.[80] Themes in his prose—especially property relations—suggest grasslands politics influenced his thought.

McAlmon's attraction to the bohemian crowd probably surprised few, but the steps that took him to the Paris expatriate community to found a publishing company did surprise his family and friends. Soon after his arrival in New York, he met and married a wealthy British steamship heir and poet-writer, Bryher, or Winifred Ellerman, already partnered with American poet H.D., or Hilda Doolittle. The marriage of convenience (and a generous allowance) allowed McAlmon to set up Contact Publishing in Paris, while Bryher went off to Switzerland and Italy a freer woman.[81] In Paris McAlmon became part of the literary scene.

McAlmon was hard to place: from where did he draw his content? Observers sometimes located McAlmon awkwardly in the Middle West tradition of new writing flowering in the first decades of the twentieth century. His work did embody some of the themes identified by the

26. Dakota- and Minnesota-raised writer Robert McAlmon (*left*) met the poet and writer William Carlos Williams and his spouse, Florence "Flossie," in 1920 through the Greenwich Village literary crowd of New York City. The two men quickly became friends over a shared writerly philosophy, though Williams was thirteen years McAlmon's senior. William Carlos Williams with Flossie Williams and Robert McAlmon, 1921, folder 1476, box 70, series 4, Beinecke Digital Collections, Beinecke Rare Book and Manuscript Library, Yale University; used by permission of the William Carlos Williams Estate, in care of the Jean V. Naggar Literary Agency, Inc. (permissions@jvnla.com).

literary scholar Ronald Weber as key to the "Midwestern moment" for literature, such as "the loss of a natural pastoral life, village mediocrity, escape to the city in search of the fullness of life, [and] rural returns touched with feelings of nostalgia, guilt, and superiority."[82] McAlmon, however, filled his stories with people from homesteading railroad towns in the Grasslands West. His colleagues seem to have understood his orientation as part of a new, beyond-the–East Coast, Middle America writing tradition that included Ernest Hemingway and Sinclair Lewis but also knew that McAlmon's work did not compare exactly in style or content. William Carlos Williams referred to McAlmon's main subjects as "the prairies and western towns."[83]

Although Ford Maddox Ford, the writer and editor of the short-lived Paris journal *Transatlantic Review*, famously classified McAlmon as "one of the worst American writers" he met in Paris, a McAlmonauthored story appeared in the first issue of that journal as a part of the tradition of "that West-Middle-West-by-West of which we have been taught to and *do* expect so much." The magazine added the disclaimer "though geography is not our strongest point" before identifying McAlmon's region. Ford also credited "the real germ of the Middle Western literary movement" in part to McAlmon's Contact Publishing. McAlmon's personal work seems to have represented something unique that at least Ford had trouble placing.[84]

McAlmon identified in part with the prairies and plains. Most scholars suggest that McAlmon's fiction about the "wild and dreary plains state," as the author once referred to the South Dakota of his boyhood, captured "the cadence of the prairie." Much of his work, according to Edward Lorusso, grew from his "memories of the wild prairies and the spare people who lived there."[85] Thinking about the body of his work in 1938, McAlmon recalled, "French commentators found me most American when writing of our land."[86] William Carlos Williams had described McAlmon's characters as "refreshingly new as literary creations": rural people of the grasslands (or the sexual underworld of Berlin) little represented in literature. In an interview McAlmon said, "I would rather write upon farming" than art.[87] Sounding very much the grasslands grown boy, he once told Williams, "A lump of dirt is liver [i.e., more alive] than a poor work of art, it will grow seeds."[88] Although he did not join a "regionalist" movement in the 1920s or 1930s, McAlmon—had his work been available to be read—might have made a contribution to the then burgeoning focus on regional cultures, much as critics saw William Faulkner's novels contributing to a modern rendering of the South, regional and national at the same time.[89]

A telling letter exchange between William Carlos Williams and McAlmon suggests some of what McAlmon might have struggled against in the publishing world. Williams referred to an unnamed text in a personal letter to McAlmon, chastising the latter's apparent ignorance of cows: "Look it up in any encyclopedia," Williams wrote. "You're a hell of a farmer. Didn't you ever hear of a cow giving 30 qts of milk, really?" He went on to explain that forty or even sixty quarts might come from a "good cow." Williams eventually answered his own inquiry, realizing, "I guess you only knew those half starved western wire-grass eating hat-racks." Indeed.[90]

No one questioned McAlmon's almost photographic depictions of places, people, and animals, yet sometimes McAlmon's work *seemed* not to ring true to his limited literary audience. McAlmon wanted to capture immediacy, in-the-moment occurrences and feelings, "as simple and pure as a recording machine."[91] Hemingway observed McAlmon's documentary impulse to be the central flaw of his fiction: "Mac worked too close to life." Hemingway felt, "You had to digest life and then create your own people."[92] An encyclopedia of the period may have even proved McAlmon's perceptions of cows to be "false," but not because he did not get the amount of milk produced correct but because his experiences with northern grasslands agriculture had not been incorporated yet into an accumulation of knowledge about American places.

A better crafting by McAlmon might have convinced a discerning reader such as Williams, but to have experiences outside the mainstream meant facing an inequality of ignorance. A professional editor could have worked with McAlmon to excise arguably obscene material for publication in the United States and to insist on the authorial "discipline" and "methods" of "artistic excellence" that even his friends thought he lacked. Perhaps the literary establishment did not know what it did not know.[93] McAlmon might have been part of an emerging modern literary Grasslands West if the mainstream could have heard the margins speaking.

McAlmon's emphasis on Scandinavian immigrants, for example, mirrors the Nebraska author Willa Cather's on the Bohemian Czechs of Nebraska. One of McAlmon's earliest unpublished short stories focuses on the farm-raised, "light-fingered" but heavy-on-her-feet "Nancy," who joyed at milking the cows and cleaning the stable; and Olaf, the "rugged faced," "big hulk" who enjoyed eating "corn beef and cabbage."[94] The short story spoke to common modern themes of consumerism and city lure but also to immigrant youth, rural culture, and real ambivalence about the countryside felt by the young people he knew in South Dakota and those he encountered in Minneapolis.

Friends most supportive of McAlmon seemed to sense his difference. In an essay published in the early 1930s, Ezra Pound used McAlmon as a case with which to criticize American publishers. The "bit of unwanted honesty that divides say McAlmon from Sinclair Lewis, and makes the latter so acceptable to the boob, whose recognized limitations he portrays, without pulling the gaff on something that affects personal vanity."[95] Responding to McAlmon's first published collections of short stories and poetry, Williams—perhaps unconsciously using regional terms—spoke about McAlmon's "antelope-like tenderness." He noted in particular the "cold sparkle of snow" in some of McAlmon's airplane poems, part of McAlmon's modern rendition of a big sky. Generally, thought Williams, "snow is all through the best part of your work in the poem book." "Here is a cold, modern style," said Williams, "bred of an attack capable of absorbing, not from a window but from the round of a circle in the open, anything in modern life pressing upon it." In another insightful remark about McAlmon's earliest work, Williams noted, "Your observation is most accurate where there is pleasure to you in the detail."[96]

Detail would be a mark of the prairie eye that learned to see in all that vastness. The literary critic Diane Quantic has suggested the "deceptively simple prose [of grasslands writing] gathers emotional power from accumulated detail until the image, the attending metaphor, and the deeper symbol become apparent."[97] Stegner's "curly" buffalo shortgrass "secretly" held "tight to the earth's skin," and his "sun walked the sky with interminable fussy slowness, like a man with a flashlight searching every blade of grass." Wilfrid Eggleston's poetry zoomed in on a single tree and one large rock; North Dakota poet Clell Gannon, on particular flowers. The comments by the older mentor Williams to the struggling McAlmon seem to get at the conundrum of details in the vastness that marks the resident versus the "passers," or, as Stegner would call the tourist, the "denizen." After time with him in Paris, Williams noted how McAlmon still seemed to keep "his own western manners and counsels."[98]

The writer Kay Boyle defended McAlmon the longest. Although she grew up in Ohio, her little-educated mother had been raised on Kansas grasslands. Despite her mother's bad health, Boyle claimed that she "prevailed, while the men of the family were effaced, line by line, a little more every year." Boyle never suggested a grasslands connection to McAlmon, but the shared history would have been there for her to see more in his work than for other critics.[99]

Northern grasslands authors of this generation sought to create new imagery to match the new storylines of a modern postfrontier world. No small task. To reach national literary achievement, aspiring grasslands writers had to shift to modern forms and subjects (still in the process of formulation) and create grasslands literary imagery that also refracted the new forms to reveal both common and particular experiences of grasslands landscapes. Works had to provide more than mere accurate descriptions that evoked authentic landscape, a task with which explorers and travelers long struggled. Grasslands fiction needed to convey sense of place: landscape and feelings, with a tangle of humanity and environment.

The Canadian prairie scholar Dick Harrison noted the place's authors "lacked the verbal traditions upon which literature builds." Writers also confronted what Thacker called "the imaginative demands of prairie space" and how to weave these compulsions into prevailing international forms. Thacker described Willa Cather's career as a classic example of "the western native ever struggling with the imaginative demands of western space." "Seemingly understood" to those who grew up in the environment, the feelings evoked remained still "strange and daunting . . . [and] ever at odds with conventional esthetics."[100]

Writers wrestled to convey grasslands senses of place. Writing about the aesthetic-artistic struggle was indeed part of a tradition that spoke to what critic Diane Quantic called the "psychological significance of open space."[101] Wallace Stegner claimed growing up on the grasslands "scored" the "geography" into him, making him respond for life to its "colors and shapes."[102] *Darkling Plain* references the artistic struggle quite openly. World War I veteran Vickers explains, "That is the magnificence of this country. It takes my breath sometimes, the sweep of it. But I can't get a flash of it into poetry that satisfies me," he felt; it was "an image too big for him." North Dakota poet Clell Gannon expressed the same: "All is so still—so big, I scarce can speak. . . . I only dare to think / Such thoughts as have no counterpart in words." McAlmon captured the challenge of perception: a young man "stood looking at the grassy prairie stretched rollingly horizonward on all sides of him," pondering the question, "Was the horizon father away, or nearer to him, because of the endlessness of space." He desired that the "wideness of space . . . fuse into his intuitions."[103]

Grasslands writers frequently described the space of the place as all-encompassing. Stegner described grasslands circling "out around, stretching in all directions from the benches to become coextensive with the disk of the world." Nell Wilson Parsons wrote of the "blinding grayness" of a storm, "no distance, only a gray wall that was land and sky in one." The roar of a creek "blended land and sky" and blue flax blossoms merged with blue sky. McAlmon wondered as he "looked to the edge of the earth / where horizon cuts it short. / If I walked that far and stepped off / I might never stop falling."[104] As would-be literary artists struggled to place the grasslands in prose and poetry, they struggled to find publishers.

The publishing scene and potential audience on the northern grasslands would have been notably sparse and unattractive to New York City and major publishers. As late as 1962, Wallace Stegner explained, "all the forces of culture and snobbery are against your *writing* by ear and making contact with your own natural audience. Your natural audience, for one thing, doesn't read—it isn't an audience." He lamented what he saw as the "deculturation" process of declining populations. The Alberta painter Annora Brown felt a similar isolation living in western Canada away from the "larger cultural centres"; she stressed a lack of community from which she might have the "benefit of constructive criticism by recognized authorities."[105] Publishers found the sparseness of the northern grasslands population with a small committed literary or artistic audience unattractive markets.

The second regional problem involved eastern literary institutional culture. McAlmon showed an early distain toward the publishing establishment when he explained in a letter to William Carlos Williams, "The idea of contact simply means that when one writes they write about something, and not to write 'literature' because it is a day of publications and publishing houses." As early as 1921, it seems

McAlmon expected to have trouble publishing his fictional portraits of northern grasslands settler society. Stegner felt "pain" and "fatal division" writing from the hinterlands. He suggested the "language of literature" learned in school seemed "unreal" because his life had always been separate. Willa Cather too felt defensive about the eastern establishment's lack of interest in the grasslands as subject matter. Yet the East of cultural criticism and acceptance pulled her to it.[106]

Modern critic Robert Thacker argued that Cather's ambivalence came from being "schooled to see the East as cultural mecca." She knew her choice of Nebraska as a setting for literature would be seen as "distinctly déclassé" by other writers. Apparently, after she published *O Pioneers!* in 1913 someone asked her, "How did you come to write about that flat part of the prairie west, . . . which not many people find interesting?" Worse, one New York critic wrote, "I simply don't care a damn what happens in Nebraska, no matter who writes about it." But residents of Cather's generation did desire a fiction set in towns and on farms and with the little details she related. Cather's literary crafting of space in settler fiction, even if partially romanticized, showed a grasslands place emergent in national culture—a project far different than vernacular "pioneer origin" stories.[107] The daily *New York Times* did publish a review of Stegner's 1943 *The Big Rock Candy Mountain*, set in part on the northern grasslands of Saskatchewan (where Vickers homesteaded in *On a Darkling Plain*). Although the reviewer called the novel "impressive," he also criticized Stegner's "jot-trot, homespun prose . . . monotonous without grace or bite or evidence of a particular personality."[108] Critic Diane Quantic has suggested the literary tradition of "direct and plain" Great Plains writing has been "often dismissed as facile or simple-minded" rather than accepted as a language of "concise, direct prose" that reflects "writers' visions of plains space."[109]

Laura Goodman Salverson, in a foreword to a 1947 edition of *Viking Heart*, mentioned struggling against "indifference to the Canadian scene."[110] Boston's Houghton Mifflin Company published the state guides produced by the Works Progress Administration's Writers Projects of the New England states in the 1930s. Washington DC authorities, however, told the South Dakota guide director that "no commercial publisher would touch North or South Dakota without a financial subsidy." In 1948 an official at the University of Minnesota Press bemoaned distribution problems in the Dakotas, though one of their regional titles "sold by the thousands" in both North Dakota and South Dakota. Accordingly, the press sold the book through "dry-goods stores, drug stores, and general stores which had never handled a book before." Apparently, whether true or not, "the Press [thought it] discovered once more that there is not a single real bookstore in the whole two states."[111] Similar to McAlmon, Stegner wanted his regional narrative to have both national critical acclaim and regional readership. As late as the early 1970s, Stegner claimed to be "testing" the establishment by keeping no residence in New York. He had been told that, by staying out of New York, he would be classified *only* as a "regional writer."[112] Despite national prizes, in the 1990s, according to one biographer, still only about one in ten Americans had even heard of the novelist and environmentalist Wallace Stegner.[113]

Settler Society, Aesthetics, and Indigeneity

The artistic expression of the grasslands-grown generation asserted regional rootedness and showed settler colonialism advancing beyond the expropriation of physical land into the realm of cultural claim. When Stegner, Eggleston, McAlmon, Salverson, Parsons, Gannon, and others embedded the grasslands and family-related experiences in their literary works, they began to "transfer" the region discursively to settler society in the United States and Canada.[114] These artistic evocations bound a broader settler population to common narratives, whether or not critics deemed them of literary value.

A collective claim to a grasslands sense of place can be seen in the turn among the postpioneer generations to words such as *our*, *my*, and *mine* when referring to particular locations and using *indigenous* and *native* as self-referential terms. When the Albertan Wilfrid Eggleston spoke of the fiction of writers Willa Cather and Hamlin Garland, he thought, "Here is the west: *our* Canadian west as well as the American west: *not as aliens* have seen it in transient visits, but as painted by a *native*, a *native* with the necessary vision and the necessary skill."

North Dakotan Clell Gannon's poem "This Land Is Mine" and his words in another poem "all of my plains" and "my prairies" assert the same settler sense of possession. Ownership comes from knowing the land's "sweet perfume," "pungent scent," and "spicy air," wrote Gannon. Waxing on over "these prairies . . . so wide, so vast," the character Thor in Salverson's *Viking Heart* tells his mother, "This is my own, my native land." In the foreword to a 1947 edition of the novel, Salverson thanked readers for "their belief in native talent."[115]

Moreover, the unconscious impulse to declare settler northern grasslands experiences as *native* showed itself in art beyond literature. A talk the Albertan painter Annora Brown gave to the Lethbridge Sketch Club emphasized the need of "close observation of the landscape of *one's own* country." One correspondent praised Brown's agricultural paintings, singling out "the animate browns of the wheat fields . . . a glowing tribute to the Western coloring so intensified by *our* distances and *our* atmosphere" and remarking, "It requires very great courage to paint the actual tones of Western scenery." The reviewer thought a "sketch of wolf willow, laden with white berries, in the moonlight, casting bluish shadows on the white snow" proved to be her "outstanding picture" and asked, "Who has not marked . . . the imagery of the wolf willow?" This reporter responded more skeptically to another painting, saying, "We are wont to regard the elevator as a graceless utilitarian thing." Yet the reporter gave Brown credit: "It is a Canadian skyline, and deserves a place in *our* art."[116]

Brown's contemporaries hungered for the imagery she produced. Although he wrote at the height of his literary crafting of the northern grasslands in *Wolf Willow*, Wallace Stegner ran out of words to convey sunlight: the sky over the grasslands produced "a light to set a painter wild, a light pure, glareless, and transparent." A column that Bismarck-born George Will wrote about the advent of fall season noted how the "colors, too, are beginning to run riot over the landscape . . . the most brilliant of the whole year." Will asked, as if words failed him, "Have you ever stopped a moment near sundown and tried to distinguish and describe to yourself the various colors present in the spectacle?" "Actually," he paused with a second thought, "a painting which faithfully depicted them would be criticized as fantastic and

27. Artist and poet Clell Gannon, here standing in 1923 on a huge rock formation near Grassy Butte, frequently hiked the landscapes of North Dakota. State Historical Society of North Dakota (00200-4x5-c-00189).

exaggerated." Dakotan Clell Gannon suggested the same, citing spring rains that "colored" the grasslands so dramatically that "it smells of paint."[117] The creative labor to depict light, color, and tone mirrored the literary struggle of northern grasslands–fiction authors to find appropriate literary imagery accepted by critics who little acknowledged the nuances the northern grasslands region might contribute, even demand, to represent the place's aesthetic environmental sensibility accurately—from the settler society's perspective.

The northern grasslands formed only a case study of the general continental situation. The modernist turn in literature aimed to convey "America"—the United States and Canada—in culture and speech. Intellectuals across North America and in expatriate Paris in the interwar period criticized American social life generally for its "emotional and aesthetic starvation." Such critics spoke of an America "still in the embryonic stage" of cultural development.[118] Perhaps this turn in literary culture to what modernist writers thought of as "native" also suggests little-noted, long, and buried reverberations of longer-established settler-colonial claims still pulsing down the generations and across the continent in regional forms.

Dakotan McAlmon, who, according to his peers "remained unmistakably American in speech and spirit," definitely hoped to encourage the type of indigeneity expressed by his northern grasslands regional contemporaries, but on the level of the continent.[119] When McAlmon moved to New York City in 1920, he had endorsed a concept he called "contact," the title of both a short-lived "little" magazine he founded with William Carlos Williams and, later, his Paris publishing company.[120] The magazine, according to its credo, desired to publish "art" representative of "indigenous . . . experience and relations." The two men expressed "faith in the existence of native artists" and wanted no "hangovers from past generations." Instead, *Contact* would foreground "native work" and "insist" on "the essential contact between words and the locality that breeds them, in this case America."[121]

Regionalists in the interwar years, with an "emphasis on *place*," most directly turned to contemporary Indigenous peoples for alternative social traditions that might mitigate standardization, consumerism, and conformity.[122] But aspiring modernist authors proved less conscious or even remained unconscious of how their fiction and poetry competed with and worked to further displace, on the plane of cultural claim, Indigenous nations from the same space. Erasing Indigenous peoples completely, citing an "invasion" of continental space only by consumer culture, Carl Van Doren referred to a novel that conveyed the "black fertile land" that "fate" had "given" Europeans when discussing the "Revolt from the Village" of small-town writers in 1921.[123] Some modernists demonstrated a rudimentary understanding that their literary claim to America *related*, if not contributed, to the dispossession of Indigenous nations living across North America. South Dakota novelist Robert McAlmon consigned Indigenous peoples to reservations inside his region as the emergent postsettlement young generation rose to create new "American" culture.[124] His friend Kay Boyle suggested the United States needed "to snap out of the red Indian open spaces stage" of (Western) mythology. Such myths of "open space" had kept the population from realizing "it had ugly houses and hideous towns and little music and no painting." Only someone who grew up in a settler colonial society, however, would analogize that experience to expatriate 1920s Paris. "A great mob of Americans are becoming settlers here, indicating how impossible that dear country is," McAlmon wrote the English poet Bryher in 1923.[125] Reality pulsed underneath critiques of myth and consumerism.

The scholar Bryce Conrad interprets William Carlos Williams's 1925 *In the American Grain* as an argument for creative writers to "giv[e] themselves full to place." American environments could become the source for breaking with English tradition and nineteenth-century literary forms. Authors must "marry the ground." In *American Grain* Williams described Daniel Boone as one who figured out, "If the land were to be possessed it must be as the Indian possessed it." He imagined Boone always seeking "to bathe in, . . . to see, to feel, to touch" the land. Considering explorer Juan Ponce de León, Williams acknowledged the conquest of North America "begins for us with murder and enslavement, not with discovery." But even in Williams's day newcomers had yet to know the land. Through Boone, Williams viewed Indigenous cultures as the "natural expression of the place, the Indian himself as 'right,' the flower of his world." Williams argued that newcomers needed to become such flowers, not simply that "Indians" romantically lived one with or as part of nature. Rather, American literature would emerge only when writers looked to the ground. "No, we are not Indians but we are men of *their* world"—or should be, he suggested.[126]

Through fictional works, poetry, and paintings, the first grasslands-grown generations of settler society created an aesthetic sensibility and new storylines for a newly conceived northern grasslands region. Their creative works conveyed a sense of place through realistic details and feelings of space by mixing memories and settler-society social experiences. These artists made the experience of native grasslands habitats transferable over the generations through literature and multiple art forms. This aesthetic expression in literature, poetry, and art—alongside more problematic "pioneer origin" stories—spoke to settler society's cultural claim to space in which Indigenous peoples persisted.[127] Cultural contests over the grasslands continued in this generation under new terms and concepts of place, aesthetics, and indigeneity.

7

"Surely, Grass Is the Great Mother of All Plains Agriculture"

Agricultural Adaptation and Grasslands Conservation

"The wind and dust were terrible," Elsie May Hammond recorded in a 1930s version of the grasslands tradition of pairing earth and sky. The "noise" of the wind struck her. Hammond made this diary entry in May 1932, a week after she and her nephew "put in 142 Caragana cuttings" designed to break the flow of the wind (and dust) on their Saskatchewan ranch. "The top blew off one of the big trees and 2 or 3 young trees were blown down." The ranch-farm system the Hammonds had configured on the semiarid grasslands near Maple Creek soon withered in the 1930s agricultural distress: "Hot again and dry," "very windy and dusty," and "still hot and dry," she wrote regularly during June 1933. "Wont last long if rain does not come soon," she recorded at the end of July, explaining, "We had to haul all water from the spring last week as both creeks are dry." Two days after touring the crops in August 1934, Elsie Hammond began to harvest weeds. "Got two wagon loads and scattered them for sheep and cows," she wrote, describing a chore once saved for oats. Since the 1890s the Hammonds had acquired additional land and modern machinery. The family over time raised horses, cows, sheep, and chickens and grew wheat, rye, and oats, as well as garden produce to sell with eggs and cream in town.[1] These products spoke to the Hammond family's efforts to adapt commercial agriculture to the northern grasslands during the prime of Elsie Hammond's life.

As so many northern grasslands agricultural operations, the Hammond ranch suffered in the 1930s, after adapting and enduring drought through many years in the 1920s, but emerged again in the

1940s. During the prime of the lives of the grasslands-grown families, settler-society communities struggled to transition to both modern "power" agriculture and to adapt agricultural life and methods to the northern grasslands environment. Many would-be permanent residents left in the 1910s, the 1920s, and the 1930s.[2] Yet many families remained, perhaps because they, like the Hammonds, owned significant acreage. Many residents "loved their land," even though "they were increasingly less secure on it." They were "willing to do all that was humanly possible to save it."[3] Residents who experienced the grasslands during these decades grew knowledge that bettered their understanding and appreciation of the northern grasslands as ecological and agricultural space.

Many grasslands-grown individuals of settler society during the prime of their lives aimed in diverse ways to solve prairie and plains problems. They desired to institutionalize a culture where profitable farm and ranch operations gave them prosperous lives and where wild grasslands, in decreasing proportions, existed for recreation and aesthetic pleasures. Individuals from this generation of settler society made a living in tough agricultural times or worked through science to help their neighbors succeed in diversified farm-ranch operations. Many of them also sought to bring awareness to native grasslands habitats by teaching Nature Study to school children, explaining ecology to adults, and preserving grasslands, wetlands, and forest habitats. By the middle of the twentieth century, the place—the natural environment—on the ground level appeared to these generations of settler society as a remix of elements favoring grain and graze lands over native grasslands.

Agricultural Adaptation

A transformative process on the northern grasslands that saw settlers pushing the limits of unaided agriculture became more complicated with the advent of World War I. Canada joined the war in 1914 and the United States in 1917. High commodity prices, rising land values (then, during the recession and drought of the 1920s, falling land values), new machinery, and encouragement to grow food to "win the war" gave impetus to farmers to mechanize and expand agricultural acreage. On "the northern Great Plains especially," wrote George Will in 1930, "power farming" had resulted in "very much larger acreages handled per man, and hence much larger farms." Even after the release of the smaller, lighter Fordson tractor in 1917, however, mechanization continued slowly. In North Dakota by 1920, for example, only about 17 percent of farmers owned a tractor; a decade later still only almost half of all farms in the state worked with tractors. Drought continued to travel through the northern grasslands, stopping at spots throughout, particularly in the first half of the 1920s. South Dakota's innovative Rural Credits loan program foreclosed on farms west of the Missouri River. When combined with international commodity-price problems, agriculturists slowed expenditures. In 1926 Saskatchewan recorded only 26,700 tractors for 119,451 farms. The goals and plans for mechanization of many agricultural operations waited for money, better weather, and higher prices, but, as Will explained, "reasonable prevision" predicted the "beginning of a new era in agriculture."[4]

Although tractor use slowed—and even declined over the 1930s in Alberta—agricultural historians have called the magnitude of these changes, apparent after 1945, the "Great Disjuncture."[5] North Dakota led the way: by then the state had a tractor for every farm and a truck for half the state's farms, if not on every farm, the highest number of any state. In South Dakota three-fourths of farmers owned tractors, although half of all farms still used horses. Historian Gerald Friesen suggested that, with the late 1940s "tractor explosion" in the Canadian prairies, agriculture "changed so much as to be almost unrecognizable to the pioneer." Elsie Hammond and her new husband, Joe Thomas, purchased a new-to-them John Deere tractor in 1942, but the Hammond family, as most families—if they hung on—spent part of the 1920s and most of the 1930s adjusting, struggling, and scheming to stay or leave.[6]

Those families who remained in the grasslands countryside continued expanding the acreage of their operations. Indeed, many expanded almost immediately after arriving, if they could. Settlers had claimed government land using multiple laws; soon their children who turned eighteen in Canada and twenty-one in the United States claimed their own government parcels. Others purchased land from rail and land companies and from the Hudson's Bay Company in Canada. In the 1920s and 1930s, departing neighbors became sources for additional purchased or rented land, creating a new agricultural business model, the "owner-tenancy," a situation in which a farmer or rancher both owned and rented land to make a viable operation.[7] Despite a struggling environment and economy, records show farm size grew across the transnational northern grasslands. The average farm size (of owned land) grew from 466 acres in North Dakota in 1920 to 600 acres by 1945. South Dakota agricultural operators owned similar acreages. Saskatchewan landowners averaged only 432 acres per farm in 1941, but operations "increased dramatically" there and in Alberta and Manitoba over the next four decades.[8]

Thorstina Jackson Walters, who grew up on a Pembina County farm in North Dakota, described continual outmigration in the state's Icelandic farming communities. Many immigrants' grown children, including herself and her husband, left the eastern Dakotas, Saskatchewan, and Manitoba to pursue other fields of work. She saw the coming of age of "young people of Icelandic extraction" who wanted to leave as part of the remedy for shifts in agriculture that encouraged expanded crop production. The need to expand required many to leave farming. The grasslands grown of settler society "took over the farms of those who went away," even if they hated to see the departure of neighbors. According to Walters's calculations, Icelandic family layouts grew from about 320 acres to 640 acres during this early twentieth-century period.[9]

The Miller family's operation grew large the same way in Montana. Lillian Miller's brothers expanded from the quarter-section ranch their father purchased to one of many thousands of acres. Until the early twentieth century, the Millers had grazed their initial eight hundred sheep on "free range" from Chinook, Montana, north to the Canadian border. The Millers purchased land from "old squaw men," as Lillian termed some of her neighbors who married Indigenous women, strategically acquiring parcels along creeks. They also took advantage of the U.S. "desert claim" law. In the 1930s her brothers purchased additional ranches acquired by the Federal Land Bank after homesteaders who came around 1910 failed. The family also leased reservation land near the Milk River, some of which they once used to graze their cattle without paying a fee.[10] Meanwhile, by the 1920s Montanan Peggy Olson Bell lived on a modest ranch near Sand Coulee.[11]

Both Lillian Miller and Thorstina Jackson Walters described a common generational shift in decision-making power regarding land use. The younger generation, Walters argued, "rather than their parents . . . felt that new farming equipment was necessary to improve and increase production."[12] Similarly, western North Dakotan Norris Hagen recalled that his father secured a Federal Land Bank loan in 1923 to buy a tractor, after "the boys finally convinced" him. The man lost everything, defaulting by 1939, but two sons nevertheless began a new "venture" in "large-scale farming." They lived on the original home base (on which the government allowed the family to remain as renters) and soon purchased and rented "many abandoned farms in the country."[13] Over many decades to the other side of 1945, the Hagen family shifted to the next generation and power farming.

In Saskatchewan, for some years, four Neatby siblings stayed on the land. Their parents and half of the siblings moved to town. The two oldest daughters, Edith and Margery, married neighbors—Swedish brothers who migrated from North Dakota—and their children "stayed on the land" through the transition of the twenties and thirties. These descendants farmed several decades later with "behemoths of tractors with enclosed air-conditioned cabs, complete with radio." The style of agriculture seemed almost unbelievable to Kate Neatby Nicoll, who recalled the "walking plough." The eldest Neatby brothers farmed as well; Alan near Birch Hills and Walter operated the original family homestead. Since he was fourteen years old, Walter Neatby had the "duties of chief executive" on what his brother Leslie described as the family's wheat operation, with thirty to forty head of livestock, horses, and poultry as "subsidiary" sources of revenue. When Walter turned eighteen he filed on a homestead. After his parents moved into Saskatoon, he sold that homestead and took over the home farm on a "crop-sharing" basis with his parents.[14]

While the Neatbys and Millers acquired land, Wilfrid Eggleston's parents left their Alberta homestead quarter section in 1925. His parents continued to own the land encumbered by government "seed and feed" liens until a Swedish immigrant neighbor offered to buy the land in 1927 for one thousand bushels of wheat, whenever he could harvest, at the market price of the time. Eggleston called those who stayed on the land "survivors."[15]

Visiting the area in 1932, Eggleston saw some sixty acres of good-looking wheat growing on his old family homestead, a much larger field than his father grew (or tried to grow) during World War I and the early twenties. The shift to power farming meant, he observed, "the acreage sown to grain was higher than before." Those who stayed also used only the "better soils . . . in the more favourable locations" for grain growing, leaving the remaining land for grazing. The new owner made the Eggleston property his home base, perhaps because of its well-known reliable water supply. It took eight years for Eggleston's neighbor to pay off his parents, but by 1951, in this way, their one-time neighbor had acquired some 2,500 acres.[16]

Elsie Hammond's daily diaries, though not reflective, allow glimpses into how one family diversified operations across the 1920s and 1930s. The now-grown Hammond children lived across an expanse of land that included town and countryside. Various family members lived and worked at the "places" of brothers Les, Bill, and Fred; field "21"; Hay Creek or the Brookside Ranch (where Elsie lived); the "farm" (where Les lived); the Hudson's Bay field; Kay's land; Kay's house in town; the "Whitten field"; and "Mom's house" in Maple Creek. With marriages, a new generation of children, education, and work situations, the Hammonds seemed to continuously reconfigure living arrangements.[17]

Over the 1920s the Hammonds raised wheat, rye, oats, and alfalfa and tried millet in 1927 and barley in 1929. Elsie's diaries record a routine of seeding the crops in May and cutting, binding, stooking, and threshing grain from August through October. Elsie recorded the purchase of the family's first Ford automobile in 1916 and a "new Ford tractor" in August 1917. But by April 1917 the Hammonds already had an "old Ford Tractor." The farm had an "irrigation ditch," and her father built ditches for additional income (he also carpentered). She attended an irrigation convention with her parents in 1922. In mid-October 1928 Elsie's father purchased a "new traction engine," and her diary highlights "tractor plowing," seeding, and binding "by tractor" the next growing season. Saskatchewan produced a memorable 312 million bushels of wheat in 1928. In 1929 the family left plowed fields "fallow" and in mid-August harvested the "gov. test wheat" when their regular stands of wheat remained "not yet fit" and "too green to cut." Her father attended "tractor school" in both 1930 and 1931.[18] Hammond's diaries suggest the family engaged regularly with developing agricultural engineering, science, and practice.

Animal production, maintenance, and management—lessons Elsie Hammond acquired during childhood—continued to be central to the family's operations. She almost always recorded her daily work, which frequently included some version of "walked all over the field to find the horses" or "fed up" the cows. Suggesting skills in forming human-animal relationships she learned as a child, when her brothers "halter broke" "Creamy," Elsie looked on "all the time" and recorded when she "touched" the horse "for the first time." Once she tended until late a "half-dead colt which had been bogged," after riding "up the creek to find the mother." To do her work she paired with particular horses, such as "Margaret" in the 1920s. Animals still took Elsie Hammond to unexpected places: "Parson's lake," "the bush," "Sheep Creek way," and far enough from the homeplace that she rode two hours morning and afternoon before "at last" she "found the cows."[19] These activities suggest continual environmental immersion and a layer of pathways in her mind's eye, all of the work building distinct muscles in her body.

Hammond had a well-honed ability to size up horses and maneuver among them, assessing their needs and field-grazing capacities. "Sis and I got in H.B. [Hudson's Bay field] horses," explained Elsie to her diary, continuing, "and when pa came from the field we cut out the mares' colts and thinner ones and put on the stubble. Then put the others back in the field." The H.B. field would be good enough for the strong, while the weak would benefit from the grain harvest just completed. Her diaries record finessing a certain cow (Sterling) into "the lead" while herding and "cutting out . . . stray steers." One time a "little black calf" and three others gave her such a "fierce time"—even with a man "in a car" who "helped drive the calves a little way"—she used "a rope for a whip" and "brought them back on the run" out of the neighbor's field through an opening made by removing a fencepost. The work was physical and dangerous. At least one time Elsie "got struck on the jaw which remained sore and swollen for a few days."[20] The automobile, fence, and road all suggested the *power* transforming land and lifeways.

The Hammond family purchase of a Ford automobile signaled the shift to come in their way of life as horse breeders. In July 1911 the Hammond men drove "20 head of horses to town." Ten years later Elsie wrote, "We all felt in the dumps by the bad luck in not selling the car load of horses, and they were driving them back." The family must have had many conversations about future directions. Horse raising continued—in 1926 Saskatchewan's 1.1 million horses outnumbered the province's human population—but soon lessened in the family's for-profit business. The shift had weighed on Elsie Hammond's mind and the community, as suggested by the "debate on car v. horse" among the juniors she taught at school.[21]

By 1923 southwestern Saskatchewan had been in some phase of drought for six years. Weeds infested and spread. The Rural Municipality of Maple Creek closed its schools—some Hammond had once taught in—from November 1922 to April 1923 for lack of funds and discussed the problem of "soil drifting" due to drought and abandoned farmlands.[22] A rumble of anxiety appeared in changing family work routines. Bill Hammond left for several days "on a car trip east to get a sale for horses" and moved north to Peace River to market the Hammond horses (he ended up living there for some years). Kay and Les made a "trip south to sell insurance and Fuller brushes." Les and his wife, Ivy, purchased a starter lot of twenty-nine sheep. Elsie imported five hundred chicks from the Pacific coast. The last horse "drive" to Maple Creek she recorded occurred in February 1928. Hammond rode east, west, and "all day in the antelope park" searching for horses. A week later several neighbors assembled for a grooming bee; Elsie described "trimming tails etc." Finally, the men "drove the 22 head to town." Elsie and the rest "went to see them load the horses" on the train for shipping to Bill at Peace River.[23]

Meanwhile, sheep production took off. Notably, although Elsie's father continued to work, Les Hammond, not his father, took the ranch in its new direction. In 1925 Les added "100 black sheep" to his herd. Now, during lambing season, Elsie recorded chasing after sheep who roamed by the dozens to the "big hill" and into neighbors' rye fields and herding "the sheep down to their new pasture," placing the animals "on the stubble" of a harvested field and shearing and "sacking wool" for sale. In the only outside labor activities Elsie ever recorded for her mother, she occasionally "took the sheep out," often accompanied by her daughter. In comments that reveal continued close observation of the land, Elsie wrote, "Ma and I moved the sheep pasture."[24]

Elsie Hammond also oversaw much of the family's "truck" gardens and poultry. She spent many summer evenings pulling hundreds of pounds of rhubarb, a specialty bundled for the Saturday market in Maple Creek. Gardens included parsnips, carrots, potatoes, beets, celery, lettuce, squash, radishes, turnips, tomatoes, grapevines, peas, beans, cucumbers, and artichokes. She also tended a strawberry patch. The Hammonds ran an irrigation system (engine, pipes, and pump) to get "water playing" in the gardens when creeks went dry.[25]

The family turned almost all of their animals into food for sale. Elsie sold cream, butter, eggs, and "dressed" meats—beef, duck, chicken, turkey, and "mutton"—to town customers. Usually father and daughter went to town together—sometimes by automobile—to "peddle," as she called it. Hens frequently kept Elsie "on the run."[26] By the end of the 1920s, the Hammonds had diversified into many agricultural products besides the wheat that probably lay at the center of their operation. The family moved into the 1930s with diversification at the heart of their operation.

Climate, drought, agricultural prices, and a world economic Great Depression soon pushed northern grasslands agricultural families to their limits and many off the land.[27] October winds in 1931 "blanketed all of southern Alberta" in "clouds of dust." Dust storms appeared that year in Saskatchewan, creating drifting soil dunes that spread across the "Regina Plains and into the extreme south-east corner" of the province.[28] In both the United States and Canada, 1934 was one of

28. Elsie Hammond's parents (*center*, both with eyeglasses) celebrated their fiftieth wedding anniversary in August 1933. Elsie, aged forty-one, stands on the far left, next to her brother Lester; her brother Bill stands fifth in the row. The setting beneath a mature sheltering tree suggests none of the drought and depression then blowing through the Hammond family's Saskatchewan farm-ranch operation. Courtesy of Joyce Hammond.

the worst drought years. South Dakota had the highest percentage of its population on relief that year, with North Dakota following right behind. Saskatchewan towns had to cancel fairs in 1934 because of "dirt in the air"; western cutworms infested the land. Grasshoppers felled some one hundred thousand square miles of plant life. Manitoba registered a rust outbreak. Hot, dry 1936 brought South Dakota its worst grasshopper plague. In North Dakota the year surpassed the previous driest year of 1934, becoming not only the driest but also the "coldest" and "hottest." Dust storms plagued North Dakota in 1935 and, reportedly, in 1936 "no prairie grass grew outside the Red River valley." Saskatchewan also recorded 1936 as one of the coldest and hottest. Montana added 1937 to 1934 and 1936 for its years of "searing droughts and frightening, dust-laden winds." Historian William Morton wrote of "driving sand" plastering rose bushes and wolf willow; Manitoba suffered one of its worst drought years in 1937.[29]

The Hammond's agricultural operation reflected 1930s regional weather patterns. In mid-April 1930 Elsie burned weeds and fox tail to help her father get ready for planting, suggesting that environmental distress was already apparent. That fall, however, Hammond visited her relatives in England, and her sister Kay took a job in Paris for a time. The following June Hammond had to keep the garden alive, irrigating "until the creek pumped dry." That August the family harvested alfalfa and recorded cutting some grain, but probably little as the Maple Creek area grew at best four bushels per acre in 1931.[30] Even as Elsie began to complain of dust and wind in 1932, she might not have understood the decade would be history making.

The thirties remain unprecedented, but drought had traveled the grasslands, leaving dust in its wake regularly. Peter Norbeck would have remembered the grasshoppers and periodic droughts of his 1870s boyhood in South Dakota. Dakotan George Will had seen drought depopulate Bismarck and Dakotan Robert McAlmon referenced "climatic hardship." Dust storms had appeared with increased row cropping in Hammond's location after the first decade of the twentieth century. She wrote in 1911, "Dust from the fields blew off in clouds." That May she could not work outside because the "wind blew about 50 miles per minute and the dust was terrible." She recorded dust in 1912 and in December 1913: "the sky was clouded with dust." The soil drifted in Manitoba on a "large scale" as early as 1917, and dust storms appeared in Montana in 1920. Hammond recorded wind and dust in 1921 and 1923.[31] Drought in the 1930s had to have called to mind prior bouts with wind and dust.

Persistent drought across the thirties and troubling top-soil erosion clarified the cyclical climate for many. Hammond made no harvest entries for 1933 and 1934. Invasive weeds became resources in 1934. "We continued with weeding," she explained, until many loads had been stored in the loft. The family started out the 1935 season with optimism, seeding wheat again, but also clover and flax. After Elsie recorded "days very hot," the Hammonds again began "cutting weeds for hay." One Sunday in July the family spread out to walk the land, eyeing conditions. While her father scanned one field, Elsie and her sister Kay walked "over all 3 quarters to see crops, weeds etc." The north half needed fencing "where page wire had to be dug out of drifted soil." In earnest they began "thistling," as Elsie eventually began calling the gathering of the "weedy stuff" they "stacked." The word "glean" entered her diary.[32]

Hammond's 1936 diaries went missing.[33] The diary that records the 1937 season began with renewed optimism. The family seeded gardens and the "2 buck pastures" with crested wheatgrass and a "little sweet clover" in one field. By the end of April, Elsie was "very weary" after finding the irrigation ditch "drying in the hot wind." Days later her throat hurt after she and her father "went to see the ditch and dig out sand." She spent many summer days "thistling" in the fields, "along the fence" and "all about the buildings." That fall Elsie "walked all over the alfalfa but could not find one good place to cut." On average between 1929 and 1938 the south and west plains, where the Hammond's lived in Saskatchewan, raised six bushels per acre, one bushel per acre above what the 1939 Prairie Farm Assistance Act would come to use as a benchmark for declaring a "disaster zone requiring aid."[34]

In May and June 1937, Elsie Hammond, her sister, and her parents left the ranch but only for road trips. The Maple Creek Rural Municipality grew zero wheat that year.[35] The Hammonds "faced wind and dust all the way" to Medicine Hat and on the way to Calgary took shelter in "some trees at a farm gate" to wait out the "black dust storm." They "watched the storm and the shingles fly.... At times the dust was so thick we could not see the roadside and once it ran down the windshield like rain." At August's end the Hammonds drove eighty-five hungry lambs to Maple Creek to be sold. Once supported by bounteous, commercial truck gardens, Les and Ivy Hammond brought "relief gifts of dry fish, cheese[,] beans and [a] sack of carrots" out to the homeplace. Elsie Hammond ended the year by watching her sister Kay succumb to cancer on 26 December. Four days later she received news of her beloved "poor black mare down and dying of starvation."[36]

There Hammond's diaries ended for five years until 1942, when a month before she turned fifty years old, she married Joe Thomas, fifteen years her junior. They stayed on Hammond property, tended the "Whitten field," and together threshed oats and wheat and stooked rye. She had less time for her diaries, but in January 1944 recorded, "Windy as H. all day and dust from fields and garden was terrible. We hardly went out." Tellingly, the next month one evening she "began to read a book on how to farm."[37] Elsie Hammond's diaries allow for glimpses into how a family stayed on the land amid insecure economic and environmental times. The Hammond family's engagement with new developments in farm cropping and animal husbandry suggest how many people made the transition by constantly working.

At the beginning of the 1930s, George Will published a second book on corn to make an argument for agricultural diversification. He believed he had found in corn an answer to viable commercial agriculture in the region, which would advance settler society and his own business. The study formed a manual for non-Indigenous farmers throughout the northern grasslands, including Canada. While he wrote with the knowledge of all he had learned from Indigenous women farmers, here Will focused on the commercial goals of settler farmers.[38] He would have approved of both the Hammond family's agricultural diversification and their small corn acreage.[39]

Pushing field corn, George Will cautioned against the expansion of monocrop wheat farming, stressing that the "basic production facts remain the same in agriculture throughout all time." He thought the "enthusiasm for power farming has in some cases outstripped probability" and warned about surpluses: "cheaper production has always brought with it increased production and lower prices." He argued that the "small farmer has never been able to succeed over any long period with all his dependence on one crop. It is unlikely that the large scale power farmer will be able to do so." The small farmer, to which Will remained committed, could not survive if monocrop production resulted in "competition between cheap land regions" that soon would "wipe out all differential profits." He prophesized that "the great wheat farms now developing in the semi-arid sections of the Great Plains" would need corn and livestock to achieve profitability. Diversification was key, corn one answer. Even though "the horse is going," he admitted, "the pig, the sheep, and the steer are still with us." Corn could serve as a commercial crop and feed for

29. The Oscar H. Will and Company in Bismarck operated a large acreage of experimental test plots to develop seeds that would grow well in North Dakota's climate. George Will took an interest especially in further developing Indigenous corn varieties. Will stands here on 14 August 1917 in a "field of Iroquois Flint and Mandan Yellowsoft." State Historical Society of North Dakota (10190-03436).

the livestock central to diversification. Postharvest cornfields also conserved moisture through the capture of snow; he pointed out this distinct northern grasslands advantage.[40]

Will seems to have thought settler-society farmers might accept the work of white corn breeders such as himself. He repeated earlier findings that at least eight "improved" Mandan and Arikara flint varieties had proven over the years to be successful across the northern grasslands in the United States and Canada at high latitudes and altitudes. He pointed to the results of his father's Dakota white flint, of "pure Mandan blood," on a Northern Pacific Railway demonstration farm near Elgin, North Dakota. Will admitted only one problem. Harvesting lacked appropriate modern machinery that could "pick corn ears low to the ground." He believed, however, that the more people who grew corn, the sooner an inventive person would solve the mechanical problem. Seeming prescient of drought years to come, Will pointed out "many a struggling homesteader in the lean years owed his home and the foundation of his success to [Indigenous corn]; when wheat failed and there was no market for other grains, flint corn and a few pigs and cattle invariably tided him over the winter." Crops of corn and alfalfa produced better than wheat and oats "nearly always," he stressed. If orders indicated Will's reach, people listened to him. Business boomed in 1930 with the "largest number of orders that have ever been received in one year."[41]

The climate situation the next year prompted Will to place an image of the "*Pioneer*" on the cover of the 1932 catalog "as a reminder that hardships and troubles are no new thing." Those "hardy settlers" lived through "troubles, dangers and trials" to raise "not only crops and livestock but communities." He lowered his prices "*materially*" on his seeds, shrubs, and trees. The situation continued to decline.[42]

The agricultural year 1934 in the Dakotas turned especially bleak. Only 9.5 inches of rain fell on average in North Dakota. Corn around Bismarck, Will admitted, "was the nearest to a total failure that we have seen in 53 years." However, Will asked his customers, "why be discouraged?" Instead of looking to the pioneers, he now asked customers to look to "the lady," an Indigenous woman farmer on the front cover, as inspiration. He explained that for at least three hundred years "her people never starved out" because they relied on adapted corn and stored surpluses for a "possible lean year," pointing to strategies he thought settler society should adopt. Will also urged maintaining a two-year supply of feed and hay, crop rotations, and "resting" pasture land. In 1935 a separate message box in the catalog indicated the company would accept government relief coupons instead of cash.[43]

In 1936 he wrote, "Perhaps we had better, to a large extent, forget the wheat which our predecessors in the land did not need, concentrate on the things which we know we can produce—corn, vegetables, feed crops, live stock, and we shall be successful in spite of drouth, rust and bugs, providing we try to help keep the proper balance of nature and do not overgraze and overcrop." While noting the "worst drouth in the history" of the region reigned in 1936, the 1937 catalog asserted, "We do not believe that permanent failure in this region is possible." Not even the cut and wire worms, the blister beetles, or grasshoppers that marred the return of rain in 1938 troubled Will. Rains replenished the "subsoil moisture." By 1946 Will understood the 1922 to 1937 "drought period" as one of the four longest in the past five hundred years. He took "considerable comfort," relying on his own interpretations of tree-ring precipitation to argue that rainfall conditions had not changed materially. With some unease about the uncertainty of drought, he looked forward to the day when settler society would "become more familiar with the region and its conditions" and might be able to "better co-ordinate with climatic conditions."[44]

Part of the answer to this new coordination and adaptation to the environment included learning from new agricultural programs at the colleges and universities of northern grasslands provinces and states. The Agricultural Experiment Station associated with the North Dakota Agricultural College in Fargo published George Will's tree-ring study. Walter and Alan Neatby had attended the University of Saskatchewan for agricultural programs, before continuing farming. While living in Saskatoon, during summers from 1921 to 1925, Leslie and Kenneth Neatby worked at the university's experimental plots. Kenneth Neatby pursued a degree in plant breeding and eventually completed graduate work. Over his career he worked at the Rust

Research Laboratory at Winnipeg; as "professor of field crops" at the University of Alberta; and after 1945 as director of "science services" for Canada's Federal Department of Agriculture.[45]

Similarly, Ralph Clifford "R. C." Russell left his family homestead near Lipton, Saskatchewan, in the 1920s to study agriculture, specifically "plant pathology," at the province's university. He continued in plant science at the University of Toronto, returned to Saskatoon, and became director of the Dominion Laboratory of Plant Pathology. Russell specialized in barley smut and helped establish a registered seed-growing district that used hot water to treat seed with a machine developed at the University of Saskatchewan. Russell's work reflected the concerns of both educational institutions and industry associations with the science and business of agriculture. Together they pushed the idea a farmer could apply the latest "scientific methods to his problems" with the "advantage of the machines that the engineer has developed," without becoming a scientist or engineer.[46]

Residents or one-time residents from this generation addressed regional problems from many directions. One North Dakotan became an agricultural engineer who "specialized in making farm machinery simpler and more efficient."[47] The businessman Peter Norbeck had long worked on the water problem by engineering well-drilling machines farmers could afford to tap below-ground artesian basins. As a politician, he worked on farm-pricing problems in the 1920s and helped shape the U.S. Agricultural Adjustment Act of 1933.[48] The research done by many in settler society raised on the northern grasslands helped the Hammond and Neatby siblings, the progeny of Icelandic immigrants to North Dakota and Manitoba, and many other farmers stay. Historian Curtis McManus has argued that the ideas embodied in Canada's Prairie Farm Rehabilitation Administration, established in the mid-1930s, emerged from a "curious mixture of settlers, scientists, 'professors of soils,' and government men."[49] Laboring in rural agriculture or agricultural science and engineering reflected settler-society attachment to the northern grasslands, despite drought and market issues.

Even experts in the United States and Canada in the thirties proposed separately the abandonment of *particular practices* on the land or shifts in production from farming to ranching, not departure from the land. The U.S. New Deal's initial Great Plains Drought Area Committee, in its August 1936 report, advised the creation of new programs to "render future droughts less disastrous" and "crushing," not the end of commercial farming in the region. Canada passed its 1935 Prairie Farm Rehabilitation Act (later Administration) (PFRA) with similar goals. The PFRA and the successor to the U.S. Drought Area Committee, the Great Plains Committee (GPC), in its *Future of the Great Plains* report, both argued for "rehabilitation" and "readjustment" to new agricultural practices in soil and water conservation. They advocated diversifying, mechanizing, irrigating, and amassing regular financial and seed reserves. Both nations passed legislation to institute new farming practices and protections for those who stayed on the land. According to historian Paula Nelson, while settlers felt anxiety about experts who criticized some land as "submarginal" and their traditional practices as unscientific, they welcomed government programs that "saved" their farms.[50]

Both the United States and Canada criticized ill-suited land law in their respective nations. The Canadian Pioneer Problems Committee grew out of an academic "frontiers" project whose authors, by the time key findings were published in the 1930s, realized their work would "make some contribution toward the development of economic and social planning in a field where the costs of planless development are peculiarly heavy." The committee study argued that to "conserve the moisture and the moisture-retaining powers of the soil" would "*permit the more efficient and dependable production of wheat*" and keep Canada's grain farmers in business. As the author phrased it, "The object is to make possible more efficient specialization in grain farming." Similarly, the U.S. Drought Area Committee suggested policies hoping to ensure that the region would be "permanently habitable." "Conservation of land and water" meant "conservation of human beings," the report made clear. The U.S. GPC report surmised that agriculture might move "east or west" according to "climate cycles" and "even" speculated that "economic and technological conditions of human occupancy" might change future calculations for grasslands agriculture.[51] In short, both nations remained committed to the advance of settler-colonial agriculture and desired the region to remain settled.

Grasslands Conservation

From the 1920s to the 1940s, as those involved in agriculture shifted operations and studied agricultural-production problems, other individuals participated in creating a wider appreciation for northern grasslands habitats. These individuals engaged in public education with the aim of conserving and preserving bits and pieces of wild grasslands and associated flora and fauna. The drought, dust, distress, and poor economic times caused some residents in town and country to see (and appreciate) grasslands anew. But they devised ways to preserve and conserve grasslands habitats consistent with their own vision of society. Eyes and ears privileged settler-society sensibilities.

Education provided a more formal scientific framework for the visceral knowledge of native grasslands habitat acquired by settler society's children. The Nature Study included in the teacher training of many in this generation helped succeeding generations of children understand the grasslands. New teachers and their students carried the knowledge and resources home to parents, siblings, and friends, spreading ideas beyond their numbers. Nature Study fertilized roots in children, so they could grow deeper by the generation. The turn to Nature Study curriculums grew in part out of the same critique of industrialism, standardization, consumerism, and urbanization that worried cultural critics of the small town and North American cultural conformity. Stegner worried about "an America that has been industrialized, regimented, bulldozed, and urbanized out of direct contact with the earth." One of the youngest of this generation, Stegner actually remembered Nature Study excursions his primary school teacher led in which his class identified Saskatchewan plants.[52] Importantly, at the same time educators in the United States and Canada encouraged teachers and children to dig themselves further into North America's land, the two nations implemented policies designed to alienate Indigenous peoples from their lands, such as sending children to boarding schools and prohibitions on rituals that used natural-habitat resources.[53]

30. In 1916 Steele County, North Dakota, voters elected Aagot Raaen as county superintendent of schools, which required her to visit schools regularly. Raaen bought a pair of skis so she could continue visiting schools in the winter, even though temperatures frequently reached well below zero. Photograph from Raaen, *Measure of My Days*, reprinted here by permission of North Dakota State University Press.

Teaching experiences suggest how this generation informed the next generation of the region's "inside," to use Stegner's phrase. Aagot Raaen, for example, placed the heading "Flowers, Weeds, and Other Things" on the front blackboard of her classroom, and she encouraged North Dakota's children to bring unidentified plants to school. During one term her students learned some forty-five wildflowers and could identify even more weeds. Raaen sent the plants they could not identify to the Mayville Normal School. Annora Brown taught a few terms in a rural school before attending art school, and she drew pictures related to the season on the blackboard and taught students to observe the colors of fields and prairies, including snow (which in truth she taught them was not white but really various shades of blue). The Regina Normal School encouraged Elsie Hammond to send plants to be identified at "Saskatoon University." One Thanksgiving she decorated her school with hawthorn branches, and one of her classes collected grasses for a book.[54]

Already by the turn of the century, theorists of Nature Study education used grasslands habitat as a good example of the delicate balance of nature gone awry. Russian thistle marked grasslands out of balance, and soon farmers "besought government aid," one 1904 textbook argued. (In November 1914 Elsie Hammond had her students burn Russian thistles.)[55] By the 1930s the United States looked to "teacher training and teacher retraining" to help disseminate new ideas about "conserving agricultural resources" such as soil and water (for better farming). A committee working on problems of the Great Plains suggested that regional schools should "at once" design a new conservation curriculum "down to the level of adolescent children," reaching out to groups such as 4-H Clubs, Future Farmers of America, Boy Scouts, and Girl Scouts. Colleges, universities, and the Extension Service of the U.S. Department of Agriculture should all become involved. Still confident of settler society's superior ways, the committee suggested distributing "edited and translated conservation education materials" to "Indian children" in both federal and nonfederal institutions.[56] From Nature Study to New Deal soil conservation and farm programs, teachers became conduits for the northern grasslands population to learn about their environment, both agricultural and native grasslands habitats.

During the 1920s Annora Brown began to both increase her awareness of grasslands terrain and look at it through eyes newly trained in formal art. She experienced more of the grasslands when she drove her Model-T from Alberta to North Dakota and via Chicago to art school in Toronto. An exhibit that hung in Macleod during the fall of 1926 suggests that Brown spent much of her summer break between art school terms filling her sketchbook with drawings of local grasslands flowers and plants. Viewers of the exhibit found the "walls of the hall . . . literally covered with sketches" of "native wild flowers and garden flowers done in both water color and oils," such as "sleepy head," sunflower, wild rose, aster, coneflower, and "wolf willow." Although Brown began teaching at the Mount Royal College of Art in Calgary in 1929, she soon found herself unexpectedly back in Fort Macleod after her mother had a stroke. Then, according to historian John Herd Thompson, "Canadian markets followed the Big Board in New York into a September slide that became an October panic," and the economies of both Canada and the United States moved almost together in a slow spiral to the bottom by 1933. Brown never returned to teaching in Calgary. Her father soon collapsed into an illness she attributed to the weight of the Great Depression and his position as town treasurer facing "desperate people begging for aid which could not be given." The town defaulted in the 1920s on interest payments on infrastructure investments made to secure Macleod's role as the wheat "hub of Southern Alberta." The 1930s economic depression rolled in with Brown herself about thirty years old.[57] But she seemed to pick up where she left off. While living in Calgary, she had started a routine of "exploring our country." Now, alone or in the company of friends, most of them women, she "wandered across the prairie." From the same bedroom sheltered by the same roof on which she had once perched, she melded her childhood with a more intellectualized sense of the prairie, transferring rough field sketches into painted compositions.[58]

Brown recalled the years of the Great Depression as times "of disappointing and grudging recognition and acceptance of her worth and work" among the general Alberta population. She sold paintings for a dollar. As if to escape the present through history, Brown sought out historical and scientific literature. The extension department at the University of Alberta in Edmonton and the Calgary Central Library loaned her government bulletins and old reports. Her notes and publications suggest that she read works by or about explorers and fur traders. She felt "privileged to read" a copy of Palliser's 1857 report "kept under lock and key in a glass case on the stairs landing of the Palliser Hotel in Calgary."[59]

Looking back on her return to Fort Macleod in 1930, Brown struggled to find words: "How to tell about this shattering period that my memory has striven so hard to blank out!" While spending many hours "crawling about on hands and knees, wiping up the layers of dust that had gathered on floor and table," she also "took myself out onto the prairie when the wind was blowing or about to blow." There she experienced what in art she knew as the sublime. "As I stood on the peaceful, sunlit prairie," she recalled, "I would see, bearing down on me from the north, a sky-high cloud of reddish-black dust. Gradually the great cloud would eat up the landscape." She recalled daily events of the 1930s: grasshoppers, dispiriting views, "flying particles," a "cloud of sand," and Russian thistle remained in her mind's eye forever. Brown looked through an artist's eyes, not the eyes of a farmer, and saw beauty in pattern and color, however. Similarly, Wallace Stegner recalled, "Even in drouth or dust storm" the grasslands are "the reverse of monotonous, once you have submitted to it with all the senses." Brown destroyed most of her dust-themed paintings, supposedly to reuse expensive paper. Some of her paintings of "huge gnarled trees" suggested to viewers the "conviction that nature has great relentless forces at work," especially the wind on the open grasslands.[60] In her memoir Brown's focus on motif and theory and her growing career as a painter diminished the calamity of 1930s drought. She suggests, however, that environmental distress led her to understand the ecology of the grasslands; individual wildflowers became "integral parts of their surroundings."[61]

Brown had researched her 1954 *Old Man's Garden* largely in the 1930s. The story of the crocus it included appeared first (and likely was her first publication) in a local newspaper in 1935, under the name "Elizabeth Forster," the first names of her parents. Brown urged readers to imagine a "green prairie meadow" and asked them to join with her: "Let us sink down into the tall grass and listen to its whisperings. Perhaps if we shut our eyes and are very quiet we may see, down vistas of time, a younger prairie, clean and vital, when men, animals and flowers lived together as friends." Brown's almost magical imaginings suggest social and environmental harmony. She may have included settler society in her notion, but the "younger prairie, clean and vital" suggested a time before commercial agriculture. Brown later recalled how she escaped through writing "to a prairie still covered with prairie wool."[62]

Old Man's Garden constituted an optimistic statement and a protoenvironmentalist public plea to preserve the northern grasslands. The book came to the public's attention in the mid-1950s as industrial agriculture hit the crucial post–World War II turning point.[63] The assault on Brown's grasslands flowers would only intensify rather than dissipate over the next few decades. To at least one reviewer it still seemed possible in the 1950s to preserve part of the grasslands: "A few acres of wilderness left on every quarter section on the prairies, small areas that would remain forever free from the plough, and the tramping feet and cropping teeth of domestic animals would not return many dollars; but would have for us the generations that follow a value far beyond gold." Using Brown's study to criticize the "tragedies of economic expansion," the suggestion might have been wishful thinking even then. This Manitoban recalled the crocuses that blossomed forty years before on a "low, dry ridge" long since planted to crops.[64]

Brown used plants as metaphors for 1930s environmental tension. Contests took place on the soil among different plant species aligned with native grasslands and commercial agriculture. Silverweed and evening primroses, both with thick nutritious roots, lost out to potatoes and other seed crops. They became "weeds that the white man hoed out with merciless determination." And the skeleton weed, in her opinion, "should have warned men against ploughing up the prairie of the dust bowl.... With deep thick roots, scanty foliage

SKELETON WEED

31. Intimate knowledge of plants made the Albertan Annora Brown question plowing the grasslands. Skeleton weed has deep and thick roots with minimal bloom and foliage, which symbolized to Brown a necessary adaptation to the "arid regions." She lamented the attitude that allowed agricultural experts to classify the wild rose as a weed. Original images from A. Brown, *Old Man's Garden*, 130, 195–97; reprinted here by permission of the Glenbow Museum, Calgary.

WILD ROSE

and even a minimum of petals, it ha[d] adapted itself [from its lush eastern counterpart] to the hard life which was too much for the softer grains." Hostility echoed in Brown's comment that provincial agricultural departments had classified wild roses as "weeds" that could be "eradicated" if one "plough[ed] very deep using a sharp share." Brown's insight might have come with her 1930s experience; after the especially tough years of 1934 and 1936, George Will observed that the skeleton weed remained the "only competitor of Russian thistle to continue survival as a live green plant." After criticizing the premier of British Columbia for his views on unemployment in 1938, a columnist went on to advise readers, "If you are weary or rushed or disillusioned, drop into the [Vancouver Art] Gallery and look at these flowers [painted by Annora Brown]. They are a tonic."[65]

Brown saw the grasslands differently as an insider. Brown "almost" titled the painting of the grain elevator purchased by Wilfrid and Lena Eggleston "It Does Rain Sometimes." She considered the "nicest puddles" depicted in *front* of the grain elevator, which appeared after a "cloudburst," to be the central element of the painting. She did not say when she painted the scene but explained to Eggleston, "At that time there were so many dustbowlish pictures of pale, barren prairie going the rounds and eastern critics were saying that the artists had caught the 'colorlessness of the prairies.' ... The idea that the prairies are colorless always infuriates me." She regretted when townspeople called grain elevators "ugly things."[66] Brown took pride in her efforts to turn Canadian public toward beauty in rural grasslands settler society.

The plant pathologist R. C. Russell also spent a lifetime charting the *Plants of Saskatchewan*, the title of a bulletin published by the University of Saskatchewan first in 1937, the worst year of the province's drought, and updated in 1944 and 1953. If the university bulletin-style scientific report differed in style to Brown's literary and artistic crafting of grasses, wildflowers, bushes, and trees, it shared at least one of her goals: to "stimulate further interest in the study and collection of the plants to be found in the vast territory covered by our province." Russell and his coauthors invited residents to "send in specimens of plants for identification." As head of the university herbarium since 1926, he collected many of the specimens while on holiday in the 1920s and 1930s. From a sense of place point of view, the list is telling: it included the wild and tame, native and imported plants, all mixed together.[67]

Russell's list—over one thousand plants—shows many extant grasses, such as prairie dropseed, porcupine grass, and little bluestem, to be found then in "hummocky bogs and meadows and on sheltered hillsides." Similarly, "dry prairie" still boasted stands of side oats and blue gramma. Plains and prairie cinquefoil still grew on dry and wet prairie, respectively. The collection also included oats, barley, and wheat cereal crops. Having "escaped" the fields, alfalfa and sweet clover cultivated for hay feed and grazing land could be found wandering the province. The Russian-introduced crested wheatgrass the Hammonds planted first in 1937 and again in 1944, "well adapted to the drier parts of the province," had also escaped. A whole host of plants could be found hanging around "cultivated fields"; imported "pigweed" and eastern couch grass, "a very persistent weed," favored farmyards. The appearance of creeping bent grass signaled the transformation of grasslands for leisure pursuits other than hunting or picking flowers: it made good greens for "our golf courses," informed Russell. His short description of sweetgrass, native to "moist prairie," suggests some of the conflict Brown highlighted, as Russell pointed out the plant's shift in status from grass to weed when found in "cultivated soil." The popular "windbreak" tree, sharpleaf willow, signaled changes overtaking the countryside: it could be "found around old deserted farmsteads."[68] In Russell's plant collection can be seen settler society's culture and its economic orientation and challenges: the remix of native grasslands and commercial agricultural plants, the stress of modern agriculture on that habitat, and the work of scientists, such as Russell, farmers, and ranchers, to find solutions to agricultural-production problems.

Not surprisingly, George Will learned "many new things about the native grasses" during the 1930s. "Almost every acre of native prairie is inhabited by twenty or thirty different species, many of which I do not even know by name," he admitted—this from a man who for over thirty years walked seven to fifteen miles on the same thirty- to forty-square-mile patch of land every Sunday of the year, in all seasons and weather, claiming "never [to have] missed more than two or three of these opportunities per year." In 1948 Will wrote he had been "too blind to observe" what appeared on the landscape before his eyes in the thirties. Now Will argued that Russian thistles and pepper grass actually "prevented, to a large extent, the worst evils of wind erosion." They "gave some protection to the apparently dead plant roots" he then understood as only dormant. Some prairie plants have the "ability to lock into their shrivelled underground roots the spark of vitality which will burst forth when the rains come again," he explained. Moreover, he saw rain-burst actions of "gullying in the draws and coulees" as natural dam building, akin, he thought, to dams newly built to help soil conservation. He described the old trails worn by bison and other animals on hills as "natural" terraces and compared these to contour plowing. Rodent burrows created subirrigation. One season's grass decayed to form a natural moisture holding and soil creating "mulch." Nature "has shown the way to those who take the time and trouble to read her lessons," he concluded.[69] The 1920s and the 1930s, along with his studies of tree rings, convinced Will, and many others, to see wet and dry cycles as an inherent part of regional climate.[70]

As Will, Russell, and Brown attempted to educate their contemporaries about the true nature of the grasslands, the Manitoban Edward Pitblado—the one who pined away for duck shooting and prairie chickens while serving in France during World War I—took up the problem of grasslands wetlands. A consciousness about the role of the grasslands in bird migration existed, as is evident in Elsie Hammond's teacher-training notes; she recorded the fly corridors on the Mississippi, Missouri, Ohio, and Red Rivers.[71] Canada produced a "crop" of some fifteen million to thirty million "young ducks" annually, more than three-fourths of North America's population. Pitblado included the statistic in an article he wrote about duck conservation; his use of the word *crop* suggests the prominent role of commercial agriculture in organizing settler society's sense of place. In the fall of 1932, spurred by the relatively recent assumption of control (since 1930) by the provinces over natural resources, Pitblado outlined a history of "game bird" resource conservation. Reduced habitat for geese, ducks, and swans began to affect overall numbers. Citing seven million hunting licenses issued in "the States" in 1930, Pitblado in part attributed the decline in shallow-water ducks, such as blue-winged teal and mallards, to the "tremendous havoc wreaked on them to the South." Pitblado estimated U.S. hunters killed thirty ducks for every one killed by Canadian shooters.[72]

Although Canadians cited American hunting zeal, drought in the 1930s certainly also affected the thinking of residents such as Pitblado. The dry weather intensified the effects of former wetlands drained for agricultural purposes. The successive droughts from 1930 to 1934 devastated the "uncounted numbers of lakes and marshes from the Dakotas northward through southern Alberta, Saskatchewan, and Manitoba," wrote one expert. This Saskatchewan observer claimed the transnational northern grasslands served as "North America's most important wildfowl breeding grounds." Precipitation in 1935 that "left sloughs full except in a small area on both sides of the North Dakota and Montana borders" allowed more ducks to nest than the previous six years.[73] But the need for action to preserve habitat continued.

Pitblado cited a 1916 migratory bird "Game Convention," held by the United States, Canada, and Great Britain, that agreed to work together on ornithological conservation.[74] The United States passed a Migratory Bird Act in 1918 that limited indiscriminate shooting. Conservationists in the United States, however, pushed for the federal establishment of "inviolate sanctuaries," as had been done in Canada. A bill had been in congressional play when the ardent conservationist Peter Norbeck began service in 1920 as a U.S. senator from South Dakota. Norbeck continued to support migratory bird–refuge legislation, which eventually passed in 1929, even though, as he told key supporters, fellow senators and office staff considered it a "joke here, . . . [along] with the general public." One of Norbeck's supporters argued the bill would fulfill "America's obligations under the Migratory Bird treaty with Canada." "I think the prairie States have suffered more from the reduced bird population than have the seaboard states," Norbeck said, explaining why some eastern congressional delegations had been lukewarm.[75]

32. South Dakotans elected Peter Norbeck governor in 1916 and to the U.S. Senate in 1920, where he advocated for migratory-bird conservation. Norbeck was still serving as senator for South Dakota in 1936, when he died. Library of Congress, Prints and Photographs Division, photograph by Harris and Ewing (LC-DIG-hec-19819).

The U.S. Congress began in 1934 to fund sanctuaries with a federal license fee for an annual hunting season, a provision Norbeck envisioned in 1928 but had been unable to secure. Norbeck felt that duck hunters "would cheerfully bear the burden" in return for a steady and secure supply of game birds.[76] The 1930s changed public opinions about many federal interventions, and hunters themselves worried as drought gripped the northern grasslands.

Pitblado and many avid shooters gladly paid fees to ensure game birds remained an annual part of their lives. By the mid-1930s Pitblado served as president of the Manitoba Game and Fish Association and attended, in 1937, the More Game Birds in America organization meeting in New York. That organization turned into Ducks Unlimited, both in the United States and Canada. Pitblado became the secretary of the Canadian organization at its founding and remained in the position for the next thirty-six years. By 1948 Ducks Unlimited had implemented some 250 conservation projects, including dams, dikes, water diversions, and protection from "grazing cattle" and fire on flyways. U.S. hunters donated the money, but first rumors about them buying up "shooting grounds" on the southern drought-stricken grasslands for private use had to be quelled. Canadians farmers and ranchers allowed the projects to be built on their land in return for the creation of "new or more permanent water areas." In a region where snowmelt meant only brief gushing creek water, these "duck factories"—as they were known—essentially extended spring. Soon Ducks Unlimited in Canada heralded U.S. hunters for providing "prairie children" with recreational opportunities—swimming, fishing, boating, and even waterskiing—and for greening "the earth" and encouraging the "bright color of wild flowers."[77]

As enthusiasts, Edward Pitblado for "shooting" and Peter Norbeck for wildlife, both exhibited wild-tame, mixed, environmental thought processes common to their generation's sense of place. A nature columnist for a Winnipeg newspaper regularly included Pitblado's sightings, such as snowy owl and whistling swan. But Pitblado was a hunter-conservationist first, an environmentalist second. When Pitblado began to take an active interest in preserving the duck population, experts estimated 85 percent of the species on the continent nested on the interior grasslands of Canada. Twenty years later some "65 per cent of waterfowl of North America raise[d] their young in these *man-made breeding grounds* through an elaborate series of artificial lakes and drainage systems." Manufactured water ponds became habitat for wild game and domestic cattle. Pitblado's vision was one where settler society could improve on and bend the environment to its engineering. In 1937, when Pitblado supported the introduction of the Himalayan "Chukor Partridge," the *Winnipeg Tribune* Wild Wings columnist warned that introductions might "decimate the native species." He asked "game associations" like Pitblado's to consider instead "preserving the environment so that native species can thrive."[78]

That Peter Norbeck's childhood experiences in southeastern South Dakota informed his legislation is suggested by a letter he received in 1928 from a boyhood friend, who wrote in support of migratory-bird legislation. The friend reminisced about the "long time since you and I played over the prairies of southern Dakota." Norbeck, however, exhibited the same wild-tame grasslands sense of place as Pitblado when he explained the benefits of the bird refuges he hoped to create: "Our farmers forget that bird life is as essential to agriculture as is soil fertility." In Norbeck's thinking wild birds remained consistent with choices that supported agriculture; insectivorous birds, for example, protected grain crops more than consumed them. Other birds ate rodents or weeds.[79] Drainage for agricultural land had endangered wild birds, but the same birds had become part of settler-society culture in aesthetics and sport. Conservation and preservation reflected an emergent wild-tame grass fusion and sensibility regarding nature growing more prevalent in the thinking of this generation of settler society.

In the wake of a general turn-of-the-century conservation movement, the region's 1920s and 1930s drought and dust, and increased understanding of the climate of the northern grasslands that came with these experiences, many in settler society began to focus on the preservation of the native grasslands habitat. Starting in the 1910s, as Lakotas began filing a lawsuit against the U.S. seizure of the Black Hills in 1877, South Dakotan Peter Norbeck worked to establish one of the largest state-owned parks, what became the Custer State Park Game Sanctuary. Almost then depleted of large game, Norbeck envisioned thousands of grasslands and mountain animals, including deer, buffalo, elk, antelope, and goats in the park, which also preserved forests. Norbeck also worked throughout the 1920s and 1930s to shape the Black Hills—including Mount Rushmore—as a tourist site that would diversify, and make more secure, the state's economy. Elsie Hammond searched for wayward horses in the "antelope park," or the Menissawok Antelope National Park, founded in 1922, south of Maple Creek to protect pronghorn. In 1942 the Old Timers' Association of Maple Creek, an organization the Hammond family supported, placed historical markers in the Cypress Hills—a forest preserve since 1906—to memorialize the North-West Mounted Police force at Fort Walsh. A glad Wallace Stegner, who saw these markers some years later, felt they helped tell the story of "rich" settler-society history. Preserved locations within the larger grasslands memorialized how settler society transformed the place to show progress and permanence. Indigenous peoples of course continued to use settler-society preserved spaces and other grasslands environments as cultural resources in ways completely unapparent to settler society. Reservations had begun to communicate the "power of Place" and "belonging" to the land generally in ways unavailable to settler society.[80]

On the Ground Level

Agriculture transformed North America's northern grasslands during the lifetimes of settler society's first grasslands-grown generations. The adaptation of modern agriculture to regional environmental constraints became these generations' contributions to settler colonialism on the ground level. The senses of place common to these residents seemed to fuse native grasslands and new agricultural landscapes. Settler society's remix of culture and nature held commercial agriculture as a determining factor. Preservation had the potential to enhance the scene, but settler society sought control of the mix of tame and wild grasses. Even as reporters lauded Annora Brown's Alberta wildflower paintings, they noted her subjects included garden flowers and grain elevators. Even as Elsie Hammond collected grasses in a book for Nature Study, she also adorned her rural Saskatchewan school blackboard with grain-field designs. One year her students took the "best of the grain," presumably from their school garden, and "made little sheaves" for decorating. The control over children's interaction with wild spaces implied in Nature Study curriculums spoke to a settler-society ethic of control over the environment. Poet North Dakotan Clell Gannon wrote of waiting for the prairie rose to show "in the prairie grass" and *magically*, the "upturned sod." Suggesting the fusion on the ground that rooted settler society, Will's 1940 customer letter read, "Agriculture and livestock, wild or tame, have supported man over most of the Great Plains for a thousand years or more." Indicative of this generation's sense of place, Will equated "wild" bison and "tame" domestic cattle and "wild" grasslands and "tame" grains.[81]

Surveying the grasslands around Bismarck a decade after the worst of the "great drought," somewhat amazed at the recovery of "entire barren patches" from the 1930s, George Will noted, "The pastures are richer and better than they have been for generations." "Surely," he concluded, "grass is the great mother of all plains agriculture and the foundation of our civilization." For him native grasses foretold steps to "civilization" that led to settler society's commercial agricultural pastures and fields. Similarly, the Saskatchewan writer Jim Wright explained in 1955, "Grass, and plants that are members of the grass family (to which wheat, oats, barley, and rye belong), may thrive where trees fail."[82] Grasslands habitat and agriculture fields became one and the same "family" in the standard postpioneer remix of nature and culture. Fusion spoke to new settler-society meanings. Residents now referred to prairies and plains without regard to the amount or even presence of native grasslands habitat within the total mix of plant species.

The grasslands grown could still look into the distance and see broad expanses of land and sky; industrial agriculture encouraged spacious sensibilities. Much native grasslands habitat, however, suddenly had seemed to disappear under expanding agriculture—to which, with no sense of irony, these first generations of settler society felt attached. When Wallace Stegner in the 1950s visited the Saskatchewan sites of his boyhood early 1910s home, he said, much of the land seemed

33. Annora Brown took pleasure in helping locals appreciate the distinct geometric designs and beauty of rural scenes, symbolized by grain elevators and agricultural fields. Brown is pictured here (in the 1950s) in front of her painting titled *Foothills Village* (oil on canvas). University of Alberta Archives (UAA-1983-116-019-001); with permission of the Glenbow Museum, Calgary, which holds the original.

"no longer wild," but nevertheless oddly "more thinly lived in, than in our time." The changes settler-society agriculture made in the details of northern grasslands grounds, accentuated by post–World War II industrialization of the occupation, crept up on this generation of residents *almost* before they knew it. Annora Brown recalled the plentiful Saskatoon berries near Fort Macleod that disappeared with the easy travel of cars and the bulldozer. Weeds replaced "turf" and prairie "took on the appearance of the after-the-battle scene." Upon hearing antelope numbers had grown in southern Alberta, Brown said, "Well I'm glad. . . . Some of the nature, the natural life is returning. I feel as if they are destroying it all over as fast as they can."[83] Who "they" were Brown did not say.

Annora Brown distanced her connections to the process of settler colonialism by conflating the arrival of her parents and a diffuse concept of the "East" with the capitalist transformation of the agricultural West. That the perspective of Indigenous peoples around her illuminated a longer view, before the early twentieth-century grasslands' context for which she pined, was evident in an adult conversation Brown recalled having with a Blackfoot acquaintance, Joe Crowshoe. After telling her a legend concerning a particular mountain area, according to Brown, he paused and said, "We are a lost and bewildered generation" pulled between two worlds: the "old people" and "their beliefs and their way of life" and what he called "the world." She agreed with him and felt "sympathy," but the two really talked past each other. Although Brown felt she also "grew up in two worlds," unlike Crowshoe's two worlds situated in the past and present, Annora's worlds both existed in the past: the "old world" of her parents and the "prairies" of her youth.[84] She sought to maintain the landscape of her youth, a rural, small-farm Grasslands West that included wild grasslands and tame agricultural landscapes.

The growth of corporate agribusiness in the post–World War II era weakened the profitability of local small agricultural seed-supply businesses such as Oscar H. Will and Company in the same way that chemical and technological innovations, requiring new investments and economies of scale, increasingly made it difficult for the farmers the Will and Company served to continue farming on a small scale. He and his customers remained tied in important ways to what Catherine McNicol Stock identified as the "traditional worldview of the small producer" on the northern plains.[85] George Will held suspect the effects of the expanding industrial "monocrop" agriculture that eventually caused his son to reorganize the family business around garden seeds.[86] Will welcomed seed breeding, technological advances that saved labor, and an expansion of production that took his settler-society agriculture to a level far removed from the agricultural system developed by Mandan women. According to historian Mary Neth, however, "urban industrial methods of capitalist production" began to edge out traditional family and community agriculture. Nevertheless, Will's ideas worked to carry out what historian Hal Barron has called the "capitalist incorporation of the countryside" occurring across North America in the first half of the twentieth century.[87]

Will, however, advocated in part a production system tied to organic small-farm adaptation to climate and environment. He argued for maintenance of "extensive" seed varieties to suit the "diversity of conditions" within the overall mercurial northern grasslands environment. A complex, ever-expanding, industrial corporate farming model edged out Will's ideal small farm in the post–World War II years. He worked with cornfields rooted in a "rectilinear-grid version of the hill-culture maize practiced by aboriginal North America," to use geographer John Hudson's description of commercial corn production in the United States until the 1950s. Hybridization; mechanization; synthetic nitrogen, herbicides, and pesticides; and fencerow-to-fencerow farming nearly eliminated Will's small family-farm world. He had embraced Indigenous corn because his deepest hope was to stay living in a prosperous settler society on the northern grasslands. Will appreciated native grasslands habitat, but small-scale settler-society agriculture rooted him in the land.[88]

As those who stayed acquired more land in the 1920s and 1930s, they absorbed the stories of "pioneer" homesteaders once located on each piece of land. The limitations of official Canadian and U.S. land policies in combination with later modern industrial-commercial agriculture ensured both the arrival and failure of many small family farms and, ironically, also made it highly probable their pioneer stories remained part of the culture. The recounting of quarter-section tracts, often by exact legal survey numbers, became an important oral tradition in northern grasslands culture that came to populate a sparsely settled land in memory if not in reality. In later years more isolated families operating larger acreages looked out across the land to see in part the peopled associations of settler society. In this way an echo of the small family farm envisioned by the Homestead Act and Dominion Lands Act persisted in the culture.

When those who stayed in southern Alberta decided to hold a reunion for "original homesteaders" and their descendants in 1969, Wilfrid Eggleston, his sister, and some two hundred "sons and daughters of the pioneers (with a sprinkling of *their* sons and daughters)" attended. Eggleston met another Swedish neighbor, one of the "originals"—then ninety-one—and he returned to his "boyish imagination," where this man "stood out as a heroic frontier type . . . enduring primitive hardships and misfortunes . . . a prototype of the original North American pioneer." Eggleston understood better than most by then the early 1900s near fraudulence of the "earliest advertisements for 'The *Best* West'" in Canada and the "doomed from the start" land policies offering homesteaders an insufficient 160 acres in both Canada and the United States. Eggleston had listened to many farmers as a member of the Rowell-Sirois Commission on Dominion-Provincial Relations, conducted in part owing to the stresses of the Great Depression.[89] Yet the pioneer stories and valorization hung on in the culture on a parallel track separate from (even his own) more realistic interpretations.

The aesthetics of a sparsely built environment combined with a frugality born in scarcity and want (that quickly repurposed the homes and outbuildings of those who left) also kept family histories of former residents alive in the cultural air. The modern northern grasslands of corporate, industrial farms, mimicked in important ways—with long horizons, waving grains, and big skies—by then plowed under and intensely grazed native grasslands habitat, making it easier for subsequent owners to retain settler-society landmarks (also evident in section lines charted by miles in both the United States and Canada). Much land remained attached to early settler owners (sometimes down the generations of stayers who had never met the people whose names they kept alive). In part, because of childhood memories, those families who used to live on the northern grassland counted on those who stayed to retain memories of their homeplaces. The retention of original pioneer stories also fulfilled a cultural need among those who stayed on the land. Stayers felt affirmed, especially as visits from those who left (or descendants) encouraged them to think the place and its history valuable. Entwined stories of "stickers" and those who "dispersed" created a larger story of the role of place in settler society that members related to even if severed from the land.[90]

Indigenous peoples maintained larger attachments to culturally defined areas of space by having woven their own stories into the landscape for many centuries. The act of attaching narratives to physical sites operated in Indigenous societies to allow for perpetuation of values, history, and culture through regular encounters with those sites. Indigenous narratives of significant events suggest land already understood as their home; stories assumed community knowledge of the details of the landscape, which members of settler society were still trying to learn. While Indigenous place-making narratives maintained landmark sites and landscape features, the physical changes to specific grasslands contours and features caused by settler-society agriculture, whether the small family farm or the industrial farm, stressed Indigenous place cultures—another, conscious or not, settler-colonial pressure for elimination of nevertheless persistent Indigenous claims.[91]

Work adapting to the region's environments helped the first generations of settler society know the place better. Now they "walked," "camped," "strolled," or drove the prairie in automobiles according to their interest and occupation. They no longer played with the imaginative power of childhood. Prior play years, however, informed their experiences of the 1920s, 1930s, and beyond. They saw the grasslands anew under times of drought with adult insight into economic problems. Grasslands patterns foreign to the original visions of settler society emerged from the struggle. These individuals sought to adapt settler society to the grasslands on a parallel with creative writers who crafted aesthetic traditions to express the place artistically.[92]

Most lived much of their lives before the dramatic industrialization of the countryside in the post–World War II era. For many the word *bulldozer* symbolized the destruction caused by intensive economic development. Such development created a built environment far from that characterized by the mix of horses and tractors, buggies and automobiles, and trains that dominated the northern grasslands cultures they lived in until the middle of the twentieth century. The grain elevators Annora Brown painted symbolized this family-farm culture. Kate Neatby Nicoll argued that a field of wheat "stooks" in Saskatchewan (or, as Americans say, "shocks") communicated the "characteristic feature of the autumn landscape" that symbolized the small family-farm senses of place she and generally her generation acquired from grasslands and grainlands. Stooks, she thought, "contributed to a particularly beautiful landscape." "As far as the eye could see stretched the shorn fields with row upon endless row of bundles of wheat tied at the center with twine," recalled North Dakotan Sophie Trupin.[93]

8

"All That Vast Region of Grass Land"
The United States, Canada, and Changing Cultural Geography

March 1944 brought Thorstina Jackson Walters of New York City at least one very good day. She flipped through her mail and found a letter from the Committee on Regional Writing at the University of Minnesota announcing a fellowship award to assist the completion of her book on Icelanders in North Dakota.[1] Under the auspices of the Rockefeller Foundation, a round of grants supported what the university called the "life and culture of the people of the Northwest." An enthusiastic David Stevens, director of the Rockefeller Foundation, wrote to Theodore Blegen, dean of the graduate school at Minnesota, "let us get manuscripts that make every reader know what is involved in living in a region."[2]

Reporting on the progress of "Regional Writing" in January 1947, Blegen boasted of the grant program's "genuine stimulus to creative work in this part of America." People from "within the region and throughout the country" had begun to understand better "what many people are *beginning* to call 'The Upper Midwest.'" Noting the regional nomenclature shift from "Northwest" to "Midwest," Blegen explained that "recently" a Minneapolis newspaper "invited the public to suggest a new name for the region." Some "10,000 persons joined in this effort." Blegen helped choose the winner. In his final report on the grant program in December 1953, Blegen still referred tentatively to "what we now call the 'Upper Midwest.'"[3] A turning point in understanding regions began in the early twentieth century and allowed "Midwest" and additional labels to displace "Northwest" for designating the place Blegen lived.

Regional writing grantee Thorstina Jackson Walters lived in many regions: Midwest, Northwest, West, and plains and prairies.

Did Walters leave the region or did the place leave her, as it had Minnesotan Theodore Blegen, although he had stayed in the same geographic space? Had the northern grasslands changed in its cultural meaning in the years since Walters's departure? The flyers the press of the North Dakota Institute for Regional Studies printed in 1953 to advertise *Modern Sagas: The Story of Icelanders in North America* claimed Walters grew up in "North America" "in the western prairies" and on the "wide level plains" in "America's West." The institute marketed Walters's study throughout the northern grasslands in the United States but also in Canada, from Winnipeg to Red Deer, Alberta.[4]

The problem of defining *the* region existed from the beginning of the regional studies grant program. University of Minnesota administrator Helen Clapesattle pondered in 1942, "Just what do we mean by *regionalism, regional culture, and the uses of regional materials*?" All answers met with "confusion and cross purposes." Practically, how did one define Minnesota's regional territory? She wondered, "Is it best grouped eastward with the states of the old Northwest Territory, or does it go better with Iowa, the Dakotas, and Montana?" All concerned agreed the project aimed to promote the study of the "significance and color . . . of the American Northwest," however defined.[5]

The emergence of new regional labels expressed a decades-long adaptation of settler society to northern grasslands environments. This chapter focuses on shifting regional nomenclature, from the Northwest to Great Plains, Prairie Provinces, and Middle West. The rise of a Prairie Provinces and the Northern Great Plains states reflected political, cultural, and environmental realities and new popular understandings of the constraints of northern grasslands environments on agriculture. The *prairies* and *plains* came to stand for politically defined provinces and states in which distinct grasslands made up only part of the environmental geography of these administrative and cultural entities. More broadly disseminated scientific understandings of climate, agriculture, and ecology caused a gradual, uneven cultural shift in the regional labels applied to the continent's northern grasslands. All the lives explored here, same as Thorstina Walters and Theodore Blegen, used a variety of terms

34. In 1929 Thorstina Jackson Walters toured in Iceland; here she sits on an Icelandic pony still boasting a long-haired winter coat. Walters lectured on Icelanders and Icelandic heritage in Canada, the United States, and Iceland. North Dakota State University Archives, Fargo, North Dakota.

to denote regional identity. Ambiguity suggests the impermanence, overlapping, and idiosyncratic nature of cultural regions growing out of diverse personal experiences in relationship to landscape and climate patterns. Change happened individual by individual, over the years and generations.

The North American Northwest

The regional label "Northwest" played different roles in incorporating North America's northern grasslands into Canada and the United States. But the common terms "Northwest," "North-West," and "Northwestern" readily circulated in the late nineteenth century and for decades into the twentieth century on both sides of the forty-ninth parallel during the youths of settler society's first grasslands-grown generations. The Northwest exerted an indirect *continental* cultural pull in association with the transnational fur trade.

English and French colonialism in North America attached the idea of the Northwest to a broad but ill-defined northern, middle North America: a "vast, vague remainder of the continent," parts of it obscure until the middle of the nineteenth century.[6] By 1870, when the Hudson's Bay Company sold its corporate land to the new nation of Canada, the entire expanse had come to be known colloquially as the "North-West Territories."[7] The "Northwest" label also grew out of the phrase "Upper Country" or *le pays d'en haut*, land north and west of Saint Lawrence River French colonial settlements since the 1600s. The Montréal Northwest Company spread the label across the grasslands, before it merged with the Hudson's Bay Company in 1821. Early French "geographical lore," according to geographer John Logan Allen, became "seminal in the development of later images of the Northwest" important to the United States. When President Thomas Jefferson sent Meriwether Lewis and William Clark in 1804 to explore the upper Missouri River "for the purposes of commerce," he referred to their entourage as the "Corps of Discovery of the Northwest."[8]

The term "Northwest" had long legal meaning in the United States as well as Canada. The 1787 U.S. Northwest Ordinance defined the statehood process for settlers living in the new nation's first official western territory. The colloquial name "Northwest Territory" persisted culturally linked to the states that emerged out of it: Ohio, Michigan, Indiana, Illinois, Wisconsin, and part of Minnesota. When setters arrived on the northern grasslands in the United States, the label "New Northwest" applied to Dakota Territory and Minnesota to distinguish the northern from central and southern Grasslands West locations.[9]

By the 1850s many settler colonials viewed the grasslands as a western destination. In this way settlers saw themselves also as "Westerners" living in the Grasslands West, whether the "Great Canadian West" or an "*Ameríku*" West, as Thorstina Jackson Walters knew the "vast areas of the central part of the American continent." The New Northwest, or the prairie or plains, specified what part of the West a person lived: for example, "a prairie-raised boy from the West." When the grasslands-grown generations left the Northwest for the East, for example, Ontarians saw them as "Westerners," or, from the perspective of politicians in Washington DC, as congressional delegations devoted to "Western agricultural interests."[10] A nineteenth-century conception of the West often also resonated in American and Canadian cultures as an unmoored, mythic West. This displaced regional West frequently had outsized influence on the "pioneer origin," family-migration narratives this generation frequently told.[11] But if one asked where one lived in the West, many individuals from the northern grasslands for well into the twentieth century answered the Northwest.

The Northwest retained elements of a *continental* conception as settler-society agriculture commenced on North America's northern grasslands. In his 1862 "Governor's Message," William Jayne, the first governor of Dakota Territory, referred to the "great North-West" and offered the "prediction," from Yankton in southeastern Dakota, "that the wheat granary of this continent will yet be found in the valley of the Red River and [the] Saskatchewan [River valley]."[12] Decades later, but still in the heady days of U.S.-Canadian competition for settlers, some Canadians attended the 1896 annual Northwestern Immigration Association convention in Minnesota. They soon left, suspecting their concerns might become a "mere adjunct to St. Paul." An editorial in the *Winnipeg Free Press* explained, "We cannot see how the Canadian Northwest and American Northwest could work together in procuring immigrants any more than the lion and lamb could hunt together for provender."[13] As late as 1934, the historian William Mackintosh, writing about early cross-border competition, asked, "Was settlement of Canada to be confined to the East, or was there a Canadian Northwest comparable in extent and promise to the United States Northwest?"[14]

Settler colonialism came to a continental northern grasslands identified with the Northwest. Saskatchewan resident Effie Laurie Storer's father originally immigrated to Winnipeg in 1869 to work in operations for the *Nor'Wester*, an early settler-colonial newspaper. The Manitoban Edward Pitblado's father recalled that at the time of Canadian Confederation in 1867, no Manitoba Province existed, only the "great undeveloped and almost unknown North West Territories."[15] Elsie May Hammond turned thirteen when the Assiniboia District of the North-West Territories became part of a larger Saskatchewan in 1905. Annora Brown turned six the same year when Alberta also became a province. Long association between the Northwest and the grasslands that became part of the Prairie Provinces kept the label alive in Canadian cultural air.

More surprising, many northern grasslands residents living south of the international border also grew up with parents who told them stories about immigrating to the Northwest. Lulu Pickler learned her parents migrated from Iowa to Dakota Territory after they read an article about the "New Northwest" in *Scribner's Magazine*.[16] North Dakotan George Will's father's company in Bismarck advertised as the "Pioneer Seed House of the Northwest."[17] The U.S. senator Peter Norbeck regularly used "Northwest" to refer to his constituency's region. Norbeck's use of the label while in the U.S. Senate in Washington DC through at least 1935 and similar use by his congressional colleagues suggest that the Northwest with reference to the northern grasslands had long national resonance in the United States as well as Canada.[18]

The term "Northwest" continued in the culture long after the decline of the fur trade and the advent of settlement. In 1904 the popular Canadian history and fiction writer Agnes Laut argued implicitly that together the explorers Pierre-Esprit Radisson, Pierre Gaultier de La Vérendrye, Meriwether Lewis, and William Clark "conquered [what] *we* have inherited. It is the Great Northwest." She linked together Manitoba and Minnesota and the Missouri and Saskatchewan Rivers. In 1908 Laut explored the "adventurers" of the Hudson's

Bay Company in *The Conquest of the Great Northwest*, explicitly referencing transnationalism. In a sixth edition—suggesting the book's popularity—she opined on James Hill's U.S. Great Northern Railroad and Donald Smith's Canadian Pacific Railway, arguing that the two men continued the conquest "story" of the "Great North-West" begun by fur-trade explorers. The use of "Northwest" by popular writers such as Laut maintained a transnational conception in northern grasslands regional culture.[19]

The term "Northwest" lingered until the middle of the twentieth century, but younger residents used the regional label less and less. The Icelandic history for which Thorstina Jackson Walters received a University of Minnesota grant made only one buried reference to the "northwestern United States." Only one of the South Dakota writer Robert McAlmon's 1920s short stories called Minneapolis the "metropolis of the Northwestern United States," the narrator explaining the city sat "between St. Paul, and farmlands." Saint Paul boasted flour mills, tractor factories, and—suggesting a direct link to the region's much older Northwest identity—"fur and skin houses." His contemporary, a decade younger, Sinclair Lewis in his 1920 novel *Main Street* located his nondescript "prairie town" on the eastern edge of the northern grasslands. But the central character, Carol Kennicott, classes the town as one of the "ugly towns here in the Northwest"—Lewis's only clear use of the label in that novel.[20]

Wallace Stegner rarely used "Northwest" and only in reference to his parents. His parents migrated to the province of Saskatchewan in 1914 with a stream of "Scandinavians moving up the migration route from the Dakotas to the Northwest." This reference came about seventy-five years after his parents moved to Saskatchewan and refers to a place that had ceased to be part of Canada's North-West Territories nine years before his parents lived there. Stegner's use of "Northwest" suggests a lingering consciousness from a family-migration narrative. North Dakotan Era Bell Thompson explained that after the Civil War her father's family left the South for a vague "great Northwest," suggesting her use also came by way of family narrative. By the middle of the twentieth century, however, Thompson used "Northwest" in reference to the state of Washington.[21]

While he did not generally identify with the Northwest personally, in 1947 Stegner collaborated with *Look* magazine on *The Central Northwest*, a volume in its regional guide series. The region included, among ten states, both Dakotas, Montana, and Wyoming, but not Minnesota. Stegner used his introduction to reflect on his boyhood in the "Montana-Saskatchewan" borderlands and a West that attached the "plains and mountains of Canada" to those of the United States. The association in the minds of the editors of *Look* suggests a lingering national memory of an older Grasslands Northwest (*The Far West* volume included Pacific coast states).[22] Nevertheless, the regional term "Northwest," but not the "West," began to fade across the decades of the twentieth century as used by Canadians, and especially Americans, in reference to the northern grasslands.

From Frost to Aridity

The term "Northwest" survived as a regional label for the northern grasslands in the United States but became increasingly anachronistic. By the middle of the twentieth century, many people referred to the space as the "Northern Great Plains." The writings of George F. Will, born in 1880s Dakota Territory, show the larger general shift from Northwest to Great Plains over time and in meaning. George Will took over the family company in 1917, after his father passed away. He claimed in his first annual letter "To Our Customers" that "no seed house can serve the Northwest better or more faithfully than can we." This 1918 catalog emphasized the firm's expertise in "developing seeds adapted to the Northwest."[23]

References to the Northwest in company literature continued throughout the 1920s with one exception, when the catalog letter in 1922 for the first time referred to the "breeding of seeds, grains and nursery stock especially adapted to the severe requirements of the Northern Great Plains." In 1924 Will also delivered an academic paper on Indigenous agriculture in "the Northern Great Plains." However, for the next ten years the Will and Company catalog letter referred *only* to the Northwest: "this great Northwest," "Northwestern Agriculture," and the "wealth of the Northwest farmer."[24] George Will grew up in a family with a business that from its start used the regional label "Northwest"; that he continued long-used company language does not surprise. The gradual appearance of the label "Great Plains," however, represented a generation's changing conception of the region.

What boundaries did George Will have in mind when he imagined the Northwest? His clearest statement appeared in his 1930 *Corn for the Northwest*. Will noted, "The territory which will be particularly in mind . . . will consist of northern Minnesota, western South Dakota, most of Wyoming, Montana, North Dakota, and Manitoba, Saskatchewan, and Alberta in western Canada." Will explained, "Within the past decade or two most of southern Minnesota and most of eastern South Dakota have come to be *just about* as much a part of the Corn-Belt territory as Iowa or Nebraska. There the altitude is low, rainfall is fairly heavy, and the season is much longer than in *most of the rest of the Northwest*." His phrasing suggests that southern Minnesota and eastern South Dakota, though "just about" part of a growing region farther east and south, remained in the Northwest. Notably, Will did not base regional divisions on national territory.[25]

In terms of the Will family seed business, the boundaries of the Northwest remained vague but distinctly transnational. Catalog sales pitches in the 1890s claim that "Will's Sugar Water Melon, Earliest Known" seed "will mature anywhere in North America south of the 50th parallel" (the border between Canada and the United States is the forty-ninth parallel). Advertising "70 Day Corn" in 1897 the company assured customers the seed "has been thoroughly tried, not only in the cold northwest, . . . [but in] Canada, [specifically] Manitoba . . . [and] the Valleys of Montana." The inside cover of the 1908 catalog—distributed to some 110,000 customers—printed testimonials from North Dakota, Montana, South Dakota, Wyoming, Minnesota, Manitoba, Saskatchewan, and Alberta. The 1913 catalog briefed customers on the Canadian-developed marquis spring wheat that "captured the cup" at Saskatchewan's 1911 fair, touting its early maturity: "Every farmer in the Northwest knows what ten days means in the maturity of the wheat crop, particularly in a cool wet season." The catalog cited bushel-per-acre statistics for Manitoba, North Dakota, and Minnesota.[26] Will conceived of the northern grasslands as one

"All That Vast Region of Grass Land" 309

transnational region for growing purposes, with its cold climate a primary concern.

In the 1930s Will studied plant growth, considering latitude without regard to the international border. He speculated that the "prairies" of North Dakota "undoubtedly" in the past appeared more like "Manitoba dotted with clumps of Aspen and Balm of Gilead" and reported—noting the synonymy of "Juneberries" and "Saskatoons"—on fruit-growing research conducted at agricultural experiment stations in South Dakota, North Dakota, and Manitoba. Will kept an eye out for quick-growing, hardy trees to import "from Canada," such as the red bark willow. He noted that box elder shade trees grew equally as well in Manitoba and North Dakota but warned against other trees, such as the Swiss stone pine, grown in Manitoba and Saskatchewan that "do not do so well with us on account of the hotter and drier conditions which we get in the summer." He pointed customers to native plants such as the buffaloberry shrub and other forest trees that survived winters. Traditionally, the company warned potential customers off "cheap Southern grown stock, sold by smooth-mouthed tree agents and slippery dealers, without responsibility." One field bean could be harvested "ten days or more earlier than any other known variety"; a selected variety of Arikara corn withstood frost and heat; and lawns grew lush with seeds "prepared for this latitude." Will now in 1939 contradicted "government authorities" who supported the Siberian or Chinese elm as a "windbreak and shelterbelt planting," explaining the tree often suffered "winter kill" in North Dakota, Saskatchewan, and Manitoba. Will stressed the "much greater length of days in the north" that—if calculated by "hours of sunlight"—resulted in packing a "much longer growing season into the same number of days."[27] In the period when the regional label of Northwest resonated most, Will understood the *northern* expansive grasslands location of settler-colonial towns and farms as transnational and distinct from the continent's central and southern grasslands.

George Will began to use "Great Plains" or "Northern Plains" more regularly in the 1930s, without explanation, suggesting the label already circulated in the regional cultural air. Will also used "northern Great Plains" or some version of "plains" throughout his

35. Oscar H. Will and Company continued to use the regional label "Northwest" in its company title until 1959. His good friend Clell Gannon painted this and many of the images of Indigenous women farmers that covered the company's catalog during the period Will served as president, from 1917 to 1955. Will's son opened a new company in 1961 called Will's Bismarck Seed House, *without* Northwest in the title but with a cover tagline that included the regional label of Northern Great Plains. North Dakota State University Archives, Fargo, North Dakota.

1930 *Corn for the Northwest.* He often intermixed label use, suggesting both synonymous and overlapping relationships. In 1935 the company urged perseverance, saying, "We have faith in the Northern Great Plains and the whole Northwest," locating the plains as part of a larger region. In 1937 Will noted the "ability of Northern Great Plains soil combined with Northern Great Plains climate to produce something under even the most adverse conditions," but he also mentioned the Northwest. Will began to reference aridity and "the question of drouth resistance" more than the latitude's short growing season. He now looked south, mentioning Canada less. In 1936 he reported on sunflowers and trees with reference to the "Great Plains from North Dakota well into Mexico." In 1939 he considered an area from North Dakota and Montana "to Texas."[28]

By the mid-1930s the U.S. government gave international publicity to the label with its New Deal report on *The Future of the Great Plains,* which suggested Congress pass special soil-conservation legislation for the "Great Plains States." A Great Plains Agricultural Council was formed.[29] Will even projected the name back to a time when few residents used that label. In 1940 he noted the previous year had been the fiftieth anniversary of North Dakota statehood; he honored the "pioneers who helped build these Great Plains states." His letter contained the words "Great Plains" five times with *no mention* of the Northwest, as if Will had gained new insight. From this point on the company, without changing its name, began to use regularly the regional label "Great Plains," often "Northern Great Plains."[30]

Precipitation became Will's primary concern. By 1944 Will asked, "Is our area definitely and gradually drying up?" Could the dry period be "merely a recurrence of conditions which have occurred before, may occur again, and may be nothing in the long time climactic record?" Will argued that bur oak tree–ring studies suggested "moisture" levels since 1405 showed "no gradual long time deterioration." However, he wrote in 1946 "In this region of the Northern Plains, where agriculture is the basic industry the presence or absence of moisture mean success or failure for the population." By 1953 the catalog referred knowingly to the "special weather conditions of *our* Great Plains."[31]

Drought in the 1930s pushed Will toward a northern plains identity, in which he now gave increasing thought to the problem of aridity in a northern growing context. The regional label of Northwest carried a *northern* climate association and emerged with the colonial fur-trade era, while the Great Plains connoted *aridity* and related historically to the advent of settler-colonial agriculture. Residents and observers shifted the way they thought of the grasslands and, if only unconsciously, the regional boundaries they drew. No moment crystalized a change. People began to divide the northern grasslands.

From Supersaturated to Dryer Air

The writer Wallace Stegner, some twenty-five years younger than George Will, over a lifetime came to identify as a "westerner" and with an "Arid West," which included northern grasslands but ambiguously. Further, by 1950 he argued, "There is no such thing as the West. There are only Wests. . . . Many regions." If he *had* to make an argument, then aridity defined *his* West. Stegner's many family moves—from Iowa, where he was born, to North Dakota, Washington, Saskatchewan, Montana, and Utah—suggest a reason to adopt "many Wests," all linked by what he called "dry country." Eventually, he drew a line of aridity at the hundredth meridian line of longitude to divide the U.S. East and West; beyond that line, when annual precipitation fell below twenty inches, agriculture grew precarious, he had learned through research.[32] Stegner's shifting ideas suggest the same patterns of gradual comprehension and lingering uncertainty about locating the northern grasslands in regional cultural geography evident in George Will's changing regional language.

Early in his literary career, Stegner drew multiple lines that conjured diverse regional conceptions rather than a West signaled strictly by the line of aridity he eventually claimed as primary. A scene in Stegner's autobiographical novel *The Big Rock Candy Mountain* (1943) provides a window into his regional thinking. Stegner's sense of the grasslands influenced by aridity shows, but so does a more diffuse expansive grasslands that flows farther east.

The novel begins in the early twentieth century with the main character, Elsa (in part modeled after Stegner's mother, from Iowa), riding a train away from her home in southern Minnesota. She travels past "trees and scattered farms, endless variations of white house, red barn [and] tufted corn" to arrive in Sioux Falls, South Dakota, where she takes another train north to a Norwegian settlement near Fargo, a place "flat as a floor and absolutely treeless." Somewhere between Sioux Falls and Fargo—traveling north—she passes "some sort of dividing line," where she sees "only a wide bare green-gold plain, pasture and unthrifty-looking cornfields." In North Dakota she looks out from a window at the "prairie running smoothly" and "watched the summer plains for a long time." She meets Bo Mason (modeled in part after Stegner's father), who lives on the "wide grasslands." The emphasis on corn's push north and west, though "unthrifty," supports George Will's 1930 observations about the crop's expansion into Minnesota and South Dakota. If "unthrifty" also signaled the stress of deficient rain, Stegner in 1943 showed a growing notion of a line based on precipitation that perhaps intersected with the stability and prosperity evident of the longer-settled Minnesota (or Iowa). Yet Stegner used "prairie," "plains," "plain," and "grasslands" without specific regard to precipitation to describe eastern tallgrass-dominant North Dakota landscapes.[33]

When the main character, Bruce, Bo and Elsa's son (and Stegner's alter ego), returns from "Minnesota" after "law school" to his parents' home in Nevada, he contemplates the meaning of "home." Is home a place where one lives or where one's family lives? Maybe home is an environment and atmosphere in which, as he later claimed in *Wolf Willow*, one's "remembering senses" are "imprisoned" whether or not one lived there? Bruce works out "home" by traveling west in an automobile, trying to mark it with his body's senses.[34]

On the road Bruce thinks, "Even if I don't know where home is, I know when I *feel* at home," and elaborates, "*Anything beyond the Missouri was close to home, at least. He was a westerner, whatever that was.*" The 1943 passage is significant to Stegner's notion of where the West begins. Bruce's road trip takes him south from Minneapolis to Albert Lea, where he turns west, encountering Blue Earth, Jackson, and Luverne, all in Minnesota. Then Bruce's car leaps known geography to continue on the same journey, heading northwest from northeastern Iowa—as if he had started from an entirely different point than Minneapolis—from the "*junction of Big Sioux* and *Missouri* [Rivers] at Sioux City, Iowa" (midway between the ninety-sixth and ninety-seventh meridians).[35] Bruce identifies himself as a "westerner" at "the moment he crossed the Big Sioux and got into the brown country where the raw earth showed, the minute the grass got sparser and the air dryer and the service stations less grandiose and the towns rattier." From the new point of departure, Bruce continues driving into South Dakota through "Yankton, Bridgewater, [and] Mitchell." "At sunset he was still wheeling *across the plains toward* Chamberlain." Bruce remarks not at all when he crosses the Missouri River at Chamberlain (near the ninety-ninth meridian), though crossing there is dramatic.[36] In 1943, in *Big Rock Candy Mountain,* Stegner seemed to have located the eastern boundary of his West near the ninety-sixth meridian (a location tallgrasses once grew). In the early 1940s Stegner wrote with uncertainty or perhaps a cultural flexibility about boundaries involving the continent's grasslands.

Stegner seems to have achieved some certainty about where to draw a boundary line for the West between 1947, when he wrote the introduction to *The Central Northwest* guide and cited the ideas of Walter Prescott Webb (who chose the ninety-eighth meridian as his arid line) and 1954, when he published a biography of John Wesley Powell (head of the U.S. Geological Survey) called *Beyond the Hundredth Meridian.* After 1945 Stegner had grown more immersed in research for what he called the "Powell project," a biography he had wanted to write since 1935 and his English PhD work. The title referred to Powell's elucidation of a line of aridity in his 1878 "Report on the Lands of the Arid Region of the United States" to the U.S. Congress, a twenty-inch precipitation line beyond which agriculture without irrigation frequently faltered. Biographer Jackson J. Benson believed, "Before he had read Powell, Stegner had only looked at the West around him; he never saw it, understood its essential nature. It was Powell who educated him." Benson argued by 1950, when Stegner began defining the West and began publishing popular articles on the conservation of public lands, "one can see that his Powell research is making a strong impression on him."[37]

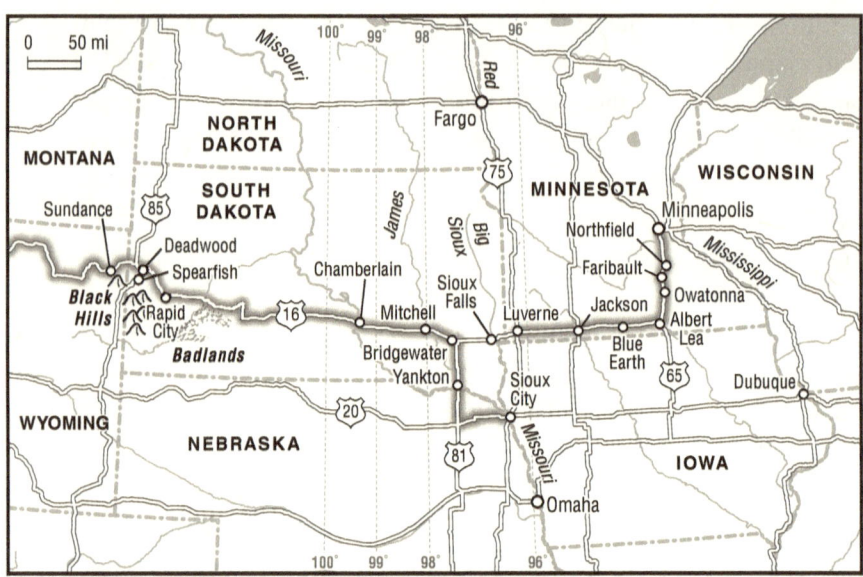

Map 7. Wallace Stegner's routes west, 1934–43. Stegner's musings about home in *The Big Rock Candy Mountain* (1943) used imaginative geography to send his character Bruce by automobile from Minneapolis–Saint Paul to Nevada. Geographic logic based on historical highways would have had Bruce cross the Missouri River in South Dakota near the ninety-ninth meridian of longitude; instead, Bruce crossed the Missouri River near Sioux City, Iowa, nearer to the ninety-sixth meridian. Stegner may have relied in part on a drive he took with his new spouse, Mary Page Stegner, during the fall of 1934. Erin Greb Cartography.

Although the title of Stegner's 1954 biography of Powell proclaimed the line boldly, Stegner with more nuance in the text cited, "the sharp change in climate that occurs *somewhere* between the 96th and 100th meridians." He noted that the "reclamation" of arid lands (for farming) began as far east as the ninety-fifth meridian. In geographic terms Stegner associated the shift at "roughly the line of the Red and the Missouri Rivers" running along Grand Forks, Fargo-Moorhead, Sioux City, and Omaha, nearer the ninety-sixth meridian, denoting a "sub-humid" zone originally theorized by Powell that leads up to the arid line. The imperceptible "line about a third of the way west in Kansas, Nebraska [near Grand Island], and the Dakotas" marked the "dividing line between *sub-humid* and arid" lands, hovering inexactly above the ninety-eighth to hundredth meridians. As Stegner phrased it in 1947, "I have never driven through Nebraska or the Dakotas without a rush of homesick recognition." Here Stegner attached political lines, also part of the culture of modern settler-colonial geographic regions, to an environmental sense of place based only in part on aridity. Steger implicitly suggested that arrival in the West would be certain at the ninety-eighth meridian and more intense at the hundredth meridian, but one would probably *feel* or begin to sense the West "shortly" after leaving Sioux City or Omaha (around the ninety-sixth meridian). East of these cities the body would be surrounded by "supersaturated warm air": more green, more trees, and more and bigger towns. Stegner also focused on observing "spaciousness" and "long-distance views" and "*seeing* . . . the forms and colors and light." Expansive views opened up before one passed the line of aridity, especially in the "sub-humid" antechamber leading to the arid line.[38] The rise of aridity in Wallace Stegner's and George Will's thinking about regions took time, research, and ground-level experience.

The Not Quite "Proper" Plains

North America's grasslands had a historical coherence of its own as an ecological biome. How could prairies and plains be so entwined in one grasslands system, yet be divided by aridity? Distinctions grew only slowly in settler culture. The problem reveals the culture involved in choosing one so-called natural element (precipitation) over another (grass) on which to base regional boundaries. To use the environmental historian Richard White's words, "Nature" is "at once a cultural construct and a set of actual things outside of us and not fully contained by our constructions."[39] Nature exists on its own but never without culture and history, which define, shape, and give it meaning. Elevating one natural feature above others to define a region *is* a cultural construction, no matter the scientific underpinning of the feature.

The language of "prairies" and "plains" had roots over two hundred years old by the advent of settler colonialism on the northern grasslands. These terms and others emerged from French, English,

Spanish, American, and Canadian contact with grasslands habitats. In the 1540s Spanish explorers moving north called southern grasslands "*Grand llanos*" and "*Llanos Estacao.*" In 1691 Henry Kelsey, an Englishman who worked for the Hudson's Bay Company, encountered while traveling south what he called a "plain running through" a country with "nothing but short Round sticky grass." Late 1600s French explorers, also traveling south, noted "prairies three, six, ten, and twenty leagues in length" with "the grass very short, and at other times, five or six feet high." By the 1720s French Illinois Country villages included commons with names such as "Prairie des Buttes" and "Grand Prairie." An Englishman traveling west in 1750 observed "beautiful natural Meadows, covered with wild Rye, blue Grass and Clover." In 1786 the future president James Monroe, traveling west out of the forest, judged the "great part" of the former French Illinois to be "miserably poor . . . extensive plains" that offered little chance of joining the new Union. Nevertheless, one 1818 Illinois English colony settled amid "rich natural meadow" and traveled through "long grass" and "brilliant flowers." Another traveler "walked . . . in the meadows, having my feet almost always in water." Knowledge of the continents' easternmost "wet" grasslands joined explorer descriptions of the westernmost grasslands as "desert." Diverse place-name terminology remained widely at play in the culture when settler colonialism came to North America's northern grasslands.[40]

Decades into the twentieth century, scientists, historians, geographers, and popular authors still utilized diverse descriptive terms for North America's grasslands. One of the first scientific maps drawn in 1898 by two Nebraska-born young men, Roscoe Pound, a botanist, and Frederic Clements, a leader in the creation of the field of ecology, depicted the grasslands continentally with geographic divisions organized under one large "Prairie Province." Suggesting the persistence of "Prairie" in regional culture, environmental historian James Malin—who moved from North Dakota to Kansas at the age of ten—called attention to the still-problematic lack of uniformity in the "use of the term prairie" *in the 1940s*. Often used as a synonym for any grasslands, "prairie" remained current for many decades. Indeed, in 1956 a prominent Nebraska botanist writing in *Grasslands of the Great Plains* called the area of his study a "magnificent prairie." He argued that, based on 1920s research, "the old terminology of mid-continental grasslands of prairie and short-grass plains" should be shifted to "the proper ecological terminology of True Prairie and Mixed Prairie association." Two years before, writing in *North American Prairie*, the same ecologist noted an unspecified point "far into the Dakotas and half way across Kansas," where an area of "drier but sparser grasslands" that *settlers* "early designated the Great Plains" became distinct from what "early settlers" called "Prairie."[41]

In 1907 the popular writer Randall Parrish published *The Great Plains*, which came out in a third edition in 1915. Parrish unsuccessfully addressed confusion in grasslands terminology. He acknowledged a "purely technical viewpoint" would define "the Plains properly" as "only a comparatively small portion of that extensive area of prairie country." Culturally, continued Parrish, the label "Great Plains" referred to "*all that vast region of grass land and arid desert* between the *valley* of the Missouri upon the north and east, and the foothills of the Rockies." The land ranged from Minnesota's "rolling, luxuriant prairie to level, sterile plain." Parrish claimed, "The most important vegetable productions of the entire region were the grasses."[42]

Scientist and laypersons alike used the label "Great Plains" *ambiguously* throughout the first decades of the twentieth century. A professional delineation of plains boundaries that George Will and Wallace Stegner might have read appeared in a series of 1923 articles on the region in the *Annals of the Association of American Geographers*. All the scientists agreed that the Rocky Mountains marked the western boundary, but each author used a specific natural feature to define the region's eastern parameters. The soil and agricultural scientists placed the boundary a "few miles *east* of the northwestern corner of Minnesota" (around the ninety-sixth meridian), which ran southward *within* Minnesota along the "South Dakota–Minnesota boundary." A climate specialist included *most* of the Dakotas and claimed that the entire area (to about the 104th meridian) received enough precipitation to practice "successful farming by ordinary methods." A botanist drew the eastern boundary of the Great Plains at the ninety-seventh meridian but noted the region included "only the western portion" of the "Tall Grass" formation, which "as a whole characterizes the great prairie region of the Mississippi Valley." This last definition of the Great Plains, then, included the western reaches of the *tall grasslands*.[43] Together these essays suggest an imprecision in grasslands regionalization among scientists in the 1920s. Moreover, notable for his influence on Stegner and others, Powell in his 1878 report to the U.S. Congress suggested the "Arid Region begins about *midway in the Great Plains*."[44]

Widespread delineations of Great Plains grasslands acknowledged regional conundrum in the culture. In his 1931 *The Great Plains*, historian Walter Prescott Webb, also influenced by Powell, argued, "The history of the Plains is the history of the grasslands." While Webb—who grew up in Texas—named the ninety-eighth meridian as the limit for successful unaided (unirrigated) commercial agriculture, the lead map ("Great Plains Environment") of his famous study defined the region more by *treelessness* than aridity, taking note of a line between grasses and timber falling between the ninety-fourth and ninety-eighth meridians (even farther east in Iowa and Illinois). Similarly, historian James Malin considered "the prairies and plains a grasslands." Malin argued further that "uniformity of vegetation" should be seen as "a positive characteristic, an evidence of completeness in nature, and not a sign of something deficient." The influential, but also perhaps the most idiosyncratic, Webb used treelessness to connect what he called the "High Plains" and the "Prairie Plains" *across* an arid line. Additionally, although Webb identified a limited "Plains proper," his "Plains" signified the *level* of geologic topography or "plane" that underlay both his "High" and "Prairie" sections of the continent's central grasslands, the primary difference between the two being the "semi-arid" (not arid) nature of Webb's "High Plains." Adding complexity, in the north Webb's *humid* "Prairie Plains" "swings westward" across the arid line "into the Dakotas." Webb generally noted a shift in average annual precipitation from east to west across the grasslands, but he also emphasized continuity in grasslands across space.[45]

In the 1930s the Canadian historian William Mackintosh at the University of Toronto also used a "Prairie Plains" concept to describe the northern grasslands above the forty-ninth parallel, but he meant

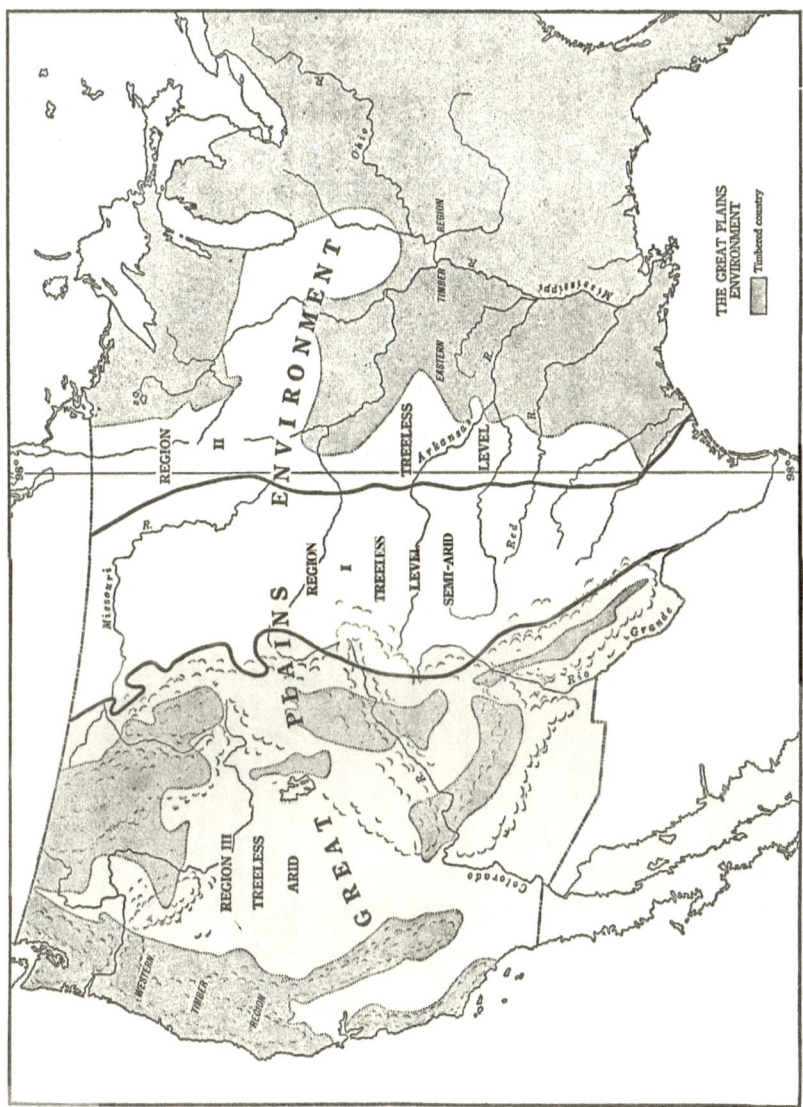

Map 8. Walter Prescott Webb's *The Great Plains Environment*, 1931. The opening map of Webb's classic history *The Great Plains* emphasized treelessness. Webb highlights grasslands as much as aridity. Courtesy of the University of Nebraska Press.

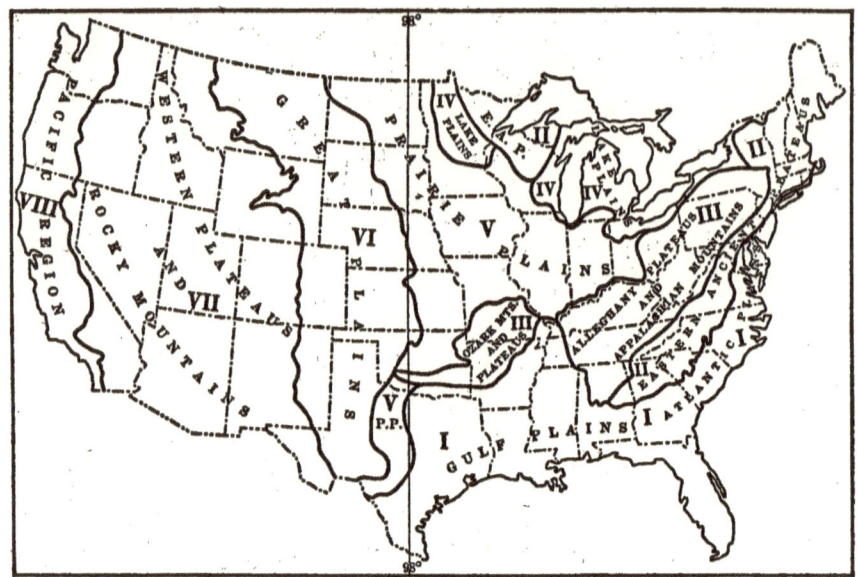

Map 9. Walter Prescott Webb's *Land Regions of the United States*, 1931. A plains concept based on topography or the idea of a general level plain or plane sloping from the Rocky Mountains to the Mississippi River gave some measure of unity to Webb's "Great Plains" and "Prairie Plains" land regions depicted on this map, included in his *The Great Plains*. Courtesy of the University of Nebraska Press.

something quite different than Walter Webb. Mackintosh used the phrase "Prairie Plains" synonymously with "semi-arid belt." For Mackintosh the Prairie Plains formed only one distinctive subregion of a larger "interior plain," on which sat three so-called Prairie Provinces, each only in part ecological grasslands. Indeed, boreal forests in the north "dwarfed" both the "dry belt" and "parkland" grasslands sectors within each of the three provinces. Unlike the United States, the most "fertile grassland" in Canada sat in a "crescent-shaped Park Belt," located in the northernmost portion of the North America's grasslands habitat, where "tall prairie-grass types" dominated. Parklands of combined patches of grasslands and "bush" or "bluffs" (clumps of trees) arched northwest across Saskatchewan and Alberta to the Rocky Mountains from a grasslands-woodlands border flowing into Manitoba from south of the international line in Minnesota. Mackintosh explained that south of the continent's northern "park belt" to the international boundary lay the land "which Canadians call the prairie, the 'true prairie,' or sometimes the 'dry belt,' a northward extension of the Great Plains region of the United States": "wholly grassland." Alfred Leroy Burt, to suggest another Canadian example, described "prairie" "grass lands" at the center of the continent "projecting into Canada" that could become "so parched that the cactus commonly takes the place of softer vegetation."[46] In a Canadian context "true prairie" meant grasslands *without* or very distant from the wooded "bluffs" or "bush" characteristic of the fertile parkland where tallgrasses grew. In this way Canadians also emphasized treelessness.

To be clear, Canada used "Prairie" as the base term, in the same way early ecologists referred to a "magnificent prairie" when referring to the grasslands overall and as consistent with area French-language precedents. Important to understanding Mackintosh's 1930s geographic conceptions is his use of an "irregular pentagon" shape (rather than "triangle") to denote explorer John Palliser's 1857 "dry-belt"; this expanded "dry-belt" included southwestern Manitoba and seemed to cover almost all the grasslands outside of what might be termed the Prairie Park Belt subregion. Palliser used the word "triangle" in his report and located the base of it on the forty-ninth parallel, from the 100th meridian (near Brandon, Manitoba) to the 114th meridian, calling the space an "arid desert." The plains in Mackintosh's "Prairie Plains" conception as used in his 1934 *Prairie Settlement* denoted Palliser's 1857 concept of expansive *treeless* grasslands (subsequently reduced by later Canadian observers). The plains in Webb's "Prairie Plains" focused more on the level "plane" topography that hosted grasslands. Mackintosh's definition held grass as primary, while Webb's elevated plane. Though they both used "Prairie Plains," the phrase described two different ways of organizing grasslands space.[47]

Scientists understood the ecology of the binational *northern* grasslands least of all. Malin argued in 1947 that the influence of climate and soil factors were "*not adequately understood* as they control northern vegetation," explaining the "boundaries between grass associations did not seem to be determined in the same manner as factors of climate and soil" in the north. Factors of evaporation, transpiration,

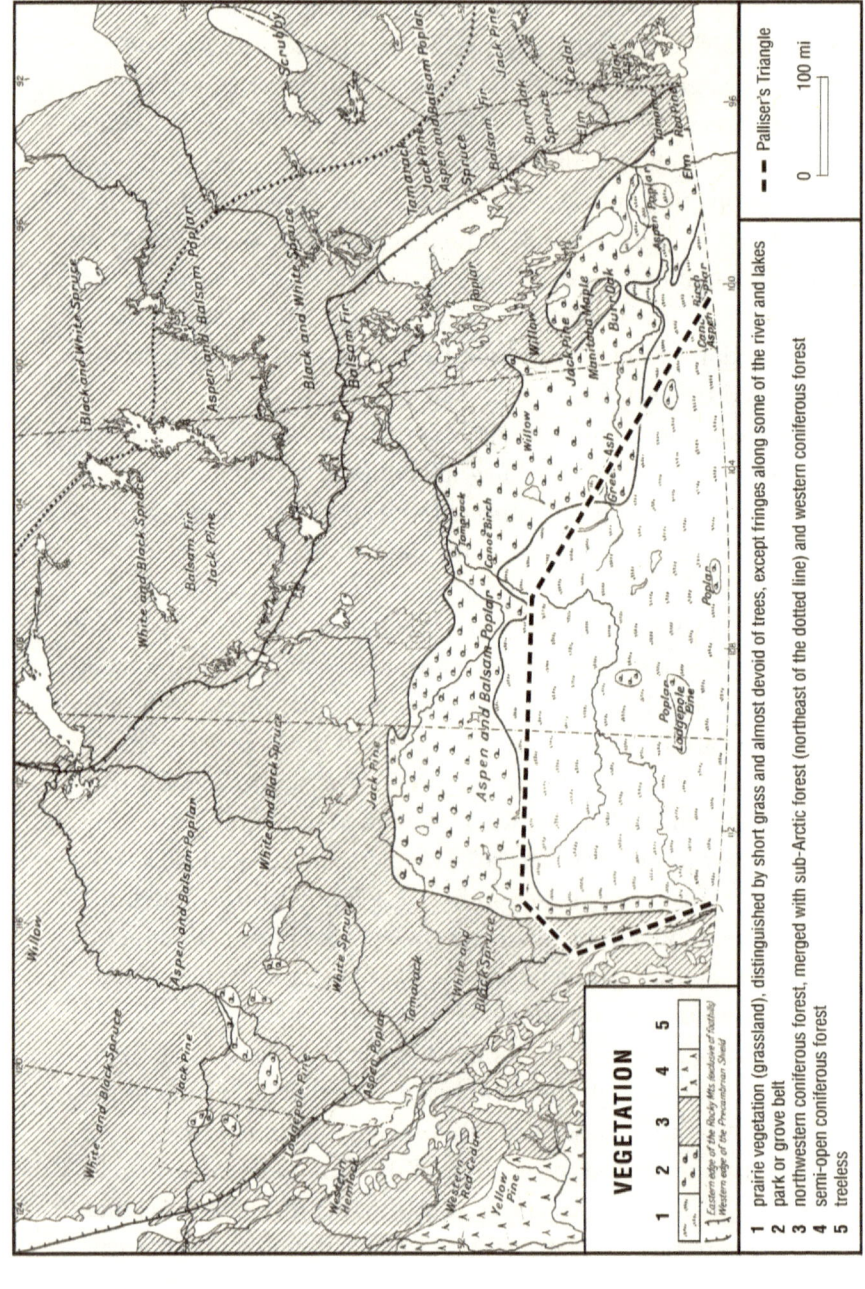

day length, snowfall, growing period, and seasonal variation in rains changed the calculus for arid lines in the Grasslands North. Malin understood the necessity of charting east-to-west "grass associations" that resulted in division by precipitation. But he also called for a north-to-south "mapping" and specifically joined Canadian and American grasslands in one transnational northern sector delimited by "latitudinal differences in light and in temperature" that separated that area from central and southern grasslands.[48]

In 1954 Wallace Stegner noted the "slight modifications"—the "peculiarly concentrated rainfall of the Dakotas"—that Powell had referenced in his 1878 "Report on the Lands of the Arid Region of the United States." In that report Powell explained that, due to greater spring and summer rain in the north, "the boundary of what has been called the Arid Region runs farther to the west," and, additionally, due to the northern latitude, "the line of possible agriculture without irrigation is carried still farther westward" another 150 miles. Winter snow added to soil-moisture levels. Powell's "Sub-humid" zone also expanded the possible area subject to aridity east into Minnesota, even as the good timing of the "rainy season" (spring and summer) in the two Dakotas expanded unaided agriculture west. The interactivity of "Sub-humid" zone climate variations with the "rainy season" likely accounts for some of the cultural distinctions in the ways settler society interpreted the northern grasslands regionally.[49] Perhaps the climate specialist in the 1923 *Annals of the Association of American Geographers* Great Plains series relied on the same information to classify "most of the Dakotas" within the range of ordinary "successful farming." The northern difference likely accounts for Webb's westward "Prairie

---

Map 10. William A. Mackintosh's *Prairie Provinces Natural Vegetation*, 1934. In *Prairie Settlement* Mackintosh used the concept "Prairie Plains" to signal the treeless "prairie vegetation (grassland)" area and also to indicate the "interior plain" on which the three provinces sit together. He superimposed a dotted line on a "Map of the Prairie Region" included in an 1880 Canadian Pacific Railway report he reproduced to outline what he called an "irregular pentagon" (today's "Palliser's triangle") of semiarid land. Mackintosh's conception of the arid area reached to the hundredth meridian at modern Brandon, Manitoba. Erin Greb Cartography; based on originals in Mackintosh, *Prairie Settlement*, 32–33.

Plains" extension in the Dakotas beyond the ninety-eighth meridian and contributes to understanding why Mackintosh identified "tall prairie-grass types" with more regard to parallels than meridians in the northernmost reaches of North America's grasslands.

Tellingly, the agricultural scientist Oliver E. Baker chose *not* to draw restrictive boundaries for the Great Plains in 1923. In part, he noted *residents* in the area "commonly" used the label "Great Plains" for a "broad belt of land" and followed their lead. More scientifically, he extended the Great Plains east into Minnesota primarily because he thought of the continuities of level geologic topography, similar to Webb. Baker noted, "If one wished to restrict the Great Plains region to those areas in which pastoral [animal] systems of farming are dominant," science would support such a boundary. However, too tight a focus on "climatic conditions" allowed "the Great Plains to be classified as a distinct agricultural region—not the topographic conditions as the term 'Great Plains' would indicate."[50] Baker defined the region considering a geologic *plane*—general level tableland—that allowed grass-covered surfaces, not aridity alone, to define a Great Plains region.

Wallace Stegner's regionalization of the continent also considered geologic topography. When relying on the underlying plane or plain, as in Webb's level land, he shifted east in his regional associations. Biographer Phillip Fradkin thought that the study of Powell led Stegner to see "watersheds," geologic drainage systems, not aridity per se, as the "most natural grouping in the West." An essay Stegner wrote on the Mississippi River (almost four decades after his 1943 *Big Rock Candy Mountain* and three after his 1954 Powell biography) conjured a region that connected grasslands across a line of aridity. Clearly thinking about his boyhood in Saskatchewan, he saw meaning in the river's drainage basin, which reached far into the west and north into Canada but flowed south to the Missouri and Mississippi Rivers, ultimately into land he considered the Middle West. Yet this region reached from eastern prairies to western plains aside the Milk River in Montana and Alberta, elevating both plane and grass with water running through rather than falling on the grasslands.[51]

Prairies and plains emerged connected when conceived in a matrix defined by geologic plane and topography. When Parrish in 1907 referred to a "level, sterile plain," he signaled the continent's interior plain. When in 1931 Webb tied together the "Great Plains" and "Prairie Plains" across the arid line, level land served as a primary point of connection. When Malin wrote of east-to-west "grass associations" charted in part by *altitude*, he indirectly referenced the geologic plane, the tableland that rose gradually from the Mississippi River Valley to a height at the foothills of the Rocky Mountains. When Mackintosh mentioned the Canadian section of the "interior plain," he referred to geological-level "steppes" gaining in height from Manitoba to the Rocky Mountains.[52]

Canadians also used "level" as a characteristic when referring to the general land on which the three grasslands provinces sit, calling the mass the "great Central Plain" or "this great plain." In this manner "plain" entered Canadian traditions of describing the grasslands. In 1916, for example, at the Normal School, Saskatchewan-born-and-raised Elsie Hammond learned that the three prairie "provinces make up the greater part of the Great Central Plains." The same plain that slopes to a low point in the Mississippi River Valley in the United States slopes to a low point at the Precambrian Shield in Canada. A divide in North America's central plain, however, created two watersheds, one flowing south to the Gulf of Mexico and another north to Hudson Bay.[53] The northern grasslands slope west to east, from high to low elevation across the international boundary. Reliance on the central-plain concept meant the "plains" and even the "Great Plains" appeared at times in Canadian cultural geography of the grasslands. The map accompanying John Palliser's report of his 1857 explorations used the label "The Great Plains" and "Plains," as did a 1955 history of Saskatchewan.[54]

Experts—ecologists, soil scientists, geologists, agronomists, and historians—worked to unlock grasslands conundrums. Over the decades they increasingly referred to "true" tallgrass prairies and plains "proper"—that is, to tighter definitions that elevated precipitation, the same factor most important to settler-colonial agriculture. Grasslands terminology—tallgrass prairie and shortgrass plains—once exhibited flexibility in its wide application across diverse spaces and as used in the everyday cultural air but became over time categorized more closely in association with precipitation and specific species of grass and flora.⁵⁵

A "Hymn of the Prairies" with "Fragmentary Feeling for the Great Plains"

The grasslands-grown generations implicitly understood the shared qualities of some native prairies and plains plants better than any settler-colonial generation—including their parents—owing to their experiences roaming the land with childhood curiosity while patches and huge expanses of diverse native grasslands habitats yet existed. In the United States the continent's native grasslands have commonly been divided into longitudinal zones of distinct predominantly tallgrass or shortgrass species, with a transitional mixed-grass zone in between. In Canada the grasslands have been divided roughly north to south in arched latitudinal patterns of shortgrasses and tallgrasses. North America's grasslands biome as a whole, however, shared plants and grasses around space in both the United States and Canada. "Indian grass" and numerous wildflowers (pasqueflower, prairie smoke, and purple prairie clover) grew throughout the grasslands. Some ecologists thought needlegrass, western wheatgrass, and June grass "did not yield to the short grasses" in the pre-1930s era and extended to the foothills of the Rocky Mountains. They believed overgrazing had caused a shift from a "Mixed Prairie association" to a dominance of shortgrass species in the grasslands' westernmost drier areas. Plants in the ever-fluctuating, transitional, "mixed" prairie association had once jumped idiosyncratically across space in any direction. Shortgrasses, such as blue grama or buffalo grass, also once grew on ridges and hill crests in otherwise predominately tallgrass terrain and often served in understories when annual climate variation produced thinner tallgrass patches. Tallgrass species (little blue stem, switchgrass, and prairie rose) existed in shortgrass-dominant areas, near rivers or when particular soil textures, such as scoria (burned clay) and drainage, as on north-facing slopes, created an abundance of water. Climate fluctuations intersected with topography to churn plant species around the entire grasslands biome—when grasslands habitats remained intact.⁵⁶

While ecologists recognized the dominant character of grasslands flora developed "under the master hand of climate," they understood that geology, topography, and soil varied the "water relations of soil and air" to "bring about changes in the groups of the dominant grasses and accompanying segregations and rearrangements of the forbs [flowers]," as two period ecologists phrased it. Rainfall was "local" and climate patterns "intricate."[57] The point to be stressed is that the greater the existence of the entire grasslands biome, the greater the potential of any one location to hold varieties of complex plant associations. Annora Brown, for example, recalled learning about "moisture-loving plants" in mudholes and "desert varieties" in sandbanks in southern Alberta.[58] Eventually, industrial commercial agriculture dramatically reduced or eliminated (especially in well-watered tallgrass areas) possibilities for idiosyncratic grasslands floral jumping.

Reflecting the cultures of larger grasslands senses of place, inexact science, and confused understandings of natural and agricultural science, grasslands-grown individuals on both sides of the forty-ninth parallel continually intermixed plains and prairies terminology. They deployed language and acted on ideas of long grasslands *cultural* traditions. Most probably understood basic distinctions between shortgrass, mixed-transitional, and tall native grasslands. Most certainly related species patterns to precipitation. Residents also understood an *unbound*, unpredictable climate threat to success in agriculture across a broad grasslands space, not necessarily limited to land with semiarid tendencies. The 1930s drought, which blanketed the Canadian and American northern grasslands without regard to the hundredth or ninety-eighth meridian, intensified perplexity in the environmental thought of this generation.

The terrain was often all "prairie" and still "plains" at the same time. According to his biographer, Gilbert Fite, when southeastern-Dakota-born-and-raised Peter Norbeck, one of the oldest in this group, led the state into the business of issuing loans to farmers in the years from 1916 to 1920, he saw the problem of turning grasslands into agricultural lands west of the Missouri River (and west of the hundredth meridian) as one of development by a "relatively new state" that "lacked sufficient capital to finance agricultural expansion" rather than as a problem of climate. Norbeck, according to Fite, "envisioned the [western] area [of South Dakota] as well cultivated and improved as Iowa." In 1928 Norbeck identified regionally with "prairie States."[59]

The grasslands-grown generations of settler society implicitly referred to lifelong experiences and their senses of place when they used "prairie" and "plains" almost interchangeably. Manitoban Laura Goodman Salverson claimed the "prairie" became a "living book" of images for her, including the "mood of the great plains that invades the heart with tender melancholy." Thorstina Jackson Walters used "Dakota plains," "Plains of the West," and "Dakota prairie." Aagot Raaen referred to the "open plains of the West" but also recalled "endless snow-covered prairies." Robert McAlmon wrote stories set in the same space called "fertile prairie states" and "fertile plains."[60] In the first line of his 1943 popular history of Montana, Joseph Kinsey Howard called the well-known folk song "Home on the Range" a "hymn of the prairies," notable for having some "fragmentary feeling for the Great Plains." Peggy Olson Bell recalled the "prairie" at night in proper plains-land Montana; fellow Montanan Lillian Miller referred to the "green prairie"; and Lula Short Asher noted hay growing "wild on the prairie" in Alberta. Elsie Hammond referred to Saskatchewan's southwestern grasslands as "prairie" in 1927 and 1928. Lulu Pickler Frad, from central Dakota, referred to the "prairie" in an 1890 letter but recalled the "plains" in the 1940s. In the 1940s Effie Storer recalled the "wide plains" and the "great expanse of prairie" of Canada's grasslands. In 1930 Will wrote of a transnational "prairie Northwest." Writing late in life, George Will described "expanses of undisturbed prairie" around Bismarck, even though he then regularly referred to the Great Plains.[61] Prairie and plains terminology reflected sensuous bodily encounters with grasslands plants and atmospheres across seasons and years. Day-to-day individual encounters with terrain mattered most, not abstract lines and boundaries.

Although he moved to Ontario in the mid-1920s, journalist Wilfrid Eggleston remained intensely interested in the northern grasslands, particularly Alberta, throughout his life. While teaching in grasslands country, Eggleston began keeping a journal in the 1919 season in which he described both "naked prairie" and "naked plains." In 1968, when he looked back on his childhood, he recalled both the "semi-arid plains" and "shortgrass prairie." Few amateurs studied longer and more diligently. Eggleston read many sources to figure out the nature of the place he spent his boyhood, including Webb's *The Great Plains*. He knew Powell's "famous report." Eggleston, like Annora Brown, consulted additional Canadian sources, such as Palliser's 1857 report on the grasslands north of the border, and like George Will, he studied Canadian policy makers and agricultural experiment-station reports. Yet in his 1982 memoir Eggleston described the shortgrass, semiarid grasslands his parents homesteaded as "arid *prairie*," a phrase Eggleston claimed as Palliser's original. Tellingly, however, Eggleston substituted "prairie" for Palliser's "plains." In 1951, after he toured the Canadian Agricultural Range Station at Manyberries near his former family homestead, he recalled, "It came to me as a great surprise to learn the exact nature of our grasslands," from soil (thin) to carrying capacity (fifty acres per cow) and plant ground cover ("quite bare"). The visit gave him a new perspective on the phrase "bald-headed prairie."[62]

After the middle of the twentieth century, scientific agriculture continued to change range and farm agriculture on the northern grasslands, and residents or one-time residents now understood a grasslands nature fully distinct from that of the nineteenth-century expectations of their parents. Settler society had one or two full generations of agricultural experience with which to come to (some) terms with the place. The grasslands grown, however, lived much of their entire lives in a state of adaptation and transition, whether they continued to follow life on the northern grasslands from within or afar. They thought of their experiences in the late nineteenth century and the first half of the twentieth century as ones of the prairie and the plains; sometimes these places distinguished, sometimes entwined.

Shifting northern grasslands regions occurred in a world that lacked clarity on a general cultural level, especially popularly in everyday common knowledge, about the nature of the ecology across space or the detailed workings of climate. Historian Paula Nelson has argued that not until the "rigors of the Depression" did the "dreams of a new Iowa on the plains" end west of the Missouri River in South Dakota. Dwellers in the plains proper only then fully shifted to the type of stock-farm ranch system for which George Will advocated generally, but on a larger scale than he envisioned. In 1966 Howard Ottoson and his colleagues, who studied in particular the transition area between the ninety-eighth and hundredth meridians, suggested that settlement "lessons" had "not yet [been] completely understood, even by its residents." Scientific knowledge about precipitation and climate had existed since the U.S Congress published John Powell's 1878 "Report on the Lands of the Arid Region of the United States" and since John Palliser reported in 1857 on the Canadian "triangle" of arid land that took his name. Spokespeople in the culture at large, however, did not present this knowledge coherently and consistently and without ambiguity or political and economic self-interest. While Powell's and Palliser's scientific frameworks suggested the trajectory of climate knowledge, it remained murky and confused in popular realms for decades. That climate, in Geoff Cunfer's words, "fluctuates more in the Great Plains than anywhere else on the continent" only accentuated indeterminacy.[63]

The grasslands-grown generations of settler society spent lifetimes reimagining and figuring out the nature of the place on terms of their own and by their neighbors' experiences. They weighed and talked over the growing sciences of the grasslands and scientific agriculture that eventually shifted attitudes and even the regional affiliations of future generations. Subsequent generations would increasingly reference abstracted geographic labels, whether West, Middle West, Prairie Provinces, or Great Plains, almost or entirely detached from personal experiences of native prairies and plains habitats. Fewer people had direct experiences with this nature, and fewer native grasslands habitats existed as parts of everyday space, profoundly changing the content and meanings of senses of place and the parameters of future choices for regional affiliation.

The Emergence of the Prairie Provinces

With degrees of shared sense of place based on transnational northern grasslands experiences, why did different settler-society regional labels emerge on opposite sides of the forty-ninth parallel? The tradition of referring to the grasslands at the center of North America as the "Prairie," whether encountered first in Illinois or in parklands with grassy openings in the northern Red River Valley of the North in Minnesota and Manitoba, had long roots in French tradition. By 1900 it made sense for early ecologists to refer to the entire grasslands biome, including Canada's share, as one "Prairie Province." The chief engineer of the Canadian Pacific Railway had included a map of the "Prairie Region" in an 1880 report.[64] Part nationalism, part language traditions, and some ecological distinctions allowed related but predominately different, yet not exclusive, regional labels to emerge. Names denoted culture as much as grasslands habitat.

A basic difference in the proportion and location of tallgrass and shortgrass associations within Canada and the United States factored into regional formation. All three of the Prairie Provinces of Canada contained ample tallgrass growth, signaling agriculturally friendly prairies. Large cities such as Winnipeg, Saskatoon, and Edmonton grew in a historical park belt, where tallgrasses once stood, perhaps sometimes hosting shortgrass understories. Although boreal and tundra landscapes dwarfed the grasslands portions of the three provinces, Canada organized the provinces primarily through settler-colonial processes aimed at the grasslands and parklands. As ecological sciences developed over the decades of the twentieth century, what became known as the semiarid "plains proper," which tended toward shortgrass predominance, occupied only parts of Alberta and Saskatchewan. This more tightly bound "scientific" plains, however, formed significant areas of Montana, Wyoming, North Dakota, and South Dakota, the states associated most with the Northern Great Plains. With a few exceptions (Minneapolis–Saint Paul, Omaha, and Denver, all on the edges of a U.S. ecological northern grasslands), only modest cities rose in these states rooted in either the easternmost boundaries of the Dakotas or in the foothills of Montana.

Clearly, the major shift in the northern grasslands regional consciousness above the international boundary came in 1905 with the consolidation of the four districts of the North-West Territories into the two new Canadian provinces of Saskatchewan and Alberta, Manitoba having achieved provincial status in 1870. In 1930, the year when all three grasslands provinces gained control of their national resources, historian Alfred Leroy Burt's *Romance of the Prairie Provinces* linked Manitoba, Saskatchewan, and Alberta in popular history to 1905, suggesting the significance of the turning point. Tellingly, Burt also extended the label to the United States, referring to "the *American prairie* where conditions were much the same as here." Also, in 1930, although George Will very much had a continental vision for the northern grasslands, his handbook for growing corn acknowledges cultural distinctions by referencing "the northwestern states and the prairie provinces of Canada."[65]

Occasional use of "plains" in Canada suggests more than one regional label alternative also existed above the international line. In 1903, for example, the Canadian prime minister Wilfrid Laurier referred to "the prairie regions of Manitoba and the Northwest," but the following year Laurier speculated that a "great population" would live "upon these western plains."[66] In 1907 the Canadian government published an agricultural census of Manitoba, Saskatchewan, and Alberta under the name *Census of Population and Agriculture of the Northwest Provinces*, suggesting the possibility of continuing that well-established regional name. Eleven years later, in 1918, however, the government labeled the same report *Census of Prairie Provinces, Population and Agriculture*.[67] The national series *Canada and Its Peoples* had published *The Prairie Provinces* in 1914. Elsie Hammond studied "The Prairie Provinces" at Normal School in Regina in 1915. Starting in 1929, the Canadian Pioneer Problems Committee published multiple "Prairie" volumes, starting with William A. Mackintosh's 1934 *Prairie Settlement* and including Arthur S. Morton and Chester Martin's 1938 *History of Prairie Settlement*.[68] Canada's government passed a Prairie Farm Rehabilitation Act in 1935 and set up an administration by the same name in 1937.[69] As with the U.S. government's speculations about the "future" of the "Great Plains" south of the forty-ninth parallel, official Canadian government action and popular publications reflected (and perhaps solidified) a cultural shift in public consciousness to conceiving of grasslands space north of the border as the Prairie Provinces.

The increasing use of the *Northern* Great Plains in the United States to acknowledge an ecological difference from southern grasslands made adoption of the Great Plains label even more problematic for Canadians. Canada's share of North America's *northern* grasslands falls in the *southern* areas of Manitoba, Saskatchewan, and Alberta. From a Canadian perspective, a *Northern* Plains region could have meaning only from a *continental* view, raising the specter of U.S. cultural annexation. In the 1920s a growing cultural nationalism worked against any dimly or unconsciously perceived threats to Canadian identity implied by regional labels. Canadian intellectuals worried with cultural critics in the United States, such as Sinclair Lewis and Robert McAlmon, about materialism and mediocrity—but also sought to distinguish Canada culturally from the United States and Great Britain. Canadians warded off *cultural* invasion with new initiatives, such as the Group of Seven painters who focused on Canadian environments (and taught Annora Brown), the formation of a Canadian Authors Association (which Wilfrid Eggleston joined), new "Canadian Clubs," and efforts to enhance Canadian content in magazines and publishing (Laura Goodman Salverson published *Viking Heart* in 1923). Canadians wished to avoid being absorbed into a general North American culture in which "Americans" from the United States already loomed large; the Northern Great Plains label formed a regional corollary, perhaps unconsciously, to threats of cultural annexation.[70]

The Spread of the Middle West

Northwest slowly and unevenly ceased to be a meaningful regional identity associated with North America's northern grasslands beyond the initial settler-colonial generation and their children. In the United States, by 1950, fewer and mostly older residents recalled a Northwest intimately attached to Canada. Over the first few decades of the twentieth century, the new Prairie Provinces and Northern Great Plains states emerged as regions that refracted grasslands environments. North America's northern grasslands also exhibited cultural flexibility that allowed for merging and mixing with neighboring regions such as the West in both the United States and Canada and the Middle West in the United States (and to an idiosyncratic degree in Canada).[71]

The rise of the Middle West across the northern grasslands signaled the spread of settler society's agriculture.

The "Middle West" with indeterminate meaning had emerged generally by the 1880s. One conception of Middle West seems to have emerged as a north-south ordering device for the continent's central grasslands biome, at the time a "western" destination for many settler colonials. The Grasslands West had three areas and the Middle West referred to the central grasslands of Kansas and Nebraska, a place distinct in historical development from northern and southern grasslands. The "Middle Western States" as a region between the East and West (or Northwest) in the United States also seems to have existed in the 1880s. Between 1902 and 1912 the east-west orientation came to dominate the spatial organization of the modern Middle West, with Chicago as its core city, according to cultural geographer James Shortridge. In the early 1920s, Norbeck compared his "Northwest" to "the East" and "the Middle States."[72]

Of the grasslands-grown residents considered here, the youngest began using "Middle West" in the early twentieth century. Only one of Robert McAlmon's 1920s stories referenced Middle West. Set in Minneapolis, the story includes an advertising executive who speaks of "middle western states" when figuring on millions of consumers. Tellingly, it is the same story in which McAlmon made his one use of the regional label "Northwest" (he used prairies and plains more). Another 1929 book-length McAlmon poem asks, "The North and South can rest, but what about the middle west?" suggesting perhaps an emergent midcontinent regional idea. In 1938 he reflected back on "writing short stories of the Middle West" and explained to readers he wrote about "Middle Western towns" while living in Paris.[73] McAlmon's increasing use of the Middle West probably reflected his distance from the grasslands, the increasing association of the phrase with metropolitan Saint Paul–Minneapolis, and the region's resonance in national culture by the late 1930s, when he wrote his autobiography.

McAlmon's acquaintance Sinclair Lewis placed his 1920 *Main Street* in the town Gopher Prairie in the "American Middlewest" (in addition to the Northwest). The literary critic Carl Van Doren definitely located Lewis in the "Middle West." Nevertheless, the diverse ways Lewis identified the general setting for his "prairie town" suggests a still-solidifying cultural shift in regional language: "Northern Middlewest," "North Middlewest," "the Northern plains" (referring to the "stinging winter"), "Middle-west," and "Middlewest" punctuate the pages of the novel with nearly synonymous meaning. Still, Carol Kennicott is conscious that her new prairie "village" home sits on the edge of a region to the west fundamentally different than the place she grew up (which was Mankato, Minnesota, located in parklands, where woods and grasslands meet). Lewis described a "breeze which had crossed a thousand miles of wheat-lands." The "Impalpable black dust far-borne from Dakota [that] covered the inner sills of the closed windows" of the Kennicott house suggests intimate connections—the smell of soil and wheat on the wind—between western Minnesota and the Dakotas.[74]

Lewis also deployed the undergirding plane or level geologic base of the land to connote an expansive northern grasslands. Carol Kennicott looks "across the silent fields to the west . . . conscious of an unbroken sweep of land to the Rockies." Another time the train heads toward the "prairie," "grumbling through Minnesota, imperceptibly climbing the giant tableland that slopes in a thousand-mile rise from hot Mississippi bottoms to the Rockies." Similar to some of McAlmon's characters, people in Gopher Prairie head west to Dakota and communicate with friends and relatives, who by then live in Alberta and Saskatchewan. As cultural observers, both Lewis and McAlmon absorbed regional and geographic relationships between the Twin Cities, western Minnesota, the Mississippi River Valley, and the Grasslands Northwest, including Canada. However, Carol and Will Kennicott merely observe the land to the west from a perch in a small town that sat in "America," defined by the industrial mass culture both Lewis and McAlmon critiqued.[75]

By the 1940s the writing of Era Bell Thompson suggests a grasslands regional affiliation in process of changing in the United States similar to—but of different personal experiences than—George Will's shift from "Northwest" to "Northern Great Plains." Thompson, who grew up in the vicinity of Bismarck, recognized the "Midwest" as her home region, at least for the purposes of securing a writing fellowship from the Newberry Library's "Midwestern Studies" grant program. The director of the library, Stanley Pargellis, called Chicago a "chief center" of the "Midwestern area" and hoped to foster interpretations of "those aspects of the Midwest's culture which are both its peculiarity and its strength." Thompson applied in 1944 to write "the story of myself, youngest of four children of a rollicking middle class Negro family, lured from the city lights of Des Moines to the prairies of North Dakota." She told grant reviewers her life story took place in "strangely beautiful" North Dakota, one of the "remote and isolated sections of the Midwest." She located herself as a member of settler society, saying, "To many, I was the First Black Child in a land . . . still burying . . . [its] First White Child." In the memoir she wrote with the grant, *American Daughter* (1946), however, she used the word "Midwest" only once and instead identified herself most with "my plains," especially "the prairies," and the West.[76]

A month after Thompson applied for a Newberry fellowship, Pargellis wrote to Helen Clapesattle at the Minnesota Historical Society to suggest that the two programs—his Midwestern, hers Northwestern, both Rockefeller Foundation sponsored—"try a bit of cooperation" in vetting regional fellowship applications. Pargellis seemed baffled by the number of applications coming "from Dakotans" and had many recommendations for writers centered in Mitchell, South Dakota—apparently a "town which teems with writers," he told Clapesattle. The "reason" for the number of Dakota applications he could not "understand, unless it be a particularly intense local patriotism." Referencing Thompson's application, as if she really would have been more appropriate for the Northwestern program, Pargellis explained of the Dakotans, "One of them we may take, because she lives in Chicago." Paternalistically, he added, "I would like to keep her under my eye as she writes." The cooperation between regional programs centered in Chicago and Saint Paul and Dakota residents who applied to both Northwestern and Midwestern Rockefeller grant programs suggests overlapping, competing regional identities and of course writers' needs for institutional support.[77]

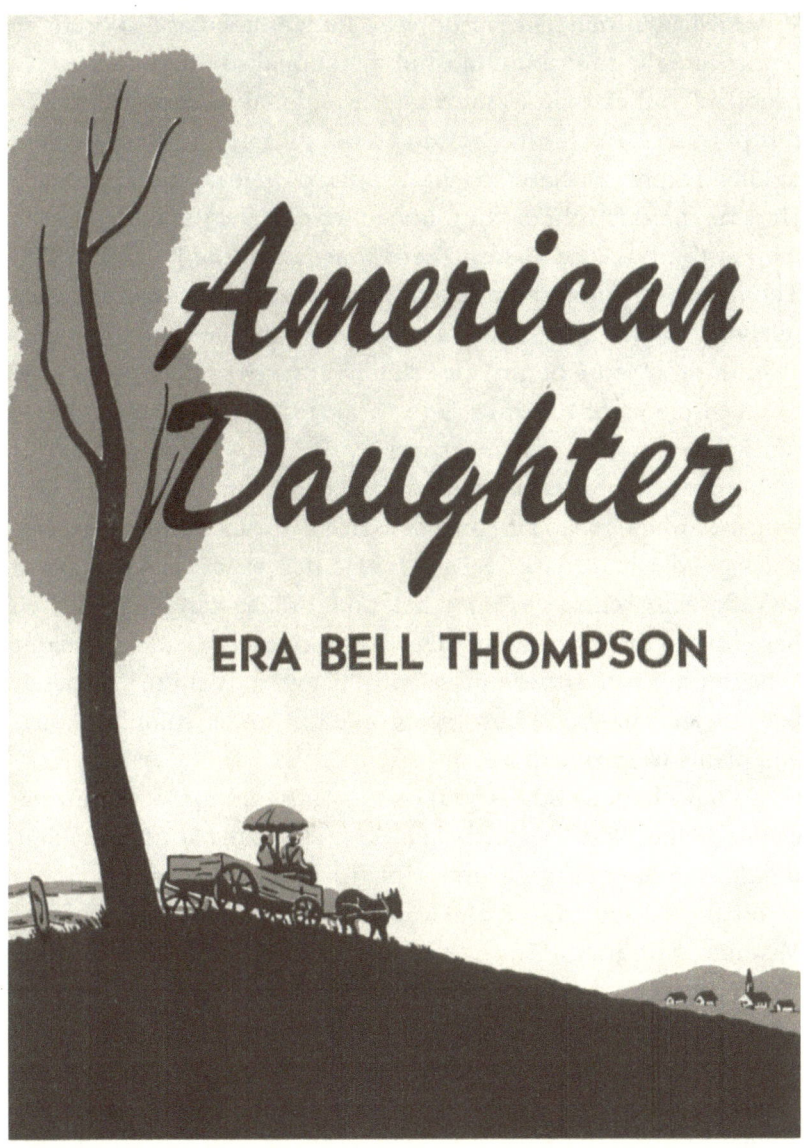

36. The University of Chicago Press design of the cover for Era Bell Thompson's 1946 autobiography, *American Daughter*, with its horse, wagon, and open skies, suggests the rural life she knew growing up on the grasslands of North Dakota. Original image from the Newberry Library Archives, Chicago; reprinted here by permission of University of Chicago Press.

Pargellis felt that Thompson, who he identified as "colored" in reports, might contribute most to a "rational solution of the race problem" rather than to midwestern regional understanding. To this purpose Pargellis had review copies of *American Daughter* sent to Lillian Smith, Richard Wright, Langston Hughes, and Zora Neale Hurston, among others, with little-to-no plan suggested by him to market the book on the northern grasslands, the place Era Bell Thompson's memoir illuminated for purposes of regional and race relations. While Pargellis seems to have thought the country needed Thompson's "sense of fun" (less "bitter" than Wright), the memoir revealed plenty of racism on the "prairies." A potential publisher praised her "tone," which "especially pleased" Thompson.[78] Her memoir documented people who stared; a "big husky boy" who screamed when he saw her; textbooks that demeaned and caricatured Black people; and "darky" stories told in her presence. A restaurant in Valley City refused to serve her, and a theater in Fargo denied her entry to the main floor.[79] The memoir indeed made a valuable contribution to northern grasslands history and culture precisely because she suggested how race worked in settler-colonial prairie and plains Western culture.

Along with many others by the mid-1940s and 1950s, Thompson claimed "the West" began at Mandan (about the 101th meridian, though she did not use scientific lingo), Bismarck's twin town west across the Missouri River. She associated regional change with the Missouri, "Mountain Time," the rodeo, and "Indians" who came "from the reservation to greet the tourist trains." Although Thompson's father quit farming soon after her three brothers left home, her memoir presented a settler-society culture focused on the transformation of the prairie grasslands into agricultural lands. She thrilled to the wheat and flax her father harvested. The memoir exuded what Michael Lansing has called "Prairie Midwest" identity. Nevertheless, according to her grant application, she thought of Mandan, North Dakota, as a place on the periphery of the Middle West. Thompson over time moved east from the Missouri River to Iowa and Chicago toward lush grain agriculture, which seems to have made the difference in her identification with a prairie Middle West.[80]

37. This portrait of Era Bell Thompson appeared on the dustjacket of *American Daughter*, written with the support of a Newberry Library "Midwestern Studies" fellowship and published by the University of Chicago Press in 1946, when she was forty-one years old. Thompson began working for *Ebony* magazine in 1949. State Historical Society of North Dakota (01085-00017).

Even George Will's sense of in-region divisions had sharpened by 1955, the year he died. That year's company catalog cover identified with the Northwest by company name, but most internal references referred to plants adapted to the Northern Great Plains. The catalog also suggested a new understanding of a division based on aridity. The Field Seed Department directed customers to choose either "Great Plains Pasture Mixture" or "Midland Pasture Mixture." The Great Plains Pasture Mixture included crested wheatgrass, "our hardiest, most drought resistant pasture grass." The Midland mixture had an extra explanation noting it should be used in "eastern North Dakota," demonstrating an awareness of a "Midland," perhaps an articulation of Middle West, association growing in North Dakota. In 1930 Will had a conception that the "milder central states" of the Corn Belt belonged to a different region and pulled parts of South Dakota and Minnesota to it.[81] By the mid-twentieth century Will's perception of regions based in crops and precipitation had strengthened.

Although Will continued to think of his home as part of a transnational place, Canadians of the northern grasslands rarely identified with the Middle West. When they did, however, the reference also resonated with agriculture. Most thought as Burt did in 1942, when he explained to Americans, "There is no Middle West in Canada," only an "enormous and largely uninhabited waste of rocks, lakes, rivers and Christmas trees." However, an unexpected example of Middle West identification appears in a 1957 work by Manitoba-born historian William L. Morton. He identified Manitoba with the prairies and plains and the West, but he also described Manitoba as a "mid-western province," attributing in part the province's identity to a public culture dominated by "Ontario-bred men" and the "metropolitan character of Winnipeg." Manitoba existed in a cultural—if not environmental—middle ground between central Canada in the east and the twinned Saskatchewan and Alberta. These provincial twins by the 1950s carried a well-known association with Palliser's arid "triangle" and shared a developmental history distinct from Manitoba.[82]

Morton made the connection between agriculture and a Middle West idea explicit. Only after Manitoba gained control of its natural resources in 1930 did the province begin "ripening towards the final form of a *cultivated* mid-western landscape." Prior to that time Canadian policy supposedly kept Manitoba from becoming a "great mid-western province." Elsie Hammond's Regina Normal School notes on the Prairie Provinces also placed Saskatchewan in the "Inland province of the Middle West," suggesting some influence of the idea on the Canadian scene as early as 1916. (Or quite possibly Elsie Hammond's teacher or textbooks came from the United States.) Hammond's notes went on to describe the diverse ecological environments of the entire province, including forests, the "great wheat plains of Regina and Moose Jaw," and the "rich mixed farming and ranching district" where she grew up.[83] The idea of Midwest had limited resonance in the Prairie Provinces of Canada, but sparse usage seemed to derive in part from the agricultural transformation of the northern grasslands.

The lead story of the popular U.S. magazine *Look* in September 1958 tellingly focused on "America's New Middle West." The "largest single feature" the magazine had "ever published" boasted an internal cover, thirteen writers, eleven photographers, and two-year planning. Journalist Joe McCarthy explained how postwar, industry—manufacturing—had begun a "deep and tremendous change" in Middle West culture. In Ohio, Illinois, Indiana, Wisconsin, and Iowa, the reporter argued, "Industry is replacing the farm as the heart and focal point of the Midwestern way of life." Signs of the change included steel production in Chicago, water-generated electric power, the existence of more industrial workers than farmers in Iowa, and in 1957 the adoption of daylight saving time in Minnesota, "which no farm-belt legislator would have dared support a few years ago." The reporter went on to explain how—over the period from 1930 to 1958—new investment in farm equipment, increase in farm size, decrease in farmers, and emergence of part-owned, part-leased operations resulted in industrialized farms. As industrial manufacturing challenged the farm image of the *eastern* Middle West, however, the existence of new industrial farming (with its plant genetics, tractors, fertilizer, and business record keeping) pulled Minnesota and the eastern Dakotas into a *western* row-crop Middle West. The infusion of industrial, power-farmed (western) terrain into the Middle West helped maintain what industrial manufacturing challenged in the old agricultural (eastern) conception of the Middle

West. The association of Saint Paul–Minneapolis with urbanization, implying a growth of manufacturing and nonagricultural populations, similar to "metropolitan" Winnipeg, also tugged the Dakotas east into Midwest consideration.[84]

Just ten years before, in 1947, in the same year the same *Look* magazine company published *The Central Northwest* guidebook introduced by Wallace Stegner, it published a volume on *The Midwest*. The introductory essay associated the "Midwest" with "endless prairies" and an "evenly distributed rainfall *which made unnecessary the expense of irrigation.*" The 1947 boundaries of *this* Midwest extended only to the western borders of Iowa and Minnesota and correlated to the potential of unirrigated agriculture and urbanization that supported manufacturing. Now, in 1958, *Look*'s map of "America's New Middle West" included Kansas, Nebraska, South Dakota, and North Dakota, as well as states to the east included in 1947, such as Ohio, Illinois, Iowa, and Minnesota.[85]

Revealing cultural ambiguity, the North Dakota–born, editor-publisher of the *Fargo Forum* newspaper, "Happy" Holgar D. Paulson, pushed back. He led 1958 *Look* journalist Chester Morrison to believe, "North Dakota doesn't consider itself as part of the Middle West. It used to be part of the Northwest until that designation was appropriated by the group of states to the westward, and for a while it was said to be on the Great Plains, but that term dropped out of usage." Morrison reported that the people of North Dakota did not "care much" about labels and that the state "will never call itself, as Minnesota does, the Upper Midwest." Paulson argued that the roads and automobiles that allowed families "to live in Fargo . . . and run to the farm" symbolized the "new [industrial] thing about what you call the New Middle West," tempting the eastern Dakotas to join.[86]

The Middle West resonated by then with younger people from the region of Era Bell Thompson's and Robert McAlmon's ages, thirty-nine and thirty-eight, respectively, when they used the regional label in formal writing (probably earlier in colloquial speech), even if they frequently also referenced prairies and plains. When seventy-five-year-old Vilhjalmur Stefansson reviewed Thorstina Walters's *Modern Sagas* in 1954, he identified the region she wrote about as the "North

American Middle West" and associated it with "pioneering" and "development." Midwestern resonated with seventy-nine-year-old Aagot Raaen, when she published the second volume of her autobiography in 1953; contemplating leaving Hawaii after teaching there for years, she "thought of the Middle West with its changing weather and heat and cold modified by winds." Nevertheless, the mixing of regional labels persisted. In a 1953 book review, Wilfrid Eggleston lauded Montanan Joseph Kinsey Howard's study of Métis culture, locating Howard in the "American North-West" and the book, *Strange Empire*, in the "mid-west."[87] A common perception that the Middle West included territory west of Minnesota and Iowa existed by 1950. Only in 1984, however, did the U.S. Census Bureau change the "North Central" region (further divided since 1900 into "East" and "West" North Central) to "Midwest" with the same interior divisions. The U.S. Census much earlier recognized "Great Plains" and "Prairie Region" as two of nineteen topographic areas.[88]

Acquisition of new regional affiliations correlates strongly with the growth of modern industrial agriculture. To the extent commercial agriculture of the Corn Belt eliminated tallgrass grasslands, many settler societies began to identify regionally, more easily, if not always, with the Middle West. Indeed, the effort to drain, often by laying underground tiles, from the 1880s to the 1920s reshaped land covered in tallgrasses too frequently wet for commercial agriculture into an "orderly appearance of large fields of regular shape," from Illinois, Iowa, and Minnesota "to the edge of the prairies" in the Red River Valley of the North. Uniformity of commercial agricultural landscapes, shaped by and for increasingly large-scale machinery, inscribed regional perception pressure points across *former* native grasslands habitat.[89] To the extent that commercial grain agriculture replaced grasslands habitats, settler societies identified regionally more easily with the Middle West. This shift, difficult to place in time, reflected industrial agriculture, generational change, and tall-grasslands habitat loss. Post–World War II intensification of industrial agriculture clarified the change.[90]

While the Precambrian Shield and Rocky Mountains more tightly contained Canada's Prairie Province region, the well-watered tallgrasses and mixed eastern grasslands of the Dakotas on the northern plains hosted a cultural capacity to merge into a modern Middle West. Looking toward Iowa and Illinois from a Mississippi River steamboat in 1979, Wallace Stegner thought of the "prairie," by then "rich farmland," with reference to the "Middle West." As early as 1950, Stegner argued that although the "Mid-West" shared cultural traits (especially speech patterns) with the West, the Middle West "doesn't share all the essentials," by which he meant aridity. Yet he located no land area in the Dakotas and Nebraska securely in the humid East. He understood in these states' climate makeup the possibilities of aligning with his arid West, even if much of their area grew crops that allowed for identity links to the Middle West.[91]

The western northern grasslands habitat of South Dakota, North Dakota, and Montana—asserting a measure of "Plains" proper identity in these states—still implicitly speak to a formerly expansive whole grasslands at North America's center, even if in diminished capacity, patched with grain and pasture fields. Plains land "proper," well before, but more clearly by 1950, formed an interior borderland between the West and the Middle West. In the words of one-time Saskatchewan-Montana borderlands' resident Stegner, plains land left settler colonials a "sense of the incompleteness of man's dominion." Agriculture had all but eliminated eastern tallgrasses, but tallgrass survival in odd spaces (in cemeteries, railroad sidings, and other spaces for contingent reasons) and within the plains proper has kept the idea of a once more expansive native grasslands habitat alive, whether called "Prairie" or "Plains."[92] The ecologically rooted labels of Prairie Provinces in Canada and Northern Great Plains states in the United States emerged in regional consciousness even as commercial agriculture began to replace or alter in increasing amounts native northern grasslands habitats. These regional labels created memory landscapes, suggesting the pull and importance of North America's wider northern grasslands to these regional cultures.

Settler-Colonial Regions and Indigenous Grasslands

Defining and dividing territory into regions named the West, Middle West, Prairie Provinces, and Northern Great Plains based on the requirements of commercial agriculture makes sense only from a settler-colonial mindset. Similar to cartography, the rise of regions in popular and official culture reflected attempts to wield power over space.[93] Lines of aridity, however "natural" in terms of precipitation patterns, suggest the broad grasslands in the interior of North America need be seen only in highly capitalized row-crop agricultural terms.[94] Nevertheless, the agricultural Mandans and Arikaras whom the La Vérendrye brothers visited along the Missouri River found social sufficiency in the broad northern grasslands. Indigenous village agriculture produced surpluses used for trade and survival in times of drought. North Dakotan George Will argued that the Missouri River and its tributaries formed the "backbone of the whole region" as Mandans, Arikaras, and Hidatsas thought of the land; this concept of space, he thought, held for "even the more distant tribes in the Plains." Will's archaeological research and interactions with Indigenous peoples led him to contemplate the differences between settler society's "state lines" and the "geological formations" they disrupted, causing him in turn to note that "prehistoric peoples and cultures" organized space by a different "force." In historical times Indigenous peoples knew grasslands resources and deployed a cycle of movement to utilize them very well.[95]

Only after the limits of (unaided, unirrigated) commercial grain agriculture became popularly accepted could a line between the Middle West and West be drawn more certainly straight through North America's northern grasslands and could prairies and plains grasses be tied to strictly defined attributes—whether in relation to precipitation or nation—that reflected new settler-colonial regions. The new definitions constituted cultural interpretations of the grasslands influenced, but not determined, by modern science and settler-society experiences from the late nineteenth century through the middle of the twentieth century. By then the lines of aridity finally apparent to so many of the descendants of settler-colonial society served to consolidate both the United States' and Canada's holds on North America, even as the lines repelled individual settler-colonial families. Settler society raised precipitation above grass, geology, and topography in modern regional definitions.

Across the grasslands, beyond the "fixity" of modern reservations, Indigenous people continued to recognize and tell stories about "where events occurred" in space and time regardless of settler-colonial national lines and the cultural regions by which settlers organized the continent. Indigenous worldviews stressed "interconnectedness and relationship between all things, between animals, land, peoples, and their languages," while settler colonials created "closed, categorized, and defined spaces." Indigenous geographic sensibilities, formed in relation to grasslands spaces, continued on in "intergenerational memory," often still "embedded in the features of the earth," anchoring Indigenous society to the place without regard to settler societies and their nations.[96]

Settler society's geographic regional labels grew from lifetimes of sensuous environmental experience to create senses of place also eventually embedded in the land alongside the survival of Indigenous places. Settler-colonial regional identities and senses of place circulated in the continent's cultural air to signal national possession of space on a cultural plane to all in the body politic, including people excluded explicitly or implicitly. The use of geographic labels to create regions became another way, perhaps unconscious in the average settler's mind, of implicitly distancing territory from Indigenous peoples for transfer to settler-society nation-states. Grasslands-grown settler-society generations shaped into regions what they sensed as children, immersed in grasslands and grainlands, experiencing considerable frustration, anguish, and joy. Their identification with cultural regions suggests their belonging to the place. Regional labels reinforced the separate claims of the United States and Canada to the continent's still-contested northern grasslands space.

Conclusion

Looking across the Line from the Prairies and Plains

"Here we have been enjoying a blizzard for 7 days," wrote Edward Pitblado to his younger sister on 26 December 1923. Ed sat stranded, not on the grasslands anchored by Winnipeg but nestled in the Swiss Alps. Pitblado had been instrumental in promoting an ice hockey team while at Oxford University and in organizing the team's between-term holiday tour. Christmas turned out to be a "very gay day at our Hotel," with people skiing and skating during the "greater part of the day," he wrote. The singular event occurred "after dinner," when "there was a masquerade dance, our Oxford team putting on a 'show' by ourselves," he boasted. "We all dressed up as Indians, with feathers, blankets and moccasins and we came into the darkened hall with a white prisoner. . . . We tied him to a tree and did a pow-wow around him with a dancer as a wild medicine man, myself as a chief with a huge butcher knife, one fat man as a squaw carrying in a papoose." He continued, "It went off very well but we had great difficulty in getting the paint off our faces. After that we changed back into evening dress and enjoyed a few dances." In this burlesque Pitblado drove down through sensibilities shaped by a place he felt had "more air than any one person could possibly breathe up" to the core of settler-colonial identity in presumed cultural and racial superiority.[1]

Edward Pitblado's racist performance of a pure fantasy "Indian pow-wow" showed little consciousness of settler-society expropriation of Indigenous land and little knowledge of the Indigenous peoples who remained on Canada's northern grasslands. Four months before the Christmas "show," he concluded in a letter, "Many many thanks for having been so successful in getting my homestead patent through. Of course it can't be viewed as a gold mine but is certainly worth something as being a piece of arable land."[2] Claiming land for many in this generation became a rite of passage, whether one wanted to make a living in agriculture or, as Pitblado planned, become a lawyer. Land led to wealth as well as sense of place. Born into settler society, he inherited that society's cultural capacity to imagine the region free of nevertheless still resident Indigenous peoples. Claiming land and "playing Indian" revealed the settler-colonial foundation of Pitblado's regional identity.[3]

What of Pitblado's Canadian identity? The famous North-West Mounted Police did not ride into the "show" to keep peace and order. For his European audience Pitblado chose to enact a North American popular mythic West identity. In England Pitblado thought of himself as a "colonial" from western Canada. One Halloween evening, for example, he told his mother, "several of we wild Colonials" set off firecrackers. He welcomed newspaper subscriptions to the provincial university's student newspaper, the *Manitoban*, and the *Winnipeg Free Press*, reasoning that they "will keep me from getting altogether Oxfordized." He played baseball with Americans and noted the "Colonial Club" hosted "the Americans as guests." Yet he also sought to distinguish himself from rowdy "Yanks" who seemed to "overrun" England with "any amount of money to throw around." He also noted "the bad habit that the people in [Great Britain] have of referring to all people from our part of the world as Americans, apparently never considering Canada at all. . . . They need educating badly as to the differences between our two countries." His love of shooting "big bags" of game birds and his discussions of grain and fresh air constituted regular expressions of regional identity. Pitblado had a distinct "colonial" British North American Canadian identity, different from "Americans" in the United States, even as he shared place connections across the international border to particular Americans who also lived on the continent's northern grasslands.[4]

Grasslands Grown has made the argument that in rooting into and growing up living day to day with native grasslands habitats, while building an agriculturally based settler society, the first generation born to settlers in Canada's Prairie Provinces and the U.S. Northern

Great Plains states shared a deep sense of place. They formed emotional senses of place by experiencing, with historical high levels of bodily immersion, a shifting mixture of existing wild native grasslands plants and commercial grains increasingly grown by settler society. The mix of grass and grain—the smells, sounds, tastes, and sights; the feel of the space in this configuration—is a distinguishing feature of this generation's sense of place. Small native animals and birds and domestic animals informed this generation's distinct rhythms of place. This settler-society generation located themselves intellectually using formal regional terms, starting with "Northwest" and "West" in both Canada and the United States and shifting increasingly across the first half of the twentieth century to "Prairie Provinces" in Canada and to the "Northern Great Plains" and "Middle West" in the United States. Identification with the "West" remained current. On both sides of the border, this generation also used "prairies" and "plains" informally, even unconsciously, as an everyday flexible cultural language that simultaneously connoted experience and location.

The angle of analytic focus on landscapes and atmosphere in *Grasslands Grown* foregrounds a continental view of the northern grasslands. This view distorts or enlarges *to reveal* a sense of place and regional identity. The elasticity of elevating part of an entire life can be seen in the two autobiographies Albertan Wilfrid Eggleston wrote. His *While I Still Remember* (1968) examined an entire journalism career with his experiences on the grasslands, discussed primarily in one chapter, but *Homestead on the Range* (1982) charted Eggleston's experiences in southern Alberta over his entire life.[5] The Canadians and Americans described here were both more—and less—than their experiences in place and region here holding center stage but too often deemphasized by the forces of nationalism that draw exclusive scholarly boundaries. Nationalism often has led to defensive caricatures of the U.S. West and indifference to valuing Canada's West, according to John Herd Thompson. Negotiating transnational history and historiography (two different tasks) can ensnare like gumbo, as historian Thomas D. Isern has said.[6] *Grasslands Grown* privileges varying amounts of time some individuals spent experiencing and thinking about North America's northern grasslands habitats.

Many of these individuals lived, or had relatives or close friends living, back and forth, on both sides of the forty-ninth parallel. Visiting across the line occurred for lifetimes. When Montana writer Dorothy Johnson crossed the border into Alberta in 1952 for the first time—perhaps surprising and also telling—border officials did not ask for identification.[7] Crossing the line for the first time suggests how long local life held sway (and Johnson had moved away from Montana for many years), and the openness of the border speaks to the fluidity of society during this period and well beyond.

As lifelong or one-time residents of North America's northern grasslands during the advent of settler colonialism, these residents shared and created an environmental sensibility known deeply from day-to-day lifeways. Many Canadians and Americans understood, and perhaps still understand, northern grasslands space in popular cliché as *the* place of "earth and sky." These generations of settler society, often unconsciously, invoked the meaning captured in the well-known phrase they also used, but by terms of experience. Wallace Stegner might say slough and rain; George Will, corn and snow; Wilfrid Eggleston, wheat and "sizzling" sun; and Robert McAlmon, "sparkle" and snow. Elsie May Hammond called it "wind and dust." Annora Brown wrote of blue snow and "blue distance." These experiences speak historically to an environmental spaciousness and envelopment that individuals first perceived and bodily absorbed while living on native grasslands habitats and over time, surrounded by commercial grain and graze fields.[8]

Most of the people discussed of course also expressed national affiliation at least in rudimentary ways. Elsie Hammond played "Britannia" in a local band in Maple Creek, Saskatchewan, honoring Canada's Dominion on 1 July 1926, and the next year she noted with special attention Canada's "60th Anniversary of Confederation." Montanan Lillian Miller recalled the "boom of cannon" and firecrackers at the 4 July celebration of U.S. national independence in her community as a "big event in our lives." Celebrating nation became ways for European immigrants to learn, as Thorstina Jackson Walters phrased it, the "essence of Democracy" in the United States. The transnational northern grassland Icelandic community, however, perhaps had their greatest attachment to Ameríku, the continent. Annora Brown recalled the British flag flying on 1 July. She appreciated Bloods and Piegans who performed in Macleod to earn money and to teach settlers, perhaps especially children, the beauty of their ceremonies. The meaning Brown took from Dominion Day suggests the role national celebratory events also played for asserting settler-society ownership of the place. The project of securing settler-society institutions in the space—amid Indigenous peoples who continued to live in the region with knowledge settler society had yet to realize—perhaps overwhelmed the need to assert Canadian and American identity or to express bold fealty to Canada or United States. These first grasslands-grown generations had a stake in securing settler society across the line first.[9]

Frequent cowboy, Mountie, and law and order or disorder references suggest these northern grasslands residents knew well U.S. and Canadian mythic West imagery. Many besides Edward Pitblado performed a popular West identity. The South Dakota writer Robert McAlmon's Paris friends spoke of his "rakish cowboy hat," "Western drawl," and propensity to deliver a "cowboy yipe" after a certain number of drinks. Wilfrid Eggleston's character in *The High Plains* fled the Royal North-West Mounted Police by crossing the border into Montana. Annora Brown retold a conversation she heard between her father and an old-timer suggestive of dueling Canadian and American Western myths: A man left Indiana for the West after the murder of his fiancée: "I come west and I was a pretty wild one." "'Dynamite' they called me and I was pretty handy with my gun—too handy with it—but that wasn't me, you know," he said, as Brown told the story. After he crossed the border into Canada he bought land, married, and helped raise two children. The shift in location from American to Canadian Wests corresponded to a change, in Brown's words, from "wild one" to upstanding man, the stereotypical U.S.-Canadian opposition. The man admitted, however, he ached for the "real man" he "left down there." A West where a damaged man renewed himself with a gun (in the United States) or one where he started over as a responsible provider (in Canada), however, are two variations of one escapist theme in which men went west to regain masculinity. The story spoke to Brown's father's "colourful past" and memorialized "the very stuff from which the country had been built," the pioneers (settlers and homesteaders) who became a primary topic for mythologizing among her own generation—on both sides of the line.[10]

The transnational grasslands grown of settler society were as likely to invoke the popular West to demythologize it as they were to play Canada and the United States against each other to express national identity. The popular West attracted readers. Members of this generation frequently included wry references to mythic Wests even as they went on to relate their more realistic personal stories. Brown might have discussed the North-West Mounted Police establishing order and peace in the Canadian West with reference to her one-time Mountie father. Instead, she focused on his economic insecurity and naivete about farming, situations that undermined the masculinity of western men. North Dakotan Era Bell Thompson undermined the dominant imagery of a West racially coded white by including Black families. By reattaching whiteness to a snowy, "frozen wilds," northern West, she also challenged popular desert depictions of the West. Further, she placed herself, a Black woman, at the center of a Western story countering a masculinist West. Finally, Thompson included Indigenous girls with whom she made friends to undercut the romantic and racist popular West ideas she herself carried to the place. North Dakotan poet Clell Gannon signaled "Wild West" with the title "The Law of Dakota" but communicated instead conflicted adaptation to the "law of the infinite space" felt by this generation of settler society: "You are going to leave certain by winter / . . . You and Winter are still in Dakota / Each wants to get out—but it can't."[11] This generation used the popular West to tell humbler, often troubled, stories that joined mythic "pioneer" narratives they also told as a part of their regional project.

The formal regional "Prairie Provinces" and "Northern Great Plains" labels used increasingly by these generations of settler society across the decades of the first half of the twentieth century almost certainly reflected growing national distinction on both sides of the forty-ninth parallel. Two incidents suggest a nationalism growing in the same decades these generations lived the prime of their lives.

A fictional account of the 1911 U.S.-Canadian Reciprocity Trade Agreement suggests how the border rose to consciousness in reference to national economic policy. In Nell Wilson Parsons's 1947 novel, *The Curlew Cried*, the Canadian-born Saskatchewan wheat farmer and horse-breeder Lane Jarvis denounces the 1911 agreement between the United States and Canada that many historical observers expected would lower tariffs on machinery Canadian farmers needed. Most farmers in Parsons's novel—and in 1911 Saskatchewan—supported the agreement. A neighbor asks Jarvis why a Canadian farmer should "pay tribute" to buy a binder. Jarvis replies, "Canada doesn't want to be annexed!" and "Perhaps some of us are willing to pay the price to remain Canadians!" Below the line the United States hoped to gain economically by opening Canadian trade to its manufacturers, but U.S. northern grasslands farmers feared their northern neighbors' grain would flood commodity markets and lower prices. National policy placed farmers worried about machinery costs against farmers uneasy about commodity surpluses. A common concern about the agricultural economy, expressed uniquely on each side of the line, however, spoke to shared insecurities associated with a changing northern grasslands agricultural sector of an international economic system. National policy operated in a realm of life different from shared day-to-day cultural features rooted in North America's northern grasslands natural environments.[12]

Conflict across the line can be seen also in the sentiment the Saskatchewan-raised Leslie Neatby recalled looking back from the 1970s, still simmering about his 1920s education. Concerned about preserving Canadian intellectual life, Neatby criticized the "Barbarian Invasion" by Americans or Canadians with doctorates from American Universities teaching in Canada, which "practically destroyed the cultural element in Canadian schooling." (Perhaps Elsie Hammond's 1916 reference to the Canadian Prairie Provinces as a "Midwest" region *did* have its origins in a U.S.-published textbook or U.S.-trained teacher!) The power of U.S. educational curriculums to overwhelm Canadian contexts, Leslie Neatby thought, made Canadian schools only "superficially . . . native." For one thing, citing a lesson on stoplights as particularly irrelevant, Neatby argued that U.S. educators taught curriculums too urban for "rural Saskatchewan" students. To him American textbooks and their "arrogant assumption of superiority" represented cultural imperialism on a par with the economic imperialism that landed "U.S. industrial enterprises on Canadian soil." At the same time, proud to have lost any inflection of the English accent he carried with him to Canada as a boy, Neatby felt affirmed in his Canadian identity, when in the 1950s he found himself annoyed with English people who believed in the "superiority of all things English." No doubt American-generated educational curriculums and schools of education thoughtlessly presumed U.S. content would work seamlessly in Canada. Teachers on the northern grasslands directly across the line from Saskatchewan in North Dakota, however, probably also felt the sting of curriculums that barely considered rural students.[13] Neatby's sentiments implicitly expressed a rural grasslands critique of an urbanizing continent *in addition* to concern for a thriving Canadian culture.

The difference in the population sizes of Canada and the United States, with the latter then and since generally ten times the size of the former, suggests the threat felt "by the sheer admitted weight of the United States," as the British poet Rudyard Kipling phrased Canadian concern about 1911 reciprocity with the United States—an election issue in Canada that year. In Parsons's novel Lane Jarvis translates Kipling's open letter about the agreement to a "warning" that "we're only nine million against America's ninety million?" At the time Canadian Conservative Party leader, Robert L. Bordon (who won causing reciprocity to fail), summed up the situation: "We must decide whether a spirit of Canadianism or of Continentalism is to prevail on the northern half of this continent." Apparently, at the time "in private, both governments recognized that something quite important had occurred and that Canadian nationalism was a factor that must in the future be taken into account." Similarly, Neatby never forgot the education professor who argued the disparity in populations across the line meant the United States "produced men of a higher order of genius" compared to "us Canadian backwoodsmen."[14]

On the ground level of northern grasslands space, however, the Prairie Provinces by the early twentieth century—depending on calculation parameters—had more population than the Northern Great Plains states. With Minnesota the Northern Great Plains states are merely twice the size of the Prairie Provinces.[15] When Canadians felt culturally threatened or ignored by the United States, they generally did not have the states of the Northern Great Plains in mind, which did not pose the same cultural threat the entire United States did to Canada and its unique cultures. Perhaps even the people of these states felt almost as inconsequential to the rest of the United States as Canadians often felt. North Dakotan Era Bell Thompson's application for a regional studies grant explained her "story" would "deal with this little known state in the Country God Forgot."[16] She felt this way, and she lived in Chicago, one-time gateway to the West, then emergent as pivotal city for a Middle West. With specific reference to the Northern Great Plains, the cultural geographer James Shortridge argued in the late 1990s, "Plains people, with their small populations, have never had much control over how others have seen them. The possibilities for distortion, misunderstanding, and general mythmaking are enormous."[17]

Still, this group of grasslands-grown individuals who grew up in settler society during its earliest decades, some living their entire lives in the Prairie Provinces or the Northern Great Plains states, attempted to express their senses of place and regional identities for wider publics to recognize. Although the individuals studied here reached for national notice, most emerged perhaps as only regional cultural elite. They became leaders in their professional and social communities. Their activities and cultural products helped build regional cultures. The regions and places they created reflected their positions of power or connections to people and organizations of power. Persistent intraregional *and* transnational regional conversations also suggest that this generation—at least these particular people—felt some measure of shared culture and had similar regional questions across the forty-ninth parallel boundary.

Not only were members of this generation on both sides of the border talking and thinking about the same issues, themes, and ideas, they were talking to one another. The similarity of the archival policies that drew in these individuals' collections perhaps should

Conclusion 357

have suggested they would run in the same social circles. Individuals with access to publishers reflected the same. However, the trail of documents left by each one alone reveals some of these Canadians reached out to some of these Americans and vice versa. They wrote one another, attended the same events, read the same materials, and drew from one another's works to enhance their own understandings of the region and place. Americans and Canadians connected across the line for particular reasons, pursuing specific elements of transnational northern grasslands culture.

The dialogue began in each country and continued across the line. When Wilfrid Eggleston wrote to fellow Albertan Annora Brown on Christmas Eve to tell her "what constant and deep pleasure we receive from daily admiration of your picture of the lone grain elevator," he explained, "We don't know one another in person, but we have heard of one another." The elevator may have seemed "graceless" to a reporter commenting on Brown's work in 1930, but by the 1950s it spoke to the place settler society built.[18] As a young journalist, Eggleston reached out to many of his contemporaries, including interviewing one of Effie Laurie Storer's brothers about the history of the area. His 1982 *Homestead on the Range* memoir used Georgina Thomson's memoir *Crocus and Meadowlark Country*. Eggleston reviewed Annora Brown's *Old Man's Garden* for the *Winnipeg Free Press*.[19] As a member of the Ottawa branch of the Canadian Writers' Foundation, Eggleston suggested providing support for the Icelandic writer Laura Goodman Salverson.[20] Eggleston may have been one of the few or the only one of these individuals to read one of Robert McAlmon's short stories included in *The Best Short Stories of 1929*.[21] When Ralph Russell published *The Carlton Trail* (1955) about a trade route that once passed some eight miles northeast of the family's Saskatchewan homestead, Leslie Neatby reached out with support: "To a resident of the Prairies who has known the contours to colours and the smells— who has seen horses forlornly grouped together in the rain—it is fascinating," he praised.[22]

South of the line, George Will knew fellow North Dakotan Vilhjalmur Stefansson from having spent time with him in the Peabody Museum at Harvard University.[23] As a historian, Leslie Neatby studied Stefansson, arguing that the explorer's Manitoba–North Dakota Icelandic community and adolescence as a "cowboy on the plains" fitted him for the work.[24] The Millennial Celebration of Iceland's "Thousand Year Old Parliament" in June 1930 brought together Thorstina Jackson Walters and U.S. South Dakota senator Peter Norbeck. Walters wrote Norbeck, who attended the celebration as part of an official delegation funded by the U.S. Congress, about the details of a Cunard excursion ship she organized, sponsored by the "Committee of American and Canadian Icelanders." Walters later sent "wonderful" photographs from the event to Lydia and Peter Norbeck.[25] The academic Theodore C. Blegen, who oversaw Thorstina Jackson Walters's regional studies grant, wrote an introduction to the second volume of Aagot Raaen's autobiography, *Measure of My Days*. In 1953 the North Dakota Institute for Regional Studies at Fargo, founded in 1950—symbolic of the institutions this generation began forming—published the Raaen volume and Walters's *Modern Sagas*. Showing broad support for Walters's history, prominent Icelanders living in North Dakota sent out "An Appeal" for donations to defray publication costs, stressing a "special significance to the Sons and Daughters of the Icelandic pioneers" as a reason to donate.[26]

A regional population received Annora Brown's *Old Man's Garden* (1954) eagerly. One reviewer described Brown's study as a key to "the flowers all we, who have lived in the west, are acquainted with by sight but certainly not as fully as we should have been." Eggleston's review admitted, "I wish it had been in existence when I was a boy on the prairie myself, and later when I taught a rural school there."[27] Georgina Thompson urged the readers of her Alberta memoir to locate Brown's *Old Man's Garden*, since they, as she, probably "had no way of knowing" wildflower names.[28] Moreover, Brown's book reflected her work in paint. She designed her paintings "to appeal to people like me who had lived amongst the wild flowers and who had loved them as I had."[29] By the 1960s, art galleries in Calgary began to sell Brown's "very fine and well known paintings of Canadian Wild Flowers" to a now eager-buying public, many who lived or once lived on Canada's grasslands.[30]

Surely, many of Brown's contemporaries across the line would have experienced reverie if they read Brown's *Old Man's Garden*.

The transnational reach of the work seemed obvious. Her publisher planned "to send review copies to the leading papers in Montana, Idaho and North Dakota" and also "circulars to various people in these states."[31] Brown's study of plants formed a popular corollary to George Will's regular review of the scientific literature issued by government experiment stations on both sides of the border.[32] Will also reached out to popular audiences; in 1928 he published "The Grandmother Who Never Dies" about Mandan sacred ceremonies and expertise in corn agriculture in the *Country Guide*, a magazine read by many prairie Canadians, including Annora Brown, who illustrated for the magazine.[33]

A telling exchange took place in 1956 between former northern grasslands residents Wallace Stegner and Wilfrid Eggleston. After reading an article by Stegner in *Saskatchewan History*, Eggleston wrote to praise Stegner by ranking him with Joseph Kinsey Howard, author of *Montana* (1943) and *Strange Empire* (1952) (a history of the Métis on the transnational northern grasslands), and "Bill" W. O. Mitchell, author of the novel *Who Has Seen the Wind* (1947).[34] (Incidentally, Mitchell owned an Annora Brown painting.)[35] Stegner cited Howard in his biography of John Wesley Powell; the latter's "plan for the plains" had also influenced Howard, who grew up in Montana and Alberta.[36] Stegner wrote back in thanks, explaining he had read one of Eggleston's articles "on the [Cypress] Hills and found it by all odds the best thing I ever saw in print about them." Eggleston had mentioned that his own novel *The High Plains* (1938) centered on a community he called "wolf willow," named after the shrub with tiny yellow flowers of "haunting fragrance"; in response Stegner admitted he "did not know" it but promised to find a copy. Stegner put Eggleston on a list to receive a copy of his next book. Eggleston's opinion mattered, Stegner explained, "as one of the few people in the world competent to judge its material."[37] When Stegner published what became *Wolf Willow* (1962)—choosing the same telling plant as Eggleston to elucidate the place—he cited Montanan Joseph Kinsey Howard's work, an author also used by Annora Brown when researching *Old Man's Garden* (1954), which of course included an entry on "Wolf Willow." She explained that wolf willow had a scent "so powerful . . . that it needs the whole prairie in which to spread itself." Brown also painted wolf willow with silver berries in the winter sun.[38] George Will agreed, and he identified the "very fragrant" "Silverberry," another name for wolf willow, as truly "of the northern plains," though according to Will, the shrub grew "much more luxuriantly in Canada" than in North Dakota.[39]

Although Stegner never mentioned his own 1940 *On a Darkling Plain*, Eggleston knew the novel. Judging Stegner's work more favorably than Eggleston's *The High Plains*, a Calgary librarian wrote Eggleston in 1941 with guarded praise, seeing positively the novel's "very faithful and true account of a period of settlement." The librarian admitted that the novel "did not warm my heart" but added that "neither has any book on prairie life that I can remember except possibly bits of Stegner's *On a darkling plain*." He cited other "prairie" women who received Eggleston's book "much more favorably" and offered, "I don't believe anyone can write a good prairie tale unless he has grown up on the prairie and come to love it and the people on it."[40] The *High River Times* reviewer of Eggleston's novel reported, "in the eyes of Western people," Eggleston "is permanently Western, with an unfailing understanding and appreciation of Western problems."[41] Stegner discussed receiving similar fan letters, saying, "I've noticed that people who did grow up on the plains nearly all feel it's a special culture."[42] Eggleston agreed; "you get it into your soul."[43]

Brown's growing book and painting market, Stegner's fans, the "prairie" women who claimed Eggleston as their own, Neatby's praise of Russell's history of the Carlton Trail, Icelanders fund-raising for Walters's history—all suggest that a larger population welcomed these bits of cultural production, even if such work received little critical acclaim or national notice. Actual and metaphoric conversations among the grasslands grown of settler society suggest their struggle to explain and express their experiences of the place. They shaped cultural memory with narratives and imagery that became regional touchpoints. They created institutions and associations through which settler society wedged their stories into the land, already associated with the history, language, memories, and sacred traditions of Indigenous peoples, from Mandans to Piegans, whose cultures have still "a different continuity and intimacy with the universe," to use the critic Elizabeth Cook-Lynn's words.[44] Region and place making was to land claiming in the settler-colonial project down the generations— that is, parents of the grasslands-grown generations acted as settler colonials by claiming homesteads under the laws of the United States and Canada; their children furthered settler colonialism by drawing boundaries and creating senses of place to express cultural ownership in atmospheric and geographic regional terms.

The shift in regional labels from "Northwest" to "Prairie Provinces" and "Northern Great Plains" states signaled the transformation of northern grasslands native habitats by settler society into grainfield and graze land and their growing identifications with Canada and the United States. The agricultural lifeways these particular generations practiced would intensify soon after the middle of the twentieth century, shifting place rhythms and regional contours. National cultures across the forty-ninth parallel of international boundary grew sharper distinctions over the next generations rising and decades passing. George Will's publications on Mandan, Arikara, and Hidatsa agricultural traditions in *North Dakota History* and Canada's *Country Guide* suggest that some residents had inklings of understanding (and some readers learned) about some of the costs of their settler society to Indigenous peoples. The agricultural transformation of the northern grasslands and the literature of memoir, fiction, poetry, and art, however, expressed settler possession of the land on the plane of regional culture. The grasslands-grown generations of settler society created places out of their emotional, physical, and intellectual experiences of prairies and plains grasses, tame and wild.

Notes

Introduction

1. DeLand, "Verendrye Explorations," 260–87, 267, 264–65, 274; Doane Robinson to Lawrence J. Burpee, 4 March 1913, folder 110; Elmer W. Anderson to State Historical Society, 18 January 1939, folder 112, both in box 3362A, DRP.
2. Wishart, *Encyclopedia*, 828–29; Paul, *Blue Water Creek*, 57–58; Ostler, *Lakotas*, 44–49, 83–84; Jonathan Ellis, "Feds Rename Harney Peak, South Dakota's Highest Point," *Argus Leader* (Sioux Falls SD), 11 August 2016.
3. DeLand, "Verendrye Explorations," 260–87, 267, 264–65, 274; G. Smith, *Explorations*, 113, 115–27.
4. Wishart, *Fur Trade*; Allen, *Lewis and Clark*, xxvi; G. Smith, *Explorations*, 3–4, 43.
5. G. Smith, *Explorations*, 113, 46, 49, 63, 109; Friesen and Young, "French Empire."
6. Meinig, *Shaping of America* (1986), 193–222, 269–70; Eccles, *French in North America*, 133–34, 268.
7. DeLand, "Verendrye Explorations," 260–87, 267, 264–65, 274, 276; Robinson, DeLand, and Libby, "Additional Verendrye Material," 371; Will, "Criticism," 296.
8. Paris archivist Pierre Margry published the La Vérendrye exploration journals in the mid-nineteenth century. Accounts of the journeys did not appear in North America or in an English version until 1888, when Francis Parkman published an article in the *Atlantic Monthly*, but the journals were vague. Parkman, "Rocky Mountains"; W. Jacobs, *Letters of Francis Parkman*, 221; DeLand, "Verendrye Explorations"; Burpee, "La Vérendrye's 1738–39 Journal"; G. Smith, *Explorations*, xv–xvi. Smith sorted through the controversies surrounding various translations.
9. D. Robinson, "Verendrye Plate"; Clark, "Historical Activities" (1915), 404; Clark, "Historical Activities" (1916), 350; "Ree Camp at Breedenhurst," 4 September 1916, folder 34, box 3360A, DRP; Libby, "Some

Verendrye Enigmas"; Robinson, DeLand, and Libby, "Additional Verendrye Material"; Will, "Criticism"; Lee, "Discovery."

10. DeLand, "Verendrye Explorations," 322 (emphasis added); Lee, "Discovery."
11. Arikaras are probably descended from Caddoans in Kansas and Nebraska. The Mandans and Hidatsas had lived together at Like-a-Fishhook village in modern North Dakota since 1845. Schell, *History of South Dakota*, 16–18, 33–34, 46, 59; E. Robinson, *History of North Dakota*, 97–98, 105, 107, 180–81; Meyer, *Village Indians*, 7–8, 13, 28, 55, 87, 101–5. See also Libby, "Some Verendrye Enigmas," 152; Robinson, DeLand, and Libby "Additional Verendrye Material," 398; Will, "Criticism." See correspondence between Orin Libby and Doane Robinson, folder 110, box 3362A, DRP.
12. Worster, "Summing Up," 271, 276–77.
13. West, "More Interesting Story," 103–11, 108.
14. M. Smith, *Sensing the Past*, 3–5; Tuan, *Space and Place*, 8–10; Tuan, *Topophilia*; Amato, *Rethinking Home*, 60–76; Rodaway, *Sensuous Geographies*, 4–10; Dorman, *Hell of a Vision*, 3.
15. Canadians called much of the northern grasslands "North-Western Territories" until 1905; see Waiser, *Saskatchewan*, 1–19. Residents of the United States knew Northwest in relation to the Old Northwest (states formed north of the Ohio River), the New Northwest (Minnesota and the Dakotas), and the Pacific Northwest (Oregon and Washington); see Shortridge, *Middle West*, 13–26; Dorman, *Hell of a Vision*, 3; and West, *Contested Plains*, xxi, 49–52, 224–28, 242.
16. White, "Trashing the Trails," 27, 29, 39; Flores, "Place," 5.
17. Veracini, *Settler Colonialism*, 33–43, 53, 96–98; Hixson, *American Settler Colonialism*, 1–4. See Veracini's list of ways settler colonialism works to "enact a variety of transfers" (33). Transfers occur, for example, "when indigenous peoples are disavowed in a variety of ways and their actual presence is not registered" (*Settler Colonialism*, 37) or "when 'settlers are also indigenous peoples' claims are made" (42–43).
18. Libby, "Some Verendrye Enigmas," 152; Robinson, DeLand, and Libby "Additional Verendrye Material," 398; Will, "Criticism," 292–93. Since at least 1908, Will and Libby had argued about distinctions of Hidatsa and Mandan sites. Will, "Bourgeois Village Site"; Dixon, "Review of Collections"; Libby, "Proper Identification."
19. Doane Robinson to Orin G. Libby, 3, 15 September 1913, folder 110; William O'Reilly (father of George O'Reilly), notarized relinquishment of claim document, 24 March 1916, folder 111; D. C. Shull to Robinson, 11 May 1916, 6 March 1917, folder 111; Robinson to Shull, 13

May 1916, folder 111; SD attorney general Royal Johnson to Robinson, 24 March 1913, folder 111, all in box 3362A, DRP; G. Smith, *Explorations*.
20. Malin, *Grassland of North America*, 75.
21. Thompson, foreword to Evans, *Borderlands*, xii–xiii; Isern and Shepard, "Duty-Free," xxviii–xxv. In *Contested Plains* West discusses the role of imagination in creating regions; see pages xix–xxii, 13–14, 54, 116–17, 122, 179, 212, 318, 326–29.
22. White, *Organic Machine*, x.
23. White, "Nationalization of Nature," 982. White quotes John H. Elliott on "notional entity," an area created as an organizational device "rather than [emerging from] the people who actually lived in it" (982); I use the label "northern grasslands" in this sense. The northern grasslands defined here includes Alberta, Manitoba, Minnesota, Montana, North Dakota, Saskatchewan, and South Dakota. Defining the area of study by national, state, and provincial lines acknowledges the political processes settler-colonial societies used to create places and regions but are not identical to the ecological boundaries, which spill beyond political lines (into western Minnesota, for example) or make up only part of a larger concern (only the southern part of Saskatchewan, for example). Continually changing ecology constantly challenges natural boundaries: an interaction of climate, topography, geology, flora, fauna, and human cultures. On mapping, see S. McManus, *Line Which Separates*.
24. Mannheim, "Problem of Generations"; Kriegel, "Generational Difference"; Spitzer, "Historical Problem of Generations"; Carl Dassbach, "The Problem of Generations Reconsidered," unpublished paper.
25. Veracini, *Settler Colonialism*, 96–104; Treaty Elders and Tribal Council, *True Spirit*, 191.
26. West, "More Interesting Story," 107–11, 110.
27. Higham and Thacker, *One West, Two Myths*; Higham and Thacker, *One West, Two Myths II*.
28. M. Jacobs, *White Mother*, xxxii, 229–30; Veracini, *Settler Colonialism*, 42–43, 46.
29. West, *Growing Up*, 42–45, 30, 130–31, 260; Shover, *First Majority*; Neth, *Preserving the Family Farm*, 5; Barron, *Mixed Harvest*, 7–16, 194; MacPherson and Thompson, "Business of Agriculture," 475–96. In *On the Great Plains* Cunfer calculates farmers left some 270 million acres unplowed, though commercial agriculture compromised all the grasslands (8).
30. Dorman, *Revolt of the Provinces*, 55–80; Thompson, *Canada*, 158–61, 175–90.

1. Parents' Choice

1. Effie Laurie Storer, "My Story," 2.3, ELSP, 1; Storer, "Queen's Printer," 1942–43, 2.4, ELSP, 1, 37; Storer, "Reverie," 1947, 2.5, ELSP, 1–2.
2. Norbeck and Norbeck, *Norbecks of South Dakota*, 3, 70, 7, 46–47, 54–62, 69–70, 81–83.
3. Veracini, *Settler Colonialism*, 33–52; Goeman, "Disrupting a Settler-Colonial Grammar," 235–38, 245.
4. Wingerd, *North Country*; Meyer, *Santee Sioux*. The four groups of "Eastern Dakotas" lived in the parkland-transition area, while the two groups of "Western Dakotas" lived on the grasslands east of the Missouri River. There has been historical confusion over whether Western Dakotas spoke Nakota or Dakota dialect. Recent linguistic work suggests Nakota is used "as a term of self-designation by the Assninboine and Stoney tribes," now north of the border in Canada. See Lakota Language Consortium, *New Lakota Dictionary*, 2.
5. Ostler, *Plains Sioux*; Ostler, *Lakotas*; Fowler, *American Indians*, 181–82; Meyer, *Village Indians*; Wingerd, *North Country*; St. Germain, *Indian Treaty-Making Policy*; Friesen, *Canadian Prairies*; St. Germain, *Broken Treaties*; Samek, *Blackfoot Confederacy*, 13.
6. Ostler, *Lakotas*, 38–41; Meyer, *Village Indians*, 103.
7. St. Germain, *Indian Treaty-Making Policy*, 6–8, 22–26, 35–46.
8. Nichols, *Indians*, 205, 207–8, 242; Friesen, *Canadian Prairies*, 131–37.
9. Allen, *Lewis and Clark*, 1; Paul, *Blue Water Creek*, 23–24, 93, 105, 107, 135, 137, 142–43, 203, 205; Wingerd, *North Country*, 301–38; Nichols, *Indians*, 215, 213–20; Ostler, *Plains Sioux*, 45–46, 50, 59, 63; St. Germain, *Indian Treaty-Making Policy*, 10–11, 27–32.
10. St. Germain, *Indian Treaty-Making Policy*, 85, 90.
11. Fowler, *American Indians*, 163; Nichols, *Indians*, 200–204.
12. Schell, *History of South Dakota*, 89.
13. See U.S. Congress, "Act for the Removal," 662–54, 819–20; Wingerd, *North Country*, 189–96, 287–345; Meyer, *Santee Sioux*, 79–88; Schell, *History of South Dakota*, 20–21, 72.
14. Meyer, *Santee Sioux*, 198–99; H. Thompson, *New South Dakota History*, 92.
15. Ostler, *Lakotas*, 58, 62–68; Prucha, "Appendix B"; St. Germain, "Appendix A"; Samek, *Blackfoot Confederacy*, 12–13, 37; Malone, Roeder, and Lang, *Montana*, 120–21.
16. Ostler, *Lakotas*, 46–51, 80–103, 65–67, 98–100; Schell, *History of South Dakota*, 138–39, 363–64; Prucha, *American Indian Treaties*, 287–88, 292–96, 300–308, 317, 324; Ostler, *Plains Sioux*, 224; Hoover, "Sioux Agreement," 58.

17. J. Miller, *Skyscrapers Hide the Heavens*, 173; St. Germain, *Indian Treaty-Making Policy*, 21–22, 81; Owram, *Promise of Eden*, 39–45, 76–77, 79–100; J. Thompson, *Forging the Prairie West*, 37; Nichols, *Indians*, 208–12, 220; Gluek, *Minnesota*, 191–219, 275–87.
18. J. Thompson, *Forging the Prairie West*, 36–42; Friesen, *Canadian Prairies*, 114–28; Sweetgrass, quoted in St. Germain, *Indian Treaty-Making Policy*, 21–22, 43, 39; Friesen, *Canadian Prairies*, 67–75, 136; Meinig, *Shaping of America* (1993), 67–69, 74; J. Miller, *Skyscrapers Hide the Heavens*, 153–55, 158–59.
19. J. Miller, *Skyscrapers Hide the Heavens*, 160–69; Friesen, *Canadian Prairies*, 135–49, 137–38; St. Germain, "Appendix 2."
20. J. Miller, *Skyscrapers Hide the Heavens*, 167–68; Ostler, *Lakotas*, 98–102, 99–100.
21. St. Germain, *Indian Treaty-Making Policy*, 44–45. Indeed, in *Skyscrapers Hide the Heavens* J. Miller attributed the reason London and Ottawa chose not to consult the peoples of Red River in 1869 when purchasing HBC land "partly" to "Canada's anxiety to annex the lands before the Americans to the south could interfere and arrange events so that the territory would fall to them as had Oregon, California, Texas, Florida and other regions the Americans had coveted in the past" (154). Minnesota politicians and businesspeople, if not the U.S. Congress or general population, dreamed of unifying the entire North American northern grasslands economically, if not politically.
22. Pike, quoted in Goetzmann, *Exploration and Empire*, 51; Pike and Long, quoted in Meinig, *Shaping of America* (1993), 76–77. On the drought tinting the Long expedition's view of the southern grasslands, see Sweeney, *Prelude*, 3–18.
23. Warren, *Explorations*, 6.
24. Hayden, quoted in Emmons, *Garden in the Grasslands*, 132, 138, 141; Goetzmann, *Exploration and Empire*, 496, also 309–10, 491–92, 527.
25. Owram, *Promise of Eden*, 61–69, 104–5, 115. The base of this arid triangle went from about the 100th to the 114th meridian along the border and angle together to a point at the 52nd parallel (152). In his 1857 study, *Climatology*, the U.S. scientist Lorin Blodgett argued the warm temperature line moved north as one moved east to west across the continent (65–67). See also Mackintosh, *Prairie Settlement*, 32.
26. Owram, *Promise of Eden*, 151–63. Hind's 40 million fertile acres "suitable for crops," under Macoun's evaluation, grew to 80 million acres in 1877 and 150 million in 1881 (163).
27. Powell, "Report on the Lands"; Emmons, *Garden in the Grasslands*, 184, 134–39, 141; Pound quoted on 138; Owram, *Promise of Eden*, 157–58; Hind quoted on 164.

28. Emmons, *Garden in the Grasslands*, 134–39, 166.
29. E. Robinson, *History of North Dakota*, 67, 120; Malone, Roeder, and Lang, *Montana*, 57, 72–74; Friesen, *Canadian Prairies*, 222.
30. Meinig, *Shaping of America* (1993), 68–69; Schell, *History of South Dakota*, 72–76; E. Robinson, *History of North Dakota*, 62–67, 72–80, 111, 113, 141; Widdis, *With Scarcely a Ripple*, 265, 255–89; Friesen, *Canadian Prairies*, 69–75, 203.
31. Malone, Roeder, and Lang, *Montana*, 57, 72–74, 64, 145–55, 94–96; Palmer, *Alberta*, 24–25, 53, 32; E. Robinson, *History of North Dakota*, 101–3; Schell, *History of South Dakota*, 66–69, 80–83; Sharp, *Whoop-Up Country*, 38–43, 51, 87–89, 128, 213, 166, 188, 224; Hildebrandt and Hubner, *Cypress Hills*, 35–39, 41, 43–47, 76.
32. Gates, *Public Land Law Development*, 219–47, 387–434; Schell, *History of South Dakota*, 170–74; E. Robinson, *History of North Dakota*, 148–49; Edwards, Friefeld, and Wingo, *Homesteading the Plains*, 25–40.
33. Martin, *Dominion Lands Policy*, 141–42, 151, 163–64, 181–89; Carter, *Imperial Plots*, 82; S. McManus, *Line Which Separates*, 40–41; Friesen, *Canadian Prairies*, 182–84, 186.
34. E. Robinson, *History of North Dakota*, 6, 12; Chapman, Ziegenhagen, and Fischer, *Valley of Grass*, 1–13; Friesen, *Canadian Prairies*, 3–9; Reaume, *Manitoba's Tall Grass Prairie*.
35. Norbeck and Norbeck, *Norbecks of South Dakota*, 45.
36. Norbeck and Norbeck, *Norbecks of South Dakota*, 3, 7, 20, 23–24, 38–40, 44–47, 54–62, 69–70, 81–82; Meyer, *Santee Sioux*, 105–6; Schell, *History of South Dakota*, 115–16, 315; Schell, *History of Clay County*, 11–12, 35; Fite, *Peter Norbeck*, 10–11; H. Thompson, *New South Dakota History*, 17–19, 30, 33, 37–38, 58, 69–70, 74–75, 89–90, 105–6; Rothrock, *Geology of South Dakota*, 26–29.
37. E. Robinson, *History of North Dakota*, 129–30, 25–27, 112, 115–16, 147; Handy-Marchello, introd. to Raaen, *Grass of the Earth*, vii–xxvii, x–xi; Raaen, *Grass of the Earth*, 15–17, 77, 102; Raaen, *Measure of My Days*, 3; Wingerd, *North Country*, 338–40; Widdis, *With Scarcely a Ripple*, 257.
38. Storer, "Queen's Printer," ELSP, 2, 4–5, 8–24, 34–35; William Laurie, "Memoir," 3.7, ELSP, 2; Hildebrandt, *Views from Fort Battleford*, 52; Owram, *Promise of Eden*, 79–84; Friesen, *Canadian Prairies*, 121.
39. S. McManus, *Line Which Separates*, 6–11.
40. Schell, *History of South Dakota*, 159; E. Robinson, *History of North Dakota*, 134; Malone, Roeder, and Lang, *Montana*, 194. Friesen, *Canadian Prairies*, 202, 220.
41. Friesen, *Canadian Prairies*, 175–81, 221; Owram, *Promise of Eden*, 161–63; J. Thompson, *Forging the Prairie West*, 52–54. Canada granted the CPR a twenty-year monopoly, ensuring no other railway would be permitted

to build lines south of the CPR; connecting lines could not be constructed within fifteen miles of the U.S. border. Malone, Roeder, and Lang, *Montana*, 177–84; E. Robinson, *History of North Dakota*, 181, 184; Schell, *History of South Dakota*, 161–63.

42. Friesen, *Canadian Prairies*, 188; Thompson and Randall, *Canada*, 56–57; Palmer, *Alberta*, 53; Waiser, *Saskatchewan*, 50; Sharp, *Whoop-Up Country*, 239; Malone, Roeder, and Lang, *Montana*, 157, 177–81, 195; Hildebrandt and Hubner, *Cypress Hills*, 78; E. Robinson, *History of North Dakota*, 184, 228.

43. Martin, *Dominion Lands Policy*, 151.

44. Malone, Roeder, and Lang, *Montana*, 148, 163–64; Voisey, *High River*, 9; J. Thompson, *Forging the Prairie West*, 64; Elofson, *Cowboys*, 9, 19, 149; Palmer, *Alberta*, 53–54; Friesen, *Canadian Prairies*, 237–38; Waiser, *Saskatchewan*, 51–52.

45. Meyer, *Village Indians*, 112–14, 136–37. In 1886 another agreement, ratified by Congress in 1891, reduced the Fort Berthold Reservation to 965,920 acres (160). E. Robinson, *History of North Dakota*, 103–6, 147–48. In 1892 the U.S. Congress requested the Turtle Mountain Chippewas (Ojibwes) formally cede the nine million acres officials seized ten years before. Wingerd, *North Country*, 340; Malone, Roeder, and Lang, *Montana*, 21, 120–21, 142–43; Samek, *Blackfoot Confederacy*, 37, 44, 107–8, 110–17; Schell, *History of South Dakota*, 299–303; Ostler, *Plains Sioux*, 217–39; Hoover, "Sioux Agreement," 63–66; H. Thompson, *New South Dakota History*, 516.

46. St. Germain, *Broken Treaties*, 44–52, 212–13; St. Germain, "Appendix B," 365–72; St. Germain, *Indian Treaty-Making Policy*, 42, 84.

47. Friesen, *Canadian Prairies*, 227–36; St. Germain, *Broken Treaties*, 246–50, 312–29.

48. Lulu [Pickler] Frad, "The Big Old House in the Little Old Town," [1949?], PFP; C. Ellis, *History of Faulk County*, 25, 61, 269; Sommer, "Pickler Family Papers," 115–20, 124; "Dakota," *Faulkton Times*, 21 December 1882, 22 February 1883, 27 December 1883, 2 October 1884; Schell, *History of South Dakota*, 165, 170, 159, 59; Alice Humphrey to Alfred Humphrey, 15 December 1884, HFP; H. Thompson, *New South Dakota History*, 69–70; Lotchin, *San Francisco*, 136, 341.

49. H. Thompson, *New South Dakota History*, 13, 18, 20, 27, 30–31, 33–34, 37–38; Rothrock, *Geology of South Dakota*, 24–26, 34–37; Hogan and Fouberg, *Geography of South Dakota*; "Dakota," *Faulkton Times*, 21 December 1882, 12 June 1884, 19 March 1885, 24 June 1886, 5 August 1886; Nellie Humphrey to Alfred Humphrey, 24 April 1885, HFP.

50. E. Robinson, *History of North Dakota*, 142, 131; Schneider, "Corn in the Crib," 3–8; annual (seventy-fifth) Oscar H. Will and Company catalog (which reprinted the 1884 catalog), 1958, OWP; George F. Will, "Auto-

biography," WFP, pt. 1, pp. 129–30, 4, 5, 7–10, 12, 206–7; Schell, *History of South Dakota*, 179–80. See also Schneider, "Oscar H. Will," 3–5.

51. Walters, *Modern Sagas*, 11–12; J. Thompson, *Forging the Prairie West*, 68; W. Morton, *Manitoba*, 162–63; Friesen, *Canadian Prairies*, 261–62; E. Robinson, *History of North Dakota*, 129, 141.
52. Walters, *Modern Sagas*, 31–32, 62–63, 164–69, 170–76, 93, 96; Friesen, *Canadian Prairies*, 204.
53. Salverson, *Confessions*, 93, and esp. chaps. 8 and 9.
54. Effie Laurie Storer, [Begins "The great expanse of prairie land"], 2.3, ELSP; Storer, "Queen's Printer," ELSP, 37–40, 59–76; Waiser, *Saskatchewan*, 142–46; Friesen, *Canadian Prairies*, 108, 223; Hildebrandt, *Views from Fort Battleford*, 52–53; J. Miller, *Skyscrapers Hide the Heavens*, 160.
55. St. Germain, *Broken Treaties*, 365–72, 211, 223–24.
56. Elsie Hammond, diary, 1887, EMHTP; "Hammond," "Perrin," and "Whitton," in Maple Creek and Area History Committee, *Maple Creek Area*. Just before her fiftieth birthday, Elsie Hammond married Joe Thomas, help hired by her father. Her maiden name is used throughout, as most of her diaries were written under that name. See Thomas, *Our Pioneers*, 47–49. Hogue, "Disputing the Medicine Line," 85–108; Treaty Elders and Tribal Council, *True Spirit*, 222; Waiser, *Saskatchewan*, 168, 464–65; Potyandi, *In Palliser's Triangle*, 19–23; Hildebrandt and Hubner, *Cypress Hills*, 106–10.
57. Julia Asher [Lula Short], "Grandma's Childhood," JAAM, 13–16, 40, 44; Voisey, *High River*, 7, 14–18, 20; Elofson, *Cowboys*, 3–22; Friesen, *Canadian Prairies*, 237–38; Samek, *Blackfoot Confederacy*, 11–15.
58. A. Brown, *Sketches from Life*, 12, 15–18, 68–70, 40; Palmer, *Alberta*, 53; Sharp, *Whoop-Up Country*, 101.
59. Bell, *Montana and I*, 1, 4, 10, 24–26; Blew, introd. to Bell, *Montana and I*, xv, xix; Samek, *Blackfoot Confederacy*, 12–13, 37; Malone, Roeder, and Lang, *Montana*, 120–21.
60. Lillian Miller, "I Remember Montana," LMC, 1, 7, 14, 223.
61. Schell, *History of South Dakota*, 159; E. Robinson, *History of North Dakota*, 134, 149; Malone, Roeder, and Lang, *Montana*, 151–57, 194; Friesen, *Canadian Prairies*, 218, 220, 202, 204, 206–7, 511; Martin, *Dominion Lands Policy*, 168–74. For Canadian acreage, the number is inexact. Martin cautions, "The acreage of homestead entries is not easily computed" (169). Breen, *Canadian Prairie West*, 61–62, 65; Elofson, *Cowboys*, 16. Canada had at least some 111,000 beeves, but this figure accounts only for concerns that operated 400 or more cattle.
62. N. Humphrey to Hale Humphrey, 14 June 1896, HFP; Schell, *History of South Dakota*, 223–24, 244–45; E. Robinson, *History of North Dakota*, 227, 229; Malone, Roeder, and Lang, *Montana*, 166–67; Waiser, *Saskatchewan*, 51.

63. On the Last Best West, see, among others, Bicha, *American Farmer*, 77–78; C. McManus, *Happyland*, 7. Eggleston discussed "The *Best* West" in *Homestead on the Range*, 93. See also Potyondi, *In Palliser's Triangle*, 63, 84–85; Palmer, *Alberta*, 76–79, 101; Elofson, *Cowboys*, 20; Schell, *History of South Dakota*, 256; E. Robinson, *History of North Dakota*, 236; and Wishart, "Land Laws and Settlement"; Malone, Roeder, and Lang, *Montana*, 241–42.
64. Bicha, *American Farmer*, 38–39.
65. Flores, "Bison Ecology," 470–71; Binnema, *Common and Contested Ground*, 17–36; Potyondi, *In Palliser's Triangle*, 12–15, 39, 86; Schell, *History of South Dakota*, 3–14; E. Robinson, *History of North Dakota*, 1–16; Malone, Roeder, and Lang, *Montana*, 6–8; Friesen, *Canadian Prairies*, 7, 108, 328, 390; L. Brown, *Grasslands*, 48–49, 56.
66. Friesen, *Canadian Prairies*, 192; Schell, *History of South Dakota*, 252–53, 256; E. Robinson, *History of North Dakota*, 236–39.
67. Gates, *Public Land Law Development*, 492–94, 520, 668; Martin, *Dominion Lands Policy*, 163–65, 169–70, 233–34; Elofson, *Frontier Cattle Ranching*, 134–35, 158, 139–40, 168; Waiser, *Saskatchewan*, 103–4.
68. In 1900 the U.S. Congress passed a "free homestead" act that applied to South Dakota that waived the fees so carefully negotiated by the Lakotas in the Sioux Agreement of 1889. Schell, *History of South Dakota*, 253; E. Robinson, *History of North Dakota*, 244; Malone, Roeder, and Lang, *Montana*, 238; Gates, *Public Land Law Development*, 504–8, 516–19. The 1911 figure was later adjusted down to only 90,768. Congress heard the number would be greater in 1912. In 1916 the U.S. Congress passed the Stock Raising Homestead Act, which allowed settlers to purchase a section of land for a minimal fee per acre and certain required improvements. See Bicha, *American Farmer*, 114.
69. St. Germain, *Indian Treaty-Making Policy*, 83–84, 97; Nichols, *Indians*, 235–39, 252–53; Schell, *History of South Dakota*, 310; Meyer, *Village Indians*, 135–38. The Three Affiliated Tribes began leaving Like-a-Fishhook village for allotments as early as 1884. See also Carter, *Lost Harvests*, 193–209; and Hurt, *Indian Agriculture in America*, 151–52, 172.
70. Samek, *Blackfoot Confederacy*, 109; Schell, *History of South Dakota*, 253–55; Nichols, *Indians*, 235–39, 252–53; Carter, *Lost Harvests*, 200.
71. Frank Oliver, quoted in Samek, *Blackfoot Confederacy*, 110.
72. Individual lots were forty acres in the Canadian system. Carter, *Lost Harvests*, 193–95, 200–203, 233–36, 247, 252; St. Germain, *Broken Treaties*, 369; Samek, *Blackfoot Confederacy*, 109–13; Carter, *Imperial Plots*, 208–9. In *Lost Harvests* Carter argues that land loss in Canada occurred especially after the Soldier Settlement Act allowed for "compulsory purchase" of "underdeveloped" agricultural land (251–52).

73. For U.S. and Canadian northern grasslands reservations and reserves, see Lavin, Shelley, and Archer, *Atlas*, 48–53; "South Dakota Reservations"; "Tribal Nations [in North Dakota]"; "Tribal Nations [in Montana]"; "Recognized Tribes in Minnesota"; Kulchyski, "Reserves in Manitoba"; Wallace, "Reserves in Saskatchewan"; Wildcat, "Reserves in Alberta."
74. Bicha, *American Farmer*, 63–64; A. Brown, *Sketches from Life*, 66.
75. Bicha, *American Farmer*, 11, 63–64, 91, 98; Walters, "Finding Aid," MSS 630, TJEWP; Parsons, *Upon a Sagebrush Harp*, 5, 2, v; Bell, *Montana and I*, 31–33, 88–89; McAlmon, *Village*, 35; Madge Pickler Hoy to Alice Pickler, 9 March 1910, PFP; Stegner, *Where the Bluebird Sings*, xx, 3, 5, 8. Waiser, *Saskatchewan*, 102, 110; Palmer, *Alberta*, 83. Bicha, *American Farmer*, also finds almost two-thirds of these immigrants, some four hundred thousand, returned to the United States not long after they entered Canada (138–41).
76. Waiser, *Saskatchewan*, 1–19.
77. Thomson, *Crocus and Meadowlark Country*, 10; "Guide to the Papers of R. C. Russell," A71, and "Pathologist R. Russell Dies," *Star Phoenix* (Saskatoon), 16 July 1964, both in RCRP; Eggleston, *While I Still Remember*, 5.
78. Bicha, *American Farmer*, 120.
79. Olseth, *Mama Came from Norway*, 11–14, 38, 45, 50–51; Trupin, *Dakota Diaspora*, 12, 23, 25–26, 31–32, 35, 149–51; F. Lewis, *Nothing to Make*, 5, 11, 26–28, 17, 32; Schell, *History of South Dakota*, 253–55.
80. Smoller, *Adrift among Geniuses*, 9–10; Johnson, *You and I*, 2; Paladin, "Introduction," xiv–xv; Guthrie, *Blue Hen's Chick*, 1–2; L. Neatby, *Chronicle*, 14, 26, 60; Nicoll, *Paths*, 1–16.
81. Schell, *History of South Dakota*, 247, 253, 300–301; Nathan Hoy to A. Pickler, 13 July 1909, [September–October 1909?], PFP; Pickler, "Family of Homesteading Women," 35; Hammond, diary, 1887, EMHTP; Hammond, diary, no. 28: 31 May 1921, EMHTP; Hagen, *Vikings of the Prairie*, 17–18, 39, 119; Raaen, *Measure of My Days*, 103, 13, 24; L. Neatby, *Chronicle*, 23; Edward Pitblado to Dad, 21 December 1916, folder 12, box 7, PFF. Peter Norbeck filed on a homestead in 1898. Fite, *Peter Norbeck*, 22.
82. Hammond, diaries, no. 71: 19 October 1949; no. 72: 19, 20, 21 October, 3, 4, 16, 29 November 1970, EMHTP. Hammond did write her history of the old-timers; see Thomas, *Our Pioneers*.
83. Walters, *Modern Sagas*, 13–15; C. Gannon, *Bunch Grass Acres*, 3; Parsons, *Upon a Sagebrush Harp*, v; Thomson, *Crocus and Meadowlark Country*, 4; Eggleston, *High Plains*, v; Olseth, *Mama Came from Norway*, 3; Trupin, *Dakota Diaspora*, iii; Johnson, *You and I*, 2.
84. Salverson, *Confessions*, 359.
85. Walters, *Modern Sagas*, 13–15, 141. See also G. E. Giesecke to Richard Beck, 21 November 1952, folder 8, box 1, TJEWP.

2. Small Worlds

1. Hale Humphrey to Alfred Humphrey, 28 February 1886; Alfred Humphrey to Nellie Humphrey, 29 November 1885; Alfred Humphrey to Alice Humphrey, 7 March 1886, HFP. Humphrey mentions three popular Victorian parlor games; "grunt" is probably a version of "Squeak, Piggy, Squeak!" See "Parlor Games."
2. See the introduction of this book for full explanations of "experience" as defined by Tuan, *Topophilia*; Tuan, *Space and Place*; and Rodaway, *Sensuous Geographies*.
3. West, *Growing Up*, 24–25; Coe, *Grass Was Taller*, esp. chap. 6.
4. Trupin, *Dakota Diaspora*, 117; Raaen, *Grass of the Earth*, 58–59.
5. Butler, "Life Review," 6; F. Davis, *Yearning for Yesterday*; Babener, "Bitter Nostalgia," 301–20.
6. A. Brown, *Sketches from Life*, 77, 46, 12.
7. Salverson, *Confessions*, 48; E. Thompson, *American Daughter*, 47; Guthrie, *Blue Hen's Chick*, 223–24.
8. Eggleston, *Homestead on the Range*, 47; Guthrie, *Blue Hen's Chick*, 22.
9. Thomson, *Crocus and Meadowlark Country*, 16–18; Salverson, *Confessions*, 9–11; Walters, *Modern Sagas*, 2.
10. Effie Laurie Storer, "Queen's Printer," 1942–43, 2.4, ELSP, 60–62, 69–70, 79; E. Thompson, *American Daughter*, 27.
11. Lulu [Pickler] Frad, "The Big Old House in the Little Town," [1949?], PFP; Trupin, *Dakota Diaspora*, 31–32; Olseth, *Mama Came from Norway*, 45.
12. Bell, *Montana and I*, 138; Stegner, *Where the Bluebird Sings*, 8–9.
13. Hale Humphrey to N. Humphrey, 3 May 1891; Alice Humphrey to Alfred Humphrey, 2 March 1886, HFP; Johnson, *You and I*, 88.
14. K. Davis, "Mental Life of Chickens," 16, 13–29.
15. Lula Short, diary, 27 August 1886; 3 April 1885; 17 April, 4 July 1886; 1, 16 April, 1, 8 May 1887; 5, 9 June 1888, SKFF; Raaen, *Grass of the Earth*, 30; K. Davis, "Mental Life of Chickens," 19; Johnson, *You and I*, 89.
16. E. Thompson, *American Daughter*, 82, 90; Alice Humphrey to N. Humphrey, 25 September [1886], 16, 25 September [1888], 7 October 1888; Alice Humphrey to Kenneth Humphrey, n.d. [enclosed with Alice's letter of 20 September 1888]; Alice Humphrey to Alfred Humphrey, 6 June 1886, HFP.
17. Bell, *Montana and I*, 127–28; McAlmon, *Hasty Bunch*, 74, 82; see also Raaen, *Grass of the Earth*, 38; McAlmon, *Post-adolescence*, 199. On the historical accuracy of Robert McAlmon's fiction, Vidal wrote, "As far as my family goes, McAlmon invents nothing. He is a literal recorder" (xi–xii); Vidal easily recognized his father, Eugene L. Vidal, in McAlm-

on's character Eugene Collins, the boyhood friend of Peter Reynalds, the teenaged character of Robert McAlmon, in the novel *Village* (ix-xiv, xi-xii). Vidal, foreword to McAlmon, *Miss Knight and Others*, ix-xiv. See also Smoller, *Adrift among Geniuses*.

18. Alice Humphrey to N. Humphrey, 22 April 1891; Hale Humphrey to N. Humphrey, 7 June 1885, [?] June [1884/85?], HFP; Lillian Miller, "I Remember Montana," LMC, 21–23; see also Stegner, *Where the Bluebird Sings*, 7–8; Walters, *Modern Sagas*, 6, 75, 2; McAlmon, *Village*, 78, 142; McAlmon, *Hasty Bunch*, 61; E. Thompson, *American Daughter*, 45–46; see also Elsie Hammond, diaries, no. 3: 19 June 1910; no. 2: 18 June 1910, EMHTP; A. Brown, *Sketches from Life*, 39–42, 186. See also Savage, *Prairie*, 119–22, 149–50, 208; and Johnsgard, *Prairie Birds*, 3–44.
19. Raaen, *Grass of the Earth*, 29; Stegner, *Wolf Willow*, 19.
20. Julia Asher [Lula Short], "Grandma's Childhood," JAAM, 57.
21. A. Brown, *Sketches from Life*, 31; Asher, "Grandma's Childhood," JAAM, 16; Eggleston, *Homestead on the Range*, 45–46.
22. L. Short, diary, 15 August 1886, SKFF; Hale Humphrey to Alfred Humphrey, 7 October 1888, HFP; Frad, "Big Old House," PFP.
23. E. Thompson, *American Daughter*, 84, 33, 141–42, 101; Walters, *Modern Sagas*, 3; Thorstina Jackson Walters to Robert E. Demme, 1 April 1947, folder 6, box 1, TJEWP. I have silently corrected the typo "ploudh."
24. Alice Humphrey to N. Humphrey, 14 April 1891, 25 September [1886]; Alice Humphrey to Hervey Humphrey, 17 July 1886, HFP.
25. Gala, "Toward a Privileging," 113, 122.
26. Will, "Autobiography," WFP, pt. 1, pp. 250–52, 265, 278.
27. Stegner, *Wolf Willow*, 35.
28. Bell, *Montana and I*, 4, 53–54, 116, 107–9.
29. Will, "Autobiography," WFP, pt. 1, pp. 250–51, 252, 248; see also McAlmon, *Village*, 88, 89; Short, diary, 18, 20, 26 November 1884, SKFF.
30. Alice Humphrey to Hervey Humphrey [included with letter from N. Humphrey to Hervey Humphrey of same date], 27 March 1887; Alice Humphrey to N. Humphrey, 16 September 1888, HFP; Short, diary, February–July, 9 December 1885; 14, 19, 20 April, 7, 31 May 1888, SKFF; Rollings-Magnusson, *Heavy Burdens*, 70–71.
31. Hale Humphrey to Alfred Humphrey, 28 March 1886; Kenneth Humphrey to Alfred Humphrey, 28 March 1886; Alice Humphrey to Alfred Humphrey, 28 March 1886, HFP.
32. Fite, *Peter Norbeck*, 12; see also Trupin, *Dakota Diaspora*, 90–91; Bell, *Montana and I*, 4, 72–73, 75, 67; Kenneth Humphrey to N. Humphrey, 26 April 1891, HFP; Walters, *Modern Sagas*, 77–78.
33. Asher, "Grandma's Childhood," JAAM, 42; Short, diary, 3, 4 August 1885; 4 March, 12, 13 April 1886; 24 June, 12, 13 July 1887; 23 April 1888, SKFF.

34. Alice Humphrey to Alfred Humphrey, 19 March 1886; Alice Humphrey to N. Humphrey, 27 April 1891 ("hered" silently corrected), HFP; McAlmon, *Hasty Bunch*, 60; Parsons, *Upon a Sagebrush Harp*, 90–91; Bell, *Montana and I*, 66–67, 72–75.
35. Alice Humphrey to N. Humphrey, 25, 26 ("diaginal" silently corrected) September 1888; Hale Humphrey to N. Humphrey, 26 September 1888, HFP; Asher, "Grandma's Childhood," JAAM, 31.
36. Bell, *Montana and I*, 225, 75–76, 104–6, 114–15, 119–20, 187.
37. Rollings-Magnusson, *Heavy Burdens*, 49, 54; Asher, "Grandma's Childhood," JAAM, 28–29, 3; Short, diary, 9 February, 6 April 1885; 31 March, 2, 3, 4 April 1886; 28 August 1887, SKFF.
38. Wetherell, *Wildlife, Land, and People*, xix, 117–57, 75–77, 252–89.
39. Stegner, *Where the Bluebird Sings*, 9; Walters, *Modern Sagas*, 75; Savage, *Prairie*, 131, 264; see also Kittie Humphrey to Hervey Humphrey, 10 May 1898, HFP; Raaen, *Grass of the Earth*, 27; Short, diary, 24 May 1885, SKFF.
40. Hammond, diaries, no. 6: 10 July 1912; no. 19: 16 February to 30 April 1919, EMHTP; Will, "Autobiography," WFP, pt. 1, pp. 250–51; Eggleston, *Homestead on the Range*, 45; Nicoll, *Paths*, 53–54; Parsons, *Upon a Sagebrush Harp*, 18.
41. Stegner, *Where the Bluebird Sings*, 8–9; Stegner, *Wolf Willow*, 275–76.
42. Sam L. Doughty to [Alfred Humphrey], 13 April 1884, HFP; Olseth, *Mama Came from Norway*, 134 ("caesarean" silently corrected).
43. Asher, "Grandma's Childhood," JAAM, 57; Short, diary, 31 October 1885, SKFF; Bell, *Montana and I*, 51–54, 107–10, 121; Will, "Autobiography," WFP, pt. 1, p. 276; see also Kenneth Humphrey to Alfred Humphrey, 5 December 1891, HFP
44. McAlmon, *Post-adolescence*, 200, 204–6; Eggleston, *Homestead on the Range*, 44–45; McAlmon, *Post-adolescence*, 205–7.
45. Stegner, *Where the Bluebird Sings*, 9.
46. Hale Humphrey to Kenneth Humphrey, 16 September 1888, HFP.
47. Wetherell, *Wildlife, Land, and People*, 174–75.
48. Asher, "Grandma's Childhood," JAAM, 43, 27; Short, diary, 24 November 1884; 20 April, 4 May 1886; 7, 12 January, 6–8, 11, 18, 19 October 1885; 14, 24, 30 September, 3, 6 October 1887, SKFF; Hammond, diaries, no. 3: 18, 24 October, 26 November 1910; no. 9: 26 October 1913.
49. Parsons, *Upon a Sagebrush Harp*, 75; Asher, "Grandma's Childhood," JAAM, 42, 57; Eggleston, *Homestead on the Range*, 41; see also Miller, "I Remember Montana," LMC, 23–24; Olseth, *Mama Came from Norway*, 58; Nicoll, *Paths*, 54; Will, "Autobiography," WFP, pt. 1, pp. 245, 250–51, 276; Will, "Autobiography," WFP, pt. 2, pp. 25, 66.
50. Stegner, *Wolf Willow*, 259; Guthrie, *Blue Hen's Chick*, 15–17; Will, "Autobiography," WFP, pt. 1, pp. 250–51, 276.

51. Hammond, diaries, no. 6: 10 July 1912; no. 11: 12, 31 October 1914; no. 13: 16, 17, 18, 19, 20 November 1915, EMHTP; see also, Bell, *Montana and I*, 121.
52. Edward Pitblado to Edith Pitblado, 27 January 1921, folder 1, 20 October 1921, folder 6, both box 8; 11 October 1923, folder 5, box 9; "Busy Winnipeg Men Enjoy Duck Shooting at Portage," *Free Press*, 23 September 1921, folder 19, box 5, all in PFF.
53. Hale Humphrey to N. Humphrey, 7 June 1885, HFP; Stegner, *Wolf Willow*, 18; Short, diary, 3, 26 May, 3, 4, 8, 9, 24, 25 September 1885, SKFF; Asher, "Grandma's Childhood," JAAM, 62, 27, 42–43; Hammond, diary, no. 17: 8 May, 9 June 1918, EMHTP.
54. Storer, "Queen's Printer," ELSP, 59–76, 65–66; Eugene F. Du Bois to Vilhjalmur Stefansson, 27 May 1947; Stefansson to Du Bois, 28 May 1947, both in folder 6, box 1, TJEWP.
55. Will, "Autobiography," WFP, pt. 1, pp. 204–7, 221; Malone, Roeder, and Lang, *Montana*, 177; E. Robinson, *History of North Dakota*, 200–201, 184–86. George Kingsbury records "a big feast" in Bismarck, as he said it was "termed in the neighborhood of Indian Country," attended by former president Grant, the German ambassador to the United States, and the president of the Northern Pacific Railway, as part of a cornerstone-laying ceremony for the new territorial capitol on 5 September 1883. See Kingsbury, *History of Dakota Territory*, 2:1308–9. It is unclear whether Indigenous guests attended both the capitol ceremony and the banquet, but they would have known of the banquet.
56. Will, "Autobiography," WFP, pt. 1, pp. 204–7, 221. Will's dates for these events include some confusion. Writing in the period, Smalley in *Northern Pacific Railroad* records that the bridge across the Missouri formally opened 21 October 1882 and was "celebrated by a banquet in Bismarck that evening" (394–95).
57. Will, "Big Game"; Palliser, *Solitary Hunter*, 89, 103, 98, 191–95; Spry, *Papers*; Owram, *Promise of Eden*, 61–65. Although Palliser published *Solitary Hunter* in 1856, the book recounts his adventures in 1847 on "the Prairies" in an area of the northern grasslands that roughly corresponds to modern North Dakota (3).
58. E. Robinson, *History of North Dakota*, 184–86; Schell, *History of Clay County*, 11–12; H. Thompson, *New South Dakota History*, 58; Isenberg, *Destruction of the Bison*, 25, 159, 164, 185; Parsons, *Upon a Sagebrush Harp*, 16; Miller, "I Remember Montana," LMC, 148; Van Nuys, *Family Band*, 83, 116; Walters, *Modern Sagas*, 74–75; Hammond, diaries, no. 16: 17 July 1917; no. 36: 18 January 1928, EMHTP; see also Storer, "Queen's Printer," ELSP, 59–76, 61, 64; Raaen, *Grass of the Earth*, 46.
59. Asher, "Grandma's Childhood," JAAM, 15; Parsons, *Upon a Sagebrush Harp*, 27; Will, "Autobiography," WFP, pt. 1, pp. 244–46; Will, "Big

Game"; Will, "Autobiography," WFP, pt. 2, p. 66; Bell, *Montana and I*, 110; Annora Brown, oral history interview by Tom Kirkham, 24 March 1982, North Saanich BC, TKOHP; Potyondi, *In Palliser's Triangle*, 116–17.
60. Will, "Autobiography," WFP, pt. 1, pp. 231, 181–84, 237–38, 275–78.
61. E. Thompson, *American Daughter*, 26.
62. Eggleston, *While I Still Remember*, 10–11; Hammond, diary, no. 14: 20, 27 February, 17, 20–21, 25 April, 2, 7, 13 May, 2, 4 June 1916, EMHTP.

3. Sensing Prairies and Plains

1. A. Brown, *Sketches from Life*, 11–12.
2. Raaen, *Grass of the Earth*, 135–36; E. Thompson, *American Daughter*, 47.
3. Tuan, *Space and Place*, 8–10; Amato, *Rethinking Home*, 30–42, 60–76; Rodaway, *Sensuous Geographies*, 4–10. Geographer Paul Rodaway has explained physical "senses are not merely passive receptors of particular kinds of environmental stimuli but are actively involved in the structuring of that information" (4); any given environment is already a "source of information, not merely raw data" (20).
4. M. Smith, *Sensing the Past*, 3–5.
5. Parsons, *Upon a Sagebrush Harp*, 19.
6. West, *Growing Up*, 25–45; Coe, *Grass Was Taller*, 33–35, 205–39.
7. A. Brown, *Sketches from Life*, 41, 42, 45, 186; see also 6, 31, 39–40, 54, 135, 172; see also Trupin, *Dakota Diaspora*, 145; Pauline Neher Diede, cited in Handy-Marchello, *Women*, 68.
8. George F. Will, "Autobiography," WFP, pt. 1, pp. 249–50.
9. Stegner, *Wolf Willow*, 8. Stegner used "tangled."
10. A. Brown, *Sketches from Life*, 6, 31; Will, "Autobiography," WFP, pt. 1, p. 250; Walters, *Modern Sagas*, 75; Stegner, *Wolf Willow*, 7; Parsons, *Upon a Sagebrush Harp*, 16.
11. Raaen, *Grass of the Earth*, 60.
12. Will "Autobiography," WFP, pt. 1, p. 223; Parsons, *Upon a Sagebrush Harp*, 20, 22; Stegner, *Wolf Willow*, 6, 8–9, 281.
13. Stegner, *Wolf Willow*, 8, 269; A. Brown, *Sketches from Life*, 42; C. Gannon, *Bunch Grass Acres*, 23.
14. Stegner, *Wolf Willow*, 6, 271; Parsons, *Upon a Sagebrush Harp*, 18–19, 41; Trupin, *Dakota Diaspora*, 31, 46, 51, 95; Lillian Miller, "I Remember Montana," LMC, 110–11; Van Nuys, *Family Band*, 187.
15. Eggleston, *Homestead on the Range*, 25, 35, 37.
16. Stegner, *Wolf Willow*, 271–73.
17. Raaen, *Grass of the Earth*, 26; Parsons, *Upon a Sagebrush Harp*, 143–44; Alice Humphrey to Nellie Humphrey, 22, 24 April 1891, HFP; Miller, "I Remember Montana," LMC, 25–26; Salverson, *Confessions*, 159–60. See also Nicoll, *Paths*, 61; Walters, *Modern Sagas*, 75.

18. Stegner, *Wolf Willow*, 6, 122; Thomson, *Crocus and Meadowlark Country*, 130–31; Parsons, *Upon a Sagebrush Harp*, 46.
19. A. Brown, *Sketches from Life*, 6, 31; A. Brown, *Old Man's Garden*, 11–12, 15, 20–21, 23–24, 128, 153–54, 188–90, 202–3; Nicoll, *Paths*, 61.
20. Lulu [Pickler] Frad, "The Big Old House in the Little Town," [1949?], PFP; Eggleston, *Homestead on the Range*, 37; see also Alice Humphrey to N. Humphrey, 16 September 1888, HFP.
21. Alice Humphrey to N. Humphrey, 14 April 1891, 25, 26 September 1886, HFP; Julia Asher [Lula Short], quoting her diary in "Grandma's Childhood," JAAM, 31.
22. Norbeck and Norbeck, *Norbecks of South Dakota*, 58–59; Miller, "I Remember Montana," LMC, 27–28, 64, 71, 163; "Pickler House Once Called Union Station; Has 20 Rooms," newspaper clipping, in Alice Mary Alt (Alice M. Pickler), box 6829, PFP; L. Neatby, *Chronicle*, 15; Hale Humphrey to Alfred Humphrey, 28 February 1886, Sam L. Doughty to Humphrey family, 12 June 1883, HFP; Will, "Autobiography," WFP, pt. 1, pp. 223–24, 225.
23. Salverson, *Confessions*, 9, 10, 12–16.
24. Salverson, *Confessions*, 29, 15, 169; Raaen, *Grass of the Earth*, 55–56, 22, 123–24, 147–48, 19–20; Walters, *Modern Sagas*, 2, 13, 74, 80–81, 134–35, 8–10, 141.
25. E. Thompson, *American Daughter*, 26, 33; Van Nuys, *Family Band*, 133, 159; Walters, *Modern Sagas*, 116–17, 13, 11; Johnson, *Indian Country*, 198; A. Brown, *Sketches from Life*, 14–15, 210–11; McAlmon, *Village*, 130.
26. McAlmon, *Village*, 89–89; Stegner, *Wolf Willow*, 278; Hewes, "Northern Wet Prairie"; Hewes and Frandon, "Occupying the Wet Prairie."
27. A. Brown, *Sketches from Life*, 11–12; Eggleston, *Homestead on the Range*, 34 ("sprawls" and "slips" made singular); Salverson, *Confessions*, 19–20, 82.
28. Eggleston, *High Plains*, 24, 165, 175; Eggleston, *Homestead on the Range*, 35.
29. E. Thompson, *American Daughter*, 141; Walters, *Modern Sagas*, 13.
30. Raaen, *Grass of the Earth*, 106; Salverson, *Confessions*, 38, 42; Will, "Autobiography," WFP, pt. 1, p. 232.
31. Eggleston, *Homestead on the Range*, 38, 70; Eggleston, *While I Still Remember*, 5.
32. A. Brown, *Sketches from Life*, 12–13; Asher, "Grandma's Childhood," JAAM, 56.
33. Raaen, *Grass of the Earth*, 58–59; Walters, *Modern Sagas*, 8.
34. Stegner, *Wolf Willow*, 18, 21–22; Van Nuys, *Family Band*, 215.
35. Raaen, *Grass of the Earth*, 23, 141; Van Nuys, *Family Band*, 215; Hale Humphrey to N. Humphrey, 3 May 1891, HFP; Parsons, *Upon a Sagebrush Harp*, 106–7; see also Will, "Autobiography," WFP, pt. 1, p. 284.
36. Elsie Hammond, diary, no. 8: 6 August 1913, EMHTP; N. Humphrey to Alfred Humphrey, 21 December 1885, HFP (emphasis added); Willard,

Story of the Prairies, 67; Parsons, *Upon a Sagebrush Harp*, 41; Miller, "I Remember Montana," LMC, 70; R. Smith, introd. to Fargo, *Prairie Chautauqua*, xix; see also McAlmon, *Village*, 47; see also E. Thompson, *American Daughter*, 50.

37. McAlmon, *Hasty Bunch*, 61 (emphasis added); Miller, "I Remember Montana," LMC, 9; Johnson, *You and I*, 2; Parsons, *Upon a Sagebrush Harp*, 17.
38. A. Brown, *Sketches from Life*, 40–45; E. Thompson, *American Daughter*, 84–85; Stegner, *Wolf Willow*, 13; see also Will, "Autobiography," WFP, pt. 1, p. 280; Will, "City of Homes."
39. A. Brown, *Sketches from Life*, 43–45; Walters, *Modern Sagas*, 6.
40. Raaen, *Grass of the Earth*, 11, 13, 26, 72; Standing Bear, *My People the Sioux*, 47; M. Jacobs, *White Mother*, xxxii, 229–80.
41. A. Brown, *Sketches from Life*, 13–14, 40, 43–45, 81. Brown explained, "Much to the annoyance of the inhabitants of Southern Alberta, bureaucrats have poked ignorant fingers into their history and recorded the name on the maps as one word, Oldman" (142).
42. Raaen, *Grass of the Earth*, 45.
43. Raaen, *Grass of the Earth*, 46–48; see also 21, 23–24, 177. For more on the Raaen sisters, see Rozum, "Indelible Grasslands," 126–32.
44. Schama, *Landscape and Memory*, 17.
45. Standing Bear, *My People the Sioux*, 47; Eggleston, *Homestead on the Range*, 37; M. Jacobs, *White Mother*, xxxii, 229–80.
46. Raaen, *Grass of the Earth*, 21–24.
47. Lula Short, diary, 25, 28 May 1885, SKFF.
48. Will, "Autobiography," WFP, pt. 1, pp. 222–23, 231.
49. Raaen, *Grass of the Earth*, 20–21; Stegner, *Wolf Willow*, 260; Walters, *Modern Sagas*, 70–71, 1.
50. A. Brown, *Sketches from Life*, 43–45, 74.
51. Alice Humphrey to Hervey Humphrey, 17 July 1886, HFP; E. Thompson, *American Daughter*, 41–42, 96; Hammond, diary, no. 28: 31 May, 4 June 1921, EMHTP.
52. A. Brown, *Sketches from Life*, 48; Eggleston, *Prairie Moonlight*, 11; Miller, "I Remember Montana," LMC, 70; Willard, *Story of the Prairies*, 62–63; Hammond, diary, no. 20: 11 May 1919, EMHTP.
53. Eggleston, *Homestead on the Range*, 28; Parsons, *Upon a Sagebrush Harp*, 21.
54. Parsons, *Upon a Sagebrush Harp*, 22; L. Neatby, *Chronicle*, 52–53; Miller, "I Remember Montana," LMC, 26.
55. Alice Humphrey to N. Humphrey, 16 September 1888, HFP.
56. Eggleston, *Homestead on the Range*, 15, 37.
57. A. Brown, *Sketches from Life*, 12–13, 41; see also 117, 142. For more on Brown, see Rozum, "Indelible Grasslands," 121–26; and Rozum, "That Understanding with Nature," 133–39.

58. A. Brown, *Sketches from Life*, 41; Trupin, *Dakota Diaspora*, 32. See also Breen, *Canadian Prairie West*; Jordan, *Cattle-Ranching Frontiers*; and Voisey, *Vulcan*.
59. A. Brown, *Sketches from Life*, 41, 12–13, 194.
60. A. Brown, *Sketches from Life*, 25–26.
61. Trupin, *Dakota Diaspora*, 81.
62. E. Thompson, *American Daughter*, 66; Van Nuys, *Family Band*, 187; E. Thompson, *American Daughter*, 70; Raaen, *Grass of the Earth*, 4, 3–9; Will, "Autobiography," WFP, pt. 1, pp. 224–26.
63. Blum, *Weather Machine*, 11–41; Riney-Kehrberg, *Nature of Childhood*, 1, 30–31.
64. Alice Humphrey to Alfred Humphrey, 27 January 1886, HFP.
65. A. Brown, *Sketches from Life*, 25–26; E. Thompson, *American Daughter*, 68; McAlmon, *Village*, 130; Raaen, *Grass of the Earth*, 5, 8; Hammond, diary, no. 10: 8 February 1914, EMHTP.
66. Parsons, *Upon a Sagebrush Harp*, 40, 73; McAlmon, *Post-adolescence*, 69–70; McAlmon, *Village*, 3, 130; E. Thompson, *American Daughter*, 67–68; see also 30; Trupin, *Dakota Diaspora*, 82.
67. Alice Humphrey to Alfred Humphrey, 17 January 1886, HFP; E. Thompson, *American Daughter*, 70; Eggleston, *Homestead on the Range*, 26; McAlmon, *Hasty Bunch*, 248; Parsons, *Upon a Sagebrush Harp*, 79.
68. Alice Humphrey to Alfred Humphrey, 19 March 1886, HFP; A. Brown, *Sketches*, 29; Stegner, *Wolf Willow*, 14.
69. E. Thompson, *American Daughter*, 103; N. Humphrey to Alfred Humphrey, 18 March 1885; Kittie Humphrey to Hervey Humphrey, 1 April 1900, HFP; Stegner, *Wolf Willow*, 242, 244; Eggleston, *High Plains*, 85 (this is a fictional account of boys on the prairies; the boys here copied their Norwegian neighbors); Raaen, *Grass of the Earth*, 105; L. Neatby, *Chronicle*, 29.
70. McAlmon, *Village*, 3, 129; Thompson, *American Daughter*, 94; Raaen, *Grass of the Earth*, 193; Trupin, *Dakota Diaspora*, 83; Alice Humphrey to Alfred Humphrey, 28 March 1886; Kenneth Humphrey to Alfred Humphrey, 5 December 1891; S. Doughty to Humphrey family, 20 January 1884, HFP; E. Thompson, *American Daughter*, 26, 68–71, 105.
71. McAlmon, *Village*, 8; A. Brown, *Sketches from Life*, 30.
72. A. Brown, *Sketches from Life*, 223; Raaen, *Grass of the Earth*, 64, 187, 233; Parsons, *Upon a Sagebrush Harp*, 18.
73. Alice Humphrey to N. Humphrey, 22, 27 April 1891; Alfred Humphrey to N. Humphrey, 29 November 1885, HFP; E. Thompson, *American Daughter*, 50; Parsons, *Upon a Sagebrush Harp*, 55.
74. E. Thompson, *American Daughter*, 47, 101; Trupin, *Dakota Diaspora*, 61, 128–29; Short, diary, 2 September 1886, 19 August, 10 September 1887,

15 March 1888, SKFF; Asher, "Grandma's Childhood," JAAM, 42, 25, 31; L. Neatby, *Chronicle*, 54–55; Nicoll, *Paths*, 43–44; Handy-Marchello, *Women*, 53–84; see also Parsons, *Upon a Sagebrush Harp*, 97. Rollings-Magnusson, *Heavy Burdens*, found that, similar to women's labor, children's labor—with tasks keyed in difficulty from four to eight, nine to eleven, and twelve to thirteen years of age to sixteen—tended to be important to agricultural success and survival but "invisible" or unrecognized (136, 143–44).

75. E. Thompson, *American Daughter*, 45, 100; Stegner, *Wolf Willow*, 258; Trupin, *Dakota Diaspora*, 118; Stegner, *Wolf Willow*, 259; Handy-Marchello, *Women*, 68.
76. L. Short, diary, 13 August, 12 December 1886, 20 August 1887, SKFF; Asher, "Grandma's Childhood," JAAM, 41–42, 23–24, 52–53; Miller, "I Remember Montana," LMC, 111; McAlmon, *Miss Knight and Others*, 91, 93; McAlmon, *Village*, 100; McAlmon, *Hasty Bunch*, 237.
77. Asher, "Grandma's Childhood," JAAM, 42; E. Thompson, *American Daughter*, 51–52.
78. E. Thompson, *American Daughter*, 57–58, 51–52; Raaen, *Grass of the Earth*, 68, 70, 72.
79. Cunfer, *On the Great Plains*, 8–14.
80. Raaen, *Grass of the Earth*, 20–21, 23, 26, 52, 66, 84, 20, 138.
81. Raaen, *Grass of the Earth*, 20–21, 23, 68, 70, 72.
82. Raaen, *Measure of My Days*, 296.
83. Gambler Tanner, quoted in Friesen, *Canadian Prairies*, 142; M. Jacobs, *White Mother*, xxxii, 229–80.

4. "The Purple Hills That Beckoned"

1. Raaen, *Grass of the Earth*, 143. Generally, Kjersti's experiences are filtered through Aagot's telling; here Raaen reprints a letter from Kjersti, presumably authentic, in her memoir. Hudson, *Plains Country Towns*, 70–85.
2. Raaen, *Grass of the Earth*, 72–73, 97, 143.
3. E. Thompson, *American Daughter*, 47, 98.
4. Cordier, *Schoolwomen*, 22–25; Rollings-Magnusson, *Heavy Burdens*, 147n4.
5. Alfred Humphrey to N. Humphrey, 3 January 1886, HFP; Effie Laurie Storer, "Queen's Printer," 1942–43, 2.4, ELSP, 83; Bell, *Montana and I*; Van Nuys, *Family Band*, 205; Elsie Hammond, diaries, nos. 2–4: 1 May 1910 to 9 May 1911, EMHTP; Thomson, *Crocus and Meadowlark Country*, 178, 239; F. Lewis, *Nothing to Make*, 151.
6. L. Neatby, *Chronicle*, 42, 56, 69; Fite, *Peter Norbeck*, 12, 14, 17; Raaen, *Grass of the Earth*, 136.
7. Nicoll, *Paths*, 96; Raaen, *Grass of the Earth*, 85, 84–89, 104–5, 136, 147, 153.

8. A. Brown, *Sketches from Life*, 6–7, 78–79; Amy J. Roe, "Countrywoman: A Personal Sketch of Annora Brown," *Country Guide*, February 1957, ABCF-GL, 59.
9. Stegner, *Wolf Willow*, 57, 114–15, 111, 121–22; Lillian Miller, "I Remember Montana," LMC, 12. See West, *Last Indian War*, 267–82.
10. Hale Humphrey to Alfred Humphrey, 25 October 1885 (enclosed with letter from N. Humphrey to Alfred Humphrey, 25 October 1885), HFP.
11. "Woman County School Superintendent Walks over County in Bitter Cold," *Fargo Forum and Daily Republican*, 22 April 1922; "Mrs. Ragnild Raaen Passed Away," clipping, [November 1923], both in folder 1, box 1, ARP; Fite, *Peter Norbeck*, 12; Salverson, *Confessions*, 179, 195, 219, 238, 242–44.
12. Walters, *Modern Sagas*, 104–6; Salverson, *Confessions*, 248–49; Nicoll, *Paths*, 88.
13. Sam L. Doughty to Alfred Humphrey, 24 June 1883, HFP.
14. Raaen, *Grass of the Earth*, 87; E. Thompson, *American Daughter*, 31–33, 109, 115–17; Salverson, *Confessions*, 195–200.
15. M. Jacobs, *White Mother*, 229; Storer, "Queen's Printer," ELSP, 92–93; E. Thompson, *American Daughter*, 128–29; Miller, "I Remember Montana," LMC, 34, 36–38.
16. E. Thompson, *American Daughter*, 47, 88, 98, 113; A. Brown, *Sketches from Life*, 40; Connerton, *How Societies Remember*; Hammond, diary, no. 6: 18 February 1912, EMHTP; see also Raaen, *Grass of the Earth*, 72–73.
17. Miller, "I Remember Montana," LMC, 177, 229; Parsons, *Upon a Sagebrush Harp*, 27.
18. Stegner, *Wolf Willow*, 27–28; Storer, "Queen's Printer," ELSP, 83; Alice Humphrey to Nellie Humphrey, 26 September [1888], HFP; Raaen, *Measure of My Days*, 51–52.
19. Hammond, diary, no. 2: 18, 19 June 1910, EMHTP.
20. Hammond, diary, no. 6: 21, 24, 25 March 1912, EMHTP.
21. Hammond, diary, no. 4: 21 April 1911, EMHTP.
22. Hammond, diary, no. 10: 17 July 1914, EMHTP.
23. Raaen, *Grass of the Earth*, 135–36, 177–80, 188, 215, 218; Aagot Raaen, "The Novelist as a Teacher," folder 1, box 3, ARP.
24. Hammond, diaries, no. 10: 12 July 1914 (emphasis added); no. 13: 1 September 1915; no. 5: 30 June 1911; no. 4: 9 May 1911; no. 6: 8 June 1912; no. 8: 24, 25 May, 15 June 1913, EMHTP.
25. Raaen, *Measure of My Days*, 37.
26. Hammond, diary, no. 6: 18 April, 18, 19, 29 July 1912, EMHTP.
27. Hammond, diaries, no. 3: 15 September 1910; no. 7: 27 April 1913; no. 30: 6 August 1922, EMHTP.
28. Hammond, diaries, no. 10: 26 September 1914; no. 12: 7 July 1915, EMHTP.

29. Ralph C. Russell, "The Old Trails of the Canadian Prairies," n.d. [circa 1955], 1.1.(h), RCRP; Hammond, diary, no. 10: 19 September 1914.
30. Eggleston, *While I Still Remember*, 7, 9, 15, 17, 20–21; Raaen, *Grass of the Earth*; on Aagot, see 108, 128–29, 137, 148–49, 185, 197; on Kjersti, see 105, 108–9, 131, 137, 141–43, 146, 158–59, 169, 170, 204; on Tosten, see 191, 195, 204, 230, 233; E. Thompson, *American Daughter*, 160, 214; Salverson, *Confessions*, 323, 329, 339, 342, 344–45, 352–53, 368–69.
31. Raaen, *Measure of My Days*, 41, 112–13, 51–52 (emphasis added).
32. E. Thompson, *American Daughter*, 169, 180–81, 230.
33. Raaen, *Grass of the Earth*, 213; Raaen, *Measure of My Days*, 46, 92.
34. Raaen, *Grass of the Earth*, 195–96, 232–33.
35. Raaen, *Measure of My Days*, 53, 149, 261.
36. Raaen, *Measure of My Days*, 52.
37. Lulu Pickler to family, 2, 3 April 1889; L. Pickler to Alice Pickler, 16, 23, 27, 31 May 1890; L. Pickler to "Grandpa and Grandma," 26 April 1889; L. Pickler to A. Pickler, 27 April 1889, all in PFP.
38. L. Pickler to A. Pickler, 16, 23 May 1890, PFP.
39. Alice Humphrey to Alfred Humphrey, 17 January 1886; Alice Humphrey to N. Humphrey, 25 September 1892; Alice Humphrey to Humphrey family, 16 October 1892, HFP; Frad, "Big Old House."
40. Hale Humphrey to N. Humphrey, 29 December 1894, 1, 6 January 1895, 16 June 1895, 8, 29 September 1895, HFP.
41. Hale Humphrey to Hervey Humphrey, 2 June 1895; Hale Humphrey to N. Humphrey, 22 December 1895, HFP; Robert McAlmon to Bryher, [1923] and [late 1923], folder 1260, box 35, BP.
42. Hale Humphrey to Kenneth Humphrey, 17 March 1895; Hale Humphrey to N. Humphrey, 22 December 1895, HFP.
43. Hale Humphrey to N. Humphrey, 17 March 1895; Hale Humphrey to N. Humphrey, 13 January 1895, HFP; E. Thompson, *American Daughter*, 117; Hale Humphrey to N. Humphrey, 24 February 1895; Hale Humphrey to Kittie Humphrey, 21 January 1895; Hale Humphrey to Kittie Humphrey, 22 January 1896; see also Hale Humphrey to N. Humphrey, 12 July 1896, 2, 16 August 1896, HFP.
44. Hale Humphrey to N. Humphrey, 12 March 1897, 14 April 1897, HFP.
45. Raaen, *Grass of the Earth*, 137–38, 140–41.
46. E. Thompson, *American Daughter*, 160, 164–65, 169, 198–200, 212–14, 218, 230–35, 249.
47. Hammond, diary, no. 12: 17 December 1914, 8, 11 June 1915, EMHTP; Smoller, introd. to McAlmon, *Nightinghouls of Paris*, xiv–xv; "Biography: Thorstina Walters," n.d., folder 1, box 1, TJEWP; "Education and Employment Record of Thorstina Jackson Walters," [circa 1950], folder 4, box 3, TJEWP.

48. Edward Pitblado to Edith, 14 May; Pitblado to family, 13 June 1916, both in folder 9, box 7, PFF.
49. Hammond, diary, no. 15: 17 July 1916, EMHTP.
50. Edward Pitblado to parents, [August 1916?]; Edward Pitblado to Dad, 28 August 1916, both in folder 10, box 7, PFF.
51. Edward Pitblado to Dad, 22 September, 11, 29 October 1916, all in folder 11; 2 December 1916, folder 12, all in box 7, PFF.
52. Edward Pitblado to mother, 24 November 1916; Edward Pitblado to Dad, 17 November 1916, both in folder 12, box 7, PFF.
53. Edward Pitblado to Dad, 2 December 1916, folder 12; Edward Pitblado to Mother, 29 January 1917, folder 13; Edward Pitblado to Dad, 5 May 1917, folder 15, all in box 7, PFF. Pitblado's World War I correspondence ends after he joined the Royal Flying Corps in February 1917 and an injury received soon after from an airplane accident in France.
54. Edward Pitblado to mother, 13 November 1921, folder 7, 12 April 1922, folder 9; Edward Pitblado to Dad, 4 April 1922, folder 9; Edward Pitblado to Edith Pitblado, 27 January 1921, folder 1; Edward Pitblado to Dad, 15 April 1921, folder 2; Edward Pitblado to Mother, 24 April 1921, folder 2, all in box 8, PFF.
55. Edward Pitblado to Mother, 24 April 1921, folder 2, box 8; Edward Pitblado to Dad, 22 October 1922, folder 11, box 8; Edward Pitblado to Edith Pitblado, 20 October 1921, folder 6, box 8, PFF. On the sport of hunting, including a class dimension, see Wetherell, *Wildlife, Land, and People*, 183–86, 191.
56. Edward Pitblado to Mother, 15 January 1921, folder 1; Edward Pitblado to Mother, 16 October 1922, folder 11, both in box 8, PFF; Eggleston, *While I Still Remember*, 88–90; Altair [Wilfrid Eggleston], "First Impressions of England," *Lethbridge Daily Herald*, June 1926; Altair, "Overseas with a Herd of Hereford: Article No. 5; And in Conclusion," *Lethbridge Herald*, 1926, vol. 25, file 1, WEF.
57. Eggleston, *While I Still Remember*, 63–64, 68–71, 75–76; Altair, "Overseas with a Herd of Hereford: Article No. 3; In Mid Ocean," *Lethbridge Herald*, May 1926, vol. 25, file 1; Altair, "Overseas with a Herd: Article No. 5"; Altair, "First Impressions of England," WEF.
58. Altair, "Overseas with a Herd: Article No. 5"; Altair, "First Impressions of England"; Altair, "First Impressions of England [cont.]," *Lethbridge Daily Herald*, 19 June 1926; Altair, "A Cycle Tour in England: Stonehenge," *Lethbridge Herald*, July 1926, all vol. 25, file 1, WEF.
59. "Biography," TJEWP; "Education and Employment Record," TJEWP; Van Nuys, *Family Band*, 244, 249; Hammond, diary, no. 5: 2 June 1911, EMHTP; Thomson, *Crocus and Meadowlark Country*, back book jacket; F. Lewis, *Nothing to Make*, interior book jacket flyleaf; L. Neatby, *Chronicle*,

75, 85–87, 59–60, 64–66; "Guide to the Papers of R. C. Russell," A71, and "Pathologist R. Russell Dies," *Star Phoenix* (Saskatoon), 16 July 1964, both in RCRP; Russell, "Cereal Smut Treatments."

60. Raaen, *Grass of the Earth*, 147, 150–53, 197, 171, 173, 184–88, 215–16, 198 (Tosten), 204–20, 233; A. Brown, *Sketches from Life*, 84; Parsons, *Upon a Sagebrush Harp*, 136–39; Hammond, dairies, nos. 10–22 for her regular teaching; see no. 10 and nos. 12–14 for her experiences and notes she took at Normal School, EMHTP; "Annora Brown," ABCF-GL; Margaret Lamb, "Alberta Had Interpreter of Its Life," [*Calgary Herald* or *Lethbridge Herald?* 1930s?], box 2, scrapbook 1, ABP; Eggleston, *While I Still Remember*, 45, 47–51; Thomson, *Crocus and Meadowlark Country*, 252; "Biography," TJEWP; "Education and Employment Record," TJEWP; Fite, *Peter Norbeck*, 14; Van Nuys, *Family Band*, 157–58, 236.
61. Raaen, *Measure of My Days*, 182, 196, 273; Raaen, *Grass of the Earth*, 207; Daniel E. Willard to "Miss Raaen," 8 January 1947, with Raaen's notations about the exchange on the backside, folder 7, box 1, ARP. See also Willard, *Story of the Prairies*.
62. A. Brown, *Sketches from Life*, 56; Raaen, *Grass of the Earth*, 209; Connerton, *How Societies Remember*; Halbwachs, *Collective Memory*.
63. Hammond, diary, no. 12: 21 January 1915, 10, 12, 24 February, 17 April 1915, EMHTP; Rose Hammond's diary (see 7–17 March 1910) is contained in Hammond, diary, no. 17: 6 October 1917 to 30 November 1918, EMHTP.
64. Hammond, diary, no. 14: Regina Normal School Nature Study notes after 21 February 1916, EMHTP; Raaen, *Measure of My Days*, 12–13; Thomson, *Crocus and Meadowlark Country*, 253; Jackman, "Nature-Study," 9.
65. Hammond, diaries, no. 13: Regina Normal School Psychology and the Physical Senses notes after 3 December 1915; no. 14: Regina Normal School Nature Study notes after 21 February, Geography after 25 April 1916, EMHTP. It is not clear whether Hammond's notes are her own or taken directly from published sources; see also Jackman, "Nature-Study," 11–12.
66. Hammond, diary, no. 14: Regina Normal School Nature Study notes after 21 February, Geography notes after 25 April 1916; 10, 11, 12 February 1915, EMHTP.
67. George F. Will, "Autobiography," WFP, pt. 2, pp. 15, 8, 20; Kroeber, "Frederic Ward Putnam."
68. Will and Spinden, "Mandans," 81–89, 93–96, 99–101, 149–51, 172–73, 176–77, 219; Will, "Autobiography," WFP, pt. 2, pp. 22–27. In "Archaeology," Will still identified the site as the "Burgois Site" but also refers internally to the "Double-Ditch site" (315) and provides the Mandan names of "Yellow Village" or "Yellow Clay Village" (316); see Walster,

"George Francis Will," 5; Will and Hyde, *Corn among the Indians*, 16; and Fenn, *Encounters at the Heart*; Fenn cites new work with "radar, magnetic gradiometry, and electrical resistivity" that has revealed there are four ditches at the "Double Ditch" site (2–4, 22–29, 83–85).
69. A. Brown, *Sketches from Life*, 84–85, 91–96, 102; Margaret Lamb, "Alberta Has Interpreter of Life," [*Calgary Herald*, 1941?], box 2, scrapbook 1, ABP.
70. Walters, *Modern Sagas*, 164–69; G. Gannon, "Strange Victory," 12.
71. A. Brown, *Sketches from Life*, 91–93, 102, 94; Geneva Lent, "Two Alberta Artists Feature in Display," [*Calgary Herald?*], [December?] 1944, scrapbook 1, ABP.
72. A. Brown, *Sketches from Life*, 86–87, 40–41, 90–91, 108–9, 126, 116, 154–55; Murray, *Best of the Group*, 15, 18; Zimon, *Alberta Society of Artists*, 76.

5. "Old Woman Who Never Dies"

1. Will and Hyde, *Corn among the Indians*, 32, 30, 301–3, 31, 33, 269. In later years Will identified himself as the "senior author" of both *Corn among the Indians* and "Mandans," written with Spinden. See Will, "Tree Ring Studies," 3. On George Hyde (1882–1968), see Lottinville, foreword to Hyde, *Pawnee Indians*; and Anderson, foreword to Hyde, *Spotted Tail's Folk*. Apparently, Will and Hyde never met, though they remained friends for some fifty years, until Will died in 1955 (xi). Will first mentioned the "Old Woman Who Never Dies" as a tale type in Will and Spinden, "Mandans," 133, 141. In the late 1920s Will began referring to the "Grandmother Who Never Dies." See Will, "Grandmother Who Never Dies."
2. "To Our Customers," Oscar H. Will and Company, annual catalog, 1919, OWP. George Will almost always wrote in the third person and signed his letters with the "OSCAR H. WILL AND COMPANY" stamp. The year before he died, in 1955, he signed his own name.
3. Will and Hyde, *Corn among the Indians*, 33; Oscar H. Will and Company, annual catalog, 1918, 1919, OWP.
4. Veracini, *Settler Colonialism*, esp. 33–52, 42–43, 46–47, on "Narrative Transfer" and "Transfer by Settler Indigenisation." Veracini notes "settler continuity" as key to the transfer of indigenization; this thinking serves to erase "the inherent difference between settler and indigenous relationship to the land" (42–43). See also Cook-Lynn, *Can't Read Wallace Stegner*, 31, 28, 30, 33, 38. Cook-Lynn suggests how the literature and history written by authors has served settler "politics of possession and dispossession" (40).
5. S. Smith, *Reimagining Indians*, 4–8, 14–15.
6. Veracini, *Settler Colonialism*, 33–52, esp. 37, on "perception transfer." Will learned to read Indigenous imprints on the land through archae-

ology. The experience led him to seek out modern Indigenous communities, and he did not consign Indigenous peoples to the past, nor claim the land "empty," as Veracini suggests is the usual case in "perception transfer" when "indigenous people are understood as part of the landscape" (37).

7. Will, "Adventures in Preserving," 78; George F. Will, "Autobiography," WFP, pt. 1, pp. 217–19. In *Corn among the Indians*, Will and Hyde vaguely suggest that his father "procured seed of the mixed flint from the Fort Berthold Indians" and that the first corn used by his father in "breeding experiments" was a "mixed flint, commonly known as Ree or squaw corn, but obtained from a Hidatsa woman" (27, 300). See also Schneider, "Corn in the Crib," 7. Anthropologist Fred Schneider, who has studied the early catalogs of Oscar H. Will and Company, concluded that before George Will began influencing the business after he returned from college, Oscar Will sold only the great northern bean, which he first obtained from Son of a Star, and what he called Will's Dakota white, a flint corn developed from the "Squaw Corn" supplied by an officer from Fort Stevenson (7).
8. Will, "Adventures in Preserving," 78; Schneider, "Corn in the Crib," 7.
9. Will, "Autobiography," WFP, pt. 1, p. 255.
10. Ostler, *Plains Sioux*, 313–16; Will, "Autobiography," WFP, pt. 1, p. 256; Kasson, *Buffalo Bill's Wild West*, 169–83.
11. Pat Dufour, "Annora: A Study in Styles," *Times-Colonist* (BC), 8 November 1981, folder 13, box 1, ABP, 25; A. Brown, *Sketches from Life*, 13–14, 38, 81.
12. Dufour, "Annora," 25; A. Brown, *Sketches from Life*, 36.
13. A. Brown, *Sketches from Life*, 36–37.
14. Salverson, *Confessions*, 38–39, 124; Salverson, *Viking Heart*, 128–34.
15. Salverson, *Confessions*, 124.
16. Walters, *Modern Sagas*, 3–4.
17. In *Settler Colonialism* Veracini describes the creation of such narratives as part of "settler territorialisation." Narratives of a "quiet peaceful idyll and disavowal of founding violence" emerged "*after* the 'closing' of the troubled frontier, the cessation of hostility, and *after* the establishment of a purportedly settled/settler order" (80).
18. E. Thompson, *American Daughter*, 42, 128–29.
19. E. Thompson, *American Daughter*, 141, 147–48.
20. Stegner, *Wolf Willow*, 49–50, 57.
21. Veracini, *Settler Colonialism*, 80.
22. Will, "Autobiography," WFP, pt. 2, p. 8; A. Brown, *Sketches from Life*, 31–33, 194–95.
23. Elsie Hammond, diaries, no. 9: 1 October 1913; no. 30: 10, 12, 13 July 1923, EMHTP; Lillian Miller, "I Remember Montana," LMC, 160; J.

Miller, *Skyscrapers Hide the Heavens*, 217–20. Julin in *Marvelous Hundred Square Miles* explores Lakota Black Elk and his performances in the 1920s and 1930s in the Black Hills of South Dakota (146–51). On stampedes, see Palmer, *Alberta*, 124–27. See also Hansen, *Encounter*, 49, 134–35; Kasson, *Buffalo Bill's Wild West*, 211–19.

24. Will, "Autobiography," WFP, pt. 2, p. 70; Will, "Adventures in Preserving," 78, 82; Will and Hecker, "Upper Missouri River Valley," 5; Will, "Archaeology," 291–92, 334; "Dr. Spinden Dead: Indian Authority," *New York Times*, 24 October 1967; Will, "New Feature," 586, 588; Will, "Unusual Group" 175; Will and Hyde, *Corn among the Indians*, 15–18.

25. Will, "Autobiography," WFP, pt. 2, pp. 78, 81–88, 86, 88; Will, "Adventures in Preserving," 78; Schneider, "Corn in the Crib," 7–8. The end of Will's unfinished autobiography begins to take the form of a diary, a list of dates with events listed (78–79).

26. Will, "Adventures in Preserving," 78, 84; Will and Hyde, *Corn among the Indians*, 31, 87, 103, 268; Schneider, "Corn in the Crib," 8.

27. Will, "Adventures in Preserving," 78, 83–84; Will, "No-Tongue," 331; Will and Hyde, *Corn among the Indians*, 16; see also 244, 268, 275.

28. Will, "Mandan Lodge at Bismarck," 38–39, 48; Will and Hyde, *Corn among the Indians*, 87–88, 102, 115–16, 160–61, 280, 291–93.

29. Will and Hecker, "Upper Missouri River Valley," 95, 99, 86–87, 89–91; Will, "Archaeology," 311, 312, 315, 323, 326–29, 332, 339.

30. Will and Hecker, "Upper Missouri River Valley," 76; Will, "Archaeology," 329; Will, "Arikara Sacred Ceremony," 265; Will, "Sleight of Hand Performances," 56, 62–63; Will, "Arikara Ceremonials," 247–48, 255–56, 263–64; Will, "Some Hidatsa and Mandan Tales," 93.

31. Hildebrandt and Hubner, *Cypress Hills*, 17–23; Friesen, *Canadian Prairies*, 141–42, 150–51; Hammond, diaries, no. 4: 7, 10 April 1911; no. 29: 28 January, 1 June 1922, EMHTP. Nekaneet, Cree signatory of Treaty 4, had died in 1897, but the band continued to resist removal north, despite the Canadian government's offer of assistance in exchange. See Waiser, *Saskatchewan*, 168, 464–65.

32. Hammond, diaries, no. 10: 9 August 1914; no. 33: 23 December 1925; no 3: 8, 13 October 1910; no. 33: 27 December 1925; no. 7: 12 May 1913; no. 19: 23 April 1919; no. 29: 28 January 1922; no. 34: 8 May 1926; no. 29: 23 November 1921; no. 33: 29 December 1925; no. 45: 19 July 1931, EMHTP; A. Brown, *Sketches from Life*, 36.

33. Hammond, diaries, no. 3: 8, 13, 16, 18, 28 October 1910; no. 16: 20 February 1917; no. 19: 10 April 1919, EMHTP.

34. Hammond, diaries, no. 16: 15 April, 1 October 1917; no. 55: 21 May 1935; no. 71: 7 February 1945; no. 20: 17 May 1919; no. 34: 8 May 1926, EMHTP; Guthrie, *Blue Hen's Chick*, 230.

35. Hammond, diaries, no. 10: 9 August 1914; no. 13: 16 December 1914; no. 33: 23 December 1925, EMHTP.
36. A. Brown, *Sketches from Life*, 197–98; Smith Mudiman, "Interpreter of the Foothills"; "Honor Native Daughter, Macleod Girl's Artistic Genius," *Lethbridge Herald*, 30 September 1926; Olive M. Ottewell to Annora Brown, [1935?]; "Macleod Artist's Work Impresses at Exhibition," *Fort Macleod Gazette*, 13 October 1930, all in box 2, scrapbook 1, ABP.
37. Annora Brown, "Prairie Totems," *Canadian Geographic Journal*, September 1941, 148–51; Annora Brown, "Heraldic Insignia on Indian Tipis Depicts Important Native Customs and Traditions," [*Calgary Herald?*], [late 1930s–early 1940s], folder 13, box 1, ABP. Brown explicitly cites McClintock's *Old North Trail* as a source; see McClintock's chapter 15, pp. 207–24.
38. A. Brown, *Sketches from Life*, 195, 197–98.
39. Samuel Henry Middleton to Annora Brown, 17 May 1949, folder 1, box 1, ABP; A. Brown, *Sketches from Life*, 196–97; see also Cardston and District Historical Society, *Chief Mountain Country*, 189–91; Palmer, *Alberta*, 170, 229.
40. A. Brown, *Sketches from Life*, 142–43.
41. Hardy, *Alberta Golden Jubilee Anthology*; Maybie, "Artist of International Fame," box 2, scrapbook 4, ABP; Robert Christie, "Dance to the Sun," *Saturday Evening Post*, 22 December 1951, folder 13, box 1, ABP, 30–31, 64–66.
42. Fisher and Tyner, *Totem, Tipi and Tumpline*, 236–63.
43. K.L. [Kenn Liddell?], review of *Old Man's Garden*, *Calgary Herald*, [1954]; Jane E. Huckvale, review of *Old Man's Garden*, *Lethbridge Herald*, [1954], both in box 2, scrapbook 3, ABP; R. Gorman, "Our Cover Artist Annora Brown," *Canadian Golden West*, Winter 1972–73, file 15, box 1, ABP, 9; Gorman refers to the 1970 reissue of Brown's book by Gray's Publishing.
44. A. Brown, *Old Man's Garden*, 3; A. Brown, *Sketches from Life*, 131–32.
45. A. Brown, *Sketches from Life*, 6–9; A. Brown, *Old Man's Garden*, 11–12; E. R. Lamm to Annora Brown, 30 December 1965; Winnifred M. C. Lamm to A. Brown, 24 October 1967; W. Lamm to A. Brown, 11 July 1968, all in folder 5, ABP. Letters from the E. R. Lamm Art Gallery in Calgary, Alberta, to A. Brown in the 1960s frequently request "crocus." See also Ken Liddell, column, [*Calgary Herald?*], 25 November 1960, ABCF-CL; Liddell discussed Brown's two hundred paintings of wildflowers commissioned by the Glenbow Foundation and reveals that Brown received about five requests for crocus paintings for one of every other flower.
46. Elizabeth Forster [Annora Brown], "How the Prairie Crocus Got Its Fur Coat," [*Fort Macleod Gazette?*], 1 June 1935, folder 13, box 1, ABP. Brown used her parents' first names as a pseudonym. Also A. Brown, *Old Man's Garden*, 13 (emphasis mine), 14, 15.

47. A. Brown, *Old Man's Garden*, 11–15, 22.
48. A. Brown, *Sketches from Life*, 135, 137, 116, 120, 126, 139–44. Later she explained how she chose the book's name: "I lived by the Old Man's River, near Old Man's Playing Ground, and I had been familiar with the thought from childhood so the title came naturally" (172). A. Brown, *Old Man's Garden*, 20–21.
49. A. Brown, *Old Man's Garden*, 21–22 (emphasis added), 58–59, 53–54; Carter, *Lost Harvests*, 69–73, 131–34.
50. A. Brown, *Old Man's Garden*, 149–51, 63–64, 51–52, 60, 57–58.
51. A. Brown, *Old Man's Garden*, 51–52.
52. A. Brown, *Old Man's Garden*, 96–97, 87–88.
53. Prayers, quoted in A. Brown, *Old Man's Garden*, 245; Will, "Arikara Sacred Ceremony," 265.
54. Rancher and other observers, quoted in Christie, "Dance to the Sun," ABP, 66.
55. Hough, review of *Corn among the Indians*; Trimble, review of *Corn among the Indians*.
56. Will, "Autobiography," WFP, pt. 1, pp. 230–31.
57. Will and Hecker, "Upper Missouri River Valley," 5–7 (emphasis mine); Will, "Grandmother Who Never Dies," 7.
58. Will and Company, catalog, 1911, 1918, 1919, OWP.
59. Will and Company, catalog, 1896, 1897 (p. 16), OWP; Will and Hyde, *Corn among the Indians*, 27.
60. Will and Hyde, *Corn among the Indians*, 75, 109, 291; Will, "Mandan Lodge at Bismarck," 38.
61. Will and Hyde, *Corn among the Indians*, 65, 66, 99, 108, 109. See also Will, "Grandmother Who Never Dies," 24.
62. Will and Hyde, *Corn among the Indians*, 78, 74–75, 76, 262, 271.
63. Will and Hyde, *Corn among the Indians*, 78–79, 93, 98–99; Will, "Grandmother Who Never Dies," 7; Will, "Mandan Lodge at Bismarck," 39, 48.
64. Will and Hyde, *Corn among the Indians*, 92, 66, 75–76, 290–91, 293.
65. G. Wilson, quoted in Will and Hyde, *Corn among the Indians*, 83–84, 293–94; Will, "Grandmother Who Never Dies," 26.
66. Will and Hyde, *Corn among the Indians*, 103; Nichols, *Indians*, 235, 235–39, 252–53. After Congress passed the Indian Reorganization Act of 1934, which ended allotments, the amount of land held by Natives in the United States dropped from 155 million acres in 1881 to 52 million in 1934. Two-thirds of allotted lands were sold; see Carter, *Lost Harvests*, 200.
67. This was in 1928. See Will, "Grandmother Who Never Dies," 26.
68. Will, "On the Road," 12, 9–10, 12–13.
69. Effie Laurie Storer, "Indian Life," 1946, 2.5, ELSP, 1, 4; Effie Laurie Storer, "Queen's Printer," 1942–43, 2.4, ELSP, 59, 24; Effie Laurie

Storer, "Chapter Red River Days, Part II," 2.5, ELSP, [2, 11]; Effie Laurie Storer, "Reverie," 1947, 2.5, ELSP, 1. On Effie's father, P. G. Laurie, see Hildebrandt, *Views from Fort Battleford*, 50–54.

70. Storer, "Queen's Printer," ELSP, 24, 83–84, 93; P. G. Laurie, quoted in Hildebrandt, *Views from Fort Battleford*, 53; Storer, "Reverie," ELSP, 1; on "constraints" on women writers, see Carter, *Capturing Women*, 116–24. I have not found any journalism written by Effie Laurie Storer but believe she wrote for a "woman's page" or "society pages."

71. Storer, "Indian Life," ELSP, 5, 2, 7, 9, 10, 14; Storer, "Queen's Printer," ELSP, 60, 59–76, 93.

72. Storer, "Queen's Printer," ELSP, 148, 156. On women as representatives of colonization, see S. McManus, *Line Which Separates*, 142–78. See also Carter, *Capturing Women*, 127–32. In "Queen's Printer" P. G. Laurie's diary is quoted in chapter 2, William Laurie's reminiscences in chapter 3, and Richard Laurie's reminiscences in chapter 6, ELSP.

73. Storer, "Indian Life," ELSP, 1–2; Storer, "Queen's Printer," ELSP, 84, 115.

74. Storer, "Indian Life," ELSP, 9, 10, 14.

75. Storer, "Indian Life," ELSP, 18, 21, 27–29.

76. Effie Laurie Storer, "Buffalo Life," 2.5, [7–8]; Storer, "Queen's Printer," ELSP, 83.

77. Walter L. Hixson, *American Settler Colonialism*, 1–4, 11. Hixson also argues (after the scholar Homi Bhaba) that settler colonials "reconciled" mixed feelings with some "distortion and denial" (11). A certain level of "denial" allowed subsequent generations of both the colonizer and the colonized to work in the "third space," where the potential for positive "hybrid" social relations occur, but violence and dispossession still resulted. In *Encounter* Hansen suggests if members of this settler generation grew up in proximity to Indigenous peoples, they at least "assumed coexistence," a small step forward (240–41).

78. A. Brown, *Old Man's Garden*, 3; Will, "Grandmother Who Never Dies," 7, 26.

79. C. Gannon, *Bunch Grass Acres*, 43–46, 79–82. On writing about American Indians as "*merely passing through*, a mere phase of history," see Cook-Lynn, *Can't Read Wallace Stegner*, 34–35, quote on 38–39.

80. Hansen, *Encounter*, 49, 54, 80, 109–11. Hansen's study of Norwegians and Dakotas living together on the Spirit Lake Reservation suggest that opportunity for contact increased with proximity and forced settlers to see Indigenous presence; however, although the two groups became neighbors, they did no "neighboring" (136).

6. "All Is So Still"

1. Ernest Hemingway to Robert McAlmon, [late January or February 1925], folder 37, box 1, RMP.

2. Pound, quoted in Smoller, *Adrift among Geniuses*, 147; Gertrude Stein to Robert McAlmon, 22 January 1925, folder 75, box 2; Ludvig Nordström to McAlmon, 24 November 1924, 6 January 1925, both in folder 61, box 2, RMP. For McAlmon Correspondence with Bryher on the creation of "Village," see also folder 1260, box 35, BP.
3. Thacker, *Great Prairie Fact*, 189. Thacker includes a section called "Inhabitants" that focuses on the postpioneer generation (185–224).
4. Newlin, *Hamlin Garland*; Woodress, *Willa Cather*; Strong-Boag and Rosa, "Some Small Legacy"; McClung, *Clearing in the West*.
5. Cook-Lynn, *Can't Read Wallace Stegner*, 40, 30, 32–33. Cook-Lynn argues that this literature aimed foremost for an "audience made up of the children and offspring of pioneer settlers" (33). This literary expression can be seen as another stage of Veracini's "narrative transfer" of the land from Indigenous hands to settler society. *Settler Colonialism*, esp. 33–52, 42–43, 46–47.
6. See Singal, *Modernist Culture*; Stansell, *American Moderns*; May, *End of American Innocence*; Dorman, *Revolt of the Provinces*; J. Thompson, *Canada*.
7. Van Doren, "Revolt from the Village," 407, 409, 410; Van Doren, *Contemporary American Novelists*, 1–4, 38–47, 113–22, 146–64.
8. Weber, *Midwestern Ascendancy*, 17. See also Stansell, *American Moderns*, 161–62.
9. Van Doren, "Revolt from the Village," 410.
10. Eggleston, *High Plains*, 135; Wetherell and Kmet, *Town Life*, 6–13, *151–55, 289–90*; Pitblado, quoted in Ann Tillenius, "Edward Bruce Pitblado Q.C.," folder 2, box 7, PFF; Quantic, *Nature of the Place*, 18, 164.
11. Altair [Wilfrid Eggleston], "Sketches of a Prairie Town I," *Lethbridge Daily Herald*, [17 March 1923], file 9, vol. 25, WEF. The townspeople turned to a dictionary authority to find out 98 percent of them erred in using *two* syllables when pronouncing "coyote."
12. C. Gannon, *Bunch Grass Acres*, 5.
13. For the "structures" railroads provided plains towns, see Hudson, *Plains Country Towns*, 15–16, 123–25; and Sandalack, "Prairie Towns," 276–84.
14. Van Doren, "Revolt from the Village," 410; Pitblado, quoted in Tillenius, "Edward Bruce Pitblado Q.C.," folder 2, box 7, PFF.
15. Parsons, *Curlew Cried*, 148, 184, 209; Salverson, *Viking Heart*, 61, 162, 107, 143, 236; Eggleston, *High Plains*, 134–50, 135–38; quotes from Altair, "Prairie Town I"; see also Altair, "Sketches of a Prairie Town IV," *Lethbridge Herald*, 7 April 1923; Altair, "Sketches of a Prairie Town V," *Lethbridge Herald*, 14 April 1923, all in file 9, vol. 25, WEF.
16. Eggleston, *High Plains*, 169.

17. Parsons, *Curlew Cried*, 156, 224–25.
18. Parsons, *Upon a Sagebrush Harp*, 141, 143–44; Parsons, *Curlew Cried*, 224.
19. Stegner, *Wolf Willow*, 287, 282; Altair, "Prairie Town I," WEF.
20. McAlmon, *Companion Volume*, 37, 45, 58.
21. See also S. Lewis, *Main Street*, 156–58.
22. McAlmon, *Companion Volume*, 37–38.
23. Quantic, *Nature of the Place*, 164.
24. Trupin, *Dakota Diaspora*, 101.
25. Stegner, *Wolf Willow*, 11, 255, 287; Will, *Corn for the Northwest*, 134.
26. Quantic, *Nature of the Place*, xix; Thacker, *Great Prairie Fact*, 3, 185–224. Thacker cites a general transnational reliance on early Canadian prairie textual analysis, especially of "prairie landscape," in conversation with a U.S. focus on western "imaginative processes" as a whole (3). Quantic argues, "Canadian prairie fiction and Great Plains fiction in the American tradition reveal the same patterns of arrival, confrontation, and transformation of mythic preconceptions" and reveal similar garden and desert dichotomies (xix).
27. Van Doren, *Contemporary American Novelists*, 39, 38–47, 117, 118, xiii, 113–22.
28. Thacker, *Great Prairie Fact*, 168.
29. Harrison, *Unnamed Country*, 100, 156; see also 98, 102–14, 121–23. Harrison's analysis in *Unnamed Country* suggests Manitoba-raised author Nellie McClung's first novel, *Sewing Seeds in Danny* (1908), about the grasslands farm and small-town hero raised in the 1880s, represents the tradition in Canada (86–88).
30. Altair, "Hamlin Garland and Other Americans," *Lethbridge Herald*, 21 April 1923; Altair, "Garland's 'Son of the Middle Border,'" *Lethbridge Herald*, 12 May 1923, both in file 1, vol. 25, WEF. Eggleston noted also the "land reform" activities of Garland served as a "precursor of such movements as our United Farmers." See also Newlin, *Hamlin Garland*, on agrarian protest (166, 104). Stegner, *Wolf Willow*, 288. Stegner also cited Sinclair Lewis's 1920 *Main Street* (285).
31. Altair, "Comments on Recent Novelists," A Reader's Journal, *Lethbridge Daily Herald*, 13 December 1924, file 3, vol. 25, WEF.
32. Altair, "A Dr. Banting of Fiction," *Lethbridge Daily Herald*, 17 October 1925, file 3, vol. 25, WEF; this review is about Lewis's novel *Arrowsmith*, but he discussed *Main Street* also. See also Altair, "Sketches of a Prairie Town II," *Lethbridge Daily Herald*, 24 March 1923; Altair, "Sketches of a Prairie Town III," *Lethbridge Daily Herald*, 31 March 1923, both in file 9, vol. 25, WEF.
33. McAlmon and Boyle, *Being Geniuses Together*, 33; the McAlmon quote continues "in those Middle Western towns."

34. McAlmon, *Village*, 13, 47, 59, 3, 11, 125, 151.
35. McAlmon, *Village*, 16–18, 54, see also 13–14, 36, 48; Quantic, *Nature of the Place*, 25–26; McAlmon, *Village*, 4–5, 8. See also Vidal, foreword to McAlmon, *Miss Knight and Others*. Vidal, whose father was McAlmon's South Dakota friend, said, "As far as my family goes, McAlmon invents nothing. He is a literal recorder" (xi–xii); McAlmon and Boyle, *Being Geniuses Together*, 33.
36. McAlmon, *Village*, 169, 125, 92–93, 99, 107, quotes from 139, 91, 13 (emphasis mine), 59, 15. Smoller in *Adrift among Geniuses* suggests McAlmon would have heard a lot of "new ideas current in politics and morality" from his older sister Victoria, "an intelligent, emancipated woman who later became vice-president of the Farmer-Labor party in Minnesota and, after being fired from the state's public school system for her politics, taught at Los Angeles City College" (15). On Henry George, see Weber, *Midwestern Ascendancy*, 39, 41.
37. McAlmon, *Village*, 151; Van Doren "Revolt from the Village," 407. Van Doren here cited specifically Edgar Lee Masters in *Spoon River Anthology*. Quote from Kay Boyle, review of Robert McAlmon's *The Indefinite Huntress and Other Stories*, William Faulkner's *Light in August*, and Dorothy Dudley's study of Theodore Dreiser, called *Forgotten Frontiers*; for a draft of the review Boyle sent to McAlmon, see folder 129, box 5, RMP; Kay Boyle to Robert McAlmon, 17 December 1932, folder 8, box 1, RMP.
38. McAlmon, *Village*, 56.
39. McAlmon, *Village*, 100–101, 78–79; Van Doren, "Revolt from the Village," 407; McAlmon in *Village* asks, "Why limit yourself?" (153, also 151).
40. McAlmon, *Hasty Bunch*, 55–67, quotes from 62, 63, 65.
41. Stegner, *Wolf Willow*, 293.
42. McAlmon, *Village*, quotes from 9, 50, 92, 6, 45, see also 191–95, 123, 45–46, 18–19, 75–76, 134–36, 137, 140–41, 37–38.
43. Walter Yust, review of *Village*, in *Philadelphia Public Ledger*, [1925], folder: "McAlmon Reviews," box 1, PRM.
44. Stansell, *American Moderns*, 275, 40–46. See Stansell's chapter "Talking about Sex," 273–308.
45. McAlmon, *Post-adolescence*, xvi, 69–70.
46. McAlmon, *Companion Volume*, 37–72, quotations and examples from 48, 40–41, 57, 55, 56, 47, 50, 40, 61, 44.
47. McAlmon, *Village*, 20, 5, 80, 145, 150, 169, 38, 159, 14, 36, 16–18, 143. See also Stegner, *Wolf Willow*, 288.
48. Eggleston, *High Plains*, i, 6, 11–22; G.H.C., [book notice] *Queen's Quarterly*, Autumn 1939, file 23, vol. 26, WEF; Eggleston, *While I Still Remember*, 68–71; Van Doren "Revolt from the Village," 410; Eggleston, *Homestead on the Range*, 6; Eggleston, *High Plains*, 159, 51, 33–34.

49. Eggleston, *High Plains*, quotations from 74, 248, see also 36, 73–75, 106, 132, 177, 209, 238–39; Eggleston, *While I Still Remember*, 68–71.
50. Eggleston, *High Plains*, 257–64, 247–48; Eggleston, *Homestead on the Range*, 70–72, 78; Palmer, *Alberta*, 118–22, 140, 209–10, 246; Jones, *Empire of Dust*, 123–26.
51. Harrison, *Unnamed Country*, 156, 165.
52. "Significant Canadian Novels," *Edmonton Journal*, 16 December 1938, file 22, vol. 26, WEF.
53. Eggleston, *Homestead on the Range*, 74.
54. Eggleston, *High Plains*, quotations from 33, 188, 86, see also 98–99, 202.
55. Parsons, *Curlew Cried*, 7, 35–36, 11, 237–38, see also 23, 217, 181, 223–24, 225.
56. Parsons, *Curlew Cried*, 47, 28, 44–45, 242–43; Parsons, *Upon a Sagebrush Harp*, 140–42.
57. Stegner, *On a Darkling Plain*, 22, 67–68, 57, 86, 72, 77–78, 14; Benson, *Wallace Stegner*, 83, 95–97, 113–14. Stegner told Etulain he thought the novel "psychologically naïve" (36) and admitted it to be autobiographical only in the "most rudimentary sense" (31). See Stegner and Etulain, *Conversations with Wallace Stegner*, 31–32, 35–37.
58. Stegner, *On a Darkling Plain*, 67, 120, 11, 4.
59. Stegner and Etulain, *Conversations with Wallace Stegner*, 32; Benson, *Wallace Stegner*, 96; Stegner, *On a Darkling Plain*, 120.
60. Honan in *Mathew Arnold* interprets the poem "Dover Beach" to convey, in part, the "modern predicament in friendship and all human relationships." Although it "opens with images of confidence and beauty and profound security," as the speaker looks across the English Channel to Calais, it uses waves as a metaphor for the "ebb and flow of misery," which "is eternal or set in life's conditions" (233–36).
61. Stegner, *On a Darkling Plain*, 121, 118–19, 16, 11; Stegner, *Wolf Willow*, 25.
62. Stegner, *Wolf Willow*, 22, 269; Stegner, *On a Darkling Plain*, 111; Thacker, *Great Prairie Fact*, 181.
63. Stegner, *Wolf Willow*, 22, 6.
64. Stegner, *Wolf Willow*, 22, 26; Stegner, *On a Darkling Plain*, 51–52; Stegner, *Wolf Willow*, 132, 24; Eggleston, *High Plains*, 194; Eggleston, *While I Still Remember*, 35–36.
65. Stegner, *Wolf Willow*, 298, 306. See also Stegner and Etulain, *Conversations with Wallace Stegner*, 33.
66. Stegner, *Wolf Willow*, 282; Harrison, *Unnamed Country*, 125–26; Stegner, *On a Darkling Plain*, 36, 13–14, 29, 131; Parsons, *Curlew Cried*, 242–46; Stegner, *Wolf Willow*, 270, 282; see also Benson, *Wallace Stegner*, 20; Eggleston, *While I Still Remember*, 70–71.
67. Salverson, *Viking Heart*, 110–12. I use a 1975 reprint of the 1947 second edition of Salverson's 1923 novel. According to Alison Hopwood, in the

1947 edition Salverson rewrote and shortened the prefatory section of the novel, which begins on page 11 (there are no pages 1–10); chapter 1 begins on page 49. See Hopwood, intro. to Salverson, *Viking Heart*, xiii–xiv.

68. Salverson, *Viking Heart*, 162, 112, 111, 108, 294. Walters, *Modern Sagas*, 191, 79, 13. On the influence of the racialized hierarchical thinking of Walters's day, see Jacobson, *Whiteness*; Higham, *Strangers in the Land*; and Palmer, "Strangers and Stereotypes," 308–34.
69. Quantic, *Nature of the Place*, 25–26; Salverson, *Viking Heart*, Nina: 273–77, Balder: 169, 236, 279, 281, Tomi: 162, 265.
70. Walters, *Modern Sagas*, 141, 46, 141–76, 79, 16, 191–92.
71. Salverson, *Viking Heart*, 305, 294, 191.
72. Smoller, *Adrift among Geniuses*, 5.
73. McAlmon, *Village*, 153 (emphasis added).
74. Ford, "Chroniques," 213.
75. Vidal, foreword to McAlmon, *Miss Knight and Others*, ix.
76. For works by McAlmon published in the United States, see his "Via Dolorosa of Art"; *Not Alone Lost*; and "Potato Picking," in O'Brien, *Best Short Stories*, 159–68.
77. Smoller, *Adrift among Geniuses*, 324, 221–29; Lorusso, introd. to McAlmon, *Village*, xvii.
78. W. Williams, foreword to Knoll, *Robert McAlmon*, vii, viii, ix; Knoll, *Lost Generation*, 5; Smoller, *Adrift among Geniuses*, 4.
79. Stansell, *American Moderns*, 41, 3, 45–46.
80. Smoller, *Adrift among Geniuses*, 15.
81. Smoller, *Adrift among Geniuses*, 34–47.
82. Weber, *Midwestern Ascendancy*, 2–3. Weber mentions McAlmon but has no discussion of his work (214–15).
83. W. Williams, "Robert McAlmon's Prose, II," 216. Williams's "towns" silently corrected to "town."
84. Yust, review, PRM; Ford, "Notes on Contributors," 98. In addition to McAlmon, Ford in *It Was the Nightingale* also gave credit for new midwestern literature to William Bird and his Three Mountains Press in Paris (341); see also 333, 335–36, 338–40, 214, 235.
85. The phrase "wild and dreary" is quoted in Smoller, *Adrift among Geniuses*, 10, from McAlmon's 1938 autobiography; Lorusso, introd. to McAlmon, *Post-adolescence*, xix; Lorusso, introd. to McAlmon, *Miss Knight and Others*, xv; Robert McAlmon to William Carlos Williams, 9 January 1939, folder 431, box 14, WCWP; McAlmon, "The Plain Tales of the Open Prairie," 43–60.
86. McAlmon and Boyle, *Being Geniuses Together*, 256.
87. McAlmon, "Questionnaire," 53; W. Williams, "Robert McAlmon's Prose," 215.

88. McAlmon to W. Williams, 5 August [1920?], folder 432, box 14, WCWP.
89. See Singal, *War Within*, on southern modernism; Boyle, review, RMP; Rexroth, review of Knoll, *Lost Generation*, 164–65; Knoll, *Robert McAlmon*, 2.
90. W. Williams to McAlmon, 11 August 1937, folder 95, box 3, RMP.
91. W. Williams, "Robert McAlmon's Prose," 361. Williams discussed the stories in McAlmon's *Hasty Bunch*.
92. Hemingway, quoted in Smoller, *Adrift among Geniuses*, 146.
93. Knoll, *Lost Generation*, 354.
94. McAlmon, "A Pastorale," typewritten piece for a short-story class, 1916, folder 129, box 5, RMP.
95. Ezra Pound, "Date Line," 82, 74–87. Pound, a lifelong supporter of McAlmon, stated boldly, "America is now teeming with printed books written by imitators of McAlmon, inferior to the original" (82).
96. McAlmon, *Hasty Bunch*, 11–27, 162–215, 268–81, esp. 248–52; W. Williams to McAlmon, 23 December 1921, folder 90, box 3, RMP; W. Williams, "Robert McAlmon's Prose," 362; W. Williams to McAlmon, 23 December 1921, folder 90, box 3, RMP.
97. Quantic, *Nature of the Place*, 168, 165.
98. Stegner, *Wolf Willow*, 6, 281; Stegner, *On a Darkling Plain*, 83, 17; Eggleston, "To See Her Walking," in *Prairie Moonlight*, 5–6, 11; C. Gannon, *Bunch Grass Acres*, 18, 70; McAlmon, *Companion Volume*, 38; Stegner, *Wolf Willow*, 283; W. Williams, quoted in Smoller, *Adrift among Geniuses*, 124.
99. McAlmon and Boyle, *Being Geniuses Together*, 20, 18–21.
100. Harrison, *Unnamed Country*, x; Thacker, *Great Prairie Fact*, 2, 187–89; see also Quantic, *Nature of the Place*, 155; Tracie, *Shaping a World*, 123–44.
101. Quantic, *Nature of the Place*, xv.
102. Stegner, *Wolf Willow*, 23, 29.
103. Stegner, *On a Darkling Plain*, 127–28, 110; C. Gannon, *Bunch Grass Acres*, 54–55; McAlmon, *Companion Volume*, 37; McAlmon, *Explorations*, 31.
104. Stegner, *Wolf Willow*, 6–7; Parsons, *Curlew Cried*, 169–70, 22; Parsons, *Upon a Sagebrush Harp*, 55; McAlmon, *Not Alone Lost*, 48; See also McAlmon, *Village*, 34.
105. Stegner, *Wolf Willow*, 26; "Annora Brown Gives Interesting Talk at Writer's Club Meeting," [*Lethbridge Herald? Calgary Herald?*], 19 October 1948; see also Albert E. Larke, "Incentives for Attractive Living," *Junior Farmer and 4-H Quarterly*, [1940s?], both in box 2, scrapbook 2, ABP.
106. McAlmon did not want people to think of their little magazine *Contact* "in terms of physical contact." McAlmon to W. Williams, [1921?], folder 431, box 14, WCWP; Stegner, *Wolf Willow*, 25, 26.
107. Thacker, *Great Prairie Fact*, 151, 188; Pratt, *Great Plains Literature*, 78–79.

108. Orville Prescott, quoted in Benson, *Wallace Stegner*, 140. The *New York Times Book Review* did publish a similarly mixed review of *Big Rock Candy Mountain* (140). The *New York Times Book Review* published reviews of neither Stegner's Pulitzer Prize nor National Book Award novels (2).
109. Quantic, *Nature of the Place*, 159, 157–59.
110. Salverson, *Viking Heart*, xv.
111. Reese, "Introduction," xxxii; "University of Minnesota Regional Writing Fellowships," in Theodore C. Blegen and Helen Clapesattle, 11 May 1948, folder 66, box 5, series 226, RG 1.1, UMRSP.
112. Stegner, quoted in Milton, "Conversations with Wallace Stegner," 115–17.
113. Benson, *Down by the Lemonade Springs*, 60; Benson, *Wallace Stegner*, ix, 3, 1, 127.
114. Such a "narrative transfer," according to the theorist Lorenzo Veracini, seeks to erase "the inherent difference between settler and indigenous relationship to the land" (43). See *Settler Colonialism*, 33–34, 41–43, 46.
115. Altair, "Hamlin Garland," 21 April 1923, WEF; C. Gannon, *Bunch Grass Acres*, 23–24, 87–88; Salverson, *Viking Heart*, 293–94; Salverson, foreword to Salverson, *Viking Heart*, xv.
116. "Alberta Artist Inspires Group at Sketch Club," [*Lethbridge Herald?*], n.d.; "Macleod Artist's Work Impresses at Exhibition," *Fort Macleod Gazette*, 13 October 1930, both in box 2, scrapbook 1, ABP.
117. Stegner, *Wolf Willow*, 7; Will, "Fall Comes to Us"; C. Gannon, *Bunch Grass Acres*, 11.
118. Dorman, *Revolt of the Provinces*, 23, 25.
119. Boyle, review, RMP; Pound, "Paris Letter."
120. Stansell in *American Moderns* explains that the phrase "vital contact" circulated in Greenwich Village (60). Proponents shifted the idea away from "religious impulses" toward "liberal political ideals," from "God" and "grace" to the "search of life" and "experience" (61–62). Robert McAlmon to W. Williams [1921?], folder 3, box 14, WCWP.
121. Quoted in Smoller, *Adrift among Geniuses*, 31–32. Smoller quotes extensively from what he calls the "editors' credo" in McAlmon and Williams's first edition of *Contact* in December 1920. Smoller suggests that McAlmon and Williams wrote jointly but that the first two sentences here contain quotations from McAlmon, while the third likely includes Williams's contributions.
122. Dorman, *Revolt of the Provinces*, 23, 25, 61–67, 78, 80. Historians list Willa Cather among the regionalists, if in her own nonpolitical category (29–35). For regionalists, "Indians" exampled "the first and only process of Americanization that has been carried to completion," and they believed Indigenous "character" came "from the soil" (64).

123. Van Doren, "Revolt from the Village," 408, 410. Van Doren here quoted terms from Edgar Lee Masters's *Spoon River Anthology* to make a larger point about how "these novels ache with the sense of a dumb confusion in America" (408). He also discusses Lewis's *Main Street* suggesting the "march of machines" had left no land "uninvaded" (410).
124. McAlmon, *Village*, 3.
125. K. Boyle to McAlmon, 17 December 1932, folder 8, box 1, RMP; Boyle, review, RMP; Robert McAlmon to Bryher, [1923], folder 1260, box 35, BP.
126. Conrad, *Refiguring America*, 107, see also 105–6, 137–39, 109, 29–40; W. Williams, *In the American Grain*, 39–42, 137–38.
127. Dorman, *Revolt of the Provinces*, 61–67, 78–80, 81–93. Dorman suggested that regionalists' appropriation of elements of Indigenous culture was "far less problematic" than the "celebration of the pioneer myths and traditions" also emerging in the interwar years because the former appropriated social values and forms "for the purposes of cultural reconstruction," while pioneer stories functioned culturally to displace Indigenous peoples from the land (61). Indeed, one group of regionalists critiqued the "pioneer" as the "agent of a triumphant capitalist ethos" (85).

7. "Surely, Grass Is the Great Mother"

1. Elsie Hammond, diaries, no. 48: 13, 21 May 1932; no. 49: 2, 7, 17–18 June 1933; no. 50: 30 July 1933; no. 52: 14, 21, 25 August 1934, EMHTP.
2. Jones, *Empire of Dust*; C. McManus, *Happyland*, 62–74, 168–69, 232–33; Worster, *Dust Bowl*, 44–63. In *Happyland* C. McManus found that in Saskatchewan some thirty thousand people left between 1914 and 1924 and forty thousand more in the 1930s (7–8).
3. Quoted in Barrows et al., *Future*, 1, see also 63, 6. On people who stayed on the land, see C. McManus, *Happyland*, 236–40; Worster, *Dust Bowl*, 140, 150–51, 161, 164–65; Voisey, *Vulcan*, 34–35, 216–17, 77–79; and Riney-Kehrberg, *Rooted in Dust*, 2–4, 96, 141, 145, 148, 164. Riney-Kehrberg argues that a "full three-quarters of the area's residents struggled on" (2).
4. J. Thompson, *Harvests of War*, 45–46, 59–63; Malone, Roeder, and Lang, *Montana*, 252, 315; Will, *Corn for the Northwest*, 134–37; Isern, *Bull Threshers and Bindlestiffs*, 176, 175–79, 182–83; E. Robinson, *History of North Dakota*, 372–73; Nelson, *Prairie Winnows*, 7, 13–14; Thompson, *Harvests of War*, 63; Waiser, *Saskatchewan*, 272; W. Morton, *Manitoba*, 357, 381, 393; Friesen, *Canadian Prairies*, 430–31; Will, *Corn for the Northwest*, 134–37.
5. Palmer, *Alberta*, 286. The phrase is from Shover, *First Majority*, xiv, xiii–xvi, 143–70; Neth, *Preserving the Family Farm*, 4–6, 147–83, 271–72; Danbom, *Born in the Country*, 233–52; Cunfer, *On the Great Plains*, 129–39.

6. E. Robinson, *History of North Dakota*, 444; Schell, *History of South Dakota*, 328; Friesen, *Canadian Prairies*, 429–31; Hammond, diary, no. 70: 22 October 1942, EMHTP. See also Malone, Roeder, and Lang, *Montana*, 315.
7. Murchie, *Agricultural Progress*, 128; Barrows et al., *Future*, 46; J. Thompson, *Harvests of War*, 61; Friesen, *Canadian Prairies*, 430.
8. E. Robinson, *History of North Dakota*, 369, 444. Farm size in South Dakota grew to 544 acres by 1940 and 674 acres in 1950. Schell, *History of South Dakota*, 327; Palmer, *Alberta*, 193, 198, 246, 286. The average Saskatchewan farm grew from 390 acres in 1926 to almost 408 acres in 1931 and to 865 acres in 1961 (273, 356). Waiser, *Saskatchewan*, 273, 356; Friesen, *Canadian Prairies*, 329, 429–30. Friesen marks the key growth period from 1941 to 1981. Malone, Roeder, and Lang, *Montana*, 283.
9. Walters, *Modern Sagas*, 177–79, 141–76.
10. Lillian Miller, "I Remember Montana," LMC, 2, 42, 79, 209–10, 214–24, 229.
11. Bell, *Montana and I*, 247. Bell later moved to Great Falls and then to a ranch near Sims, Montana (250).
12. Walters, *Modern Sagas*, 177.
13. Hagen, *Vikings of the Prairie*, 186, 204; Hansen, *Encounter*, 225–26.
14. L. Neatby, *Chronicle*, 14–16, 23, 42, 51–52, 56, 60–65; Nicoll, *Paths*, 15, 17, 18, 20–21, 106, 120.
15. Eggleston, *Homestead on the Range*, 77, 78–81.
16. Eggleston, *Homestead on the Range*, 81, 85.
17. Hammond's diaries continually report on the movements of people and where they lived and worked. See Hammond, diaries, no. 2: 19 May, 9, 13 July 1910; no. 13: 25, 26 July 1915; no. 28: 16, 31 May, 1 July 1928; no. 31: 16, 28 August 1923; no. 32: 4 March 1924; no. 33: 24 December 1924; no. 34: 9 May 1926; no. 35: 25 December 1926; no 48: 18 March 1932; no. 42: 12 April 1930; no. 50: 25 July 1933; no. 51: 20 March 1934; no. 62: 22, 26 April 1937; and no. 71: 15 April 1948, EMHTP.
18. Hammond, diaries, no. 12: August 1917; no. 17: 14 November 1917, 13 April 1918; no. 30: 27 July 1922; no. 32: 24 May 1924; no. 35: 17 September, 10–15 October 1927; no. 36: 26, 28 October, 4 November 1927; no. 37: 6–10 August, 16 October 1928; no. 39: 30 May, 3–27 June, 12 July, 12–14 August 1929; no. 40: 19, 20, 23 September 1929; no. 42: 11 March 1930; no. 45: 29 January 1931, 22, 25–28 June 1931; EMHTP. C. McManus, *Happyland*, 118. The substance of her father's irrigation work is unclear. See Downing, "George R. and Ada (Cook) Hammond."
19. Hammond, diaries, no. 17: 5 September 1918; no. 4: 6 June 1911; no. 28: 14 March, 22 April, 22 May, 24 June 1921; no. 5: 5, 21 August 1911; no. 6: 2 April, 12 June 1912; no. 26: 16 October 1920; no. 55: 5 August 1935; no. 29: 3 January 1922; no. 54: 31 March 1935, EMHTP. Elsie Hammond

records activities with her horse Margaret from 1921 to 1937 (see no. 28: 14 March 1921 and no. 64: 22 August 1937).

20. Hammond, diaries, no. 6: 11 May 1912; no. 17: 8 October 1917; no. 5: 21 August 1911, EMHTP. On the development of power farming, see Will, *Corn for the Northwest*, 134; L. Neatby, *Chronicle*, 58; Eggleston, *Homestead on the Range*, 81.

21. Hammond, diaries, no. 5: 18 July 1911; no. 28: 2, 19 August 1921; no. 35: 5 April 1927, EMHTP; Waiser, *Saskatchewan*, 256, 272; Friesen, *Canadian Prairies*, 430–31. Although a decline is suggested, the Hammonds still sold some horses.

22. C. McManus, *Happyland*, 83, 54–55, 63. Hammond taught in Hay Creek School and Aylesford School. The soil-drifting discussion took place in February 1923.

23. Hammond, diaries, no. 30: 1, 14 August 1923; no. 31: 28 August 1923; no. 34: 8 April 1926; no. 36: 1, 3, 6, 14, 17 February 1928, EMHTP.

24. Hammond, diaries, no. 31: 28 August 1923; no. 33: 2, 3, 9 January 1926; no. 34: 5, 6 September 1926; no. 35: 25–31 October 1926, 25 March, 19, 21–22 April, 17–21 May, 26 August 1927; no. 38: 7, 9 November 1928, EMHTP. See Dooks, "George Lester and Ivy Madaline Amelia (Rex) Hammond."

25. Hammond, diaries, no. 28: 20 July 1921; no. 29: 24 March 1922; no. 30: 16 August 1929; no. 34: 9 May 1926; no. 37: 9 June, 19 July, 27 October 1928; no. 46: 5, 6 November 1931; no. 48: 4, 16 May 1932; no. 54: 12, 16, 17 May 1935; no. 55: 14 June, 23 September 1935; no. 32: 24 May, 11 October 1924; no. 45: 24, 27 April, 16 May, 25, 26, 27, 28 June, 28 July 1931; Hammond, diaries, nos. 22–65, EMHTP.

26. Hammond, diaries, no. 34: 2 August 1926; no. 35: 21, 28 March, 15–20 August 1927; no. 37: 27–31 August 1928; no. 36: 27 November 1927; no. 42: 14 May 1930; no. 48: 14 May, 5 November 1932; no. 49: 3–6 May 1933; no. 40: 13 November 1929, EMHTP; Riney-Kehrberg, *Rooted in Dust*, 77–78, 95–96.

27. Worster, *Dust Bowl*, 118–38.

28. C. McManus, *Happyland*, 114, 118; Palmer, *Alberta*, 252.

29. Schell, *History of South Dakota*, 283, 292, 295; Waiser, *Saskatchewan*, 294–96; Friesen, *Canadian Prairies*, 386–88; W. Morton, *Manitoba*, 421, 430; E. Robinson, *History of North Dakota*, 398, 400, 374; Malone, Roeder, and Lang, *Montana*, 292; C. McManus, *Happyland*, 202.

30. Hammond, diaries, no. 42: 11, 12 April 1930; no. 42: 25 June, 2 July 1930; no. 44: 7 November 1930; no. 45: 26–28 June, 21–23 July 1931; no. 46: 3, 22, 24 August, 2 September 1931; no. 48: 13 April, 21 May 1932, EMHTP; C. McManus, *Happyland*, 114.

31. Schell, *History of South Dakota*, 118–19, 223, 257; George F. Will, "Autobiography," WFP, pt. 1, p. 230; McAlmon, *Village*, 11, 125; Hammond,

diaries, no. 4: 13 March, 6 May 1911; no. 9: 7 December 1913; no. 29: 26 September 1921; no. 31: 24 November 1923, EMHTP; Malone, Roeder, and Lang, *Montana*, 280–85; W. Morton, *Manitoba*, 357.

32. Hammond, diaries, no. 52: 7, 12, 15, 21, 23, 25 August 1934; no. 55: 1, 11, 12, 13, 14, 17, 19 June, 7, 11 July, 27, 28, 29, 30, 31 August 1935; no. 64: 1, 2 September 1937, EMHTP.

33. The missing periods from Elsie Hammond's diaries include the late summer of 1930, again from the fall of 1935 to the spring of 1937, and finally from January 1938 to July 1942. The complete set of diaries is numbered sequentially, so it appears Hammond did keep diaries during these years.

34. Hammond, diaries, no. 62: 12, 16, 26, 29 April, 30 July, 26, 27, 28, 30 August, 17, 18 September 1937, EMHTP; C. McManus, *Happyland*, 113.

35. C. McManus, *Happyland*, 114, 202; Friesen, *Canadian Prairies*, 386–88; Waiser, *Saskatchewan*, 294–96.

36. Hammond, diaries, no. 62: 11 May, 2 June 1937; no. 64: 8, 11 September 1937; no. 65: 25 November, 25–26, 30 December 1937, EMHTP. Hammond's diaries from January 1938 through July 1942 do not exist. Elsie Hammond made the last entry for her horse Margaret on 22 August 1937 (no. 64); it is not clear if the horse who starved to death is the same one. C. McManus, *Happyland*, 205–6, 210.

37. Hammond, diaries, no. 69: 10 September 1942; no. 70: 20 November 1942, 2–4, 22 August 1943, 7–12 August 1944; no. 69: 2–6, 25 August 1942; no. 70: 4–5, 25 September 1944, 17 January 1944, 20 February 1944, EMHTP. In the summer of 1948, Les Hammond and his family and eighty-eight-year-old father moved to British Columbia. Her mother had passed away in 1946; her father passed in the fall of 1949. See Hammond, diaries, no 71: 26 July 1948, 27 April 1946; 4, 8, 9 September 1949, EMHTP. On her birthday, 19 October 1949, Elsie made her last diary entry for twenty-two years until her seventy-eighth birthday.

38. Will, *Corn for the Northwest*, 9–12; Will and Hyde, *Corn among the Indians*, 19–33.

39. Hammond, diaries, no. 39: 13 July 1929; no. 46: 18 November 1931; no. 45: 20–21 May 1931; no. 46: 14–15 September 1931; no. 55: 14 June 1935, EMHTP. In 1925 farmers in Saskatchewan planted some eighty-seven thousand acres to corn (Will, *Corn for the Northwest*, 67). In the 1920s, according to Paula Nelson in *Prairie Winnows*, farmers living west of the Missouri River in South Dakota grew corn, used for feed, more than any other crop; corn made a profit about half of the time (18–25).

40. Will, *Corn for the Northwest*, 134–36; W. Morton, *Manitoba*, 393.

41. Will and Hyde, *Corn among the Indians*, 27–29, 31; Will, *Corn for the Northwest*, 72, 75–76, 114–15, 124–25, 138–41, 143, 146, 147, 151; Oscar H. Will and Company, annual catalog, 1931, OWP.

42. Will and Company, catalog, 1932, OWP.
43. E. Robinson, *History of North Dakota*, 398; Will and Company, catalog, 1937, 1935, OWP.
44. Will and Company, catalog, 1936, 1937, 1939, OWP; Will, "Tree Ring Studies," 18, 23–24.
45. L. Neatby, *Chronicle*, 14, 23, 60–61, 64–66; Nicoll, *Paths*, 120–21.
46. "Pathologist R. Russell Dies," *Star Phoenix* (Saskatoon), 16 July 1964, RCRP; Russell, "Cereal Smut Treatments"; T. J. Harrison, quoted in Russell, Lewis, and Clark, *Smut Control of Barley*, 1, 9, 19–21; R. C. Russell, "The College of Agriculture," unpublished paper, [1959?], RCRP, 7, 1–8. Russell worked at or in affiliation with University of Saskatchewan from the mid-1920s until he retired in 1961.
47. Walters, *Modern Sagas*, 161, 160–63.
48. Norbeck and Norbeck, *Norbecks of South Dakota*, 75; Fite, *Peter Norbeck*, 14–16, 18–21, 101–42, 158–67. See also "Peter Norbeck"; and Leuchtenburg, *Franklin D. Roosevelt*, 48–52.
49. C. McManus, *Happyland*, 213–15.
50. Bennett et al., *Report*, 2, 4, 6, 15–17; Barrows et al., *Future*, 6, 1, 2, 63, 4, 5, 89. On the PFRA, see C. McManus, *Happyland*, 213–15, 221, 242; and for discussion of new farming methods, see 204, 116–17, 216–17. The Canadian government passed the PFRA in 1935, an administration emerged in 1937, and the Prairie Farm Assistance Act passed in 1939 (221). The U.S. Congress passed the Agricultural Adjustment Act in 1933 (and other programs). "Government subsidies" in the United States, starting with the 1930s New Deal Farm Programs, argues Sweeney in *Prelude*, have been "absolutely mandatory to maintain a high permanent population on the plains" (221). Quoted in Nelson, *Prairie Winnows*, 159, 149, see also 163, 189, 198; Stock, *Main Street in Crisis*, 10, 207–9, 217; Riney-Kehrberg in *Rooted in Dust* argues that New Deal farm legislation encouraged persistence among larger farmers (147).
51. Mackintosh, *Prairie Settlement*, viii, ix, xv, 135, see also 180, 116, 124–35; Murchie, *Agricultural Progress*, 126–27. Grasslands failure would signal "national failure," Bennett and the U.S. Drought Area Committee report argued and would "endanger our democracy" (15, 16). Barrows et al., *Future*, 1, 2–6, 63. Saskatchewan's official policy of "non-evacuation," according to Curtis McManus in *Happyland*, aimed to "ensure that no one abandoned their land and left the province" (though many did leave, many with government help) (142, see also 72, 204–5). Indeed, in the United States, Sweeney in *Prelude* argues that only government subsidies have allowed a relatively high population to live permanently on the southern plains (217–25).
52. Benson, *Wallace Stegner*, 26; Stegner, *Wolf Willow*, 23.

53. See M. Jacobs, *White Mother*, xxxii, 229–80; Nichols, *Indians*, 227–30; J. Miller, *Skyscrapers Hide the Heavens*, *198*.

54. Stegner, *Wolf Willow*, 57; Raaen, *Measure of My Days*, 20, 25–26; Annora Brown, oral history interview by Tom Kirkham, 24 March 1982, North Saanich BC, TKOHP; Hammond, diary no. 12 records Elsie's experiences at Regina Normal School from 2 January to 1 May 1915; diaries no. 13 and no. 14 include class notes as well as diary entries for 1915 and 1916. See Hammond, diary, no. 14: Regina Normal School Nature Study notes after 21 February 1916 and after 3 July 1916; see also no. 17: 6 October 1918; no. 10: 26 June 1914; no. 28: 24 June 1921; no. 37: 28 July 1928, EMHTP.

55. Hammond, diary, no. 12: 30 November 1915, EMHTP. See also Jackman, "Nature-Study," 23, 20.

56. Barrows et al., *Future*, 125–26, 122–23; Leuchtenburg, *Franklin D. Roosevelt*, 172–73.

57. "Honor Native Daughter, Macleod Girl's Artistic Genius," *Lethbridge Herald*, 30 September 1926, box 2, scrapbook 1, ABP; J. Thompson, *Canada*, 193–95; A. Brown, *Sketches from Life*, 90–91, 98, 126–28; History Book Committee, *Fort Macleod*, 35–37, 102–3, 350–51. The town's bonded indebtedness would not be paid in full until 1974, a decade after Annora Brown retired (351).

58. A. Brown, *Sketches from Life*, 40–41, 119–20, 139–42.

59. Albert E. Larke, "Incentives for Attractive Living," *Junior Farmer and 4-H Quarterly*, [1940s?], box 2, scrapbook 2; "Ken Liddell's Column," *Calgary Herald*, [May 1965], box 2, scrapbook 4; research notes, folder 11, box 1, both ABP; A. Brown, *Sketches from Life*, 141–42, 120, 123; Annora Brown to Ross M. Waldron, 4 May 1976, folder 1, box 1, ABP. She referenced Alexander MacKenzie, Daniel W. Harmon, and Katherine Parr Trail and papers from the Smithsonian Institution. She read an edition of W. B. Cheadle's *The North-West Passage by Land* during the 1860s and Howard's 1943 *Montana*. Brown relied most heavily for much of her writing about the Blackfoot, Blood, and Piegan peoples on Walter McClintock's 1910 London-published *Old North Trail*. "Annora Brown Gives Interesting Talk at Writers' Club Meeting," 19 October 1948, box 2, scrapbook 2, [*Calgary Hearald?*], ABP; A. Brown, *Old Man's Garden*, vii–viii.

60. A. Brown, *Sketches from Life*, 127, 130–33, 155–56; Smith Mudiman, "Interpreter of the Foothills," 1, 10; "Canvasses Review Alberta History," [*Calgary Herald*], [early 1940s?]; Margaret Lamb, "Alberta Has Interpreter of Its Life," [*Calgary Herald*, 1941?], all box 2, scrapbook 1, ABP; Stegner, *Wolf Willow*, 8.

61. A. Brown, *Sketches from Life*, 215, 219–20.

62. Elizabeth Forster [Annora Brown], "How the Prairie Crocus Got Its Fur Coat," [*Fort Macleod Gazette?*], 1 June 1935, folder 13, box 1, ABP; A. Brown, *Old Man's Garden*, 149; A. Brown, *Sketches from Life*, 171–72.
63. Shover in *First Majority* argues this process commenced quickly after World War II, when a "Great Disjuncture" occurred based on technological and scientific changes in agriculture and rural life (xiii–xiv, 148).
64. C.V., "They Please the Mind and Eye," *Winnipeg Free Press*, 27 March 1954, box 2, scrapbook 3, ABP.
65. A. Brown, *Sketches from Life*, 6–9; A. Brown, *Old Man's Garden*, 59, 53–54, 130, 195–97; Will, "Some Unusual Uses," 5; Constance Errol, "The Women's View," *Federationist*, 4 August 1938, box 2, scrapbook 1, ABP.
66. Annora Brown to Wilfrid and Lena Eggleston, 29 December 1951, vol. 16, file 20, WEF; A. Brown, *Sketches from Life*, 8, 130.
67. Fraser and Russell, *Annotated List*, iii; Fraser and Russell, *List of the Flowering Plants, 1*. Note that Fraser died while he and Fraser worked on the first edition of this list.
68. Fraser and Russell, *Annotated List*, 4–8, 14, 17, 18, 24, 27.
69. Will, "Grass"; Will, "Strolls of a Scientist"; Will, "Nature's Conservation Methods."
70. Stock, *Main Street in Crisis*, 207.
71. Hammond, diary, no. 14: Regina Normal School Nature Study notes after 21 February 1916, EMHTP.
72. Ann Tillenius, "Edward Bruce Pitblado Q.C.," folder 2, box 7, PFF; Edward Pitblado, "Wild Duck Life: Wither Bound," [*Actimist*, September 1932], box 17, PFF, 5.
73. Unidentified source and Reuben Lloyd, quoted in "Field News and Notes: Items of Interest to Practical Conservationists," clipping, [1936/7?], scrapbook 1932–51, box 17, PFF.
74. Pitblado, "Wild Duck Life," box 17, scrapbook 1932–51, PFF, 5; Wetherell, *Wildlife, Land, and People*, 212–19.
75. Peter Norbeck to Robert D. Jones, 18 February 1929; Barrington Moore to Norbeck, 23 February 1928: Norbeck to C. R. Tinan, 27 March 1928, all in folder 6, box 74, PNP.
76. Norbeck to Tinan, 27 March 1928, folder 6, box 74, PNP; Fite, *Peter Norbeck*, 144–48.
77. "West Duck Projects Get $325,000 Grant," *Winnipeg Tribune*, 8 April 1948; "Ducks Unlimited Sees Conditions Good for Hatch," *Winnipeg Free Press*, 8 April 1948; "Ducks Unlimited Approves $350,000 Breeding Project," clipping, 1949; "Mr. Huntington Addresses Manitoba Annual Meeting," *Western Angles and Hunters*, May 1937; all in box 17, scrapbook 1932–51, PFF. "The Story of Ducks Unlimited," *Wildlife Crusader*, June–July 1956, folder 15, box 19, PFF, 4; "Ducks Unlimited: Sportsmen

Who Care," *TribFocus*, 13 May 1978, folder 16, box 19, PFF, 10; L. F. Earl, "Engineering Giant That Ducks Made," *Financial Post*, 9 March 1963, box 17, scrapbook 1963–69, PFF.

78. "Ducks Unlimited Sets $458,000 Goal," *Reno Evening Gazette*, 16 April 1955 ("yer cent" silently corrected to per cent; emphasis mine), scrapbook 1952–60, PFF; Wild Wings, column, *Winnipeg Tribune*, November 1948, box 17, scrapbook 1932–51; Wild Wings, column, *Winnipeg Tribune*, 5 November 1937, folder 15, box 19, PFF.

79. Paul Mason to Peter Norbeck, 1 June 1928; Norbeck to Mason, 4 June 1928, folder: "Migratory Bird Bills," box 75b, PNP; Norbeck to C. R. Tinan, 20 April 1928, folder 6, box 74, PNP; Fite, *Peter Norbeck*, 144; Wetherell, *Wildlife, Land, and People*, 88–89.

80. Fite, *Peter Norbeck*, 74–77; Ostler, *Lakotas*, 128–38; Hammond, diary, no. 36: 3 February 1928; Potyondi, *In Palliser's Triangle*, 116–17; Waiser, *Saskatchewan*, 465; Stegner, *Wolf Willow*, 111–13; Basso, *Wisdom Sits in Places*, 31–34, 50–69; Hansen, *Encounter*, 220, 141, 241–42.

81. "Macleod Artist's Work Impresses," box 2, scrapbook 1, ABP; Pat Dufour, "Annora: A Study in Styles," *Times-Colonist* (BC), 8 November 1981, folder 13, box 1, ABP, 25; Hammond, diary, no. 13: 5, 10 August 1915, EMHTP; C. Gannon, *Bunch Grass Acres*, 18–19, 70–71; Will and Company, catalog, 1940, OWP. See Riney-Kehrberg, *Nature of Childhood*, 104; Rozum, "Spark That Jumped," 133–44; and Tracie, *Shaping a World*, 91, 95–97.

82. Will, "Grass"; Wright, *Saskatchewan*, 8.

83. Stegner, *Wolf Willow*, 10–11; A. Brown, *Sketches from Life*, 43–44; A. Brown, interview, TKOHP.

84. A. Brown, *Sketches from Life*, 198–201, 6–9; A. Brown, *Old Man's Garden*, vii–viii.

85. Stock, *Main Street in Crisis*, 7, 5, 10, 207–8.

86. Rozum, "Nature Rarely Establishes."

87. Neth, *Preserving the Family Farm*, 5; Barron, *Mixed Harvest*, 7–16, 194.

88. Will, *Corn for the Northwest*, 26, 70–71; Hudson, *Making the Corn Belt*, 198, 154, 171–72, 196–201; Shover, *First Majority*, xiii–xiv, 148. See Lansing, *Insurgent Democracy*, on the capitalist alternative in North Dakota, the Nonpartisan League, which would have been active in the years Will took over the Will Company (240, 258–65, 275). I am unaware of Will's opinion of the NPL; he critiqued growing big businesses, but he believed in the utility of trained agricultural experts.

89. Eggleston, *Homestead on the Range*, 77–78, 80–81, 85, 90–91, 93, 96; Eggleston, *Road to Nationhood*, xii–xiv, 35–39.

90. Nicoll, *Paths*, 36, 121; Rozum, "It's Weathered Many," 352–67; Tracie, *Shaping a World*, 74–75; Stegner, *Wolf Willow*, 299; Stegner, *Big Rock Candy Mountain*, 63, 251, 667; Eggleston, *High Plains*, 161, 162.

91. Basso, *Wisdom Sits in Places*, 10, 32–33, 55, 57, 60, 62. Basso studied the Western Apaches but suggests "general similarities do exist" among Indigenous peoples (63). See also Tracie, *Shaping a World*, 80, 91, 96–97; Goeman, "Disrupting a Settler-Colonial Grammar," 235–38, 245.
92. A. Brown, *Sketches from Life*, 14, 67–69, 137–39, 141–43; Will, "Early Summer Walk"; Fraser and Russell, *Annotated List*; Hammond, diaries, no. 14: 28 May, 2 June 1916; no. 15: 30 September 1916, EMHTP.
93. A. Brown, *Sketches from Life*, 44, 7, 130; Stegner, *Wolf Willow*, 23; Nicoll, *Paths*, 62, 44; Trupin, *Dakota Diaspora*, 129; Sandalack, "Prairie Towns," 272–73, 278–80. From nearly 6,000 grain elevators in the Canadian Prairie Provinces in the 1930s, only 1,498 remained by 1992 (280).

8. "All That Vast Region of Grass Land"

1. Helen Clapesattle to Thorstina Jackson Walters, 25 March 1944, folder 4, box 1, TJEWP.
2. Walter C. Coffey to David Stevens, 13 March 1943; Malcom M. Willey to Stevens, 21 December 1943; Stevens to Theodore Blegen, 20 July 1943, all in folder 63, box 5, series 226, RG 1.1, UMRSP.
3. Blegen to Stevens, 22 January 1947, folder 65 (emphasis added); Blegen to John Marshall, 8 December 1953, folder 67, both in box 5, series 226, RG 1.1, UMRSP.
4. "Modern Sagas," flyer, [1956?], folder 10, box 4; Leo Hertel to Thorstina Jackson Walters, 9 February 1956, folder 10, box 1, TJEWP. For more on Walters, see Rozum, "That Understanding with Nature," 147–55.
5. Clapesattle, quoted in Margaret S. Harding to Walter C. Coffey, 30 September 1942, folder 62, box 5, series 226, RG 1.1, UMRSP.
6. Meinig, *Shaping of America* (1993), 59, 62; Allen, *Lewis and Clark*, 1; J. Thompson, *Forging the Prairie West*, 10.
7. A. Morton, *Canadian West*, 1. See also *Royal Charter*; "British North America Act"; and "Schedule A."
8. Kellogg, *Early Narratives*, 3, 32–33; DeVoto, *Course of Empire*, 140; G. Smith, *Explorations*, 2–5, 43, 55, 50, 58; Allen, *Lewis and Clark*, xix, 2, 4–5, 126; Meinig, *Shaping of America* (1993), 68–69, 75–76; J. Thompson, *Forging the Prairie West*, 32–43; Jefferson's instructions, 20 June 1803, quoted in Allen, *Lewis and Clark*, xix; Coues, *New Light*, ix, xvii, 1, 5, 185, 225, 227, 93, 228, 287.
9. Borchert, *America's Northern Heartland*, 3–4; Shortridge, *Middle West*, 14–16, 23.
10. Salverson, *Viking Heart*, 22; Salverson, *Confessions*, 356; Walters, *Modern Sagas*, 14, 41. For "Ameríku," see Thorstina Jackson, *Saga Íslendinga*, and the first volume of a three-volume compilation of the histories of

Icelandic immigration to North America: *Brot af landnámassögu*, written by her father, Thorleifur Jóakimsson [Jackson]. The individual or family entries always indicate immigration to "Ameríku," not only Canada or the United States, and entries indicate frequent cross-border moves. See also George F. Will, "Autobiography," GWP, pt. 2, p. 16; A. Brown, *Sketches from Life*, 146, 155; Eggleston, *Homestead on the Range*, 74, 78; Peter Norbeck to William Roy Ronald, 27 December 1921, folder 12, box 105, PNP.

11. Higham and Thacker, *One West, Two Myths*; Higham and Thacker, *One West, Two Myths II*; H. Smith, *Virgin Land*.
12. "Governor's Message, Dakota, 1862," WJC. Jayne's conception of the Northwest focuses specifically on the Great Lakes and the Mississippi and Missouri Rivers, but this speech suggests he saw the grasslands as one transnational wheat region.
13. *Free Press*, quoted in Bicha, *American Farmer*, 44.
14. Mackintosh, *Prairie Settlement*, 1, 2–3.
15. Isaac Pitblado, "Manitoba Club," 21 March 1957, folder 36, box 6, PFF; Effie Laurie Storer, "Queen's Printer," 1942–43, 2.4, ELSP; Owram, *Promise of Eden*, 79–84.
16. C. Ellis, *History of Faulk County*, 111; A. Pickler, "Family of Homesteading Women," 29.
17. Oscar H. Will and Company, annual catalog, 1896, 1897, 1908, OWP.
18. Peter Norbeck to Stitzel X. Way, 29 August 1921, folder 12, box 50; Norbeck to Ronald, 27 November 1923, folder 12, box 105; "Senator Peter Norbeck's Speech at Yankton, Thursday Evening, November 24, 1930," notice, folder 15, box 36; Ray Johnson to Norbeck, 7 January 1935, folder 6, box 36; Norbeck to C. T. Johnson, 29 January 1935, folder 13, box 37, all PNP; Olger B. Burtness, "The One Thousandth Anniversary of the Althing in Iceland," speech, reprinted from *Congressional Record*, 11 June 1929, folder 28, box 2, TJEWP.
19. Laut, *Pathfinders of the West*, x, xvi, xxvii, 234, 333 (emphasis mine); Laut, *Conquest*, x, xi, xiii, xiv, xix; "Agnes Christina Laut."
20. Walters, *Modern Sagas*, 3; McAlmon, *Companion Volume*, 256–57; S. Lewis, *Main Street*, 21, 435.
21. Stegner, *Where the Bluebird Sings*, 7, 3–21; E. Thompson, *American Daughter*, 14, 285.
22. Stegner, *Central Northwest*, 9, 14. The "Central Northwest" also included Kansas, Nebraska, Colorado, Idaho, Utah, and Nevada.
23. Will and Company, catalog, 1918, OWP.
24. Will and Company, catalog, 1926, 1924, 1927, see also 1919, 1920, 1921, 1922, 1923, 1924, 1925, 1928, 1929, 1930, 1931, OWP. In 1932 the company catalog letter referenced both Northwest and Great Plains. Will

first used "the Plains" with reference to Indigenous peoples. Will, "Indian Agriculture," 204; Will and Hyde, *Corn among the Indians*, 60.

25. Will, *Corn for the Northwest*, 11, 5, 9. Will cites a "Biological Survey of the United States" as a source for his regional boundaries (41–42). Will and Hyde, *Corn among the Indians*, 22–24.
26. Will and Company, catalog, 1896, p. 5; 1897, p. 14; 1908, pp. 11, 79; 1911; 1913, p. 62; 1933, OWP. The company sent its eighty-four-page fiftieth anniversary 1933 catalog to 230,000 people.
27. Will, "Trees of the Dakotas," no. 8, p. 88; Will, "Fruit in North Dakota"; Will, "Trees of the Dakotas," no. 9; no. 11, 124; Will and Company, catalog, 1896 (p. 9, back cover, p. 13), 1897 (p. 14), OWP; Will, "Trees of the Dakotas," no. 10; Will, "Our Wealth"; Will, *Corn for the Northwest*, 73.
28. Will, *Corn for the Northwest*, 135, 134, 55, also 153, 53, 56; Will and Company, catalog, 1932, 1935, 1937, OWP; Will, "Drouth Resistant Shrubs," 3; Will, "Adventures," 82; Will, "Trees of the Dakotas," no. 10, p. 112.
29. Barrows et al., *Future*, 10; Ottoson et al., *Land and People*, 87–89.
30. Will and Company, catalog, 1940, OWP.
31. Will, "Value of Historical Societies," 276–77; Will, "Tree Ring Studies," 19, 23–24; Will and Company, catalog, 1953, 1938–61, OWP. The company catalog letter omitted Northwest for the first time in 1938, although that regional label continued as part of the company brand. Northwest did not appear in the annual catalog letter again until 1959, the last year of the original company's operation. George Will died in 1955, and his son George Will Jr. reorganized the company in 1960 and issued the first Will's Bismarck Seed House catalog in 1961.
32. Stegner, *Marking the Sparrow's Fall*, 98–99; Stegner, *Where the Bluebird Sings*, 17–19. Stegner argued that the ninety-eighth meridian is the significant dividing line between the East and West in his 1947 introduction to the *Central Northwest*.
33. Stegner, *Big Rock Candy Mountain*, 35, 1–4, 8–9.
34. See Stegner, *Big Rock Candy Mountain*, 519–27; Stegner, *Wolf Willow*, 277.
35. Stegner, *Big Rock Candy Mountain*, 526, 519. Stegner stressed that, while his novels frequently contained autobiographical elements, the particular actions, timing of events, and individual choices did not always or tightly match up to those of his life. Stegner (loosely, the story's Bruce), for example, enrolled in a graduate program in English at the University of Iowa, not in law school in Minneapolis. See Stegner and Etulain, *Conversations with Wallace Stegner*, 41. See also Benson, *Wallace Stegner*, 61.
36. Stegner, *Big Rock Candy Mountain*, 519, 526–27. Going by the town names Stegner mentions, Bruce turned west presumably on Highway 16 (modern I-90). *If* Stegner's character continued straight west on the

route implied, Bruce would have been propelled to Mitchell—without geographic jump to Iowa—and crossed the Missouri River only once at Chamberlain. Bruce would have crossed the Big Sioux River at Sioux Falls, South Dakota.

37. Stegner, *Central Northwest*, 14, 16, 30; Webb, *Great Plains*, 4, 8, 27, 419–22; Benson, *Wallace Stegner*, 119, 122, 224, 159–61. See also Fradkin, *Wallace Stegner*, 169–71, 174–75.

38. Stegner, *Beyond the Hundredth Meridian*, 399–400 (emphasis mine), 353, 409, 221; Stegner, *Marking the Sparrow's Fall*, 99; Stegner, *Beyond the Hundredth Meridian*, 399–400 (emphasis mine), 409, 221; Stegner, *Central Northwest*, 10, 14–16, 34; Stegner, *Marking the Sparrow's Fall*, 97, 102, 105, 215, 219; Stegner and Stegner, *American Places*, 95, 47.

39. White, *Organic Machine*, x.

40. Meinig, *Shaping of America* (1993), 59, 62, 75–77; Bolena and Flores, "Prairie Wetlands"; Warkentin, *Kelsey Papers*, vii, xiv–xvii, 12, 20, 22, 25, 27, 7–9; Louis Jolliet, quoted in Dondore, *Making of Middle America*, 22; Ekberg, *French Roots*, 60, 64, 79; Christopher Gist, quoted in Transeau, "Vanishing Prairies of Ohio," 61; P. F. X. de Charlevoix and Morris Birkbeck, both quoted in D. Williams, "Reconstruction," 84; Hamilton, *Writings of James Monroe*, 117–18; Morris Birkbeck, quoted in Jordan, "Forest and the Prairie," 213. See also Hudson, *Making the Corn Belt*, 27–30; Faragher, *Sugar Creek*, 61–75; Prince, *Wetlands*, 117–40, 161–74; Goetzmann, *Exploration and Empire*, 51.

41. Pound and Clements, "Vegetation Regions"; Malin, *Grassland of North America*, 2, 80; Weaver and Albertson, *Grasslands*, 3, 18; Weaver, *North American Prairie*, 3; Meinig, *Shaping of America* (1993), 62–65, 76–77.

42. Parrish, *Great Plains*, 17–18, 24–25. Parrish's boundaries seem confused; he also divides the region into "three distinct belts" of "about" equal size: from the 95th to the 98th meridian; the next, to the 101st; and the third, to the 104th, but excludes Montana, only to suggest the region ultimately extends west until one "approached closer to the mountains" (20–21).

43. Marbut, "Soils," 43 (emphasis mine); Baker, "Agriculture," 112; Kincer, "Climate," 68–70; Shantz, "Natural Vegetation," 97. Marbut excluded the southeastern corner of South Dakota. Kincer estimated that successful agriculture required fifteen to twenty inches of precipitation, but climate factors "operated more favorably in the northern half" of the plains. See also Fenneman, "Physiographic Boundaries," 90, 135–34, 114–19. In 1914 Fenneman provided one of the first scientific descriptions of the physiographic Great Plains, showing a division between the Great Plains and prairies. Three pages of unpaginated maps also accompanied the article at the end.

44. Powell, "Report on the Lands," 11 (emphasis added).
45. Webb, *Great Plains*, 32, 319, 34 (map); Malin, *Grassland of North America*, 261, 1–2, iii; Webb, *Great Plains*, 3–7, 353, 34 (map). Webb identified the "plains environment" with "the region west of the Mississippi River" (4). He called his third division "Western Plateaus and Rocky Mountains" (34, map); it shared only treelessness with his two other divisions. The Great Plains includes a specific physiographic "High Plains," according to Fenneman ("Physiographic Boundaries"), consisting of an uneroded area of a formerly much larger "uniform smooth surface" (116), but Webb's use of "High Plains," "Prairie Plains," and "Plains proper" seems in part to be his own (6–7).
46. Mackintosh, *Prairie Settlement*, 86, 19–20; Sandwell, *Canada's Rural Majority*, 110; Burt, *Romance*, v, 1, 5–7.
47. Mackintosh, *Prairie Settlement*, 32, 86; Spry, *Papers*, 9. See Owram, *Promise of Eden*, for an analysis of early discussions of the extent, expansion, and contraction of aridity on the Canadian grasslands (68–69, 61–63). Mackintosh cited the *Annals of the Association of American Geographers'* 1923 Great Plains issue.
48. Malin, *Grassland of North America*, 75, 2, 80. Malin explains he published this 1967 *Grassland* book originally in 1947 (399).
49. Stegner, *Beyond the Hundredth Meridian*, 224, 221; Powell, "Report on the Lands," 12–14. Stegner suggested that Powell first called this zone "sub-arid" and also located the zone between the ninety-seventh to the hundredth meridian (224). In *Great Plains* Webb seemed to use "semi-arid" and "sub-humid" interchangeably; he wrote of subhumid but labeled his map semiarid (6). Powell, in his "Report on the Lands," explained that agriculture supported by fifteen inches of annual precipitation in the Dakotas required twenty inches in Texas (in Stegner, *Arid Lands*, 12); for distribution of rain, see pages 61–65. Powell coined the phrase "Sub-humid Region" to refer to a "broad belt" that "separates the Arid Region of the West from the Humid Region of the east" (13), from the twenty-inch rainfall line to the twenty-eight-inch rainfall line in Minnesota—"beautiful prairie country throughout, lacking somewhat in rainfall" (14). Powell thought that a "much more extended series of rain-gauge records than we now have is necessary before this line constituting the eastern boundary of the Arid Region can be well defined" (13). The hundredth meridian stood "in a general way" for the line but "should by no means be exaggerated," he said, adding, "On this point it is impossible to speak with certainty" (13).
50. Baker, "Agriculture," 110, 114, 110.
51. Fradkin, *Wallace Stegner*, 182; Stegner and Stegner, *American Places*, 59, 63–64, 68, 74.

52. Parrish, *Great Plains*, 18; Webb, *Great Plains*, 34 (map); Malin, *Grassland of North America*, 80; Mackintosh, *Prairie Settlement*, 86.
53. Sandwell, *Canada's Rural Majority*, 105; Elsie Hammond, diary, no. 14: Regina Normal School Geography notes after 25 April 1916, EMHTP.
54. Wright, *Saskatchewan*, vi, 2–3, 7–8; Wright also refers to "prairies" (262, 269); Spry, *Papers*.
55. Weaver and Albertson, *Grasslands*, 3, 18; L. Brown, *Grasslands*, 20–23, 30–63; Parrish, *Great Plains*, 17; Webb, *Great Plains*, 6–7.
56. My general interpretation relies on the following historical and recent studies but with some specific pages noted: Weaver and Albertson, *Grasslands*, 3, 18–21 (quote from 18), 321–26, 340–41; Weaver, *North American Prairie*, 10, 11, 15–16; L. Brown, *Grasslands*, 62–63, 52–53; Barkley, Brooks, and Schofield, *Flora*; Weaver and Fitzpatrick, "Prairie," 113, 129, 165.
57. Weaver and Fitzpatrick, "Prairie," 113 (quote), 129, 165; Barrows et al., *Future*, 3, see also 23, 2–3.
58. A. Brown, *Sketches from Life*, 68.
59. Fite, "Rural Credit System," 223–24, 269; Norbeck to C. R. Tinan, 27 March 1928, folder 6, box 74, PNP.
60. Salverson, *Confessions*, 359, 360, 13; Walters, *Modern Sagas*, 89, 97, 116, 132, 135, 136; Raaen, *Measure of My Days*, 290, 205, 52, 315; Raaen, *Grass of the Earth*, 72, 69; McAlmon, *Village*, 11, 13, 130, 39, 3; McAlmon, *North America*, 34–36; McAlmon, *Companion Volume*, 37, 72.
61. Howard, *Montana*, 1, 8; Bell, *Montana and I*, 4, 50, 121, 133, 209; Lillian Miller, "I Remember Montana," LMC, 70; Lula Short, diary, 13 August 1886, 12 December 1886, 20 August 1887, SKFF; Julia Asher [Lula Short], "Grandma's Childhood," JAAM, 28, 35, 41–42, 23–24, 52–53; Hammond, diary, no. 35: 19 April 1927, 15 January 1928, EMHTP; Lulu [Pickler] Frad, "The Big Old House In the Little Old Town," [1949?], PFP; L. Pickler to Mother, 23 May 1890, PFP; Storer, "Queen's Printer," ELSP, 2–3, 37–40, 59–77; Will, "Grass"; Will, *Corn for the Northwest*, 14; Will, "Autobiography," WFP, pt. 1, pp. 228, 276.
62. Eggleston, *Homestead on the Range*, 68, 36; Eggleston, *While I Still Remember*, 5, 8–9; Eggleston, *Homestead on the Range*, 93, 75 (emphasis added), 87, see also 93–96, 24, 62–68, 86–88; Eggleston, *Road to Nationhood*; Spry, *Papers*, 9, 18; Owram, *Promise of Eden*, 67.
63. Nelson, *Prairie Winnows*, 200; Ottoson et al., *Land and People*, 3, 5, 8; Cunfer, *On the Great Plains*, 235, 234–37. Cunfer suggests that the range, rather than average, of annual precipitation is key.
64. Meinig, *Shaping of America* (1993), 76–77; Pound and Clements, "Vegetation Regions"; Canadian Pacific Railway report, quoted in Mackintosh, *Prairie Settlement*, 32.
65. Burt, *Romance*, v, 253 (emphasis added), 256; Will, *Corn for the Northwest*, 9.

66. Laurier, quoted in Conway, *West*, 28, 13.
67. *Census of Population*; *Census of Prairie Provinces*.
68. Shortt and Doughty, *Canada and Its Provinces*. Hammond, diary, no. 14: Regina Normal School Geography notes after 25 April 1916, EMHTP.
69. Stewart, "Prairie Farm Rehabilitation Programme"; Marchildon, "Prairie Farm Rehabilitation Administration"; C. McManus, *Happyland*, 213–15, 221, 242; Waiser, *Saskatchewan*, 321.
70. Thompson and Randall, *Canada*, 103–5, 112, 115–28; J. Thompson, *Canada*, 158–92; Owram, *Promise of Eden*, 67, 68, 157.
71. For the importance of the neglected Middle West to U.S. culture, see Lauck, *Lost Region*.
72. Shortridge, *Middle West*, 14–16, 23, 13–26. Shortridge found the phrase "Middle West" in general use by the 1890s and believed it emerged at least in the 1880s (16) to distinguish the north-south space from "New Northwest" (Dakotas and Minnesota) and "Southwest" (Oklahoma and "Indian Territory"). For a late 1880s early appearance of the second east-west conception uttered in Montana, see *Proceedings and Debates*, 802, 804. Norbeck to Ronald, 17 November 1923, folder 12, box 105, PNP.
73. McAlmon, *Companion Volume*, 238–39, 256–57; McAlmon, *North America*, 8; McAlmon and Boyle, *Being Geniuses Together*, 33, 226, 157–58.
74. S. Lewis, *Main Street*, 17, 22, 39–40, 97, 99, 144, 158, 126, 17, 165; Van Doren, "Revolt from the Village," 410. See also Walter Yust, review of *Village*, in *Philadelphia Public Ledger*, [1925], folder: "McAlmon Reviews," box 1, PRM; Yust assumes a "Middle West" location for McAlmon's novel. In 1917 Lewis used "Middle West" in *Job* (33, 53–54, 95, 101, 131).
75. S. Lewis, *Main Street*, 470, 40, 35, 215, 198, 16. Stegner quotes the same Lewis phrase in reference to Eastend, Saskatchewan, in his *Wolf Willow*, 285.
76. Newberry Library announcement, folder 93; Stanley Pargellis to John Marshall, 8 March 1944, folder 91, both box 3; Era Bell Thompson to Pargellis, 24 May 1944, folder 136, box 4; all RG 3, SG 5, series 3, all in SPP; E. Thompson, *American Daughter*, 276, 67, 88, 113, 199, 26, 145, 152, 278. For more on Thompson, see Rozum, "That Understanding with Nature," 139–47.
77. Pargellis to Clapesattle, 29 June 1944; Clapesattle to Pargellis, 7 July 1944; Clapesattle, quoted in Willey to Pargellis, 8 July 1944; Pargellis to Leland D. Case, 5 July 1944, all in folder 93, box 3, all RG 3, SG 5, series 3, SPP.
78. Pargellis to David H. Stevens, 16 September 1944, folder 91, box 3; Pargellis to Stevens, 28 February 1947, folder 93, box 3; "Promotion Report," for "Era Bell Thompson: American Daughter," folder 94,

box 3; untitled report ("About a year ago Miss Thompson applied"); "REPORT on Era Bell Thompson, *American Daughter*"; [Rosemary York] to Era Bell Thompson, 5 March 1945; 10 March 1945, all folder 136, box 4, all RG 3, SG 5, series 3, all in SPP.

79. E. Thompson, *American Daughter*, 151, 139–43, 117.
80. E. Thompson, *American Daughter*, 145, 25–26, 50, 100, 117, 274, 276; Era Bell Thompson to Pargellis, 24 May 1944, folder 136, box 4, RG 3, SG 5, series 3, SPP; Lansing, "American Daughter in Africa."
81. Will and Company, catalog, 1955, OWP; Will and Hyde, *Corn among the Indians*, 22; Will, *Corn for the Northwest*, 11; Rozum, "Nature Rarely Establishes."
82. Burt, *Short History*, 4; W. Morton, *Manitoba*, 396–97.
83. W. Morton, *Manitoba*, 411 (emphasis mine), 406; Hammond, diary, no. 14: Regina Normal School Saskatchewan notes after 25 April 1916, EMHTP; Neatby, *Chronicle*, 79–81.
84. "America's New Middle West," 23; McCarthy, "New Middle West"; "The Most American Part of America," 108; Morton, *Manitoba*, 396–97, 408, 413, 420, 472.
85. Bromfield, *Midwest*, 9–10 (emphasis added); "America's New Middle West," 23. See also Stegner, *Central Northwest*; in 1947 *Look* placed both Dakotas with Wyoming, Montana, Kansas, Nebraska, Colorado, Idaho, Utah, and Nevada.
86. Morrison, "Editor with No Problems," 99–101; "The Most American Part of America," 108.
87. Vilhjalmur Stefansson, review of Walters, *Modern Sagas*, *Saturday Review*, 14 August 1953, folder 10, box 4, TJEWP; Raaen, *Measure of My Days*, 315, 261; Wilfrid Eggleston, Causerie, column, [*Winnipeg Free Press*?], 24 January 1953, vol. 39, file 24, WEF.
88. Bureau of the Census, *Geographic Areas Reference Manual*, chaps. 6–2, 15–18. Montana has been associated with the Mountain West since 1900. West North Central included the states of North Dakota, South Dakota, Nebraska, Kansas, Minnesota, Iowa, and Missouri, while East North Central included the states of Wisconsin, Illinois, Indiana, Michigan, and Ohio.
89. Prince, *Wetlands*, 233, 231–33, 288, 30, 296; Hudson, *Making the Corn Belt*, 13, 138–40. Shortridge's argument that the Middle West became a "general label for all parts of the interior that were characterized by a prosperous rural economy" aligns with what these voices suggest about shifting regional affiliation (*Middle West*, 26).
90. Shover, *First Majority*, xiii–xiv, 148. As early as 1936, the U.S. government speculated that technology might ease the impact of aridity. Barrows et al., *Future*, 2.

91. Stegner and Stegner, *American Places*, 59, 63–64, 68, 56–79, 57–50 (Stegner traveled the Mississippi River in 1979; see page 63); Stegner, *Marking the Sparrow's Fall*, 99, 215; Stegner, *Beyond the Hundredth Meridian*, 399–400, 221, 353.
92. Stegner, *Central Northwest*, 30; Jacobson, Albrecht, and Bolin, "Wildflower Routes"; Schennum, "Comprehensive Survey." According to Cunfer in *On the Great Plains*, one-third of the Great Plains but 80 percent of Corn Belt grasslands have been plowed (237).
93. Short, *Cartographic Encounters*, 12, 41.
94. Danbom, *Born in the Country*, 233–52.
95. Will and Hyde, *Corn among the Indians*, 34, 174, 171; Will, "Resume," 151, 154–55; Kaye, *Goodlands*, 5, 20–21; West, *Contested Plains*, 18–32.
96. Porter, *Land and Spirit*, 5, 31; Goeman, "Disrupting a Settler-Colonial Grammar," 235–38, 245; Basso, *Wisdom Sits in Places*, 32–34. Basso's study examines Western Apache traditions, but his survey of "modern Indian writers," including Vine Deloria Jr., suggests "general similarities do exist" in the traditions of other Indigenous groups (63).

Conclusion

1. Edward Pitblado to Edith Pitblado, 26 December 1923, folder 6, box 9; Edward Pitblado to Mother, 16 October 1922, folder 11, box 8, both in PFF.
2. Edward Pitblado to Isaac Pitblado, 20 August 1923, folder 4, box 9, PFF.
3. Deloria, *Playing Indian*, 2–3, 7–8, 183. Deloria concludes that "aboriginal Indianness made one a citizen, not of an impermanent government, but of the land itself" (183). Pitblado also fits Deloria's description of the phenomenon as a predominately white male performance of "domination and power" (186).
4. Edward Pitblado to Mother, 13 November 1921, folder 7; 1 January 1922, folder 8, both in box 8; Edward Pitblado to Mother, 17 January 1923, folder 1, box 9; Edward Pitblado to Isaac Pitblado, 26 March 1921, folder 2; Edward Pitblado to Mother, 12 February 1921, folder 1; Edward Pitblado to I. Pitblado, 4 May 1921, folder 3; 20 November 1922, folder 12; 27 June 1921, folder 3, all in box 8; Edward Pitblado to I. Pitblado, 27 October 1923, folder 5; 21 December 1923[?], folder 6, both in box 9; Edward Pitblado to Mother, 16 October 1922, folder 11, box 8, all in PFF.
5. Eggleston, *While I Still Remember*; Eggleston, *Homestead on the Range*.
6. Thompson, foreword to Evans, *Borderlands*, xii–xiii; Isern and Shepard, "Duty-Free," xxix, xxxiii.
7. See, for example, Nicoll, *Paths*, 18, 9; Eggleston, *Homestead on the Range*, 13, 16–18; L. Lillian Miller, "I Remember Montana," LMC, 169; Raaen, *Grass of the Earth*, 234–35, 130–31; Raaen, *Measure of My Days*, 127–28, 313–17; and Johnson, *You and I*, 153.

8. Stegner, *Wolf Willow*, 7–8; Will, *Corn for the Northwest*, 136; Eggleston, *Homestead on the Range*, 52, 37, 70; McAlmon, *Companion Volume*, 37; McAlmon, *Hasty Bunch*, 248–52; William Carlos Williams to Robert McAlmon, 23 December 1921, folder 90, box 3, RMP; Elsie Hammond, diary, no. 46: 3 August 1931, EMHTP; A. Brown, oral history interview by Tom Kirkham, 24 March 1982, North Saanich BC, TKOHP; A. Brown, *Sketches from Life*, 31, 139.
9. Hammond, diaries, no. 34: 30 June, 1 July 1926; no. 35: 1 July 1927, EMHTP; Miller, "I Remember Montana," LMC, 175; Walters, *Modern Sagas*, 118, 41, 13–16; see also note 10 in chapter 8 on Icelanders who tended to immigrate to "Ameríku," not merely Canada or the United States. See also A. Brown, *Sketches from Life*, 31–33.
10. Smoller, *Adrift among Geniuses*, (W. Williams quoted on) 28, 109, (F. Ford quoted on) 190; Eggleston, *High Plains*, 177, 106–9, 129–33, 88; A. Brown, *Sketches from Life*, 37, 210–12, 66, 69, 11, 71. Brown uses the phrase "good citizen," though probably reference to an "upstanding" member of the community makes more sense in constructions of mythic nationalist-opposition sensibility. See Carter, "Transnational Perspectives"; and H. Smith, *Virgin Land*.
11. L. Mitchell, "Whose West," 139–51; A. Brown, *Sketches from Life*, 14–18; E. Thompson, *American Daughter*, 26, 7, 13–14, 21–22, 26–27, 30, 42, 47, 86, 128, 149, 152, 190, 194–95, 294. On Thompson, see also Rozum, "That Understanding with Nature," 139–47; and C. Gannon, *Bunch Grass Acres*, 37–39.
12. Parsons, *Curlew Cried*, 189–90, 206–8, 154–55; L. Ellis, "Northwest," 56; Waiser, *Saskatchewan*, 133–38, 210, 225, 264. While a U.S. Congress representative at the time bloviated about increasing U.S. possessions, Bothwell in *Your Country, My Country* suggests the U.S. government had hoped only to draw Canada's "various parts" to "American neighbors" across the line, away from "the orbit of the British Empire" through economic ties, not territorial acquisition (193, see also 148–54).
13. L. Neatby, *Chronicle*, 71, 79–80, 86, 71–80; Hammond, diary, no. 14: Regina Normal School Geography notes after 25 April 1916, EMHTP.
14. Kipling, quoted in Bothwell, *Your Country, My Country*, 152, 148–54; Borden, quoted in Wright, *Saskatchewan*, 154; Parsons, *Curlew Cried*, 207; and L. Neatby, *Chronicle*, 71–72.
15. Manitoba, Saskatchewan, and Alberta had a combined population of 1,956,082 in 1921, while Montana, North Dakota, and South Dakota together registered at 1,832,308 in 1920. Including Minnesota's 1920 population raised the U.S. side to a total population of 4,219,433, doubling the size of the Prairie Provinces' population, but not reaching ten times the size. Including Wyoming in 1920 would have added

another 194,402 people. Comparable figures for 1951 and 1950 show the same trend; only Manitoba, Saskatchewan, and Alberta had increased their population advantage over Montana, North Dakota, and South Dakota. The three Prairie Provinces grew by more than a half million people, while the three northern plains states considered here together added only about 30,000 people. The U.S. total in 1950 for Montana, North Dakota, and South Dakota equaled 1,863,400; the Prairie Provinces hosted 2,647,770 people in 1951. Adding Minnesota to the U.S. northern grasslands side of the border in 1950 brings the total population to 4,845,883. Wyoming would add only about another 290,000 to the 1950 population total. Indeed, the Prairie Provinces made three of ten Canadian provinces, while the Northern Great Plains states, considering Montana, North Dakota, and South Dakota, made up one-sixteenth of the United States and, considering these three along with neighbors Wyoming, Nebraska, and Minnesota, one-eighth of the states. For U.S. census data, see "Census of Population"; for Canadian census data, see "InfoGuide: Historical Resources."

16. Thompson to Pargellis, 24 May 1944, folder 136, box 4, RG 3, SG 5, series 3, SPP.
17. Shortridge, "Expectations of Others," 115.
18. Wilfrid Eggleston to Annora Brown, 24 December 1951, box 2, scrapbook 2; "Macleod Artist's Work Impresses at Exhibition," *Fort Macleod Gazette*, 13 October 1930, box 2, scrapbook 1, ABP.
19. Altair [Wilfrid Eggleston], "Wheat-fields and White-Caps," [*Lethbridge Herald*], [1926?], vol. 25, file 1, WEF; Eggleston, *Homestead on the Range*, 37; Thomson, *Crocus and Meadowlark Country*; Wilfrid Eggleston, Causerie, column, [*Winnipeg Free Press?*], 17 April 1954, vol. 39, file 25, WEF.
20. It is unclear whether the Writer's Foundation provided Salverson with an "allowance" under a program the organization apparently had for "writers who have not been able to provide for their old age," but Eggleston asked the organization to consider it. Joy Tranter to Wilfrid Eggleston, 18 July 1957; "Terry" to Eggleston, 6 August 1957; Eggleston to Tranter, 9 August 1957, vol. 2, file 7, WEF.
21. Eggleston was familiar with the modern literature series edited by literary critic Edward J. O'Brien; the 1929 volume included McAlmon's "Potato Picking." Smoller, *Adrift among Geniuses*, 199. In *Canadian Letters*, Eggleston cited a 1935 article by O'Brien (35).
22. Leslie Neatby to Ralph C. Russell, 5 July 1959, RCRP; Russell, *Carlton Trail*, 3.
23. George F. Will, "Autobiography," WFP, pt. 2, pp. 27, 31, 29, 37.
24. L. Neatby, *Conquest*, 365.
25. Olger B. Burtness, "The One Thousandth Anniversary of the Althing in Iceland," speech, reprinted from *Congressional Record*, 11 June 1929;

"The Althing" program; "1930 Millennial Celebration of the Icelandic Parliament," Cunard brochure, all folder 27, all in box 2, TJEWP; Thorstina Walters to Peter Norbeck, 9 November 1929; Norbeck to Walters, 23 November 1929, folder 1; Thorstina Jackson Walters to Norbeck, 26 February 1930; Norbeck to Walters, 17 March 1930, folder 2; Thorstina Jackson Walters to Lydia Norbeck, 7 December 1930; Peter Norbeck to Walters, 9 December 1930, folder 3, all in box 12, PNP.

26. Gudmundur Grimson et al., "An Appeal," folder 29, box 2, TJEWP.
27. See reviews: B.M., *Crag and Canyon* [Banff National Park], 30 April 1954, box 2, scrapbook 3, ABP; Eggleston, Causerie, column, 17 April 1954, WEF.
28. Thomson, *Crocus and Meadowlark Country*, 130.
29. A. Brown, *Sketches from Life*, 215.
30. Leslie Agghazy to Annora Brown, 2 August 1969; see also Joannie Bartlett to A. Brown, 16 July 1973; Store Manager [Quest, in Banff, Alberta] to A. Brown, 13 August 1973, all in folder 2, box 1; see also letters, esp. 30 September 1965, and receipts from J. Patrick Cowan to A. Brown, August–October 1965, folder 4, box 1, ABP.
31. W. G. Stephens [of J. M. Dent] to Annora Brown, 5 May 1954, box 2, scrapbook 3, ABP.
32. Will, *Corn for the Northwest*, 15, 35, 55–58, 73, 84; Will, "Trees of the Dakotas," no. 11, p. 124.
33. Will, "Grandmother Who Never Dies." For an example of Annora Brown's illustrations, see Ralph Hedlin, "The Little Hunter," *Country Guide*, April 1957, folder 13, box 1, ABP, 58.
34. Wilfrid Eggleston to Wallace Stegner, 25 October 1956, vol. 23, file 9, WEF. The Stegner article "Quiet Earth, Big Sky" originally appeared in *American Heritage*.
35. Marleen Hayes, "Annora Brown Says Macleod Good Artistic Background," *Fort Macleod Gazette*, 2 January 1958, ABCF-GL.
36. Stegner, *Beyond the Hundredth Meridian*, 350; Howard, *Montana*, 32, 31–37; Howard, *Strange Empire*, 11–19; Eggleston, Causerie, column, 24 January 1953, WEF.
37. Stegner to Eggleston, 16 November 1956, vol. 23, file 9, WEF; Eggleston, *High Plains*, 51.
38. Stegner used Howard's *Strange Empire* (in *Wolf Willow*, 60–61) and *Montana* (in *Beyond the Hundredth Meridian*, 399); Annora Brown used Howard, *Montana*. See research notes, folder 11, box 1, ABP; A. Brown, *Old Man's Garden*, 228–29; "Macleod Artist's Work Impresses."
39. Will, "Our Wealth."
40. Alexander Calhoun to Eggleston, 18 September 1941, vol. 26, file 23, WEF. Calhoun cited the approval of "Miss Thomson," probably Geor-

gina, "who has lived on the open prairie"; see Thomson, *Crocus and Meadowlark Country*.
41. "Writer from West Does First Novel," *High River Times*, 28 April 1938, WEF.
42. Stegner and Etulain, *Conversations with Wallace Stegner*, 1.
43. Eggleston to Stegner, 25 October 1956, vol. 23, file 9. In 1960 Eggleston claimed Stegner's 1943 novel *Big Rock Candy Mountain* for his nation's "prairie literature," after he discovered a "Canadian novelette embedded in this American novel." Eggleston, Causerie, column, 30 January 1960, vol. 39, file 25, WEF.
44. Cook-Lynn, *Can't Read Wallace Stegner*, 30; Basso, *Wisdom Sits in Places*, 40–69.

Bibliography

Archives

ABCF-GL. Annora Brown Clippings File. Glenbow Library and Archives. Archives and Special Collections, University of Calgary, Alberta.

ABP. Annora Brown Papers. University of Alberta Archives, Edmonton.

ARP. Aagot Raaen Papers. Institute for Regional Studies. North Dakota State University Libraries, Fargo.

BP. Bhryer Papers. Yale Collection of American Literature. Beinecke Rare Book and Manuscript Library, Yale University, New Haven CT.

DRP. Doane Robinson Papers. State Archives Collection. South Dakota State Historical Society, Pierre.

ELSP. Effie Laurie Storer Papers. Provincial Archives of Saskatchewan, Regina.

EMHTP. Elsie May Hammond Thomas Papers. Provincial Archives of Saskatchewan, Regina.

HFP. Humphrey Family Papers. State Archives Collection. South Dakota State Historical Society, Pierre.

JAAM. Julia Anna Asher [Lula Short] Memoir. Archives of Manitoba, Winnipeg.

LMC. Lillian M. Miller Collection. Montana State Historical Society Archives, Helena.

OWP. Oscar Will Papers. Institute for Regional Studies. North Dakota State University Libraries, Fargo.

PDC. Pioneer Daughters Collection. State Archives Collection. South Dakota State Historical Society, Pierre.

PFF. Pitblado Family Fonds. Archives and Special Collections, University of Manitoba Libraries, Winnipeg.

PFP. Pickler Family Papers. State Archives Collection. South Dakota State Historical Society, Pierre.

PNP. Peter Norbeck Papers. Richardson Archives. University of South Dakota Libraries, Vermillion.

PRM.   Pamphlets by and about Robert McAlmon, including newspaper clippings, articles in periodicals, and other ephemera. Beinecke Rare Book and Manuscript Library, Yale University, New Haven CT.
RCRP. R. C. Russell Papers. Saskatchewan Archives Board, Regina.
RMP.   Robert McAlmon Papers. Yale Collection of American Literature. Beinecke Rare Book and Manuscript Library, Yale University, New Haven CT.
SKFF. Short, Knupp Family Fonds. Glenbow Library and Archives. Archives and Special Collections, University of Calgary, Alberta.
SPP.   Stanley Pargellis Papers. Office of the President. Newberry Library Archives, Chicago.
TJEWP. Thorstina Jackson/Emile Walters Papers. Institute for Regional Studies. North Dakota State University Libraries, Fargo.
TKOHP. Tom Kirkham Oral History Project. Glenbow Library and Archives. Archives and Special Collections, University of Calgary, Alberta.
UMRSP. University of Minnesota Regional Studies Papers. Rockefeller Foundation Records. Rockefeller Archive Center, Sleepy Hollow NY.
WCWP. William Carlos Williams Papers. Yale Collection of American Literature. Beinecke Rare Book and Manuscript Library, Yale University, New Haven CT.
WEF.   Wilfrid Eggleston Fonds. Library and Archives Canada, Ottawa.
WFP.   Will Family Papers. North Dakota State Historical Society Archives, Bismarck.
WJC.   William Jayne Collection. State Archives Collection. South Dakota State Historical Society, Pierre.

Published Works

"Agnes Christina Laut." Canada's Early Women Writers, Canadian Writing Research Collaboratory. 18 May 2018. www.cwrc.ca/islandora/object/ceww%3Acafde280-35b5-4a46-a741-a4acc253dccf.

Akin, Wallace E. *The North Central United States*. Princeton NJ: Van Nostrand, 1968.

Alderson, Patricia A. "Annora Brown: Forming a Regionalist Sensibility." MA thesis, University of Calgary, Alberta, 2005.

Allen, John Logan. *Lewis and Clark and the Image of the American Northwest*. New York: Dover, 1975.

Amato, Joseph A. *Rethinking Home: A Case for Writing Local History*. Berkeley: University of California Press, 2002.

"America's New Middle West." *Look* 22, no. 20 (1958): 23.

Anderson, Harry H. Foreword to Hyde, *Spotted Tail's Folk*, v–xiii.
Ayers, Edward L., Patricia Nelson Limerick, Stephen Nissenbaum, and Peter S. Onuf. *All Over the Map: Rethinking American Regions*. Baltimore: Johns Hopkins University Press, 1996.
Babener, Liahna. "Bitter Nostalgia: Recollections of Childhood on the Midwestern Frontier." In West and Petrik, *Small Worlds*, 301–20.
Baker, Oliver E. "The Agriculture of the Great Plains Region." *Annals of the Association of American Geographers* 13, no. 3 (1923): 109–67.
Barkley, Theodore M., Ralph E. Brooks, and Eileen K. Schofield, eds. *Flora of the Great Plains*. Lawrence: University Press of Kansas, 1986.
Barron, Hal S. *Mixed Harvest: The Second Great Transformation in the Rural North, 1870–1930*. Chapel Hill: University of North Carolina Press, 1997.
Barrows, Harlan H., Hugh H. Bennett, L. C. Gray, Francis C. Harrington, Richard C. Moore, John C. Page, Harlow S. Person, and Morris L. Cooke. *The Future of the Great Plains*. Washington DC: U.S. Government Printing Office, 1936.
Basso, Keith H. *Wisdom Sits in Places: Landscape and Language among the Western Apache*. Albuquerque: University of New Mexico Press, 1996.
Bell, Margaret. *When Montana and I Were Young: A Frontier Childhood*. Edited by Mary Clearman Blew. Lincoln: University of Nebraska Press, 2002.
Bennett, Hugh H., Frederick H. Fowler, Francis C. Harrington, Harry L. Hopkins, Richard C. Moore, John C. Page, Rexford G. Tugwell, Henry A. Wallace, and Morris L. Cook. *Report of the Great Plains Drought Area Committee*. Washington DC: U.S. Government Printing Office, 1936.
Benson, Jackson J. *Down by the Lemonade Springs*. Reno: University of Nevada Press, 2001.
———. *Wallace Stegner: His Life and Work*. New York: Viking, 1996.
Bicha, Karel Denis. *The American Farmer and the Canadian West, 1896–1914*. Lawrence KS: Coronado, 1968.
Binnema, Theodore. *Common and Contested Ground: A Human and Environmental History of the Northwestern Plains*. Norman: University of Oklahoma Press, 2001.
———. "How Does a Map Mean? Old Swan's Map of 1801 and the Blackfoot World." In *From Rupert's Land to Canada*, edited by Theodore Binnema, Gerhard J. Enns, and Rod C. Macleod, 201–24. Edmonton: University of Alberta Press, 2001.
Blew, Mary Clearman. Introduction to Bell, *Montana and I*, ix–xxx.
Blodgett, Lorin. *The Climatology of the United States and the Temperate Latitudes of the North American Continent*. Philadelphia: Lippincott, 1857.
Blum, Andrew. *The Weather Machine: A Journey inside the Forecast*. New York: HarperCollins, 2019.

Bogue, Allan G. "James C. Malin: A Voice from the Grasslands." In Etulain, *Writing Western History*, 215–43.

Bolena, Eric G., and Dan L. Flores. "Prairie Wetlands of West Texas: The History and Ecology of Playa Lakes." In *The Prairie: Roots of Our Culture; Foundation of Our Economy: Proceedings of the Tenth [1986] North American Prairie Conference*, edited by Arnold Davis and Geoffrey Standford. Austin: Native Prairie Association of Texas, 1993.

Borchert, John R. *America's Northern Heartland: An Economic and Historical Geography of the Upper Midwest*. Minneapolis: University of Minnesota Press, 1987.

Bothwell, Robert. *Your Country, My Country: A Unified History of the United States and Canada*. New York: Oxford University Press, 2015.

Boyle, Kay. Review of *Robert McAlmon, Expatriate Publisher and Writer*, by Robert E. Knoll. *Prairie Schooner* 34, no. 1 (1960): 1–41.

Breen, David H. *The Canadian Prairie West and the Ranching Frontier, 1874–1924*. Toronto: University of Toronto Press, 1983.

Briggs, Harold E. "An Appraisal of Historical Writing on the Great Plains Region since 1920." *Mississippi Valley Historical Review* 34, no. 1 (1947): 83–100.

———. *Frontiers of the Northwest*. New York: Appleton-Century, 1940.

"The British North America Act, 1867." Department of Justice, Government of Canada. Accessed 5 December 2020. www.justice.gc.ca/eng/rp-pr/csj-sjc/constitution/lawreg-loireg/p1tl1.html.

Bromfield, Louis. *The Midwest*. With the Editors of *Look*. Boston: Houghton Mifflin, 1947.

Brown, Annora. *Old Man's Garden*. Toronto: Dent and Sons, 1954.

———. *Sketches from Life*. Edmonton: Hurtig, 1981.

Brown, Lauren. *Grasslands*. New York: Knopf, 1985.

Bureau of the Census. *Geographic Areas Reference Manual*. Washington DC: U.S. Department of Commerce, Economics and Statistics Administration, 1994.

Burpee, Lawrence J. "La Vérendrye's 1738–39 Journal." *Canadian Historical Review* 23 (1942): 407–11.

Burt, Alfred Leroy. *The Romance of the Prairie Provinces*. Toronto: Gage, 1930.

———. *A Short History of Canada for Americans*. Minneapolis: University of Minnesota Press, 1942.

Butler, Robert. "The Life Review: An Interpretation of Reminiscence in the Aged." *Psychiatry* 26 (1963): 65–76.

Cardston and District Historical Society. *Chief Mountain Country*. Calgary: Friesen, 1978.

Carter, Sarah. *Capturing Women: The Manipulation of Cultural Imagery in Canada's Prairie West*. Montreal: McGill-Queen's University Press, 1997.

———. *Imperial Plots: Women, Land, and the Spadework of British Colonialism on the Canadian Prairies.* Winnipeg: University of Manitoba Press, 2016.

———. *Lost Harvests: Prairie Indian Reserve Farmers and Government Policy.* Montreal: McGill-Queen's University Press, 1990.

———. "Transnational Perspectives on the History of Great Plains Women: Gender, Race, Nations, and the Forty-Ninth Parallel." *American Review of Canadians Studies*, no. 4 (2003): 565–96.

Census of Population and Agriculture of the Northwest Provinces: Manitoba, Saskatchewan, Alberta, 1906. Ottawa: Dawson, 1907.

"Census of Population and Housing." United States Census Bureau. Accessed 25 September 2020. www.census.gov/prod/www/decennial.html.

Census of Prairie Provinces, Population and Agriculture: Manitoba, Saskatchewan, Alberta, 1916. Ottawa: De Labroquerie Taché, 1918.

Chapman, Kim Alan, Mary Ziegenhagen, and Adelheide Fischer. *Valley of Grass: Tall Grass Prairie and Parkland of the Red River Valley.* St. Cloud MN: North Star, 1998.

Clark, Dan E. "Historical Activities in the Trans-Mississippi Northwest, 1914–1915." *Mississippi Valley Historical Review* 2 (1915): 384–406.

———. "Historical Activities in the Trans-Mississippi Northwest, 1915–1916." *Mississippi Valley Historical Review* 3 (1916): 347–67.

Clow, Richmond L. "General William S. Harney on the Northern Plains." *South Dakota History* 16, no. 3 (1986): 229–48.

Coe, Richard N. *When the Grass Was Taller: Autobiography and the Experience of Childhood.* New Haven: Yale University Press, 1984.

Connerton, Paul. *How Societies Remember.* Cambridge: Cambridge University Press, 1989.

Conrad, Bryce. *Refiguring America: A Study of William Carols Williams' "In the American Grain."* Urbana: University of Illinois Press, 1990.

Conway, John F. *The West: The History of a Region in Confederation.* Toronto: Lorimer, 1983.

Cook-Lynn, Elizabeth. *Why I Can't Read Wallace Stegner and Other Essays: A Tribal Voice.* Madison: University of Wisconsin Press, 1996.

Cordier, Mary Hurlbut. *Schoolwomen of the Prairies and Plains: Personal Narratives from Iowa, Kansas, Nebraska, 1860s–1920s.* Albuquerque: University of New Mexico Press, 1992.

Coues, Elliott, ed. *New Light on the Early History of the Greater Northwest: The Manuscript Journals of Alexander Henry and of David Thompson, 1799–1814.* 2 vols. 1897. Reprint, Minneapolis: Ross and Haines, 1965.

Courtwright, Julie. *Prairie Fire: A Great Plains History.* Lawrence: University Press of Kansas, 2011.

Cronon, William. *Nature's Metropolis: Chicago and the Great West.* New York: Norton, 1991.

Cunfer, Geoff. *On the Great Plains: Agriculture and Environment*. College Station: Texas A&M University Press, 2005.
Danbom, David B. *Born in the Country: A History of Rural America*. Baltimore: Johns Hopkins University Press, 1995.
Davis, Fred. *Yearning for Yesterday: A Sociology of Nostalgia*. New York: Free Press, 1979.
Davis, Karen. "The Mental Life of Chickens as Observed through Their Social Relationships." In Smith and Mitchell, *Experiencing Animal Minds*, 13–29.
DeLand, Charles E. "The Verendrye Explorations and Discoveries, Leading to the Planting of the Fort Pierre Tablet." *South Dakota Historical Collections* 7 (1914): 99–322.
Deloria, Philip J. *Playing Indian*. New Haven: Yale University Press, 1998.
DeVoto, Bernard. *The Course of Empire*. Boston: Houghton Mifflin, 1952.
Dixon, Roland B. "Review of Collections of the State Historical Society of North Dakota." Vol. 2. *American Anthropologist* 2, no. 3 (1909): 498–503.
Dondore, Dorothy Anne. *The Prairie and the Making of Middle America: Four Centuries of Description*. Cedar Rapids IA: Torch, 1926.
Dooks, Phyllis M. (Hammond). "George Lester and Ivy Madaline Amelia (Rex) Hammond." In *Maple Creek Area: Where Past Is Present*, edited by Maple Creek and Area History Committee, 555–56. Altona MB: Friesens, 2000.
Dorman, Robert L. *Hell of a Vision: Regionalism and the Modern American West*. Tucson: University of Arizona Press, 2012.
———. *Revolt of the Provinces: The Regionalist Movement in America, 1920–1945*. Chapel Hill: University of North Carolina Press, 1993.
Downing, Iris Rosina (Hammond). "George R. and Ada (Cook) Hammond." In *Maple Creek: Where Past Is Present*, edited by Maple Creek and Area History Committee, 554–55. Altona MB: Friesens, 2000.
Dudley, Dorothy. *Forgotten Frontiers: Dreiser and the Land of the Free*. New York: Smith and Haas, 1932.
Eccles, William J. *The French in North America, 1500–1763*. East Lansing: Michigan State University Press, 1998.
Edwards, Richard, Jacob K. Friefeld, and Rebecca S. Wingo. *Homesteading the Plains: Toward A New History*. Lincoln: University of Nebraska Press, 2017.
Eggleston, Wilfrid. *The Frontier and Canadian Letters*. Toronto: Ryerson, 1957.
———. *The High Plains*. Toronto: Macmillan, 1938.
———. *Homestead on the Range*. Ottawa: Borealis, 1982.
———. *Prairie Moonlight and Other Lyrics*. N.p.: privately printed, 1927.
———. *Prairie Symphony*. Ottawa: Borealis, 1978.
———. *The Road to Nationhood*. Toronto: Oxford University Press, 1946.
———. *While I Still Remember: A Personal Record*. Toronto: Ryerson, 1968.

Ekberg, Carl J. *French Roots in the Illinois Country: The Mississippi Frontier in Colonial Times.* Urbana: University of Illinois Press, 1998.
Eliot, T. S., ed. *Literary Essays of Ezra Pound.* 1934. Reprint, New York: New Directions, 1968.
Ellis, Caleb H. *History of Faulk County, South Dakota.* 1909. Reprint, Aberdeen SD: North Plains, 1973.
Ellis, L. Ethan. "The Northwest and the Reciprocity Agreement of 1911." *Mississippi Valley Historical Review* 26, no. 1 (1939): 55–66.
Elofson, Warren M. *Cowboys, Gentlemen and Cattle Thieves.* Montreal: McGill-Queen's University Press, 2000.
———. *Frontier Cattle Ranching in the Land and Times of Charlie Russell.* Montreal: McGill-Queen's University Press; Seattle: University of Washington Press, 2004.
Emmons, David M. *Garden in the Grasslands: Boomer Literature of the Central Great Plains.* Lincoln: University of Nebraska Press, 1971.
Etulain, Richard W., ed. *Writing Western History: Essays on Major Western Historians.* Albuquerque: University of New Mexico Press, 1991.
Evans, Sterling, ed. *Borderlands of the American and Canadian Wests: Essays on Regional History of the Forty-Ninth Parallel.* Lincoln: University of Nebraska Press, 2006.
Faragher, John Mack. *Sugar Creek: Life on the Illinois Prairie.* New Haven: Yale University Press, 1986.
Fargo, Lucile F. *Prairie Chautauqua.* 1943. Reprint, Dell Rapids SD: Smith, 1991.
Faulkner, William. *Light in August.* London: Smith and Haas, 1932.
Fenn, Elizabeth A. *Encounters at the Heart of the World: A History of the Mandan People.* New York: Hill and Wang, 2014.
Fenneman, Nevin M. "Physiographic Boundaries within the United States." *Annals of the Association of American Geographers* 4 (1914): 84–134, plus 3 pages of maps.
"First Nations and Treaty Areas in Manitoba." Indigenous and Northern Affairs, Government of Canada. 15 September 2020. www.aadnc-aandc.gc.ca/eng/1100100020576/1100100020578.
"First Nations in Alberta." Indigenous and Northern Affairs, Government of Canada. 15 September 2020. www.aadnc-aandc.gc.ca/DAM/DAM-INTER-AB/STAGING/texte-text/fnamarch11_1315587933961_eng.pdf.
"First Nations in Saskatchewan." Office of the Treaty Commissioner. Indian and Northern Affairs Canada, Saskatchewan Region. Accessed 5 December 2020. www.otc.ca/ckfinder/userfiles/files/fnl_1100100020617_eng.pdf.
Fisher, Olive, and Clara Tyner. *Totem, Tipi and Tumpline: Stories of Canadian Indians.* Toronto: Dent and Sons, 1955.

Fite, Gilbert C. "The History of South Dakota's Rural Credit System." *South Dakota Historical Collections* 24 (1949): 220–75.

———. *Peter Norbeck: Prairie Statesman.* 1948. Reprint, Pierre: South Dakota State Historical Society Press, 2005.

Flores, Dan. *American Serengeti: The Last Big Animals of the Great Plains.* Lawrence: University Press of Kansas, 2016.

———. "Bison Ecology and Bison Diplomacy: The Southern Plains from 1800 to 1850." *Journal of American History* 78 (1992): 465–85.

———. "Place: An Argument for Bioregional History." *Environmental History Review* 18 (1994): 1–18.

Ford, Madox Ford. "Chroniques." *Transatlantic Review* 2, no. 2 (1924): 213.

———. "Communications." *Transatlantic Review* 1, no. 5 (1924): 359–60.

———. *It Was the Nightingale.* Philadelphia: Lippincott, 1933.

———. "Notes on Contributors." *Transatlantic Review* 1, no. 1 (1924): 96–98.

Fort Macleod History Book Committee. *Fort Macleod: Our Colourful Past, a History of the Town of Fort Macleod, from 1874 to 1924.* Calgary: Friesen, 1977.

Fowler, Loretta. *American Indians of the Great Plains.* New York: Columbia University Press, 2003.

Fradkin, Philip L. *Wallace Stegner and the American West.* New York: Knopf, 2008.

Francis, R. Douglas, and Howard Palmer, eds. *The Prairie West: Historical Readings.* Edmonton: University of Alberta Press, 1992.

Fraser, William P., and Ralph C. Russell. *An Annotated List of the Plants of Saskatchewan.* Revised by Ralph C. Russell, George F. Ledingham, and Robert T. Coupland. Rev. ed. Saskatoon: University of Saskatchewan, 1953.

———. *List of the Flowering Plants, Ferns and Fern Allies of Saskatchewan.* Saskatoon: University of Saskatchewan, 1937.

———. *A Revised, Annotated List of the Plants of Saskatchewan.* University of Saskatchewan, 1944.

Friesen, Gerald. *The Canadian Prairies: A History.* Toronto: University of Toronto Press, 1987.

———. *River Road: Essays on Manitoba and Prairie History.* Winnipeg: University of Manitoba Press, 1996.

Friesen, Gerald, and Kathryn Young. "La Vérendrye and the French Empire in Western North America." In Friesen, *River Road: Essays on Manitoba and Prairie History*, 13–16.

Gala, Argent. "Toward a Privileging of the Nonverbal: Communication, Corporeal Synchrony, and Transcendence in Humans and Horses." In Smith and Mitchell, *Experiencing Animal Minds*, 111–28.

Gannon, Clell G. *Ever and Always I Shall Love the Land*. New York: Vantage, 1965.
———. *Songs of the Bunch Grass Acres*. Boston: Gorham, 1924.
Gannon, Grael Brian. "Strange Victory of Clell Gannon." In C. Gannon, *Ever and Always*, 11–15.
Gates, Paul W. *History of Public Land Law Development*. Washington DC: U.S. Government Printing Office, 1968.
Gluek, Alvin C., Jr. *Minnesota and the Manifest Destiny of the Canadian Northwest: A Study in Canadian-American Relations*. Toronto: University of Toronto Press, 1965.
Goeman, Mishuana R. "Disrupting a Settler-Colonial Grammar of Place." In *Theorizing Native Studies*, edited by Audra Simpson and Andrea Smith, 235–65. Durham: Duke University Press, 2014.
Goetzmann, William H. *Exploration and Empire: The Explorer and the Scientist in the Winning of the American West*. New York: Norton, 1966.
Greene, Jerome A. "The Sioux Land Commission of 1889: Prelude to Wounded Knee." *South Dakota History* 1, no. 1 (1970): 41–72.
Guthrie, Alfred B., Jr. *The Big Sky*. New York: Sloane Associates, 1947.
———. *The Blue Hen's Chick: An Autobiography*. 1965. Reprint, Lincoln: University of Nebraska Press, 1993.
Hagen, Norris C. *Vikings of the Prairie: Three North Dakota Settlers Reminisce*. New York: Exposition, 1958.
Halbwachs, Maurice. *The Collective Memory*. 1950. Reprint, New York: Harper and Row, 1980.
Hall, Jacquelyn Dowd. "'You Must Remember This': Autobiography as Social Critique." *Journal of American History* 85, no. 2 (1998): 439–65.
Hamilton, Stanislaus Murray, ed. *The Writings of James Monroe*. Vol. 1, *1778–1794*. New York: Putnam's Sons, 1898.
Handy-Marchello, Barbara. Introduction to Raaen, *Grass of the Earth*, vii–xxvii.
———. *Women of the Northern Plains: Gender and Settlement on the Homestead Frontier, 1870–1930*. St. Paul: Minnesota Historical Society Press, 2005.
Hansen, Karen V. *Encounter on the Great Plains*. New York: Oxford University Press, 2013.
Hardy, William G., ed. *The Alberta Golden Jubilee Anthology*. McClelland and Stewart, 1955.
Harrison, Dick. *Unnamed Country: The Struggle for a Canadian Prairie Fiction*. Edmonton: University of Alberta Press, 1977.
Hewes, Leslie. "The Northern Wet Prairie of the United States: Nature, Sources of Information, and Extent." *Annals of the Association of American Geographers* 41, no. 4 (1951): 307–23.

Hewes, Leslie, and Phillip E. Frandon. "Occupying the Wet Prairie: The Role of Artificial Drainage in Story County, Iowa." *Annals of the Association of American Geographers* 42, no. 1 (1952): 24–50.

Hicks, John D. "The Constitutions of the Northwest States." *University Studies* 22, nos. 1–2 (1923): 1–162.

———. "The Western Middle West, 1900–1914." *Agricultural History* 20, no. 2 (1946): 65–77.

Higham, Carol, and Robert Thacker, eds. *One West, Two Myths: A Comparative Reader*. Calgary: University of Calgary Press, 2004.

———, eds. *One West, Two Myths II*. Calgary: University of Calgary Press, 2007.

Higham, John. *Strangers in the Land*. 1955. Reprint, New Brunswick: Rutgers University Press, 1998.

Hildebrandt, Walter. *Views from Fort Battleford: Constructed Visions of an Anglo-Canadian West*. Regina SK: Canadian Plains Research Center, 1994.

Hildebrandt, Walter, and Brian Hubner. *The Cypress Hills: The Land and Its People*. Saskatoon SK: Purich, 1994.

"Historical Palmer Drought Indices: Maps." National Centers for Environmental Information. National Oceanic and Atmospheric Administration. Accessed 5 December 2020. www.ncdc.noaa.gov/temp-and-precip/drought/historical-palmers/psi/193401-193412.

Hixson, Walter L. *American Settler Colonialism: A History*. London: Palgrave Macmillan, 2013.

Hogan, Edward Patrick, and Erin Hogan Fouberg. *The Geology of South Dakota*. 3rd ed. Sioux Falls: Augustana College Center for Western Studies, 2001.

Hogue, Michael. "Disputing the Medicine Line: The Plains Cree and the Canadian-American Border, 1876–1885." In Higham and Thacker, *One West, Two Myths*, 85–108.

Honan, Park. *Matthew Arnold: A Life*. New York: McGraw-Hill, 1981.

Hoover, Herbert T. "The Sioux Agreement of 1889 and Its Aftermath." *South Dakota History* 19, no. 1 (1989): 56–94.

Hopwood, Alison. Introduction to Salverson, *Viking Heart*, ix–xiv.

Hough, Walter. Review of *Corn among the Indians of the Upper Missouri*, by George F. Will and George E. Hyde. *American Anthropologist* 21 (October–December 1919): 448.

Howard, Joseph Kinsey. *Montana: High, Wide, and Handsome*. 1943. Reprint, Lincoln: University of Nebraska Press, 1983.

———. *Strange Empire: A Narrative of the Northwest*. 1952. Reprint, St. Paul: Minnesota Historical Society Press, 1994.

Hudson, John C. *Making the Corn Belt: A Geographical History of Middle-Western Agriculture*. Bloomington: Indiana University Press, 1994.

———. *Plains Country Towns*. Minneapolis: University of Minnesota Press, 1985.
Hurt, R. Douglas. *Indian Agriculture in America: Prehistory to the Present*. Lawrence: University Press of Kansas, 1987.
Hyde, George E. *The Pawnee Indians*. 1951. Reprint, Norman: University of Oklahoma Press, 1974.
———. *Spotted Tail's Folk*. 1961. Reprint, Norman: University of Oklahoma Press, 1974.
"InfoGuide: Historical Resources." Statistics Canada. Accessed 30 December 2020. www.statcan.gc.ca/eng/library/historical#a2.
Isenberg, Andrew C. *The Destruction of the Bison: An Environmental History, 1750–1920*. Cambridge: Cambridge University Press, 2000.
Isern, Thomas D. *Bull Threshers and Bindlestiffs: Harvesting and Threshing on the North American Plains*. Lawrence: University Press of Kansas, 1990.
Isern, Thomas D., and R. Bruce Shepard. "Duty-Free: An Introduction to the Practice of Regional History along the Forty-Ninth Parallel." In Evans, *Borderlands*, xxvii–xxxv.
"'I Shall Love the Land': The Art of Clell Gannon." *North Dakota History* 76, nos. 1–2 (2010): 26–33.
Jackman, Wilbur S. "Nature-Study." Pt. 2. In *The Third Yearbook of the National Society for the Scientific Study of Education*, edited by Manfred J. Homes, 1–96. Chicago: University of Chicago Press, 1904.
Jackson, Thorstina. *Saga Íslendinga í Norður-Dakota* [History of the Icelanders in North Dakota]. Winnipeg: City, 1926.
Jacobs, Margaret. *White Mother to a Dark Race: Settler Colonialism, Maternalism, and the Removal of Indigenous Children in the American West and Australia, 1880–1940*. Lincoln: University of Nebraska Press, 2009.
Jacobs, Wilbur R., ed. *Letters of Francis Parkman*. Vol. 2. Norman: University of Oklahoma, 1960.
Jacobson, Mathew Frye. *Whiteness of a Different Color: European Immigrants and the Alchemy of Race*. Cambridge MA: Harvard University Press, 1998.
Jacobson, Robert L., Nancy J. Albrecht, and Kathryn E. Bolin. "Wildflower Routes: Benefits of a Management Program for Minnesota Right-of-Way Prairies." *Proceedings of the Twelfth North American Prairie Conference* 12 (1990): 153–58.
Jóakimsson [Jackson], Thorleifur. *Brot af landnámassögu Nyja Islands* [Partial history of New Iceland]. Vol. 1. Winnipeg: Prentsmiðja Columbia Press, 1919.
Johnsgard, Paul A. *Prairie Birds: Fragile Splendor in the Great Plains*. Lawrence: University Press of Kansas, 2001.
Johnson, Dorothy M. *Beulah Bunny Tells All*. New York: Morrow, 1942.
———. *Indian Country*. Lincoln: University of Nebraska Press, 1995.

———. *When You and I Were Young, Whitefish.* 1982. Reprint, Helena: Montana Historical Society Press, 1997.
Jones, David C. *Empire of Dust: Settling and Abandoning the Prairie Dry Belt.* Edmonton: University of Alberta Press, 1987.
Jordan, Terry G. "Between the Forest and the Prairie." *Agricultural History* 38 (October 1964): 205–16.
———. *North American Cattle-Ranching Frontiers.* Albuquerque: University of New Mexico Press, 1993.
Julin, Suszanne Barta. *A Marvelous Hundred Square Miles: Black Hills Tourism, 1880–1941.* Pierre: South Dakota State Historical Society Press, 2009.
Kasson, Joy S. *Buffalo Bill's Wild West.* New York: Hill and Wang, 2011.
Kaye, Frances W. *Goodlands: A Meditation and History on the Great Plains.* Edmonton: Athabasca University Press, 2011.
Kellogg, Louise Phelps, ed. *Early Narratives of the Northwest, 1634–1699.* New York: Scribner's Sons, 1917.
Kincer, Joseph B. "The Climate of the Great Plains as a Factor in Their Utilization." *Annals of the Association of American Geographers* 13, no. 2 (1923): 67–80.
Kingsbury, George Washington. *History of Dakota Territory.* Vol. 2. Chicago: Clarke, 1915.
Knoll, Robert E., ed. *McAlmon and the Lost Generation: A Self Portrait.* Lincoln: University of Nebraska Press, 1962.
———. *Robert McAlmon: Expatriate Publisher and Writer.* Lincoln: University of Nebraska Press, 1957.
Koupal, Nancy Tystad, ed. "Lydia Norbeck's 'Recollections of the Years.'" *South Dakota Historical Collections* 39 (1979): 1–147.
Kraenzel, Carl Frederick. *The Great Plains in Transition.* Norman: University of Oklahoma Press, 1955.
Kriegel, Annie. "Generational Difference: The History of an Idea." *Daedalus* 107 (Fall 1978): 23–38.
Kroeber, Alfred L. "Frederic Ward Putnam." *American Anthropologist* 17 (1915): 712–18.
Kulchyski, Peter. "Reserves in Manitoba." The Canadian Encyclopedia. Historica Canada. 30 September 2020. www.thecanadianencyclopedia.ca/en/article/reserves-in-manitoba.
Lakota Language Consortium. *New Lakota Dictionary.* 2nd ed. Bloomington: Lakota Language Consortium, 2011.
Lamar, Howard R. "Comparing Depressions: The Great Plains and Canadian Prairie Experiences, 1929–1941." In *The Twentieth-Century West,* edited by Gerald D. Nash and Richard W. Etulain, 175–206. Albuquerque: University of New Mexico Press, 1989.

Lansing, Michael J. "An American Daughter in Africa: Land of My Fathers; Era Bell Thompson's Midwestern Vision of the African Diaspora." *Middle West Review* 1, no. 2 (2015): 1–28.

———. *Insurgent Democracy: The Nonpartisan League in North American Politics*. Chicago: University of Chicago Press, 2015.

Lauck, Jon K. *The Lost Region: Toward a Revival of Midwestern History*. Iowa City: University of Iowa Press, 2013.

Laut, Agnes C. *The Conquest of the Great Northwest: Being the Story of the Adventures of England Known as the Hudson's Bay Company, New Pages in the History of the Canadian Northwest and Western States*. 6th ed. 1908. Reprint, New York: Doran, 1918.

———. *Pathfinders of the West, Being the Thrilling Story of the Adventures of the Men Who Discovered the Great Northwest: Radisson, La Vérendrye, Lewis and Clark*. 1904. Reprint, London: Macmillan, 1907.

Lavin, Stephen J., Fred M. Shelley, and J. Clark Archer. *Atlas of the Great Plains*. Lincoln: University of Nebraska Press, 2011.

Lee, Thomas. "The Discovery of La Vérendrye's Inscribed Leaden Plate." *Nation* 99, no. 2559 (1914): 71.

Leloudis, James L. *Schooling the New South: Pedagogy, Self, and Society in North Carolina, 1880–1920*. Chapel Hill: University of North Carolina Press, 1996.

Leuchtenburg, William E. *Franklin D. Roosevelt and the New Deal, 1932–1940*. New York: Harper Perennial, 1963.

———. *The Perils of Prosperity, 1914–1932*. 2nd ed. Chicago: University of Chicago Press, 1993.

Lewis, Faye Cashatt. *Nothing to Make a Shadow*. Ames: Iowa State University Press, 1971.

Lewis, Sinclair. *The Job*. New York: Grosset and Dunlap, 1917.

———. *Main Street*. 1920. Reprint, New York: Signet, 2008.

Libby, Orin G. "The New Northwest." *Mississippi Valley Historical Review* 7, no. 4 (1921): 332–47.

———. "The Proper Identification of Indian Village Sites in North Dakota: A Reply to Dr. Dixon." *American Anthropologist* 12 (1910): 123–28.

———. "Some Verendrye Enigmas." *Mississippi Valley Historical Review* 3, no. 2 (1916): 143–60.

Licht, Daniel S. *Ecology and Economics of the Great Plains*. Lincoln: University of Nebraska Press, 1997.

Limerick, Patricia Nelson, Clyde A. Milner II, and Charles E. Rankin, eds. *Trails: Toward a New Western History*. Lawrence: University Press of Kansas, 1991.

Lorusso, Edward N. S. Introduction to McAlmon, *Miss Knight and Others*, xv–xxvi.

———. Introduction to McAlmon, *Post-adolescence*, xi–xxiii.
———. Introduction to McAlmon, *Village*, v–xviii.
Lotchin, Roger W. *San Francisco, 1846–1856: From Hamlet to City*. 1974. Reprint, Urbana: University of Illinois Press, 1997.
Lottinville, Savoie. Foreword to Hyde, *Pawnee Indians*, v–vii.
Mackintosh, William A. *Prairie Settlement: The Geographic Setting*. With A. B. Clark, G. A. Elliott, and W. W. Swanson. Toronto: Macmillan Company of Canada, 1934.
MacPherson, Ian, and John Herd Thompson. "The Business of Agriculture: Prairie Farmers and the Adoption of 'Business Methods,' 1880–1950." In Francis and Palmer, *Prairie West*, 475–96.
Malin, James C. *The Grassland of North America, Prolegomena to Its History*. 1947. Reprint, Gloucester MA: Smith, 1967.
Malone, Michael P., Richard B. Roeder, and William L. Lang. *Montana: A History of Two Centuries*. Seattle: University of Washington Press, 1991.
Mannheim, Karl. "The Problem of Generations." In *Essays on the Sociology of Knowledge*, 276–320. London: Routledge and Kegan Paul, 1952.
Maple Creek and Area History Committee, ed. *Maple Creek Area: Where Past Is Present*. Altona MB: Friesens, 2000.
"Map of the Numbered Treaties." Treaty Relations Commission of Manitoba. Accessed 5 December 2020. www.trcm.ca/treaties/treaties-in-manitoba/view-pdf-interactive-map-of-numbered-treaties-trcm-july-20-entry/.
Marbut, Curtis F. "Soils of the Great Plains." *Annals of the Association of American Geographers* 13, no. 2 (1923): 41–66.
Marchildon, Gregory P. "The Prairie Farm Rehabilitation Administration: Climate Crisis and Federal-Provincial Relations during the Great Depression." *Canadian Historical Review* 90, no. 2 (2009): 275–301.
Martin, Chester. *Dominion Lands Policy*. 1938. Reprint, Millwood NY: Kraus, 1974.
Masters, Edgar Lee. *Spoon River Anthology*. New York: Macmillan, 1915.
May, Henry F. *The End of American Innocence: A Study of the First Years of Our Own Time, 1912–1917*. 1959. Reprint, New York: Columbia University Press, 1992.
McAlmon, Robert. *A Companion Volume*. Paris: Contact, 1923.
———. *Explorations*. London: Egoist, 1921.
———. *A Hasty Bunch*. Paris: Contact, 1922.
———. *Miss Knight and Others*. Edited by Edward N. S. Lorusso. Albuquerque: University of New Mexico Press, 1992.
———. *The Nightinghouls of Paris*. Edited by Sanford J. Smoller. Urbana: University of Illinois Press, 2007.
———. *North America: Continent of Conjecture*. Paris: Contact, 1929.
———. *Not Alone Lost*. Norfolk CT: New Directions, 1937.

———. "The Plain Tales of the Open Prairie." In McAlmon, *Not Alone Lost*, 43–60.

———. *Post-adolescence: A Selection of Short Fiction*. Edited by Edward N. S. Lorusso. 1923. Reprint, Albuquerque: University of New Mexico Press, 1991.

———. "Potato Picking." In O'Brien, *Best Short Stories*, 159–68.

———. "Questionnaire." *Little Review*, May 1929, 52–53.

———. "The Via Dolorosa of Art: White Males, Today's Music, Form Destructionist-Sculptor." *Poetry* 17, no. 3 (1920): 117–29.

———. *Village: As It Happened through a Fifteen Year Period*. Edited by Edward N. S. Lorusso. 1924. Reprint, Albuquerque: University of New Mexico Press, 1990.

McAlmon, Robert, and Kay Boyle. *Being Geniuses Together, 1920–1930*. 1938. Reprint, London: Hogarth, 1984.

McCarthy, Joe. "The New Middle West." *Look* 22, no. 20 (1958): 27–28.

McClintock, Walter. *The Old North Trail: Life, Legends and Religion of the Blackfeet Indians*. 1910. Reprint, Lincoln: University of Nebraska Press, 1992.

McClung, Nellie. *"Clearing in the West" and "The Stream Runs Fast": The Complete Autobiography*. Edited by Veronica Strong-Boag and Michelle Lynn Rosa. Peterborough ON: Broadview, 2003.

———. *Sowing Seeds in Danny*. Toronto: Briggs, 1908.

McManus, Curtis R. *Happyland: A History of the "Dirty Thirties" in Saskatchewan, 1914–1937*. Calgary: University of Calgary Press, 2011.

McManus, Sheila. *The Line Which Separates: Race, Gender, and the Making of the Alberta-Montana Borderlands*. Lincoln: University of Nebraska Press, 2005.

Meinig, Donald. W. *The Shaping of America: Atlantic America, 1492–1800*. New Haven: Yale University Press, 1986.

———. *The Shaping of America: Continental America, 1800–1867*. New Haven: Yale University Press, 1993.

———. *The Shaping of America: Transcontinental America, 1850–1915*. New Haven: Yale University Press, 1998.

Meyer, Roy W. *History of the Santee Sioux: United States Indian Policy on Trial*. Rev. ed. 1967. Reprint, Lincoln: University of Nebraska Press, 1993.

———. *The Village Indians of the Upper Missouri: The Mandans, Hidatsas, and Arikaras*. Lincoln: University of Nebraska Press, 1977.

Miller, Jim R. *Skyscrapers Hide the Heavens: A History of Indian-White Relations in Canada*. Rev. ed. Toronto: University of Toronto Press, 1991.

Milton, John. "Conversations with Wallace Stegner." *South Dakota Review* 23, no. 4 (1985): 107–18.

Mitchell, Lee Clark. "Whose West Is It Anyway?" In Higham and Thacker, *One West, Two Myths II*, 139–51.

Mitchell, W. O. *Who Has Seen the Wind*. Toronto: Macmillan, 1947.

Moorehead, Ethel. Review of *Village: It Happened through a Fifteen Year Period*, by Robert McAlmon. *This Quarter* 1, no. 1 (1925): 266–70.
Morrison, Chester. "An Editor with No Problems." *Look* 22, no. 20 (1958): 99–101.
Morton, Arthur S. *A History of the Canadian West to 1870–71*. 1939. Reprint, Toronto: University of Toronto Press, 1973.
Morton, Arthur S., and Chester Martin. *History of Prairie Settlement and Dominion Lands Policy*. Toronto: Macmillan Company of Canada, 1938.
Morton, William L. *Manitoba: A History*. 1957. Reprint, Toronto: University of Toronto Press, 1967.
"The Most American Part of America." *Look* 22, no. 20 (1958): 108.
Murchie, Robert Welch. *Agricultural Progress on the Prairie Frontier*. Toronto: Macmillan Company of Canada, 1936.
Murray, Joan. *The Best of the Group of Seven*. Toronto: McClelland and Stewart, 1984.
Neatby, Blair. "The Saskatchewan Relief Commission, 1931–34." *Saskatchewan History* 3, no. 2 (1950): 51–56.
Neatby, Leslie H. *Chronicle of a Pioneer Family*. Saskatoon SK: Western Producer Books, 1979.
———. *Conquest of the Last Frontier*. Athens: Ohio University Press, 1966.
Nelson, Paula M. *Prairie Winnows Out Its Own: The West River Country of South Dakota in the Years of Depression and Dust*. Iowa City: University of Iowa Press, 1996.
Neth, Mary. *Preserving the Family Farm: Women, Community, and the Foundations of Agribusiness in the Midwest, 1900–1940*. Baltimore: Johns Hopkins University Press, 1995.
Newgard, Thomas P., and William C. Sherman, eds. *African Americans in North Dakota: Sources and Assessments*. Bismarck ND: University of Mary Press, 1994.
Newlin, Keith. *Hamlin Garland: A Life*. Lincoln: University of Nebraska Press, 2008.
Nichols, Roger L. *Indians in the United States and Canada: A Comparative History*. Lincoln: University of Nebraska Press, 1998.
Nicoll, Kate Neatby. *Paths They Have Not Known*. Princeton NJ: privately printed, 1978.
Norbeck, Peter, and George Norbeck. *The Norbecks of South Dakota*. South Dakota: privately printed, 1938.
O'Brien, Edward J. *The Best Short Stories of 1929*. New York: Dodd, Mead, 1929.
Olseth, Olaf H. *Mama Came from Norway*. New York: Vantage, 1955.
Ostler, Jeffrey. *The Lakotas and the Black Hills*. New York: Penguin Books, 2010.

———. *The Plains Sioux and U.S. Colonialism from Lewis and Clark to Wounded Knee.* Cambridge: Cambridge University Press, 2004.
Ottoson, Howard W., Eleanor M. Birch, Philip A. Henderson, and A. H. Anderson. *Land and People in the Northern Plains Transition Area.* Lincoln: University of Nebraska Press, 1966.
Owram, Doug. *Promise of Eden: The Canadian Expansionist Movement and the Idea of the West, 1856–1900.* Toronto: University of Toronto Press, 1980.
Paladin, Vivian. "Introduction to the 1997 Edition." In Johnson, *You and I,* ix–xxx.
Palliser, John. *The Solitary Hunter, or Sporting Adventures in the Prairies.* London: Routledge, 1856.
Palmer, Howard. *Alberta: A New History.* With Tamara Palmer. Edmonton: Hurtig, 1990.
———. "Strangers and Stereotypes: The Rise of Nativism, 1880–1920." In Francis and Palmer, *Prairie West,* 308–34.
Parkman, Francis. "The Discovery of the Rocky Mountains." *Atlantic Monthly* 61 (March 1888): 783–93.
"Parlor Games." Accessed 26 December 2020. www.victoriaspast.com /ParlorGames/parlor_games.htm.
Parrish, Randall. *The Great Plains: The Romance of Western American Exploration, Warfare, and Settlement, 1527–1870.* Chicago: McClurg, 1907.
Parsons, Nell Wilson. *The Curlew Cried.* Seattle: McCaffrey, 1947.
———. *Upon a Sagebrush Harp.* Saskatoon SK: Western Producer, 1969.
Paul, Eli. *Blue Water Creek and the First Sioux War, 1854–1856.* Norman: University of Oklahoma Press, 2004.
"Peter Norbeck: Well Driller, Statesman." *Water Well Journal* 28, no. 10 (1974): 35–37.
Peters, Bernard C. "Oak Openings or Barrens: Landscape Evaluation on the Michigan Frontier." *Proceedings of the Association of American Geographers* 4 (1972): 84–86.
Pickler, Alice. "A Family of Homesteading Women." In *Daughters of Dakota,* vol. 2, *Stories from the Attic,* edited by Sally Roesch Wagner, 26–36. Yankton SD: Sky Carrier, 1990.
Porter, Joy. *Land and Spirit in Native America.* Santa Barbara CA: Praeger, 2012.
Potyondi, Barry. *In Palliser's Triangle: Living in the Grasslands, 1850–1930.* Saskatoon SK: Purich, 1995.
Pound, Ezra. "Date Line." 1934. In Eliot, *Literary Essays,* 74–87.
———. "Paris Letter." *Dial* 72, no. 2 (1922): 192.
Pound, Roscoe, and Frederic E. Clements. "The Vegetation Regions of the Prairie Province." *Botanical Gazette* 25 (June 1898): 382–94.
Powell, John Wesley. "Report on the Lands of the Arid Region of the United States." In *Arid Lands,* edited by Wallace Stegner, 1–195. 1878. Reprint, Lincoln: University of Nebraska Press, 2004.

Pratt, Linda Ray. *Great Plains Literature.* Lincoln: University of Nebraska Press, 2018.

Prince, Hugh. *Wetlands of the American Midwest: A Historical Geography of Changing Attitudes.* Chicago: University of Chicago Press, 1997.

Proceedings and Debates of the Constitutional Convention Held in the City of Helena, Montana, July 4, 1889, August 17, 1889. Helena MT: State, 1921.

Prucha, Francis Paul. *American Indian Treaties: The History of a Political Anomaly.* Berkeley: University of California Press, 1994.

———. "Appendix B: Ratified Indian Treaties." In Prucha, *American Indian Treaties*, 446–502.

Quantic, Diane Dufva. *The Nature of the Place: A Study of Great Plains Fiction.* Lincoln: University of Nebraska Press, 1995.

Raaen, Aagot. *Grass of the Earth.* 1950. Reprint, St. Paul: Minnesota Historical Society Press, 1994.

———. *Measure of My Days.* Fargo: North Dakota Institute for Regional Studies, 1953.

Reaume, Tom. *Manitoba's Tall Grass Prairie.* Winnipeg: Manitoba Naturalists Society, 1993.

"Recognized Tribes in Minnesota." Office of the Minnesota Secretary of State. Accessed 21 December 2020. www.sos.state.mn.us/about-minnesota/minnesota-government/tribal-government/.

Reese, Lisle. "Introduction: Memoirs of a State Director." In *A South Dakota Guide*, xxi–liv. 1938. Reprint, Pierre: South Dakota Historical Society Press, 2005.

Rexroth, Kenneth. Review of *McAlmon and the Lost Generation*, edited by Robert E. Knoll. *Nation* 95 (1962): 164–65.

Riney-Kehrberg, Pamela. *The Nature of Childhood: An Environmental History of Growing Up in America since 1865.* Lawrence: University Press of Kansas, 2014.

———. *Rooted in Dust: Surviving Drought and Depression in Southwestern Kansas.* Lawrence: University Press of Kansas, 1994.

Robinson, Doane. "The Verendrye Plate." *Proceedings of the Mississippi Valley Historical Association* 7 (1914): 244–53.

Robinson, Doane, Charles E. DeLand, and Orin G. Libby. "Additional Verendrye Material." *Mississippi Valley Historical Review* 3, no. 3 (1916): 368–99.

Robinson, Elwyn B. *History of North Dakota.* Lincoln: University of Nebraska Press, 1966.

Rodaway, Paul. *Sensuous Geographies: Body, Sense and Place.* London: Routledge, 1994.

Rollings-Magnusson, Sandra. *Heavy Burdens on Small Shoulders: The Labour of Pioneer Children on the Canadian Prairies.* Edmonton: University of Alberta Press, 2009.

Ross, Earle D. "A Generation of Prairie Historiography." *Mississippi Valley Historical Review* 33 (December 1946): 391–410.

Rothrock, Edgar P. *A Geology of South Dakota.* Pt. 1, *The Surface.* State Geological Survey. Bulletin 13. Vermillion SD, 1943.

The Royal Charter for Incorporating the Hudson's Bay Company, A.D. 1670. London: Causton and Son, 1816.

Rozum, Molly P. "The Great Plains and the Middle West in 'Middle America': Historiographical Reflections." *Middle West Review* 4, no. 1 (2017): 71–84.

———. "Indelible Grasslands: Place, Memory, and the 'Life Review.'" In *Toward Defining the Prairies: Region, Culture, and History,* edited by Robert Wardhaugh, 119–35. Winnipeg: University of Manitoba Press, 2001.

———. "'It's Weathered Many a Storm': The Enduring Sod House in Northwestern South Dakota." *South Dakota History* 47, no. 4 (2017): 295–368.

———. "'Nature Rarely Establishes Sharp Boundaries': Settler Society Agriculture Adaptation in the Great Plains Northwest." In *The Greater Plains: Rethinking a Region's Environmental Histories,* edited by Brian Frehner and Kathleen A. Brosnan, 253–75. Lincoln: University of Nebraska Press, 2021.

———. "'The Spark That Jumped the Gap': North American's Northern Plains and the Experience of Place." In Higham and Thacker, *One West, Two Myths,* 133–47.

———. "'That Understanding with Nature': Region, Race, and Nation in Women's Stories from the Modern Canadian and American Grasslands West." In *One Step over the Line: Toward a History of Women in the North American Wests,* edited by Elizabeth Jameson and Sheila McManus, 129–64. Edmonton: University of Alberta Press/Athabasca University Press, 2008.

Russell, Ralph C. *The Carlton Trail: The Broad Highway into the Saskatchewan Country from the Red River Settlement, 1840–1880.* Saskatoon SK: Modern, 1955.

———. "Cereal Smut Treatments." BA thesis, College of Agriculture, University of Saskatchewan, 1924.

Russell, Ralph C., Hartford A. Lewis, and Stan Clark. *Smut Control of Barley.* Bulletin 3. Winnipeg: Barley Improvement Institute, [1953?].

Salverson, Laura Goodman. *Confessions of an Immigrant's Daughter.* Toronto: Ryerson, 1939.

———. Foreword to Salverson, *Viking Heart,* xv–xvi.

———. *The Viking Heart.* 1923. Reprint, Toronto: McClelland and Stewart, 1975.

Samek, Hana. *The Blackfoot Confederacy, 1880–1920: A Comparative Study of Canada and U.S. Indian Policy.* Albuquerque: University of New Mexico Press, 1987.

Sandalack, Beverly A. "Prairie Towns: Process and Form." In *Place and Replace: Essays on Western Canada*, edited by Adele Perry, Esyllt W. Jones, and Leah Morton, 271–97. Winnipeg: University of Manitoba Press 2013.

Sandwell, Ruth W. *Canada's Rural Majority: Households, Environments, and Economics, 1870–1940*. Toronto: University of Toronto Press, 2016.

Savage, Candace. *Prairie: A Natural History*. Vancouver: Greystone Books, 2011.

Schama, Simon. *Landscape and Memory*. New York: Knopf, 1995.

"Schedule A, 'Address to Her Majesty the Queen from the Senate and House and Commons of the Dominion of Canada,' Called the 'Rupert's Land and North-Western Territory Order[-in-Council].'" Department of Justice, Government of Canada. Accessed 5 December 2020. www.justice.gc.ca/eng/rp-pr/csj-sjc/constitution/lawreg-loireg/plt32.html.

Schell, Herbert S. *History of Clay County, South Dakota*. Vermillion SD: Clay County Historical Society, 1976.

———. *History of South Dakota*. With John E. Miller. Rev. ed. 1975. Reprint, Pierre: South Dakota State Historical Society Press, 2004.

Schennum, Wayne E. "A Comprehensive Survey for Prairie Remnants in Iowa." *Proceedings of the Ninth North American Prairie Conference* 9 (1984): 163–68.

Schneider, Fred. "'Corn in the Crib Is Like Money in the Bank': George F. Will and the Oscar H. Will and Company, 1917–1955." *North Dakota History* 76, nos. 1–2 (2010): 2–25.

———. "Oscar H. Will: North Dakota's Pioneer Seedman." *North Dakota History* 68, no. 1 (2001): 2–19.

Shantz, Homer L. "The Natural Vegetation of the Great Plains Region." *Annals of the Association of American Geographers* 13, no. 2 (1923): 81–107.

Sharp, Paul F. *Whoop-Up Country*. 1955. Reprint, Helena: Historical Society of Montana, 1960.

Short, John Rennie. *Cartographic Encounters: Indigenous Peoples and the Exploration of the New World*. London: Reaktion Books, 2009.

Shortridge, James R. "The Expectations of Others: Struggles toward a Sense of Place in the Northern Plains." In *Many Wests: Place, Culture, and Regional Identity*, edited by David M. Wrobel and Michael C. Steiner, 114–35. Lawrence: University Press of Kansas, 1997.

———. *The Middle West: Its Meaning in American Culture*. Lawrence: University Press of Kansas, 1989.

Shortt, Adam, and Arthur G. Doughty, eds. *Canada and Its Provinces*. Vol. 20, *The Prairie Provinces*. Toronto: Edinburgh University of Press, 1914.

Shover, John L. *First Majority–Last Minority: The Transforming of Rural Life in America*. Dekalb: Northern Illinois University Press, 1976.

Singal, Daniel Joseph, ed. *Modernist Culture in America*. Belmont CA: Wadsworth, 1991.
———. *The War Within: From Victorian to Modernist Thought in the South, 1919–1945*. Chapel Hill: University of North Carolina Press, 1982.
Smalley, Eugene Virgil. *History of the Northern Pacific Railroad*. New York: Putnam's Sons, 1883.
Smith, G. Hubert. *The Explorations of the La Vérendryes in the Northern Plains, 1738–43*. Lincoln: University of Nebraska Press, 1980.
Smith, Henry Nash. *Virgin Land: The American West as Symbol and Myth*. 1950. Reprint, Cambridge: Harvard University Press, 1978.
Smith, Julie A., and Robert W. Mitchell, eds. *Experiencing Animal Minds: An Anthology of Animal-Human Encounters*. New York: Columbia University Press, 2012.
Smith, Mark M. *Sensing the Past: Seeing, Hearing, Smelling, Tasting, and Touching in History*. Berkeley: University of California Press, 2007.
Smith, Rise L. Introduction to Fargo, *Prairie Chautauqua*, vii–xxiv.
Smith, Sherry L. *Reimagining Indians: Native Americans through Anglo Eyes, 1880–1940*. New York: Oxford University Press, 2000.
Smith Mudiman, Freda. "Interpreter of the Foothills." *Calgary Herald Magazine*, 17 October 1942.
Smoller, Sanford J. *Adrift among Geniuses: Robert McAlmon, Writer and Publisher of the Twenties*. University Park: Pennsylvania State University Press, 1975.
———. Introduction to McAlmon, *Nightinghouls of Paris*, xiv–xv.
Sommer, Linda M. "The Picker Family Papers and the Humphrey Family Papers at the South Dakota State Historical Society." *South Dakota History* 24, no. 2 (1994): 115–34.
"South Dakota Reservations." St. Joseph's Indian School. Accessed 21 December 2020. www.stjo.org/native-american-culture/oceti-sakowin-seven-council-fires/south-dakota-reservations/.
Spitzer, Alan B. "The Historical Problem of Generations." *American Historical Review* 78 (December 1973): 1353–85.
Spry, Irene M., ed. *The Papers of the Palliser Expedition, 1857–1860*. Toronto: Champlain Society, 1968.
Standing Bear, Luther. *My People the Sioux*. 1928. Reprint, Lincoln: University of Nebraska Press, 1975.
Stansell, Christine. *American Moderns: Bohemian New York and the Creation of a New Century*. New York: Holt, 2000.
Stegner, Wallace, ed. *The Arid Lands: John Wesley Powell*. Lincoln: University of Nebraska Press, 2004.
———. *Beyond the Hundredth Meridian: John Wesley Powell and the Second Opening of the West*. 1954. Reprint, New York: Penguin. 1992.

———. *The Big Rock Candy Mountain*. New York: Penguin, 1943.
———. *The Central Northwest*. With the Editors of *Look*. Boston: Houghton Mifflin, 1947.
———. Introduction to Stegner, *Arid Lands*, xiii–xxxi.
———. *Marking the Sparrow's Fall: The Making of the American West*. New York: Holt, 1998.
———. *On a Darkling Plain*. New York: Harcourt, Brace, 1940.
———. "Quiet Earth, Big Sky." *American Heritage* 6, no. 6 (1955): 22–27.
———. *Where the Bluebird Sings to the Lemonade Springs: Living and Writing in the West*. New York: Penguin, 1992.
———. *Wolf Willow: A History, a Story, and a Memory of the Last Plains Frontier*. New York: Penguin, 1962.
Stegner, Wallace, and Page Stegner. *American Places*. 1981. Reprint, New York: Penguin, 2006.
Stegner, Wallace, and Richard W. Etulain. *Conversations with Wallace Stegner on Western History and Literature*. Salt Lake City: University of Utah Press, 1983.
Stewart, Andrew. "The Prairie Farm Rehabilitation Programme." *Canadian Journal of Economics and Political Science* 5, no. 3 (1939): 310–24.
St. Germain, Jill. "Appendix 2: Comparison of Terms in the Numbered Treaties." In St. Germain, *Indian Treaty-Making Policy*, 175–84.
———. "Appendix A: 1868 Treaty with the Sioux." In St. Germain, *Broken Treaties*, 353–63.
———. "Appendix B: 1876 Treaties at Forts Carlton and Pitt." In St. Germain, *Broken Treaties*, 365–72.
———. *Broken Treaties: United States and Canadian Relations with the Lakotas and the Plains Cree, 1868–1885*. Lincoln: University of Nebraska Press, 2009.
———. *Indian Treaty-Making Policy in the United States and Canada, 1867–1877*. Lincoln: University of Nebraska Press, 2001.
Stock, Catherine McNicol. *Main Street in Crisis: The Great Depression and the Old Middle Class on the Northern Plains*. Chapel Hill: University of North Carolina Press, 1992.
Strong-Boag, Veronica, and Michelle Lynn Rosa. "Some Small Legacy of Truth: Introduction." In McClung, *"Clearing in the West,"* 9–22.
Stuckey, Ronald L., and Karen J. Reese, eds. *The Prairie Peninsula: In the "Shadow" of Transeau; Proceedings of the Sixth [1978] North American Prairie Conference*. Columbus: College of Biological Sciences, Ohio State University, 1981.
Sweeney, Kevin Z. *Prelude to the Dust Bowl: Drought in the Nineteenth-Century Southern Plains*. Norman: University of Oklahoma Press, 2016.

Thacker, Robert. *The Great Prairie Fact and Literary Imagination*. Albuquerque: University of New Mexico Press, 1989.
Thomas, Elsie May Hammond, comp. *Our Pioneers*. With Gwen Pollock. Maple Creek SK: Southwest Saskatchewan Old Timer's Association, 1975.
Thompson, Era Bell. *American Daughter*. 1946. Reprint, St. Paul: Minnesota Historical Society Press, 1986.
Thompson, Harry F., ed. *A New South Dakota History*. 2nd ed. Sioux Falls SD: Augustana College Center for Western Studies, 2009.
Thompson, John Herd. *Canada, 1922–1939: Decades of Discord*. With Allen Seager. Toronto: McClelland and Stewart, 1985.
———. Foreword to Evans, *Borderlands*, xi–xiv.
———. *Forging the Prairie West*. Toronto: Oxford University Press, 1998.
———. *The Harvests of War: The Prairie West, 1914–1918*. Toronto: McClelland and Stewart, 1978.
Thompson, John Herd, and Stephen J. Randall. *Canada and the United States: Ambivalent Allies*. Athens: University of Georgia Press, 1994.
Thomson, Georgina. *Crocus and Meadowlark Country: The Story of an Alberta Family*. Edmonton: Institute of Applied Art, 1963.
Tracie, Carl J. *Shaping a World Already Made: Landscape and Poetry of the Canadian Prairies*. Regina SK: University of Regina Press, 2016.
Transeau, Edgar Nelson. "The Prairie Peninsula." *Ecology* 16 (July 1935): 423–37.
———. "The Vanishing Prairies of Ohio." In Stuckey and Reese, *Prairie Peninsula*, 61–62.
Treaty Elders and Tribal Council. *The True Spirit and Original Intent of Treaty 7*. With Walter Hildebrandt, Dorothy First Rider, and Sarah Carter. Montreal: McGill-Queen's University Press, 1996.
"Tribal Nations." Montana Governor's Office of Indian Affairs. Accessed 21 December 2020. www.tribalnations.mt.gov/tribalnations.
"Tribal Nations." North Dakota Indian Affairs. Accessed 21 December 2020. www.indianaffairs.nd.gov/tribal-nations.
Trimble, William. Review of *Corn among the Indians of the Upper Missouri*, by George F. Will and George E. Hyde. *Mississippi Valley Historical Review* 4 (March 1918): 531.
Trupin, Sophie. *Dakota Diaspora: Memoirs of a Jewish Homesteader*. Berkeley CA: Alternative, 1984.
Tuan, Yi-Fu. *Space and Place: The Perspective of Experience*. Minneapolis: University of Minnesota, 1977.
———. *Topophilia: A Study of Environmental Perception, Attitudes, and Values*. Englewood Cliffs NJ: Prentice-Hall, 1974.

U.S. Congress. "An Act for the Removal of the Sissetons, Wahpaton, Medawkanton, and Wahpakoota Bands of Sioux or Dakota Indians, and for the Dispossession of Their Lands in Minnesota and Dakota." *Statutes at Large, 1789–1875.* Vol. 12, *1859–1963.* Library of Congress. Accessed 5 December 2020. www.loc.gov/law/help/statutes-at-large/37th-congress/session-3/c37s3ch119.pdf.

Van Doren, Carl. *Contemporary American Novelists, 1900–1920.* New York: Macmillan, 1922.

———. "Revolt from the Village." *Nation* 113, no. 2936 (1921): 407–12.

Van Nuys, Laura Bower. *The Family Band: From the Missouri to the Black Hills, 1881–1900.* Lincoln: University of Nebraska Press, 1961.

Veracini, Lorenzo. *Settler Colonialism: A Theoretical Overview.* London: Palgrave Macmillan, 2010.

Vidal, Gore. Foreword to McAlmon, *Miss Knight and Others,* ix–xiv.

Voisey, Paul. *High River and the Times: An Alberta Community and Its Weekly Newspaper, 1905–1966.* Edmonton: University of Alberta Press, 2004.

———. *Vulcan: The Making of a Prairie Community.* Toronto: University of Toronto Press, 1988.

Waiser, Bill. *Saskatchewan: A New History.* Calgary: Fifth House, 2005.

Wallace, Sarah Isabel. "Reserves in Saskatchewan." The Canadian Encyclopedia. Historica Canada. 16 January 2019. www.thecanadianencyclopedia.ca/en/article/reserves-in-saskatchewan.

Walster, Harlow Leslie. "George Francis Will, 1884–1955." *North Dakota History* 23, no. 1 (1956): 4–25.

Walters, Thorstina. *Modern Sagas: The Story of the Icelanders in North America.* Fargo: North Dakota Institute for Regional Studies, 1953.

Warkentin, John, ed. *The Kelsey Papers.* Regina SK: Canadian Plains Research Center, 1994.

Warren, Gouverneur K. *Explorations in the Dacota Country in the Year 1855.* Washington DC: Nicholson, 1856.

Weaver, John E. *North American Prairie.* Lincoln NE: Johnsen, 1954.

Weaver, John E., and Frederick W. Albertson. *Grasslands of the Great Plains.* Lincoln NE: Johnsen, 1956.

Weaver John E., and Thomas J. Fitzpatrick. "The Prairie." *Ecological Monographs* 4, no. 2 (1934): 113–295.

Webb, Walter Prescott. "The American West, Perpetual Mirage." *Harper's Magazine,* May 1957, 25–31.

———. *The Great Plains.* 1931. Reprint, Lincoln: University of Nebraska Press, 1981.

Weber, Ronald. *The Midwestern Ascendancy in American Writing.* Bloomington: Indiana University Press, 1992.

West, Elliott. *The Contested Plains: Indians, Goldseekers, and the Rush to Colorado.* Lawrence: University Press of Kansas, 1998.

———. *Growing Up with the Country: Childhood on the Far Western Frontier.* Albuquerque: University of New Mexico Press, 1989.

———. *The Last Indian War: The Nez Perce Story.* New York: Oxford University Press, 2009.

———. "A Longer, Grimmer, but More Interesting Story." In Milner, Limerick, and Rankin, *Trails,* 103–11.

West, Elliott, and Paula Petrik, eds. *Small Worlds: Children and Adolescents in America, 1850–1950s.* Lawrence: University Press of Kansas, 1992.

———. "Walter Prescott Webb and the Search for the West." In Etulain, *Writing Western History,* 167–91.

Wetherell, Donald G. *Wildlife, Land, and People: A Century of Change in Prairie Canada.* Montreal: McGill-Queen's University Press, 2016.

Wetherell, Donald G., and Irene R. A. Kmet. *Town Life: Main Street and the Evolution of Small Town Alberta, 1880–1947.* Edmonton: University of Alberta Press, 1995.

White, Richard. "The Nationalization of Nature." *Journal of American History* 86, no. 3 (1999): 976–86.

———. *The Organic Machine: The Remaking of the Columbia River.* New York: Hill and Wang, 1995.

———. "Trashing the Trails." In Milner, Limerick, and Rankin, *Trails,* 26–39.

Widdis, Randy William. *With Scarcely a Ripple: Anglo-Canadian Migration into the United States and Western Canada, 1880–1920.* Montreal: McGill-Queen's University Press, 1998.

Wildcat, Matthew. "Reserves in Alberta." The Canadian Encyclopedia. Historica Canada. 5 March 2020. www.thecanadianencyclopedia.ca/en/article/reserves-in-alberta.

Will, George F. "Adventures in Preserving and Improving Indian Food Plants." *North and South Dakota Horticulture* 9, no. 7 (1936): 78–84.

———. "Archaeology of the Missouri Valley." *Anthropological Papers of the American Museum of Natural History* 22 (1924): 285–344.

———. "Arikara Ceremonials." *North Dakota Historical Quarterly* 4, no. 4 (1930): 247–65.

———. "An Arikara Sacred Ceremony." *North Dakota History* 16, no. 4 (1949): 265–68.

———. "Big Game in North Dakota." *North and South Dakota Horticulture* 21, no. 4 (1948): 58.

———. "The Bourgeois Village Site." *American Anthropologist* 12, no. 3 (1910): 473–76.

———. "The Burr Oak." *North and South Dakota Horticulture* 22, no. 4 (1949): 58.

———. "A City of Homes Is Built." *North and South Dakota Horticulture* 19, no. 11 (1946): 174.

———. *Corn for the Northwest.* St. Paul MN: Webb, 1930.

———. "Criticism of 'Some Verendrye Enigmas.'" *American Anthropologist* 19, no. 2 (1917): 291–97.

———. "Dr. Melvin Randolph Gilmore." *North Dakota Historical Quarterly* 8, no. 3 (1941): 179–83.

———. "Drouth Resistant Shrubs and Plants." *North and South Dakota Horticulture* 2, no. 12 (1930): 3–4.

———. "Early Summer in Dakota." *North and South Dakota Horticulture* 20, no. 4 (1947): 60.

———. "An Early Summer Walk." *North and South Dakota Horticulture* 21, no. 7 (1948): 106.

———. "Fall Comes to Us." *North and South Dakota Horticulture* 20, no. 11 (1947): 172.

———. "Fruit in North Dakota." *North and South Dakota Horticulture* 21, no. 3 (1948): 42.

———. "The Grandmother Who Never Dies." *Country Guide*, 15 December 1928, 7, 24–26.

———. "Grass." *North and South Dakota Horticulture* 20, no. 3 (1947): 44.

———. "Heart of the World." *North and South Dakota Horticulture* 23, no. 10 (1950): 154.

———. "In Defense of the Cottonwood." *North Dakota Outdoors* 12, no. 3 (1949): 19.

———. "Indian Agriculture at Its Northern Limits in the Great Plains Region of North America." *Annaes do XX Congresso Internacional de Americanistas* 1 (1924): 203–5.

———. "Indian Vegetables." *North and South Dakota Horticulture* 8, no. 8 (1935): 90.

———. "Magical and Sleight of Hand Performances by the Arikara." *North Dakota Historical Quarterly* 3, no. 1 (1928): 50–65.

———. "The Mandan Lodge at Bismarck." *North Dakota Historical Quarterly* 5, no. 1 (1930): 38–48.

———. "Nature's Conservation Methods." *North and South Dakota Horticulture* 21, no. 11 (1948): 154.

———. "A New Feature in the Archeology of the Missouri Valley in North Dakota." *American Anthropologist* 13, no. 4 (1911): 585–88.

———. "North Dakota Sunsets." *North and South Dakota Horticulture* 21, no. 6 (1948): 91.

———. "No-Tongue, a Mandan Tale." *Journal of American Folk-Lore* 26, no. 102 (1913): 331–37.

———. "On the Road to Civilization: A Visit to the Fort Berthold Reservation." *North Dakota History* 15, no. 1 (1948): 4–13.
———. "Our Wealth of Native Shrubs." *North and South Dakota Horticulture* 12, no. 6 (1939): 64.
———. "A Resume of North Dakota Archaeology." *North Dakota Historical Quarterly* 7, nos. 2–3 (1933): 150–61.
———. "Some Hidatsa and Mandan Tales." *Journal of American Folk-Lore* 25, no. 95 (1912): 93–94.
———. "Some Unusual Uses of Plants by Our Indians." *North and South Dakota Horticulture* 10, no. 1 (1937): 4–5, 10.
———. "The Strolls of a Scientist." *North and South Dakota Horticulture* 21, no. 5 (1948): 74.
———. "Tree Ring Studies in North Dakota." *Agricultural Experiment Station Bulletin* 338 (April 1946): 1–24.
———. "Trees of the Dakotas." *North and South Dakota Horticulture* 12, no. 8 (1939): 88, 93.
———. "Trees of the Dakotas." *North and South Dakota Horticulture* 12, no. 9 (1939): 100.
———. "Trees of the Dakotas." *North and South Dakota Horticulture* 12, no. 10 (1939): 112.
———. "Trees of the Dakotas." *North and South Dakota Horticulture* 12, no. 11 (1939): 124, 126.
———. "An Unusual Group of Mounds in North Dakota." *American Anthropologist* 23, no. 2 (1921): 175–79.
———. "The Value of Historical Societies in the Plains States." *North Dakota Historical Quarterly* 11, no. 4 (1944): 272–81.
Will, George F., and George E. Hyde. *Corn among the Indians of the Upper Missouri.* 1917. Reprint, Lincoln: University of Nebraska Press, 1964.
Will, George F., and Herbert J. Spinden. "The Mandans: A Study of Their Culture, Archaeology and Language." *Papers of the Peabody Museum of American Archaeology and Ethnology, Harvard University,* August 1906, 79–219.
Will, George F., and Thad C. Hecker. "Upper Missouri River Valley Aboriginal Culture in North Dakota." *North Dakota Historical Quarterly* 11, nos. 1–2 (1944): 5–126.
Willard, Daniel E. *The Story of the Prairies, or The Landscape Geology of North Dakota.* 1902. Reprint, Chicago: Rand, McNally, 1923.
Williams, Donald L. "Reconstruction of Prairie Peninsula Vegetation and Its Characteristics from Descriptions before 1860." In Stuckey and Reese, *Prairie Peninsula,* 83–86.
Williams, William Carlos. Foreword to Knoll, *Robert McAlmon,* vii–ix.

———. *In the American Grain*. 2nd ed. 1925. Reprint, New York: New Directions, 2009.
———. "Robert McAlmon's Prose." *Transatlantic Review* 1, no. 5 (1924): 361–64.
———. "Robert McAlmon's Prose, II." *Transatlantic Review* 2, no. 2 (1924): 215–17.
Wingerd, Mary Lethert. *North Country: The Making of Minnesota*. Minneapolis: University of Minnesota Press, 2010.
Wishart, David J., ed. *Encyclopedia of the Great Plains*. Lincoln: University of Nebraska Press, 2004.
———. *The Fur Trade of the American West, 1807–1840: A Geographical Synthesis*. 1979. Reprint, Lincoln: University of Nebraska Press, 1992.
———. "Land Laws and Settlement." In Wishart, *Encyclopedia*, 240.
Woodress, James. *Willa Cather: A Literary Life*. Lincoln: University of Nebraska Press, 1987.
Worster, Donald. *Dust Bowl: The Southern Plains in the 1930s*. New York: Oxford University Press, 1979.
———. *Nature's Economy: A History of Ecological Ideas*. 1977. Reprint, Cambridge: Cambridge University Press, 1994.
———. "Summing Up: Grounds for Identity." In *Centennial West: Essays on the Northern Tier States*, edited by William L. Lang, 265–80. Seattle: University of Washington Press, 1991.
Wright, Jim. *Saskatchewan: The History of a Province*. Toronto: McClelland and Stewart, 1955.
Zimon, Kathy E. *Alberta Society of Artists*. Calgary: University of Calgary Press, 2000.

Index

Page numbers in italics refer to illustrations.

acculturation, 21, 141, 214
adolescence, 142, 232–33
adult perspectives, 59–60, 66. *See also* parents
aesthetics, 197–98, 220–21
Agreement of 1877, 22–23, 25
Agricultural Adjustment Act of 1933, 277, 403n50
Agricultural College at Brookings, 155, 165
Agricultural Experiment Station, 276
agriculture: and access to pasture grasslands, 36; and adaptation, 261–79; and animals, 60–61, 68, 73, 87; and aridity, 312–17; and children, 125–29; and climate, 275–76; and commercial grain, 345, 347; and cultural differences, 198–99; and diversification, 273–75; and economics, 355; and grain crops, 162–63; and grain stooks, *127*, 299–300; and haying, 126–29; and Indigenous peoples, 186–88, 201–9, 215; and modern agriculture, 87, 199, 242, 287, 293, 297; and one-one-one lease system, 36; and owner-tenancy business model, 264; and potential of the grasslands, 25–28, 31, 46; and power farming, 262–63, 265–66, 273; and prairie and plains terminology, 327–28; and programs at colleges and universities, 276–77; and ranch-farm systems, 29, 44, 200, 261–62, 332; and R. C. Russell, 287; and regional labels, 302; and rocks, 115–20; and science, 166, 277, 331–32; and sheep production, 269; and shortgrass, 333; and stock farming, 27, 29; and tallgrasses, 345–46; and tame grasses, 125–29; and tractors, 263, 266–67; and transformation of the grasslands, 12–13, 86, 215, 293–300, 343; and transnational traffic, 30; and village tribes, 185. *See also* commercial agriculture

Alberta, Canada: and agricultural adaptation, 264; and the Big Move Out, 236–37; and the cattle industry, 36; and the Fiftieth Jubilee, 193–94; and Fort Macleod, 43, 59, 106–7, 110–12, 118–19, 179, 282–83; immigrants to, 51–52; and the Last Best West, 45–47; and the Northwest, 306; and Palliser's Triangle, 27; and post–World War II, 297–98; reserves in, 49; and rocks, 116; and woods, 111

449

alienation, in literary expression, 223, 237
alienation, land, 99, 131
Allen, John Logan, 304
Allied effort in World War I, 176
allotments, 48–49, 188, 371n69, 390n66
American Daughter (Thompson), 338–41, *339*
American literature, 259
American publishers, 251
American social life, 258
animals: and agriculture, 60–61, 68, 73, 87; cattle, 36, 47, 68, 75–76; and children, 57–58, 62–76, 81, 87–90, 91, 190, 267–68; collage of drawings of, *64*; coyotes, 79–80; and Elsie Hammond, 267–69; and extermination, 76–81; as extinct or endangered, 87–90; as free grazing, 36, 74; and herding, 73–74, 76; historical grasslands, 58, 87–90; horses, 68–71, 75–76, 190, 267–68; and nostalgic remembering, 58–60, 155, 157–58; and senses of place, 60–62, 74–75, 91; and sexuality, 231; and transport, 61–62, 72; as wild game, 81–86; and work, 72–76, 190
Annals of the Association of American Geographers (journal), 319, 325
antisemitism, 52
appropriation, 198, 217, 399n127
archaeological sites, 171, 177, 188
aridity, 312–17, 320, 326, 342, 346–47, 414n90
arid plains, 26–28, 367n25
Arikaras, 3–5, 7, 20, 176, 200, 209, 215, 347, 364n11
Arnold, Matthew, 239

Art Institute of Chicago, 172
Asher, Julia "Lula" Short: and agricultural tasks, 126, 128; and animals, 63, 67–68, 72–74, 76, 88; and experience of grasslands, 102; and extermination efforts, 79; and family migration story, 43; and prairie and plains terminology, 330; and water, 107; and wild game, 81–82, 84; and woods, 114
assimilation, 21, 140–41, 181, 189
Assiniboia, Saskatchewan, 42, 45
Assiniboines, 20, 24
associations of place. *See* senses of place
astronomy courses, 167–68
atmospheres, 59, 95–96, 122–24, 155–59
autobiographical writing, 209–14, 219–20
automobile travel, 90–91, 268

backwoodsmen, 204
badlands, 46
Baker, Oliver E., 326
banquets and settler ceremonies, 54, 81, 85–88, 183, 376nn55–56
Barron, Hal, 296
Battleford, Saskatchewan, 42, 140, 211–13
Battle of Greasy Grass (Battle of Little Big Horn), 22
Bell, Peggy Olson: and animals, 62, 65–66, 71, 75–76; education of, 135; and extermination efforts, 79; and family migration story, 44, 51; and land use, 265; and prairie and plains terminology, 330
Benson, Jackson J., 239, 315

berries, 115, 129–30
Big Foot, 178
Big Move Out, 236–37
The Big Rock Candy Mountain (Stegner), 254, 313–17
Big Sioux River Valley, 29, 38
birds, 66–67, 159–63, 288–92
Bismarck ND, 4, 29, 40–41, 85, 105, 271
bison, 20, 25, 46, 87–89, 113
Black communities, 158–59, 340
Blackfeet (United States), 20, 22, 37, 44, 48, 118, 192
Blackfoot Confederacy (Canada), 20, 24–25, 37–38, 43, 49, 111–12, 118, 120, 184, 191–92, 193–94, 198, 215–16, 296, 404n59
Black Hills, 22–23, 46, 88, 292–93
Blackness, 151–52
Blegen, Theodore, 301–2, 359
Blodgett, Lorin, 367n25
Blood Reserve, 43, 193, 200
Bloods, 179, 200, 215, 353
bohemians, 247
Boone, Daniel, 259
boosterism, 26–28, 225
Bordon, Robert L., 356
Bothwell, Robert, 416n12
Bower, Laura. *See* Van Nuys, Laura Bower
Bowman ND, 52
Boyle, Kay, 251–52, 259
"A Boy's Discovery" (McAlmon), 231–33
Bozeman Trail, 21
bracken fern, 198–99
Brandon, Manitoba, 42
British Columbia, Canada, 23
British North American Act of 1867, 23
Brookings SD, 155, 165

Brown, Annora: and agricultural tasks, 125; and animals, 66–67, 89; and berries, 115; and cultural ownership, 256; education of, 136–37, 171–73; and elastic meanings, 167; and environmental experiences, 352; and experience of grasslands, 95–97, 100–101; and family migration story, 43–44; and geography of home, 141; *Indian Encampment, 184;* and Indigenous peoples, 179–81, 183, 190–201; and isolation, 253; and national affiliation, 353–54; and native grasslands habitats, 329; and the Northwest, 306; and nostalgic remembering, 59; *Old Man's Garden,* 194–201, *196,* 283–86, *285,* 359–61; and painting, 171–73, 191–94; photograph of, *119, 172, 295;* and return to Fort Macleod, 282–83; and rocks, 116, 118–20; and social hybridity (Hixson), 214–17; and soil, 93; and stories, 104, 106–7; and teaching, 166, 281; and transformation of grasslands, 293, 295–96, 299; and transnational dialogue, 359–61; and water, 105, 106–7; and winter, 123; and woods, 110–12
Bryher (Winifred Ellerman), 247
Buffalo Bill Cody, 178–79
built environments, 121–22, 125, 130, 136, 164–65, 299
Burt, Alfred Leroy, 323, 334, 342

Calgary, Canada, 35
Calgary Herald Magazine, 191–92
Calgary Stampede, 192

Index 451

Canada: and agricultural diversification, 273; Americans immigrating to, 51; and competition for settlers, 306–7; and conservation, 278; and drought, 269–70; and Grasslands West, 28; and Indigenous peoples, 20, 23–25; international border of, 35; and land laws, 30–31, 36, 47; and land ownership, 263–64; and the Last Best West, 45–53; and the Middle West, 343; and native grasslands habitats, 328; and the Northwest, 304; and opposition to the United States, 353–57; and ornithological conservation, 289–92; and prairie and plains terminology, 323; and regional identity, 12–13, 349–50; and regional labels, 333–35; and reserves, 37, 47–48; and settlement boom, 35–45; and shared continental experiences, 8–9; and transcontinental status of northern grasslands, 20–21, 23; and transnational origins of settler colonialism, 28–35; and treaties, 20, 24–25, 37–38, 48–49; and World War I, 262

Canada and Its Peoples (series), 334
Canadian Authors Association, 335
Canadian Clubs, 335
Canadian Northern Railway, 46
Canadian Pacific Railway (CPR), 29, 35, 38, 46, 88–89, 307, 368n41
Canadian Pioneer Problems Committee, 278, 334
The Carlton Trail (Russell), 358
Cather, Willa, 226–27, 250, 252, 254, 255, 398n122
cattle, 36, 47, 68, 75–76

CCC (Civilian Conservation Corps), 188
census (1880/1881), 35
census (1890/1891), 44
Census of Population and Agriculture of the Northwest Provinces, 334
Census of Prairie Provinces, Population and Agriculture, 334
The Central Northwest (Stegner), 308, 315, 344
Champlain Society of Toronto, 4
Cheyenne River Reservation, 37, 48
Cheyennes, 23
Chicago and North Western Railway, 46
Chicago pemmican tests, 85
Chicago World's Fair, 70
children: and agriculture, 125–29; and animals, 57–58, 62–76, 81, 87–90, 91, 190, 267–68; and built environments, 136; and experiences of grasslands, 6, 12, 57–58, 61–62, 79, 91, 93–102, 104–31, 141–48, 150; and extermination efforts, 76–81; and geography of home, 141–48; and herding, 73–74, 76; and horses, 68–71, 75–76, 190, 267–68; and Indigenous peoples, 177–85, 194–98; and maturity, 126, 144, 232; and nostalgic remembering, 58–60, 150–58; and parents, 54–56, 59–60, 71, 77–78, 121, 180–82, 244–45; and schools, 134–41; and sexuality, 230–33; and soil, 93–94; and stories, 102–4; and wild game, 81–86; and work, 72–76, 148–50, 190, 267–68, 381n74
Choteau MT, 53
Civilian Conservation Corps (CCC), 188
civilization, 211, 216

452 *Index*

Clapesattle, Helen, 302, 338
class distinctions, 139
Clements, Frederic, 318
climate, 26–27, 288, 323–25, 332
Climatology (Blodgett), 367n25
Collections (South Dakota State Historical Society), 4
colonization, 7, 25, 215–17
Colorado militia massacre, 21
comfort, 103, 151–52, 160–62
commercial agriculture: and agricultural diversification, 273; and agricultural transformation of northern grasslands, 12–13, 215; and animals, 60–61, 68, 73; and droughts, 278; and environmental tension, 284–87; and flora, 329; and Great Plains grasslands, 320; and horses, 68–71; and Indigenous peoples, 206–8, 214; and monocrop agriculture, 273–75, 296; and ranch-farm systems, 261–62; and regional affiliations, 345–47; and rocks, 119–20; and settler colonialism, 23; and tame grasses, 126–29; and transformation of grasslands, 293–94; and water, 109
commercial grain agriculture, 345, 347
Committee of American and Canadian Icelanders, 359
congressional commission on settler-Indigenous conflict, 21
The Conquest of the Great Northwest (Laut), 307
Conrad, Bryce, 259
conservation, 278–93, 312
consumerism, 221, 242, 250, 258–59
Contact (magazine), 258
Contact Publishing Company, 219, 247, 249

Contemporary American Novelists (Van Doren), 221
continental northern grasslands, 4, 6, 9, 305–6
Cook-Lynn, Elizabeth, 221, 362
corn, 175–76, 201–9, 215, 273–76, 297, 314, 387n7, 402n39
Corn among the Indians of the Upper Missouri (Will and Hyde), 175, 201–9, 387n7
Corn for the Northwest (Will), 309–12
corporate agribusiness, 296
Coteau de Missouri, 40
country-born populations, 24, 34
Country Guide (magazine), 360, 362
coyotes, 79–80
CPR (Canadian Pacific Railway), 29, 35, 38, 46, 88–89, 307, 368n41
creative play, 112–14, 118
Crees, 37–38, 120, 189, 211–13
Crocus and Meadowlark Country (Thomson), 358
Crow Creek Reservation, 22
Crowshoe, Joe, 296
culture: and atmosphere, 156–57; and cultural conformity, 239, 242, 279; and cultural exchanges, 3, 8, 185–94; and cultural ownership, 8, 13, 18, 98–99, 137, 237–38, 255–60, 362; and cultural pluralism, 208, 216; and differences, 177, 182, 198–99; of Indigenous nations, 113, 183–85, 201–9; and nationalism, 335; and patterns of cultural expression, 12–13, 125; and prairie and plains terminology, 329; and regions, 302–3, 313, 317, 325, 347–48; of settler-colonial societies, 7–8; and settler-Indigenous connections, 215–16; of small towns, 221–22

Index   453

The Curlew Cried (Parsons), 223–24, 238, 355
Custer, George A., 22
Custer State Park Game Sanctuary, 293
Cypress Hills, Saskatchewan, 36, 43, 46, 147, 189, 293

Dakotas, 19, 21–22, 48, 113, 366n4
Dakota Territorial University, 153
Dakota Territory, 22, 28–29, 33, 35, 37, 38–42, 45, 85, 115, 304–5
Davis, Rosie, 192
Dawes Act of 1887, 48, 188, 206–8
Dawson, George, 27
deculturation, 241, 253
DeLand, Charles, 3–6
Deloria, Philip J., 415n3
Department of Agriculture (Canada), 27
Department of Indian Affairs (Canada), 48–49
Department of the Interior (Canada), 47
depopulation, 166
desert claim law, 264
Desert Land Act of 1877, 36
diffuse area, 141
distant grasslands, 62, 148, 174
diversity in schools, 139–41
Dixon, Roland B., 171
Dixon Business College, 155–56
Dominion Day, 183, 352–53
Dominion Lands Act of 1872, 30–31, 36, 43, 47, 297
Dominion of Canada, 23–24
Doolittle, Hilda, 247
Dorman, Robert L., 399n127
Doughty, Sam, 139
drainage, 292
droughts, 263, 268–72, 276, 278, 289–91, 313

ducks, 162, 288–92
Ducks Unlimited, 291
dust storms, 237, 261, 269–71, 272–73, 279, 283–84, 286, 288, 337, 352

Eagle, Dan, 188
Earl Grey, Saskatchewan, 53
earth and sky, 96–98, 261, 352
Eastend, Saskatchewan, 51, 110, 182, 226, 241
east-west orientation of the Middle West, 336
ecology of northern grasslands, 12–13, 77, 86, 90, 102, 112–13, 176, 215, 283, 323–25. *See also* environment
economics, 22, 25–28, 282, 299, 355
Edmonton Journal, 237
education, 134–41, 150–51, 165–73, 279, 355–56
Eggleston, Wilfrid: and agricultural adaptation, 265–66; and animals, 68; and automobiles, 90; and cultural ownership, 98–99; and detail, 251; and environmental experiences, 352; and experience of grasslands, 101; and extermination efforts, 78; and family migration story, 52; and Hamlin Garland, 227, 255; literature of, 222–25, 236–38, 239, 241–42, 251; and the Middle West, 345; and nostalgic remembering, 60; and parental pioneers, 55; photograph of, 235; and pioneer origin stories, 297–98; and prairie and plains terminology, 330–31; and regional identity, 351; and rocks, 116, 118; and Sinclair Lewis, 228; and teaching, 166;

and transnational dialogue, 358–61; and travel away from home place, 163–65; and water, 105, 106; and West identity, 353; and wild game, 82; and Willa Cather, 255; and winter, 123; and woods, 113; and work, 148
Ellerman, Winifred, 247
Elliott, John H., 365n23
Emmons, David M., 28
engineering, 86, 277
England, 163–64
English tradition, 259
Enlarged Homestead Act, 47
Enoch/Stony Plains Reserve, 49
environment: and bodily retellings, 144; built, 121–22, 125, 130, 136, 164–65, 299; and children, 58–59, 73, 75, 104–31, 150–55; and conservation, 292; and cultural exchanges, 8; disruption of, 77; and environmental tension, 284–87; and experiences with grasslands, 104–29, 150–55, 267, 352; and fires, 102; and immersion, 93–98, 106, 124, 130, 267; and Indigenous peoples, 216, 293; knowledge of, 75, 77, 102, 146–48, 170; and lifeways, 352; and literary tradition, 220; and nostalgic remembering, 150–58; and regional identities, 9–13; and regional labels, 302; and rocks, 115–20; and sensual awareness, 6, 95–98, 129–31, 176, 377n3; and snow, 120–25; and tame grasses, 125–29; and water, 104–9; and woods, 109–15
Etulain, Richard, 239
European immigrants, 51, 141
evening primroses, 284

Ever and Always (Gannon), 89
expropriation of Indigenous land, 8, 36–37, 181, 349–50
extermination efforts, 76–81
extinct or endangered animals, 87–90

Fair Day, 183
family economy, 72–73
family migration stories, 18, 38–45, 51–56, 103, 305
famine years, 198
farm size, 264, 400n8
Faulkton SD, 40, 53, 57, 75, 109, 135, 142, 153–56
Faulkton Times, 40
Federal Land Bank, 264–65
festivals, 183–85
fires, 75, 101–2
First Majority (Shover), 405n63
fish, 83–84
Fite, Gilbert, 329–30
Fitzgerald, F. Scott, 246
flora, 31, 98, 100–101, 107, 145, 153, 169, 194, 195–99, *196*, 284–86, *285*, 293, 328–29, 359–61
folk characters, 103–4
folk floral taxonomies, 100–101
foodways, 84–86, 199, 205
Ford, Ford Maddox, 248–49
foreign corporate investments, 36
Fort Benton MT, 29–30
Fort Berthold Reservation, 4, 37, 48, 175, 185–88, 207, *207*, 369n45
Fort Laramie Treaty of 1851, 20
Fort Laramie Treaty of 1868, 22
Fort Macleod, Alberta, 43, 59, 106–7, 110–12, 118–19, 179, 282–83
Fort Pierre SD, 1–3, 7, 21
Fort Randall NE, 21
Fort Totten ND, 37, 179

Index 455

Fort Walsh, Saskatchewan, 36, 293
forty-ninth parallel, 35, 45–53, 323
Foster, Harriet May "Hattie," 1–8, *2*
Frad, Lulu Pickler: and animals, 68–69; education of, 153–55; and experience of grasslands, 101; and family migration story, 38–40; and horses, 91; and the Northwest, 306; photograph of, *154*; and prairie and plains terminology, 330; and travel away from home places, 153–55
Fradkin, Phillip, 326
free grazing animals, 36, 74
"free homestead" act, 371n68
French colonialism, 2–3, 7
Frenchman River, 107, *108*
freshwater springs, 108–9
Friesen, Gerald, 28–29, 45, 263
frontiers project, 278
fur trade, 20, 30, 178, 304
The Future of the Great Plains (report), 278, 312

The Gambler. *See* Tanner, Gambler
game birds, 159–63, 289–92
Game Convention, 289
Gannon, Clell: and animals, 89; and cultural ownership, 256–57; and detail, 251; *Ever and Always*, 89; and experience of grasslands, 97; and painting, 172; and parental pioneers, 55; photograph of, *203, 257*; "Redmen," 215–16; and regional literary expression, 223; and senses of place, 252–53; and transformation of grasslands, 294; *Village of Corn Growing Indian Tribe in North Dakota*, 202; and West identity, 354
gardens, 269. *See also* modern agriculture

Garland, Hamlin, 226–27, 255
gender roles, 126–27, 204–5, 211–14
General Land Office, 37
generation concept, 10
geographic determinism, 246
geography of home, 141–48, 169–70
geologic topography, 326
George, Henry, 230
Germany, 150
Gimli, Manitoba, 180
Glyndon MN, 41
gold and silver strikes, 29
Gold Creek MT, 85
Goodman, Laura. *See* Salverson, Laura Goodman
Goose River, 34, 106, 111, 150–51
"Gopher Prairie" (Lewis), 228
gophers, 67–68, 77–79
GPC (Great Plains Committee), 278
grain crops, 162–63
grain stooks, *127*, 299–300
Grand Forks ND, 151
"The Grandmother Who Never Dies" (Will), 360
Grand Trunk Pacific Railway, 46
Grant, Ulysses S., 85–86
grasshopper plague, 270
Grasslands North, 325
Grasslands Northwest, 308
Grasslands of the Great Plains (Weaver and Albertson), 318–19
Grasslands West, 23, 28, 50, 220, 227–45, 296, 305, 336
Great American Desert, 26
Great Britain, 3, 23, 36, 289, 335
Great Depression, 269–70, 282–83, 298
Great Disjuncture, 263
Great Falls MT, 53, 240
Great Northern Railway, 35, 46, 307
Great Northern region, 36
Great Northern Reservation, 22

The Great Plains (Parrish), 319
The Great Plains (Webb), 320
Great Plains Agricultural Council, 312
Great Plains Committee (GPC), 278
Great Plains Drought Area Committee, 278
The Great Plains Environment (Webb), *321*
Great Plains literature, 225–26, 237, 254
Great Plains region, 319–28, 334–35, 345, 411n45
Great Reserve. *See* Indian Territory
Great Sand Hills, Saskatchewan, 43
Great Sioux Reservation, 22–23, 37, 48
Greenwich Village, 232–33, 246–47, 398n120
Grinnell, George Bird, 185
Gros Ventre, 22
Group of Seven, 172–73, 335
gumbo, 105
Guthrie, Alfred, 53, 60, 82–83, 190

habitat. *See* native grasslands habitat
Hagen, Norris, 53, 265
Hammond, Bill, 268, 270
Hammond, Elsie May: and agricultural adaptation, 261–63, 266–73; and animals, 88, 267–69; and automobiles, 90; and environmental experiences, 352; and extermination efforts, 77–78; and family migration story, 42–43; and geography of home, 141–48; and Indigenous peoples, 183, 189–91; and the Middle West, 343; and Nature Study course, 281; and the Northwest, 306; and parental pioneers, 54; photograph of, *270;* and prairie and plains terminology, 327, 330, 334; and preserved spaces, 293; and rocks, 116; and social hybridity (Hixson), 214–15; and teaching, 166, 169–70; and transformation of grasslands, 293–94; and water, 109; and wild game, 82–84; and winter, 122. *See also* Thomas, Joe
Hammond, Fred, 165
Hammond, Kay, 146, 166, 169
Hammond, Les, 268–69, *270*
Hammond, Rose, 83
Happyland (McManus), 403n51
Harney, William S., 1, 7
Harney Hill, 1–2
Harrison, Dick, 227, 237, 242, 252, 393n29
Hartley, Marsden, 233
Harvard University, 171
Hatton ND, 133–34
Hay Creek, Saskatchewan, 43
Hayden, Ferdinand V., 26–28
haying, 126–29
HBC (Hudson's Bay Company), 20, 23, 31, 34, 36, 264, 304, 306–7
H.D. (Hilda Doolittle), 247
Helena MT, 133–34
Hemingway, Ernest, 219, 246, 250
herding, 73–74, 76
heroic-male narrative tradition, 234
Hidatsas, 4, 7, 20, 188, 347, 364n11
The High Plains (Eggleston), 224, 236–38, 241, 353, 360
High River, Alberta, 43, 102
Hildebrandt, Walter, 34
Hill, James, 307
Hind, Henry Youle, 26–28
historical grasslands animals, 58, 87–90
historical imagery, 142, 245

Index   457

Hixson, Walter L., 214–17, 391n77
Holding Eagle, James, 185–86, 207, 208, 214
Holmes, Robert, 173
Home Harvest picnic, 81
home places, 141, 150–53, 174
Homestead Act of 1862, 30–31, 40, 47–48, 297
Homestead on the Range (Eggleston), 351, 358
homesteads, 30–31, 40, 44, 47–48, 371n68
Honan, Park, 395n60
horses, 68–71, 75–76, 190, 267–68
Houghton Mifflin Company, 254
Howard, Joseph Kinsey, 330, 345, 360
"How the Prairie Crocus Got Its Fur Coat" (Brown), 195–97
Hoy, Madge Pickler, 53
"HP" brand, 43
Hudson, John, 297
Hudson's Bay Company (HBC), 20, 23, 31, 34, 36, 264, 304, 306–7
human-animal relationships. *See* animals
human body, 94, 97, 121–22, 124, 129–30, 144
Humphrey, Alfred, 126
Humphrey, Alice: and agricultural tasks, 126; and animals, 63–66, 69, 72–75, 155; and experience of grasslands, 100, 101–2; and extermination efforts, 80; and geography of home, 142; and rocks, 115, 117; and travel away from home places, 155; and winter, 122–23
Humphrey, Ira "Hale": and animals, 57–58, 62–63, 68, 73, 75; and collage, *64*; education of, 138, 155–58; and fish, 83; and hunting, 66; and rocks, 117; and water, 108–9; and wild game, 81

Humphrey, Kenneth, 73, 124
Humphrey, Kittie, 124
Humphrey, Nellie, 109, 123–24
hundredth meridian, 313, 317, 323, 325, 329, 332, 411n49
hunting, 66, 81–86, 162, 289–91
Hutton, Gwen, 193
Hyde, George, 175, 185, 188, 201–9, 387n7

Icelandic immigrants, 41–42, 88, 242–45, 264, 352–53
I. G. Baker, 36
imagery, 142, 151–52, 224, 245, 252, 256–58, 353–54
imaginative play, 112–14, 118
immersion, 93–95, 106, 124, 130, 267
immigrants, 28, 34, 35, 41–42, 47, 51, 88, 138–39, 180
import duties, 36
Indian Bureau, 37
Indian Encampment (Brown), *184*, 191
Indian Industrial School, 140
Indian Legend of Autumn Leaves (Brown), 191
"Indian Life" (Storer), 209–14
Indian Reorganization Act of 1934, 390n66
Indian Stanley, 214
Indian Territory, 21–23
indigeneity, 12, 221, 258
Indigenous nations of the northern grasslands, 19–25, 113
Indigenous peoples: and agriculture, 186–88, 201–9, 215; and Annora Brown, 179–81, 183, 190–201; and artifacts, 193; and banquets, 85–88; and children, 177–85, 194–98; and corn, 175–76, 201–9, 215, 273–76, 297; and

cultural exchanges, 185–94; and cultural history, 146–47, 180–83, 188–89, 193, 298–99; diets of, 198–99; displacement of, 18, 31; and education, 140–41; and Edward Pitblado, 349–50; and Effie Laurie Storer, 209–14; and Elsie May Hammond, 183, 189–91; and the environment, 216, 293; and Era Bell Thompson, 181–82; and expropriation of land, 8, 36–37, 181, 349–50; and the famine years, 198; and George F. Will, 177–79, 183, 347; history of, in schools, 137; and horses, 190; and Indigenous children, 111–13, 131, 139–40, 181–82; infantilization of, 180–81; and knowledge, 177, 216; and land rights, 23–25, 131; and Laura Goodman Salverson, 180; and the La Vérendryes, 3–4; and lifeways, 101, 217; and Lillian Miller, 183; and modernists, 258–59; and narrative traditions, 221, 299; and nation-to-nation incidents, 118; and Nature Study course, 279; and oral traditions, 7, 188–89; and place names, 99; and preserved spaces, 293; racist attitudes about, 140–41, 176–77, 180–81, 202–9, 211–13, 216, 349–50; and regional labels, 347–48; and religious values, 200–201; removal of, 12; and reserves and reservations, 22, 37, 48–49; and resistance to colonial interventions, 186; and Robert McAlmon, 258; and rocks, 118–20; and settler-colonial society, 10, 38, 140–41, 175–94, 198–201, 214–17; and social hybridity (Hixson), 214–17; and spirituality, 112; territorial claims of, 20, 221; and Thorstina Jackson Walters, 181; and traditions, 190, 208; and transformation of grasslands, 296; and treaties, 20, 24–25, 37–38, 48–49, 131; and Wallace Stegner, 182; and women, 175, 178, 201, 203–8, 215, 273

industrial agriculture, 284, 294–95, 297, 343, 345

industrialization, 174, 241–42, 299

industrial manufacturing, 86, 343–44

infantilization of Indigenous peoples, 180–81

interactions with Indigenous peoples, 175–94, 209–17

intergenerational memory, 348

international border, 35

international colonialism, 19

In the American Grain (Williams), 259

invasive weeds, 271–72

inviolate bird sanctuaries, 289

involuntary cession, 37

irrigation, 28, 36, 269

Isern, Thomas D., 9, 351

isothermal lines, 27

Jackman, Wilbur S., 169

jack rabbits, 80

Jackson, Thorstina. *See* Walters, Thorstina Jackson

Jayne, William, 305

Johnson, Dorothy, 53, 55, 63–65, 104, 110, 166, 352

Kelsey, Henry, 318

kept objects, 101

Kincer, Joseph B., 410n43

Kingsbury, George, 376n55
Kipling, Rudyard, 356

Lake Agassiz, 31
Lakotas, 19, 21–23, 25, 37, 53, 111, 113, 178
land cessions, 20, 37
land claims, 52–53, 98–99, 176, 263–65, 350
land grants, 24, 47
land laws, 30–31, 36, 47–49, 206–8, 264–65, 277–78, 297–98
Land Regions of the United States (Webb), 322
Lansing, Michael, 340
Last Best West, 45–53
Laughing Joe, 180
Laurentian Shield, 116
Laurier, Wilfrid, 334
Laut, Agnes, 306–7
La Vérendrye, François and Louis-Joseph, 1–8, 363n8
lead plate, 1–8
Lemmon SD, 47, 53
Lethbridge Daily Herald, 222–23
Lethbridge Herald, 164
Lethbridge Sketch Club, 256
Lewis, Sinclair, 221–22, 227–29, 307, 336–37
Lewis Cashatt, Faye, 52, 135, 165
Lipton, Saskatchewan, 52
Lismer, Arthur, 173
literary tradition: and alienation, 223, 237; and Grasslands West stories, 220, 227–45; and Great Plains literature, 225–26, 254; and imagery, 151–52, 224, 252, 256–58; and Indigenous narrative traditions, 221, 299; and modern literature, 226–45, 258–59; and narrative transfer, 392n5; and new literature of place, 220–21; and place identity, 245–55; and railroads, 222–26; and senses of place, 255–58; and small-town culture, 221–26
locality, 133–34, 138, 141–53
Long, Steven, 26
Look (magazine), 308, 343–44
Lorusso, Edward, 249
Lower Brulé Reservation, 37, 48
Loy, Mina, 233
lumber houses, 122

Mackintosh, William, 305–6, 320–23, 326–27
Macoun, John, 27–28
Madison SD, 52–53
Main Street (Lewis), 221–22, 227–28, 307, 336–37
Main Travelled Roads (Garland), 226
Malin, James, 318–20, 323–25, 327
Mandan agricultural village site, *170*
Mandan ND, 159, 340
Mandans, 4, 7, 20, 175–76, 185–89, 202, 205, 208–9, 215–16, 347, 364n11
Manitoba, Canada, 24, 29, 30–31, 34, 35, 42, 45, 49, 53, 100, 180, 264, 270, 342–43
Manitoba Act of 1870, 24
Manitoba Game and Fish Association, 291
Maple Creek, Saskatchewan, 36, 43, 88, 183, 268
Maple Creek Rural Municipality, 272
"Map of the Prairie Region" (Mackintosh), 324
Marbut, Curtis F., 410n43
Margry, Pierre, 363n8
masculinity, 231–34
massacre at Wounded Knee Creek, 178–79
Mathew Arnold (Honan), 395n60

460 *Index*

maturity, 126, 144, 232
Mayville ND, 150–51, 167
McAlmon, Robert: and animals, 66; and atmosphere, 156; autobiographical writing of, 219–20; and contact concept, 258; and drought, 271; and environmental experiences, 352; and Ernest Hemingway, 219, 246, 250; and extermination efforts, 80–81; and family migration story, 51–53; and Indigenous peoples, 258; and the literary establishment, 220–21, 247, 253–54; literature of, 225, 227–35, 245–54; and the Middle West, 336–37, 344; and the Northwest, 307; photograph of, 229, 248; and prairie and plains terminology, 330; and Sinclair Lewis, 228–29; and stories, 104; and transnational dialogue, 358; *Village*, 219; and West identity, 353; and winter, 122–23, 125; and woods, 110
McCarthy, Joe, 343
McManus, Curtis, 277, 403n51
Measure of My Days (Raaen), 359
mechanization, 263, 297
Medawkantons, 19, 21
memoirs, 59
memory. *See* nostalgic remembering
Menissawok Antelope National Park, 293
meridian lines, 313–17
Merry Horse, Eddie, 192, 214
Métis peoples, 24, 34, 37–38, 42, 141, 181–82, 189–90
Middleton, Samuel Henry, 193
Middle West region, 335–46, 413n72, 414n89
migration stories, 18, 38–45, 51–56
Migratory Bird Act, 289

military forts, 21
Miller, J. R., 25, 367n21
Miller, Lillian: and agricultural adaptation, 264–65; and agricultural tasks, 128; and animals, 66, 88; education of, 137, 140–41; and experience of grasslands, 98; and family migration story, 44; and geography of home, 141; and Indigenous peoples, 183; and national affiliation, 352; and prairie and plains terminology, 330; and racial superiority, 140–41; and rocks, 116–17; and stories, 102; and water, 109
Milwaukee Railway, 46, 53
Minneapolis–Saint Paul MN, 158–59, 316, 336, 344
Minnesota, 28–29, 301–2, 304–5
Mississippi Valley Historical Association, 3
Missouri River, 22, 29, 46, 86, 106, 155, 175, 185, 188, 347
Mitchell, "Bill" W. O., 361
Mitchell SD, 338
modern agriculture, 87, 199, 242, 287, 293, 297
modern literature, 246–47, 258–59
moderns, 233
Modern Sagas (Walters), 55–56, 302, 344–45, 359
monocrop agriculture, 273–75, 296
Monroe, James, 318
Montana, 22, 29, 36, 37, 44–45, 47, 52, 264, 270–71, 414n88
Montana Territory, 35, 45
Montréal Northwest Company, 304
Moore, Marianne, 233
More Game Birds in America, 291
Morrison, Chester, 344
Morton, William L., 270, 342–43
Muscowpetungs, 49

Index   461

mythic West, 73–74, 176, 225–26, 305, 350, 353–54

naming landmarks, 99
Nanton, Alberta, 51
narrative transfer, 386n4, 387n17, 392n5, 398n114
Nation (magazine), 4, 221
national identity, 20, 25, 245, 354
nationalism, 335, 351–56
national literature, 245
National Policy of Canada, 23, 35
national sovereignty, 25, 177, 216
nation-to-nation incidents, 118
native grasslands habitat, 77–78, 224–25, 262, 279, 284–87, 292–98, 328–32, 345–46, 362
natural elements, 142, 317
Nature Study course, 169–70, 262, 279–81, 294
Neatby, Alan, 276
Neatby, Hilda, 165–66
Neatby, Kate. *See* Nicoll, Kate Neatby
Neatby, Kenneth, 276–77
Neatby, Leslie: and agricultural programs, 276; and agricultural tasks, 126; education of, 135–36, 165, 355–56; and parental pioneers, 53; photograph of, *117*; and rocks, 116–17; and transnational dialogue, 358–59, 361; and winter, 124
Neatby, Walter, 53, 116–17, *117*, 265, 276
Nebraska, 19, 21, 26–27, 250, 254, 336, 346
Nelson, Paula, 278, 331–32
Neth, Mary, 296
Newberry Library, 338
newcomers, 10, 259
New Deal, 278, 312

New France, 3
New Northwest region, 304–5
New York NY, 246–47, 258
New York Times, 254
New York Zoological Park, 88
Nichols, Roger L., 20
Nicoll, Kate Neatby, 53, 78, 96, 101, 103, 124, 139, 265, 299–300
nighttime, 62, 70, 79, 96–97, 101, 152, 226
nineteenth-century literary forms, 259
ninety-eighth meridian, 315–17, 320, 326, 329, 332, 409n32
ninety-ninth meridian, 40, 316
Nixon River, 40
nonagricultural employment sectors, 166
non–home places, 135
Nonpartisan League, 406n88
Norbeck, George, 18, 56
Norbeck, Peter: and agricultural engineering, 277; and animals, 73, 88; and conservation, 289–93; and drought, 271; education of, 136, 138; and grasslands stories, 102; and the Middle West, 336; and the Northwest, 306; and parental pioneers, 56; photograph of, *290*; and pioneer origin stories, 17–18, 33; and prairie and plains terminology, 329–30; and transnational dialogue, 359
Nordström, Ludvig, 219
Normal School, 150, 167–69
North American Prairie (Weaver), 319
North Dakota: and agricultural adaptation, 263–64; archaeological sites in, 188; and ecology, 112–13; and extermination efforts, 77; and extinct or endangered animals, 88; and the Great

462 *Index*

Depression, 270; immigration from, 51; and involuntary cession of Indigenous territories, 37; and literary establishment, 255; and the Middle West, 342, 344; and population growth, 46; and precipitation, 275; and railroads, 46–47; and rocks, 119; and settlement boom, 34, 44–45; and tame grasses, 125; and water, 106–7; and woods, 111

North Dakota Agricultural College, 276

North Dakota History (journal), 208, 362

North Dakota Institute for Regional Studies, 302, 359

North Dakota Pioneer Agriculturalist (catalog inset), 203

"A North Dakota Surveying Party" (McAlmon), 234

northern grasslands: and aesthetic expression, 220–21; and agricultural adaptation, 261–62; agricultural potential of, 25–28, 31, 46; agricultural transformation of, 12–13, 86, 215, 293, 343; and animals, 62–76, 87–90; and Annora Brown's *Old Man's Garden*, 194–201, 283–86; and arrival of settler society, 7; and childhood experiences, 6, 12, 57–59, 61–62, 73, 75, 79, 91, 93–102, 104–31, 141–48; climate of, 26–27; and climate patterns, 166; and colonization, 7; commercial transformation of, 118; and conservation, 278–93, 312; and cultural boundaries, 315; and cultural development, 258; and cultural ownership, 8, 12–13, 18, 98–99, 113, 137, 237–38, 255–60, 362; and deculturation, 241; and drought, 263; ecology of, 12–13, 77, 86, 90, 102, 112–13, 176, 215, 283, 323–25; economics of, 22, 25–28, 282, 299, 355; and education, 134–41, 150–51, 165–73, 279, 355–56; and Effie Laurie Storer's "Indian Life," 209–14; and extermination efforts, 76–81; and failure, 403n51; and fires, 75, 101–2; geologic assessments of, 26–27; geopolitical importance of, 19–25; and George Will's *Corn among the Indians*, 201–9, 387n7; and grasslands plants, 194–200; and the Great Plains, 319–28, 334–35; and homesteads, 30–31, 40, 47–48, 371n68; and Indigenous corn, 175–76; and Indigenous cultures, 175–77; Indigenous nations of, 19–25, 113; and land laws, 30–31, 36, 47–49, 206–8, 264–65, 277–78, 297–98; and La Vérendrye routes, 5; literary tradition of, 221–60, 392n5, 393n26; and the Middle West, 335–46; and New Northwest region, 304–5; and Northern Great Plains, 9, 308–13, 335, 346, 354, 357, 362; and Northwest region, 6, 304–8, 335, 362; and nostalgic remembering, 58–60, 150–58; and notional entity, 365n23; and ornithological conservation, 288–92; and painting, 171–73, 191–94; and place identity through literature, 245–55; and prairie and plains terminology, 317–28; and Prairie Provinces region, 9, 306, 318, 332–35, 343, 346, 354, 356–57, 362, 416n15; privitization of, 30; and regional identity, 6,

northern grasslands (*cont.*)
9–13, 56, 136, 164, 245, 303, 335, 338, 348, 349–51, 357; and regionalism, 11–13; and regional knowledge, 173–74; and regional labels, 6, 9–10, 302–13, 319, 326–27, 332–36, 344–48, 354–55, 362; and regional space, 148, 153; and reserves and reservations, 37, 47–49; and rocks, 115–20; and settlement boom, 35–45, *39*, 52; and settler-society culture, 163; and snow, 120–25; and social hybridity (Hixson), 214–17; and stories, 102–4; and tame grasses, 125–29; and taste, 81–87, 115, 162–63; as transnational, 28–35; and transnational dialogue, 357–62; and transportation network, 72; and uplands, 46; and water, 104–9; and wetlands, 288–89; and wild game, 81–86; and winter, 120–25; and woods, 109–15. *See also* environment
Northern Great Plains region, 9, 308–13, 335, 346, 354, 357, 362
Northern Pacific Railway, 35, 37, 46, 85–86, 88
north-south settlement, 29–33
Northwestern Immigration Association convention, 305
Northwestern Territory, 20
North-West Mounted Police, 30, 36, 212–13, 293, 350, 353, 354
Northwest Ordinance of 1787, 304–5
Northwest Passage, 2
Northwest Rebellion of 1885, 37–38, 212–13
Northwest region, 6, 304–8, 335, 362, 364n15, 408n12, 409n31
North-West Territories, 24, 30–31, 35, 42, 45, 211, 304–8, 333–34

Norwegian settlements, 33–34, 391n80
Nor'Wester (newspaper), 34, 306
nostalgic remembering, 58–60, 143–44, 150–58
notional entity, 365n23
Numbered Treaties, 24–25, 37, 42–43, 49

Oak Grove High School, 151
Ojibwes, 20, 24, 33, 37, 113, 131, 369n45, 381n83
Oklahoma, 22
Oldman River, 43, 111, 179
Old Man's Garden (Brown), 194–201, *196*, 283–86, *285*, 359–61
Old Timers' Association of Maple Creek, 293
Old Timer's Banquet, 54, 88
Olseth, Olaf, 52, 55
Olson, Peggy. *See* Bell, Peggy Olson
On a Darkling Plain (Stegner), 238–42, 252, 361
One of Ours (Cather), 227
one-one-one lease system, 36
Ontarians, 24, 305
Ontario College of Art, 171–73
oral traditions, 7, 188–89, 297
O'Reilly, George, 2
ornithological conservation, 288–92
Oscar H. Will and Company, 114–15, 171, 175–76, 202–3, 296, 308–9, *311*, 409n31
Ostler, Jeffrey, 25
Ottoson, Howard, 332
outdoor spaces, 142
outmigration, 264
Overland Trail, 21, 28
owner-tenancy business model, 264
Oxford University, 162

painting, 171–73, 191–94

Palliser, John, 26–27, 87, 323, 327, 332, 342, 376n57
Palliser's Triangle, 26–27, 367n25
parents, 54–56, 59–60, 71, 77–78, 121, 180–82, 244–45
Pargellis, Stanley, 338–40
Parkman, Francis, 5, 363n8
Parrish, Randall, 319–20, 326–27, 410n42
Parsons, Nell Wilson: and agricultural tasks, 126; and animals, 75, 88; and economics, 355–56; and experience of grasslands, 94, 96–98, 99–100; and extermination efforts, 78; and family migration story, 51; and geography of home, 141–42; literature of, 223–25, 227, 238, 239, 242, 253; and parental pioneers, 55; and rocks, 116; and teaching, 166; and water, 109; and wild game, 82; and winter, 123; and woods, 110
Pasquah, 49
Passpasschase Reserve, 49
pastures, 36
Paulson, Holgar D. "Happy," 344
Pembina ND, 29, 41, 88, 181
perception transfer, 386n6
PFRA (Prairie Farm Rehabilitation Act), 278, 334, 403n50
Pickler, Dale, 53
Pickler, Lulu. See Frad, Lulu Pickler
Piegan Reserve, 43
Piegans, 49, 179, 191–92, 215
Pike, Zebulon, 25–26
Pine Ridge Reservation, 37, 48
pioneer origin stories, 12–13, 17–18, 54–56, 220, 254, 260, 297–98, 305, 354
Pitblado, Edward: and hunting, 83; and Indigenous peoples, 349–50; and the Northwest, 306; and ornithological conservation, 288–92; and parental pioneers, 53; photograph of, *160*; and railroads, 222–23; and regional game birds, 159–63; West identity of, 353; and World War I, 159–63
Plains Crees, 20, 42, 182
plant names, 100–101. *See also* flora
plant pathology, 277
Plants of Saskatchewan (Russell), 286
population, 28–29, 35–46, 356–57, 416n15
Populism, 247
Post-adolescence (McAlmon), 233–34
post–World War II, 295–99, 345
potatoes, 198
Potts, Jerry, 179
Pound, Ezra, 219, 251
Pound, Roscoe, 27–28, 318
poverty, 139
Powell, John Wesley, 28, 315–16, 320, 325–26, 331–32, 360, 411n49
power farming, 262–63, 265–66, 273
prairie and plains terminology, 317–31, 334
prairie anemone, 195–97, *196*
Prairie Chicken Dance (Brown), 193–94
prairie chickens, 161–62
prairie-dog villages, 145
Prairie Farm Assistance Act, 272, 403n50
Prairie Farm Rehabilitation Act (PFRA), 278, 334, 403n50
Prairie Farm Rehabilitation Administration, 277
Prairie Park Belt subregion, 323
Prairie Plains, 320–27, 345
"Prairie Plains" (Webb), 323

Prairie Provinces, 9, 306, 318, 332–35, 343, 346, 354, 356–57, 362, 416n15
Prairie Settlement (Mackintosh), 323
Prairie Winnows (Nelson), 402n39
prayer, 200
precipitation, 31, 46, 312–15, 320, 327, 329, 347, 410n43, 411n49
Preemption Act of 1841, 30
prejudices, 182
preservation, 292–93
preserved spaces, 215, 279–93
primitivism, 208
privatizing grasslands, 30
Proceedings (Mississippi Valley Historical Association), 3
pronghorn antelope, 88–89, 293
protectionist tariffs, 35–36, 355
public declarations of residency, 40
publishers, 251, 253–55
Purchased Homestead Act of 1908, 47
Putnam, Frederic, 171

Quantic, Diane, 225, 229, 244, 251, 252, 254, 393n26
"The Queen's Printer" (Storer), 17

Raaen, Aagot: and agricultural tasks, 125; and animals, 67; education of, 136, 138–39, 150–51; and experience of grasslands, 96–97, 99, 129–30; and geography of home, 142, 144–45; and the Middle West, 345; and Nature Study course, 281; and nostalgic remembering, 150–52; photograph of, *168*, *280*; and pioneer origin stories, 33–34; and prairie and plains terminology, 330; and soil, 93; and stories, 103; and teaching, 165–69; and train travel, 134; and transnational dialogue, 359; and travel away from home places, 150–53; and water, 106–7; and winter, 121, 122; and woods, 111, 112–15; and work, 148–51
Raaen, Kjersti: and animals, 63, 67; education of, 136, 139; and experience of grasslands, 96–97, 99; and nostalgic remembering, 158; photograph of, *149*; and train travel, 133–34; and woods, 111, 112–15; and work, 148–50
Raaen, Tosten, 124, 150, 166
race, 140–41, 176–77, 180–81, 202–9, 211–13, 216, 244, 340, 349–50, 354
railroads, 29, 35, 46–47, 86, 133–34, 220, 222–26
ranch-farm systems, 29, 44, 200, 261–62, 332
Rapid City SD, 35
Red Deer, Alberta, 93
Red River, 29, 31–33, 106
Red River Colony, 24, 34
Red River Resistance of 1869–70, 34, 37, 209
Red River Valley, 33–34, 38, 41, 113, 145
Regina Normal School, 169–70, 281
regional affiliations, 332, 337–38, 345–47
regional boundaries, 165
regional cultural geography, 137–38, 313–17
regional identities, 6, 9–13
regionalization, 317–28
regional labels, 6, 9–10, 302–13, 319, 326–27, 332–36, 344–48, 354–55, 362
regional language, 223, 313–17, 337

regional narratives. *See* family migration stories
regional school consolidation, 166
regional weather patterns, 271
regional writing grants, 301–2, 337–41
Reid, Russell, *187, 203*
religious values, 200–201
"Report on the Lands of the Arid Region of the United States" (Powell), 315, 325, 332
reserves and reservations: and belonging, 293; Blackfeet Reservation, 48; Blood Reserve, 43, 193, 200; Cheyenne River Reservation, 37, 48; Crow Creek Reservation, 22; and the Dawes Act of 1887, 206–8; and education, 139–41; Enoch/Stony Plains Reserve, 49; Fort Berthold Reservation, 4, 37, 48, 175, 185–86, 207; Great Northern Reservation, 22; Great Sioux Reservation, 22–23, 48; and homestead laws, 47–48; and Indigenous lifeways, 101; Lower Brulé Reservation, 37, 48; and national sovereignty, 177; and nation-to-nation incidents, 118; Piegan Reserve, 43; Pine Ridge Reservation, 37, 48; Rosebud Reservation, 37, 48, 52; and segregation, 216; and settler-colonial presence, 37–38; Standing Rock Reservation, 37, 48
revision, 247
"Revolt from the Village" (Van Doren), 221
Riel, Louis, 24, 34, 212
River Crows, 22
rivers, 106–7
river trees, 144–45
Robinson, Doane, 3, 5

Robinson, Elwyn, 88
Rockefeller Foundation, 301
rocks, 115–25
Rocky Mountains, 38, 104–5, 114, 319
Rodaway, Paul, 377n3
rodents, 76–81
Rollings-Magnusson, Sandra, 76
Romance of the Prairie Provinces (Burt), 334
Roosevelt, Theodore, 88
Rosebud Reservation, 37, 48, 52
Rough-Surface, Abe, 188
Rowell-Sirois Commission on Dominion-Provincial Relations, 298
Running Horse, Priscilla, 182
Rupert's Land, 23
Rural Credits loan program, 263
rural culture, 231, 242
rural teaching, 166–69, 279–82
Russell, Ralph Clifford "R.C.," 51–52, 147, 166, 277, 286–87, 358, 361

Saint Paul MN, 29–30, 336
Salverson, Laura Goodman: and animals, 61; and cultural ownership, 256; education of, 138–39; and experience of grasslands, 100; and family migration story, 41–42; and Indigenous peoples, 180; and literary establishment, 254–55; literature of, 223–24, 227, 242–45; and parental pioneers, 55; photograph of, *243*; and prairie and plains terminology, 330; and stories, 103; and transnational dialogue, 358; and water, 105, 106; and work, 150; and the Writer's Foundation, 417n20

Index 467

Sand Creek, 21
Saskatchewan, Canada: and agricultural adaptation, 263–64, 267–73; and drought, 270, 272; and homestead laws, 47; immigrants to, 51; and the Middle West, 343; and the Neatby family, 265; and non-evacuation, 403n51; and the Northwest Rebellion, 37–38; and the North-West Territories, 306; and Numbered Treaties, 49; and Palliser's Triangle, 26–27; and the settlement boom, 45
Saskatchewan Herald, 17, 212
Saskatchewan History (journal), 360
Saturday Evening Post, 200
Scandinavian immigrants, 33, 234, 250, 307
Scattered Corn, 186–88, *187*, 202, 204, 206, 207
Schneider, Fred, 387n7
schools, 134–41
Scottish colony, 29
Scribner's, 246
Seattle WA, 88
segregation, 216
Selkirk, Manitoba, 100
senses of place: and agricultural transformation, 293; and animals, 60–62, 74–75, 91; and aridity, 317; and childhood experiences of grasslands, 6, 12, 57–58, 61–62, 79, 91, 93–102, 104–31, 141–48; and commercial agriculture, 288; and cultural ownership, 8, 13, 98–99, 113, 255–60, 362; and culture of the grasslands, 162–63; and education, 134–41; and food culture, 84–85; and geography of home, 141–48; and Grasslands West stories, 220, 227–45; and Hattie Foster's story, 4–6; and home places, 141, 150–53, 174; and immersion, 93–95, 106, 124, 130, 267; and literature, 220–21, 252–53; and locality, 133–34, 138, 141–53; and naming landmarks, 99; and native grasslands habitats, 332–35; and prairie and plains terminology, 329–30; and regional identities, 9–13, 56, 348; and regional sensibilities, 134; and reserves and reservations, 49; and rocks, 115–20; and sensual awareness, 6, 95–98, 129–31, 176, 377n3; and snow, 120–25; and stories, 102–4, 107; and taste, 81–87, 115, 162–63; and transnational dialogue, 357–62; and water, 104–9; and wild-tame grasslands, 291–92; and winter, 120–25; and woods, 109–15
sensual awareness, 6, 95–98, 129–31, 176, 377n3
sentimental comedy, 237
Settler Colonialism (Veracini), 364n17; and narrative transfer, 386n4, 387n17, 392n5, 398n114; and perception transfer, 386n6
settler-colonial societies: and aesthetic expression, 220–21; and agriculture, 25–28, 31, 46, 261–79; and the allotment process, 48; and animals, 62–76, 87–90; arrival of, 7; and banquets, 54, 81, 85–88, 183, 376nn55–56; and Canada, 23; and childhood experiences of grasslands, 6, 12, 57–58, 61–62, 79, 91, 93–102, 104–31, 141–48; and claim to land, 176; and climate, 325; and commercial agriculture, 12–13, 288; and conservation, 278–93, 312; and cultural crosscurrents, 178–85;

and cultural development, 258; and cultural exchanges, 185–94; and cultural geography, 313–17; and cultural norms, 112; and cultural ownership, 8, 12–13, 18, 98–99, 113, 137, 237–38, 255–60, 362; and culture, 162–63; and denial, 391n77; and depictions of Indigenous peoples, 193–94; and education, 134–41, 150–51, 165–73, 279, 355–56; and environmental experiences with grasslands, 104–29, 150–55, 267, 352; and environmental knowledge, 75, 77, 102, 146–48, 170; and extermination efforts, 76–81; and family migration stories, 18, 38–45, 51–56, 103; first generations of, 10–12; and food culture, 84–85; and generational divergence in understanding, 202; and geography of home, 141–48; and Grasslands West stories, 220, 227–45; and historical grasslands animals, 58, 87–90; and hunting, 66, 81–86, 162, 289–91; and identity, 176; and immigrants, 180; and Indigenous conflicts, 21, 137, 198–201; and Indigenous corn, 175–76; and Indigenous nations, 19–25, 113; and Indigenous peoples, 20, 36–38, 52, 111, 175–94, 209–17; and Indigenous women, 205–8; and the Last Best West, 45–53; and the Middle West, 335–47; and modern agriculture, 199; and the mythic West, 225–26; and nationalism, 351–56; and native grasslands habitats, 328–32; and north-south settlement, 29–30; and the Northwest, 306; and nostalgic remembering, 58–60, 150–58; and parents, 54–56, 59–60, 71, 77–78, 121, 180–82, 244–45; and pioneer origin stories, 12–13, 54–56, 220, 254, 260, 297–98, 305, 354; and prairie and plains terminology, 317–18, 330; and race, 140–41, 176–77, 180–81, 211–13, 216, 244, 340, 349–50, 354; and railroads, 86; and regional identity, 6, 9–13, 56, 136, 164, 245, 303, 335, 338, 349–51, 357; and regionalism, 11–13; and regional labels, 6, 9–10, 302–13, 319, 326–27, 332–36, 344–48, 354–55, 362; and rocks, 115–20; and schools, 134–41; and settlement boom, 35–45, 39, 52; and singfests, 104; and snow, 120–25; and social hybridity (Hixson), 214–17, 391n77; and stories, 102–4; and storytelling, 58; and teaching, 166–69, 279–82; and transfers, 386n4, 386n6, 387n17, 392n5, 398n114; and transformation of grasslands, 293–300; and the transnational northern grasslands, 28–35; and travel, 28–29, 90–91, 133–35, 145–55, 158–59, 163–65, 268; and water, 104–9; and wealth, 230; and winter, 120–25; and woods, 109–15; and work, 148–50

sexuality, 230–34
sheep production, 269
Shepard, R. Bruce, 9
shooting tradition, 81–84, 162
Short, Julia "Lula." *See* Asher, Julia "Lula" Short
shortgrass, 333
Shortridge, James, 336, 357
Shover, John L., 405n63
silverweed, 198, 284

singfests, 104
Sioux City IA, 29
Sioux nations, 19, 33, 179
Sissetons, 19, 21
Sitting Bull, 85–86, 178–79
skeleton weed, 284–86, *285*
Skyscrapers Hide the Heavens (Miller), 367n21
small family farms, 297
Smith, Donald, 307
Smith, Mark, 94
Smoller, Sanford, 245, 247, 398n121
snow, 120–25
snowmelt, 105–6
social and moral values, 195–97, 221
social hybridity (Hixson), 214–17, 391n77
soil, 31–33, 93–94, 278, 312, 323–25
Solitary Hunter (Palliser), 87, 376n57
Son of a Star, 177
South Dakota: and agricultural adaptation, 263–64; and archaeological sites, 188; and the Crow Creek Reservation, 22; and drought, 270–71; and homesteaders, 52, 371n68; and Last Best West land taking, 53; and literary establishment, 254–55; and population growth, 46; and railroads, 47; and settlement boom, 44
southern grasslands, 22, 26–27, 121, 318
species control, 76–81
Spirit Mound, 33
sporting narratives, 115
Squaces, 212, 214
stagecoach travel, 29
stampedes, 183
Standing Rock Reservation, 37, 48
Stanfield, Herbert, *172*
Stansell, Christine, 233, 247

State Historical Society of North Dakota, 4, 7–8, 185
steamboat service, 29
Stefansson, Vilhjalmur, 85, 344–45, 358–59
Stegner, Wallace: and agricultural tasks, 127–28; and animals, 62, 67, 70–71; and autobiographical writing, 409n35; and berries, 115; *The Big Rock Candy Mountain*, 313–17; and climate, 325; and detail, 251; education of, 137; and environmental experiences, 352; and experience of grasslands, 96–98, 99–100; and extermination efforts, 77–78, 81; and family migration story, 51; and geography of home, 142; and geologic topography, 326; and Indigenous peoples, 182; literature of, 226, 227, 238–42, 251, 252–56, 313–17; and the Middle West, 344, 346; and Nature Study course, 279; and the Northwest, 307–8; photograph of, *108*, *240*; and preserved spaces, 293; and sexuality, 232; and the sublime, 283; and transformation of grasslands, 294–95; and transnational dialogue, 360–61; and water, 104, 107; and wild game, 82, 83–84; and winter, 124; and woods, 110
Stein, Gertrude, 219
Stevens, David, 301
St. Germain, Jill, 21, 25, 48
Stock, Catherine McNicol, 296
stock farming, 27, 29
Stock Raising Homestead Act, 371n68
Storer, Effie Laurie: and animals, 61; autobiographical writing of,

209–14; education of, 135, 140; and family migration story, 42; and geography of home, 142; "Indian Life," 209–14; and Indigenous peoples, 209–14; and the Northwest, 306; and parental pioneers, 55–56; photograph of, *210*; and pioneer origin stories, 17, 34; and race, 216; and wild game, 84–85
Stories of Canadian Indians (Brown), 194
storytelling, 58, 102–4, 107
Strange Empire (Howard), 345
sublime, 283
Sun Dance, 200
sweet grass, 198
Sweetgrass (chief), 24
swimming, 109

tallgrasses, 328, 333, 345–46
tame grasses, 125–29
Tanner, Gambler, 131
tariffs, 35–36, 355
taste, 81–87, 115, 162–63
teaching experiences, 166–69, 279–82
teepee symbolism, 192
territorial claims by Indigenous peoples, 20, 221
Thacker, Robert, 220, 227, 241, 252, 254, 393n26
Thirst Dance, 212–13
"This Land Is Mine" (Gannon), 256
Thomas, Elsie May Hammond. *See* Hammond, Elsie May
Thomas, Joe, 263, 272–73, 370n56
Thompson, Era Bell: and agricultural tasks, 126–27, 128–29; and animals, 61–62, 65–66, 68–69; education of, 139–40, 151–52; and geography of home, 141; and Indigenous peoples, 181–82; and the Middle West, 337–40, 344; and the Northwest, 307; and nostalgic remembering, 157; photograph of, *69*, *140*, *341*; and regional studies, 357; and rocks, 115–16; and soil, 93–94; and stories, 104; and travel away from home places, 151–52, 158–59; and water, 105–6; and West identity, 354; and winter, 121–23, 125; and woods, 110; and work, 150
Thompson, John Herd, 9, 282, 351
Thomson, Georgina, 51, 55, 61, 100, 135, 165, 166, 169, 358, 359
Thomson, Tom, 172
Thousand Year Old Parliament, 359
Three Affiliated Tribes, 205, 206, 371n69
Three Stories and Ten Poems (Hemingway), 219
Timber Culture Act of 1878, 30
Tongue River, 41, 106, 111
topography, 61–62
Toronto, Canada, 171–73
town naming, 223
tractors, 263, 266–67
trade, 35–36
Transatlantic Review (journal), 248–49
transcontinental status of northern grasslands, 20–21, 23
transfers, 364n17, 386n4, 386n6, 387n17, 392n5, 398n114
transnationalism, 307
transnational northern grasslands, 28–35, *32*, 45–53, *50*, 264, 289, 310, 354–62
transportation and animals, 61–62, 72
travel, 28–29, 90–91, 133–35, 145–55, 158–59, 163–65, 268
treaties, 20, 24–25, 37–38, 48–49

treelessness, 25–26, 320, 323
trees, 109–15, 144–45
trench living, 159
Trupin, Sophie, 52, 55, 98, 119, 120–21, 123, 126–27, 226, 300
Tuan, Yi-Fu, 94

United States: and boosterism, 26–28; and the Census Bureau, 345; and competition for settlers, 49–51, 305; and Congress, 36, 48, 291, 403n50; and drought, 269–70; and educational curriculums, 355–56; and the Great Plains Drought Area Committee, 278; and homestead laws, 30–31, 47–48, 371n68; and hunting, 289, 291; and Indigenous peoples, 19–25, 47–48, 139–41, 188–89, 206–8; and land alienation, 99, 131; and land laws, 30–31, 36, 47–49, 188, 206–8, 264–65, 277–78, 297–98; and lines of aridity, 347; and the Middle West, 335–46; and modernist literature, 258–59; and native grasslands habitat, 328, 333; and the New Deal, 278, 312; and the Northwest, 304–8; and opposition to Canada, 353–57; and Prairie Provinces, 332–35; and regional labels, 348, 362; and reservations, 37, 47–48; and settlement boom, 35–45, 52; and transnational origins, 28–35; and treaties, 19–25; and trees, 110; and the U.S.-Canadian Reciprocity Trade Agreement, 355–56; and the U.S.-Dakota War, 21–22; and the U.S. Indian Office, 206
University of Minnesota, 150, 301–2
University of Minnesota Press, 255
University of Saskatchewan, 276–77, 286–87
University of Wisconsin, 150–51
Unnamed Country (Harrison), 393n29
uplands, 46
Upper Country, 304
urbanization, 159, 241–42, 344
Uses His Arrow, Bede, 188–89

Van Doren, Carl, 221–23, 227, 230, 258–59, 336–37, 399n123
vanishing trail, 147–48
Van Nuys, Laura Bower, 88, 104, 107–8, 121, 135, 165, 166
Veracini, Lorenzo, 176, 364n17, 386n4, 386n6, 387n17, 392n5, 398n114
Vermillion SD 153
veterans of World War I, 49
The Viking Heart (Salverson), 223–24, 242–45, 254–55, 256
Village (McAlmon), 219, 228–35, 245–46
Village of Corn Growing Indian Tribe in North Dakota (Gannon), 202–3
Villard, Henry, 85

Wahpekute Dakotas, 19, 21
Wahpetons, 19, 21
Walters, Emile, 41, 172
Walters, Thorstina Jackson: and agricultural adaptation, 264–65; and animals, 61, 69, 88; and berries, 115; education of, 138, 165; and experience of grasslands, 96; and extermination efforts, 77; and family migration story, 41, 51; and Indigenous peoples, 181; literature of, 244–45; and national affiliation, 352–53; and

the Northwest, 307; and parental pioneers, 54–56; photograph of, *303*; and prairie and plains terminology, 330; and regional writing, 301–2; and stories, 103–4; and teaching, 166; and transnational dialogue, 359; and water, 106–7; and woods, 111; and World War I, 159
Ward, Birlea, 79–80, 171
Warren, Kemble, 26
water: and conservation, 278, 291–92; and experiences of the grasslands, 104–9; and flora, 328–29; and freshwater springs, 108–9; and research, 277; and watersheds, 33, 326–27
Webb, Walter Prescott, 315, 320–22, 323, 325–27
Weber, Ronald, 221, 248
West, Elliott, 5, 11
western myths, 11, 353–54. *See also* mythic West
While I Still Remember (Eggleston), 351
White, Richard, 9, 317, 365n23
white people, 202–9, 211–13, 244
wild game, 81–86, 89
wild rose, *285*
Will, George F.: and animals, 70, 72, 87–89; and archaeological sites, 171, 177, 188; and aridity, 314, 317; *Corn among the Indians of the Upper Missouri*, 201–9, 387n7; and cultural exchanges, 185–89; and drought, 271; and environmental experiences, 352; and experience of grasslands, 95–97; and extermination efforts, 78, 79–80; and family migration story, 40–41; and Indigenous corn, 175–76, 273–76, 314; and

Indigenous peoples, 177–79, 183, 347; and James Holding Eagle, 207, 208; literature of, 256–57; and the Middle West, 342; and the Northern Great Plains, 308–12; and the Northwest, 306; and photographs, *170, 203, 274*; and plant species, 286–88, 310; and post–World War II farming, 296–97; and power farming, 263; and prairie and plains terminology, 330, 334; and religious values, 200; and social hybridity (Hixson), 214–17; and stories, 102; and transformation of grasslands, 294; and transnational dialogue, 360–62; and water, 106; and wild game, 85–86; and winter, 121; and woods, 114–15
Willard, Daniel E., 167
Williams, Flossie, *248*
Williams, William Carlos, 246–51, *248*, 259
Williston ND, 53, 145
Willow Bunch, Saskatchewan, 51
Wilson, Gilbert, 185, 206
Wilson, Nell. *See* Parsons, Nell Wilson
Wind Cave National Park, 88
Winnipeg, Canada, 29–30, 34, 38, 42, 105, 159, 180, 306
Winnipeg Free Press, 305
Winnipeg Tribune, 292
winter, 120–25
Wolf Willow (Stegner), 241, 256, 314
wolf willows, 95, 107, 224, 236, 256, 270, 282, 360–61
women, 31, 83, 126–27, 175, 178, 201, 203–15, 231, 234, 273
Woodland Park, 88
woods, 109–15
Woods Crees, 20

Index 473

work, 72–76, 148–51, 190–91, 267–68, 381n74
Works Progress Administration's Writers Projects, 254
World War I, 159–61, 176, 262
Worster, Donald, 4–5
Wounded Knee Creek, 178–79

Wright, Jim, 294

Yanktonais, 19, 22
Yanktons, 19, 48
Yankton SD, 29
Your Country, My Country (Bothwell), 416n12

www.ingramcontent.com/pod-product-compliance
Lightning Source LLC
Chambersburg PA
CBHW030559230426
43661CB00053B/1778